Marbury Versus Madison

Landmark Events in
U.S. History Series

The Declaration of Independence: Origins and Impact
Scott Douglas Gerber, Editor

The Louisiana Purchase: Emergence of an American Nation
Peter J. Kastor, Editor

Marbury Versus Madison: Documents and Commentary
Mark A. Graber and Michael Perhac, Editors

Marbury Versus Madison
Documents and Commentary

Mark A. Graber and Michael Perhac, Editors

CQ PRESS

A Division of Congressional Quarterly Inc.
Washington, D.C.

CQ Press
1255 22nd Street, N.W., Suite 400
Washington, D.C. 20037

202-729-1900; toll-free: 1-866-4CQ-PRESS (1-866-427-7737)

www.cqpress.com

Printed and bound in the United States of America

06 05 04 03 02   5 4 3 2 1

☉ The paper used in this publication meets the minimum requirements of the American National Standard for Information Sciences—Permanence of Paper for Printed Library Materials, ANSI Z39.48-1992.

Cover design: Debra Naylor

Library of Congress Cataloging-in-Publication Data

Marbury Versus Madison : documents and commentary / edited by Mark A. Graber and Michael Perhac.
        p. cm.
Includes bibliographical references and index.
   ISBN 1-56802-719-2 (alk. paper)
   1. Judicial review—United States—History.   2. Separation of powers—United States—History.   3. Marbury, William, 1761 or 2–1835—Trials, litigation, etc.   4. Madison, James, 1751–1836—Trials, litigation, etc.   I. Title: Marbury versus Madison.   II. Graber, Mark A.   III. Perhac, Michael.
   KF4575 .M37 2002
   347.73'12—dc21

2002015932

Contents

Preface

Marbury v. Madison is possibly the most famous and yet the most obscure judicial decision in U.S. history. Chief Justice John Marshall's 1803 opinion is generally credited with establishing "judicial review"—the judicial power to declare the actions of state and federal governments unconstitutional. The Supreme Court based several subsequent decisions on *Marbury,* including the famous rulings that struck down the Income Tax Act of 1894, demanded that Arkansas officials desegregate their schools, required President Richard M. Nixon to turn over incriminating Watergate tapes, and negated congressional efforts to provide broad remedies for violence against women. Anyone glancing at the actual opinion may justly wonder what all the fuss was about. Litigants asked the Court to decide whether William Marbury, a local Federalist politician, was entitled to a commission as a justice of the peace for the District of Columbia, whether his commission was valid when sealed or when delivered, and whether the law declared unconstitutional gave the Supreme Court original jurisdiction in a matter over which the Constitution vested that tribunal with appellate jurisdiction. These seem unlikely issues to spawn a landmark judicial decision.

This volume helps to explain why a dispute over a minor office has had an enduring impact on U.S. constitutional and political development. One of the book's aims is simply to introduce students and citizens unfamiliar with legal argument to *Marbury.* Chief Justice Marshall wrote in early nineteenth-century legal English, a dialect bearing only a family resemblance to contemporary American English. Numerous twists in *Marbury* cannot be appreciated by laypersons without considerable explanation. A second purpose, aimed at ordinary readers and scholars alike, is to provide context for the enduring interest in the case. *Marbury* is often introduced or discussed as if the idea of judicial review sprang fully born from Marshall's head in 1803. The essays and documents in this book demonstrate that, rather than being a novel concept, judicial review had been the subject of discussion in the United States for at least the previous twenty years and had antecedents that reached back more than two thousand years. Virtually all the crucial claims in Marshall's opinion could have been lifted from the congressional debates over the repeal of the Judiciary Act of 1801. Hardly anyone, including the litigants in *Marbury,* was concerned about the questions of constitutional civil procedure that occupy most of the opinion. The central issue of *Marbury* was the relationship between a Federalist-controlled judiciary, potentially armed with the right to declare laws unconstitutional, and the Jeffersonian-controlled elected branches of government.

Marbury highlights judicial review in its full ambiguity. The Federalist judiciary in 1803 asserted the power to declare Jeffersonian measures unconstitutional, while never actually voiding any Jeffersonian measure. This pattern would be repeated throughout history. Judicial review, the following essays and documents suggest, serves more often than thwarts popular political interests. Federalists may have championed the judiciary as the institution that would protect the rights of unpopular political minorities, but the unpopular minorities the courts have protected have been slaveholders and the wealthiest Americans as often as they have been the poor and downtrodden.

The materials in this volume are divided into three sections. The first consists of essays by the leading contemporary students of judicial review. Each essay introduces a major area of controversy surrounding the *Marbury* opinion and makes an original scholarly contribution to that debate. The second contains numerous documents that cast light on the questions raised by the essays. They range from analogues to judicial review in ancient Greece to contemporary exercises of that judicial practice. The final section consists of three appendices: an annotated version of the case that explains to laypersons the arguments in *Marbury* and some of the controversial legal aspects of the opinion, a record of all the Supreme Court decisions that specifically refer to the case, and a list of all the cases cited in this volume.

We wish we could supply definitive answers to the numerous questions that persist about judicial practice, or at least answers on which the editors of this book could agree. That not being possible, we will rest content with our efforts to compile materials that will interest readers in *Marbury* and help them to develop more informed answers to the central questions raised by the judicial power to declare laws unconstitutional.

Acknowledgments

Mark A. Graber would like to apologize to Larry Kramer for not taking more of his useful suggestions; to Naomi Graber, Abigail Graber, Rebecca Graber, Rebecca Cole, and Emily Sutton for cutting the section that involved their research; to Michael Perhac for sending him to the library repeatedly after claiming "we now have all the documents we need"; to Christopher Anzalone, Debbie Hardin, and Talia Greenberg for being obsessive and missing numerous deadlines; and to Julia Frank for generally being too distracted. This volume exists because of their kindness and patience.

Michael Perhac would like to thank Mark A. Graber for giving him the opportunity to coedit this book, and his wife, Valerie, for providing support and encouragement while he was working on this project.

This book is dedicated to Rogers M. Smith, in gratitude from his first advisee and on the occasion of the first publication by a grand-advisee. Given his spirit, we have no doubt there will be many more publications in the future.

Mark A. Graber
Michael Perhac
September 2002

1

The Myth of *Marbury v. Madison* and the Origins of Judicial Review

SCOTT DOUGLAS GERBER

The most authoritative citation in American law is *Marbury v. Madison* (1803). Indeed, in two cases that had the potential to shake the foundation of American government to its core, *Cooper v. Aaron* (1958) and *United States v. Nixon* (1974), the Supreme Court invoked *Marbury* to quell the threat. In *Cooper,* a challenge by Arkansas state officials to the binding effect of the landmark desegregation decision in *Brown v. Board of Education* (1954), a unanimous Court thundered,

Article VI of the Constitution makes the Constitution the "supreme Law of the Land." In 1803, Chief Justice [John] Marshall, speaking for a unanimous Court, referring to the Constitution as "the fundamental law of the nation," declared in the notable case of *Marbury v. Madison,* 1 Cranch 137, 177, that "It is emphatically the province and duty of the judicial department to say what the law is." This decision declared the basic principle that the federal judiciary is supreme in the exposition of the law of the Constitution, and that principle has ever since been respected by this Court and the Country as a permanent and indispensable feature of our constitutional system.

In *Nixon,* a case that found a sitting president challenging the power of a court to order him to produce certain tapes and documents

relating to alleged criminal activity by him and his staff, the Supreme Court—again unanimously—also turned to the most famous decision in the history of American law to resolve the dispute:

In the performance of assigned constitutional duties each branch of the Government must initially interpret the Constitution, and the interpretation of its powers by any branch is due great respect from the others. The President's counsel . . . reads the Constitution as providing an absolute privilege of confidentiality for all Presidential communications. Many decisions of this Court, however, have unequivocally reaffirmed the holding of *Marbury v. Madison,* 1 Cranch 137 (1803), that "[i]t is emphatically the province and duty of the judicial department to say what the law is."

Significantly, the president—the commander in chief of the most powerful military in the world—complied with the Court's decision and turned over the incriminating materials. He resigned from office shortly thereafter.

The purpose of this chapter is to explore the background of *Marbury v. Madison* by tracing the origins of the doctrine of judicial review: the power of a court to hold unconstitutional and hence unenforceable any law, any official

The author thanks Henry Abraham, George Billias, Bill Casto, and Wythe Holt for reading a draft of this chapter.

action based on a law, or any other action by a public official deemed in conflict with the Constitution of the United States. As will be seen, this awesome power did not spring full-blown—like Athena from the forehead of Zeus—with Marshall's opinion in that great case. In fact, Chief Justice Marshall himself, the person most often credited with "inventing" judicial review, did not believe he was doing anything unusual when he struck down the statute in question in the case.

From Legislative Supremacy to Judicial Review

Legislative supremacy is the central tenet of the British theory of government. This doctrine stems from the Glorious Revolution of 1688 and the efforts therein to limit the power and authority of the crown. As a result of the successful culmination of the Glorious Revolution, Parliament, or more formerly the crown-in-Parliament, is supreme over every other governmental body, including the crown and the crown's appointed officials. Judges are largely limited to the ministerial task of ensuring that the procedures mandated by particular legislative acts have been properly followed in specific cases. As Sir William Blackstone's classic statement on the matter makes clear, under the British doctrine of legislative supremacy judges do _not_ enjoy the power of judicial review in the American sense of striking down legislation they deem in conflict with the Constitution. In Blackstone's famous language:

[I]f the parliament will positively enact a thing to be done which is unreasonable, I know of no power that can control it: and the examples usually alleged in support of this sense of the rule do none of them

prove, that where the main object of a statute is unreasonable the judges are at liberty to reject it; for that were to set the judicial power above the legislative, which would be subversive of all government. (Blackstone 1765–1769, vol. 1, 91)

The notion that judges are without significant authority has not gone unchallenged in British history. The first claim by a court to enjoy the power of judicial review is usually said to be the 1610 opinion of Sir Edward Coke, then the Lord Chief Justice, in _Dr. Bonham's Case_. At issue in the case was Parliament's claim of an exclusive right to control the licensing of physicians. Coke considered the claim contrary to the common law. In now legendary language, he planted the seed for the American doctrine of judicial review: "[W]hen an act of Parliament is against common right and reason, or repugnant, or impossible to be performed, the common law will controul it and adjudge such an act to be void" (_Bonham_ 1610, 652). However, by promptly reenacting the disputed statute, Parliament rejected Coke's claim of judicial review for British courts. Indeed, Coke's decision in _Dr. Bonham's Case_ played no small part in his subsequent removal from the bench. The idea that British judges are without authority to set aside acts of Parliament, a matter definitively settled by the Glorious Revolution, has continued ever since.

Given that the American colonists were British subjects, it was natural that they initially subscribed to British ideas on government. The colonists' commitment to the principle of legislative supremacy is well illustrated by the strength of their resentment of the royal governors' consistent attempts to frustrate this principle in practice. Historian Allan Nevins aptly remarked during the first quarter of the twentieth century that "the beginnings of the Revolution were first discerned in a clash between the [colonial] legislature[s] and the royal officers" (Nevins 1924, 26). With respect to the courts specifically, a key source of friction during the dawn of the American Revolution was the dispute between the colonial legislatures and the royal governors over who should control the courts. This was a point included in the Declaration of Independence's list of grievances against the king: "He has made Judges dependent on his Will alone, for the tenure of their offices, and the amount and payment of their salaries."

The first state constitutions adopted after the Declaration of Independence were organized around the doctrine of legislative supremacy. Although a few of the early constitutions contained an explicit declaration of the separation of powers, none provided for judicial review and all made the elected legislature the dominant branch of government. Judges of the day understood this arrangement well. Judge Daniel Chipman of Vermont wrote,

> [W]hen [the first state constitutions] constituted the legislature, they considered that its power was necessarily supreme and uncontrollable, and that all constitutional restrictions upon their power were merely directory. No idea was entertained that an act of the legislature, however repugnant to the constitution, could be adjudged void and set aside by the judiciary, which was considered by all a subordinate department of government. (Chipman 1824, book 2, 22)

The colonists' initial commitment to the doctrine of legislative supremacy did *not* mean they were unconcerned about protecting individual rights—the principal function of government in a liberal state such as America. (In the language of the Declaration of Indepen-

dence, "To secure these rights, governments are instituted among men.") Rather, it reflected the conventional wisdom that the security of individual rights depended on the power of the legislature to check the power of the executive—an idea that the colonists' disputes with the royal governors had brought sharply into focus. In fact, the chief task of the legislative branch was not to legislate; it was to protect rights.

That the legislature was charged, above all else, with protecting individual rights will undoubtedly strike modern Americans strangely, accustomed as we are to a powerful judicial check on the legislative and executive branches alike in the sacred realm of individual rights. Nevertheless, the colonists were initially committed to that idea. The cry "no taxation without representation" symbolized not only the colonists' dispute with the British in general but their belief that the protection of rights depended specifically on representative government. The first state constitutions reflected this faith in the power of representation to protect rights, attempting as they did to limit as much as possible the distance between constituents and representatives through structural devices such as annual elections, rotation in office, the right of instruction, equitable apportionment, and a broad franchise.

In time, however, the colonists came to realize that even a reformed system of representation provided inadequate security for individual rights. This sentiment was well reflected in Thomas Jefferson's famous remark, "[A]n *elective despotism* was not the government we fought for" (Jefferson 1975, 164). Mobilization for the War of Independence and reorganization of society and government after the war required that the new American state legislatures govern actively, something to which the newly independent American people were unaccustomed. Most notably affected by the increased legislative activity were private property rights. Fighting a war and rebuilding a society in its aftermath are expensive propositions, and the colonists were not spared from this reality. State legislatures imposed a host of taxes and other economic restraints. The specific impact of those measures on private property rights was certainly resented. More important, though, the measures and the overall increased legislative activity caused the colonists to rethink their position on the broader question of the power of representation to protect individual rights. After all, the scope of the legislative function had changed and the colonists realized that their faith in representation must change as well.

As a consequence of their diminishing faith in representation to protect individual rights, the colonists attempted more and more to limit legislative power. The proliferation of written constitutions during the early days of the American republic was directly attributable to this perceived need to limit the legislature. In those written constitutions, not only did grants of power to the legislature become more specific, but formal exemption of certain rights from the legislature's reach through a bill of rights became commonplace. Virginia, for example, adopted a bill of rights in 1776. Most other states soon followed suit.

Emerging concurrently with the attempts to limit the legislative branch through the enumeration of particular legislative powers and the constitutional exemption of specific rights was one of the most significant American contributions to constitutional theory: the idea that judges had the authority to protect individual rights from infringement by the forces of representation through the power of judicial review. Before judicial review took root, however, one last attempt was made to reform representation, this time at the national level.

For the delegates to the Constitutional Convention who met in Philadelphia during the summer of 1787, the ultimate objective was to establish a form of government that would provide better security for individual rights than was then occurring under the Articles of Confederation (the young nation's first attempt at a national constitution). In the words of James Madison, the so-called father of the Constitution, "[T]he necessity of providing more effectually for the security of private rights, and the steady dispensation of Justice. Interferences with these were evils which had more perhaps than any thing else produced this convention" (Farrand 1911, vol. 1, 134).

What was the cause of the insecurity of individual rights under the Articles of Confederation? In the minds of most delegates to the Constitutional Convention, the answer could be found in the failure of representation in the state assemblies. As Maryland delegate John Mercer explained, "What led to the appointment of this Convention? The corruption and mutability of the Legislative Councils of the States" (Farrand 1911, vol. 2, 288).

Although those who met in Philadelphia agreed that a new national constitution was needed to better secure individual rights, considerable disagreement arose over how to frame it. As Mercer's remarks reflect, most of the delegates had lost faith in representation at the _state_ level. However, several in attendance thought a reformed system of representation at the *national* level could provide the requisite security for the people's rights. Madison was the foremost proponent of this view.

Madison arrived in Philadelphia prepared to set the terms of the debate. Before the Convention began, he drafted a plan of government that went far beyond simply revising the Articles of Confederation. Madison's plan, commonly known as the Virginia Plan, envisioned a strong national government with sweeping powers to check state legislative assemblies. Those sweeping national powers were lodged principally in the national legislature by way of a veto power over laws passed in the state assemblies. For Madison, all faith in representation was not lost. But his faith depended on a different kind of legislator serving in the national assembly than those then serving in the state assemblies. Put directly, legislators in Congress had to be far more resistant to the pressures of self-interest than their counterparts in the states had proved to be. Madison's influential vision of an extended federal republic came to the fore.

An extended federal republic was important to Madison for several reasons. The most widely recognized reasons were because majority factions would be less likely to exist in a large territory and would find it more difficult to organize if they did. An often overlooked reason was because an expanded pool of potential representatives would be created, thereby making it more probable that meritorious representatives would emerge—representatives who would be more respectful of the people's rights.

When all was said and done, however, even the Virginia Plan showed only modest faith in the power of representation to secure individual rights. Most notable in this regard was Madison's call for a council of revision, consisting of the national executive and several federal judges, that would have the authority to veto acts of the national legislature. The reason Madison wanted a national veto over state laws was because he distrusted representation at the state level. But the reason he wanted a council of revision was because he did not have full confidence in representation at the national level. As Madison advised the convention:

[The council of revision] would . . . be useful to the Community at large as an additional check agst. a pursuit of those unwise & unjust measures which constituted so great a portion of our calamities [under the Articles of Confederation]. . . . Experience in all the States had evinced a powerful tendency in the Legislature to absorb all power into its vortex. This was the real source of danger to American Constitutions; & suggested the necessity of giving every defensive authority to the other departments that was consistent with republican principles. (Farrand 1911, vol. 2, 28)

Despite Madison's repeated efforts to convince the Convention of the need for both a national veto over state laws and a council of revision, he could obtain passage of neither. The national veto failed primarily because of the potent political argument that the states would not accept such an arrangement. The council of revision was rejected chiefly because it would give the Supreme Court a double negative over laws passed by Congress. Maryland delegate Luther Martin's remarks typified this latter concern: "[A]s to the Constitutionality of laws, that point will come before the Judges in their proper official character. In this character they have a negative on the laws. Join them with the Executive in the Revision and they will have a double negative" (Farrand 1911, vol. 2, 28).

If not by representation at the national level, how were individual rights to be protected? The answer was by the courts. In place of the congressional veto over state laws emerged the supremacy clause, under which state courts are required to strike down state laws that violate the federal Constitution. With respect to the council of revision, that proposal was rejected, as was just noted, because many of the delegates did not want to involve the Supreme Court in reviewing congressional acts twice. Indeed, as historian Charles Beard demonstrated nearly a century ago, the evidence from Philadelphia, especially that surrounding the council of revision, suggests that the Constitution commissions the Court with the power to void unconstitutional federal and state legislation alike. Admittedly, the evidence is not unambiguous. For example, the text of the Constitution that the framers finally agreed on does not expressly provide for judicial review. However, any doubt about the Supreme Court's authority to exercise judicial review is dispelled when the ratification debates are consulted. James Wilson, who was second only to Madison in terms of contributions at the Constitutional Convention, informed the Pennsylvania ratifying convention:

If a law should be made inconsistent with those powers vested by this instrument in Congress, the judges, as a consequence of their independence, and the particular powers of government being defined, will declare such law to be null and void. For the power of the Constitution predominates. Anything therefore that shall be enacted by Congress contrary thereto will not have the force of law. (Elliot 1901, vol. 2, 489)

There are also the observations of Marshall in the Virginia ratifying convention. Marshall's remarks are particularly interesting, given the role he was to play in *Marbury v. Madison:*

Has the government of the United States power to make laws on every subject? . . . Can they make laws affecting the mode of transferring property, or contracts, or claims between citizens of the same state? Can they go beyond the delegated power? If they were to make a law not warranted by any of the powers enumerated it would be considered by the judges as an infringement of the Constitution which they are to guard. They would consider such a law as coming under their jurisdiction. They would declare it void. (Elliot 1901, vol. 3, 553)

Finally, there is Alexander Hamilton in *The Federalist Papers,* the landmark series of newspaper essays written by Hamilton, Madison, and John Jay in support of the Constitution's ratification. Hamilton wrote in one of the most important of those essays, No. 78:

The interpretation of the laws is the proper and peculiar province of the courts. A constitution is, in fact, and must be, regarded by the judges as fundamental law. It must, therefore, belong to them to ascertain its meaning, as well as the meaning of a particular act proceeding from the legislative body. If there should happen to be an irreconcilable variance between the two, that which has the superior obligation and validity ought, of course, to be preferred, or in other words, the Constitution ought to be preferred to the statute, the intention of the people to the intention of their agents.

This is but a sampling of the historical evidence supporting a strong judicial check on the forces of representation—evidence that reveals how far the founders had moved from their original faith in the power of representation to secure individual rights. Indeed, some opposed ratification precisely because the Constitution had, in their judgment, moved too far from the doctrine of legislative supremacy. Most notable in this regard was Robert Yates, who feared that the Supreme Court's power of judicial review and its independent status under the Constitution would make the Court despotic. As the discussion in this section suggests, however, Yates's continued faith in representation was a minority view.

The Judicial Precedents

The previous section chronicled the movement from legislative to judicial protection of individual rights in American constitutional theory. This fundamental change in how the founders viewed the *theory* of constitutional law would not have been possible without an emerging *practice* to which they could turn for support. This section examines that emerging practice: the judicial precedents that eventually would lead to *Marbury v. Madison*. Although the reporting of judicial decisions during the early days of the American republic was far from the science it is today, sufficient documentation exists to make plain that Chief Justice Marshall's opinion in *Marbury* had a strong line of precedent behind it.

The first recorded statement of judicial review in America was made by James Otis before the Massachusetts Superior Court, in 1761, in the famous writs of assistance case, *Paxton v. Gray*. According to a young John Adams, who chronicled the case, in dispute was a request by the royal customs office that the court issue general search warrants, or writs of assistance, because particular search warrants had proved ineffective in the customs office's efforts to curb smuggling. Nothing was more repugnant to the colonists' conception of liberty than general searches, violating as they did the cherished maxim that "a man's house is his castle." Otis was so strongly opposed to the idea of general search warrants that he not

only refused to argue the case on behalf of the customs office, as was his charge as the king's advocate in the province, but he decided to represent the local merchants instead. Significantly, Otis's argument against the general search warrants—an argument that relied heavily on Coke's opinion in *Dr. Bonham's Case*—centered on the power of a court to void legislation that conflicts with the constitution. In Otis's words: "As to acts of Parliament. An act against the Constitution is void; an act against natural equity is void; and if the act of Parliament should be made, in the very words of the Petition, it would be void. The executive Courts must pass such acts into disuse" (Adams 1850–1859, vol. 2, 522).

When Otis argued the writs of assistance case, the doctrine of legislative supremacy held sway. It should therefore come as no surprise that he lost the case. This fact notwithstanding, Otis's argument for judicial review was a milestone in American history, portending as it did events to come. According to Adams, Otis's argument about the unenforceability of legislative acts that contravene the constitution was so influential that with it "the child of independence was born" (Adams 1850–1859, vol. 10, 248).

Robin v. Hardaway (1772) is another noteworthy pre-Revolution case in the development of judicial review. In that case, George Mason, an influential Virginia lawyer, argued that a 1682 Virginia law giving slave traders the right to sell the descendants of Native Americans as slaves violated the Native Americans' natural rights—the philosophical foundation of individual rights in liberal political theory—and was, therefore, void. In Mason's words:

[A]ll acts of the legislature apparently contrary to natural right and justice, are, in our laws, and must be in the nature of things, considered as void. The laws of nature are the laws of God; whose authority can be superseded by no power on earth. A legislature must not obstruct our obedience to him from those whose punishments they cannot protect us. All human constitutions which contradict his laws, we are in conscience bound to disobey. Such have been the adjudications of our courts of justice.

A forceful advocate, Mason no doubt overstated the frequency with which judges in 1772 were striking down legislation they deemed violative of higher law. In fact, the judges in *Robin v. Hardaway* worked hard to avoid passing on the legitimacy of the statute in question. In a maneuver reflective of the still widespread commitment to legislative supremacy, the judges concluded that the statute had been repealed in 1705. They were not, therefore, required to assess the statute's constitutionality as Mason had requested. Nevertheless, Mason's argument, like Otis's before it, is representative of a growing willingness on the part of the Bar to challenge legislative power by invoking the power of a court to curb it. This trend continued after the colonists declared independence.

Records survive of five state court precedents for judicial review before the Constitution went into effect. These precedents illustrate the judiciary's *emerging* role as the guardian of the people's rights. *Commonwealth v. Caton* (1782) is the first reported case in the United States in which a court openly exercised judicial review.[1] At issue was the constitutionality of a 1776 Virginia statute that moved the pardon power from the executive to the legislature. The statute was before the Virginia Court of Appeals, the state's highest tribunal, because a dispute arose when the lower legislative house pardoned three men con-

demned to death for treason and the upper house refused to concur. The attorney general, seeking to enforce the death sentences, insisted that the pardons were ineffective because the statute required the assent of both legislative houses. The condemned men disagreed, arguing that the statute granted the pardoning power to the lower house alone or it was unconstitutional.

The judges sided with the attorney general. More important, they held that they had the power to strike down laws that violated the constitution. Although individual rights were at stake—the condemned men's right not to be killed—*Caton* was chiefly about the allocation of governmental power—specifically, about where the pardon power resided. Judge George Wythe's opinion in the case—the practice in those days was for each judge to issue his own opinion—offers a revealing glimpse into the developing conception of the judicial function as guardian of individual rights. Of special interest are Wythe's observations about the threat legislative power poses to the rights of individuals and about the responsibility of judges to protect against that threat. He wrote,

[I]f the whole legislature, an event to be deprecated, should attempt to overleap the bounds, prescribed to them by the people, I, in administering the public justice of this country, will meet the united powers, at my seat in this tribunal; and, pointing to the constitution, will say to them, here is the limit of your authority; and hither, shall you go, but no further.

Earlier in his opinion, Wythe—who had taught the law to Marshall (more on this later)—favorably invoked the Cokean notion that it is the duty of a judge to "protect the rights of the subject."

One of the most intriguing of the early state court cases is *Rutgers v. Waddington* (1784), argued by Alexander Hamilton. At issue was whether Hamilton's client, a British citizen named Joshua Waddington, committed a trespass by occupying plaintiff Elizabeth Rutgers's property during the American Revolution. Rutgers sued Waddington pursuant to a New York statute that entitled any person who vacated his or her property under threat of the war to recover in trespass against any person who occupied or destroyed the property.

Hamilton, like Otis and Mason before him, emphasized in his argument to the court the need for the judiciary to protect his client's individual rights. He said, "The enemy having a right to the use of the Plaintiffs property & having exercised their right through the Defendant & for valuable consideration he cannot be made answerable to another without injustice and a violation of the law of Universal society."

The court was fully aware of the thrust of Hamilton's argument. The judges noted that Hamilton's defense centered on the claim that "statutes against law and reason are void." And the court appeared to accept Hamilton's position:

[W]e profess to revere the rights of human nature; at every hazard and expence we have vindicated, and successfully established them in our land! and we cannot but reverence a law which is their chief guardian—a law which inculcates as a first principle—that the amiable precepts of the law of nature, are as obligatory on nations in their mutual intercourse, as they are on individuals in their conduct towards each other; and that every nation is bound to contribute all in its powers to the happiness and perfection of others! (Hamilton 1964, vol. 1, 395, 400)

Despite this strong language about the importance of protecting individual rights, the court upheld the statute, explicitly acknowledging the supremacy of the legislature. The court did, however, deny the plaintiff relief. What the court's inconsistent actions suggest is that the judges were torn between their increasing awareness of the need for judges to protect individual rights and their lingering commitment to the doctrine of legislative supremacy.

In a Connecticut decision the following year such inconsistency was conspicuously absent. The *Symsbury Case* (1785) involved a land dispute between two neighboring Connecticut towns. Originally, title to the land was held by the town of Symsbury. Subsequently, the town of New Hartford surveyed the land and found that the land was located within the New Hartford town limits. The state legislature agreed and granted title to New Hartford. The proprietors of the town of Symsbury sued, demanding that title to the land be returned to them. The court ruled in favor of Symsbury. In the court's judgment, the act of the state legislature granting title to New Hartford "could not legally operate to curtail the land before granted to the proprietors of the town of Symsbury, without their consent" (*Symsbury*, 447).

Brief though it is, the court's decision in the *Symsbury Case* is important for two related reasons. The first is that the decision is plainly an early example of judicial review. The second is that the decision is additional evidence of a growing awareness among judges that they must serve as a check against legislative power when rights are at stake, such as the right to property involved in the dispute before the Connecticut court.

Trevett v. Weeden (1786) is another landmark case in the development of judicial review. As is so often true of cases from the early days of the American republic, the opinion of the court has not been found. A widely read account of the case by James Varnum, the lead defense attorney, is available, however.[2] At issue was a controversial Rhode Island statute that required local merchants to accept paper money as legal tender—a requirement that, given the inflationary pressures of the day, the merchants opposed. Merchants who refused to accept paper money were subject to arrest and to trial without the benefit of a jury. Varnum's client was one such merchant.

Varnum made a variety of arguments in defense of his client but, according to Varnum himself, "[B]y far the most important" was a direct challenge to the statute's constitutionality. Varnum claimed both that the statute was unconstitutional and that the judges had to declare it so. "The true distinction lies in this," he said, "that the legislative have the uncontrollable power of making laws not repugnant to the constitution; the judiciary have the sole power of judging of those laws, and are bound to execute them; but cannot admit any act of the legislative as law, which is against the constitution" (Varnum 1787, 11, 25).

Just as important as Varnum's comments about the *existence* of the power of judicial review was his argument about *why* that power should be exercised: to protect individual rights. Varnum's substantive attack on the statute was that trial by jury is an "unalienable right" that the legislature cannot justly infringe, and his argument to the court was replete with references to the sanctity of individual rights and to the fact that the American regime was founded to secure them.

Unfortunately, because the court's opinion has not been found, the court's reaction to Varnum's argument is somewhat unclear. Newspaper reports suggest that most judges were re-ceptive to Varnum's position. Resolutions passed by the Rhode Island legislature condemning the judges' handling of the case provide additional evidence of this fact.

The most famous of the early state court precedents for judicial review is *Bayard v. Singleton* (1787). Like most states during the American Revolution, North Carolina confiscated property held by individuals who remained loyal to the British. At issue in the case was a statute that required judges to dismiss, without regard to merit, any action brought by an individual seeking to recover title to confiscated property. In a short opinion, the Supreme Court of North Carolina unanimously declared the statute unconstitutional on the ground that an individual seeking to recover title to confiscated property was entitled to a jury trial on the merits of his or her claim.

The court was undoubtedly influenced in its decision by a widely discussed letter "To the Public" published in a local newspaper before the outcome of the litigation. The letter was written by James Iredell, the plaintiff's co-counsel. Iredell emphasized the need to curb the legislature, and he did so by drawing on the lessons of the American Revolution:

It was, of course, to be considered how to impose restrictions on the legislature, that might still leave it free to all useful purposes but at the same time guard against the abuse of unlimited power, which was not to be trusted, without the most imminent danger, to any man or body of men on earth. We had not only been sickened and disgusted for years with the high and almost impious language of Great Britain, of the omnipotent power of the British Parliament, but had severely smarted under its effects. We felt in all its rigor the mischiefs of an absolute and unbounded authority, claimed by so weak a creature as man, and should have been guilty of the basest breach of trust, as well as the grossest folly, if the moment when we spurned at the insolent despotism of Great Britain, we had established a despotic power among ourselves. (Iredell 1857–1858, vol. 2, 145)

After the court's decision declaring the confiscation statute unconstitutional—the direct check on legislative overreaching for which Iredell had argued—Richard Dobbs Spaight, then serving as a North Carolina delegate to the Constitutional Convention in Philadelphia, wrote a letter to Iredell severely criticizing him for encouraging the court to engage in such a "usurpation" of power. Iredell held his ground. He responded to Spaight in a letter that expanded on his earlier letter "To the Public." More specifically, Iredell insisted that judicial review was necessary because without it individual rights like the right to property would not be adequately protected.

The Court before John Marshall

Iredell's contributions to public life did not end with *Bayard v. Singleton*. Not only was he to become one of the leading proponents of the Constitution in the North Carolina ratifying convention, he went on to serve as an original member of the Supreme Court after the Constitution went into effect. Importantly, Iredell was not the only member of the early Court who contributed to the development of judicial review. All of the justices who served on the Supreme Court before Marshall played a significant role in the establishment of the doctrine—a doctrine that remains synonymous to this day with the "great chief justice's" opinion in *Marbury v. Madison*.[3]

Many of the early justices championed judicial review long before they were appointed

to the Supreme Court. For example, even before independence was declared, William Cushing was charging grand juries in Massachusetts that courts had the authority to declare acts of Parliament unconstitutional; John Blair participated in at least three early cases involving judicial review in Virginia, including *Commonwealth v. Caton* (1782), the first of the state court precedents; John Rutledge, despite fighting hard in the Constitutional Convention of 1787 to protect the power of state courts, both expected and supported federal judicial review of the sort exercised in *Marbury;* and Oliver Ellsworth, who preceded Marshall as chief justice of the United States, endorsed the doctrine at the Connecticut ratifying convention. Ellsworth in particular could not have been clearer on the matter. He reassured his Connecticut colleagues: "If the general legislature should . . . make a law which the Constitution does not authorize, it is void; and the judicial power, the national judges . . . will declare it to be void" (Jensen et al. 1976–1997, vol. 3, 553).

Perhaps most important, as the previous section suggested, Iredell articulated on several occasions before the Constitution went into effect a strong argument in favor of judicial review. Indeed, Iredell's biographer, Willis Whichard, maintains that Iredell's analysis of the doctrine was superior even to Hamilton's more celebrated treatment in *Federalist* No. 78 and that Marshall was familiar with, and drew on, Iredell's musings on the subject to craft his famous opinion in *Marbury*.

As sitting justices, the men who preceded Marshall to the Supreme Court continued to advocate judicial review. The best-known examples of this are William Paterson's jury charge in *Vanhorne's Lessee v. Dorrance* (1795), a property dispute, and Samuel Chase's jury charge in the 1800 trial of James Callender for seditious libel. (Supreme Court justices had rigorous circuit-riding responsibilities during the early years—responsibilities that often included presiding over jury trials.) These widely reported jury charges helped pave the way for public acceptance of judicial review. Paterson's charge—issued eight years before *Marbury v. Madison*—is particularly revealing, given that he instructed the jury in no uncertain terms that it was unconstitutional to take private property from an individual without just compensation. Paterson said,

What is a Constitution? It is the form of government, delineated by the mighty hand of the people, in which certain first principles of fundamental laws are established. The Constitution is certain and fixed; it contains the permanent will of the people, and is the supreme law of the land. . . . Whatever may be the case in other countries, yet in this there can be no doubt, that every act of the Legislature, repugnant to the Constitution, is absolutely void. (*Vanhorne* 1795, 304, 308)

Likewise, James Wilson, who rivaled Iredell for the most scholarly member of the pre-Marshall Court, presented the case for judicial review in his famous law lectures of 1790 to 1792—lectures that influenced generations of American lawyers and judges. Wilson, like Paterson and like the judges in the early state court cases discussed in the previous section, emphasized the need to check legislative encroachments on individual rights. As Wilson put it, judicial review would help prevent self-interested majorities from acting out of "passions" and "prejudices" that are "inflamed by mutual imitation and example" (Wilson 1967, vol. 1, 291).

The justices who made up the Supreme Court before Marshall did more than simply advocate judicial review: They practiced it. Barely a year after the establishment of the federal courts, Chief Justice John Jay and Associate Justice Cushing, on circuit, declared several state laws unconstitutional. In April 1791, Jay and Cushing voided, pursuant to the supremacy clause of the new federal Constitution, a Connecticut statute that conflicted with a provision in the Treaty of Peace with Great Britain ratified in 1783; in May 1791, they struck down a Rhode Island legal tender law as inconsistent with the "gold and silver" clause of Article I, Section 10; and in June 1792, they invoked the contracts clause and adjudged another Rhode Island prodebtor statute unconstitutional. Then there is *Ware v. Hylton* (1796), in which Justices Chase, Cushing, Paterson, and Wilson, sitting together as the Supreme Court, struck down a Virginia statute on the ground that it was inconsistent with a federal treaty and, hence, the supremacy clause of the Constitution.[4] And Bushrod Washington, who spent most of his career on the Court during Marshall's chief justiceship, asserted in *Cooper v. Telfair* (1800) that the Court possessed the power of judicial review—a position echoed by Justices Chase, Paterson, and Cushing in that case, as well as in *Pennhallow v. Doane's Administrators* (1795) some five years earlier.

The pre–Marshall Court justices exercised judicial review over federal law as well. (*Marbury* itself involved the constitutionality of a federal law.) The first clear occasion in which this occurred was *Hayburn's Case* (1792), wherein Justices Wilson and Blair, on circuit, declared the Invalid Pensioners Act of 1792 unconstitutional. The Court as a whole, in the then-unreported *United States v. Yale Todd* (1794), appears to have concurred with Wilson's and Blair's position.[5] (Marshall himself, and in *Marbury v. Madison* no less, made note of another unreported case, *Chandler v. Secretary of War* [1794], in which the Court appears to have invalidated an executive act.) Perhaps most important, in *Hylton v. United States* (1796), the Court reviewed a congressional tax on carriages to determine whether the tax was constitutional. The Court concluded that it was, but the justices nevertheless asserted their power to declare otherwise. Indeed, when John Wickham, the counsel for the government, offered at the circuit level to address the issue of judicial review, Justice Wilson told him to sit down and be quiet because the issue had "come before each of the judges in their different circuits, and they all concurred in the opinion" that the Court could declare congressional statutes unconstitutional.

Conclusion

More examples of pre-*Marbury* incidents of judicial review can be discussed, but it should be clear by now that early American lawyers and judges—including the individuals who served on the Supreme Court before Marshall—understood the concept of judicial review, argued for it, and practiced it. Moreover, there is ample evidence that Marshall himself was both fully aware of and substantially influenced by these early precedents. Stephen Presser, Chase's biographer, suggests, for example, that Marshall was in the audience when Chase delivered his jury charge in the Callender trial, and that Marshall later adopted some of Chase's language in his *Marbury* opinion; and Whichard, as mentioned earlier, points out in his biography of Iredell that Marshall's opinion in *Marbury* drew on Iredell's well-known views on judicial review. It also should be recalled that Marshall was trained in the law by Wythe, the Virginia jurist who played such a leading role in *Commonwealth v. Caton* (1782), the first state court precedent for judicial review—a precedent Marshall heard announced from the bench. Most telling, the self-confident tone in which Marshall wrote *Marbury* suggests that *he* knew he was not breaking new ground with the decision. At the beginning of the discussion of judicial review in that case, Marshall declared, to resolve the "question, whether an act repugnant to the constitution, can become the law of the land . . . [i]t seems only necessary to recognise certain principles, supposed to have been long and well established" (*Marbury* 1803, 137, 176).

Why, then, does Marshall's opinion in *Marbury v. Madison* occupy such mythical status in the annals of American law? A still compelling essay written by F. W. Grinnell in 1917 offers three explanations for why this might be so:

First, the habit of looking for a precedent, rather than a principle, has led men to rely on Chief Justice Marshall's opinion in *Marbury v. Madison;* although he himself looked for the principle without worrying about the precedents. Second and third, the combined forces of Anti-Federalist "politics" on one side, and the American tendency to self-glorification on the other, stepped in and asserted that it was exclusively an American idea invented by Chief Justice Marshall. The fact that there were few printed law reports before 1803 when *Marbury v. Madison* was decided helped this myth. Recent researches have uncovered a mass of buried information showing that the principle was neither exclusively American nor invented by Marshall. (Grinnell 1917, 442)

Although through these "researches" scholars have come to realize that judicial review was not "invented" by Marshall in *Marbury v. Madison*, *Marbury*'s role in the development of the doctrine still eclipses everything else to this day. From basic textbooks on American government to more advanced treatises on the judicial process, judicial review remains synonymous with Marshall's opinion for the Court in *Marbury*. This chapter has argued that the origins of judicial review are more complicated than that. There is no question that *Marbury* is a landmark case. However, the case simply established, once and for all, a doctrine that has deep roots in early American constitutional theory and practice.

Bibliography

Adams, John. *The Works of John Adams*. Edited by Charles F. Adams. 10 vols. Boston: Little, Brown, 1850–1859.

Beard, Charles A. *The Supreme Court and the Constitution*. New York: Macmillan, 1912.

Blackstone, William. *Commentaries on the Laws of England*. Edited by Stanley Nader Katz. 4 vols., 1765–1769; facsimile. Chicago: University of Chicago Press, 1979.

Boyer, Allen Dillard. " 'Understanding, Authority, and Will': Sir Edward Coke and the Elizabethan Origins of Judicial Review." *Boston College Law Review* 39 (December 1997): 43–93.

Casto, William R. *The Supreme Court in the Early Republic: The Chief Justiceships of John Jay and Oliver Ellsworth*. Columbia: University of South Carolina Press, 1995.

Chipman, Daniel. *Vermont Reports*. Middlebury, Vt.: D. Chipman & Sons, 1824.

Elliot, Jonathan, ed. *The Debates in the Several State Conventions on the Adoption of the Federal Constitution, as Recommended by the General Convention at Philadelphia*. 2d ed. 5 vols. 1836. Reprint, Philadelphia: J. B. Lippincott, 1901.

Farrand, Max, ed. *The Records of the Federal Convention of 1787*. 3 vols. New Haven: Yale University Press, 1911.

Gerber, Scott Douglas. *To Secure These Rights: The Declaration of Independence and Constitutional Interpretation*. New York: New York University Press, 1995.

———, ed. *Seriatim: The Supreme Court before John Marshall*. New York: New York University Press, 1998.

Grinnell, F. W. "The Anti-Slavery Decisions of 1781 and 1783 and the History of the Duty of the Court in Regard to Unconstitutional Legislation." *Massachusetts Law Quarterly* 2 (May 1917): 437–462.

Hamilton, Alexander. *The Law Practice of Alexander Hamilton: Documents and Commentary*. Edited by Julius Goebel Jr. 4 vols. New York: Columbia University Press, 1964.

Hamilton, Alexander, et al. *The Federalist*. Edited by Clinton Rossiter. New York: New American Library, 1961.

Iredell, James. *Life and Correspondence of James Iredell*. Edited by Griffith J. McRee. 2 vols. New York: Appleton, 1857–1858.

Jefferson, Thomas. *The Portable Thomas Jefferson*. Edited by Merrill D. Peterson. New York: Penguin Books, 1975.

Jensen, Merrill, John P. Kaminski, and Gaspare J. Saladino, eds. *The Documentary History of the Ratification of the Constitution*. 18 vols. Madison: State Historical Society of Wisconsin, 1976–1997.

Nevins, Allan. *The American States during and after the Revolution, 1775–1789*. New York: Macmillan, 1924. Reprint, New York: Augustus M. Kelley, 1969.

Presser, Stephen B. *The Original Misunderstanding: The English, the Americans and the Dialectic of Federalist Jurisprudence*. Durham, N.C.: Carolina Academic Press, 1991.

Treanor, William Michael. "The Case of the Prisoners and the Origins of Judicial Review." *University of Pennsylvania Law Review* 143 (December 1994): 491–570.

Varnum, James Mitchell. *The Case, Trevett Against Weeden: On Information and Complaint for Refusing Paper Bills in Payment for Butcher's Meat, in Market, at Par with Specie*, 1787.

Whichard, Willis. *Justice James Iredell.* Durham, N.C.: Carolina Academic Press, 2000.

Wilson, James. *The Works of James Wilson.* Edited by Robert G. McCloskey. 2 vols. Cambridge: Belknap Press of Harvard University Press, 1967.

Wood, Gordon S. "The Origins of Judicial Review Revisited, or How the Marshall Court Made More out of Less." *Washington and Lee Law Review* 56 (summer 1999): 787–848.

Notes

1. There is some evidence that two years earlier, in *Holmes v. Walton* (1780), the New Jersey Supreme Court invalidated a state statute mandating the use of six jurors in certain cases instead of the traditional twelve. The evidence includes a series of petitions introduced in the New Jersey legislature denouncing the court's invalidation of the statute. However, because the court's opinion in *Holmes* has never been found, I credit *Caton* with being the first recorded state case of judicial review. *Josiah Philips's Case* (1778) is also frequently mentioned as an early state precedent for judicial review. Like *Holmes v. Walton,* the opinion in *Josiah Philips's Case* has never been found. As such, I begin with *Commonwealth v. Caton.*

Readers should be aware that scholars disagree about the status of the early state cases as precedent for judicial review.

2. The contemporaneous accounting of the case by one of the principals makes *Trevett v. Weeden* more reliable than *Holmes v. Walton* and *Josiah Philips's Case.*

3. Little information survives about the judicial careers of Thomas Johnson and Alfred Moore, two of the twelve individuals who served on the Supreme Court before Marshall arrived in 1801. Therefore, I will not address what contributions they made, if any, to the development of judicial review.

4. Iredell had been one of the judges in the lower circuit court that adjudicated the case. As a consequence, he did not participate in the Supreme Court's decision. He did take the unusual step of reading into the record his thoughts on the matter. Ellsworth, who was not serving on the Supreme Court at the time *Ware* was decided, voiced his agreement with the decision in *Hamilton v. Eaton* (1796).

5. As was the case with the state court precedents described in the previous section, scholars disagree about the Court's holding in *Yale Todd.*

2 The Politics of *Marbury*

JAMES M. O'FALLON

The narrowing vision of doctrinalism, perhaps a necessary evil in law, can afflict historians. The consequence is often an anachronistic account of a judge's purpose, crediting him or her with foresight that would honor an oracle. So it has been with *Marbury v. Madison* (1803).

In the world of doctrine, *Marbury* stands for the proposition that courts are authorized to review acts of Congress for constitutionality. As the foundation of the most distinctive aspect of our government (judicial review), *Marbury* is studied and criticized for introducing the principle of judicial review. One standard criticism, clearly sound from a doctrinal perspective, takes Chief Justice John Marshall to task for considering and deciding a number of issues irrelevant to the decision's ultimate holding: The Court was without jurisdiction in the case, so the argument holds.

This chapter rejects the traditional view of *Marbury* as a statesmanlike opinion that clearly established the Supreme Court's authority as the final arbiter of the Constitution while distracting the Republicans' attention and avoiding a conflict with the executive branch. A reading of *Marbury* in context reveals that the case was born of the bitter political battle of its time. Chief Justice Marshall's

concern with judicial review has been exaggerated by the desire of legal scholars for a strong foundation for this doctrine.

Historians have accepted the view that *Marbury* concerns judicial review and that Marshall's discussion of William Marbury's right to his commission and the authority of the courts to examine the executive's discharge of legal duties was, strictly speaking, unnecessary, and therefore improper. In an influential analysis of *Marbury,* Robert McCloskey (2000, 25) argued that Marshall's opinion is a "masterwork of indirection, a brilliant example of Marshall's capacity to sidestep danger while seeming to court it, to advance in one direction while his opponents are looking in another." This interpretation is an important element of Marshall's apotheosis, the creation of a judicial statesman fit to stand alongside George Washington and Abraham Lincoln, Daniel Webster and Henry Clay, securing the judiciary's status as a coequal branch of government.

Marbury arose when Federalist president John Adams, in the waning days of his administration, nominated Marbury and several others to be justices of the peace. The formal commissions had not been delivered when Thomas Jefferson took office. The new president refused to deliver them. Marbury and others brought a writ of mandamus to compel Secretary of State James Madison to act.

One consequence of the marriage of history to doctrine embodied in McCloskey's interpretation is that *Marbury*'s place as a text engaging the political discourse of its time has been obscured. Historians have noted the controversy embroiling the judiciary during Jefferson's first term, highlighted by the struggle over repeal of the 1801 Judiciary Act and the Republican effort to impeach Justice Samuel Chase. That controversy frames the account of *Marbury* that centers on judicial review. However, the use of context to illuminate Marshall's political motives has not been accompanied by an appropriately informed reading of Marshall's text. The result caricatures Marshall and impoverishes our understanding of the clash of political beliefs that underlay the conflict over the judiciary.

From the outset, Marshall's *Marbury* opinion displays a striking ambivalence toward the claims of doctrinalism, with its implicit restrictions on the judiciary's political function. At the beginning of his opinion, Marshall stated that "[t]he peculiar delicacy of this case, the novelty of some of its circumstances, and the real difficulty attending the points which occur in it, require a complete exposition of the principles on which the opinion to be given by the court is founded" (*Marbury* 1803, 154). It would appear that Marshall anticipated the criticism of his opinion. Yet the justification he offered, referring to the "delicacy" of the case and the "novelty" of its circumstances, suggests that the claims of doctrinalism have their limits: that sometimes courts must step beyond the confines that doctrinalism seeks to establish.

Marshall's proffer of justification should alert us that the normative assumptions of doctrinalism are not a given in *Marbury* but are in fact at issue in the case. They are part of a critical tension between the contending conceptions of the American political order that animated the debate swirling around the Court. To understand *Marbury* fully, we must appreciate the decision not simply as deciding a legal dispute between Marbury and Madison but as a political act contributing to the establishment of a discourse of constitutionalism in which the realms of law and politics merge. This understanding demands a close reading of *Marbury* in light of the circumstances that gave it delicacy and novelty.

The second part of this chapter describes the bitter clash between Federalists and Republicans over repeal of the 1801 Judiciary Act and the conflicting views of the parties over the proper role of the federal government and the federal courts. The third part describes how the Federalists turned to the courts after the act was repealed. The fourth part analyzes *Marbury* in the context of these political battles. The fifth part explains *Marbury*'s current significance.

The Politics of Repeal

The national judiciary during the late 1790s had earned the enmity of Jeffersonian Republicans by aggressively favoring the government in prosecutions under the Alien and Sedition Act. When, in the waning days of John Adams's presidency, the Federalists pushed the 1801 Judiciary Act through Congress, thereby creating sixteen new circuit court judgeships immediately filled by Adams with loyal Federalists, they ensured that the judiciary would be a focal point of partisan conflict under the entering Jefferson administration.

Jefferson's Message

President Jefferson did not disappoint. His first annual message suggested that the judiciary system, especially as augmented by the new circuit courts, was unnecessary for the limited business federal courts performed. With his remarks, Jefferson placed the judiciary squarely in the middle of a great ideological struggle between Federalist defenders of a strong national government and Jeffersonian champions of the primacy of the states. In Jefferson's view, the expanded judiciary created by the 1801 act did more than merely threaten to displace state courts from their rightful role. It also exemplified a practice—the creation of sinecures to secure the loyalty of those appointed to fill them—that displayed the corruption of the Federalists. That Jefferson viewed the matter in this light is confirmed by a letter written ten days after his annual message, on the day the Supreme Court issued its show-cause order in *Marbury*. He wrote that the Federalists "have retired into the Judiciary as a stronghold . . . and from that battery all the works of Republicanism are to be beaten down and erased" (Jefferson 1903, 302).

The Congressional Response

Jefferson may have hoped to avoid a bitter partisan struggle over repeal of the 1801 act. Events, including the Supreme Court's decision to entertain Marbury's suit against the secretary of state, conspired against him. Republicans in Congress moved with alacrity to push for repeal. A warning of what was to come appeared in a request to the president of the Senate from the editor of the *National Intelligencer,* asking that he be permitted to occupy a position on the floor of the Senate chamber to facilitate the taking of notes of the debate. The request was approved and was duly noted in that staunchly Jeffersonian journal with the comment that the decision to admit the press complied with the true principles of Republican institutions. The legislative debate was quickly defined in terms of two issues: the necessity or expediency of the judicial system established by the 1801 act and the constitutionality of its repeal.

The Uses of the Circuit Courts. Republicans insisted that there was not enough work to occupy the judicial establishment erected by the Federalists, nor was the workload likely to grow to the point of requiring thirty-eight federal judges. Even if the business that fit the constitutional description of the judicial power were to grow, no need existed for an elaborate federal judicial establishment. The state courts would be competent to handle most of the nation's legal business. John Breckenridge, who introduced the repeal motion in the Senate, argued that the judicial powers given to the federal courts were not intended to embrace subjects of litigation that could be left with the state courts. Their jurisdiction was intended for great national and foreign concerns. Abraham Baldwin of Georgia counted among the chief defects of the revised judiciary system that it attempted to draw off business from the state courts to the federal courts. Only by keeping the concerns of the nation few and tightly focused could the experiment with the federal government hope to succeed, Baldwin argued.

The lack of a real need for the new judgeships created by the 1801 act provided the foundation for the claim that its actual purpose was to provide patronage for the president and a position in government from which the Federalists could continue to exert their pernicious influence. Senator Breckenridge spoke for those who were concerned that the creation and manipulation of new courts would corrupt the government. He raised the possibility that those in power would combine to provide handsomely for their friends by creating courts and filling them with those friends.

Although Breckenridge was content to suggest archly that a future corrupt government might abuse the power to create and fill judgeships, Rep. William Giles was less restrained. He characterized the Federalists as people attached to the principle of patronage, in contrast to the Republican adherence to the general interests and attachment to the people at large. Giles saw the 1801 act as a direct Federalist reaction to their anticipated defeat in the presidential election of 1800, an election not fully settled until ten days after the Judiciary Act was passed.

Federalists insisted that the national judiciary was badly organized under the 1789 Judiciary Act. By requiring Supreme Court justices to ride circuit, with all the hazards that travel presented to the health of the traveler as well as to his or her schedule, the 1789 act ensured that the federal circuits would often not sit for a year or more. Litigants were greatly inconvenienced and constrained to submit their federally cognizable disputes to state courts. According to Federalists, the revisions of 1801 were necessary to render the national judiciary capable of undertaking that caseload, which was sure to increase with the growth of the country's commercial activities. Some, like

Gouverneur Morris, went so far as to insist that the Constitution required the creation of inferior federal courts in which American citizens could exercise their right to have cases falling within the national judicial power heard by the national courts.

The circuit duties of the Supreme Court justices provided proponents of the 1801 reform with two additional arguments. First, justices had complained from the outset of the rigors laid on them by circuit riding. Some had resigned. Others declined appointment, citing the difficulty of travel. Morris stated that candidates for the bench required less the learning of a judge than the agility of a postboy. Second, the old circuit system was flawed because it required judges to sit on appeals of cases in which they had presided at trial. Although the Supreme Court had informally adopted a practice by which justices would not participate in appeals of cases in which they had been involved originally, it was sometimes necessary for all available justices to participate to have a quorum. In any event, the closeness of the association among the judges made it unlikely that they would reverse a decision of one of their number.

The Constitutionality of Repeal. The constitutional argument centered on the Federalist claim that repeal, with the consequent removal of the sixteen newly commissioned circuit judges from office, would violate the constitutional guarantee of good behavior tenure for judges. Morris presented the core of the Federalist position to the Senate in a speech that set the emotional tone of the debate. Repeal would have the effect of subjecting judges to the will and pleasure of the legislature. It would sacrifice the check against unconstitutional laws that the Constitution had vested in the courts.

For Morris, the repeal effort was not simply a legislative initiative of dubious constitutionality. It was the spearhead of a program designed to break down the carefully constructed constitutional barriers to factional politics. The checks built into the electoral process, originally intended to ensure that only the best individuals would be chosen to serve in the elective branches, had already failed. Only the judiciary remained, holding the threat of a veto of legislative or executive overreaching.

Morris might not have denied the Jeffersonian claim that the Federalists had retreated into the judiciary. However, he would have insisted that this was the right thing to do. The judiciary represented the last hope for preserving the Constitution against the onslaught of the Jeffersonian faction. He would certainly dispute the implicit charge that the Federalists were acting as a faction, pursuing narrow self-interest rather than the interest of the whole.

The Republican rejoinder to the charge of unconstitutionality took various forms. Breckenridge, anticipating the charge, insisted in his opening remarks that the 1801 act itself had established a legislative construction of the Constitution by abolishing existing inferior courts and establishing new ones, implicitly supporting the authority of Congress to abolish judicial offices. Federalists resisted this reasoning, insisting that the 1801 act gave no authority to remove any judge from office. But to the degree that the analogy was persuasive it allowed Breckenridge to argue that either Congress had the power to abolish judicial offices or the 1801 act itself was unconstitutional and so should be repealed.

Breckenridge and others also argued that the good-behavior tenure guarantee was intended only as a check on the president's power to remove judges and not as a limit on the exercise of legislative power. In the House John Randolph of Virginia took the position that the constitutionality of the repeal depended on the motivation of the legislature. Only if the intent of the repeal was to get rid of the particular judges was it problematic. So long as it was directed at abolishing useless offices it was unexceptionable.

Senator Baldwin of Georgia objected that the Federalists were relying improperly on arguments from the abuse of power. A Congress bent on overwhelming the independence of the judges had other means at hand, including the power to assign onerous duties and thereby force resignations. All that the present bill involved was an exercise of ordinary legislative power to fashion a judiciary well adapted to the circumstances of the country. Baldwin was willing to concede a salary for life to the judges whose offices were eliminated, if that was what the Constitution required.

By establishing a connection with the argument for protecting the independence of judges, Federalist opponents of repeal made judicial authority to review acts of Congress for constitutionality an important theme of the repeal debates. For the most part, both argument and voting on repeal of the Judiciary Act followed strictly partisan lines. A closely divided Senate, where the Republican victory in the 1800 elections had less effect owing to the six-year term of office, passed the bill 16 to 15. In the House, where the Jefferson–Burr ticket's coattails swept broadly, the bill carried 59 to 32. Opinion on the nature of judicial review, however, did not follow party lines.

Competing Theories of Judicial Review

Of those who spoke to the question, a clear majority, including many Jeffersonians, acknowledged that courts could legitimately declare an act of Congress unconstitutional. In some instances, this took the form of denying that judges could declare a law null and void while admitting that they could legitimately refuse to execute a law that they thought to be unconstitutional. By drawing this distinction some Republicans suggested that the Federalists were advocating a general judicial superintendence of legislative action, not necessarily tied to a judge's duty to decide a case. Whether they actually believed this or were making the suggestion for political effect is not clear.

Even if opinion on judicial review did not divide along strict party lines, it was nonetheless deeply divided. The division is nowhere better displayed than in an exchange between Breckenridge and Morris near the end of the Senate debate. Breckenridge began by challenging the claim that the Constitution gave the courts authority over the acts of the legislature. He asked where the courts got the power and who was to check the courts. No clause of the Constitution granted the power. A power of such significance should not rest on construction.

Morris, a master of melodrama, according to Henry Adams, seized the opportunity to respond to Breckenridge's remarks. He insisted the power of the courts came from an authority higher than the Constitution. It was implicit in the very nature of law. Those who denied that could also be expected to violate the very specific provisions of the Constitution, such as the prohibitions on bills of attainder and ex post facto laws. Denial of judicial authority was an endorsement of unconstrained legislative supremacy.

Thus, the line of battle was drawn between a judiciary armed with the power of construction reaching out to subjugate the legislature and thereby assume direction of the government and a legislature untrammeled by constitutional limits, overwhelming the states and usurping the sovereignty of the people. Senator Baldwin's stricture against arguments from abuse fell on deaf ears on both sides of the aisle. The assumption that virtue would give way to self-seeking, that power would be abused, was too deeply embedded in the foundations of American political thought to be swayed by mere adjuration.

Each side claimed the final authority to interpret the Constitution, and metonymically the Constitution itself, for the branch within its own control. Each painted the other branch with the sins of the faction that supported it. The evils that would attend the wrong resolution of this dispute faithfully reflected each side's view of the particular political vice represented by the other.

The Role of Classical Republican Thought

From the beginning of the Republic, Federalists and Republicans had drawn on the common inheritance of classical republican thought to characterize the dangers posed by the other side. To each side, the other represented faction—what Madison called the "Republican disease." On the Jeffersonian account, the Federalists represented the forces of monarchism. For John Taylor of Caroline, an important spokesperson for the opposition in the 1790s, the Federalists constituted a "party," a confederation of individuals concerned to benefit themselves rather than being committed to the public good.

The Republican critique of Federalism was carried forward into Jefferson's legislative program. He moved to repeal internal taxes, reduce the military and the diplomatic corps, and set the course for early repayment of the national debt. Repeal of the 1801 Judiciary Act was just a piece of the attack on the Federalists' corrupt and corrupting edifice of government.

The Federalist account of abuses to be expected from a legislature unchecked by judicial review closely tracks the litany of state legislative abuse that fired the movement for adoption of the Constitution. Widely acknowledged weaknesses in the Confederation government provided the occasion for calling the Constitutional Convention, but the "excesses of democracy" that characterized the state governments provided the most compelling reason for the choice of a strong national government as the means of rectifying the Confederation weaknesses. Prominent among the "excesses of democracy" were paper money acts, stay laws, and other forms of debtor-relief legislation.

The Federalists had hoped that structural characteristics would protect the national government from the ravages of democracy. The success of the Jeffersonians in the 1800 election had dashed that hope. The judiciary alone remained, and the independence that kept it free from democratic taint was threatened by the repeal of the 1801 Judiciary Act. In making the case for judicial review, Federalists described the constitutional violations that could be expected from an unchecked legislature. These examples tied their case for judicial review to their fear of democracy and its consequences—

factional warfare and the abandoned pursuit of popular favor through measures that sacrificed private rights. The Federalists gave prominent place in their arguments to the possibility of legislative impositions of bills of attainder and ex post facto laws, as well as suspension of habeas corpus. Each of these protections had found its way into the Constitution as a response to the factional wars that had sundered British society. Equally prominent were fears of laws impairing the obligation of contracts or violating the public faith, which meant laws interfering with either public or private debt.

The Federalist charge that an unchecked legislature would violate private rights was not allowed to rest as a speculative possibility. It was made part of the Federalist case against repeal in a more direct way. The Federalists claimed that the judges who were to be displaced by the repeal held their positions by contract. To deprive them of their compensation and life tenure would not only transgress a specified limitation on legislative power but would violate private rights. The Republicans claimed that the power to eliminate the courts was simply an instance of the general principle that whatever one legislature can do, another can undo; no legislature can bind its successor. The Federalists flatly denied this principle.

This element of the argument has special significance for understanding the form of Marshall's opinion in *Marbury*. By treating the constitutional provisions securing the tenure and salary of judges as contractual terms, the Federalists were playing on the connection, settled in Republican political thought, between the security of property and the capacity to function as a virtuous, independent member of the political community. Identification of the judges' claim as contractual had practical, as well as ideological, significance. Breaches of contract were the stuff of lawsuits. The Federalists contemplated a legal challenge to the repeal, should it pass.

Another ideological element of the Federalist defense of judicial review is suggested by arguments that they did not make, or made only in muted fashion. The Bill of Rights made only one significant appearance in the Federalist catalogue of legislative violations to be feared. Ironically, it came when Rep. Benjamin Huger from South Carolina enlisted St. George Tucker, a noted Republican legal scholar, in the defense of the 1801 Judiciary Act. Tucker was quoted for the proposition that the courts alone could relieve citizens from the effect of laws invading rights of religious exercise, free speech, assembly, or bearing arms.

Despite the force of this Federalist argument, the most prominent use of the Bill of Rights in the debate was by the Republicans. The latter used the judicial role in enforcing the Alien and Sedition Act as a taunting symbol of the fecklessness of relying on judges to defend against tyranny.

Federalist deployment of federalism arguments—arguments that cited the importance of judicial review as a means of preserving the states against national encroachments—were common in the House. Nevertheless, the use of such arguments was probably more a matter of political expedience than deep conviction. Likewise, in the Senate debate, Morris first raised the fear of a national legislature overwhelming the states in his response to Breckenridge on the last day of the debate. These words ring hollow in the mouth of the great nationalist, who in the Constitutional Convention had said, "State attachments, and State importance have been the bane of this Country. We cannot annihilate; but we may perhaps take out the teeth of the serpents" (Madison 1966, 241).

States' rights would become a preserve of the Federalists as they tried on the garb of not-so-loyal opposition to Jefferson's embargo and Madison's war. Perhaps Morris's newfound solicitude for the future of the states reflected a realization, as the result of the debate became clear, of the end of Federalist control in national councils.

If the Federalist defense of judicial review exhibited their fear of partisan, democratic politics—faction in Jeffersonian dress—the Republican opposition similarly reflected their fear of corrupted and dependent partisans in office—faction in Federalist garb. Those Jeffersonians opposing judicial review clearly feared that the judges whose positions had been secured by corrupt party action would use the bench to pursue the aggrandizement of the national government at the expense of the states and Federalist projects to the detriment of republicanism.

Republicans, like Federalists, had to rethink their arguments as the atmosphere changed. Their rejection of the notion of constitutional interpretation resting in the hands of a Federalist judiciary must have had another significant dimension for Jeffersonians. From their resistance to Alexander Hamilton's fiscal plan in the early 1790s, Jeffersonians had claimed strict construction of the Constitution as the justification for their actions.

In the repeal debate, the Republicans now were the party of power rather than the party of opposition. They were being challenged on grounds that they hitherto had considered their own. The Republicans had indulged in some "wire-drawn constructions" when defending against the Federalist claim that repeal would violate the judicial-tenure provisions of the Constitution. They were experiencing what J. G. A. Pocock described as "the recurrent problem of all Country parties[:] that they could not take office without falsifying their own ostensible values" (Pocock 1975, 409). The conceit of each party was the belief that it was the true representative of the public good, and that with power in its hands exercised for the common good there would be no legitimate opposition. Were the Constitution to fall into the hands of Federalist judges, the Federalists would secure the benefit of a kind of legitimacy that had been the cornerstone of the Jeffersonian opposition. It is not surprising, then, that a key element of Jeffersonian opposition to judicial review was the principle of "responsibility," understood to require political accountability.

Although Federalists claimed that judicial review by an independent judiciary was necessary to protect the people from their own worst enemies—themselves—they also appealed to the people as authors of the Constitution that established limits on the authority of their agent, the legislature. They reinforced this appeal by relying on examples of constitutional violations by the legislature where no interpretation was apparently required to ascertain the violation: bills of attainder and ex post facto laws, suspension of *habeas corpus,* and clearly prohibited taxes and export duties.

Responsibility, Common Law, and Federalism

Republicans responded by asserting that representatives of the people were to be trusted much more than unelected and only remotely responsible judges with interpreting the "people's statute." Rep. Robert Williams of North Carolina made the point that mistakes by elected officials could be corrected at the next election. Mistakes by judges, protected for life in their jobs, could be corrected only by resort to revolutionary principles.

Judicial performance in enforcing the Alien and Sedition Act provided the cautionary example for the Republican case. As Representative Randolph described it, far from protecting the people against unconstitutional fettering of the press, the courts had reached out to the common law of England to extend the coverage of the act.

The issue of responsibility connected the matter of judicial review to the question of whether the common law of England should apply in federal courts, even if properly adapted for American circumstances. The willingness of some federal judges to apply the common law of seditious libel in instances not covered by the Alien and Sedition Act had infuriated Republicans, whose newspapers were the primary target of Federalist prosecutions. Virginia representative Philip Thompson said that he had no great fear of usurpation by the legislative or executive branches because they were both periodically responsible to the people for their offices. But he insisted that a judiciary armed with the power to declare laws null and void and with the common-law powers of English judges would render the legislature powerless.

Rep. John Milledge of Georgia read into the record a letter from John Dickinson, the "Pennsylvania farmer," denouncing the common law as a source of "sophistical argumentations" that had insulted the understanding of America and would "turn judges into legislators, and trustees into usurpers" (*Annals of Congress* 1802, 796).

Federalists might insist, echoing Hamilton's argument in *Federalist* No. 78, that the judiciary, having neither purse nor sword, was not to be feared. To the Republicans, if the judges wielded a general common-law authority, they were sufficiently armed to be dangerous. Such common-law authority made plausible the Republican claim that the Federalists had retreated into the judiciary to do battle against Jeffersonian Republicanism.

Introducing Marbury

The case of *Marbury v. Madison* then pending in the Supreme Court was the object of some discussion in the repeal debate. Republicans cited the issuance of a show-cause order in the case as evidence of judicial ambition. Federalists argued that not to issue the order would place the president above the law, while cautioning that the show-cause order was only preliminary, deciding nothing.

Enactment of the repeal act did not, by any means, end the debate. Congress returned to the subject of the judiciary at the end of the legislative session. The announced objective was to address the details of transition from the system created by the 1801 act back to the 1789 system. One of these "details" modified the terms of the Supreme Court so it would meet annually in February rather than twice a year in June and December. The Republican majority implemented the change by canceling the Court's upcoming June term. The next meeting of the Court would be after the justices had to decide whether to resume their circuit-riding duties. Federalists charged that the change was actually designed to deny the

Court an early opportunity to consider challenges to the constitutionality of the repeal. It has been supposed that the Republicans wished to delay a decision in *Marbury*. There is no evidence in the debates, however, that either side believed that *Marbury* would provide the vehicle for a challenge to the repeal.

Federalist Attacks on Repeal

True to their principles, the politically defeated Federalists turned to the courts for vindication. In the months between passage of the repeal act and the convening of the Supreme Court for the February 1803 term, Federalist strategists attempted to bring the constitutionality of the repeal before the Court in three ways. Each device failed.

The Federalists first attempted to recruit their allies on the Court as active participants in this challenge by inducing them to refuse to resume their circuit-riding duties. Oliver Wolcott of Connecticut, one of the dispossessed circuit judges, outlined the strategy. The Supreme Court justices would refuse to perform the duty of circuit judges. The circuit judges would then sit to hear argument on whether they had been abolished. That would set the stage for a final decision of the Supreme Court on appeal.

At first, Marshall assured other Federalists that the justices of the Supreme Court would stand firm if the matter of the circuit judges were brought before them. However, after extensive correspondence, in which Justice Chase argued most aggressively against resumption of circuit-riding duties, the justices concluded that congressional authority to assign the duties of judges, and the constitutionality of Supreme Court justices holding circuit courts, had been decided by the practice of the Court since 1789 and could not now be challenged. This conclusion was crucially dependent on Marshall's position that the only constitutional question involved the authority of Congress to assign circuit duties to Supreme Court justices. A separate constitutional issue, unaddressed by Marshall, centers on the constitutionality of displacing circuit judges—a question that certainly was not settled by earlier practice. With the justices' decision to take up their circuit duties, one avenue of attack on the repeal collapsed.

A second effort involved challenges to the jurisdiction of the reconstituted circuit courts in cases that initially had been brought in the circuit courts created under the 1801 Judiciary Act. This effort was laid to rest by the Supreme Court's decision in *Stuart v. Laird* (1803), handed down one week after *Marbury*. It was actually defeated, however, by the justices' rejection of the challenge in their capacities as circuit judges. Marshall himself had rejected the argument in *Stuart* at the circuit level and did not participate formally in the Supreme Court's adjudication of the issue.

The third effort to challenge the constitutionality of the repeal sought redress from the very Congress that had done the dirty deed. A widely circulated essay protesting the repeal, written by Richard Bassett, paved the way. Bassett was a judge of the Third Circuit and the father-in-law of Federalist stalwart congressman James Bayard. The essay was followed by a memorial to Congress, signed by eleven of the dispossessed judges. The memorialists sought to be assigned duties consistent with their commissions as judges and an opportunity to submit to judicial resolution their claims for compensation.

The House of Representatives gave short shrift to the memorial, rejecting it on the very day it was submitted. The Senate, however, took the puzzling step of referring it to a committee consisting of Morris, Jonathan Dayton, and James Ross, all strong Federalists. The committee returned a proposal that the attorney general be directed to institute an action in the nature of *quo warranto,* testing the claim to office of the judges and their right to compensation. This proposal heaped insult on injury. It suggested that Congress had acted unconstitutionally in eliminating the circuit courts. It also triggered Republican sensitivities to the common-law pretensions of the federal courts. By directing the attorney general to act, the proposal appeared to involve Congress in the same kind of intrusion into the affairs of another branch that had brought Republican fire to bear on Marbury's mandamus action. After a day of debate, the Senate rejected the proposal on a party-line vote.

Marbury

By the time Marbury's petition was heard, the battle over repeal had been lost. There remained only the formal announcement, due the next week in the Court's affirmance of Marshall's action in *Stuart v. Laird* (1803). There were signs, however, that the problems for the embattled Federalist judges were only beginning. Congress had initiated the impeachment of district judge John Pickering. The common understanding was that Pickering's impeachment would be a test of strength for a Republican effort to cleanse the judiciary of the taint of Federalist irredentists. That threat would later prove sufficiently worrisome to lead Marshall, in the throes of the Chase impeachment, to suggest that the doctrine of impeachment should give way to legislative review of judicial decisions.

By February 1803, the office of justice of the peace in the District of Columbia, to which Marbury had been appointed, was a sorry little thing. It had been stripped of many of its functions, as well as the power to demand compensation for services rendered, by the act organizing a government for the District. Even the claimants acknowledged that if not for principle, they would hardly be interested in the job.

However, the case was a different matter. It was identified with the repeal issue, primarily because of Republican insistence that, in issuing a show-cause order, the Court had demonstrated its willingness (that of the Federalist judges) to intrude improperly on the functions of the executive. From the Federalist perspective, certainly from Marshall's perspective, Jefferson's way of dealing with the undelivered commissions was of a piece with sweeping away judges in the repeal act—a willful disregard of private right in service to a political purpose.

The administration's participation in the case was marginal and came grudgingly. The secretary of state was not represented by counsel. Marbury's effort to prove the status of his commission was made difficult by the reluctant and partial testimony of State Department officials and by the Senate's refusal to provide a copy of its journal showing consent to his appointment.

Jefferson had let it be known that he considered all Adams's appointments made after Adams knew the outcome of the presidential elections on December 12, 1800, to be an outrage. Except for those judges holding life appointments and therefore not removable, Jefferson indicated his intention to treat the appointments as nullities. These pronouncements were certainly sufficient to alert the Court to the possibility that any order to the administration on Marbury's behalf might be ignored.

According to one widely held view, Marshall made a virtue of necessity. Rather than simply announcing the Court's lack of jurisdiction, Marshall used the potential conflict between Court and president to draw attention away from his real objective—the establishment of judicial review. This account, however, is inconsistent with Marshall's timorousness regarding conflict with the other branches, as reflected in his cautious action respecting the repeal of the Judiciary Act. The voice that sounds most insistently in the early passages of *Marbury* is that of Marshall's devoutly Federalist colleague, Chase.

"Has the Applicant a Right to the Commission He Demands?"

According to the common account, the Court's discussion of Marbury's right to the commission was a gratuitous but strategic tweaking of Jefferson. Others have viewed it as a demonstration of the necessity of judicial review. Either reading obscures how the initial part of the opinion pursues an aggressively Federalist line of constitutional interpretation in which judicially protected rights displace an arguably legitimate claim to executive political authority.

Marshall's opinion establishing Marbury's right to the commission exemplifies the kind of judicial performance that the Jeffersonians found most objectionable. The opinion consists of little more than bare assertions, heavily camouflaged by constitutional reference and common-law analogy. The structure of Marshall's argument, which determines the existence of a right before examining the question of remedy, is not simply a statement of the proper ordering of judicial reasoning. The action is for mandamus, the essence of which is to delineate the border between law and politics. The first question is whether Marbury's commission, having been signed and sealed, passed from the domain of politics and discretion into the realm of legal right. The answer to Marshall's first question will inexorably draw with it the answer to the second: whether Marbury has a remedy.

Had Madison been represented before the Court, his argument would likely have reflected the position that Jefferson later took in describing *Marbury* as "not law." It is well known that Jefferson chided Marshall for discussing the merits of the case after deciding that the Court was without jurisdiction. But Jefferson's fire was not limited to the breach of judicial propriety. He was equally concerned with denouncing the substance of the decision.

Jefferson grounded his criticism in what he perceived as the strict independence of the three branches of government. He fixed on delivery as the point of effectiveness of a commission, drawing an analogy to the common-law requirement of delivery for an effective deed, but he defended that position on the ground that the Constitution intended that the three great branches of the government should be coordinate and independent of each other. The absence of any constitutionally provided means for compelling the executive to deliver or to record a commission demonstrated, Jefferson believed, that the judiciary was to have no control over the executive in such matters. Less mischief would result from respecting the independence of each branch in its own domain than from giving any branch control over the others.

Perhaps abetted by Madison's absence, the Court completely abstracted Marbury's claim of a right to the commission. Despite the early nod to the "peculiar delicacy" and "novelty" of the circumstances of the case, there was little in the part of the opinion concerning Marbury's right to the commission to suggest that the Court appreciated that it was examining the conduct of a coordinate branch of government rather than that of private parties.

The circumstances of Marbury's case—particularly the dissatisfaction of a new president with the last appointments of a predecessor—are about the only circumstances in which one can imagine the problem arising. The great virtue of Jefferson's position was not his insistence on the radical independence of the branches of government (a stance fraught with difficulties for the effective functioning of government) but its practical usefulness in avoiding conflict over matters of little significance. The Court expressed some concern that if delivery were required for effectiveness, a president would be unable to make an appointment without the cooperation of others. But this was not a case in which the president was being denied an appointment by a renegade clerk in the secretary of state's office, and it is hard to imagine that as a problem requiring judicial intervention. As the Court well knew, Marbury's commission was being withheld at the direction of the president.

Similar objections may be levied against the Court's facile dismissal of the possibility that the justices of the peace were removable at the president's discretion. In arguing that Marbury and the others were beyond the president's control, Charles Lee claimed first that they were judicial officers holding office for five years independent of the will of the president, and then proceeded to claim that they held their appointments forever under the Constitution. The importance of their independence lay in the fact that they exercised most of the day-to-day legal authority in the District of Columbia. Lee emphasized that the people of the District were worried by the stretch of power by the secretary of state in exercising control over the justices.

Profound difficulties inhered in Lee's argument that justices of the peace were Article III judges enjoying life tenure. Not only was the justices' term of office limited by the statute creating the office, the same statute also authorized the president to appoint such number of justices as he should from time to time think necessary. If the justices were Article III judges, this could be thought to effectively delegate to the president the power reserved to Congress to create inferior courts. Furthermore, the statute had not provided for compensation of the justices beyond empowering them to charge for services rendered, and that authority had been withdrawn before the hearing in *Marbury*. Finally, the assigned responsibilities of the justices well-exceeded ordinary judicial duties—the only proper function of Article III judges, according to the invalid pensioner cases.

Marshall's apparent conclusion that the judicial appointment for a term of years barred removal was also problematic. In 1789 Congress had implicitly acknowledged the power of the president to remove executive appointees from office, but only after some assiduous parliamentary maneuvering by Madison. The scope of the so-called decision of 1789 was indeterminate, but Marshall elected to ignore that well-known instance of congressional resolution of a constitutional issue. Marshall simply presumed that Congress intended, by setting the term of the justices at five years, to limit the president's removal power. If the independence of the justices was the primary concern of Congress, then some security of tenure, even if only five years, was a rational provision. Yet both the failure to provide for compensation other than from the parties and the President's carte blanche authority to create more justices suggest that independence was not of paramount concern to Congress. Why else might Congress fix a term for the justices, other than to limit the president's discretionary power of removal? Perhaps it was to make clear that it was not creating an inferior U.S. Court, whose appointees would be entitled to the protections of Article III, or perhaps to ensure a regular review of the performance of these officers who exercised a significant degree of political power. If Congress did not intend to limit the president's removal power by limiting the terms of the justices, Marshall's resolution of the constitutional issue was, as critics have recognized, both unduly casual and gratuitous.

Marshall's primary argument concerning Marbury's right to the commission was based on a constitutionally derived distinction between the president's appointing and commissioning powers. The separate mention of the two powers was made to order for Marbury's situation. Marshall drove a wedge between appointment and commission by noting that the president may be required to commission officers he does not appoint. He then inferred that the commission must be evidence of the appointment, rather than the appointment itself, and moved out in search of the act that actually constitutes the appointment. He asserted that the appointment must be complete once the president performs the last required act, signing the commission. This conclusion rested not on analysis of reasons for the distinction between appointment and commission but on bare assertion.

Marshall's justification for this conclusion was announced in the next paragraph. "Some point of time must be taken, when the power of the executive over an officer, not removable at his will, must cease" (*Marbury* 1803, 157). Of course that is true, lest the concept of "not removable" lose all meaning. But there is little to recommend the particular time chosen by the Court, over, say, the delivery of the commission to the appointee. The Court's choice carried with it the potential for serious proof problems and invited a battle the Court seemed destined to lose.

The framing assumption for Marshall's analysis of Marbury's claim was the notion that the commission, and ultimately the office, is a species of property. The footprints of the repeal controversy are all over this assumption. In finding a right to the commissions, against the claim of political authority implicit in Jefferson's withholding of the commissions, the Court drew a parallel with the cases of the circuit judges "dispossessed" by the political decision to abolish their offices. The Federalists had finally settled on the property rights of the judges as the best ground on which to challenge the repeal but had failed in their efforts to secure a forum to hear their claims. Marbury's case provided the vehicle for vindicating the principles that, from a Federalist perspective, condemned the repeal.

The rights of the circuit judges provided the last line of Federalist defense against the Jeffersonian attack on the judicial system. These rights symbolized the generality of rights that the Federalists fully expected to be trampled in the stampede of unprincipled politicians seeking popular favor. As the foundation of judicial independence, they were also the last remaining barrier to the stampede.

The issue was equally freighted on the other side. As the Republicans viewed it, the appointments of the justices were among the last desperate efforts of a corrupt and dying regime to maintain a position of power. Should the "rights" of the justices prevail, it would be yet another example of the capacity of courts to manipulate the law in ways subversive of justice and the public good.

"Do the Laws of His Country Afford Him a Remedy?"

The parallel between the cases of the justices and the circuit judges extends powerfully into the next section of the *Marbury* opinion. The question there was whether the law provided a remedy for the right denied by withholding the commissions. Lest anyone be misled into believing that the case involved just a minor squabble over an insignificant office, Marshall made clear what was really at stake.

The very essence of civil liberty certainly consists in the right of every individual to claim the protection of the laws, whenever he receives an injury. . . .

The government of the United States has been emphatically termed a government of laws, and not of men. It will certainly cease to deserve this high appellation, if the laws furnish no remedy for the violation of a vested legal right. (*Marbury* 1803, 163)

Given the Court's conclusion that Marbury had a remedy, albeit not from the court to which he had applied, the heavy portentousness of these passages seems out of place. However, the question of a remedy for the circuit judges had been before the Senate in the days immediately preceding the Court's consideration of *Marbury*. On February 3, 1803, the Senate received a report from the committee appointed to consider the memorial of the circuit judges, who sought assignment to judicial duties and provision for their salaries. The committee proposed a resolution to the president, asking for institution of a legal proceeding in the nature of *quo warranto*, a common-law writ, against Bassett, to try his right to the office and salary that he claimed. Notwithstanding Morris's insistence to the Senate that there were other ways to bring the question before the courts, the absence of an appropriate forum for judicial examination of the repeal act was a major problem for the Federalists.

When the justices of the Supreme Court deliberated about how to respond to the repeal, particularly the requirement that they resume riding circuit in place of the ousted circuit judges, the lack of a remedy for the circuit judges was a prominent consideration in Justice Chase's efforts to convince his colleagues to refuse to hold the circuit courts. In a letter to Marshall, Chase wrote that the repealing act, to the degree that it affected the appoint-

ment, commission, office, or salary of the circuit court judges, was contrary to the Constitution and therefore void. If the issue could be brought before the Supreme Court by an appropriate action, he would so hold. Unfortunately, the laws passed by Congress had not authorized an appropriate action, leaving the circuit court judges without a remedy.

The reason for the defect of remedy returns to one central issue of the repeal debate: whether the federal courts could have recourse to the common law. The Morris committee's recommendation, proposing an action in the nature of *quo warranto*, raised this specter. The Jeffersonians were quick to respond. As they saw it, a resort to common-law remedies in this case was the first step toward a regime of judge-made law of the sort the American Revolution had left behind.

Set against this background, Marshall's argument stands forth as yet another iteration of the basic Federalist position, captured by one partisan in the sobriquet, "There must be much law or there will be no justice" (Kerber 1970, 171). The common law was precisely what Marshall had in mind as the necessary insurance of the reputation of the country's jurisprudence. William Blackstone, that oracle of Tory principles, was called to witness for the fundamental right to appeal to the common law "for all possible injuries whatsoever" (*Marbury* 1803, 163, citing William Blackstone).

Marshall, however, quickly set aside the question of the availability of common-law remedies. *Marbury* did not require resort to the common law. The appropriate remedy was available by legislative provision. Marshall then turned his attention to the issue that had aroused disputants since the issuance of the show-cause order: whether the proceeding improperly intruded on the domain of executive action. As was the case in the repeal debates, the battle would be fought on the terrain of anticipated abuses of power.

The Republican position had been articulated a few weeks before, in the Senate debates over whether to grant Marbury's request for a copy of the Senate journal showing his confirmation. According to Sen. Robert Wright, the certificate of the journal entry was requested in an audacious attempt to pry into executive secrets by a tribunal with no authority. It was an effort by enemies of the president to enable the judiciary to exercise authority over the president.

These charges echoed an argument advanced in the repeal debate, where the issuance of the show-cause order in *Marbury* was linked explicitly to claims of judicial authority to review acts of the legislature for constitutionality, as well as claims to common-law jurisdiction. Jeffersonians viewed the claims as demonstrating the judiciary's thirst for power.

The general tone of Marshall's response was conciliatory. Here, and again in his discussion of mandamus, he posited a distinction between discretionary functions of the executive, for which the president is accountable only politically, and legislatively imposed duties, for which he may be held accountable at law. Marshall disclaimed judicial authority to examine acts in the domain of executive discretion. As he entered into the analysis of mandamus, he explicitly noted that in the circumstances of the case, some considered the suit "an attempt to intrude into the cabinet, and to intermeddle with the prerogatives of the executive," but he strongly denied any such "absurd and excessive" pretensions (*Marbury* 1803, 170).

Notwithstanding the conciliatory move, Marshall's adherence to core Federalist doctrine was unwavering. The line between discretion and duty was to be drawn by law, and law is the province of the judiciary. The reach of Marshall's claim to authority was belied by the examples he offered: a secretary of war refusing to place on the pension list an invalid whose entitlement to the pension he had previously certified; a secretary of state withholding a land patent granted by the president. Neither example presented a claim of independent executive authority. Yet the Court asserted a right to decide just such a claim, and did so, in *Marbury.*

Earlier in the opinion, Marshall had given the impression that the secretary of state's duties concerning the commissions were statutorily prescribed. The two examples he used to demonstrate the amenability of cabinet officers to legal process both involved statutorily imposed duties. But the duty involved in *Marbury* was not, as Marshall admitted, statutorily prescribed. It was the product of judicial inference from arguable constitutional premises.

That Marshall thought necessary to note the absence of a statutory mandate suggests its importance. If one were inclined to be concerned about both the potential for unconstrained executive officers trampling the rights of innocent citizens and an unbridled judiciary insinuating itself in executive matters, limitation of the mandamus remedy to violations of statutorily prescribed duty might appear an inviting solution. But Marshall gave not one inch as he insisted that the determination of rights was the special prerogative of the judiciary.

It has often been remarked that the immediate response to *Marbury* attended more to the Court's treatment of the commission than to its assertion of judicial review. In the view of some, this is evidence of Marshall's genius for distracting the opposition while stealing a march. But properly understood, there was no distraction at all. Both the question of Marbury's right to the commission and the question of the Court's jurisdiction involved conflict with another branch's claim of authority. Of the two questions, the conclusion regarding the Judiciary Act could easily be seen as involving less of a reach by the Court both because it was necessary to the result in the case and because it involved the Court's view of a matter—jurisdiction—which even many critics of the Court's ambitions conceded to be within its authority. Far from distracting the Jeffersonians from their target, it served to sustain a degree of fear and hatred that culminated in the impeachment of Justice Chase.

"Is It a Mandamus Issuing from This Court?"

Twenty-one pages into a twenty-eight-page opinion, Marshall finally came to the jurisdictional issue on which Marbury's case foundered. His interpretations of Section 13 of the Judiciary Act of 1789 and Article III of the Constitution yielded the conclusion that the Court was without jurisdiction. Marbury was left to seek his remedy elsewhere.

It is widely assumed that this particular conjunction of labored readings was in service of Marshall's dual objectives of establishing judicial review while avoiding direct conflict with Jefferson over enforcement of the Court's mandate. The statutory reading was necessary to reach the constitutional issue. The constitutional reading was necessary to avoid the con-

flict and provided the occasion for the Supreme Court's first pronouncement of its authority to review acts of Congress for constitutionality.

In light of the controversy in which *Marbury* was so deeply embedded, this is certainly a plausible account of Marshall's strategy. It does not, however, require that Marshall be credited as a visionary. The immediate stakes for the Federalists in judicial review were very high, and not simply because they had an entrenched position in the judiciary. The Constitution, in the years leading up to the electoral "revolution" of 1800, had become a mainstay of Jeffersonian political criticism. By wrapping themselves in the Constitution, outspoken critics blunted charges of disloyalty.

The opposition to judicial review was grounded on an appeal to the electorate as the ultimate authority on the meaning of the Constitution. Stated otherwise, the Jeffersonian counter to the doctrine of judicial review was not a claim to legislative supremacy but the doctrine of legislative responsibility to the people. Judicial review provided the Federalists with a way to drive a wedge between the people and the Constitution, as well as between the legislature and the Constitution. In so doing, it preserved a critical purchase for Federalist participation in the political life of the country.

There is also a more mundane explanation for the particular approach that Marshall took to the statutory and constitutional issues regarding jurisdiction. It has been supposed that Marshall sacrificed judicial power through his reading of Article III, and this has been credited to his tactical genius. But the hand of Justice Chase is particularly evident in this portion of the opinion. Chase's letter to Marshall regarding the action that the justices should take in response to the repeal of the 1801 Judiciary Act strongly prefigured aspects of Marshall's argument in *Marbury*. It also suggests reasons why these issues may have had special importance for the Court.

Chase began his argument against the constitutionality of the repeal by insisting that Congress had a duty to create inferior federal courts for the trial of all cases within the Article III definition of the judicial power, albeit a duty without remedy if Congress should fail to act. Integral to his view of congressional duty was the premise that the Supreme Court could not be vested with original jurisdiction in any cases except the few enumerated in Article III. He insisted that the specific vesting of appellate jurisdiction in "all the other Cases before mentioned" (U.S. Constitution, Art. III, sec. 2, para. 2) compelled the conclusion that the Constitution intended to restrict original jurisdiction to the few cases explicitly mentioned.

Chase anticipated the position ultimately taken by the justices—that the constitutionality of Supreme Court justices sitting circuit was settled by past practice—by noting that there was a new element to be considered: The justices would be complicit in the unconstitutional removal of the judges appointed to the circuit courts. Beyond that, Chase claimed not to have given serious consideration to the circuit issue previously, having acted on the basis of his predecessors' practice.

Marshall's argument on the jurisdictional issue in *Marbury* began with a statement verging on Chase's claim that Congress must create inferior federal courts:

The constitution vests the whole judicial power of the United States in one supreme court, and such inferior courts as congress shall, from time to time, ordain and establish. This power is expressly extended to all cases arising under the laws of the United States; and consequently, in some form, may be exercised over the present case; because the right claimed is given by a law of the United States. (*Marbury* 1803, 173–174)

This statement need mean only that Congress must somehow provide, in either original or appellate form, a federal forum for Marbury's claim. But, as Justice Joseph Story would later show in *Martin v. Hunter's Lessee* (1816), it is also amenable to an interpretation making the creation of inferior federal courts mandatory.

The quoted paragraph is a seemingly irrelevant part of the opinion. Nothing turns on it; its only apparent value is as gratuitous advice to Marbury's lawyers. But when joined with the conclusion that Congress cannot add to the original jurisdiction of the Supreme Court, it stands ready, as Chase had shown, to assist the courts if they were confronted with even more serious attacks by a partisan legislature.

At another point in his letter, Chase anticipated such attacks. Having acknowledged the extensive legitimate authority of Congress over the courts, he cautioned that Congress might impose on them unreasonable duties for the purpose of compelling them to resign their offices. During the repeal debates, Republicans had seized on Congress's acknowledged power over the courts as evidence that the Federalist theory of a radically independent judiciary was without merit. If the Court believed that Congress was prepared to launch additional assaults on judicial independence, by manipulation of jurisdiction or other regulation of the workload of the Court, the decision in *Marbury* could provide a valuable precedent in an effort of self-defense. At the very least, it might provide a basis for rejecting additions to the original jurisdiction designed to overwhelm the Court with trivial cases.

This view of the Court's purpose helps to explain, if not justify, two aspects of the Court's treatment of the jurisdictional issue. First, Marshall ignored the "exceptions and regulations" language of Article III. It is true that the clause appears in a sentence referring to the appellate jurisdiction. As Professor William Van Alstyne (1969, 32) has noted, however, that language would have supported a plausible argument that Congress had "excepted" certain cases from the appellate jurisdiction by placing them in the original jurisdiction.

Second, Marshall ignored the Court's own practice in entertaining original mandamus actions and that the Judiciary Act was a product of the First Congress, which generally received deference for its understanding of the Constitution. Oversight is an unlikely explanation. As Bloch and Marcus (1986) have noted, Marshall cited the relevant precedent only a few paragraphs earlier, as he made the case for the propriety of the mandamus remedy. In *Stuart v. Laird*, decided only a few days after *Marbury*, the Court emphasized the interpretive authority of the First Congress and the acquiescent practice of the Court in upholding the constitutionality of the justices sitting on circuit courts. But if *Stuart* was on the Court's mind, it might have served best to remind the justices of the difficulty that antecedent practice, established during a period of friendly relations among the branches, could cause when things turned nasty. The Court's ability to respond adequately to the plight of the circuit judges was limited by that practice, and a number of justices lamented that they had simply followed the practice without thinking. The justices effectively committed themselves to the decision in *Stuart* when they took up their circuit duties. But additional developments, and the opportunity for close consultation, may have convinced them of the need to place some distance between themselves and their predecessors. In a circumspect fashion, that was accomplished by the pointed omissions of *Marbury*.

The political struggle between Federalists and Republicans was powerfully at work as Marshall moved to the closing act of *Marbury*, the defense of judicial review. Marshall introduced his treatment of the issue by remarking that whether an act of Congress contrary to the Constitution could become law was a matter of great interest but "not of an intricacy proportioned to its interest" (*Marbury* 1803, 176). This was a fair indicator of the seriousness that he would accord to arguments against the practice. His vindication of judicial review was the hackneyed litany of the Federalists in the repeal debates, shorn of its rhetorical flair. His examples were of a legislature suffused with power, ignoring its constitutional responsibilities and running roughshod over its enemies with bills of attainder, ex post facto laws, and relaxed evidentiary requirements for treason. His fixation on the abuse of power makes sense only in a political culture rooted in the expectation of declension. Senator Baldwin had cautioned against such arguments in the course of the repeal debates. His caution had fallen on deaf ears on both sides of the aisle then, and the same tenor of argument prevailed in the Court.

To appreciate fully the import of Marshall's argument, it is necessary to consider the position of those who challenged the Court's authority. The most prominent Republican argument was of a piece with the Federalist argument in that it focused on the potential for abuse of judicial power. The Republicans insisted that a judiciary armed with the authority to nullify acts of Congress, and both insulated and isolated from political responsibility, would become the tyrant, bending the nation to its will. Experience with the Alien and Sedition Act provided the exemplar for the Republican vision. It demonstrated a judiciary willing to reach into the common law for ammunition to use against political enemies and the perils of relying on courts to protect constitutional rights.

There was, however, a more moderate Republican argument, voiced effectively by Senator Baldwin in the same speech in which he cautioned against reliance on arguments premised on abuse of power. Marshall's argument was premised on the clear restraints that the Constitution imposed on legislative power. His examples—ex post facto laws, bills of attainder, taxes on exports—all fit the model of abuse of legislative power. According to Marshall, the primary purpose of a written constitution is the imposition of such restraints, and without judicial review these restraints would be destroyed.

Senator Baldwin started from a very different position. He affirmed the great value of written laws and constitutions, while acknowledging that they were not perfect. Although settling many issues, they unavoidably left others afloat, subject to honest differences. Without denying the courts' authority to nullify acts of Congress, Baldwin commended the practice of the government, which had been to settle constitutional issues through legislative constructions. Baldwin's confidence in the political settlement of constitutional issues was tied to a more general confidence in the political process. In countering Federalist charges that the repeal was part of a design to destroy the independence of the judiciary, Baldwin argued that a legal system satisfactory to the people would not be easily changed for political advantage.

The persistent notion, echoing a theme frequently voiced by Republicans in the repeal controversy, was reliance on the good sense of the people as the sustaining force of the Constitution. If the Federalists rested their hopes on the restraints and limits imposed by the Constitution, the Republicans placed their faith in an engaged and vigilant electorate.

In the Federalist lexicon, the people were "their own worst enemies." They would be driven by their passions to the election of demagogues (such as Jefferson, according to the Federalists) who would lead an assault on the rights of the stable and virtuous members of the community (by undermining a national judiciary that was the best guarantor of these rights). Marshall's opinion in *Marbury* was loyal to this vision. He was more politic than Morris, eschewing the "people their own worst enemies" language, but the thought was the same. In the repeal debate, Morris spoke of the ratification of the Constitution as occurring in a moment when "[t]he passions of the people were lulled to sleep" (*Annals* 1802, 40). For Marshall, it was a great exertion of the people, which neither could nor *ought* to be frequently repeated.

The convenient fiction of the sovereign people had served the Federalists well in the ratification debates, as they responded to charges that the new Constitution would substitute a consolidated government for the sovereignty of the states. In *Marbury,* with no apparent appreciation for the irony, the people's sovereignty became the mechanism for dismissing them from a role in preserving (or, given the correctness of Baldwin's observation on the number of structural issues left unresolved by the Constitution, constituting) the fundamental structure of their government. After their mighty exertion, the people should be allowed to slumber.

Marshall and the Federalists were unable or unwilling to see that there was a difference between a legislature that had the final word on constitutional issues and a legislature unchecked by constitutional restraints. Theirs was a bleak view of human nature, epitomized by Morris's proclamation that governments were made "to provide against the follies and vices of men," for "if mankind were reasonable, they would want no Government" (*Annals* 1802, 38). Positing a few absurd examples of a legislature maddened by a hunger for power and indifferent to consequences, the Federalists prepared to ride the frail barque of judicial review into the storm. Only if they were dead wrong in their premises would their vessel have any chance of survival.

Conclusion

Marbury was born out of political defeat. One would expect as much: Victors are not the likely authors of restrictions on their success. Even as *Marbury* attempts to persuade us of the timeless necessity of its reading of the Constitution, it prominently displays the marks of the political struggle within which it was situated.

Because we are all losers at one time or another, *Marbury* remains a central text of American politics. It stands as an assurance that the stakes of the political game will not get too high; that however threatening matters may appear, we rarely have everything at stake. Perhaps the single most profound failure of *Marbury*'s promise, *Dred Scott v. Sandford* (1857), failed on just that count. The black man was without rights, the Congress without power, opponents of slavery without recourse. Lincoln found a way to save the Court from itself, reminding that there is always another day and another case.

When we tell the story of constitutional law, *Marbury* is the beginning. Like most beginnings, however, it is also an ending, a point of transition that sums up the understandings of the past as it opens on to the future. The very fact that we have chosen it as our beginning ensures that its own story, the one of which it is a self-conscious telling, will not be our story, of which it was necessarily ignorant.

The world for which *Marbury* was written was rapidly disappearing. It was a world in which the political energy of the masses could be held in check through an elaborate structure of suffrage limitations and remote representations, wedded to a culture of deference. As Joyce Appleby (1987, 803) has said of the elements of classical republicanism found in eighteenth-century writings, the implicit political vision of Marshall's *Marbury* opinion "attest[s] to the persistence of ideas no longer capable of illuminating reality."

The new reality would involve the normalization of factional politics. The Court would play an important role in legitimating the ideological tools that nationalist politicians would use to construct a conceptual nation in the absence of a strong national government. In the political struggles that provided the context for Marshall's most enduring contributions to American constitutionalism, *Marbury* was an irrelevancy. But that is another story.

Bibliography

Annals of Congress. Vol. 11. Washington, D.C.: U.S. Government Printing Office.

Appleby, Joyce. "The American Heritage: The Heirs and the Disinherited." *Journal of American History* 74 (1987): 798–813.

Bloch, Susan L., and Maeva Marcus. "John Marshall's Selective Use of History in *Marbury v. Madison.*" *Wisconsin Law Review* (1986): 301–337.

Jefferson, Thomas. *The Writings of Thomas Jefferson*. Vol. 10. Edited by Andrew A. Lipscomb. Washington, D.C.: Thomas Jefferson Memorial Association, 1903.

Kerber, Linda K. *Federalists in Dissent: Imagery and Ideology in Jeffersonian America*. Ithaca: Cornell University Press, 1970.

Madison, James. *Notes of Debates in the Federal Convention of 1787*. Athens: Ohio University Press, 1966.

McCloskey, Robert G. *The American Supreme Court*. 3d ed., rev. Edited by Sanford Levinson. Chicago: University of Chicago Press, 2000.

Pocock, J. G. A. *The Machiavellian Moment: Florentine Political Thought and the Atlantic Republican Tradition*. Princeton: Princeton University Press, 1975.

Van Alstyne, William W. "A Critical Guide to *Marbury v. Madison.*" *Duke Law Journal* 1 (1969): 1–47.

3

The Strategic John Marshall (and Thomas Jefferson)

LEE EPSTEIN AND JACK KNIGHT

Chief Justice John Marshall's decision in *Marbury v. Madison* (1803) has generated no shortage of commentary. Everyone from former presidents to current members of the Court to legal academics and social scientists has an opinion. Some reactions are highly critical, but many more are replete with accolades, deeming Marshall's writing "brilliant" (McCloskey 1960, 40–41), a "tour de force" (Urofsky 1988, 183), "shrewd" (Jackson 1941, 24), and "extraordinary" (Corwin 1911, 292).

We understand the lavish praise. By ruling against William Marbury, Marshall avoided a potentially devastating clash with President Thomas Jefferson. By exerting the power of judicial review, he sent a clear signal to the new president that the Court has a major role to play in American government.

Nonetheless, we disagree with the general characterization of *Marbury* as a "brilliant" strategic move by Marshall in the face of overwhelming political opposition. Marshall was able to write the opinion he did, to establish judicial review, because it was a politically viable step at the time. Jefferson favored the establishment of judicial review and Marshall realized this. The chief justice simply took the rational course of action. He denied Marbury his commission (ruling as Jefferson wanted) and justified judicial review (a move of which Jefferson also approved).

To develop our claim we invoke game theory. Game theory provides a potent set of tools for examining situations involving strategic behavior, situations in which the outcome is the product of the interdependent choices of at least two actors. In the case of *Marbury*, those key actors were a president, Thomas Jefferson, and a chief justice, Marshall, with the outcome of their interactions producing, among other norms, judicial review.

Jefferson Versus Marshall: A Chronology of Key Events

In the next section we have much more to say about our use of game theory to study *Marbury*. For now, though, we turn to an analysis

A grant from the National Science Foundation's Law and Social Sciences Program (SES-9024640) facilitated our research, which we adapt and adopt from Knight and Epstein 1996. We are also grateful to Robert Lowry Clinton, Carol Mershon, William M. O'Barr, George Tsebelis, and members of the Departments of Political Science at the University of Minnesota, SUNY Stony Brook, Texas A&M University, and the University of Virginia for providing useful suggestions.

of the key historical events unfolding during the early 1800s. We do so for two reasons. First, even though the story we tell may be familiar to sociolegal scholars (see Clinton 1994 for a brief review), various accounts often leave out events they do not deem critical. Many studies of *Marbury* fail to discuss *Stuart v. Laird* (1803), in which Marshall (on circuit) upheld the Repeal Act—a decision the full Court later affirmed. Second and even more important, without an appreciation of the key events that structured Jefferson's and Mar-

shall's behavior, we would be unable to construct the games designed to explain those very behaviors. Readers would be unable to follow and assess our analyses.

Box 3-1 briefly lays out the chronology of those events. But the story requires some elaboration. The saga began with the 1800 election, a watershed as the Federalist Party lost control of the executive and the legislature. To retain some presence in government, the Federalists sought to pack the judiciary. President John Adams appointed his secretary of state,

Box 3-1 Chronology of Key Events

December 3, 1800	Presidential election of 1800
January 20, 1801	Adams (a Federalist) nominates Secretary of State John Marshall for chief justice
February 11, 1801	Tie in election between two Democratic-Republican candidates, Burr and Jefferson
February 13, 1801	Adams signs Judiciary Act of 1801
February 17, 1801	House chooses Jefferson as president; Federalists lose control of Congress and executive branch
February 27, 1801	Federalist Congress passes an act concerning the District of Columbia
March 3, 1801	Adams makes "midnight appointments" to ensure a Federalist presence in the courts
March 1801	Jefferson inaugurated president; refuses to deliver five commissions of Adams's appointments
December 7, 1801	New Congress meets
December 18, 1801	Marbury asks Court to hear his case; Court agrees (*Marbury v. Madison*)
January 8, 1802	Jefferson asks Congress to repeal the 1801 Judiciary Act
March 31, 1802	Congress passes the Repeal Act, negating the 1801 Judiciary Act
April 29, 1802	Congress passes the Amendatory Act
December 2, 1802	Marshall—on circuit—dismisses challenge to the Repeal Act (*Stuart v. Laird*)
February 1803	Jefferson initiates impeachment against Federalist Judge Pickering
February 9–12, 1803	Oral arguments in *Marbury* (orals in *Stuart* about the same time)
February 24, 1803	Marshall delivers unanimous opinion of the Court in *Marbury*
March 2, 1803	House impeaches Pickering
March 2, 1803	Full Court upholds the Repeal Act in *Stuart v. Laird*
May 2, 1803	Justice Chase condemns the Democratic–Republican Party in a grand jury charge
January 4, 1804	Senate begins Pickering trial
January 5, 1804	At Jefferson's request, House begins an investigation of Chase
March 12, 1804	Senate impeaches Pickering; House impeaches Chase
February 1805	Senate begins Chase trial
March 1, 1805	Senate dismisses charges against Chase

Marshall, as chief justice. Congress passed the 1801 Judiciary Act, which restructured the court system by creating independent circuit courts (justices no longer would ride circuit),[1] along with other legislation, which provided the lame-duck Senate and president with many new positions to fill. And so they did (or at least they thought they did) with "midnight" appointments—judicial commissions filled in the waning days of the Adams administration.

Enter the Jefferson administration. Although Jefferson's preferences about judicial supremacy remain ambiguous, he and his party clearly viewed the Federalists' attempts to pack the judiciary with disdain. To Jefferson and his colleagues, the bills passed in the waning days of the Adams administration were "iniquitous party measures designed by the defeated Federalists to entrench themselves and their discredited political doctrines in the judiciary—a measure 'as good to the party as an election' " (Haskins and Johnson 1981, 127; see also Warren 1926, 189). The Jeffersonians (especially the new president) had nothing but contempt for the new chief justice, whom they viewed as a "subtly calculating enemy of the people" (Brown 1966, 185), a man "of strong political ambitions, capable of bending others to his will, determined to mobilize the power of the court by craftiness, by sophisticating the law to his own prepossessions, and by making its opinion those of a conclave which he would dominate" (Boyd 1971, 158). Marshall had no love lost for the Republicans and, in particular, for Jefferson. He refused a request by Alexander Hamilton to support Jefferson over Aaron Burr in the 1800 election, writing that because Jefferson would "sap the fundamental principles of the government," he could not "bring

[himself] to aid Mr. Jefferson" (Dewey 1970, 41–42). Marshall and Jefferson "despised each other" (Dewey 1970, 29).

It is not wholly surprising that Republicans plotted to undermine the Federalist judiciary even before Jefferson took office. Some partisans argued for wholesale impeachments of Federalist judges and justices (Beveridge 1919, 20; Stites 1981, 82). Jefferson's views on the impeachment strategy, at least initially, were ambiguous at best and contradictory at worst. Another plan favored by some Republicans involved repealing the Judiciary Act of 1801 to rid the judiciary of some Federalist appointees. Historical records provide mixed evidence on Jefferson's initial reaction to this suggestion.

In the end, the following steps were taken. First, Jefferson refused to deliver some judicial commissions. As Jefferson told the story:

I found the commissions on the table of the Department of State, on my entrance into the office, and I forbade their delivery. Whatever is in the Executive offices is certainly deemed to be in the hands of the President, and in this case, was actually in my hands, because when I countermanded them, there was as yet no Secretary of State. (Warren 1926, 244)

This was a move over which Marshall immediately expressed "infinite chagrin." He believed that once the commissions had been sealed Jefferson lacked discretion over their delivery. He also thought that "some blame may be imputed to [Marshall]" as he was Secretary of State at the time the commissions should have been delivered (Stites 1981, 84). Marshall's reaction aside, Jefferson's failure was challenged when some of those who were owed their commissions—including Marbury—brought suit in the Supreme Court under Section 13 of the Judiciary Act of 1789.

In December 1801, the justices granted Marbury's motion for a ruling on whether the executive branch must deliver his commission.

The Court's decision to hear *Marbury* received attention in the partisan presses of the day and generated a good deal of speculation about the Court's motives. It also may have precipitated the administration's second step: Jefferson's initiation of legislation designed to repeal the 1801 Judiciary Act. Although this idea had been considered earlier, some historical accounts indicate that the Court's decision to hear *Marbury* "excited widespread indignation and was the immediate cause for the repeal of the 1801 Judiciary Act" (Stites 1981, 86; see also Malone 1970). Marshall's action was cited in the debate over repeal. As one Jeffersonian representative put it: "Think, too, of what Marshall and the Supreme Court have done! They have sent a . . . process leading to a mandamus, into the Executive cabinet to examine its concerns" (Beveridge 1919, 78). Other historians saw repeal as inevitable. They have argued that Jefferson intimated the need for repeal in his inaugural address, delivered ten days before the Court's decision to grant Marbury's request (Haskins and Johnson 1981, 153–154). In that address, Jefferson presented "statistics," indicating that the extra judges and circuits were not necessary. This money-saving approach was a strategy that Jefferson continued to pursue as Congress debated (and eventually passed) repeal of the 1801 Judiciary Act. Almost all analysts agree that Jefferson's "political motives are too palpable to require elaboration, for proof is clearly laid out in the debates recorded in the *Annals of Congress*" (Haskins 1981, 11). He was "obsessed with the idea that federal judges should fall in line with Republican views, and a prime objective of his policies . . . was to remove or replace Federalist judges" (Haskins 1981, 22).

Another step taken by Jefferson and his party was passage of the Amendatory Act, which had the effect of prohibiting the Court from meeting for fourteen months (December 1801 to February 1803). The president viewed this as necessary because he (and his party) worried that the Court might strike down the Repeal Act as a violation of the Constitution. His concern reflected congressional debates over repeal in which the question of judicial power arose on several occasions. Some Republicans who had supported judicial review before this point (indeed, some of the very same members of Congress who had wanted the Court to strike down the Alien and Sedition Acts) now argued that the Court did not have this power. These turnabouts were not missed by members of the Federalist congressional delegation. One pointed out that "it was once thought by gentlemen who now deny the principle, that the safety of the citizen and of the States rested upon the power of the Judges to declare an unconstitutional law void" (Warren 1926, 218). Whatever position the president took on the subject of judicial review, he was concerned enough that the Court might strike down the Repeal Act that he pushed for passage of the Amendatory Act, despite cautions from members of his own party that the Amendatory Act was itself unconstitutional. In a letter to Jefferson (dated five days before passage of the Amendatory Act), Monroe wrote, "If repeal was right, we should not shrink from the discussion in any course which the Constitution authorizes, or take any step which argues a distrust of what is done or apprehension of the consequences." He added that the Amendatory Act may be "considered an unconstitutional oppression of the judiciary by the legislature, adopted to carry a preceding measure which was also unconstitutional" (Malone 1970, 132).

Federalist leaders were in an uproar. One asked, "May it not lead to the virtual abolition of a Court, the existence of which is required by the Constitution? If the function of the Court can be extended by law for fourteen months, what time will arrest us before we arrive at ten or twenty years?" (Warren 1926, 223). The Federalist press concurred, widely circulating reports that the abolition of the Supreme Court would soon follow (Dewey 1970, 69). Not surprisingly (and just as the Jeffersonians had predicted), Federalists immediately initiated several lawsuits challenging the Repeal Act's constitutionality.

Chief Justice Marshall was more than a bit concerned. Historical accounts of his reaction to the Repeal and Amendatory Acts are mixed. Garraty (1987, 13) claimed that repeal "made Marshall even more determined to use the *Marbury* case to attack Jefferson." Stites (1981, 87) wrote that "Marshall was less upset than many Federalists by the Repeal Act." Still, Marshall clearly was worried about the "survival of the institution" (Haskins 1981, 5). As a secondary matter, he did not want to resume circuit court duty, which the Repeal Act mandated.[2] Yet Marshall would not take this step "without a consultation of the Judges." Accordingly, he corresponded with the associate justices to see if they should ignore the act and refuse to sit on circuit, while meeting as a Supreme Court. In a letter to Justice William Paterson, he wrote,

I confess I have some strong constitutional scruples. I cannot well perceive how the performance of circuit duties by the Judges of the supreme court can be supported. If the question was new I should be willing to act in this character without a consultation of the Judges; but I consider it as decided & that whatever my own scruples may be I am bound by the decision. I cannot however but regret the loss of the next June term. I could have wished the Judges had convened before they proceeded to execute the new system. (Haskins and Johnson 1981, 169)

How to interpret this and other letters has been a matter for scholarly debate. Some analysts (e.g., Malone 1970, 134) think that Marshall wanted the justices to perform circuit duty and that "he favored peaceful acceptance of the situation." Others (e.g., Dewey 1970, 71) assert that the letters represented an attempt "to persuade his brethren . . . to risk a show of force against the Jeffersonians by refusing to resume their circuit duties." What we do know is that all of the associate justices (except Samuel Chase) thought the consequences too grave if they did not sit.

In 1802 the justices rode circuit, with three hearing Federalist challenges to the constitutionality of the Repeal Act. When all three justices, including Marshall, dismissed these challenges, the Federalist attorney (Charles Lee) who had argued the case Marshall heard (*Stuart v. Laird*) appealed to the Supreme Court. This was not Lee's only pending suit; he also was the attorney who represented Marbury and colleagues.

While these cases awaited Court action, Jefferson took yet another step against the judiciary. Whatever qualms Jefferson had about the impeachment strategy before his ascension to the presidency apparently had dissipated.[3] He now asked Congress to remove a Federalist judge, John Pickering. Jefferson even supplied Congress with incriminating information against Pickering. The timing of his request was probably no coincidence. Beveridge (1919, 112) noted,

Everybody . . . thought the case would be decided in Marbury's favor and that Madison would be ordered to deliver the withheld commissions. It was upon this supposition that the Republican threats of impeachment were made. The Republicans considered Marbury's suit as a Federalist partisan maneuver and believed that the court's decision and Marshall's opinion would be inspired by motives of Federalist partisanship.

But whether Pickering was targeted because he was an easy mark (he was aged, mentally incompetent, and an alcoholic) or, as Beveridge (1919, 112) argued, because he was being used to "test the [impeachment] waters" is an open question. What is clear is that the Federalists believed Jefferson was out to "destroy the judiciary by removing all Federalist judges" (Turner 1949, 487). They thought "definite plans were . . . afoot to impeach . . . [Justice Samuel] Chase, as a prelude to impeaching Marshall himself" (Haskins 1981, 7).

As the House considered the Pickering case, the Court—all too aware of the doings in Congress[4]—busied itself with *Marbury* and *Laird*. In both cases, counsel asked the justices to exert the power of judicial review and strike down or uphold acts of Congress. Attorney Lee, who represented Marbury, specifically argued that Section 13 of the Judiciary Act of 1789, under which his client had brought suit, was constitutional (*Marbury* 1803, 148),[5] whereas in *Stuart* (1803, 303) Lee asserted that the Repeal Act violated the Constitution.[6] Lee lost both cases.

In *Marbury,* Marshall (and the Court) had two different, though related, sets of decisions

to make: (1) whether to uphold Section 13 of the Judiciary Act of 1789 and (2) whether to give Marbury and his colleagues their commissions. In the end, Marshall denied the commissions while striking the law—a move contemporary scholars regard as tactically brilliant.

But "why the Court decided the case as it did . . . [is a] question to which there can be no certain answer, only reasoned conjecture" (Hobson 1990, 164). A standard response comes from Dewey (1970, 117), who wrote that "[p]olitics were not far from Marshall's mind as he composed the *Marbury v. Madison* decision. The most frequently borrowed description of the opinion is . . . Corwin's judgment that this was a 'deliberate partisan coup.' " Haskins (1981, 10) provided yet another answer: Marshall was "genuinely fearful that Jefferson, with the firm 1800 electoral mandate behind him, would declare himself and his officers to be above the law." For this reason, as Haskins and Johnson (1981, 195) argued, Marshall chose to "echo . . . certain positions taken in the *Federalist Papers*, including those of Madison himself."

Whatever the explanation for the *Marbury* decision, we do know that the Court handed down *Stuart* just six days later and that this was a much clearer ruling. The Court merely affirmed Marshall's decision on circuit and upheld the Repeal Act.

According to some historical accounts, the Republican press (at least initially) was "delighted by the Jeffersonian victories in these two cases" (Dewey 1970, 100). Haskins and Johnson (1981, 217) even maintained that a major reason why *Marbury* "did not evoke greater hostility" was because of the surprise ruling in *Stuart.* Many Jeffersonians thought the Court would strike down the Repeal Act and were overjoyed when the Court upheld it. Only later did Jefferson and his colleagues realize the magnitude of the *Marbury* ruling. Whether Jefferson objected to Marshall's assertion of judicial review is not clear. At the very least, he sorely resented Marshall's implication that, had the Court had jurisdiction, he would have been legally bound to deliver the commissions.[7]

Attempts to remove Federalist judges continued. On the same day that the Court handed down *Stuart,* the House impeached Pickering. Just two months later, the Jeffersonians turned their sights on Justice Chase. Marshall was so concerned about his (and the Court's) political survival that he suggested that Congress should have appellate jurisdiction over Supreme Court decisions—a suggestion that might have effectively gutted *Marbury.* In a letter to Chase, he wrote, "I think the modern doctrine of impeachment should yield to an appellate jurisdiction in the legislature. A reversal of those legal opinions deemed unsound by the legislature would certainly better comport with the mildness of our character than (would) a removal of the Judge who has rendered them unknowing of his fault" (Jackson 1941, 28). But this proved unnecessary. The Senate acquitted Chase.

Why Jefferson was able to prevail in the Pickering impeachment only to lose in Chase's has been the subject of scholarly inquiry. One answer is that Jefferson's "managers" did a poor job in handling the case (Murphy 1962, 14). Another comes from McCloskey (1960, 47):

Mismanagement by the impeachment leaders undoubtedly contributed to this result. But the essential explanation is that many members of the Senate, including some Republicans, were not yet incensed enough with the judiciary to vote to destroy its independence. And their wrath was moderate or nonexistent because the Court under Marshall had really done so little to incite it. The charge that the judiciary was tyrannically imposing a Federalist will on a Republican-minded nation did not square with the immediate facts of judicial behavior, whatever suspicions might be entertained about Marshall's long-term aspirations.

In other words, the decisions in *Marbury* and *Stuart* indicated to some Jeffersonians that the Court was not the enemy they had anticipated. Those decisions failed to provide sufficient grounds to take aim at Marshall, who was—in some scholars' estimation—the real target. With diminishing reasons to remove Marshall, enthusiasm for Chase's impeachment also waned.

A Game-Theoretic Analysis of the Jefferson–Marshall Conflict

This brief description of the events during the early Jefferson administration highlights the emergence of a "game" pitting Jefferson against Marshall. We are not the first to depict the Marshall–Jefferson interaction in these terms. At least since Corwin (1910, 1911) and Beveridge (1919, 21), commentators have invoked the intuitions of game theory to describe these events. With one exception (Clinton 1994), these intuitions have never been put to the test. Even in the Clinton paper the researcher stopped short of examining all key decisional points.

Our historical review highlights this point. We know what happened, but we do not know *why.* Why did the actors take the strategic paths that they did? To "test" various historical answers to this question, we use game theory.

Two aspects of this statement require elaboration. The first centers on game theory and its application to legal phenomena, such as the Marshall–Jefferson dispute. The second concerns the notion of using game-theoretic analysis to test historical answers to our question. We discuss these conceptual points and then turn to the steps necessary to set up the games.

Applying Game Theory to Legal Phenomena

A number of tools are available to address legal questions. Their appropriateness is largely dependent on the nature of the phenomena under investigation. Game theory provides a potent set of tools to examine a particular kind of phenomena, social situations involving strategic behavior. In these situations, the social outcome is the product of the interdependent choices of at least two actors (Elster 1986). "Politics" is in large part about such strategic interactions. Regardless of whether they are motivated by self-interest, the public good, impartial principle, or some combination of these or other motivations, political actors usually engage in strategic decision making when they interact with others to derive a solution to a political problem. *To the extent that some legal phenomena contain a political dimension, game theory provides an appropriate approach to explaining their strategic components.*

The use of game theory in legal studies remains controversial. Some scholars argue that game theory involves a reductionist research program that extracts out much of what is essential to understanding social and political events. Others believe that rational choice models inherently mischaracterize the fundamental motivations on which political behavior is based. To these charges, we offer a simple response. The use of such models has often produced inadequate explanations, but the weaknesses in these explanations are a product of how game theory was used rather than a function of inherent limitations in the approach.

Game-theoretic models are not sufficient to produce persuasive explanations of most political competitions. Strategic decision making is only one feature of most social situations; another is the social context in which they occur. Adequate explanations of legal events must locate strategic choice in its appropriate social context. To accomplish this, scholars must combine game-theoretic analysis with other theoretical and empirical approaches (see Johnson 1991; Knight 1992).[8]

Using Game Theory to "Test" Historical Answers

The value of any method or approach rests with its ability to clarify and to illuminate the mechanisms that affect social and political life. Game theory provides the appropriate tools to shed light on the political conflict between Marshall and Jefferson over the nature and structure of the American judicial system. Through the use of game-theoretic models, we can "test" the plausibility of different historical claims about why the Marshall–Jefferson conflict produced the outcome that it did.

We use the idea of "testing" loosely. Our study takes advantage of how game theory involves counterfactual analysis.[9] The solutions to these models entail claims about what actors will do under certain conditions and what they would have done differently had the conditions been different. By varying the relevant conditions in the game, we can assess the relative merits of the historical counterfactuals that underlie the different explanations of this period.

Our primary focus is on those conditions inducing equilibrium behavior that replicate historical events. If a model induces behavior similar to the historical choices we observe, then it highlights the importance of the conditions that produced the behavior. If a model fails to reconstruct previously observed events, then it calls into question explanations based on the conditions embedded in it. Although replication alone does not definitively answer the question of why an event occurred, it can lend strong support to the explanation at hand.[10]

Setting Up the Games

Let us turn to the steps necessary to set up the games. We started with historical materials, reading case records, secondary accounts, letters of the key participants, newspaper articles, and congressional hearings. In so doing, we had four goals in mind. First, we wanted to determine whether the events depicted in Box 3-1 were part of the same game or whether they were discrete decision points requiring separate analyses. We concluded that they were all part and parcel of one game, largely between Jefferson (the president) and Marshall (the Court).[11]

Second, we needed to identify the alternative courses of action the actors *thought* they had at the time (not just those we now know in retrospect) at each key decisional point. Figure 3-1 reflects these determinations: It shows all the major decision points as part of one game, and it lays out the possible courses of action or "paths of play."[12] Although most of the key points displayed in the figure are obvious, such as Marshall's decision on whether or not to strike the Repeal Act, one deserves a bit of

elaboration. By *impeachment* we mean that Jefferson sought to have Marshall removed from office. But in demarcating the points at which history reveals the possibility of this occurring we do not suggest that Jefferson would have succeeded had he sought to have Marshall impeached. Indeed, as we detail later, our model explicitly takes into account the actors' beliefs about the probability of success and failure.

Third, we establish the actors' preferences over the various outcomes displayed in Figure 3-1. We posit two classes of motivations—the political and the institutional. By *political* we mean that the actors care about the advancement of their partisan causes and their parties. In this context, there are two relevant political factors. The first involves the resolution of the problem of the appointments and presents two alternatives: appointments going to the Democratic–Republicans (as desired by Jefferson) or to the Federalists (as desired by Marshall). The second—involving the consequence of Jefferson's use of the impeachment strategy—also presents two alternatives: success or failure on Jefferson's part if he tried to invoke it. By *institutional* we mean that the actors are concerned with the relative power and authority of the political branches of government. Two aspects of the judiciary were at issue: its structure (the Repeal and Amendatory Acts) and its supremacy (judicial review). On the structural dimension, the alternatives were the successful establishment of the Repeal Act, the status quo,[13] and the unsuccessful attempt to establish the Repeal Act. On the judicial review dimension, the alternatives were establishment of judicial review, status quo, and failure to establish judicial review.

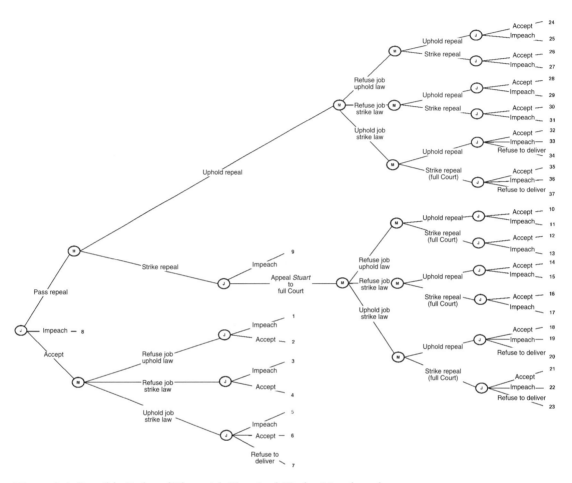

Figure 3-1 Possible Paths of Play with Terminal Nodes Numbered

Our extensive review of the historical record suggests that Marshall and Jefferson were differentially concerned about these things (see, for example, Beveridge 1919; Haskins and Johnson 1981; Malone 1970; Warren 1926). Marshall cared most about judicial supremacy, then judicial structure, and least about the political dimension. Jefferson was most concerned with structure, then the advancement of his party, and finally supremacy. These form assumptions under which we operate. Their reasonableness can be assessed, in part, by working through the games.

With these assumptions in mind, we constructed utility functions, mathematical representations of how the various goals of the actors combine to create an overall value for each of the possible outcomes of the game (Osbourne and Rubinstein 1994) for Jefferson and Marshall. We let U_m represent the value for Marshall and U_j the value for Jefferson. Because we analyze two separate games that differ in the assumed preferences for Jefferson (discussed in full later), we use superscripts A and B to distinguish Jefferson's utility value in the two games. The functions are as follows:

$$U_m = 2I_1 + 3I_2 + I_3 + I_4$$
$$U_J^A = -3I_1 - I_2 - 2I_3 - I_4$$
$$U_J^B = -3I_1 + I_2 - 2I_3 - I_4$$

where

$$I_1 = \begin{cases} -1 \text{ if Repeal Act established} \\ 0 \text{ if status quo} \\ 1 \text{ if no Repeal Act established} \end{cases}$$

$$I_2 = \begin{cases} -1 \text{ if no judicial review established} \\ 0 \text{ if status quo} \\ 1 \text{ if judicial review established} \end{cases}$$

$$I_3 = \begin{cases} -1 \text{ if appointment for Democratic–} \\ \quad\text{Republican Party} \\ 0 \text{ if status quo} \\ 1 \text{ if appointment for Federalist Party} \end{cases}$$

$$I_4 = \begin{cases} -1 \text{ if impeachment succeeds} \\ 0 \text{ if status quo} \\ 1 \text{ if impeachment fails} \end{cases}$$

Two features of these functions require explanation. The first involves the differences in the functions for games A and B: They are the same for Marshall but not Jefferson. In game A, we assume that Jefferson has opposing preferences from Marshall on the judicial review dimension; in game B, we assume that he shares Marshall's preferences on this dimension. The reason for this seeming discrepancy is that analysts claim genuine uncertainty about how Jefferson felt about judicial review: The historical evidence, particularly Jefferson's writings and letters, is quite mixed (see, for example, Haskins and Johnson 1981).[14] Setting it up this way is sensible and has the additional benefit of allowing us to investigate Jefferson's preferences over judicial review.

The other feature of the functions in need of discussion is the method of weighting the dimensions. For each actor we weighted his most important dimension by a factor of 3, his next most important dimension with a 2, and his least important dimension with a factor of 1. For Marshall, an outcome that establishes judicial review (3), eradicates the Repeal Act (2), gains an appointment (1), and results in no impeachment attempt (0) receives a value of 6 in both games. For Jefferson, the outcomes differ. In game A, an outcome that upholds repeal (3), that gains an appointment (2), that does not establish judicial review (1), and results in no impeachment attempt (0) yields a value of 6. In game B, a value of 6 is achieved if judicial review is established. (A complete definition of the payoffs for the two games is available from the authors.)

Finally, we wanted to incorporate the fact that the Jefferson–Marshall conflict takes place in a political context in which the actions of Congress affect the likelihood that either actor will successfully achieve his goals. Any node that ends with Jefferson choosing to impeach Marshall is characterized by a distribution of possible outcomes. Whether Jefferson will be successful in these attempts depends on the political actions of members of Congress. Neither Jefferson nor Marshall know with certainty what Congress will do if Jefferson attempts impeachment. Rather, they have a belief that there is a particular probability that Jefferson would be successful.

To capture these probabilities, we distinguished two states of the world at these nodes: a political environment in which Jefferson will be successful in his impeachment effort (probability p) and a political environment in which he will fail (probability $1 - p$). The greater the value of p, the more favorable the political environment for Jefferson. To put it somewhat differently, we can interpret the value of p as a measure of the relative bargaining power of the actors. In assessing the relative merits of various strategies available to them, both Jefferson and Marshall must base their decisions on assessments of these probabilities.

Solving the Games

To solve the games we used the subgame perfect-equilibrium solution concept. Invoking the logic of backward induction, we identified the equilibrium behavior that would be induced by different beliefs about the political context in which the Jefferson–Marshall interaction takes place. The basic intuition is a simple one: Strategic actors will peer into the future to see the implications of their present actions. If the time horizon of the future is fairly short, they should be able to establish reasonably good expectations about how their present actions will affect their future choices. If they can do so, they will take account of those future implications in deciding what to do at earlier stages of the game. In analyzing the Jefferson–Marshall interaction, we assume that both the president and chief justice will choose to act at any point in the game in such a way as to maximize the value of their future choices.

Our discussion begins on the next page with game A, which assumes that Marshall and Jeffer-

son have different preferences over judicial review. We then turn to game B, which has the actors agreeing over judicial review. In both cases, we characterize equilibrium behavior based on the actors' beliefs about the probability of Jefferson winning and losing. Here we present the various possible subgame perfect-equilibria outcomes of the two games. Given the complexity of the games we do not present all of the out-of-equilibria choices that would be part of a complete characterization of these equilibria. We restrict our characterizations to the equilibrium paths of play that are induced by the different range of beliefs about the state of the political environment in which the executive–judiciary game takes place.

Discussion of the Results

What do we learn from these games? Before addressing that core question, we must make some determination about whether the actors believed that the political environment substantially favored Jefferson over Marshall. The story we tell about these games depends on our response to that question, because equilibria are quite distinct under the various beliefs. Our answer is simple. Based on scholarly commentary, historical accounts, and empirical evidence, it seems clear that the actors thought the environment overwhelmingly favored Jefferson. Just as Marshall ascended to the chief justiceship, Jeffersonians had taken control of the government (except for the judiciary). Their impressive victory in the elections of 1800 posed a threat to Marshall that is sometimes obscured in the political science literature. He believed (and rightly so) that many followers of Jefferson and, perhaps, Jefferson himself would seek to take control of the judiciary

Game **A**

The equilibrium paths of play differ depending on the actors' beliefs about the state of the political environment. They are as follows.

1. If 0 < p < .25, meaning that the actors believe that the political environment strongly favors Marshall, then the following are equilibrium paths of play:

Jefferson ACCEPTS Marshall's decision to hear the *Marbury* case,

Marshall REFUSES JOB and STRIKES LAW,

Jefferson ACCEPTS.

Or Jefferson ACCEPTS Marshall's decision to hear the *Marbury* case,

Marshall UPHOLDS JOB and STRIKES LAW,

Jefferson REFUSES TO DELIVER.

2. If .25 < p < .50, meaning that the actors believe that the political environment generally favors Marshall, then the following are equilibrium paths of play:

Jefferson ACCEPTS Marshall's decision to hear the *Marbury* case,

Marshall UPHOLDS JOB and STRIKES LAW,

Jefferson REFUSES TO DELIVER.

3. If .50 < p < .70, meaning that the actors believe that the political environment generally favors Jefferson, then the following are equilibrium paths of play:

Jefferson PASSES REPEAL ACT,

Marshall (circuit) STRIKES REPEAL ACT,

Jefferson APPEALS,

Marshall REFUSES JOB and STRIKES LAW,

Marshall STRIKES REPEAL ACT,

Jefferson IMPEACHES.

Or Jefferson PASSES REPEAL ACT,

Marshall (circuit) UPHOLDS REPEAL ACT,

Marshall REFUSES JOB and STRIKES LAW,

Marshall STRIKES REPEAL ACT,

Jefferson IMPEACHES.

4. If .70 < p < 1, meaning that the actors believe that the political environment strongly favors Jefferson, then the following are equilibrium paths of play:

Jefferson PASSES REPEAL ACT,

Marshall (circuit) STRIKES REPEAL ACT,

Jefferson APPEALS,

Marshall REFUSES JOB and UPHOLDS LAW,

Marshall UPHOLDS REPEAL ACT,

Jefferson IMPEACHES.

Or Jefferson PASSES REPEAL ACT,

Marshall (circuit) UPHOLDS REPEAL ACT,

Marshall REFUSES JOB and UPHOLDS LAW,

Marshall UPHOLDS REPEAL ACT,

Jefferson IMPEACHES.

(continued on next page)

Game B

Again, equilibrium paths of play differ depending on the actors' beliefs about the state of the political environment.

1. If 0 < p < .5, meaning that the actors believe that the environment favors Marshall, then the following are equilibrium paths of play:

Jefferson ACCEPTS Marshall's decision to hear the *Marbury* case,

Marshall REFUSES JOB and STRIKES LAW,

Jefferson ACCEPTS.

Or

Jefferson ACCEPTS Marshall's decision to hear the *Marbury* case,

Jefferson UPHOLDS JOB and STRIKES LAW,

Jefferson REFUSES TO DELIVER.

2. If .5 < p < 1, meaning that the actors believe that the environment favors Jefferson, then the following are equilibrium paths of play:

Jefferson PASSES REPEAL ACT,

Marshall (circuit) UPHOLDS REPEAL ACT,

Marshall REFUSES JOB and STRIKES LAW,

Marshall UPHOLDS REPEAL ACT,

Jefferson ACCEPTS.

Or

Jefferson PASSES REPEAL ACT,

Marshall (circuit) STRIKES REPEAL ACT,

Jefferson APPEALS,

Marshall REFUSES JOB and STRIKES LAW,

Marshall UPHOLDS REPEAL ACT,

Jefferson ACCEPTS.

---

through impeachment. This so-called impeachment strategy had already taken hold in the states.[15] To Marshall, there was little reason to believe it would not succeed on a federal level.

Marshall cared deeply about judicial supremacy and power. But he knew he could not achieve critical institutional goals if Jefferson impeached him. Indeed, he was so concerned about that possibility (and Jefferson's probability of success) that, during the impeachment proceedings of his colleague, the ardent Federalist justice Chase, he offered to repudiate the doctrine of judicial review (Jackson 1941, 27–28). To argue that the actors did not believe

the environment overwhelmingly favored Jefferson is to take a position well at odds with virtually all of the evidence.

If this is so, then we ought to give our closest attention to the equilibrium paths supported by belief 4 in game *A* and belief 2 in game *B*. These represent the beliefs most closely approximating those Marshall and Jefferson held: that the political environment so strongly favored Jefferson that the president would succeed in any decision he made, be it impeachment, acceptance, or so forth. From this representation of beliefs, we can analyze the strategic choices of the actors to see what we can learn about the executive–judicial conflict over the courts.

The most obvious lesson is that the behavior induced by the preferences attributed to Jefferson and Marshall in game *A* are at odds with the historical record, whereas the behavior induced in game *B* (at least under belief 2) replicates history. This has an important implication for Jefferson's preferences over judicial review: If we treat them as the same as Marshall's, at least in this game, we obtain an outcome that is more in line with the historical events. In other words, our results indicate that Jefferson *favored* judicial review and that Marshall knew this.

For some readers, this conclusion is significant because it suggests a resolution to a long-standing debate about Jefferson's preferences. And it would be enough to reject game *A,* because it does not mirror history. Although we agree on both scores, game *A*—alone and juxtaposed with game *B*—carries important information that we should not neglect. In general, it shows us the outcome that would have resulted had Jefferson not preferred the doctrine of judicial review: *Marbury* would not have established the doctrine; Jefferson would have obtained repeal of the 1801 Judiciary Act; and Marshall would have been removed from office. In both games, *Stuart v. Laird* was the more important of the decisions to Jefferson, as evidenced by the fact that Marshall's impeachment was all but ensured regardless of what he did in *Marbury*. The reason is simple. As long as he obtained repeal, Jefferson—wanting to attain the payoff with the highest value and viewing the political environment in his favor—would almost certainly have sought impeachment. Had this occurred, a norm of

impeachment might have been established, a norm that could have indelibly altered the nature of the Court and its relationships with the other institutions of government.

Game *B,* which induced behavior consistent with history, also reflects the importance of *Laird*. Marshall's decision saved him from impeachment, not the ruling in *Marbury*. Jefferson could cope with *Marbury* because he shared Marshall's preference for the establishment of judicial review. He would have attempted impeachment had Marshall struck down the Repeal Act in *Laird*. Marshall, apparently believing that Jefferson would have been successful in this attempt, opted out by upholding the law.

Taking this step—that is, upholding the Repeal Act—was *not* Marshall's preferred position. He probably would have been devastated to learn that decades would pass before Congress relieved the justices of "riding" circuit. Nor, to a lesser extent, was denying Marbury his commission his sincere desire. But—given the sequence of events—these were the courses of action Marshall thought he had to take to avoid impeachment. To put it differently, Marshall acted in a sophisticated fashion. Had his unconstrained preferences driven his behavior, he would have given Marbury his commission and struck down Section 13 and the Repeal Act. But, as a strategic actor, he could not—given his beliefs about the political environment—vote naively.

Game *B* also suggests the importance of relative bargaining power as reflected in the social context in which the conflict occurred. In this game, after the Court issued its decision in *Marbury*, Marshall might have struck down the Repeal Act had he perceived Jefferson's position to have been only slightly weaker. But, given his beliefs about the state of the political environment, this was not a step Marshall (nor any rational actor) was willing to take. This is especially so because he perceived the consequences—the loss of his job—to be the gravest of all.

Marshall was not the only actor in this drama to consider context. Jefferson did so too. Game *B* suggests that had Jefferson perceived the strength of his political clout as more uncertain, he would not have proposed the Repeal Act in the first place. *Marbury* would have been decided as it was and the game would have ended. Historically, this would have meant that the 1801 Judiciary Act would have gone into effect. Politically, it would have led to the (almost) successful culmination of the Federalist plan to stack the judiciary. That party would have ruled the circuits throughout the United States.

Implications of the Study

We could end our analysis of the struggle between Jefferson and Marshall. But the story tells us much more; it provides us with important insights into how to study other interactions between courts and presidents, be they of historical moment (such as the struggle between Franklin Roosevelt and the Court in 1936 to 1937) or of future concern (such as those that may ensue in newly established democracies in Eastern Europe). First, our examination demonstrates that politicians—even those who lack an electoral connection—are strategic actors. Had Marshall not been a strategic actor, he simply would have voted his unconstrained preferred positions in *Marbury* (strike the law and provide the commission) and in *Laird* (strike the Repeal

Act). He rejected these steps not because his unconstrained preferences over the outcomes changed. Given his beliefs about Jefferson and the political environment, he acted in a sophisticated manner to maximize his expected utility.

Our results lend support to the growing number of scholars (e.g., Epstein, Knight, and Martin 2001; Eskridge 1991a, 1991b; Spiller and Gely 1992) who argue that justices do not need an electoral connection to act strategically. Members of the Court know that other institutions wield an impressive array of weapons, weapons that can at minimum move the state of the law away from their preferred position and at maximum can jeopardize their political survival. By the same token, our study shows that presidents (and, we suspect, Congress) must act strategically when dealing with the Court. If they do not, as Jefferson knew, they can face severe political penalties.

A second implication of our study is that despite differences between legal and political actors, all politicians—be they presidents or justices—consider the environment under which they are operating. Rational responses depend not just on actors' preferences and their beliefs about those of their opponents but on the decision-making context. In our study, Jefferson and Marshall clearly believed that the political environment of the day favored Jefferson's interests. Had this not been the case, Jefferson would never have sought repeal of the 1801 Judiciary Act and the Federalists would have remained firmly entrenched in the nation's judiciary. Justices may not follow the election returns as carefully as, say, members of Congress, but they must make calculations about their political clout relative to that of the other institutions. If they do not, as the Marshall–

Jefferson games indicate, the results may be costly. We think a reconsideration of other defining moments in judicial development would bear this out.

The general lesson is a simple one. In situations in which uncertainty over outcomes abounds—that is, in most political situations—we ought to incorporate considerations about the actors' beliefs about the possible states of the world in which they interact. This is something that the actors do, and we would be remiss to ignore. So, too, it helps us to make sense of seemingly incomprehensible political events.

Conclusion

We end where we started, with the question of the institutionalization of judicial review. At the time the Constitution was framed, the role of the judiciary in the three-branch structure of American democracy was underdeveloped. The major long-term consequence of the Jefferson–Marshall interaction was a restructuring of the institutional division of labor among the branches. This was, in large part, a result of the short-term political interests of the two major political parties. The Supreme Court's authority for judicial review emerged, as we claimed at the onset and as we have now demonstrated, not because of some complex intentional design and not because of some brilliant strategic move by Marshall in the face of overwhelming political opposition but merely because it was politically viable at the time.

Bibliography

Alfange, Dean, Jr. "Marbury v. Madison and Original Understandings of Judicial Review: In Defense of Traditional Wisdom." *Supreme Court Review* (1994): 329–446.

Beveridge, Albert J. *The Life of John Marshall—Volume III.* Boston: Houghton Mifflin, 1919.

Boyd, Julian P. "The Chasm that Separated Thomas Jefferson and John Marshall." In *Jefferson,* Adrienne Koch, ed. Englewood Cliffs, N.J.: Prentice-Hall, 1971.

Brown, Stuart Gerry. *Thomas Jefferson.* New York: Washington Square Press, 1966.

Clinton, Robert Lowry. "Game Theory, Legal History, and the Origins of Judicial Review: A Revisionist Analysis of *Marbury v. Madison." American Journal of Political Science* 38 (1994): 285–302.

Corwin, Edward S. "The Establishment of Judicial Review—I." *Michigan Law Review* 9 (1910): 102–125.

———. "The Establishment of Judicial Review—II." *Michigan Law Review* 9 (1911): 283–316.

Dewey, Donald O. *Marshall Versus Jefferson: The Political Background of Marbury v. Madison.* New York: Knopf, 1970.

Elster, Jon. *Rational Choice.* New York University Press, 1986.

Epstein, Lee, Jack Knight, and Andrew D. Martin. "The Supreme Court as a *Strategic* National Policy Maker." *Emory Law Journal* 50 (2001): 583–611.

Eskridge, William N., Jr. "Overriding Supreme Court Statutory Interpretation Decisions." *Yale Law Journal* 101 (1991b): 331–417.

———. "Reneging on History? Playing the Court/Congress/President Civil Rights Game." *California Law Review* 79 (1991a): 613–684.

Garraty, John A. "The Case of the Missing Commissions." In *Quarrels that Have Shaped the Constitution.* Rev. ed. Ed. John A. Garraty. New York: Harper and Row, 1987.

Haskins, George L. "Law Versus Politics in the Early Years of the Marshall Court." *University of Pennsylvania Law Review* 130 (1981): 1–27.

Haskins, George Lee, and Herbert A. Johnson. *History of the Supreme Court of the United States—Volume II—Foundations of Power: John Marshall, 1801–15.* New York: Macmillan, 1981.

Hobson, Charles F., ed. *The Papers of John Marshall.* Chapel Hill: University of North Carolina Press, 1990.

Jackson, Robert H. *The Struggle for Judicial Supremacy.* New York: Vintage Books, 1941.

Johnson, James. *Symbol and Strategy*. Ph.D. dissertation, University of Chicago, 1991.

Knight, Jack. *Institutions and Social Conflict*. Cambridge: Cambridge University Press, 1992.

Knight, Jack, and Lee Epstein. "On the Struggle for Judicial Supremacy." *Law and Society Review* 30 (1996): 87–120.

Malone, Dumas. *Jefferson the President: First Term, 1801–1805*. Boston: Little, Brown, 1970.

McCloskey, Donald. "Counterfactuals." In *The New Palgrave: A Dictionary of Economics,* John Eatwell, Murray Milgate, and Peter Newman, eds. New York: Stockton, 1987.

———. *The American Supreme Court*. University of Chicago Press, 1960.

Murphy, Walter F. *Congress and the Supreme Court*. University of Chicago Press, 1962.

O'Brien, David M. *Storm Center: The Supreme Court in American Politics*. New York: Norton, 1990.

Osbourne, Martin J., and Ariel Rubinstein. *A Course in Game Theory*. Cambridge: MIT Press, 1994.

Proctor, L. B. "Jefferson Contempt of Chief Justice Marshall's Opinions." *Albany Law Journal* 44 (1891): 342–343.

Rehnquist, William H. *Grand Inquests*. New York: Morrow, 1992.

Spiller, Pablo T., and Rafael Gely. "Congressional Control of Judicial Independence: The Determinants of U.S. Supreme Court Labor-Relations Decisions, 1949–1988." *RAND Journal of Economics* 23 (1992): 463–492.

Stites, Francis N. *John Marshall—Defender of the Constitution*. Boston: Little, Brown, 1981.

Turner, Lynn W. "The Impeachment of John Pickering." *American Historical Review* 54 (1949): 485–507.

Urofsky, Melvin I. *A March of Liberty*. New York: Knopf, 1988.

Warren, Charles. *The Supreme Court in United States History*. Vol. 1. Boston: Little, Brown, 1926.

Endnotes

1. The 1789 Judiciary Act required the justices to perform circuit duty. This involved traveling long distances by horseback or carriage—which they loathed—to hear appeals (along with district court judges) from trial courts (see O'Brien 1990, 135–138).

2. As O'Brien (1990, 138) noted, riding circuit was "not merely burdensome; it also diminished the Court's prestige, for a decision by a justice on circuit court could afterward be reversed by the whole Court."

3. After the midnight appointments, Jefferson was "determined that this 'outrage on decency should not have this effect, except in life appointment [judges] which are irremovable' " (Stites 1981, 84). This position is consistent with the general tenor of letters he wrote in 1788 and 1789 criticizing the impeachment of judges. But by 1803, "[p]olitical expediency and accession to power helped to bring about a change in Jefferson's early views on the independence of the judiciary. Now, and throughout the remainder of his life, the idea that judges were irremovable became progressively more abhorrent to him" (Haskins and Johnson 1981, 208).

4. Even Malone (1970, 148), who is always quick to defend Jefferson, notes that although there was much "loose" talk about impeachments and "there is no way of proving that [Marshall] was in actual danger," the chief justice clearly thought he was.

5. In Lee's words, "Congress is not restrained from conferring original jurisdiction in other cases than those mentioned in the Constitution" (*Marbury* 1803, 148).

6. Lee argued that the act "is unconstitutional, inasmuch as it goes to deprive the courts of all their power and jurisdiction, and to displace judges who have been guilty of no misbehavior in their offices" (*Stuart* 1803, 303).

7. Indeed, throughout his lifetime, Jefferson took every opportunity to criticize Marshall and his ruling in *Marbury*. As late as June 1822, after the Supreme Court decided *Cohens v. Virginia* (1821), Jefferson wrote, "There was another case I recollect, more particularly as it bore upon me." He then described *Marbury* and wrote, "But the chief justice went on to lay down what the law would be had they jurisdiction of the case, to wit: they should command the delivery. Besides the impropriety of

this gratuitous interference, could any thing exceed the perversion of the law. Yet this case of *Marbury v. Madison* is continually cited by bench and bar as if it were settled law, without any animadversion of its being merely an *obiter* dissertation of the chief justice" (Proctor 1891, 343).

8. Increasingly, scholars are offering ways to bring context into strategic explanations. See Johnson (1991) and Knight (1992) for discussions of efforts to incorporate factors such as institutions and culture into rational-choice explanations.

9. For an excellent and informative discussion of the role of counterfactual reasoning in game theoretic analysis, see McCloskey 1987.

10. It is important to note that when we use game theory to assess the merits of historical explanations, the key to the analysis is the way in which we define the conditions of the game (including the definition of the actors' preferences). From the very logic of this form of analysis it follows that the solutions to games will be sensitive to changes in the conditions that are posited in the particular model. Thus, a valid criticism of the kind of analysis we present would not rest on the fact that the solution of any model is sensitive to changes in the parameters. Rather, an appropriate criticism would focus on weaknesses in the historical claims that we incorporate in the definitions of the conditions of the game.

11. Most scholars (e.g., Clinton 1994) consider only three moves as crucial: Jefferson's failure to deliver the commissions, Marshall's decision in *Marbury,* and Jefferson's response. Our review of the relevant historical materials, particularly the letters and the biographies of the key players, shows that this reading is too simple and that it does not fully encapsulate the concerns of the day. In any case, the assumption that Marshall and Jefferson viewed all the events detailed in Box 3-1 as part of a long chain of closely related occurrences is one our analysis allows us to test.

Also embedded in this statement is the notion that Jefferson and Marshall were actors who represented their respective institutions. This is an assumption under which Clinton (1994) worked and one we think is reasonable to make.

12. We begin the games with Jefferson having to decide what to do after the Supreme Court agreed to hear the *Marbury* case. Previous attempts to solve the games show that the president would always fail to deliver the commissions and that the justices would always agree to hear the *Marbury* case, regardless of their beliefs about the political environment.

13. We use the term "status quo" to mean no change on the particular dimension.

14. Even within individual sources confusion abounds. For example, in his seminal biography of Jefferson, Malone (1970, 133) at one point asserted that Jefferson's "general attitude toward the judiciary can be described with confidence. Unquestionably he wanted to keep it within what he regarded as proper bounds, and the doctrine of absolute judiciary supremacy was to him another name for tyranny. . . ." Later, Malone wrote (1970, 151) that "Jefferson's fears of judicial power varied with circumstances." Today, prevailing sentiment seems to be that Jefferson's views—like those of the framers of the Constitution—are not known with certainty, though Clinton (1994) makes a good case for the position that the president supported judicial review.

15. By a straight party vote the Pennsylvania legislature impeached Federalist judge Alexander Addison in 1803. Apparently, though, talk of impeachment of federal judges and justices was, as Haskins (1981, 213) wrote, "contemplated even before the 1801 Act had been repealed."

4

The Idea of Judicial Review in the Marshall Era

STEPHEN M. GRIFFIN

Judicial review as established by Chief Justice John Marshall and the Supreme Court in *Marbury v. Madison* (1803) was quite different from judicial review as it exists today. Unfortunately, the widespread use of the term "judicial review" to describe both eighteenth- and twenty-first-century practice promotes the idea that when we debate the role the Supreme Court should have in American government and politics, we are continuing a debate begun two centuries ago. Legal scholars, political scientists, and historians all use "judicial review" to refer to the practice advocated by Alexander Hamilton in *Federalist* No. 78 and by Chief Justice Marshall in *Marbury*. Looking at it from another angle, however, it is a mistake to use "judicial review" to refer to the practice advocated by Hamilton and Marshall. This is true in the trivial sense that neither Hamilton nor Marshall used the term itself. But it is also true in the important sense that the practice they advocated does not match the twenty-first-century institution with which we are familiar. The eminent historian Gordon Wood has stated this point of view forcefully. He argued that to ask whether the founding generation intended to establish judicial review is

anachronistic because "no one meant to establish what eventually became judicial review; it could scarcely have been imagined. Like most developments in history, judicial review was unplanned and unintended" (Wood 1988, 1295).

In this chapter I will follow these suggestive remarks by demonstrating that the founding generation did not advocate or establish some of the most important contemporary elements of the power of judicial review. The founding generation was committed to an understanding of the scope of judicial review that is no longer accepted. These contentions lead naturally to the question of how and when judicial review assumed its contemporary shape. I close this chapter by providing a few suggestions about how this question can be answered. The particular point I want to emphasize is that to use the term "judicial review" to describe both present practice and practice in the early republic ignores the crucial issue of what *conditions* were attached to the exercise of judicial review. Focusing on the issue of conditions will help us understand the early debate over the judicial power and how the Supreme Court eventually acquired the power we call judicial review.

The Elements of Judicial Review

The practice we currently call "judicial review" that is the focus of contemporary debate over the role of the Supreme Court is more a creation of the twentieth century than an accepted idea of the era in which Chief Justice Marshall lived. The contemporary debate is about whether the Court's exercise of judicial review is justified or is legitimate in light of our constitutional tradition and democratic principles. The influence the Court wields over American law, politics, and society, however, does not derive simply from the discrete power that Hamilton in *Federalist* No. 78 referred to as "the right of the courts to pronounce legislative acts void" (Hamilton 1961, 524).

The contemporary power of judicial review consists not only of the practice Hamilton defended (which I will call the "voiding power") but also of other important elements. Some of these elements were present in the Constitution when it was signed in 1787, but others were acquired over time. Two elements present in the Constitution were judicial independence and life tenure, both of which are just as important to the contemporary power of judicial review as the voiding power. If, for example, justices served for a nonrenewable six-year term or were elected, the power of judicial review would be affected significantly. Judicial review is thus a complex institution composed of a number of elements, not just a discrete power. Another key element of the contemporary power of judicial review that only developed over time is the doctrine of judicial supremacy, the idea that the Supreme Court is the final authority in matters of constitutional interpretation. When the legitimacy of judicial review was debated in the twentieth century, the doctrine of judicial supremacy was part of the institution under debate. Yet the voiding power defended by Hamilton and Chief Justice Marshall is analytically distinct from judicial supremacy.

The use of the term "judicial review" to denote both what I have called the voiding power and the complex contemporary institution of judicial review thus introduces an important ambiguity that has affected the inquiry into the origins of the power of the Supreme Court. When we inquire into the origins of judicial review, are we concerned with the voiding power or with judicial review considered as a whole? The contemporary power of judicial review consists of a number of elements. Although some of them were present in the early republic, others were not. If we are to understand how the contemporary power of judicial review differs from judicial review in the early republic, we must take care to identify these elements as clearly as possible. In the discussion that follows I will distinguish among (1) those elements that existed in the early republic and continue to exist today, (2) those that existed in the early republic but no longer exist, and (3) those that were created by later developments.

Judicial Review in the Early Republic

Three elements of judicial review that existed in the early republic continue to exist today: (1) judicial independence, (2) the voiding power, and (3) life tenure. As argued first by Wood and, more recently, by historian Jack Rakove, the most overlooked element on this list is judicial independence. Before the founding generation could properly consider what sort of power the judiciary should have, they first had to conceive it as a truly separate, co-equal branch of government. Unfortunately, as Wood noted, "[W]e still have no history of the emergence of what Americans called an 'independent judiciary' at the end of the eighteenth century and the beginning of the nineteenth century—perhaps because we take a strong independent judiciary so much for granted" (Wood 1993, 157).

Many scholars have seen Hamilton's famous argument justifying judicial review in *Federalist* No. 78 as a forerunner of the argument Chief Justice Marshall provided in *Marbury*. But Hamilton's argument also well-illustrates how all three of these elements were important to the founding generation. Hamilton's general topic is judicial independence. After briefly defending life tenure, Hamilton begins his discussion of "the right of the courts to pronounce legislative acts void" by stating, "The complete independence of the courts of justice is peculiarly essential in a limited constitution" (Hamilton 1961, 524). The Constitution is limited in that it "contains certain specified exceptions to the legislative authority; such for instance as that it shall pass no bills of attainder, no *ex post facto* laws, and the like." Hamilton declares that it is the duty of the courts "to declare all acts contrary to the manifest tenor of the constitution void" (Hamilton 1961, 524).

Hamilton denied the charge that this kind of judicial independence makes the judiciary superior to the legislature. Hamilton's denial rests on the character of the Constitution as a fundamental or supreme law and the doctrine of popular sovereignty. The power of the people in establishing the Constitution is superior to both the legislative and judicial powers. If a legislative act is contrary to the Constitution, it therefore must be invalid. The courts are in a good position to enforce the will of the people as "an intermediate body between the people and the legislature, in order, among other things, to keep the latter within the limits assigned to their authority." This is confirmed by the idea that the "interpretation of the laws is the proper and peculiar province of the courts" (Hamilton 1961, 525).

Although Hamilton argued in favor of judicial independence and life tenure, it is understandable that scholars have seen his argument in favor of the voiding power as the most significant part of *Federalist* No. 78. For all practical purposes, the judicial duty to declare unconstitutional acts void seems equivalent to what we call judicial review. But making this easy equivalence would be a serious error. The critical point that is missed is that Hamilton's idea of the voiding power might have certain limiting conditions attached to its exercise that would make it quite remote from the contemporary institution of judicial review. To see the force of this point, we must consider the possibility that there were elements of judicial review in the early republic that no longer exist.

The Forgotten Elements of Judicial Review

Recent scholarship on judicial review has been concerned with exploring the idea that there were important elements to the institution of judicial review in the early republic that are no longer accepted. There are three candidates: (1) the doubtful case rule, (2) a much different understanding of the relationship between law and politics, and (3) the limitation of the voiding power to instances where the legislative and executive branches encroached on the power of the judiciary. I will argue that the first two points are largely correct and did constitute conditions on the exercise of judicial review but that the third is misguided.

Sylvia Snowiss's study (1990) of the origins of judicial review played an instrumental role in bringing the relevance of the doubtful case rule back to the attention of scholars. This was the "rule of administration" cited by James Bradley Thayer in his famous article (Thayer 1893, 140) arguing for what is now called judicial restraint. Thayer by no means presented all the evidence that this rule was part of the debate over the judicial power in the early republic. As Snowiss argued, the debate over judicial power in the late eighteenth century "reflected the understanding that this power was confined to the concededly unconstitutional act. This understanding was expressed on the U.S. Supreme Court by repeated use of the doubtful case rule. Under this rule legislation could be overturned only if there was no doubt about its unconstitutionality" (Snowiss 1990, 60).

Hamilton's discussion of judicial review in *The Federalist Papers* and Chief Justice Marshall's argument in *Marbury* both reflect the assumption that the voiding power be exercised only in a clear case. Hamilton argued that the judiciary has a duty to strike down any law contrary to the "*manifest* tenor of the constitution." His examples all involve absolutely clear cases of constitutional violation. In *Marbury*, Marshall argued that because "[i]t is emphatically the province and duty of the judicial department to say what the law is," a statute conflicting with the Constitution must be held invalid. Marshall

stated that any other result would allow the legislature to do "what is expressly forbidden." Marshall then gives three examples of legislation clearly violating a provision of the Constitution. For instance, he commented that the Constitution "declares that 'no bill of attainder or *ex post facto* law shall be passed.' If, however, such a bill should be passed and a person should be prosecuted under it; must the court condemn to death those victims whom the constitution endeavors to preserve?" (*Marbury* 1803, 179). Of course, there is only one answer to Marshall's rhetorical question. When a provision of the Constitution is expressly violated, the judiciary must take cognizance of the case that results and uphold the Constitution's status as supreme law.

Marshall endorsed the doubtful case rule in important cases such as *Fletcher v. Peck* (1810), *McCulloch v. Maryland* (1819), *Dartmouth College v. Woodward* (1819), and *Brown v. Maryland* (1827). Nevertheless, the idea that the doubtful case rule was an important element of judicial review in the early republic is not free from difficulty. Legal scholar William Treanor has questioned its importance based on his review of the arguments of Edmund Randolph and St. George Tucker in the 1782 *Case of the Prisoners* (1782) in Virginia (better known as *Commonwealth v. Caton*). As Treanor himself noted, however, Randolph's argument provides support for the doubtful case rule. In addition, Treanor does not contest the substantial evidence produced by Thayer, Snowiss, and others that the doubtful case rule was part of the context in which the institution of judicial review took shape. On balance, the evidence is clear that the rule played an important role in debates over judicial review in the early republic.

This rule is not part of the contemporary institution of judicial review. Once it is accepted that the judiciary has the duty to interpret and enforce the Constitution in ordinary cases, the rule becomes very problematic. As a practical matter, the rule counsels the judiciary to ignore probable cases of constitutional violation. In contemporary terms, the rule threatens judicial independence by asking for extraordinary deference to the legislature. The rule does not ask so much for judicial restraint as judicial abdication.

The different understanding the founding generation had of the relationship between law and politics is another good candidate for an element of judicial review in the early republic that no longer exists. This understanding had several overlapping dimensions. One was that the judiciary had no power to resolve all the constitutional questions that might arise. The judiciary could hear only legal cases, not political disputes. As Marshall stated in a largely overlooked speech to the House of Representatives in March 1800: "[T]he constitution had never been understood, to confer on that department [the judiciary], any political power whatever" (Hobson 1990, 95). Marshall's discussion of "political questions" in *Marbury* reflected this view. To some extent, Marshall was making the point, familiar to constitutional lawyers, that the judiciary could consider only concrete cases and controversies. Implicit in his remarks, however, was the idea that there was some sort of additional limit on the kind of cases the judiciary could hear. Presumably the Supreme Court should refrain from hearing a political dispute masquerading as a properly brought case.

A second dimension of the relationship of law to politics was that judges were not understood to be making law. From the perspective of the eighteenth century, the law was not the product of individual will but of general reason. This point is quite important but can be difficult to understand. We are used to the idea that in some cases, the justices of the Supreme Court change the law. For the founding generation, the very idea of changing the law through judicial decisions was almost unthinkable. As legal historian William Nelson commented, "They understood law as fixed and immutable, not as something that government could change in response to shifting conceptions of social good" (Nelson 2000, 7). In the specific case of constitutional law, members of the founding generation, such as Hamilton, believed that judges did not make new law by enforcing the Constitution; they merely implemented the will of the people.

The third dimension of the relationship of law to politics had to do with the method the judiciary used to decide cases. This point has been illuminated by Nelson's study of *Marbury*. Nelson argued, "[I]n *Marbury v. Madison*, Chief Justice John Marshall drew a line, which nearly all citizens of his time believed ought to be drawn, between the legal and the political" (Nelson 2000, 8). Marshall implemented this understanding by distinguishing

between political matters, to be resolved by the legislative and executive branches in the new democratic, majoritarian style, and legal matters, to be resolved by the judiciary in the government-by-consensus style that had prevailed in most eighteenth-century American courts. (Nelson 2000, 59)

The Court would attempt to refrain from entering the political fray by focusing on values, such as protecting property rights, on which there was widespread agreement.

None of these understandings of the law–politics distinction survives today in any meaningful fashion. The Court does not avoid issues just because they might be politically controversial. One favorite contemporary argument for judicial review is that the Court can act to solve significant social problems when the political branches are paralyzed. Although some defend the distinction between law and politics by emphasizing the differences between how the legislative and judicial branches make decisions, no one defends the eighteenth-century view that judges do not change the law but simply declare it. To put the point another way, the sharp distinction the founding generation drew between reason and will no longer holds.

Robert Clinton claimed a third condition for the exercise of judicial review. This was that it could be exercised only to defend the judiciary against encroachments by the other branches. This view arises largely from two sources: remarks at the Federal Convention and the fact that *Marbury* concerned a jurisdictional statute. In the Federal Convention, Elbridge Gerry stated that the judiciary "will have a sufficient check agst. encroachments on their own department by their exposition of the laws, which involved a power of deciding on their Constitutionality" (Farrand 1937, vol. 1, 97). Arguably, *Marbury* simply followed up on this understanding in holding unconstitutional section 13 of the Judiciary Act of 1789.

This view of *Marbury* is not borne out by the opinion that Marshall wrote. Limiting judicial review to defenses against encroachment is not suggested by anything in Marshall's actual argument. Although Marshall's examples of unconstitutional actions may be limited to clear cases of violation, they are not limited to statutes that pertain to the judiciary. Such a doctrine is not supported by the early practice of the Supreme Court in entertaining claims that acts of Congress were unconstitutional no matter what their subject. Gerry's suggestion to limit the voiding power to cases of encroachment was simply that: one possible future for judicial review that did not come to pass.

Two elements of judicial review in the early republic no longer exist. Scholars have been slow to appreciate the significance of this point. They have long noted the absence of any controversy over the power of judicial review after the Supreme Court rendered judgment in *Marbury*. They have also cited statements made in support of judicial review during the founding period. Consider this statement of Oliver Ellsworth, made in the Connecticut ratifying convention:

[I]f the general legislature should at any time overleap their limits, the judicial department is a constitutional check. If the United States go beyond their powers, if they make a law which the Constitution does not authorize, it is void; and the judicial power, the national judges, who to secure their impartiality are to be made independent, will declare it to be void. On the other hand, if the states go beyond their limits, if they make a law which is an usurpation upon the general government, the law is void, and upright independent judges will declare it to be so. (Bailyn 1990, 252)

This is apparently a comprehensive statement in favor of judicial review. Ellsworth endorsed Supreme Court review of state laws. He made plain that laws made by Congress are subject to being ruled void by the Court. But it would be a mistake to conclude from this that Ellsworth and others of like mind supported judicial review in a contemporary sense. It is possible that Ellsworth did not favor the doubtful case rule and that he shared none of the understandings of the distinctions between law and politics just reviewed. That is very unlikely. The evidence from the founding period supports the conclusion that because of these conditions on the exercise of judicial power, the institution of judicial review in the early republic, as ratified by Chief Justice Marshall in *Marbury*, was very different from the contemporary institution of judicial review.

The New Elements of Judicial Review

The final category is those elements of the contemporary institution of judicial review that have been acquired since the days of the early republic. The most obvious candidate is the doctrine of judicial supremacy, the idea that the Supreme Court is the final authority in matters of constitutional interpretation, especially with respect to the other two branches of the federal government. Marshall never claimed supremacy for the Court in *Marbury*. The opinion ends with Marshall saying that courts have an *equal* right to the other departments in interpreting the Constitution. The Court committed itself explicitly to judicial supremacy only relatively recently. In *Cooper v. Aaron,* for example, the Court stated that the "federal judiciary is supreme in the exposition of the law of the Constitution" (1958, 18).

A less obvious candidate for an important element of contemporary judicial review is the near-total control the Supreme Court has over its own docket. The Court achieved substantial control over its docket only in the twentieth century following passage of the Judiciary Act of 1925. This control contributed to the sense of the justices that the Court has a special mission that differentiates it from other courts. Chief Justice Vinson stated that

[t]he Supreme Court is not, and never has been, primarily concerned with the correction of errors in lower court decisions. . . . To remain effective, the Supreme Court must continue to decide only those cases which present questions whose resolution will have immediate importance far beyond the particular facts and parties involved. (Perry 1991, 36)

In effect, Vinson was saying that the Court did not exist to provide justice to individuals (as many Americans believe) but to decide broad matters of legal policy.

Combined with the expansion of the Court's jurisdiction in the decades following the Civil War, the result has been to transform the Court into a roving commission seeking out important constitutional questions. The Court can deliberately avoid cases that are poor vehicles for new constitutional rules and seek out cases that are good vehicles. The ability to select cases also means that the Court can respond relatively quickly to a public demand to resolve an important constitutional issue.

The Supreme Court did not have this ability in the early republic. Chief Justice Marshall's Court was a common-law court. The Court had control over its docket only in the sense that there were not that many cases to decide. It would have never occurred to Marshall to use the Court as a policymaking body in the way described by Vinson. This would have undermined the law–politics distinction that Marshall strove to maintain. Vinson's Court was confident of its status as a truly coequal branch of government and comfortable with the idea that its decisions would have significant policy consequences and might be politically controversial. Marshall's Court had none of these characteristics.

When understanding the differences between the contemporary institution of judicial review and judicial review in the early republic, it is important to keep in mind the precarious state of the federal judiciary in the early nineteenth century. There was widespread agreement on the legitimacy of judicial review in the founding period. This agreement did not necessarily have any implications for the legitimacy of the judiciary once it actually began to wield power. It is easy to agree to a practice that sounds desirable when it is considered in the abstract. Once the Court began making decisions, the question of judicial review moved into the realm of practical politics. In this realm, the legitimacy of judicial review could be seriously threatened by whether the Court's decisions advanced or retarded important political interests.

This is exactly what occurred during Chief Justice Marshall's tenure. Leslie Goldstein declared

that a particular state at one time explicitly endorsed federal judicial authority was no guarantee that some issue in the future would not arouse passions so strong as to evoke resistance by that same state to federal authority. (Goldstein 1997, 155–156)

During the period 1790 to 1859, according to Goldstein, there were thirty-two instances of defiance by a state of the interpretation of a law by a federal court, twenty instances of rejection of the authority of the federal courts to interpret law, thirty-two instances of defiance of the evident meaning of federal law, twenty-one instances of formal acts of nullification of

federal law, and sixteen instances of defiance of a federal court order. This is not a description of a polity that has placidly accepted judicial review. Rather it describes a situation in which the federal judiciary is struggling to achieve even the kind of routine enforcement of court orders that we now take for granted.

The power of the federal judiciary was a contested point in the early decades of the nineteenth century, particularly during the 1820s. This poses the interesting problem of determining when the contemporary institution of judicial review, and in particular the doctrine of judicial supremacy, began to take shape. There was not a single point in time at which government institutions and the public agreed that judicial review in the contemporary sense was legitimate. There is evidence of respect for the Supreme Court and deference to its interpretation of the Constitution before the Civil War. Alexis de Tocqueville noted the prestige of lawyers and judges in antebellum America in a section of *Democracy in America* (1850) titled, "The Temper of the American Legal Profession and How It Serves to Counterbalance Democracy" (Tocqueville 1850/ 1969, 263). He commented that "[a]n American judge, armed with the right to declare laws unconstitutional, is constantly intervening in political affairs" and famously concluded, "There is hardly a political question in the United States which does not sooner or later turn into a judicial one" (Tocqueville 1850/ 1969, 269–270). Tocqueville claimed that the power of state and federal judges to declare legislation unconstitutional "is recognized by all the authorities; one finds neither party nor individual who contests it" (101). With regard to the doctrine of judicial supremacy, however, historian Phillip Paludan contended that before the Civil War, "[T]he idea that only Supreme Court justices could declare the meaning of the Constitution had not yet been established" (Paludan 1994, 13).

An analysis that focuses on the interplay of government institutions is useful in understanding how the contemporary institution of judicial review took shape. The power and activity of the Supreme Court assumed modern proportions only after the Civil War. This is true both in terms of the number of state and federal laws ruled unconstitutional and the increase in institutional capacity provided to the federal judiciary through various jurisdictional grants from Congress. Before 1860, only two federal laws were held unconstitutional, along with thirty-five provisions of state and local law. After 1860, the pace at which state and local laws were held unconstitutional picked up considerably and invalidation of federal laws became common. The ratification of the Civil War Amendments, especially the Fourteenth Amendment, was one important reason for the increase in the activity of the Court. Also important, however, were the Jurisdiction and Removal Act of 1875 and the Judiciary Acts of 1891 and 1925. These acts increased the jurisdiction of the Court under Article III and gave it greater institutional capacity to control its caseload and direct its attention to constitutional cases.

Considered in the abstract, a number of institutional factors have always worked to the Supreme Court's advantage, even in the early republic. When decisions striking down state statutes enhanced the authority of the federal government as a whole, the elected branches were likely to support the Court. This guarantees the existence of the power to review acts of state and local governments and places it on an especially firm footing.

Matters are considerably more complex in the case of holding acts of the elected branches unconstitutional. The Supreme Court can build goodwill among the branches by ruling that their actions are constitutional. Holding actions unconstitutional may not provoke the other branches if the decision is perceived as a narrow or technical one that does not have important policy implications. Even if there are important policy implications, the Court can still escape damage if it is allied with political forces or one of the branches that objected to the legislation. These allies can protect the Court by using the checks and balances the Constitution provides. The legislation may have passed over a presidential veto or become unpopular over time. However, it is also possible that the Court may rule legislation unconstitutional when the elected branches and the public have agreed that the law in question is desirable. In this situation, the Court may be overruled by a constitutional amendment or it may back down in a subsequent ruling. The effects of a fragmented political system filled with checks and balances thus work to the Court's advantage, along with its ability to move quickly if need be to reverse itself.

Another positive source of the Supreme Court's power is that it can take advantage of the legalistic aspects of American ideology and identify itself closely with the Constitution in a patriotic sense. We should keep in mind that after the Civil War the Supreme Court did not stand in an unmediated relationship to the public and the elected branches. As the status of lawyers increased and they grew more self-conscious as a profession, they saw the Court as a strong ally and as an expression of their highest sentiments. Any hostility toward the Court during the formative period of judicial supremacy in the late nineteenth century was thus mediated by the legal profession. There is a strong relationship between the growing importance of lawyers to American life and the doctrine of judicial supremacy. Support, respect, and reverence for the Supreme Court remain strong today among American lawyers and constitute one of the main pillars of the Court's power.

These remarks are, of course, only preliminary. We need a better understanding of how the contemporary institution of judicial review came to be established. Such an understanding must be grounded in a disaggregation of "judicial review" into its constituent elements. As Mark Graber has emphasized, exploring how these different elements came together (while others were discarded) involves exploring "the broader struggles between the partisan forces that supported and opposed the federal judiciary at different times in American history" (Graber 1995, 91). Despite all the work on judicial review in the early republic, we still lack a panoramic view of the development of the federal judiciary as an institution—one that would provide Wood's missing history of the origins of judicial independence and include material on partisan politics. Also surprising is the lack of a history of the popular response to federal judicial power, especially before the Civil War. The great interest in what the founding generation accomplished has in many ways stifled inquiry into more fruitful approaches to understanding the development of judicial review as an institution.

This chapter describes some differences between the contemporary institution of judicial review and judicial review in the early republic. The agenda of contemporary constitutional theory has been formed out of the acknowledgment that judicial review in the twentieth century was a more controversial institution than was true in the era of Chief Justice Marshall. This is a result in part of the abandonment of the doubtful case rule, but has more to do with the very different understandings of the distinctions between law and politics that came to prevail in the twentieth century and continue to prevail in the twenty-first century. The questions raised about the legitimacy of the contemporary institution of judicial review therefore cannot be answered by looking to the arguments that prevailed in *Marbury*. Those questions remain unanswered.

Bibliography

Alfange, Dean, Jr. "Marbury v. Madison and Original Understandings of Judicial Review: In Defense of Traditional Wisdom." In *The Supreme Court Review 1993*. Chicago: University of Chicago Press, 1994.

Bailyn, Bernard. *Faces of Revolution: Personalities and Themes in the Struggle for American Independence*. New York: Knopf, 1990.

Baum, Lawrence. *The Supreme Court*. 7th ed. Washington, D.C.: CQ Press, 2001.

Bickel, Alexander M. *The Least Dangerous Branch*. New York: Bobbs-Merrill, 1962.

Casto, William R. "James Iredell and the American Origins of Judicial Review." *Connecticut Law Review* 27 (1995): 329–363.

Clinton, Robert Lowry. Marbury v. Madison *and Judicial Review*. Lawrence: University Press of Kansas, 1989.

Ellis, Richard E. *The Jeffersonian Crisis: Courts and Politics in the Young Republic*. New York: W. W. Norton, 1971.

Farrand, Max, ed. *The Records of the Federal Convention of 1787*. Vols. 1–3. New Haven: Yale University Press, 1937.

Goldstein, Leslie Friedman. "State Resistance to Authority in Federal Unions: The Early United States (1790–1860) and the European Community (1958–94)." *Studies in American Political Development* 11 (1997): 149–189.

Graber, Mark A. "The Passive-Aggressive Virtues: *Cohens v. Virginia* and the Problematic Establishment of Judicial Power." *Constitutional Commentary* 12 (1995): 67–92.

_____. "The Problematic Establishment of Judicial Review." In *The Supreme Court in American Politics: New Institutionalist Interpretations.* Edited by Howard Gillman and Cornell Clayton. Lawrence: University Press of Kansas, 1999.

Griffin, Stephen M. *American Constitutionalism: From Theory to Politics.* Princeton: Princeton University Press, 1996.

Hamilton, Alexander, James Madison, and John Jay. *The Federalist.* Edited by Jacob E. Cooke. Reprint, Middletown, Conn.: Wesleyan University Press, 1961.

Hobson, Charles F. *The Papers of John Marshall.* Vol. 4. Chapel Hill: University of North Carolina Press, 1990.

_____. *The Great Chief Justice: John Marshall and the Rule of Law.* Lawrence: University Press of Kansas, 1996.

Kammen, Michael. *A Machine That Would Go of Itself: The Constitution in American Culture.* New York: Knopf, 1986.

Kramer, Larry D. "Foreword: We the Court." *Harvard Law Review* 115 (November 2001): 4–169.

Kutler, Stanley I. *Judicial Power and Reconstruction Politics.* Chicago: University of Chicago Press, 1968.

Lasser, William. *The Limits of Judicial Power: The Supreme Court in American Politics.* Chapel Hill: University of North Carolina Press, 1988.

Nelson, William E. Marbury v. Madison: *The Origins and Legacy of Judicial Review.* Lawrence: University Press of Kansas, 2000.

Newmyer, R. Kent. *The Supreme Court under Marshall and Taney.* Arlington Heights, Ill.: Harlan Davidson, 1968.

_____. *Supreme Court Justice Joseph Story: Statesman of the Old Republic.* Chapel Hill: University of North Carolina Press, 1985.

Paludan, Phillip Shaw. *The Presidency of Abraham Lincoln.* Lawrence: University Press of Kansas, 1994.

Perry, H. W., Jr. *Deciding to Decide: Agenda Setting in the United States Supreme Court.* Cambridge: Harvard University Press, 1991.

Purcell, Edward A., Jr. *Litigation and Inequality: Federal Diversity Jurisdiction in Industrial America, 1870–1958.* New York: Oxford University Press, 1992.

Rakove, Jack N. *Original Meanings: Politics and Ideas in the Making of the Constitution.* New York: Knopf, 1996.

_____. "The Origins of Judicial Review: A Plea for New Contexts." *Stanford Law Review* 49 (1997): 1031–1064.

Ross, William G. *A Muted Fury: Populists, Progressives, and Labor Unions Confront the Courts, 1890–1937.* Princeton: Princeton University Press, 1994.

Smith, Jean Edward. *John Marshall: Definer of a Nation.* New York: Holt, 1996.

Snowiss, Sylvia. *Judicial Review and the Law of the Constitution.* New Haven: Yale University Press, 1990.

Thayer, James B. "The Origin and Scope of the American Doctrine of Constitutional Law." *Harvard Law Review* 7 (1893): 129–156.

Tocqueville, Alexis de. *Democracy in America.* Translated by George Lawrence. 1850. Reprint, Garden City, N.Y.: Doubleday, 1969.

Treanor, William Michael. "The *Case of the Prisoners* and the Origins of Judicial Review." *University of Pennsylvania Law Review* 143 (1994): 491–570.

Van Alstyne, William W. "A Critical Guide to *Marbury v. Madison.*" *Duke Law Journal* 1969: 1–47.

Warren, Charles. *The Supreme Court in United States History.* Vol. 1. Boston: Little, Brown, 1926.

White, G. Edward. *The Marshall Court and Cultural Change, 1815–35.* New York: Macmillan, 1988.

Wood, Gordon S. "The Origins of Judicial Review." *Suffolk University Law Review* 22 (1988): 1293–1307.

_____. "Judicial Review in the Era of the Founding." In *Is the Supreme Court the Guardian of the Constitution?* Edited by Robert A. Licht. Washington, D.C.: AEI Press, 1993.

5

Marbury v. Madison, Judicial Review, and Constitutional Supremacy in the Nineteenth Century

ROBERT LOWRY CLINTON

Marbury v. Madison (1803) is now widely regarded by legal scholars as the leading precedent for the authority of the U.S. Supreme Court to invalidate, or "strike down," national laws that violate the Constitution. In *Marbury*, for the first time in a unanimous decision with a fully reasoned opinion, the Court refused to enforce an act of Congress because of constitutional problems in the act. Since the early twentieth century, this authority has been known as the power of "judicial review." The phrase "judicial review" was not used in the nineteenth century to stand for the Court's power to strike down laws on constitutional grounds. The first use of the phrase by a prominent constitutional commentator to stand for constitutional review of legislation did not occur until 1910 (Corwin 1910, 102). Before that, the phrase was used almost exclusively in the field of administrative law to stand for court review of executive agency action.

The present prominence of the Supreme Court in our constitutional system results from the Court's possession and use of constitutional judicial review. Because the American judicial system is based largely on English common law, in which court decisions are normally expected to be based on previous court decisions, called "precedents," one might expect that *Marbury* would have been a prominent precedent throughout all of American constitutional history. This is not the case. *Marbury v. Madison* was almost completely irrelevant for most of the nineteenth century. To understand this astonishing fact about *Marbury*, it is necessary to examine some features of the case that are often misunderstood or even ignored. These features can be brought to light only by careful rereading of *Marbury* and careful reconsideration of its historical background.

Today, the *Marbury* case is usually portrayed as a simple "political" struggle between President Thomas Jefferson and Chief Justice John Marshall. Politics was involved in the case, but if we want to understand how it was understood in the nineteenth century, we will have to look at it in a less simplified way. We must begin by realizing that the case did raise serious legal and constitutional issues regarding the Court's jurisdiction, the legal status of unconstitutional acts, the role of the judiciary in making determinations of constitutionality, the circumstances under which judicial orders could be appropriately directed to executive branch officials, the precise point at which judicial appointments become final, the kinds of duties that may be properly imposed on administrators by Congress, and the extent to which executive officials are entitled to withhold information or testimony from courts and parties to lawsuits.

The Case

Marbury v. Madison arose in 1801 when William Marbury and three others—Dennis Ramsay, Robert Townsend Hooe, and William Harper[1]—were appointed justices of the peace for the District of Columbia by outgoing ("lame duck") Federalist president John Adams, who had lost the election of 1800 to Republican Jefferson. The offices to which the four would-be judges were appointed had been created by an act of Congress passed on February 27, 1801. Because there was so little time between the appointments and Adams's departure from office, the judges failed to receive their commissions, which were left undelivered on the eve of Jefferson's inauguration. The new administration refused to deliver or produce the commissions on request. On December 17, 1801, the four sued for a writ of mandamus[2] in the U.S. Supreme Court to force newly appointed secretary of state James Madison to produce them. Political infighting developed over these and other last-minute Federalist judicial appointments in the months after Jefferson assumed office. This infighting led to the Republican Senate's refusal to produce records of the confirmations and to congressional suspension of the Court's 1802 terms, causing Marbury's case not to be tried until February 1803.

Before initiating the suit, at least three of the plaintiffs applied to the secretary of state and the secretary of the Senate for information regarding the commissions. The application to the secretary of state is confirmed in the *Marbury* opinion. None of the witnesses examined at trial questioned the existence or the validity of the commissions.[3] According to the testimony of Jacob Wagner, a subpoenaed witness from the State Department, Marbury and Ramsay had been referred to him by the secretary of state. Wagner told the applicants that "two of the commissions had been signed but the other had not." Wagner then stated that this fact had been communicated to him by others but declined to reveal the identity of the informants. A second employee of the State Department, Daniel Brent, testified that he was "almost certain" that Marbury's and Hooe's commissions had been completed, but not Ramsay's, and that he (Brent) had "made out the list of names" that the clerk had used to draft the documents (*Marbury* 1803, 142–143).

The only other administration witness called was Attorney General Levi Lincoln, who had been acting secretary of state (Madison was out of town) when Marbury and Ramsay first made their application to the department. At first, Lincoln declined to answer questions because he "did not think himself bound to disclose his official transactions while acting as secretary of state" and "ought not to be compelled to answer any thing which might tend to criminate himself." Later, Lincoln agreed to entertain several questions, though he stated that he would not answer the crucial question as to "what had been done with the commissions" (*Marbury* 1803, 143–145). Lincoln's change of heart was apparently in response to an argument made by Charles Lee, Marbury's lawyer. In this argument, Lee distinguished between two kinds of duty that had been laid on the secretary of state by Congress in two separate enactments passed in 1789 (*Marbury* 1803, 139–142, 144).

The first of these acts had been passed on July 27, 1789, and had created the Department of Foreign Affairs, with the secretary of state as its head. Under this act, the secretary was to "perform and execute such duties as shall from time to time be enjoined on, or entrusted to him by the President." The act was explicitly confined to matters "respecting foreign affairs," as the title of the agency suggested. Lee conceded that, in regard to "the powers given and the duties imposed by this act, no mandamus will lie," since the secretary is here "responsible only to the President" (*Marbury* 1803, 139–140).

The second act was passed on September 15, 1789. Its purpose was to provide for the safekeeping of official documents of the United States. This act changed the name of the Department of Foreign Affairs to the Department of State and charged the secretary with the duty to publish, print, preserve, and record all bills, orders, resolutions, and notes of Congress that have been signed by the president and to "make out," "record," and "affix the seal of the United States to all civil commissions, after they have been signed by the President." The act also stated that all copies of official documents, including commissions, "shall be as good evidence as the originals." According to Lee, the duties of the secretary embodied in this act, unlike those in the earlier act, must be performed independently of the president, and

may therefore be compelled by mandamus in the case of nonperformance, "in the same manner as other persons holding offices under the authority of the United States" (*Marbury* 1803, 140–141).

The last-quoted phrase is a clear reference to Section 13 of the Judiciary Act of 1789, which enacted that the Supreme Court "shall have power to issue . . . writs of mandamus, in cases warranted by the principles and usages of law, to any courts appointed, *or persons holding office, under the authority of the United States*" (1 Stat. 81, quoted in *Marbury* 1803 at 148; emphasis added). Lee interpreted this phrase concerning mandamus as pertaining to the Court's original, or trial, jurisdiction. This explains why Marbury and the other plaintiffs brought their complaint directly to the Supreme Court in reliance on Section 13 rather than taking their case to a lower court first. After quoting Section 13 during oral argument, Lee remarked that "Congress is not restrained from conferring original jurisdiction *in other cases than those mentioned in the constitution*" (*Marbury* 1803, 148; emphasis added). The Court would ultimately disagree with Lee's statement on this point and thus deny Marbury's application for a writ of mandamus.

Failing in their application to the State Department, the plaintiffs also sought aid from the Senate. Evidence of the application of Marbury, Hooe, and Ramsay for copies from the Senate journal reflecting its "advice and consent to the appointments" is found in the *Debates and Proceedings of the Congress of the United States* for 1803 (34–50). On January 31, 1803, the Senate considered the following motion: "That the Secretary of the Senate be directed to give an attested copy of the proceedings of the Senate of the 2d and 3d of March, 1801, so far as they relate to the nomination and appointment of William Marbury, Robert T. Hooe, and Dennis Ramsay, as justices of the peace for the counties of Washington and Alexandria, in the territory of Columbia, on the application of them or either of them" (*Debates and Proceedings* 1803, 34). After a lengthy debate, in which proponents of the motion advanced the simple justice and reasonableness of the application, opponents urging the need for secrecy and privacy in Senate proceedings and expressing fears that the motion constituted a veiled attack on the executive branch, the motion was defeated by a vote of 15 to 13.

The Opinion

Chief Justice Marshall's opinion for the Court in *Marbury v. Madison* was announced on February 24, 1803. The first, and longest, section of the opinion dealt with Marbury's right to receive his commission and the appropriate legal remedy to enforce the right (*Marbury* 1803, 154–173). The Court's rulings on these points were that Marbury had been duly appointed, that delivery of the commission was unnecessary to validate the appointment, that the secretary of state did not have the right to withhold the commission, that it is a duty of any government of laws to supply remedies for violated rights, and that a writ of mandamus was an appropriate legal remedy for resolution of Marbury's dilemma.

The second section of the opinion dealt with the power of the Court to issue the requested order (*Marbury* 1803, 173–180). The Court's answer was negative. One of the acts on which

Marbury relied, Section 13 of the Judiciary Act of 1789, authorized the Court to issue writs of mandamus in original (trial) jurisdiction to *any* "persons holding office under the authority of the United States." This impermissibly enlarged the Court's jurisdiction beyond the terms of Article III, Section 2, of the Constitution, which restricts the Court's original jurisdiction to cases involving ambassadors, public ministers, consuls, or states. Although Marbury had a legal right to his commission that was violated by Madison's failure to perform a ministerial duty assigned by Congress in the act of September 15, 1789, the Court could not provide the requested relief. The provision of the Judiciary Act of 1789 extending the Court's trial jurisdiction to cases involving all federal officials was unconstitutional. Marbury was entitled to his commission, applied for an appropriate legal remedy, but could not get it from the Supreme Court.

In the final pages of his *Marbury* opinion, Chief Justice Marshall justified the Court's constitutional analysis, arguing that the courts must "say what the law is," that the Constitution is "superior," "paramount" law, and that a legislative act (a "statute") in conflict with the Constitution is void (*Marbury* 1803, 176–177). After establishing the principle that unconstitutional legislative acts are void, Marshall carefully restricted the Court's power to invalidate such acts to cases in which the Court is *forced* to ignore either the Constitution or the statute to decide the case before it (177–180). *Marbury*-style judicial review is very limited in scope. This is one of the main reasons why the case was largely ignored by courts and legal commentators as a precedent for judicial review until the late nineteenth century.

The First Section of the Opinion

The first section of Marshall's opinion dealt with Marbury's right to receive his commission and the appropriate remedy that attaches to this kind of right. Several serious issues were confronted by the Court in this section of the opinion:

1. The precise point at which judicial appointments become final—in other words, whether "delivery" is required or the president's signature is enough;
2. The kinds of duties that may be properly imposed on administrators by Congress;
3. The circumstances under which judicial orders may appropriately be directed to executive branch officials;
4. The extent to which executive officials are entitled to withhold information or testimony from courts and parties to lawsuits;
5. The nature and extent of the Court's trial and appellate jurisdiction, especially whether Congress may enlarge the trial jurisdiction of the Court.

In the second section of the opinion, the following two issues were addressed:

6. The legal status of unconstitutional acts, or whether an unconstitutional legislative act is void;
7. The role of the judiciary in making determinations of constitutionality, or whether the Court has the authority to overturn an unconstitutional act.

The most interesting historical fact about these issues is that only those pertaining to the first section of the opinion (1–5) were noticed by the Court and by commentators throughout most of the nineteenth century. Those pertaining to the second section of the opinion (6–7) were hardly noticed at all.

Many contemporary commentators treat the issues addressed in the first section of the *Marbury* opinion as uninteresting, given the overriding importance of the constitutionality of laws and judicial review (6 and 7) in modern times. But constitutional judicial review was not an issue of overriding importance in Marshall's time. The issue of how courts could protect individual rights afforded by law under the new Constitution was of overriding importance.

Marbury's case provides an excellent illustration of this point. As William E. Nelson (2000, 60) noted in a book on *Marbury*, the narrow, technical ruling on issue 1, that the president's signature on a judicial commission completes the appointment and entitles the appointee to delivery of the commission, was crucially important to lawyers of Marshall's time. This kind of entitlement creates a vested property right analogous to a right to land. If a subsequent administration could withhold a judicial commission signed by a previous president merely because it did not like the appointee, the appointee's political party, or the previous president, then what would prevent such an administration from withholding a land patent or a lease merely because it did not like the assignee or the lessee?

The seriousness of this matter comes into fuller focus when we consider issue 2: the kinds of duties that may be properly imposed on administrators by Congress. It is often said that *Marbury* arose when the secretary of state failed to "deliver" the commissions to Marbury and the other appointees, as if delivery of a commission was analogous to delivering a summons—which is required if a lawsuit is to proceed. This suggests that the cause of action arose when the *previous* (Adams) administration failed to do something that was required to complete the appointment and then that the *subsequent* (Jefferson) administration merely ratified that initial failure. The Jefferson administration's failure was much more serious, even bordering on the unlawful, as Attorney General Lincoln suggested by "taking the Fifth" when called on to testify.

This point is almost always overlooked in contemporary discussions of *Marbury*. Marbury's notorious "right" is not to *delivery* of his commission but rather to a mere *copy* from the record on demand. The administration did not merely refuse to send someone across town on horseback with papers to the plaintiffs; it refused to produce copies of those papers (commissions) that it had been *required by law* to produce. That law was the act of September 15, 1789, which imposed on the secretary of state a ministerial duty to "make out," "record," and "affix" the seal of the United States to all civil commissions (*Marbury* 1803, 158). It does not impose on the secretary the obligation to deliver a commission, "but it is placed in his hands for the person entitled to it; and cannot be more lawfully withheld by him, than by any other person" (173). Marbury's claim "respects a paper, which according to law, is upon record, and to a copy of which the law gives a right, on the payment of ten cents" (170).

Marbury's claimed right is *statutory*, not constitutional, arising directly from the duty imposed by Congress on the secretary to do a certain act affecting the absolute rights of individuals, in the performance of which he is not placed under the particular direction of the President, and the performance of which, the President cannot lawfully forbid, and therefore is never presumed to have forbidden. (*Marbury* 1803, 171)

The secretary's duty is to perform a purely "ministerial" act not within executive discretion. It is within the power of a court to supply a remedy for an individual who has been harmed by a public minister's failure to do his or her duty. This is the main reason why "delivery" of a commission cannot be considered essential to the completion of an appointment: "The transmission of the commission, is a practice directed by convenience, but not by law. It cannot therefore be necessary to constitute the appointment which must precede it, and which is the mere act of the President" (*Marbury* 1803, 160).

The Court's rulings on these points, taken together, constitute a classic example of good statutory interpretation, emphasizing the distinction between the two congressional acts creating and structuring the State Department—one assigning "discretionary" and the other assigning "ministerial" duties. Any other interpretation would have violated the plain meaning of one or the other statute, defeating its purpose and intended effect. Any other interpretation would have denied Congress the power to impose ministerial duties on executives and would have moved the republic at least a step toward executive supremacy. Any other interpretation would have denied to aggrieved individuals a judicial forum to challenge the arbitrary acts of administrators impairing vested rights. This issue (issue 3 in the previous discussion) concerning the circumstances in which judicial orders might be appropriately directed to executive branch officials was especially critical for a Court trying to establish its authority to enforce and apply the law in a new government trying to work out the details of a constitutional separation of powers. Any other interpretation would have blurred the line that Marshall and his fellow justices were trying to draw between "law" and "politics." This line is described by Nelson (2000, 61):

[Marshall's] central task in *Marbury* was to specify when law bound the political branches and when it did not. To do so, he and the Court distinguished between political matters, such as foreign policy, as to which the legislature and executive were accountable only to the electorate, and matters of individual rights, which the courts would protect by adhering to fixed principles. In Marshall's own words, "political" subjects "respect[ed] the nation, not individual rights" and were governed by a political branch whose decisions were "never . . . examinable by the courts" but "only politically examinable." In contrast, there were cases where "a specific duty [was] assigned by law, and individual rights depend[ed] upon the performance of that duty." In such cases involving "the rights of individuals," every officer of government was "amenable to the laws for his conduct; and [could not] at his discretion sport away . . . vested rights," and a person, such as Marbury, who possessed a vested right was entitled to a remedy. In Marshall's own words, "The very essence of civil liberty certainly consist[ed] in the right of every individual to claim the protection of the laws, whenever he receives an injury."

Drawing this line clearly between matters for which the government would be accountable to the electorate and matters governable by "fixed principles" and so accountable to the law was vital for Marshall and his colleagues. They knew that on this effort would depend the success of the framers' goal of allowing the government to control the governed and, at the same time, obliging it to control itself. The *Marbury* Court even invoked William Blackstone, the most prominent legal writer of the eighteenth century, citing Blackstone's rule against presuming that the government, at least in the person of its highest executive authority, might have arbitrarily violated the vested rights of an individual. According to Blackstone (1979, 255): "[I]njuries to the rights of property can scarcely be committed by the crown without the intervention of its officers, for whom the law, in matters of right, entertains no respect or delicacy; but furnishes various methods of detecting the errors and misconduct of those agents, by whom the king has been deceived and induced to do a temporary injustice" (*Marbury* 1803, 165).

The same point had been made by Sen. James Hillhouse of Connecticut during the Senate debate on Marbury's request for a copy of relevant portions of the Senate journal. After noting certain situations requiring Senate–executive cooperation (e.g., treaties), Hillhouse remarked (*Debates and Proceedings* 1803, 38) that "[i]n all these cases the President may be deceived; the Secretary of the Senate may by mistake or fraud certify . . . the ratification of a treaty, when the fact is otherwise; and where, but to the journals of the Senate, can we resort to correct the error?"

Regarding issue 4, the extent to which executive officials are entitled to withhold information or testimony from courts and parties to lawsuits, the *Marbury* situation must have been very disturbing to the Court. With the Court trying to establish its authority to protect individual rights created by national laws reflecting the sentiments of democratic majorities against official attempts to abridge those rights, the justices would have understandably been upset over the apparent "stonewalling" of the administration. The secretary of state had refused to make an appearance to "show cause why a mandamus should not issue" (*Marbury* 1803, 153–154). The attorney general, who did appear, sought refuge in the Fifth Amendment. The separation of powers doctrine of the Constitution surely enabled the Court to defend itself against such a brazen attempt by a coordinate branch of government to impair the capacity of the judiciary to perform its functions properly. Such a concern was probably the framers' main rationale for judicial review in the first place, as reflected in their narrowing of the power to decide cases "arising under the Constitution" to those "of a Judiciary nature," of which *Marbury* is a classic example. According to Madison, the framers accepted the extension of federal judicial power to cases "arising under the Constitution, Laws, and Treaties of the United States" only after it had been "generally supposed that the jurisdiction given was constructively limited to cases of a Judiciary nature" (Clinton 1991, 88–89). Constitutional judicial review, as the framers understood it, was designed to allow the courts to prevent legislative or executive interference with the proper performance of judicial duties.

The *Marbury* situation is somewhat like that in *United States v. Nixon* (1974). There the Court unanimously held that documents in the custody of executive officials, including the president, are subject to judicial process (subpoena) whenever such documents are essential to appropriate adjudication of the rights and duties of parties to a case pending in federal court, at least in the absence of a clear showing that exempting the documents from judicial scrutiny is absolutely necessary for reasons of national security. There are some important differences between the two cases. In *Nixon*, the president was directly named as an unindicted coconspirator in a criminal prosecution. In *Marbury*, a civil action, the president was a background figure, though later he confessed to having ordered the secretary to refuse delivery of the commission. However, despite these and other differences, in both cases important documents needed by a court were withheld without any showing of necessity. In *Marbury*, there was not even a pretense of necessity. Moreover, in *Marbury* the administration's intransigence had occurred in the face of an act of Congress that not only *required* that the requested information be produced but whose stated purpose was to *ensure* that such information be produced when needed by a court. The Court's effort to declare the law respecting whether, and in what circumstances, someone in Marbury's position possessed a valid claim of legal right deserving of judicial remediation must be understood against this threatening background.

This brings us to issue 5, the nature and extent of the Court's trial and appellate jurisdiction—specifically whether Congress may enlarge the trial jurisdiction of the Court. Perhaps the most frequent criticism that has been leveled by modern commentators at the *Marbury* opinion is the claim that, because the Court declined to issue the writ of mandamus on jurisdictional grounds in the last analysis, it should simply have dismissed the case without opinion, without attending to the issues that we have been discussing at all. The Court should not have addressed issues 1 through 4, because in the end it decided not to require the secretary of state to produce Marbury's commission for constitutional reasons. In other words, the Court should not have decided at which point a judicial appointment becomes effective, or whether—and in what circumstances—Congress may impose nondiscretionary duties on executive officials, or whether—and in what circumstances—courts may order administration officers to perform duties assigned to them by Congress, or whether—and in what circumstances—executives are entitled to withhold from the courts information that is needed to resolve cases.

This ignores the historical context of *Marbury*. Nowadays we expect courts—at least most of the time—to refrain from considering the substantive issues in a case that is going to be dismissed on jurisdictional grounds. However, this approach was not developed until the late nineteenth and early twentieth centuries. It was developed to place limits on an ever-increasing constitutional policymaking authority in the courts unknown (and probably unimagined) in the time of Marshall. Early American courts handled such issues in a much more flexible manner in the interest of doing justice to the claims of litigants in particular cases. This charge also reflects a serious misunderstanding of the jurisdictional aspects of the case, because the Court's jurisdiction over the issues treated in the first section of the *Marbury* opinion had nothing to do with the Court's authority to issue a writ of mandamus. To disentangle these issues, we must consider the following points.

First, the judicial power of the United States is expressly extended in Article III, Section 2, of the Constitution to all cases arising under the laws of the United States; and the right claimed by Marbury is a *statutory* (not a constitutional) right given by a law of the United States, the congressional act of September 15, 1789 (not the Judiciary Act of 1789). Chief Justice Marshall explicitly stated the basis of the Court's jurisdiction in the *Marbury* opinion. He said that the case is one to which the judicial power of the United States applies, because this power "is expressly extended to all cases arising under the *laws* of the United States; and consequently, in some form, may be exercised over the present case; because the right claimed is given by a *law* of the United States" (*Marbury* 1803, 173–174). This law was the act of September 15, 1789, imposing on the secretary of state the duty to keep records of all civil commissions and produce copies of them for parties in lawsuits as well as for other lawful purposes. In this instance, a specific duty had been "assigned by law" and "individual rights depend upon the performance of that duty" (*Marbury* 1803, 166). Under these conditions, the secretary "is so far an officer of the law; is amenable to the laws for his conduct; and cannot at his discretion sport away the vested rights of others" (166).

Second, the appropriateness of the writ of mandamus as a remedy to enforce the statutory right claimed by Marbury was an issue requiring interpretation of the common law (not statutory or constitutional interpretation), which was regarded in the early 1800s and before as based on natural justice and equity and so could not be inconsistent with natural law. Aristotle, in *Nicomachean Ethics* (1998, 95), defined equity as "the correction of that, wherein the law (by reason of its universality) is deficient." Blackstone, in his *Commentaries*

(1979, 62), the most influential law book of Marshall's time, quoted this passage approvingly. Referring to the attitudes of early Anglo-American lawyers and judges on this point, William R. Casto stated,

Blackstone wrote that God had ordained a system of "external immutable laws of good and evil," Human laws—especially the common law—"derive all their force, and all their authority" from this universal natural law and are invalid if they are contrary to it. . . .

Under this theory, judges do not make laws. They are not legislators. They are, to use Blackstone's phrase, "the living oracles" of a common law that preexists in nature. Reasoning in humans was a process bestowed by God that enabled them to detect the subtleties of the preexisting natural law; judges, through their talent, experience, and wisdom, were supposed to use their reasoning to discern the law in the cases that came before them. . . . Under this almost Platonic vision of the common law, a particular judicial determination was proper only to the extent that it approximated natural law that had an existence outside and independent of the court. (Casto 1995, 34–35)

These beliefs would have made it very difficult for the Marshall Court simply to have dismissed Marbury's claim without expressing an opinion on the common-law and equitable aspects of the case. Thus the question of whether the Court should have dealt with issues 1 through 5 before reaching the constitutionality of Section 13 (issue 6) and judicial review (issue 7) is a question that could not (and should not) have been addressed with wooden legal formulas in the context of early nineteenth-century jurisprudence.

Marshall ruled straightforwardly that the duty of a government of laws is to supply remedies for violated rights (*Marbury* 1803, 162–168) and that the writ of mandamus is an appropriate remedy for resolving a problem like Marbury's (168–173). Here Marshall follows closely the lines of argument laid down by attorney Lee in his presentation of Marbury's case, though Lee went farther than Marshall was willing to go. According to Lee, because the secretary was acting merely as recorder of laws, deeds, letters patent, and commissions, he was controlled only by the laws imposing such duties and was subject to indictment for refusing to perform them: "A prosecution of this kind might be the means of punishing the officer, but a specific civil remedy to the injured party can only be obtained by a writ of mandamus" (*Marbury* 1803, 149–150). Lee then cited a series of English cases designed to show that mandamus is appropriate where there is "no other adequate, specific, legal remedy," thereby rendering the use of the writ consistent with "the principles and usages of law," as had been required by Section 13 of the Judiciary Act of 1789 (151–153). The only other remedy available was a prosecution, which, under the circumstances of the case, would have been a "remedy" in name only. Moreover, Marshall was unwilling to charge directly that the secretary had committed a crime.

The equitable considerations are crucial. Though it is often argued that summary disposition of the case would have been appropriate, this approach would have been disingenuous on the part of the Court. Marbury had relied in good faith on a presumptively valid act of Congress. Had the Court chosen to deny Marbury his remedy without apprising him of his right, whether that apprisal is conceived as a right to pursue the cause in another court or merely as a declaration of the law, Marbury's fate would have, in effect, been determined by something we call nowadays a "legal technicality," which seems inconsistent with the fairness expected of courts when they give judgment on the rights of individuals. On the other hand, the Court could not have reached the constitutional issues without ruling on these questions. It was necessary for the Court carefully to distinguish the acts of a subordinate official that are assumed to be the *acts of the executive itself* from the acts of such an official *operating on his own*. Otherwise, the Court could rightly have been charged with disrespect toward a coordinate agency of government. In the case that Section 13 was void and the writ could not be issued, the Court would have acquiesced in an executive usurpation of judicial functions, because the outcome would have been dependent on the mere arbitrary will of a subordinate executive official. In the case that Section 13 was valid and the writ could be issued, the Court would have intruded on the prerogatives of the president by issuing the writ when it was unclear whether the "failure to show cause" was properly within executive discretion or not.

Third, the power of the Court to issue a mandamus to the secretary of state is a remedial power entirely separate from Marbury's right to his commission or the appropriateness of the remedy sought. The jurisdiction to decide on Marbury's right and the appropriate remedy is entirely separate from the jurisdiction to issue a mandamus to the secretary of state. The Court's jurisdiction to decide the legal and equitable issues involved in discerning the *existence* of Marbury's right and the appropriate remedy is based on the act of September 15, 1789, imposing ministerial duties on the secretary of state. The jurisdiction to decide whether the Court is *empowered* to

award the precise remedy called forth by the existence of the right is given by an entirely different act of Congress, Section 13 of the Judiciary Act of 1789.

Let us explore for a moment what this might have meant to the judges of Marshall's time. The distinction between trial and appellate jurisdiction was not viewed in the same way in the first decade of the nineteenth century as today. We tend to view the distinction as a textbook division, defined in such as way as to give an absolute answer to any court considering whether to reach the merits of a case. It is as if there were, for any court, two "baskets" on the bench, one labeled "original" and the other "appellate." If a case appears in the "wrong" basket, then the court discards it, usually without opinion. But in 1803, before the establishment of sharp jurisdictional distinctions and a highly bureaucratized court system, things were viewed differently.

In the pre-*Marbury* era, long before a formal system of intermediate appellate courts declaring its own procedural law was established, most "appeals" were essentially de novo (new) trials. As Nelson (2000, 61–62) put it, following Marbury's counsel Lee and Alexander Hamilton in *Federalist* No. 81, "the concept of appeal had not yet assumed its relatively narrow and precise modern meaning." This meant that "the word 'appellate' [was] not to be taken in its technical sense, . . . but in its broadest sense, in which it denotes nothing more than the power of one tribunal" to have "by reason of its supremacy . . . the superintendence of . . . inferior tribunals and officers, whether judicial or ministerial." The question was, what kind of "superintendence" are we talking about here? As Nelson pointed out, if the Court were to issue the writ, then either Congress has power to "grant original jurisdiction to the Supreme Court in cases in which the Constitution denie[s] it" or "an action for mandamus in the Supreme Court [is] not the commencement of an original proceeding but a form of appeal against the official against whom the writ [is] being sought."

Issuing the writ would have required the Court either to acquiesce in a congressional violation of the Constitution—thus violating the Constitution itself—or to involve itself in reviewing executive acts—thus bringing itself into the political arena. Either way, the Court would compromise its ability to perform its most important function: to discover, declare, and apply the fixed, immutable principles of the law without the distraction of involvement in the policymaking processes of the government.

Marbury in Nineteenth-Century Citation and Commentary

To the degree that *Marbury v. Madison* was noticed at all during the remainder of the nineteenth century—which was not to a very large degree—the aspects of the case discussed in the previous section of this chapter are the only ones that commanded the attention of judges, lawyers, and commentators. The issues of constitutionality and judicial review dealt with in the second section of the *Marbury* opinion were almost entirely unnoticed, as is evident from subsequent commentary on the case, both on and off the bench. Marshall's most prominent progressive-era biographer, Albert J. Beveridge (1916, 153), was "dumbfounded by the apparent disinterest in the case." Bev-

eridge complained that Marshall's first great decision "received scant notice at the time of its delivery. The newspapers had little to say about it. Even the bench and bar of the country, at least in the sections remote from Washington, appear not to have heard of it, or if they had, to have forgotten it."

Such newspaper coverage that there was tended to be in the nature of mere reportage rather than editorial commentary, as is exemplified by articles in the *National Intelligencer* and the *Washington Federalist,* the most prominent Republican and Federalist newspapers, respectively, in the District of Columbia. To the extent that the public paid heed to the decision, the focus was primarily on Marshall's indication that courts had power to issue writs of mandamus to executives in some circumstances. For the most part, the Court's refusal to enforce Section 13 of the Judiciary Act of 1789 was either approved without comment or ignored altogether (Clinton 1991, 102).

There was even a fair amount of misunderstanding about the opinion in the immediate aftermath of its announcement. The following statement, appearing in the *Alexandria Gazette* and several other newspapers the day after the opinion was announced, is a graphic example: "The judges of the Supreme Court have given it as their opinion, in the case of the Mandamus, that the justices are entitled to their commissions, but, that they have not the power to issue a mandamus in the District of Columbia, it not being a State" (Clinton 1991, 102–103).

Some scholars, such as Donald O. Dewey (1970, 136–138), have suggested that such statements reflect a general public failure to understand the opinion, and that such a failure explains why there was so little controversy about it. Others have suggested that *Marbury* was uncontroversial because it was consistent with the Constitution, with existing legal precedent, and with the general political philosophy held by most early nineteenth-century Americans (Clinton 1991, chap. 6). Nelson (2000, 73) noted that *Marbury* was a "modest" decision that "withdrew the courts from politics rather than inserting judges into the political maelstrom."

The Supreme Court, throughout most of the nineteenth century, must have agreed with this view of *Marbury*. During the remainder of Marshall's tenure as chief justice, ten separate opinions contain references to the case. Nine are purely jurisdictional in nature, supporting the distribution of jurisdiction contained in Article III (Clinton 1991, 266 n. 1). The remaining reference is made to support the ruling that writs of mandamus may be issued to executive officials only when such officials are engaged in the performance of purely ministerial duties (Clinton 1991, 266, n. 2).

The pattern established during the remainder of the Marshall era continues during the period of Chief Justice Roger Taney as well. Between 1835 and 1865, *Marbury* is cited in fifteen separate Supreme Court opinions. The largest number of citations is in the jurisdictional area (Clinton 1991, 268, n. 15). Six concern nuances in the mandamus remedy (Clinton 1991, 268, n. 16). One, found in *Carroll v. Carroll* (1853, 287), quotes a well-known passage in an 1821 Marshall opinion, *Cohens v. Virginia* (1821, 399), where Marshall clarified some loose language in *Marbury* unnecessary to the decision

in that case and thus was regarded as *dicta*. In this passage, Marshall provided the classic definition of *dictum* in a judicial opinion:

It is a maxim not to be disregarded that general expressions in every opinion are to be taken in connection with the case in which these expressions are used. If they go beyond the case, they may be respected, but ought not to control the judgement in a subsequent suit, when the very point is presented. The reason of this maxim is obvious. The question actually before the court is investigated with care, and considered in its full extent; other principles which may serve to illustrate it are considered in their relation to the case decided, but their possible bearing on all other cases is seldom completely investigated. (*Cohens* 1821, 399)

Again, there is not even a hint of a critical attitude toward *Marbury* or any of its holdings in these citations, nor are the issues of constitutionality (issue 6) or judicial review (issue 7) mentioned in connection with the case.

During the Taney era, the Court did invalidate an act of Congress for the second time, in *Dred Scott v. Sanford* (1857, 450), where the Court, among other things, struck down the Missouri Compromise of 1820. The most interesting aspect of *Dred Scott* is the Court's striking failure to cite *Marbury v. Madison* as precedent for its exercise of judicial review. Nor did the Court cite *Marbury* in any of the next twenty cases in which national laws were invalidated between 1865 and 1894 (Clinton 1991, 269, n. 33). During this period, *Marbury* was cited in twenty-four separate U.S. Supreme Court opinions. Most of the citations refer either to jurisdictional issues (Clinton 1991, 269, n. 34) or to the mandamus remedy (Clinton 1991, 269–270, n. 35). A few references are to the distinction between "political" and "ministerial" acts of administrators (Clinton 1991, 270, n. 36). Two refer to the technical finality of acts within the executive's discretion (Clinton 1991, 270, n. 37). One quotes the equitable "right/remedy" maxim announced in the first section of the *Marbury* opinion (Clinton 1991, 270, n. 38). One mentions the *Cohens v. Virginia* (1821) clarification of *Marbury* dicta (Clinton 1991, 270, n. 39).

Marbury v. Madison is first cited as precedent for the idea that courts may enforce constitutional limitations on legislative bodies in *Mugler v. Kansas* (1887, 661). Perhaps the Court had been reminded of the *Marbury* case three years before *Mugler* in *Juilliard v. Greenman* (1884, 431), when *Marbury* had been cited in oral argument for the first time before the Supreme Court. In *Juilliard*, the plaintiff's counsel theorized that *Marbury* held the question of whether Congress had exceeded its constitutional authority to be a "judicial" question, suggesting that throughout most of the nineteenth century, this question had been regarded as "nonjudicial."

The *Mugler* citation is significant because it involves two important misrepresentations of *Marbury*. First, the Court uses *Marbury* to support not its power to invalidate a national law but rather its power to invalidate a state law on grounds of Fourteenth Amendment substantive economic due process (*Marbury* 1803, 661). Moreover, it does so in a passage that is essentially *obiter dicta*, because the actual decision in *Mugler* merely upheld a state prohibition on manufacture and sale of intoxicating beverages. Second, and more important for our purpose of understanding the nineteenth-century *Marbury*, the *Mugler* Court asked, quoting from the *Marbury* opinion (*Marbury* 1803, 176):

To what purpose . . . are powers limited, and to what purpose is that limitation committed to writing, if these limits may, at any time, be passed by those intended to be restrained? The distinction between a government with limited and unlimited powers is abolished, if those limits do not confine the persons on which they are imposed, and if acts prohibited and acts allowed are of equal obligation. (Mugler 1887, 661)

This segment of Marshall's argument is used in *Marbury* to support the conclusion that legislative acts contrary to the Constitution are void, *not that courts have the power to refuse to apply them*. But the *Mugler* Court uses the passage to propose that

the courts must obey the Constitution rather than the lawmaking department of government, and must, upon their own responsibility, determine whether, in any particular case, these limits have been passed. (Mugler 1887, 661)

This confusion of the two issues addressed by Marshall in the final pages of his *Marbury* opinion is the key to the difference between the nineteenth-century understanding of *Marbury* and the twentieth-century understanding of the case. This confusion generates modern judicial supremacy, the idea that the Court is entitled to invalidate any act of a coordinate agency of government with final, conclusive authority if a majority of the justices believe—rightly or wrongly—that the law is inconsistent with the Constitution. In the second section of Marshall's opinion, two issues were addressed: issue 6, the legal status of unconstitutional acts, specifically whether an unconstitutional act is void; and issue 7, the role of the judiciary in making determinations of constitutionality, specifically whether courts are entitled to invalidate an unconstitutional act.

Again, the most interesting historical fact about these issues is that not until 1887 were these issues noticed at all by the Supreme Court, and when they were noticed by the Court in *Mugler*, the issues were utterly confused. Let us now turn to an examination of these issues.

The Second Section of the Marbury Opinion

After the Court's rulings on Marbury's appointment, the duties of the government in regard to it, and the appropriateness of mandamus as a remedy, Marshall turned to the power of the Court to issue the requested writ (*Marbury* 1803, 173–180). The Court's answer is negative, on the ground that issuing the writ would require the Court to exercise its Article III trial jurisdiction in a type of case not mentioned in the Constitution. Marbury brought suit in the Supreme Court in the first place because, in the opinion of his lawyer, Congress had attempted to extend the Court's trial jurisdiction to cases involving federal officials in general. Yet Article III of the Constitution states that the original jurisdiction of the Court extends only to ambassadors, public ministers, consuls, and states, not to all federal officials.

The argument supporting the Court's refusal to issue the writ, and thereby its refusal to enforce Section 13 of the Judiciary Act of 1789, contains two subarguments. The first subargument supports the conclusion that "an act of the legislature, repugnant to the constitution, is void" (*Marbury* 1803, 176–177). The second subargument supports the altogether different conclusion that the "courts, as well as other departments, are bound by that instrument [the constitution]" (177–180). Marshall clearly distinguishes between a law *being a nullity* as a re-

sult of incompatibility with the Constitution and the Court *having the power to nullify* such a law once it is determined to be unconstitutional. Marshall distinguishes clearly between issue 6 (the issue of constitutionality) and issue 7 (the issue of judicial review).

The nullity of unconstitutional laws stems primarily from the Constitution's democratic foundation, being drawn from the original right of the people "to establish, for their future government, such principles as, in their opinion, shall most conduce to their own happiness" (*Marbury* 1803, 176). The steps in this subargument are these: (1) the government of the United States is a government of strictly "defined and limited" powers; (2) the Constitution is a law of "superior obligation"; and (3) the nullity of invalid laws is a theory "essentially attached to a written constitution" (176–177). Though none of these steps are repeated in the argument for judicial review, they are obviously necessary to the Court's ultimate result.

Marshall's first conclusion follows from a straightforward argument. The Constitution is clearly a "law of superior obligation" *if* the people do in fact have a right to establish binding rules for their future government *and* the set of these rules is the Constitution. If the law of superior obligation is a written one that defines and limits legislative power, is one whose legislative authority is purely delegated, then any legislative act against that superior law is as a result void—by the mere fact that its passage has occurred before authorization by a constitutional delegation. If any legislative act is void before constitutional authorization, then the proposition that legislative acts in violation of the Constitution are void is a mere truism. That is why Marshall said in *Marbury* that "the question, whether an act, repugnant to the constitution, can become the law of the land, is a question . . . not of an intricacy proportioned to its interest" (176).

The subargument that leads to Marshall's second conclusion, that courts as well as other departments are bound by the Constitution, begins with a rhetorical question left unanswered at the close of the first subargument: "If an act of the legislature, repugnant to the constitution, is void, does it, notwithstanding its invalidity, bind the courts, and oblige them to give it effect" (*Marbury* 1803, 177)? The answer commences with Marshall's famous declaration that the Court is required to "say what the law is," even in situations in which conflicting constitutional and statutory provisions are simultaneously applicable to a particular controversy that the Court must decide. If an act in violation of the Constitution is not law (the conclusion of the first subargument—issue 6) and the Court's duty is to apply law in particular cases, then the direct application of an unconstitutional statute would violate the judge's oath to support the Constitution. Because the judicial power extends to cases arising under the Constitution and the laws (by Article III), and because only those laws made "in pursuance" of the Constitution have constitutional status (by Article VI), courts may prefer constitutional over conflicting statutory provisions when operating within their authority to resolve particular disputes. In other words, they are not bound to "close their eyes on the constitution, and see only the law" (178–180).

It is important to note carefully the real import of Marshall's conclusion. It is *not*, as so often has been said, that the Court is the "ultimate" arbiter of constitutional questions or possesses an "exclusive" authority to interpret the fundamental law or a "final" authority to enforce the Constitution against coordinate agencies of government. The coequality of Congress's role in constitutional interpretation is explicitly asserted in Marshall's reiteration of his conclusion on the final page of the *Marbury* opinion: "It is apparent, that the framers of the constitution contemplated that instrument, as a rule for the government of courts, *as well as of the legislature*" (179–180). The rulings in the second section of the *Marbury* opinion are that the Constitution is law, that legislative acts against the Constitution are not law, and that the Court, when faced with a conflict between the Constitution and an unconstitutional act, has the power to apply the Constitution, which entails disregarding the unconstitutional act.

No judicial power to "strike down" laws is claimed in the *Marbury* opinion. This fact was recognized throughout most of the nineteenth century, at least until the eve of the *Mugler* dictum. Quoting from the Court's opinion in *Ex parte Siebold* (1880), Justice Antonin Scalia noted in *Reynoldsville Casket Co. v. Hyde* (1985) that what a court does with regard to an unconstitutional law is simply to *ignore* it. It decides the case "disregarding the [unconstitutional] law" because a law repugnant to the Constitution "is void, and is as no law" (Clinton 1999, 18). In other words, the power of constitutional review claimed by the Court in *Marbury* is a power of *discretion* to disregard existing laws in the decision of particular controversies, provided that the constitutional and statutory provisions involved are, like those in Article III and the Judiciary Act, addressed to the Court itself. If the provisions are not addressed to the Court, then the Court will not be *compelled* to choose between them to decide the case. This means that there must be a distinction between acts violating the Constitution and acts requiring invalidation by the Court, which is exactly what Marshall says in *Marbury*.

These reflections cast light on the meaning of Madison's well-known statement about the Constitutional Convention's extension of Article III federal judicial power to cases arising under the Constitution, laws, and treaties. As noted previously, the framers extended federal judicial power to such cases only after it had been generally agreed "that the jurisdiction given was constructively limited to cases of a Judiciary nature" (Clinton 1991, 18). The general agreement of the founders that Madison reported is based on the same distinction that Marshall draws in *Marbury* between unconstitutional acts and acts appropriate for judicial invalidation. Madison expounds this distinction most clearly in his remarks of June 17, 1789, during the 1789 congressional debates over the president's removal power (Hobson and Rutland 1979, 234). In these remarks, Madison flatly denies the power of *any* branch of the national government (including the judicial) to "determine the limits of the constitutional division of power." Arguing in support of vesting the removal power solely in the president and responding to the charge that the legislature had no right to interpret the Constitution (through vesting of the power by statute), Madison stated the following:

I acknowledge, in the ordinary course of government, that the exposition of the laws and constitution devolves upon the judicial. But, I beg to know, upon what principle it can be contended, that any one department draws from the constitution greater powers than another, in marking out the limits of the powers of the several departments. The constitution is the charter of the people to the government; it specifies certain great powers as absolutely granted, and marks out the departments to exercise them. If the constitutional boundary of either be brought into question, I do not see that any one of these independent departments has more right than another to declare their sentiments on that point. . . . There is not one government on the face of the earth, so far as I recollect, there is not one in the United States, in which provision is made for a particular authority to determine the limits of the constitutional division of power between the branches of the government. In all systems there are points which must be adjusted by the departments themselves, to which no one of them is competent. If it cannot be determined in this way, there is no resource left but the will of the community, to be collected in some mode to be provided by the constitution, or one dictated by the necessity of the case. (Hobson and Rutland 1979, 234)

There can be little doubt about Madison's meaning. Among the "points which must be adjusted by the departments themselves" are all questions pertaining to "the limits of the constitutional division of power between the branches of the government." Because no single department "draws from the constitution greater powers than another, in marking out the limits of the powers of the several departments," the founders' restriction of the "arising under" jurisdiction of federal courts to cases "of a Judiciary nature" must be read as a straightforward denial of the power of courts to issue final constitutional pronouncements in cases involving interpretations of the constitutional powers of coordinate agencies. Cases *not* of a judiciary nature that *also* arise under the Constitution are those that require determination of the constitutional authority of the legislative or executive branch. *Appropriate cases for judicial review are those that do not require such a determination.*

Under this view, only in cases that involve constitutional provisions directly addressed to the courts is the Supreme Court's refusal to apply relevant law necessarily "final." In cases involving constitutional provisions addressed to other branches of government (e.g., the Art. I, sec. 8, necessary and proper clause), the Court may surely refuse to apply the law, but it may not do so with "finality" in the strict sense. Even though the Court's decision may bind the parties in a particular case, Congress may nonetheless choose to disregard the Court's constitutional ruling and provide for executive enforcement of the statute. Congress might even use its power to regulate the Court's appellate jurisdiction to discourage or prevent future appeals on the question of the law's constitutional validity. In such instances, it is the judgment of Congress, not of the Court, that will be "final." On the other hand, if the case involves such a constitutional provision as that in the Sixth Amendment's right to confront one's accusers in a federal criminal trial, then the Court's decision on the constitutional question will necessarily be final, because carrying on any federal criminal trial requires a court, and federal trial courts are bound by rulings of the Supreme Court.

The Madisonian–Marshallian theory of constitutional review partitions constitutionally defective laws into two categories. One category includes those instances in which judicial review is appropriate, because the authority for final refusal to apply an unconstitutional act rests in the courts by virtue of the judicial function itself. The most obvious example is an act that operates "unconstitutionally" on a court's performance of its own duties. In the other category, constitutional judicial review is inappropriate because the performance of judicial duty in those instances is unaffected by the constitutional infirmity of the law. Taking the Madison–Marshall partition seriously is absolutely fatal to any doctrine of judicial supremacy. *Marbury* affords no basis for inferring that the Court should disregard a statutory provision in conflict with the Constitution except in that relatively small number of instances in which the Constitution furnishes a direct rule for the courts.

Where does the Constitution furnish direct rules for the courts? Most provisions of this type may be found in three places: Article III, Amendments 4 through 8 of the Bill of Rights, and some provisions of Article I, Section 9. The classic example is one that Marshall himself used in *Marbury*: the treason clause of Article III, Section 3, which requires either a confession or the testimony of two witnesses in open court to the same overt treasonable act. For an obvious example from the Bill of Rights, one only need add the requirement of the Fifth Amendment that such a confession be uncoerced. Suppose that Congress, in a zealous attempt to suppress subversion, amends the federal rules of criminal procedure to make it possible for the government to obtain a conviction on a charge of treason on the basis of a coerced confession. Much like the situation that the Court believed it was facing in *Marbury*, this situation presents a clear-cut case "of a judiciary nature" because *the Court cannot apply the statutory provision without at the same time violating the Constitution.*

Reformulating the emphasized portion of the previous section as a question allows formulation of a rule that will help to determine whether any particular case is one of a judiciary nature. In each case, one may ask, "Can the Court apply the law in question without itself violating the Constitution?" If the answer to this question is negative, then the case is "judiciary" in nature, and the Court will have no sensible alternative but to disregard the law. If, on the other hand, the answer is positive, then the case is "nonjudiciary" in nature, and the Court will be entitled to apply the law, *whether or not the judges believe that the law itself violates the Constitution.*

Thus the only notion of "final" constitutional authority that may be drawn from the *Marbury* opinion is that the statutory provision disregarded in the case pertains to the Court's performance of its own functions. The Court's pronouncement on the unconstitutionality of the mandamus provision of Section 13 is final and binding on the other departments only because the section is a jurisdictional provision that the Court alone can exercise. The Court's refusal to apply the law left the coordinate branches of government no alternative but to comply with its decision (i.e., to do nothing) because the Court, by enforcing a constitutional restriction on judicial power, essentially *did nothing.* Its decision amounted to a "final," or "ultimate," interpretation of the Constitution. Moreover, because the provision invalidated in *Marbury* was one that *enlarged* the Court's jurisdiction, it is plausible to argue that *Marbury* entitles the Court to disregard laws only when such laws violate constitutional *restrictions* on judicial power (Clinton 1991, 17–18). This would be the correct reading of the constitutional holding by Marshall's own maxim, stated in *Cohens v. Virginia* (1821, 399) that "expressions in every opinion are to

be taken in connection with the case in which these expressions are used."

The Second Section of *Marbury* and Constitutional Review in the Nineteenth Century

This is the authentic *Marbury*, the historical *Marbury*, the nonmythical nineteenth-century *Marbury*. Far from being the case in which Marshall appropriated the Constitution for the Supreme Court and fashioned a doctrine of judicial supremacy, the historical *Marbury* was the case in which Marshall carefully circumscribed the power of the Court by narrowing the range of judicial discretion to cases directly affecting the performance of judicial functions, thereby taking the Court out of the policy-making arena and empowering the national democracy. For most of the nineteenth century the Court and the country accepted Marshall's approach, seeing no necessary connection between issue 6, the question of whether a legislative act violating the Constitution is void, and issue 7, the question of whether the Court has the power to nullify an invalid law. Holding fast to Marshall's sharp distinction between these two issues means that some unconstitutional acts should not be invalidated by courts. Such acts are those that violate constitutional provisions addressed to other branches of government and that are not subject to final enforcement by the courts. Marshall's approach, like Madison's, implies a "coordinate" or "departmental" theory of constitutional review, in which each branch of the national government is expected to "police" its own constitutional territory by ensuring that its policies do not circumvent or contravene the Constitution.

This approach is everywhere in evidence throughout the first half of the nineteenth century. Before the Civil War, all three branches of the national government regularly engaged in the activity we now call "constitutional interpretation." Most of the great debates in Congress during the antebellum period were over the meaning of important constitutional provisions. The antebellum congressional record is filled with speeches asserting the duty of legislators to interpret the Constitution rightly and in accord with accepted canons of construction. Early presidential vetoes of congressional acts were exercised almost solely on constitutional grounds. Most of these were accompanied by explicit, uncontested assertions of executive authority to interpret the fundamental law. From the time the Constitution went into effect until 1832, when Andrew Jackson vetoed the bill renewing the charter of the Second Bank of the United States, presidents employed the executive veto nine times, in every instance claiming that the vetoed legislation violated the Constitution (Clinton 1991, 113). Chief Justice Taney later confirmed Jackson's position regarding the constitutional interpretive authority of the executive (Clinton 1991, 113).

A quarter-century after Jackson's veto message, Abraham Lincoln expounded a similar view of constitutional authority in his response to the notorious *Dred Scott* decision. Focusing on the constitutional role of Congress and the appropriate response of a legislator to the Court's holding that slavery could not be constitutionally prohibited in the territories, Lincoln promised that "[i]f I were in Congress, and a vote should come up on a question whether slavery should be prohibited in a new territory, in spite of that *Dred Scott* decision, I would vote that it should" (Basler 1953, 495). Lincoln also tacitly approved the constitutional basis for Jackson's bank veto, reminding Stephen Douglas and his audience that Douglas also had supported the veto on the same ground:

Do not gentlemen here remember the case of that same Supreme Court, some twenty-five or thirty years ago, deciding that a national bank was constitutional? . . . Such is the truth, whether it be remembered or not. The Bank charter ran out, and a re-charter was granted by Congress. That re-charter was laid before General Jackson. It was urged upon him, when he denied the constitutionality of the bank, that the Supreme Court had decided that it was constitutional; and that General Jackson then said that the Supreme Court had no right to lay down a rule to govern a co-ordinate branch of the government, the members of which had sworn to support the Constitution—that each member had sworn to support that Constitution as he understood it. I will venture here to say, that I have heard Judge Douglas say that he approved of General Jackson for that act. (Basler 1953, 496)

In the face of these considerations, it should not be difficult to understand why the second section of Chief Justice Marshall's opinion in *Marbury v. Madison* was uncontroversial in its own day. Nelson (2000, 72) noted that not even Jefferson criticized the decision at the time it was handed down, or the Republican press, or Congress—which was in session at the time: "[T]here was a general consensus that the Court had correctly decided . . . *Marbury v. Madison.*" Nor should there be great difficulty in understanding why the second section of the *Marbury* opinion was hardly noticed throughout most of the nineteenth century, before the *Mugler* Court's grotesque misreading of the decision in the 1880s. The implications of *Mar-*

bury with regard to the status of unconstitutional laws (issue 6) and the judiciary's role in applying or disregarding such laws (issue 7) were perfectly consistent with the prevailing constitutional principles of the period. We have difficulty understanding these things now only because we no longer subscribe to those principles and have revised American constitutional history to make *Marbury* seem compatible with our current views.

The Declaratory Theory of Law

The jurisprudential world view shared by the American legal community from before the time of the founding until the mid- to late nineteenth century has often been referred to as the "declaratory theory of law." It is really a tradition and not a theory. The tradition has ancient roots but was given modern formulation by such seventeenth- and eighteenth-century jurists as Hugo Grotius, Samuel Pufendorf, Emerich de Vattel, and William Blackstone. Judges and lawyers of Marshall's day believed, with Blackstone, that all human laws were based on "external immutable laws of good and evil" (Casto 1995, 34–35). For these early American judges and lawyers, all human-made law was necessarily drawn from underlying principles of order, ethics, and morality. Human laws must be just, fair, equitable, and made in pursuit of the common good. They must be consistent with "universal natural law" and are "invalid if they are contradictory to it" (Casto 1995, 34–35).

This means that the substance or essence of the law *pre-exists* its "declaration" by courts or other interpreters; hence, the designation "declaratory theory." When a court applies the

law to resolve a case, it must first "find" or "discover" that law, which includes determining its consistency with the underlying principles of natural justice and natural law. The court then "declares" the law, or "says what the law is," to use Marshall's famous phrase in *Marbury*. The declaratory theory ascribes to the law an underlying unity, a *ratio legis* or "reason of the law," that goes beyond any particular application. According to Edward Coke, the great English common lawyer, judge, and exponent of the declaratory theory, "legal rules are many but legal reason is one" (Stoner 1992, 54). Blackstone reflected this conception of the law when he held that precedents (previous decisions) found to be "absurd" or "unjust" are not merely "bad law," they were never "law" at all (Blackstone 1979, 70). Blackstone also clearly distinguished between laws "declaratory of natural rights and duties" and laws "determinative of things indifferent." He distinguished between laws targeting acts that are "wrong in themselves" (for example, laws against murder) and laws targeting acts that are wrong only because the law says so (for example, traffic laws). He then added that, for acts "wrong in themselves," human laws add *nothing* to the obligations already imposed by natural or divine law (Blackstone 1979, 54).

According to this approach, the law exists independently of courts, legislatures, constitutional conventions, or any other set of human lawgivers. The law is an objective reality, which human lawgivers try, imperfectly, to capture as best they can in their efforts to legislate, and which courts try to discover, as best they can, in their efforts to decide cases. This effort to capture or discover the law that exists behind the veil of our ignorance is the activity we call "interpretation," the activity of discerning the meaning of the law. It is this conception of a "true" but invisible law, a law infused with meaning that we are continually trying to discern and make visible, that gives the law its objectivity and gives us a reason to obey it. Without this objectivity, according to which judges "discover" and "declare" the law rather than "make" it, the law becomes merely an instrument of raw power. The law becomes whatever the legislature, court, or tyrant says it is. Without this objectivity, the law becomes a mere empirical fact, losing its normative force, and failing to carry sufficient moral obligation to bind the subject in obedience.

Applying this reasoning to the constitutional jurisprudence of early American courts, we understand better why Marshall's sharp distinction between an unconstitutional law being void (issue 6) and the judicial power to invalidate such a law (issue 7), leading to "coordinate" or "departmental" constitutional review, was agreed to by all. Under the influence of the declaratory theory of law, *no other constitutional approach was possible.* The reason is that, under the declaratory theory, the Constitution is not, and cannot be, "what the Court says it is." The law is not something "made up" by judges, legislators, or presidents. The law is an intelligible reality, an "idea" that exists entirely independent of, and wholly distinct from, any human effort to capture, interpret, or apply it. It is an immaterial object of thought, a "will" or "intention" of the lawgiver, a "design," "purpose," "object," or "end" of the written constitutional provision or legislative act. It is an idea accessible by intelligent beings, yet never fully or absolutely so.

It is not an agglomeration of rules, practices, or principles devised by human beings in any judicial or political capacity. Nor is it a set of "interpretations" given over time by the Supreme (or any other) Court. It is rather the source, rule, and measure of all such rules, practices, principles, and interpretations. This means that a judicial declaration of the law is not the law itself but merely a statement of it, maybe even an erroneous one. The judicial invalidation of a law on constitutional grounds is not constitutional law itself but merely a statement of it, maybe even an erroneous one. When a judge "says what the law is," to use Marshall's famous phrase one more time, he or she is formulating or applying a rule or principle that he or she hopes will capture the underlying essence of the law insofar as that is possible in the circumstances of the case. Because the judge can always get it wrong, his or her statement of the law cannot be the law itself.

This is the historical–jurisprudential context of the early Supreme Court. Its decisions and opinions become much more easily understandable if we attend to the fact that the justices regarded the Constitution as an attempt to capture a "true" underlying set of meanings rather than as a wooden set of formulas. It becomes easier to understand the interplay of text, tradition, common law, natural law, natural justice, and equity jurisprudence in these opinions, including that in *Marbury v. Madison,* as efforts to "find" or "discover" the "true" equitable, legal, or constitutional principle(s) underlying the text. We have to remember that the justices of the early Court believed that their job was to "find" and then "declare" the law. That law always preexisted any written text, whether constitution, statute, will, or contract. This meant that the law was higher than, and thus independent of, judges and courts. Judges and courts were in continual danger of getting law wrong.

Demise of the Declaratory Theory

We no longer see the legal world in the way just described. This is largely because of the onset and acceptance of several ideologies essentially unknown in the time of Marshall and *Marbury*. The natural law interpretive tradition and the declaratory theory that complements it contrast sharply with ideologies such as skepticism, positivism, and utilitarianism—all of which came into prominence in the United States *only after the Civil War*. Pre–Civil War American constitutional jurisprudence, including that of the Marshall Court, was based on the earlier tradition. That tradition began to disappear from the American scene and from American law writing after the Civil War and has since been largely ignored by contemporary legal historians and commentators (Clinton 2000, 946). This disappearance has had a huge impact on our contemporary understanding of the early Supreme Court and its decisions, including *Marbury*.

The first of these modern ideologies is legal positivism. Although the roots of positivism in the law are certainly much older, its formulation as a comprehensive theory was accomplished by the English philosopher John Austin in the 1830s (Austin 1832) and became generally accepted in the United States only in the late-nineteenth and early-twentieth centuries. Austin formulated his original analysis as a jurisprudence derived from the relationship or "position" that exists between "superiors" and "inferiors"—hence the designation "posi-tivism," meaning "derived from position." Although Austin did not deny the existence or importance of other kinds of legal experience such as divine or natural law, Austin's philosophical descendants tended to advance legal positivism as a hardened ideological position denying legal reality to any rules except those "posited" as commands of a "superior" with power to inflict pain and suffering on disobedient "inferiors." The law becomes nothing more than the "command" of any person or group able to gain control of a sovereign government. Rather than "might" having to be based on "right," "might" instead *makes* "right." The judicial process is no longer conceived as an effort to discover the "reason of the law" and then to "declare" it when deciding cases. The declaratory theory at the heart of the natural law interpretive tradition of the early Supreme Court gives way to the positivist idea of the judge as a "lawmaker."

In constitutional law, one effect of legal positivism was to advance a notion of a "self-contained" legal order organized under a Constitution that articulates an authoritative power structure in society. Eric Voegelin (1991, 28) cited, disapprovingly, the positivistic "pure theory" of his teacher Hans Kelsen, which

orders the members of society to behave in conformity with the norms deriving ultimately from the constitution. The power structure articulated in the constitution is the origin of the legal order . . . . Whatever power establishes itself effectively in a society is the law-making power . . . whatever rules it makes are the law. The classic questions of true and untrue, of just and unjust order do not belong in the science of law. . . .

Kelsen's theory is a sophisticated variant of what has come to be known as "analytical legal positivism," a theory of law developed by Austin's disciples in the late nineteenth and early twentieth centuries. Such theories were unknown and probably unimaginable in Marshall's time and throughout most of the nineteenth century. Yet under the name of "legal pragmatism" or "legal instrumentalism," positivism has become the dominant theory of law in modern times.

The second of the modern ideologies, closely related to and strongly complementing legal positivism, is mechanistic materialism, which came to prominence in the Gilded Age. Materialism is the view that all is matter and that everything explicable must be explained by physical causes. It is an ancient world view, but its modern formulation originated in the philosophy of Thomas Hobbes in the mid-seventeenth century. Though Hobbes's views became highly influential two centuries later, they were rejected at the time by the English legal profession. Their reception on the western side of the Atlantic was even less favorable. Early American common lawyers, trained largely (and often solely) by reading and rereading books like Blackstone's *Commentaries*, shared the view of their English counterparts that the basis of law was custom, tradition, and reason, developed and refined by habit, discoverable by learned judges, and pointing to a more comprehensive legal reality that transcends particular societies and cultures.

The third of the modern ideologies is progressivism, initially formulated by John Stuart Mill and his disciples in England and manifested most prominently in the United States by the progressive historians in the early decades of the twentieth century. The progressive historians, looking to the future rather than the past

in their writing of history, devalued and distorted much of the Court's early history—not to mention much of the history of the founding itself. The founders were recast by the progressives as a dominant socioeconomic elite bent on safeguarding wealth and social position. The early Supreme Court, consisting entirely of Federalists, was to be the judicial organ of this dominant class—the institution that would construct and develop legal safeguards for its members and their property. Along with this new view of the Constitution and the early Court came a new view of Marshall and a new view of his most famous decision as well. Legal progressives revised the history of *Marbury v. Madison*, claiming that Marshall had, in *Marbury*, illegitimately appropriated the power of judicial review so that he could use that power to protect the property interests of the wealthy against depredation by the states. The view suggested by this reading of *Marbury* holds that the landmark decisions of the Marshall Court (including *Marbury* itself) were founded on an unjustified usurpation of legislative authority by the Court, were politically motivated, and were essentially unprecedented. The progressive historians denied the jurisprudential foundation of these decisions and made it possible for future generations of legal scholars to reinterpret them in the light of modern concerns.

Conclusion

General acceptance of positivism, materialism, and progressivism by large segments of the legal community in the late-nineteenth and early-twentieth centuries brought about a monumental change in American attitudes toward law and government. Our immersion in

the jurisprudence that follows from these beliefs has taken us far from the constitutional
world view of antebellum courts. We now tend
to believe that laws, and even constitutions, are
mere tools of powerful political or economic
interests. We read the decisions of the early
Supreme Court as if they were apologies for
such interests. We tend to believe that laws are
merely the "commands" of a sovereign, so we
think it strange, or even "disingenuous," for
Chief Justice Marshall to run on about the ma-
jestic generalities of the Constitution as if they
could be thought about apart from the concerns of the moment. We tend to think that all
is matter, so we think that when Marshall regards a judicial appointment as a special case
of "the sanctity of private property," his "real"
concern must have been the "property" and
not the "sanctity." We tend to think of constitutional cases as political "games" rather than
principled controversies, so we have great difficulty taking seriously the high-toned discussions in *Marbury* or many of Marshall's other
famous constitutional opinions.

Because we find difficult to believe that objective truth exists, we find difficult to believe
that "the law" has an existence outside and independent of legislatures and courts, and thus
find difficult to believe that there is any such
thing as "correct" constitutional interpretation. If recent discussions in constitutional
theory are representative, we seem to have lost
our ability to think clearly about "interpretation" at all. Because we now think that judges
do not "discover" the law but instead "make"
it, we read the early Court's opinions, like that
in *Marbury v. Madison*, as judicial legislation.
Some find that the Court legislated well; others
find that it legislated badly. Because we now

believe that judges "really" make decisions
based not on reason and law but rather on the
basis of nonlegal "policy preferences" or even
"personal predilections," we look for, and
easily find, all kinds of "base," "unconscious,"
or "subconscious" motives lurking between
the lines of the early Court's opinions.

We read the opinions of the early Court as
exercises in judicial lawmaking rather than as
attempts to discover and declare a preexisting
constitutional consensus. We read these cases
as if they had been decided by judges who believed that the normative force of law is derived solely from the command of a sovereign
rather than from a dictate of reason. We read
the cases as if they had been decided by judges
who believed that society was inevitably and
continually "progressing" to a better state and
that their role as judges was to help society get
there as fast as possible. We read the cases as if
they had been decided by monistic materialist
judges who believed that the social good was
quantitative in character and that economic
motives determined the law of the Constitution. The judges of Marshall's time believed
none of these things. Neither did the judges
and lawyers who lived and worked during
much of the remainder of the nineteenth century. That is why the twentieth-century *Marbury* is so different from the nineteenth-century
Marbury.

Marshall's careful and clear distinction between issue 6 (the status of an unconstitutional
law) and issue 7 (the authority of a court to
dispense with an unconstitutional law) is now
largely invisible to us. We are legal positivists
and so believe that judges are lawmakers. We
have difficulty even imagining a court failing to
strike down any law or policy that a majority

of its judges believe to be constitutionally infirm. The reasons why Marshall and his colleagues chose to address the legal validity of Marbury's appointment, the nature of the rights flowing from that appointment, and the appropriateness of the requested remedy, even though they were going to decline to award that remedy in the last analysis, are likewise largely invisible to us. We have forgotten that modern jurisdictional rules designed to protect later generations against judicial usurpation of legislative authority were not in play during Marshall's time.

One of Marshall's favorite rules of interpretation, stemming from the jurisprudence of Emerich de Vattel, was the "no surplusage" rule (Clinton 2000, 956). No provision in the Constitution or laws should be read in such a way as to deny effect to another provision. Marshall was a "harmonizer," and fortunately so. The unprecedented task confronting the Supreme Court in its early years was that of interpreting the new written Constitution so as not to disturb the settled framework of preexisting law. How was the Court to accomplish this? Would the Constitution be treated as a legal document subject to the same interpretive rules that govern statutes, contracts, wills, and the like? If not, then how would the instrument be made effective in its object of controlling the government? If the Constitution was to be subject to traditional rules of interpretation or construction, a task naturally performed by courts, then how would that other object—to enable the government to control the governed—be fully ensured?

The solution was finally reached by the Marshall Court in its establishment of coordinate constitutional review in *Marbury* and its subsequent development in other cases. Government would control the governed via an expansive reading of national power. At the same time, the Constitution would control the government in a limited range of cases—including most prominently, *Marbury v. Madison*—touching on the rights of individuals, the separation of powers, and the judicial function. Marshall and his colleagues successfully "legalized" the Constitution by emphasizing the intimate relationship between the Constitution and other sources in the legal tradition.

The constitutional judicial authority that resulted from Marshall's solution was so confined in its scope as to be largely unimaginable to modern observers. The modern American mind, conditioned by at least a half-century of judicial supremacy, can hardly help but regard the judicial branch as a coequal partner in the public policymaking process, as just another rulemaking agency of the government. But it was to prevent such participation by judges in policymaking that the Constitution's framers circumscribed the jurisdiction and power of courts so narrowly. And it was to prevent being dragged into such processes that Marshall and other early American judges used constitutional review to safeguard their independence—both by resisting legislative or executive encroachment on legitimate judicial functions, as in *Marbury*, and by refusing to intrude themselves on domains they (and the framers) regarded as better left to others.

Beginning in the 1880s, when the case was first cited as a precedent for judicial review (of *state* laws) by the Supreme Court, *Marbury* began its meteoric rise to prominence as a symbol in the progressive-era controversy over the constitutional role of the courts. During this era the Court began to invalidate acts of Congress with greater frequency, and Marbury's case became a useful precedent for justifying a more aggressive constitutional role for the judiciary. Near the end of the nineteenth century, in the Income Tax Case (*Pollock v. Farmer's Loan & Trust Co.*, 1894, 554), the Court first used *Marbury v. Madison* to justify its power to invalidate a *national* law. Since that time, *Marbury* has become an icon of American constitutional law. During the twentieth century, the case would be cited not only with increasing frequency but often in support of sweeping declarations of judicial supremacy that contrast sharply with the more modest *Marbury* of Marshall's Court. Two examples are (1) *Cooper v. Aaron*, the Little Rock school desegregation case (1958) in which the Court used *Marbury* in support of its claim to be the "supreme" expositor of the Constitution; and (2) *City of Boerne v. Flores* (1997), in which the Court used *Marbury* in support of its declaration that Congress was without authority to determine the substantive meaning of constitutional provisions (Clinton 1999, 14–15). Such claims and declarations would have seemed (and been) absurd to the judges that decided *Marbury v. Madison*.

The *Marbury* of present times is largely a myth, fashioned in the late nineteenth century and developed in the twentieth to justify an emerging doctrine of judicial supremacy that had little, if any, support during the eras of Marshall or Taney. This transformation of an obscure case into the "landmark" precedent of American constitutional law could not have been accomplished without the earlier-described changes in the jurisprudential world view of legal professionals during the nine-teenth century. Absent progressivism, materialism, positivism, and their complements, we would look on *Marbury* in a very different light—if we looked on it at all. If the strange career of *Marbury v. Madison* proves anything, it is that when we do our constitutional history, we must do more than merely chronicle the events of the past. We must try to understand what the people who lived in bygone eras actually believed, what their fundamental principles were. If we do not, we will invariably and inevitably interpret their events and experiences as if they believed what we believe, as if their fundamental principles were ours. We can hardly help believing what we believe; but if we really want to understand the past, we must suspend our beliefs when we do our history and tell the truth about our ancestors. We will get only mythology if we insist on reading their history through the fog of our present concerns.

Bibliography

Aristotle. *Nicomachean Ethics*. D. P. Chase, trans. Mineola, N.Y: Dover, 1998.

Austin, John. *The Province of Jurisprudence Determined*. London: John Murray, 1832.

Basler, Roy P., ed. *The Collected Works of Abraham Lincoln*. 9 vols. New Brunswick, N.J.: Rutgers University Press, 1953.

Beveridge, Albert J. *The Life of John Marshall*. 4 vols. Boston: Houghton Mifflin, 1916.

Blackstone, William. *Commentaries on the Laws of England*. Facsimile of 1769 edition. 4 vols. Chicago: University of Chicago Press, 1979.

Casto, William R. *The Supreme Court in the Early Republic: The Chief Justiceships of John Jay and Oliver Ellsworth*. Columbia: University of South Carolina Press, 1995.

Clinton, Robert Lowry. Marbury v. Madison *and Judicial Review*. Lawrence: University Press of Kansas, 1989.

_____. "How the Court Became Supreme." *First Things* 89 (1999): 13–19.

_____. "Classical Legal Naturalism and the Politics of John Marshall's Constitutional Jurisprudence." *John Marshall Law Review* 33 (2000): 935–971.

Corwin, Edward S. 1910. "The Establishment of Judicial Review." *Michigan Law Review* 9 (1910): 102–125.

Debates and Proceedings of the Congress of the United States. 1803. Washington, D.C.: Gales & Seaton, 1851.

Dewey, Donald O. *Marshall Versus Jefferson: the Political Background of* Marbury v. Madison. New York: Knopf, 1970.

Hobson, Charles F., and Robert A. Rutland, eds. *The Papers of James Madison.* 15 vols. Charlottesville: University of Virginia Press, 1979.

Nelson, William E. Marbury v. Madison: *The Origins and Legacy of Judicial Review.* Lawrence: University Press of Kansas, 2000.

Simon, James F. *What Kind of Nation: Thomas Jefferson, John Marshall, and the Epic Struggle to Create a United States.* New York: Simon and Schuster, 2002.

Stoner, James R., Jr. *Common Law and Liberal Theory: Coke, Hobbes, and the Origins of American Constitutionalism.* Lawrence: University Press of Kansas, 1992.

Voegelin, Eric. "The Nature of the Law and Related Legal Writings." In *The Collected Works of Eric Voegelin,* vol. 27. Robert Anthony Pascal et al., eds. Baton Rouge: Louisiana State University Press, 1991.

Notes

1. "Certainly neither Marbury nor the other litigants sued because they were reliant on the office for their sustenance. Besides being a successful land speculator, Marbury was a principal in the Potomac Company, an ambitious venture led by George Washington. . . . Hooe, speculated in land in [D.C.] and elsewhere and owned more than a hundred thousand acres in the state of Kentucky. . . . Ramsay, was the former mayor of Alexandria [Virginia]. . . . Harper . . . was also a large landowner and had long standing ties to George Washington. . . ." (Simon 2002, 175).

2. A writ of mandamus is a judicial order to a government official ordering that official to perform a duty that has been assigned by law.

3. James Marshall, John's brother, who "had been rewarded by Adams with a judicial appointment to the new circuit court for the District of Columbia, recalled that he had taken a batch of commissions to the newly appointed justices of the peace in . . . Alexandria." An affidavit to this effect was entered into the record. (See Simon 2002, 174, 180, 182).

6 "To Support This Constitution": Judicial Supremacy in the Twentieth Century

KEITH E. WHITTINGTON

Judicial supremacy in the twentieth century began in the nineteenth century. But it is possible to push origins even further back. The story of judicial supremacy in the twentieth century might begin in the 1860s and 1870s, when the Supreme Court dug out from the Civil War and the ignominy of the *Dred Scott* decision (Graber 2000). Or it might begin earlier, with *Dred Scott* or the nationalist decisions, such as *McCulloch v. Maryland,* of the Marshall Court in the 1820s (Whittington 2001). It might have begun with *Marbury v. Madison* (1803) and the Court's first nullification of a provision of federal law as contrary to the Court's own reading of the Constitution (Snowiss 1990). Or it might be found even earlier, in the "higher law background" of the Constitution and the development of the British common law (Corwin 1955). But the late nineteenth century is a particularly good place to start. The Court's twentieth-century struggle for judicial supremacy took its most characteristic form during the waning days of the 1800s.

In the 1890s the Supreme Court firmly established itself as an important player in many central debates of American politics. With the increasing nationalization of the American economy in the late nineteenth and early twentieth centuries, the federal government became increasingly important as a regulator and promoter of the economic arena. The courts had long been one of the strongest and most active components of nineteenth-century American government, at both the state and national levels. Accordingly, the federal judiciary was on the leading edge of the national government's response to the economic and social transformations of the late nineteenth century. Federal judges became important actors shaping the growth of the railroads, resolving labor disputes, putting down labor unrest, and defining the rules of economic competition (Berk 1994; Forbath 1991; Freyer 1979; Letwin 1965). Congress turned to the federal judiciary as a central vehicle for national policy making and implementation. Congress bolstered the federal courts with additional personnel and resources. Courts were authorized to hear new kinds and larger numbers of cases and were vested with the discretion to resolve those cases as the judges thought appropriate (Gillman 2002). By the opening of the twentieth century, federal courts had come to occupy an important place in American life.

The federal judiciary, particularly the Supreme Court, took on greater constitutional responsibilities at the same time that those tribunals took on enhanced administrative and policymaking duties. The active exercise of judicial review quickly became a routine part of the Court's business. By the first decade of the twentieth century, the Court was voiding on constitutional grounds nearly one congressional statute and more than three state statutes per year. The last time that the Supreme Court completed a term without striking down a state law was in 1893. There have been distinct periods of relative activism and restraint in the Supreme Court's exercise of judicial review in the twentieth century, but the overall trend has been toward greater activity (see Figure 6-1).

Marbury Comes of Age

In the twentieth century the Court asserted for itself the final authority to interpret the Constitution and give voice to the fundamental law that all other government officials must follow. Although occasional challenges to such judicial assertions took place, the Court was successful to a remarkable degree in sustaining its claims. The Supreme Court increasingly viewed itself, and was viewed by others, as the ultimate guardian of the Constitution.

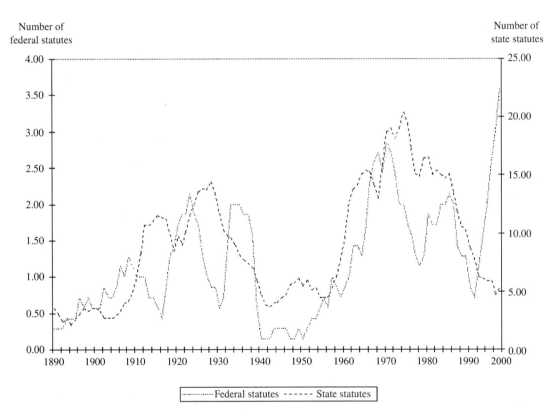

Figure 6-1   Acts of Government Struck Down by Supreme Court (Seven-Year Moving Average)

The Court's assertion of judicial review in *Marbury* gained new significance in the twentieth century. Not until the early twentieth century was a specific term, *judicial review,* coined to refer to the power of courts to invalidate legislation for it being contrary to the requirements of the Constitution (Corwin 1909).[1] Tracing the rise of the "American Doctrine of Judicial Supremacy," one prominent commentator of the period observed that through the power of judicial review "the judiciary, a coordinate branch of government, becomes the particular guardian of the terms of the written constitution" (Haines 1914, 5). For "most practical purposes, the judiciary exercises supreme power in the United States" by possessing the "sole right to place an authoritative interpretation upon the fundamental written law" (Haines 1914, 11). The power of judicial review had become too important to ignore or to relegate to a mere background feature of the American constitutional system.

As the century wore on, the Supreme Court emphasized the importance of *Marbury* for judicial power and its centrality to American constitutionalism. Over the course of the nineteenth century, the justices of the Supreme Court cited *Marbury* only twice for the proposition that the courts may enforce constitutional limitations against other government officials, once in 1887 and again in 1894 (Clinton 1989, 120–121). By contrast, the Court referred to *Marbury* as the touchstone of the power of judicial review on seven occasions in the first half of the twentieth century. Such references exploded in the second half of the twentieth century (Clinton 1989, 122–123).

A turning point in judicial rhetoric came in 1958, when Chief Justice Earl Warren pre-sented the unanimous opinion of the Court in *Cooper v. Aaron* (1958), which offered a fresh interpretation of Chief Justice John Marshall's famous sentence in *Marbury* declaring the judicial duty to "say what the law is." In response to state government officials who questioned the judicial authority to define constitutional meaning, the chief justice noted that "it is only necessary to recall some basic constitutional propositions which are settled doctrine" (*Cooper* 1958, 17). The Court instructed,

This decision [of *Marbury*] declared the basic principle that the federal judiciary is supreme in the exposition of the law of the Constitution, and that principle has ever since been respected by this Court and the Country as a permanent and indispensable feature of our constitutional system. It follows that this interpretation of the Fourteenth Amendment enunciated by this Court in the *Brown* case is the supreme law of the land. (*Cooper* 1958, 18)

Warren concluded, "Every state legislator and executive and judicial officer is solemnly committed by oath pursuant to Art. VI, cl. 3, 'to support *this* Constitution'" (*Cooper* 1958, 18, emphasis added).[2] Marshall similarly concluded his *Marbury* opinion by appealing to the constitutional oath. His emphasis, however, was that judges took the same oath as legislators to support the Constitution and, therefore, could not willingly become instruments of its violation (*Marbury* 1803, 180). In *Marbury*, the oath imposed a responsibility on each government official to read the Constitution for him- or herself and act accordingly. *Cooper* executes an ironic reversal of *Marbury*, transforming the oath into a command to government officials to "close their eyes to the Constitution, and only see the law" (*Marbury*

1803, 179). Four years later, in the context of state legislative apportionment, the Court again explained to the state governments that the Supreme Court is the "ultimate interpreter of the Constitution" (*Baker v. Carr* 1962, 211). Within a decade the Court had repeated those words first to Congress, in reviewing the congressional refusal to seat one of its members, and then to the president, in response to a claim of executive privilege over documents desired by judicial officers (*Powell v. McCormack* 1969, 521; *United States v. Nixon*, 1974, 704). The justices have insisted that the power to interpret the meaning of the Constitution "can no more be shared with the Executive Branch than the Chief Executive, for example, can share with the judiciary the veto power" (*Nixon* 1974, 704).

This strong language raises interesting questions about how the justices reached this point and why they expected other government officials to accede to their authority. The implicit questions raised by such tough talk by the Court can be made even more pointed by considering the influential analysis of political scientist Robert Dahl. Dahl (1957, 279, 281) set out to examine the Court as a "political institution" that must routinely "choose among controversial alternatives of public policy" and do so based on considerations that cannot be strictly deduced from traditional legal materials such as precedent or constitutional text. Dahl was concerned with whether the Court "acted in some special way as a protection of minorities against tyranny by majorities," a role he thought unlikely in a generally democratic political system (Dahl 1957, 282). Given that justices are appointed by presidents and confirmed by senators with

policy consequences in mind, and that vacancies occur regularly on the Supreme Court, Dahl (1957, 285) expected that "the policy views dominant on the Court are never for long out of line with the policy views dominant among the lawmaking majorities of the United States."

Dahl reinforced this suggestion by considering how often and under what circumstances the Supreme Court struck down laws recently passed by Congress (and therefore, laws presumably still supported by political majorities), and how Congress responded to the Court's action. Dahl found that the Court rarely struck down recent, important legislation. When such laws were declared unconstitutional, Congress almost always found some means for getting around the Court's objections in fairly short order (Dahl 1957, 290). Numerous cases in which the Court held such policies unconstitutional occurred during "short-lived transitional periods" when the views of the Court lagged behind the views of political branches affected by sudden electoral change (Dahl 1957, 293).

Dahl's central conclusion was that the Court should normally be fairly passive and restrained when exercising judicial review. Under most circumstances, the Court is "part of the dominant national alliance" and can be expected to act accordingly—by upholding the policies approved by its coalition partners in the other branches of government (Dahl 1957, 293). Dahl's conclusion seemed quite plausible in 1957, especially when the focus was on the extraordinary circumstances of the New Deal and the subsequent judicial deference to Congress in the 1940s and 1950s. The Court, however, embarked on a new period of constitutional activism immediately after the publication of Dahl's article, which seemed to call his conclusions into question. Reconsiderations of his analysis highlighting state laws or making somewhat different assumptions about when legislation enjoyed continued legislative support complicates the story (Beck 1976; Canon and Ulmer 1976; Casper 1976; Funston 1975). Nonetheless, a number of studies following Dahl have similarly concluded that the Court does not generally behave in a strongly countermajoritarian fashion (Flemming and Wood 1997; Friedman 1993; Graber 1993, 1998; Klarman 1996; Mishler and Sheehan 1993; Rosenberg 1992; Stimson, MacKuen and Erikson 1995). In any case, Dahl's basic, quite plausible, argument seems to run counter to the Court's increasing political presence in the twentieth century.

This apparent discrepancy between Dahl's conclusion and the general twentieth-century experience suggests the need for further consideration of the political foundations of the expanding judicial role. If it seems politically anomalous in a democratic political system for justices selected by a political appointment process to actively use the power of judicial review to strike down policies adopted by elected legislative majorities, then this apparent anomaly requires explanation. One clue might be found in one of Dahl's (1957, 281) opening questions: "What groups are benefited or handicapped by the Court and how does the allocation by the Court of these rewards and penalties fit into our presumably democratic political system?" The Court may be "most likely to succeed against a 'weak' majority." Democratic politics in the twentieth century may have presented more opportunities for the Court to make its mark (Dahl 1957, 286). In addition, contrary to Dahl's assumption, elected officials may sometimes desire an activist Court. The justices may sometimes act as free agents, rather than as partners with elected officials, and demonstrate more independence in rendering constitutional judgments than Dahl expected.

The Supreme Court at the Turn of the Century

In the first months of 1895 the Court issued three important decisions with constitutional implications that expanded judicial power and propelled the Court into presidential politics. The Supreme Court upheld the broad power of the federal courts to issue injunctions preventing labor unrest from disrupting interstate commerce when sustaining the jailing of socialist leader Eugene V. Debs for violating such an injunction during a railway worker strike (*In re Debs*, 1895). A few months earlier, the Court allowed a merger to proceed that gave a single company control of 98 percent of the national market in refined sugar. This ruling that federal regulatory power did not extend over manufacturing sharply limited the scope of the 1890 Sherman Antitrust Act (*United States v. E. C. Knight Co.*, 1895). In the American system of federalism, the Court held, state governments had exclusive responsibility for regulating the actual production of goods. The national government was limited to regulating the transportation and exchange of goods across state boundaries. Responding to an appellate lawyer's charge that the 1894 income tax was "communistic in its purposes and tendencies," the Court narrowly struck down most of that law as beyond the taxing power granted to Congress (*Pollock v. Farmer's Loan and Trust Co.*, 1895, 532). The Constitution, a judicial majority noted, was designed "to prevent an attack upon accumulated property by mere force of numbers" (*Pollock* 1895, 583). Federal taxes on income had rarely been levied before 1894, but they were not unprecedented and had gained some support from the Court in the past. Congress in 1894 included a largely symbolic income tax on the wealthy as part of a larger tax package raising tariff duties, which fell most heavily on the working class. Still, the tax that was declared unconstitutional was distinctive and had been heavily promoted by a growing populist wing of the Democratic Party. Over the previous several years the Court had also struck down a number of state laws concerned with business regulation and taxation, most of which had emerged from Democratic and Populist strongholds in the West and South (Gates 1992, 63–68).

These decisions helped set the stage for the presidential contest of 1896. In that year William Jennings Bryan and his populist allies wrested control of the Democratic Party from the incumbent conservatives and mounted a radical challenge to the Republicans. According to the insurgent Democrats, such decisions by the "judicial oligarchy" would "rob the people of the powers of self-government" (Stephenson 1999, 125, 127). They launched what would become the distinctive twentieth-century critique of the Supreme Court and the federal judiciary—that the Court was "countermajoritarian" or antidemocratic (Bickel 1962, 16). The Court was increasingly denounced by populists and progressives not for making decisions regarded as substantively wrong or legally unjustified but for striking

down policies favored by democratic majorities. The central problem, for these critics, was that the "Supreme Court as at present constituted does not spring from the people, and therefore does not properly represent the people," that the power of judicial review was a "menace to democratic government" (Friedman 2001, 1439–1440, 1441).

Although Bryan in his acceptance speech for the Democratic presidential nomination carefully insisted that the party made "no suggestion of an attempt to dispute the authority of the Supreme Court" and recognized "the binding force" of judicial decisions, Republicans seized the opportunity to highlight their growing differences with Democrats and to paint their opponents as extremists (Schlesinger 1971, 2:1853). Republicans made respect for the courts a central theme of the campaign of 1896. In his letter accepting the Republican presidential nomination, William McKinley swore to defeat "the sudden, dangerous and revolutionary assault upon law and order" (Ross 1994, 36). Observing the Democratic convention, former president Benjamin Harrison told his fellow Republicans in New York City, "I cannot exaggerate the gravity and the importance of this assault upon our constitutional form of government" and the threat to "the high-minded, independent Judiciary that will hold the line on questions between wealth and labor, between rich and poor" (Stephenson 1999, 127). The prominent Republican politician and railroad executive Chauncey DePew accused Bryan of wanting to "abolish the Supreme Court and make it a creature of the party caucus" (Stephenson 1999, 127). McKinley's campaign manager declared the Democratic platform to be a "covert threat to pack the Supreme Court of the United States" (Stephenson 1999, 126). A breakaway convention of conservative Democrats adopted a platform condemning "all efforts to degrade that tribunal or impair the confidence and respect which it has deservedly held" (Ross 1994, 36).

After twenty years of close electoral competition between the two parties, the Republicans won a crushing victory in 1896. For the first time since General Ulysses S. Grant's reelection in 1872, a presidential candidate won a solid popular majority. Equally important, urban voters throughout the North and upper Midwest swung decisively into the Republican camp, where they would stay until shaken loose by the Great Depression (Sundquist 1983, 154–169). The Republican victory was widely interpreted in newspaper editorials as a "determination on the part of the people everywhere to maintain the dignity and supremacy of the courts" (Westin 1959, 38). The image of the Democrats as the party of "radicalism" was entrenched (Sundquist 1983, 165). The Court had thrown its weight behind "the constitutional position of the most conservative wing of the Republican party," and that coalition emerged from 1896 in firm control of its party and the elected branches of the federal government (Gates 1992, 68).

It might be expected, following Dahl, that the Court would become less active after the electoral success of its ideological allies. In fact, the Court became more active. The very public support of conservative Republicans helped bolster the authority of the Court to promote aggressively its own understanding of constitutional requirements. After 1896 the Court continued to monitor state governments, especially in the West and the South, for legislation that imposed excessive restrictions on business. At the same time, the justices struck down an increasing number of politically less important congressional statutes covering a variety of issues (Gates 1992, 78–83).

During this period the Court developed some characteristic constitutional doctrines that guided its work during the early twentieth century. In 1897 the Court broke new constitutional ground in *Allgeyer v. Louisiana*, finding a "liberty of contract" in the due process clause of the Fourteenth Amendment. In doing so, the Court formally adopted an interpretation of the Fourteenth Amendment that had been vigorously argued by the dissenters in the Reconstruction-era *Slaughterhouse Cases* (1873). Four justices in *Slaughterhouse* contended that the Fourteenth Amendment's protections of the liberty and property of persons and the "privileges and immunities" held in common by all citizens barred the Louisiana legislature from creating a slaughterhouse monopoly in New Orleans that restricted the ability of independent butchers to pursue their livelihood. In 1873, the judicial majority responded that the Fourteenth Amendment had only the narrow effect of securing "the freedom of the slave race" and did not create a new supervisory role for the federal courts to oversee the general relationship between the state governments and their citizenry (*Slaughterhouse* 1873, 71). A quarter of a century later the Court, in *Allgeyer*, took up another case originating in Louisiana in which the state had prohibited a New York company not licensed by Louisiana from selling marine insurance for goods being shipped from the port of New Orleans. In addition to blocking Louisiana's protectionist effort to bar out-of-state insurance companies from competing for business associated with the state's busy ports, the unanimous Court emphasized that "pursuing an ordinary calling or trade, and . . . acquiring, holding, and selling property, is an essential part of [an individual's] rights of liberty and property, as guarantied by the fourteenth amendment" (*Allgeyer* 1897, 590). Louisiana had pushed the Court too far. By contrast, the next year the Court upheld a Utah law limiting miners to working eight hours per day. The justices observed that government could appropriately place reasonable restrictions on the liberty of contract in the case of occupations especially "dangerous or unhealthful," given that the state "still retains an interest in [an individual's] welfare, however reckless he may be" (*Holden v. Hardy* 1898, 386, 396).

The Court became increasingly mistrustful of governmental motives in passing such regulations (Gillman 1993). In the first decade of the twentieth century, the Court still upheld the vast majority of the state laws challenged on due process grounds, but the number of cases in which the Court struck down such laws rose substantially. Most important, the Court claimed for itself the right to determine what constituted "reasonable" economic legislation and when such legislation was instead "arbitrary" or "unjust." Most famously, the Court in *Lochner v. New York* (1905) narrowly rejected a state law that limited bakers to working ten hours per day. The special circumstances that justified government interference with the general liberty "to purchase or to sell labor" in the case of miners (or, as the Court found in 1908, women) did not apply in the case of bakers (*Lochner* 1905, 53; *Muller v.*

Oregon, 1908). To prevent states from circumventing the Fourteenth Amendment on a mere "pretext," the Court reasoned, justices must be prepared to examine whether the legislation at issue is

a fair, reasonable, and appropriate exercise of the police power of the state, or is it an unreasonable, unnecessary, and arbitrary interference with the right of the individual to his personal liberty, or to enter into those contracts in relation to labor which may seem to him appropriate or necessary for the support of himself and his family. (*Lochner* 1905, 56)

The majority admitted that courts must avoid making mere policy judgments.

If the act be within the power of the state it is valid, although the judgment of the court might be totally opposed to the enactment of such a law. But the question would still remain: Is it within the police power of the state? and that question must be answered by the court. (*Lochner* 1905, 57)

The Court found that the trade of baker was not commonly regarded to be unusually risky or unhealthy. If the legislature could impose limits on the freedom to contract in the case of such relatively normal occupations as bakers, then "there would seem to be no length to which legislation of this nature might not go" and everyone "on that account, [would be] at the mercy of legislative majorities" and "no trade, no occupation, no mode of earning one's living, could escape this all-pervading power" (*Lochner* 1905, 59). The justices found it "impossible for us to shut our eyes to the fact that many laws of this character, while passed under what is claimed to be the police power for the purpose of protecting the public health or welfare, are, in reality, passed from other motives" (*Lochner* 1905, 64).

Those "other motives" were not hard to find, but substantial disagreement existed about whether those other motives were constitutionally illegitimate and how they might be related to general welfare. Dissenting in *Lochner* (1905, 68), Justice John Marshall Harlan argued that such other motives were irrelevant to the judicial decision unless the government's actions were "beyond question, plainly and palpably in excess of legislative power." The statute had "a real or substantial relation to the protection of health," and the Court should not "presume that the state of New York has acted in bad faith" (*Lochner* 1905, 69, 73). More famous—and more important—Justice Oliver Wendell Holmes asserted that the Constitution "is made for people of fundamentally differing views," that the Court should not attempt to prevent "the natural outcome of a dominant opinion," no matter how "injudicious, or if you like as tyrannical" it might seem (*Lochner* 1905, 76, 75). For Holmes, and a growing group of progressive reformers, democratic majorities had broad power to intervene in the social and economic relations of individuals, even when the government was primarily seeking to benefit some individuals at the expense of others.

This growing sensibility favoring relatively unfettered democratic power gained strength in both the Democratic and Republican Parties in the late-nineteenth and early-twentieth centuries. Reformers adhering to this democratic view disagreed with the Supreme Court's substantive understanding of the Constitution. For such progressives and populists, not only was the federal judiciary interfering with policy matters best left to elected representatives and citizens but the courts were also voicing economic and political understandings increasingly incompatible with the demands of the twentieth century. The Court seemed both out of step with contemporary needs and bent on imposing its antiquated ideas on popular majorities.

The Court against "The Tumultuous Ocean of Democracy"

As both the state and federal courts more actively struck down or sharply curtailed legislation, many reformers questioned the value of judicial review and an independent judiciary. An active scholarly debate emerged over whether the power of judicial review was, as one commentator concluded, a "dangerous innovation" or a practice intended by the founders and embedded in the original constitutional design (Smith 1907, 103). Although most concluded that some form of judicial review was inherent in the Constitution, many argued that the growth of judicial review at the turn of the century was nonetheless "revolutionary" (Boudin 1911, 242). Theodore Roosevelt became vocally critical of the courts after he left office in 1908. When he returned to the public stage in the years leading up to his independent run for the White House in 1912, Roosevelt gave voice to the more radical criticisms of the courts that were gaining increased prominence. Roosevelt called the "right of the people to rule" the "first essential in the Progressive program" (Stephenson 1999, 128). That commitment was in clear tension with active judicial review. In the 1911 speech announcing his new campaign for the presidency,

Roosevelt declared that judicial rulings invalidating laws on constitutional grounds "should be subject to revision by the people themselves" through a "right to recall" individual judicial decisions (Ross 1994, 135). Asserting "I believe in pure democracy," Roosevelt argued, "If the courts have the final say-so on all legislative acts, and if no appeal can lie from them to the people, then they are the irresponsible masters of the people" (Ross 1994, 136). The Progressive Party platform in 1912 demanded "such restrictions on the power of the courts as shall leave to the people the ultimate authority to determine fundamental questions of social welfare and public policy" (Stephenson 1999, 129). The Socialist Party, led by Eugene V. Debs, called for the "abolition" of the "usurped" power of judicial review (Stephenson 1999, 129). Roosevelt's Progressive Party collected a little more than 27 percent of the popular vote for president in 1912. Debs's Socialist Party collected another 6 percent.

Roosevelt's proposal was vigorously denounced by various commentators and influential members of the Republican Party. The *New York Times* called one of Roosevelt's early essays criticizing the courts "the craziest article every published by a man of high standing and responsibility in the Republic" (Ross 1994, 134). Roosevelt's assault on the Court provided an opportunity for the Republican Party to insist on greater deference to judicial authority. President William Howard Taft, Roosevelt's successor, was a firm supporter of the courts. His formerly close relationship with Roosevelt grew increasingly bitter during Taft's term of office as the new president cast his lot with the conservative wing of the party. Taft had served as a federal appellate court judge

through much of the 1890s, and Roosevelt sneered at the "lawyers' administration" (Cooper 1983, 144). In 1911, Taft vetoed statehood for Arizona and New Mexico in part because those territories had adopted recall provisions that the president regarded as "destructive of the independence of the judiciary," "injurious to the cause of free government," and encouraging of "tyranny of a popular majority" (Stephenson 1999, 301 n. 100). Roosevelt's speeches hit Taft "like a bolt out of a clear sky." Taft denounced Roosevelt's proposals as "absolutely impossible" and thought Roosevelt was becoming "not unlike Napoleon" in his impatience with the law (Cooper 1983, 151). Roosevelt's crusade against the courts turned even centrist Republicans against him, while motivating Taft to seek renomination and reelection. In letters, Taft avowed, "I represent a safer and saner view of our government and its Constitution than does Theodore Roosevelt, and whether beaten or not I mean to labor in the vineyard for those principles." Taft was convinced that he "represent[ed] a cause that would make it cowardly for me to withdraw now" (Cooper 1983, 157). More important than winning the election, Taft and his supporters were convinced, was "retain[ing] the regular Republican party as a nucleus for future conservative action" (Cooper 1983, 159). In campaign speeches, Taft denounced Roosevelt for planting the seeds of "tyranny" and he expressed confidence that the American people would "never give up on the Constitution" (Ross 1994, 138). The Democratic nominee Woodrow Wilson remained largely silent on the judiciary, though occasionally expressing opposition to judicial reform. Roosevelt de-emphasized it as the presidential campaign of 1912 progressed. Taft continued insisting that the Constitution was "the supreme issue" of the election and that the "Republican Party stands for the Constitution as it is" (Ross 1994, 149). After leaving the presidency, Taft accepted a position teaching constitutional law at Yale to continue the fight. Once the Republicans reclaimed the White House, Taft was rewarded for his service with an appointment to the Supreme Court as chief justice.

Unlike 1896, the election of 1912 was not a clear victory for the courts. Roosevelt had the best showing of any third-party candidate in the twentieth century and outpolled Taft by more than 600,000 votes. Nonetheless, the Court was able successfully to exercise judicial review at an even greater rate over the next two decades. Antijudicial sentiment was unable to coalesce into a political majority. The Wilson administration did not support such measures as the recall, and conservatives retained control of the national Republican Party apparatus. Progressives inside and outside of Congress were as divided among themselves over the appropriate response to the courts as they were in other matters of politics and policy. Their hostility to the courts ensured that conservatives would continue to regard the preservation of judicial authority as a priority—as the "only breakwater . . . against the tumultuous ocean of democracy," in the words of one American Bar Association president (Dillon 1892, 211). The fragmented nature of the antijudicial forces ensured that their challenges were not politically serious. Chief Justice Taft observed in 1923, "[T]he truth is that the so-called radicals are vastly more noisy than they are important" (Ross 1994, 217).

Meanwhile, the substantive policy successes of progressive forces in both Congress and the states gave the conservative courts plenty of opportunities to exercise their constitutional veto. Because the Court's conservative ideological allies could not dominate the policymaking process, the Court was faced with a steady stream of laws conservatives regarded as constitutionally dubious. Because the Court's ideological foes could not dominate national, and especially presidential, politics, they could not bring the Court to heel. The weakness of the political majority both motivated and facilitated expanded judicial activity.

This political situation endured until the onset of the Great Depression. Wilson's victory against a divided Republican Party proved a temporary interruption to general Republican dominance of national politics. The Supreme Court reached unprecedented levels of activism against the federal government in the 1920s while continuing through the mid-1930s to strike down increasing numbers of state laws. In the 1924 elections Progressive candidate Robert M. La Follette offered expected criticisms of the courts but downplayed the judicial issue in favor of other campaign themes. A Republican senator from Wisconsin, La Follette had long been a leading spokesperson for the progressive movement and a visible critic of the conservative judiciary. The Republican and Democratic candidates again took the opportunity to bolster judicial authority. Calvin Coolidge argued, "Majorities are notoriously irresponsible," and judicial review was essential to prevent political majorities from voting away even the "most precious rights." One New York political reporter observed that the Republicans "did not want to permit La

Follette to escape from the Supreme Court issue if it could be forced on him"(Ross 1994, 268). The Democratic presidential nominee was John W. Davis, a Wall Street attorney, past president of the American Bar Association, and no friend of court curbing. His nomination found favor with Chief Justice Taft, who was confident that Davis would hold to the "preservation of constitutional principles and the dignity and influence of the Court" (Ross 1994, 259). Coolidge won in a landslide, despite La Follette's relatively strong showing in the popular vote. Many observers attributed Republican success in part to La Follette's perceived opposition to the Supreme Court (Ross 1994, 282–283).

The Court continued developing constitutional doctrines that hampered the success of progressive plans to strengthen the power of the state and federal governments to intervene in the economy. The "substantive due process" understandings developed in the *Lochner* line of cases remained an important obstacle to extensive new economic regulations, especially at the state level. In 1923, the Court struck down a minimum-wage law for women and children in Washington, D.C. The judicial majority argued that the law was simply a "compulsory extraction from the employer for the support of a partially indigent person," which unconstitutionally shifted the burden to care for the poor from "society as a whole" to individual employers (*Adkins v. Children's Hospital of the District of Columbia*, 1923, 557, 558). In 1932 the Court struck down an Oklahoma statute prohibiting new companies from engaging in the manufacturing or sale of ice unless the company could prove to a state commission that the new business was necessary.

The state violated the Fourteenth Amendment by "denying or unreasonably curtailing the common right to engage in [an otherwise] lawful business practice" (*New State Ice Co. v. Liebmann*, 1932, 278). In 1918 the Court ruled that a federal law prohibiting the interstate shipment of goods produced with child labor exceeded the congressional power to regulate only the transportation of goods but not their production (*Hammer v. Dagenhart*, 1918). That decision provoked a long political struggle to circumvent the Court's ruling by statute or constitutional amendment.

The ground shifted under the Court's feet in 1932. Democrat Franklin D. Roosevelt trounced incumbent President Herbert Hoover at the polls as the nation remained mired in the Great Depression. Roosevelt finally broke the loyalty of urban voters to the Republican Party while retaining the traditional Democratic base in the South and West. A veteran of progressive politics, Roosevelt was backed by huge Democratic majorities in Congress. During his first presidential campaign Roosevelt (1938, 837) departed from a prepared text to observe that the "Republican Party was in complete control" of the federal judiciary, but unsurprisingly his campaign focused on the Depression not the courts. In doing so, Roosevelt articulated a vision of positive government sharply at odds with the more limited state the Court had insisted on for three decades. Roosevelt's "new deal for the American people" required a government committed to the "greatest good to the greatest number" and that bore "responsibility for the welfare" of the people (Roosevelt 1938, 659, 650, 745). As the administration provided first mass relief and then fundamental economic reform, it came into increasing conflict with the Supreme Court.

Roosevelt (1938, 4:16, 5:234) pledged himself to fight "undue private power" and "economic royalists." Although his opponents might hide behind the "flag and the Constitution," the president reminded his foes that those symbols "stand for democracy, not tyranny; for freedom, not subjection," and that "freedom is no half-and-half affair" that could tolerate "economic slavery" (Roosevelt 1938, 5:234, 233). Roosevelt's (1938, 5:233) effort to align government against "economic tyranny" ran headlong into the Supreme Court's long-held understanding of the Constitution. In some instances, the Court upheld innovative legislative efforts to prop up prices and address the economic emergency. The Court narrowly approved a New York milk price-fixing scheme and a Minnesota moratorium on mortgage payments, as well as congressional nullification of private and public contractual provisions requiring payments in gold (*Nebbia v. New York,* 1934; *Home Building and Loan Association v. Blaisdell,* 1934; *United States v. Bankers' Trust Co.,* 1935). In ten major cases before the Court involving the New Deal in 1935 and 1936, however, the government lost eight (Kelly, Harbison, and Belz 1991, 475–480). Important congressional statutes were rejected for delegating excessive legislative authority to executive-branch regulators, for exceeding congressional regulatory and taxation authority, for violating the property rights of creditors, and for interfering with state sovereignty. In some instances, the justices were in agreement. When confronted by the National Recovery Administration's use of private business groups to write economic regulations fixing prices and limiting competition, even the progressive Justice Benjamin Cardozo thought, "This is delegation running riot" (*A. L. A. Schechter Poultry Corporation v. United States*, 1935, 553). In others cases, the justices were sharply divided. Justice Owen Roberts held the swing vote in 5-to-4 majorities striking down a congressional statute requiring railroads to create a federally managed pension program and a New York minimum wage law (*Railroad Retirement Board v. Alton Railroad Co.* 1935; *Morehead v. People of the State of New York ex rel. Tipaldo* 1936). To the Court, as well as a sizable number of conservatives off the bench, both the basic principles and the particular details of Roosevelt's program were contrary to the Constitution.

In the face of judicial resistance, the president took the offensive. In a lengthy press conference following some early decisions against the New Deal, Roosevelt (1938, 4:209, 210) denounced the Court for pitching the nation back into the "horse and buggy age" and for failing to view the Constitution "in the light of present-day civilization." In his annual message to Congress after his first successful reelection campaign in 1936, Roosevelt declared, "Means must be found to adapt our legal forms and our judicial interpretation to the actual present national needs of the largest progressive democracy in the modern world" (Roosevelt 1938, 5:639–640). The judiciary was being "asked by the people to do its part in making democracy successful" (Roosevelt 1938, 5:641). Against those who would use "the Constitution as a cloak to hide their real designs" of putting "their own interest above the general welfare," Roosevelt (1938, 6:332, 331) affirmed his belief in "democracy—and more democracy."

"Majority rule . . . [is] the safeguard of both liberty and civilization" (Roosevelt 1938, 6:333). The Court had an obligation to fall in line.

Unlike earlier progressive critics of the Court, Roosevelt occupied the presidency. Soon after the election of 1936, the president unveiled his plan to "reorganize" the federal judiciary. His proposal called for the immediate presidential appointment of as many as six additional justices, one for each sitting justice over the age of seventy who would not resign from the bench. Roosevelt had not had the opportunity to appoint even a single justice during his first term of office, despite the advanced age of the "nine old men," especially the conservative "Four Horsemen" (Pierce Butler, James McReynolds, George Sutherland, Willis Van Devanter) who formed the core of the antiprogressive coalition on the Court. The administration feared that the conservative justices would "outlive it" (Jackson 1941, 187). Disingenuously, the president suggested that the elder justices might be "impaired" and in need of additional justices to "accelerate the work of the court" (Roosevelt 1938, 6:56, 55). But in his initial message to Congress, he was also more forthright: "A constant and systematic addition of younger blood will vitalize the courts and better equip them to recognize and apply the essential concepts of justice in the light of the needs and the facts of an ever-changing world" (Roosevelt 1938, 6:55). This theme was emphasized in later weeks when Roosevelt (1938, 6:133, 127, 129) stumped for a "reinvigorated, liberal-minded Judiciary" that understood the "present-day sense of the Constitution" and could be trusted not to "override the judgment of the Congress on legislative pol-

icy." As Justice Robert Jackson (1941, xiv), who had served as an assistant attorney general during the Court-packing fight, later wrote, "What we demanded for our generation was the right consciously to influence the evolutionary process of constitutional law, as other generations have done," to loosen the "firm grip" of a "past that was dead and repudiated."

The Court-packing plan, as Roosevelt's judicial reorganization bill immediately became known, sparked a political firestorm. Republicans, who might be expected to be critical of the plan, remained largely silent to avoid turning the dispute into a partisan contest and allowed conservative Democrats to lead the opposition to the bill. The administration had decided against one traditional Court-curbing proposal that would seek to limit or eliminate the power of judicial review in favor of the more innovative and indirect plan of adding justices. In many ways, this was an important acknowledgment of the heightened status of judicial review by the 1930s. The administration hoped to harness the power of the Court, not destroy it. The administration's proposal exploited the widespread concern that life-tenured judges could be out of touch and infirm, while appealing to the undoubted right of Congress to alter the size of the Supreme Court and create new judicial offices. That congressional power had fallen into disuse, however, and the size of the Court had remained at nine since 1869. Roosevelt's political intent to "pack" the Court with more sympathetic justices was obvious. Surprisingly, Sen. Burton Wheeler, a staunch progressive and former running mate of La Follette's, came out in opposition to the plan. Wheeler produced a letter from Chief Justice Hughes denying that the proposed bill would improve judicial efficiency (Leuchtenburg 1995, 140–141). The Court further weakened support for the plan in the spring of 1937 by releasing its decisions upholding minimum wage in Washington, the National Labor Relations Act (NLRA), and the Social Security Act (*West Coast Hotel v. Parrish* 1937; *National Labor Relations Board v. Jones & Laughlin Steel Corp.* 1937; *Steward Machine Co. v. Davis* 1937). The Court had clearly turned a corner, with Justice Roberts switching sides to ease restrictions on government power. With the approval of the NLRA, unions lost interest in Court packing. Public opinion turned decisively against the plan (Caldeira 1987). In May, one of the Four Horsemen, Justice Willis Van Devanter, resigned, giving FDR his first vacancy on the Court. A bipartisan Senate Judiciary Committee report denounced the plan as "an invasion of judicial power such as has never been attempted in this country" (U.S. Senate 1937, 10). Undaunted, the president pressed forward with his plan and launched an aggressive lobbying campaign to shore up congressional support. The sudden death of the Senate majority leader, Joseph Robinson, in the midst of the summer debates on the bill was the final blow. Support for the plan evaporated.

The fate of the Court-packing plan was a testament to the Court's strength and to its vulnerability. Even a popular president, fresh from a landslide electoral victory, backed by overwhelming partisan majorities in Congress, and faced with stern judicial resistance to his policy program in the midst of economic crisis could not win passage of a relatively tempered proposal to tamper with the Court. The public and political opposition to the Court-packing plan demonstrated the substantial authority the Court still possessed, even among those who disagreed with many of its substantive decisions. Many distrusted a plan that seemed to consolidate further power in the presidency. Congressional New Dealers rhetorically asked how they would have been expected to respond to such a proposal had a Republican president made it (Leuchtenburg 1963, 234–235). As the Court grew more accommodating over the course of the spring of 1937, affected interests such as labor unions were split off from the antijudicial coalition. Although those close to the president who could foresee future potential conflicts with the Court, such as Democratic Party chair Jim Farley, might ask, "Why compromise?" others who had already had their particular policies upheld, such as Sen. James Byrnes, began to wonder, "Why run for a train after you've caught it?" (Leuchtenburg 1995, 144). The huge Democratic majorities won in the previous elections also papered over basic divisions within the New Deal coalition that the Court-packing fight began to lay bare. A substantial group of conservative Democrats, especially from the South, concerned about the direction of the party and the government, were unwilling to concede more power to the president. In the future, FDR would attempt to purge or circumvent such conservatives, but the "Conservative Coalition" became an important and enduring constraint on liberalism for decades (Milkis 1993; Patterson 1967). Although powerful, the Democratic majority had limits. The Court had found them.

After the Revolution:
The Court at Midcentury

The "constitutional revolution" of 1937 was dramatic, even if the Court emerged unscathed (Corwin 1941). The revolution turned on the switch of Justice Roberts and, to a lesser extent, Chief Justice Hughes from the conservative wing of the Court to its more progressive wing. The revolution was foreshadowed by the increasing complexity of the Court's earlier case law, especially the 1934 *Nebbia* decision in which Roberts voted to uphold the New York milk law (Cushman 1998). Roberts's final switch became known in the decisions announced in the spring of 1937, but his crucial vote was cast before FDR released his judicial reorganization proposal. Soon thereafter the president was able to make his first appointment to the Court. Roosevelt eventually named nine justices, achieving his own majority on the bench in 1940. Over the ten terms beginning in 1937, the Court overturned thirty-two of its own earlier decisions, including eight precedents that had originally been adopted unanimously, some that had just been established a few years earlier, and others that had endured since Reconstruction (Leuchtenburg 1995, 233). After rejecting thirteen federal laws between 1934 and 1936, the Court struck down only two congressional statutes over the next fifteen years. The Court struck down thirty state laws between 1934 and 1936, but averaged half that rate in the 1940s (though this was still above the rate achieved in any decade in the nineteenth century).

A particularly notable feature of the New Deal Court's constitutional jurisprudence was its new deference to the elected branches of gov-

ernment. The so-called *Lochner* Court had emphasized judicial skepticism of political decisions if constitutional liberties were to be protected. The New Deal Court embraced Justice Holmes's belief that democratic majorities should be given substantial latitude to make their own political choices. The substantive due process doctrine of the *Lochner* era that required government neutrality in the social conflict between economic interests was scrapped. In upholding Washington's minimum wage, Chief Justice Hughes expanded "public interest" in the economy to include a wide range of activities that the state might choose to regulate. "The Constitution does not speak of freedom of contract," he wrote. "It speaks of liberty . . . necessarily subject to the restraints of due process" (*West Coast Hotel* 1937, 391). The chief justice noted that the Court "must take judicial notice of the unparalleled demands for relief," "the evils of the 'sweating system,'" and the "selfish disregard of the public interest" by "unconscionable employers." "The Legislature is entitled to its judgment" (*West Coast Hotel* 1937, 399). To the dissenting Justice George Sutherland, the Court's refusal to "say the final word as to the validity of a statute assailed as unconstitutional" was a "betrayal of the trust" (*West Coast Hotel* 1937, 401). By refusing to exercise their constitutional duty, Sutherland thought, the majority of the justices had effectively amended the Constitution "under the guise of interpretation" (1937, 404). Less than a year later Justice Sutherland left the Court. In upholding a law banning the sale of filled milk (evaporated skimmed milk supplemented with vegetable oils) in 1938, the Court concluded, "regulatory legislation affecting ordinary commercial transactions" was held to be valid unless the Court could not find any "rational basis" for the law (*United States v. Carolene Products Corp.* 1938, 152). In reversing a rare postwar lower court decision finding a state economic regulation unconstitutional, the New Deal Justice William O. Douglas reminded the trial judge, "For protection against abuses by legislatures the people must resort to the polls, not to the courts" (*Williamson v. Lee Optical Co.* 1955, 488).

At the same time the Court adopted the new "rational-basis" test for state and federal economic legislation, the justices sustained an expanded national government relative to the states. In upholding the NLRA that even Roosevelt's attorney general thought "of rather doubtful constitutionality," the chief justice delivered good news to the White House (Leuchtenburg 1995, 217). In 1937 the Court still believed that the "distinction between what is national and what is local . . . is vital to the maintenance of our federal system" (*Jones & Laughlin Steel* 1937, 30). But whereas the previous year the Court had found that "the relation of employer and employee . . . in all producing occupations is purely local in character," the majority of the justices now could not "shut our eyes to the plainest facts of our national life," including that labor relations were "a matter of the most urgent national concern" (*Carter v. Carter Coal Co.* 1936, 303; *Jones & Laughlin Steel* 1937, 41). Over the next few years the holdover justices continued to believe that the Court had a vital role in "policing the boundary between the local and the national, of making the final determination of whether the activity of a particular enterprise fell within the domain of federal regulatory authority" (Cushman 1998, 188). By 1941, the justices ap-

pointed by FDR held a majority and abandoned that role entirely, no matter how "tenuous, speculative or remote" from interstate commerce a particular national economic regulation might be.[3] In a pair of important decisions, the Court declared that Congress may regulate any activity with a "substantial effect" on interstate commerce (*Wickard v. Filburn* 1942; *United States v. Darby* 1941). Citing Chief Justice Marshall, Justice Jackson declared for the Court that in federalism cases the "effective restraints on its [the Federal commerce power] exercise must proceed from political rather than from judicial processes" (*Wickard* 1942, 120). Even if an "activity be local and though it may not be regarded as commerce, it may still, whatever its nature, be reached by Congress" without judicial intervention (1942, 125). Privately, Jackson wrote that for the Court to act in the future against the use of federal power "the relation between interstate commerce and the regulated activity would have to be so absurd that it would be laughed out of Congress." The "commerce clause is what the Congress says it is" (Cushman 1998, 218).

Consistent with the core commitments of the New Deal coalition, the Supreme Court in 1937 loosened the previously recognized constitutional restrictions on the government's power to intervene in the economy and to regulate broad swaths of what had previously been regarded as the "private" life of citizens. Roosevelt's (1938, 6:133) more "liberal-minded judiciary" had become more acquiescent to the desires of legislative majorities. The subversion of judicial authority was not complete, however. As the political reaction to the Court-packing plan indicated, many progressives as well as conservatives saw a continuing role for judicial review. The editor of the *Nation*, for example, wrote, "If I were a Negro I would be raging and tearing my hair over this [Court-packing] proposal" (Leuchtenburg 1963, 235). Others pointed to the value of the Court in protecting free speech and religion (Leuchtenburg 1995, 139). As Jackson argued, the key demand of the New Dealers was for "influence" in the Court, not the abandonment of the power of judicial review itself.

The pre–New Deal Court launched some constitutional initiatives that the New Dealers regarded as worth continuing. Edward S. Corwin (1941, 110, 111), who was a Princeton constitutional scholar and one architect of the Court-packing plan, thought judicial "self-abnegation" would be "less laudable in the long run" in such areas as extending against the states "certain rights which the Bill of Rights protects in more specific terms against Congress." The "enlargement of judicial review" had "its best justification" when the "Court empowered itself to give voice to the conscience of the country in behalf of poor people against local prejudice and unfairness." He singled out "freedom of speech and press and the right to a fair trial" (Corwin 1941, 111–112). As Corwin's phrasing suggested, such a judicial initiative promised to appeal to the substantive interests and constituencies of the New Deal coalition while attending to the procedural mechanisms of democracy rather than challenging substantive policy outputs.

The Court hinted at this broader constitutional agenda in various decisions. In the early 1930s the Court intervened in some racially charged and particularly unjust southern cases to extend criminal procedure guarantees against the states (*Powell v. Alabama* 1932;

Norris v. Alabama 1935; *Brown v. Mississippi* 1936). In the 1920s the Court struck down state laws burdening the rights of parents to guide the education and upbringing of their children (*Meyer v. Nebraska* 1923; *Pierce v. Society of Sisters* 1925). Also in the 1920s, in the aftermath of the "Red Scare" of the previous decade, the Court recognized free speech as among the "fundamental personal rights and 'liberties'" protected by the Fourteenth Amendment from state encroachment, though it was not until the 1930s that the Court actually overturned state actions as inconsistent with the requirements of free speech (*Gitlow v. New York* 1925, 666; *Stromberg v. California* 1931; *Near v. Minnesota* 1931). Progressive scholars and activists urged the Court to offer greater protection to political dissenters who might contribute to the democratic process and the creation of new popular majorities (Graber 1991). Beginning in 1937 the Court became more sympathetic to labor movement arguments for enhanced constitutional protection of such activities as picketing, the distribution of handbills, and the holding of public rallies (*Senn v. Tile Layers Union* 1937; *Hague v. Committee for Industrial Organization* 1939; *Thornhill v. Alabama* 1940). The particular religious practices of the Jehovah's Witnesses often ran afoul of these same sorts of government restrictions (*Lovell v. Griffin* 1938; *Schneider v. Irvington* 1939; *Murdock v. Pennsylvania* 1943). Given that the New Deal coalition was itself "an extraordinary assemblage of such traditional outgroups" as organized labor, Catholics, Jews, and blacks, it is not surprising that the political representatives of that coalition found new value in free speech and similar civil liberties (Klarman 1996, 44).

The Court and constitutional commentators viewed various particular rights as part of the same package of fundamental liberties protected by the Fourteenth Amendment and the Bill of Rights. Some progressives would subordinate individual rights in general to democratic majorities, adopting a judicial posture of general deference to legislative decisions. Others sought to distinguish between different forms of liberty and to dedicate the judiciary to enforcing the "preferred freedoms" that were "indispensable conditions of a free society" in contrast to those that "derived merely from shifting economic arrangements" (Frankfurter 1938, 51; see also Mason 1956).

One approach to distinguishing preferred from less preferred freedoms was procedural, or what constitutional scholar John Hart Ely (1980) later called "representation-reinforcing." The classic expression of this view was hidden away in a crucial footnote in the 1938 *Carolene Products* case upholding the Filled Milk Act. Having announced the deferential "rational-basis" test for upholding laws regulating "ordinary commercial transactions," the Court explained in a footnote the conditions under which there would be "more exacting judicial scrutiny." Those conditions include apparent violation of "specific" textual prohibitions in the Constitution, legal restrictions on the political process, and "prejudice against discrete and insular minorities" that might likewise leave some unprotected by the normal political process (*Carolene Products* 1938, 152 n. 4). The Court's role was not to second-guess the judgment of legislatures but to ensure that the "remedial channels of the democratic process remain open and unobstructed" (*Minersville School Dist. v. Gobitis* 1940, 599).

An alternative approach to identifying preferred freedoms was substantive, exercising judicial judgment to determine which freedoms were simply too sacred to be infringed. The progressive justice Benjamin Cardozo gave eloquent statement to this approach in 1937. When rejecting the claim to a privilege against double jeopardy in state criminal trials, Cardozo articulated a judicial mission to protect rights that are "of the very essence of a scheme of ordered liberty" and whose loss would "violate a 'principle of justice so rooted in the traditions and conscience of our people as to be ranked as fundamental' " (*Palko v. Connecticut* 1937, 325). To all the justices, the "guaranties of civil liberty are but guaranties of freedom of the human mind and spirit and of reasonable freedom and opportunity to express them," as was "protection against torture" (*Gobitis* 1940, 604; *Palko* 1937, 326). Such formulations did not solve all problems or satisfy those who would regard the rights of property as fundamental, but they indicated a continuing judicial role in securing the "constitutional protection of the liberty of small minorities to the popular will" (*Gobitis* 1940, 606).

Dahl would question the political viability of such judicial promises to protect "small minorities" from "the popular will," or what Holmes often called the "dominant opinion" (*Lochner* 1905, 75). Yet such opinions laid the groundwork for the judicial "rights revolution" of the 1960s and a resurgence in the active exercise of judicial review. Corwin (1941, 111) was prescient in specifying that the Court might act "against *local* prejudice and unfairness." National conservatives in the Republican Party in the first decades of the twentieth century had welcomed judicial monitoring of the states for progressive legislation that violated their constitutional understandings, so national liberals in the Democratic Party in the middle decades of the twentieth century welcomed judicial action against conservative states that violated liberal constitutional commitments. The federal judiciary was a useful watchdog of national political majorities against local majorities.

The Warren Court and After

The most notable achievements of the Warren Court in the 1950s and 1960s came against the state governments. There is a remarkable geographic concentration in the Court's work during these years. The vast majority of politically important exercises of judicial review was aimed at the Southern and border states. Nearly all the remaining cases came from Republican states (Gates 1992, 153; Powe 2000, 489–494).

After the initial successes of the New Deal, progressives in the national government were frustrated. The liberal reform agenda had bogged down in the face of mounting opposition from the Conservative Coalition of Southern Democrats and Republicans. As one prominent commentator observed in the early 1960s, "Paradoxically, while the congressional Democrats have broadened their grip on political machinery over the last quarter century, the scope of their policy interests has narrowed" (Burns 1963, 314). In particular, "most Southern heartland congressmen have reverted to solid opposition to presidential Democratic programs," which remained liberal (Burns 1963, 315). Meanwhile, the presi-

dential wing of the Republican Party had been dominated by a centrism that was "balanced in its rhetoric, . . . [and] liberal on specifics" (Burns 1963, 290). As a consequence of these divisions among elected officials, national policymaking tended toward compromise and moderation, with conservatives unable to roll back the New Deal and liberals unable to extend it.

Race was a major sticking point for national policy making and ultimately a central concern of the Warren Court. The "party of Lincoln" continued to hold liberal views on racial civil rights in the postwar period, though Roosevelt had successfully pulled some of the black vote away from the Republican Party. Northern liberals in the Democratic Party were likewise committed to civil rights, and the Democratic electoral base in the urban North made such a position increasingly politically attractive. The Democratic Solid South, where the black vote was suppressed, was implacably opposed to civil rights reform. Senior legislators from the South were well-positioned to block new civil rights statutes. One response to this legislative impasse was unilateral action by the executive branch. During his 1948 reelection campaign, President Harry Truman issued executive orders desegregating the military and establishing a board to investigate complaints of racial discrimination within the executive branch (Dudziak 2000, 25–27).

Another response was judicial. At the turn of the century, the Court had a rather unattractive record on racial civil rights. The justices had ruled that blacks could not be excluded from juries but had done little to make that ruling effective (*Strauder v. West Virginia* 1880). In the nineteenth century, the Court approved Jim Crow segregation in the states while blocking Congress from addressing racial discrimination by private persons (*Plessy v. Ferguson* 1896; *Civil Rights Cases* 1883). In the twentieth century, the Court gradually became more critical of Jim Crow, encouraged in part by the aggressive efforts of the National Association for the Advancement of Colored People (NAACP) and support from the U.S. Department of Justice (Kluger 1975; Tushnet 1994). In 1915, the Court struck down an Oklahoma state constitutional amendment that imposed special voting restrictions on blacks, and in 1927 struck down a Texas law that excluded blacks from the Democratic Party primary (*Guinn v. United States* 1915; *Nixon v. Herndon* 1927). Progress became more rapid over time. The Court began its march toward the desegregation of schools in 1938 in a case involving law school admissions (*Missouri ex rel. Gaines v. Canada* 1938). In subsequent decades, the pace quickened on school desegregation and other fronts of the civil rights struggle. Most famously, the Court in *Brown v. Board of Education* (1954) finally abandoned the principle of "separate but equal" in the face of the evident inequality in practice of segregated institutions.

The civil rights struggle was both a test of and a triumph for judicial review and supremacy in the mid-twentieth century. The Court's rejection in principle of racial segregation, and in the sensitive context of primary education, touched off a firestorm of protest in the South. On the one hand, the courts made relatively little headway in achieving actual desegregation in primary and secondary education in the decade after the *Brown* decision. The Supreme Court largely left the federal trial

courts to their own devices in implementing desegregation. State governments and local school boards proved both creative and persistent in obstructing and circumventing those efforts, denying practical effect to the Supreme Court's constitutional decision. Significant progress in achieving real desegregation was not accomplished until after the political success of the civil rights movement and the policy efforts of Congress and the executive branch in the 1960s (Peltason 1971; Rosenberg 1991). On the other hand, resistance to the courts in the South provoked renewed rhetorical support for the judiciary in Washington, D.C. Most dramatically, in 1957 Gov. Orval Faubus of Arkansas defied the federal courts and threatened to use force to prevent black children from attending white Little Rock schools. President Dwight Eisenhower, who otherwise showed little interest in school desegregation, responded by sending federal troops to Arkansas to back up the judicial order. Eisenhower repeatedly emphasized that "the responsibility and authority of the Supreme Court to interpret the Constitution are very clear" and all other political actors had a duty to obey the Court regardless of whether they agreed with its decisions (Dudziak 2000, 132). Events in Little Rock moved a unanimous Court, a year later, to issue its most forceful pronouncement on behalf of judicial supremacy to that date in *Cooper v. Aaron*. In an opinion largely written by Justice William Brennan and read aloud by Chief Justice Warren, both Eisenhower appointees, the Court instructed, "Every state legislator and executive and judicial officer is solemnly committed by oath pursuant . . . 'to support *this* Constitution,'" the Constitution as the U.S. Supreme

Court had interpreted it (*Cooper* 1958, 18, emphasis added). Ultimately, the success of the civil rights movement retrospectively gave new moral authority to the Supreme Court, which had made such a strong public defense of racial equality when the elected branches seemed incapable of action.

The political and legal struggle for racial civil rights had spillover effects in less obvious areas of constitutional law. Many early cases in which the Supreme Court extended federal constitutional protections to state criminal trials arose from "the national scandal of racist Southern justice" (Cover 1982, 1306). These early cases laid the foundation for cases arising in the 1960s and beyond that had a more national reach. Although *Gideon v. Wainwright* (1963), which established that states must provide counsel to poor criminal defendants, did not involve a black defendant, only a handful of states in the Deep South did not routinely provide such assistance (Lewis 1964, 132–133). By the mid-1960s, as President Lyndon Johnson was launching the War on Poverty, race and poverty were increasingly intermingled in the minds of the justices and others. The initial draft of the 1966 *Miranda v. Arizona* decision constraining police interrogations included an explicit reference to race and "illegal official action in the southern states" (Schwartz 1983, 591).

Racial concerns gave new impetus to the Court's protection of free speech in the 1960s. The efforts of Southern states to harass and stifle the civil rights movement provoked the Court into developing new constitutional doctrines protecting protest activities and speech. In cases involving the NAACP, the Court enhanced constitutional protections for "freedom of assembly" that included the right of activists to remain anonymous and restricted legislative investigations that might have a "chilling effect" on speech (*NAACP v. Alabama* 1958; *Bates v. Little Rock* 1960; *NAACP v. Button* 1963). One prominent free-speech case placing new high barriers against the ability of public figures to bring libel cases against the media arose after an Alabama police commissioner claimed to be defamed by an advertisement placed by civil rights activists in the *New York Times* (*New York Times v. Sullivan* 1964). When finding new constitutional limits on the previously well-established law of libel, the Court asserted "a profound national commitment to the principle that debate on public issues should be uninhibited, robust, and wide-open" and to the "unfettered interchange of ideas" (*Sullivan* 1964, 270, 269).

The New Deal coalition, especially as it morphed into the Great Society coalition of the 1960s, empowered many who had previously been outside the political mainstream. The Court gave voice to their concerns. The geographic apportionment of seats in the state legislatures had not kept up with the rapid urbanization of America during the first half of the twentieth century. In a stark reversal of precedent and intervention into what had previously been regarded a "political question," the Court in 1962 found such malapportioned legislatures to violate the right of individual voters to be treated equally (*Baker v. Carr* 1962; *Reynolds v. Sims* 1964). The decision immediately benefited the urban electorate central to the New Deal coalition while tapping into widely held beliefs about proper democratic ideals. The social beliefs of elite lawyers within the New Deal political coalition were visibly represented on the Court when the justices worked to remove traditional religious and moral concerns from the political arena. The Court acted to remove religion from the public schools and other public arenas (*Engle v. Vitale* 1962; *Abingdon School District v. Schempp* 1963). Although deeply controversial and often ignored in practice, the Court's decisions on school prayer and other related issues reflected what had become "a dominant view shared by the well-educated—and therefore the justices of the Court—that religion was a private matter, best left to the home and the churches" (Klarman 1996, 46–62; Powe 2000, 358). Through the 1960s, the Court facilitated the sexual revolution by imposing increasingly difficult obstacles on government censorship and regulation of obscenity, most notably striking down Connecticut's anticontraceptive law as an invasion of privacy (*Griswold v. Connecticut* 1965).

The Supreme Court in the 1960s may have been in partnership with the Democratic majority that controlled Congress and the White House, but it was not inactive. The Court increasingly exercised judicial review against the states on matters of substantial political concern on both a regional and national level, particularly after national elected officials were unable or unlikely to take action on their own. Although Republican candidate Barry Goldwater attempted to make the Supreme Court's decisions an important issue in the 1964 presidential election, his critical message appeared to win few supporters outside the South. He lost in a landslide.

Although the Warren Court's most important constitutional decisions were directed against the states, the justices increasingly struck down federal statutes. The Court struck down more acts of Congress in the 1960s than in any previous decade, including the 1930s. In almost every case, the Court invalidated laws passed in the early 1950s or laws that had a distinctly conservative cast. Congress pointedly chastised the Court after it struck down a handful of anticommunist security measures in 1957, and the justices retreated from that still volatile issue (Murphy 1962). As the 1960s wore on, the Court returned to that and similar issues, striking down a 1950 prohibition on members of the Communist Party from being employed in the defense industry, the criminal conviction of activist Timothy Leary for failing to register and pay a tax required by the 1954 Marihuana Tax Act, and a 1952 law providing for the loss of American citizenship by those who vote in foreign elections (*United States v. Robel* 1967; *Leary v. United States* 1969; *Afroyim v. Rusk* 1957). Although congressional votes to repeal such laws even in the late 1960s might have been politically costly and legislatively time-consuming, the Democratic Congresses of the Johnson years were unlikely to initiate and pass such statutes or regard them as politically important. The Court that challenged Congress over the constitutionality of its laws during this period was working well within the bounds of dominant political opinion.

The Court became even more active striking down state legislation in the 1970s and early 1980s, but pulled back somewhat from activism against federal statutes. Rulings against Congress also changed. The Court foreshadowed the new tendency in a 1969 case striking down a residential waiting period for receipt of welfare benefits in Washington, D.C., as well as similar restrictions in the states (*Shapiro v. Thompson* 1969). That decision was followed in the early 1970s by similar rulings removing legal obstacles to illegitimate children and cohabitating unmarried couples receiving government benefits (*Jimenez v. Weinberger* 1974; *Department of Agriculture v. Moreno* 1973). Later in the decade, the Court identified and struck down various legal rules that made gender-based distinctions when granting benefits such as Social Security and military pensions (*Frontiero v. Richardson* 1973; *Califano v. Goldfarb* 1970). In the budding culture war launched in the 1960s, the Court had chosen sides, tending to favor greater access to government benefits and less governmental favoritism affecting lifestyle choices than Congress. Such actions mirrored moves the Court was making against state laws.

Although wading into more current political controversies with such cases, the Court nonetheless was choosing battles in which it could count on numerous allies. Republican Richard Nixon won the presidency in 1968 riding law-and-order campaign themes aimed as much against the Warren Court as against the incumbent Democratic administration, more successfully using the "Southern strategy" that Goldwater had pioneered four years earlier. Goldwater's and Nixon's examples of harsh public criticism of the federal courts were followed, with varying degrees of intensity, by Republican presidents and presidential candidates through the last decades of the twentieth century. Such conservative criticism of particular constitutional decisions usually stopped well short of the more general challenge to judicial authority to interpret the Constitution and exercise the power of judicial

review made by progressive critics of the courts early in the twentieth century.

Recent Republican presidential candidates have been relatively successful at the polls, yet the Court remains fairly active and secure in its constitutional status. Part of the reason for the persistence of this state of affairs is divided government. Nixon was the first president since 1848 to come to power without carrying either chamber of Congress for his party. This episode of divided government did not soon resolve itself, with a single party capturing control of both elected branches of government. Republicans remained relatively successful at the presidential level but generally frustrated at the congressional level. At the end of the twentieth century, divided government was the norm rather than the exception. Unlike their predecessors, Republican presidents could neither win over the Court through appointments (because they usually had to compromise with a Democratic Senate) nor overcome the Court through credible threats of legislative sanctions (because their partisans did not control Congress). Since the 1960s Republicans have been able to pull the Court in their direction, but they have not been able to convert that tribunal into a reliable coalition partner. In recent decades, the Court has enjoyed substantial political space within which to pursue its own constitutional understandings with relatively little interference from the other branches. The Court could ally with one branch of government against the other, as when it advanced the Watergate investigation by upholding a subpoena of White House tapes or unravel fragile legislative coalitions, as when it struck down on separation of powers grounds provisions of the Gramm-Rudman-

Hollings deficit control measures, with little fear of lasting political damage (*United States v. Nixon* 1974; *Bowsher v. Synar* 1986). In the late 1990s the Rehnquist Court struck down recently enacted federal laws at a historically blistering pace, while making emphatic assertions about its own role as the ultimate constitutional interpreter.

The power declared in *Marbury*, the power of the Supreme Court to give legally effective meaning to the terms of the Constitution and to strike down the acts of elected officials in the name of the Constitution, took on new significance in the twentieth century. In the twentieth century the Court has routinely found both state and federal laws to be at odds with the requirements of the Constitution. The Supreme Court is understood as having the opportunity to be heard on many controversial and important political issues of the day. The federal courts have sometimes initiated new political debates, shifted the terms of old debates, or stood squarely against the ideals and desires of democratic majorities and political leaders. Accompanying the twentieth-century growth in the constitutional role of the Court was vocal criticism of judicial review as antidemocratic.

The triumphs of the Court stand on political foundations. The Court can achieve influence only if others are prepared to listen. The justices are selected by a political process and must operate within a political environment. As Justice Cardozo (1921, 168) once noted, "The great tides and currents which engulf the rest of men do not turn aside in their course and pass the judges by." The exercise of judicial review implies a degree of conflict with democracy, but that power could not be maintained if it were not ultimately accountable to democracy. The apparent growth of judicial review in the twentieth century is not an illusion, but that growth depends on a supportive political environment. The Court cannot simply be obstructionist (at least not for very long), but it can still be activist.

The Court has found numerous opportunities in the twentieth century to exercise the power of judicial review. Even when members of the political majority have shared the Court's understanding of the Constitution, there have been opportunities for the Court to act. The decentralized structure of the American political system creates many openings for those who cannot win national elections to exercise political power. At times, such dissenters can impede the progress of national political majorities, as did Southern Democrats in the post–New Deal Congress. The judiciary may be an alternate vehicle for advancing the majority's political goals. At times, such dissenters may gain power at the state and local level and adopt policies that national political leaders regard as unwise and unconstitutional, as conservatives viewed much of the early progressive legislation. The federal judiciary may be an effective and efficient instrument for monitoring and correcting state governments. The justices of the Supreme Court may have their own political and constitutional priorities, such as the protection of free speech after World War II, and seize opportunities provided by a distracted, divided, or superannuated political majority to advance their own goals. The Court's capacity to command others to support "this Constitution" has limits, but within those limits the Court can and has played an important role in defining the content of American constitutionalism.

Bibliography

Beck, Paul Allen. "Critical Elections and the Supreme Court: Putting the Cart before the Horse." *American Political Science Review* 70 (1976): 930–932.

Berk, Gerald. *Alternative Tracks*. Baltimore: Johns Hopkins University Press, 1994.

Bickel, Alexander M. *The Least Dangerous Branch*. Indianapolis: Bobbs-Merrill, 1962.

Boudin, Louis B. "Government by Judiciary." *Political Science Quarterly* 26 (1911): 238–270.

Burns, James MacGregor. *The Deadlock of Democracy*. Englewood Cliffs, N.J.: Prentice-Hall, 1963.

Caldeira, Gregory A. "Public Opinion and the U.S. Supreme Court: FDR's Court-Packing Plan." *American Political Science Review* 81 (1987): 1139–1153.

Canon, Bradley, and S. Sidney Ulmer. "The Supreme Court and Critical Elections: A Dissent." *American Political Science Review* 70 (1976): 1215–1218.

Cardozo, Benjamin N. *The Nature of the Judicial Process*. New Haven: Yale University Press, 1921.

Casper, Jonathan D. "The Supreme Court and National Policy Making." *American Political Science Review* 70 (1976): 50–63.

Clinton, Robert Lowry. Marbury v. Madison *and Judicial Review*. Lawrence: University Press of Kansas, 1989.

Cooper, John Milton, Jr. *The Warrior and the Priest*. Cambridge: Harvard University Press, 1983.

Corwin, Edward S. "The Supreme Court and the Fourteenth Amendment." *Michigan Law Review* 7 (1909): 643–672.

———. *Constitutional Revolution, Ltd*. Claremont, Calif.: Claremont College, 1941.

———. *The "Higher Law" Background of American Constitutional Law*. Ithaca: Cornell University Press, 1955.

Cover, Robert. "The Origins of Judicial Activism in the Protection of Minorities." *Yale Law Journal* 91 (1982): 1287–1316.

Cushman, Barry. *Rethinking the New Deal Court*. New York: Oxford University Press, 1998.

Dahl, Robert A. "Decision-Making in a Democracy: The Supreme Court as a National Policy-Maker." *Journal of Public Law* 6 (1957): 279–295.

Dillon, John F. "Address of the President." In *Report of the Fifteenth Annual Meeting of the American Bar Association*. Chicago: American Bar Association, 1892.

Dudziak, Mary L. *Cold War Civil Rights*. Princeton: Princeton University Press, 2000.

Ely, John Hart. *Democracy and Distrust*. Cambridge: Harvard University Press, 1980.

Flemming, Roy B., and B. Dan Wood. "The Public and the Supreme Court: Individual Justice Responsiveness to American Public Moods." *American Journal of Political Science* 41 (1997): 468–498.

Forbath, William E. *Law and the Shaping of the American Labor Movement*. Cambridge: Harvard University Press, 1991.

Frankfurter, Felix. *Mr. Justice Holmes and the Supreme Court*. Cambridge: Harvard University Press, 1938.

Freyer, Tony Allan. *Forums of Order*. Greenwich, Conn.: JAI Press, 1979.

Friedman, Barry. "Dialogue and Judicial Review." *Michigan Law Review* 91 (1993): 577–682.

———. "The History of the Countermajoritarian Difficulty, Part Three: The Lesson of *Lochner*." *New York University Law Review* 76 (2001): 1383–1455.

Funston, Richard. "The Supreme Court and Critical Elections." *American Political Science Review* 69 (1975): 795–811.

Gates, John B. *The Supreme Court and Partisan Realignment*. Boulder: Westview Press, 1992.

Gillman, Howard. *The Constitution Besieged*. Durham: Duke University Press, 1993.

———. "How Political Parties Can Use the Courts to Promote Their Agendas: Federal Courts in the United States, 1875–1891." *American Political Science Review* 96 (2002).

Graber, Mark A. *Transforming Free Speech*. Berkeley: University of California Press, 1991.

———. "The Nonmajoritarian Difficulty: Legislative Deference to the Judiciary." *Studies in American Political Development* 7 (1993): 35–73.

———. "Federalist or Friends of Adams: The Marshall Court and Party Politics." *Studies in American Political Development* 12 (1998): 229–266.

_____."The Jacksonian Origins of Chase Court Activism." *Journal of Supreme Court History* 25 (2000): 17–39.

Haines, Charles Grove. *The American Doctrine of Judicial Supremacy.* New York: Macmillan, 1914.

Jackson, Robert H. *The Struggle for Judicial Supremacy.* New York: Vintage, 1941.

Kelly, Alfred H., Winfred A. Harbison, and Herman Belz. *The American Constitution.* New York: W. W. Norton, 1991.

Klarman, Michael J. "Rethinking the Civil Rights and Civil Liberties Revolution." *Virginia Law Review* 82 (1996): 1–67.

Kluger, Richard. *Simple Justice.* New York: Vintage, 1975.

Letwin, William. *Law and Economic Policy in America.* New York: Random House, 1965.

Leuchtenburg, William E. *Franklin D. Roosevelt and the New Deal.* New York: Harper and Row, 1963.

_____. *The Supreme Court Reborn.* New York: Oxford University Press, 1995.

Lewis, Anthony. *Gideon's Trumpet.* New York: Vintage, 1964.

Mason, Alpheus Thomas. "The Core of Free Government, 1938–1940: Mr. Justice Stone and 'Preferred Freedoms.'" *Yale Law Journal* 65 (1956): 597–628.

Milkis, Sidney M. *The President and the Parties.* New York: Oxford University Press, 1993.

Mishler, William, and Reginald S. Sheehan. "The Supreme Court as a Countermajoritarian Institution? The Impact of Public Opinion on Supreme Court Decisions." *American Political Science Review* 88 (1993): 87–101.

Murphy, Walter F. *Congress and the Court.* Chicago: University of Chicago Press, 1962.

Patterson, James T. *Congressional Conservatism and the New Deal.* Lexington: University of Kentucky Press, 1967.

Peltason, J. W. *58 Lonely Men.* Urbana: University of Illinois Press, 1971.

Powe, Lucas A., Jr. *The Warren Court and American Politics.* Cambridge: Harvard University Press, 2000.

Roosevelt, Franklin D. *Public Papers and Addresses of Franklin D. Roosevelt.* Samuel I. Rosenman, ed. 6 vols. New York: Random House, 1938.

Rosenberg, Gerald N. *The Hollow Hope.* Chicago: University of Chicago Press, 1991.

_____. "Judicial Independence and the Reality of Political Power." *Review of Politics* 54 (1992): 369–398.

Ross, William G. *A Muted Fury.* Princeton: Princeton University Press, 1994.

Schlesinger, Arthur, Jr., ed. *History of American Presidential Elections, 1789–1968.* 4 vols. New York: Chelsea House, 1971.

Schwartz, Bernard. *Super Chief.* New York: New York University Press, 1983.

Smith, J. Allen. *The Spirit of American Government.* New York: Macmillan, 1907.

Snowiss, Sylvia. *Judicial Review and the Law of the Constitution.* New Haven: Yale University Press, 1990.

Stephenson, Donald Grief, Jr. *Campaigns and the Court.* New York: Columbia University Press, 1999.

Stimson, James A., Michael B. MacKuen, and Robert S. Erikson. "Dynamic Representation." *American Political Science Review* 89 (1995): 543–565.

Sundquist, James. *Dynamics of the Party System.* Washington, D.C.: Brookings Institution, 1983.

Tushnet, Mark V. *Making Civil Rights Law.* New York: Oxford University Press, 1994.

U.S. Senate, Committee on the Judiciary. *Reorganization of the Judiciary.* 75th Cong., 1st sess., S. Rept. 711, 1937.

Westin, Alan Furman. "The Supreme Court, the Populist Movement, and the Campaign of 1896." *Journal of Politics* 15 (1959): 3–41.

Whittington, Keith E. "The Road Not Taken: *Dred Scott,* Constitutional Law, and Political Questions." *Journal of Politics* 63 (2001): 365–391.

Notes

1. Matthew Franck has traced the earlier scattered use of the term, but Princeton constitutional historian Edward Corwin seems to have popularized it in a series of influential law review articles on the subject beginning in 1909.

2. It is interesting that the Court quotes the language of the oath in *Cooper.* In most other cases in which the Court makes reference to this

clause of the Constitution, it normally paraphrases it as an oath to support *the* Constitution.

3. Justices Hugo Black and Felix Frankfurter convinced Justice Harlan Fiske Stone to drop such language from a 1939 opinion because it might "imply an approval of that decision [*Schechter*] and I [Black] do not wish to approve it even by implication" (Cushman 1998, 187).

7 Beyond the American Experience: The Global Expansion of Judicial Review

RAN HIRSCHL

Judicial review—broadly defined as the courts' authority to hold unconstitutional and therefore unenforceable any law, statute, administrative decree, legislative and executive practice, or any action by a public official on the grounds that the challenged statute, act, or practice is in conflict with a polity's constitution or basic law (Abraham 1986, 292)—has become one of the most powerful and commonly practiced ideas of our times. It is based primarily on judicial interpretation of constitutionally entrenched provisions, or quasi-constitutional principles and conventions that define the principles of federalism and the separation of powers, administrative due process, and the fundamental rights and entitlements of the members of a given polity. Armed with judicial review procedures, courts throughout the constitutional–democratic world have become key policymaking bodies determining a range of matters: from the scope of expression, religious freedoms, privacy and reproductive rights to intergovernmental and electoral disputes; from the conformity of legal norms with international treaties to public policies concerning education, immigration, criminal justice, property, commerce, welfare, consumer protection, and regulation of the environment (to name but a few heavily judicialized policy realms). Increasingly, courts throughout the world—both at the national and at the supra-national levels—have expanded the scope of their jurisprudence to deal with macroeconomic policies and regulation, fundamental nation-building processes, restorative justice dilemmas, and matters of political transformation and regime change. Examples of the dramatic public policy consequences of the global expansion of judicial review are abundant and widely documented, whether in the United States (where the legacy of active judicial review is nearing its bicentennial anniversary and where courts have long played a significant role in policymaking), or in newer constitutional democracies that have established active judicial review mechanisms only in the past few decades.

I thank Mark A. Graber for his encouragement, Alexei Trochev for his efficient research assistance, and Helen Moffett for her valuable editorial assistance. Special thanks are due to Ayelet Shachar for her illuminating comments and useful suggestions. The discussion in the first section of this essay is drawn from Ran Hirschl, *Towards Juristocracy: A Comparative Inquiry Into the Origins and Consequences of the New Constitutionalism* (Cambridge: Harvard University Press, 2003), chap. 1.

This chapter goes beyond the traditional discussion of the foundation, practice, and consequences of judicial review in the United States to discuss a few fundamental aspects of the proliferation of judicial review in the "new constitutionalism" world. The chapter is divided into four major sections. I begin by providing a rough taxonomy of the seven most common scenarios of judicial empowerment through the constitutionalization of rights and the establishment of judicial review in the post–World War II era. Next, I survey various models of judicial review prevalent in the new constitutionalism world, as well as innovative mechanisms aimed at mitigating the "counter-majoritarian" difficulty and the "democratic deficit" embedded in rigid constitutionalism and judicial review. Third, I discuss several *Marbury v. Madison*–like foundational judgments by national high courts striving to exercise their newly acquired judicial review powers within an often mistrustful political sphere. I conclude by discussing the transformative effect the expansion of judicial review has had on constitutional rights jurisprudence and the judicialization of politics in the new constitutionalism world.

The Global Expansion of Judicial Review

Most scholars of constitutional politics agree that there is a strong correlation between the recent worldwide expansion of the ethos and practice of democracy and the contemporaneous global expansion of judicial power. Indeed, with a few notable exceptions (such as Egypt and Pakistan, which maintain surprisingly autonomous and influential national high courts),

the expansion of judicial power has taken place primarily in democratic polities. Over the past three decades, three major waves that established and consolidated democracy took place: in Southern Europe in the late 1970s; in Latin America in the 1980s; and in Central and Eastern Europe in the early 1990s. These movements brought with them an expansion of judicial power in most of these new democracies, primarily through the constitutionalization of rights and the establishment of relatively autonomous judiciaries and supreme courts armed with judicial review practices.

Indeed, by its very nature, the existence of a democratic regime implies the presence of a set of procedural governing rules and decision-making processes to which all political actors are required to adhere. The persistence and stability of such a system, in turn, requires the existence of at least a semiautonomous, supposedly apolitical judiciary that serves as an impartial umpire in dealing with disputes that may arise concerning the scope and nature of the fundamental rules of the political game. Similarly, judicial review is a prerequisite of viable distribution of legislative powers between the central government and states/provinces in federal countries (for example, the United States, Germany, Canada, India, and Australia), as well as in emerging supranational polities (for example, the European Union). Moreover, the transition to and consolidation of democracy entails the establishment of some form of separation of powers, both between the major branches of government and between the central and provincial–regional legislatures. In short, the existence of a relatively independent and active judiciary appears almost to be a necessary condition for, and an inevitable by-product of, the proliferation of democracy during the second half of the twentieth century.

Also, there appears to be a close affinity between judicial activism by a polity's judiciary and the existence of a constitutional catalogue of rights in that polity. If the constitution does not list tangible and defensible rights that individuals hold against the state, then judicial review is based on limited *ultra vires* (going beyond the powers granted by authority or by law) principles and is generally confined to procedural matters. In these circumstances, intervention by the judiciary in fundamental moral controversies or in highly political or politicized issues is generally unlikely. On the other hand, the existence of a constitutional catalogue of rights provides the necessary institutional framework for courts to become more vigilant in their efforts to protect the fundamental rights and liberties of a given polity's residents. It also enables them to expand their jurisdiction to address salient moral dilemmas and political controversies fundamental to that polity. Therefore, in countries where bills of rights have been adopted one can expect a significant change in the frequency and scope of exercise of judicial review and a corresponding intrusion by the judiciary into the prerogatives of both legislatures and executives. Moreover, in "Westminster," or "British," style democracies, these processes may involve a transition from the traditional governing principle of parliamentary sovereignty and judicial restraint to one of constitutional and judicial supremacy.

Seven broad scenarios of judicial empowerment through the constitutionalization of rights and the establishment of judicial review have been commonly seen in the post–World War II era.

1. *The "reconstruction" wave of constitutionalization, in which judicial empowerment was a by-product of political reconstruction in the wake of World War II.* Examples include the 1946 introduction of a revised constitution in Japan; the introduction of a new constitution in Italy in 1948 and the consequent implementation of the Italian Constitutional Court in 1956; the adoption of the German Basic Law in 1949 and the establishment of the Federal Constitutional Court; and the 1958 adoption of the French Constitution and the consequent establishment of the Constitutional Council (*Conseil Constitutionnel*).

2. *The "independence" scenario, in which the constitutionalization of rights and the establishment of judicial review were part of decolonization processes, primarily in former British colonies.* A classic example of this pattern was the 1950 proclamation of the new Indian constitution and the establishment of the Supreme Court of India, the foundations of which had been laid out by the Indian Independence Act of 1947. Although for many years Britain was unwilling to incorporate the provisions of the European Convention on Human Rights into its own legal system (let alone enact a constitutional bill of rights of its own), it enthusiastically promoted the entrenchment of Convention rights in the "independence constitutions" of newly self-governing African states, as devices for protecting established interests from the "whims" of independent majoritarian politics. The constitutionalization of rights in the Gold Coast (Ghana) in 1957, Nigeria

in 1959, and Kenya in 1960 (to mention only three examples) followed this pattern.

3. *The "single transition" scenario, in which the constitutionalization of rights and the establishment of judicial review are the by-products of a transition from a quasi-democratic or authoritarian regime to democracy.* South Africa adopted an interim bill of rights in 1993 and a final Bill of Rights in 1996, along with a Constitutional Court in 1995, as part of its transition to full democracy in the mid-1990s. Almost all the newer democracies in Southern Europe (Greece in 1975, Portugal in 1976, Spain in 1978) and Latin America (Nicaragua in 1987, Brazil in 1988, Colombia in 1991, Peru in 1993, Bolivia in 1994) adopted bills of basic rights as part of their new constitutions, as well as establishing some form of active judicial review.

4. *The "dual transition" scenario, in which constitutionalization is part of a transition to both a Western model of democracy and a market economy.* Obvious examples of this scenario include the numerous constitutional revolutions of the postcommunist and post-Soviet countries. The most significant of these were the pioneering establishment of the Polish Constitutional Tribunal in 1986; the establishment of the Hungarian Constitutional Court in 1989 to 1990 and the Russian Constitutional Court in 1991; and the inauguration of judicial review in the Czech Republic and Slovakia in 1993.

5. *The "incorporation" scenario, in which constitutionalization is associated with the incorporation of international and trans- or supranational legal standards into domestic law.* Important examples include the 1994 incorporation of ten international treaties and covenants protecting fundamental human rights and civil liberties into Argentina's domestic law; the incorporation of the European Convention on Human Rights into Denmark's domestic law in 1993 and Sweden's domestic law in 1995 (Sweden had already adopted judicial review in 1979); and the passing in Britain of the Human Rights Act in 1998, which effectively incorporated the provisions of the European Council of Human Rights (ECHR) into British constitutional law—the first rights legislation in the United Kingdom for three hundred years.

6. *The "no-apparent-transition" constitutionalization scenario, in which constitutional reforms have neither been accompanied by, nor resulted from, any apparent fundamental changes in political or economic regimes.* Some examples are the adoption of the Canadian Charter of Rights and Freedoms in 1982; the 1979 amendment of the Swedish constitution to allow for active judicial review; the enactment of the New Zealand Bill of Rights Act in 1990; and the adoption of two new Basic Laws in Israel protecting a number of core rights and liberties.

7. *The establishment of judicial review at the supranational level through the proliferation of supranational courts and quasi-judicial tribunals, panels, and commissions dealing with international governance, trade and monetary affairs, as well as international human rights issues.* The European Court of Justice (ECJ), for

example, is the supreme court of the European Union (EU). It has been given increasingly important status by legislators, executives, and judiciaries in member states of the EU dealing with interstate legal and economic disputes. The ECJ interprets the treaties on which the EU is founded and hears appeals on matters brought by member countries, the European Commission, the Council of Ministers, or private citizens. The court's decisions are final and binding on all parties involved, including the member governments. Meanwhile, the European Court of Human Rights in Strasbourg, the judicial arm of the forty-one-member Council of Europe, has in effect become the final court of appeal on human rights issues for most of Europe. The judgments of both these supranational European courts carry great weight and have forced many countries to incorporate transnational legal standards into their domestic legal systems. Similarly, the advisory reports of the United Nations Human Rights Commission and the International Court of Justice, although not legally binding (any nation that seeks a ruling from the latter forum must agree to accept the court's decision), carry great symbolic weight and have forced numerous countries to amend their laws and practices in accordance with the recommendations of these tribunals. Present calls for the adoption of a global constitution and for the establishment of an international tribunal for war crimes and human rights violations also suggest that courts and judicial review processes are becoming key factors in international politics as well.

Models of Judicial Review

Models of judicial review used by leading constitutional democracies vary significantly in their procedural characteristics—a fact that has important implications for the scope and nature of judicial review in these countries. A few fundamental distinctions between various structural features of judicial review used by new constitutionalism countries should be mentioned. To begin with, there is the distinction between *a priori* and *a posteriori* review and the distinction between *abstract* and *concrete* review. *A priori* versus *a posteriori* review refers to whether the constitutionality of a law or administrative action is determined before or after it takes effect. Abstract versus concrete review refers to whether a declaration of unconstitutionality can be made in the absence of an actual case or controversy—in other words, hypothetical "what if" scenarios ("abstract" review) or only in the context of a specific legal dispute ("concrete" review).

In the United States, only *a posteriori* judicial review is allowed. Judicial review of legislation, whether exercised by lower courts or by the Supreme Court, is a power that can only be exercised by the courts within the context of *concrete adversary litigation*—in other words, when the constitutional issue becomes relevant and requires resolution in the decision of the case. In France, judicial review is limited to an *a priori* or abstract judicial review. The *Conseil Constitutionnel*, which was established by the 1958 constitution of France's Fifth Republic, has only preenactment constitutional review powers. The principal duty of the council has been to control the constitutionality of legislative bills passed by the parliament but not yet promulgated by the president of the republic. In addition, the council ensures the regularity of presidential and parliamentary elections and rules on disputes concerning the constitutionality of laws before they are promulgated, if requested by the president, the premier, the president of the houses of the legislature, or (since an amendment in 1974) sixty members of either house. Unlike the courts in the United States or Germany, the French *Conseil Constitutionnel* has no power to nullify a law after it has been enacted by the legislature.

A number of leading democracies that have joined the trend toward constitutionalization over the past few decades feature combined *a priori* and *a posteriori*, abstract *and* concrete review systems, which effectively blur the distinct public policy effects of each of these models. Judicial review in Canada, for example, is not limited to review within the context of concrete adversary litigation. The reference procedure allows both the federal and provincial governments in Canada to refer proposed statutes or even questions concerning hypothetical legal situations to the Supreme Court or the provincial courts of appeal for an advisory (abstract) opinion on their constitutionality. A system that permits *a priori* and abstract review would appear to have a greater potential for generating high levels of judicialized policymaking using the process of constitutional review. National high courts in such countries could outlaw a statute before it was formally enacted on the basis of hypothetical constitutional arguments about its effect. Moreover, unlike in the United States, most *a priori* and abstract review models allow public officials, legislators, cabinet members, and heads of state to initiate judicial scrutiny of proposed laws and hypothetical constitutional scenarios, thereby providing a constitutional framework hospitable to the judicialization of politics and the politicization of the judiciary. With that said, Neal Tate is right to point out that "the apparently more restrictive combination of *a posteriori* and concrete review has hardly relegated the U.S. Supreme Court to a minor policy role" (Tate 1992, 6).

Another important distinction is that between *decentralized* (all courts) and *centralized* (constitutional court) review. The United States uses a decentralized system of judicial review whereby ordinary judicial courts may determine the constitutionality of laws. Under this system of judicial review, there is no special body empowered to decide on the constitutionality of state action. Thus, almost all courts—state courts, federal courts, and, of course, the Supreme Court—have the power of judicial review of constitutionality, which in this system can be exercised over all acts of Congress, state constitutions and statutes, and acts of the executive and the judiciary itself. Even the constitutional validity of treaties and legislation based on treaties may be the subject of judicial inquiry. In short, according to the decentralized system, judicial review is an inherent competence of all courts in any type of case and controversy.

The centralized judicial review system (often referred to as "constitutional review") is characterized by having only a single state organ (a separate judicial body in the court system or an extrajudicial body) acting as a constitutional tribunal. This model of judicial review has been adopted by many European countries that follow various branches of the civil law tradition (such as Germany, Austria, Italy, and

Spain), as well as by almost all new democracies in postcommunist Europe.

In Germany, for example, a separate judicial body—the Federal Constitutional Court—fulfills the sole function of constitutional review (Kommers 1997). Its jurisdiction includes interpreting the Basic Law in disputes by parties with rights vested under it; settling public law disputes between the federation and the states and between and within the states; and settling election disputes. In addition, any person who claims that a state action violated his or her constitutional rights may, after exhausting all other legal remedies, file a constitutional complaint in the Federal Constitutional Court. All state actions may be attacked, especially executive actions, court decisions, and laws even before their application, provided the complainant is affected directly and immediately.

Some new constitutionalism countries (such as Bulgaria, Portugal, Mozambique, and Peru) use a combined decentralized–centralized model of judicial–constitutional review. The decentralized elements of the Portuguese constitution, for example, require all the courts of the country to refrain from applying unconstitutional provisions or principles. Statutes, decrees, executive regulations, regional or any other state acts are thereby subject to review by the courts. Because this ability is given as a judicial duty, the courts have ex officio power to raise constitutional questions. Issues can also be raised by a party in a concrete case or by the public prosecutor. Parallel with the decentralized system of judicial review, the Portuguese constitution has also established a centralized system that can review both enacted and proposed legislation. The Portuguese Constitutional Court exercises a preventative control over constitutionality with regard to international treaties and agreements and other laws when so requested by the president of the republic. The constitutionality of enacted legislation can also be the object of abstract scrutiny by the Constitutional Court.

Other variables being equal, the impact of the judiciary on public policy outcomes is likely to be more significant under a decentralized, all-court review system. As Tate pointed out, "[R]estricting the power to declare legislation and regulations unconstitutional to a constitutional court ... sharply reduces the number of occasions and range of policy issues on which courts can be invited (or can invite themselves) to exercise judicial review" (1992, 7). Administrative review, however limited, is always available to the courts in most centralized review countries. Moreover, the symbolic importance of landmark high court decisions in such countries is at least as significant as that of national high court rulings in countries using a decentralized review system. Germany's Federal Constitutional Court and the youthful Hungarian Constitutional Court are perhaps the most frequently mentioned examples of centralized judicial bodies that not only fulfill the sole function of judicial review in their respective countries but have also become crucial policymaking bodies at the national level over the past few years (Kommers 1997; Sólyom and Brunner 2000; Schwartz 2000, 75–108).

Another important aspect of judicial review is the question of standing (locus standi) and access rights: who may initiate a legal challenge to the constitutionality of legislation or official action and at what stage of the process a given polity's supreme court may become involved.

In the United States, standing rights traditionally have been limited to individuals who claim to have been affected by an allegedly unconstitutional legislation or official action. The U.S. Supreme Court will not hear a challenge to the constitutionality of legislation unless all other possible legal paths and remedies have been exhausted. Moreover, the Court has full discretion over which cases it will hear—its docket therefore consists of "discretionary leave" cases, rather than appeals by right. However, constitutional democracies that use *a priori* and abstract judicial review (such as France) allow for, and even encourage, public officials and political actors to challenge the constitutionality of proposed legislation.

Several polities authorize their constitutional court judges, in an ex-officio capacity, to initiate proceedings against an apparently unconstitutional law. Other countries (South Africa, for example) impose mandatory referrals of constitutional questions by lower courts to a constitutional tribunal. Other countries allow private-person constitutional grievances to be submitted directly to their respective high courts.

The Supreme Court of Israel, for example, has jurisdiction as appellate court over appeals from the district courts in all matters, both civil and criminal. In addition, it is a court of first instance (sitting as a high court of justice) in direct actions launched by individual stakeholders against public authorities in matters where the court considers it necessary to grant relief in the interests of justice, which are not normally within the jurisdiction of any other court or tribunal. Originally, the court demanded that a petitioner show possible harm to a direct and material personal interest. Since 1988,

however, the court has significantly liberalized the rules of standing pertaining to direct individual petitions, effectively recognizing standing rights of public petitioners and lowering the barrier of nonjusticiability.

Since the mid-1970s, the Supreme Court of India has also been entertaining matters in which interests of the public at large are involved, in addition to its appellate and advisory jurisdiction. In this "epistolary" jurisdiction, often referred to as "public interest litigation," the Court can convert a letter from a member of the public highlighting a question of public importance into a writ petition. Any member of the public or social action group can apply on behalf of an individual or class unable to do so on its own; access to judicial redress may therefore be obtained without a lawyer or even the filing of formal paperwork (Baar 1992, 79).

Naturally, extending direct private person access to a country's supreme court provides an important institutional channel through which ordinary citizens can challenge what they regard as infringements on their constitutionally protected rights before the country's highest judicial body. This therefore increases the efficacy of judicial review by enhancing the rule of law through close monitoring of legislatures and public officials. On the other hand, generous standing rights and lowered barriers of nonjusticiability also entail ever-expanding caseloads, as well as less judicial control over the docket and issue agenda. These concerns are not merely theoretical: Over the past two decades, the numbers of cases before the Israeli and Indian Supreme Courts have skyrocketed.

Finally, an interesting feature of judicial review in a number of leading democratic polities is the existence of innovative mechanisms designed to address and mitigate the tension between rigid constitutionalism and judicial activism on the one hand and fundamental democratic governing principles on the other. Precisely because many recent constitutional revolutions have taken place in established democracies, the framers of the new constitutional arrangements in these countries could not ignore the countermajoritarian tendency embedded in constitutionalism and judicial review. Persisting political traditions of parliamentary sovereignty had to be taken into account by those who initiated the constitutionalization of rights and judicial review in Britain, Canada, Israel, South Africa, and New Zealand (to mention only a few). The result has been the development of a variety of innovative institutional mechanisms aimed at compensating for the countermajoritarian problem presented by judicial review. Consider the following examples.

The rights protected by the Canadian Charter of Rights and Freedoms are subject to two important limitations. First, the charter contains an explicit limitation clause (section 1), which states that the rights protected by the charter are subject to "such reasonable limits prescribed by law as can be demonstrably justified in a free and democratic society." In other words, if any limits are to be put on such rights, then the government must establish to the satisfaction of the courts that these limits can be justified in a free and democratic society. In its landmark judgment of *R. v. Oakes* (1986), the Supreme Court of Canada introduced a two-pronged approach to interpreting the charter's "limitation clause." First, the *Oakes* test asks whether the challenged law or

conduct violates, denies, or infringes any right. This requires an analysis of the scope and definition of the right, as well as the purpose and effect of the legislation and conduct. The second investigates whether there has been a justifiable limitation on the right concerned. Some of the criteria a justifiable limitation on a charter right would have to meet to be held valid are (1) the limitation must protect a sufficiently important objective; (2) there must be a rational connection between the limiting law and that objective; (3) the least drastic means should be used—in other words, the law must impair the right no more than is necessary to accomplish the objective; and (4) proportional effect must be observed—the law must not have a disproportionately severe effect on the persons to whom it applies.

Another significant limitation to rights and freedoms lies in section 33, the "notwithstanding clause." This clause enables elected politicians, in either the federal parliament or the provincial legislatures, to legally limit rights and freedoms protected by section 2 (fundamental freedoms) and sections 7–14 (due process rights) and section 15 (equality rights) of the charter by passing a renewable overriding legislation valid for a period of up to five years. This means that any invocation of section 33 essentially grants parliamentary fiat over these rights and freedoms. This in turn means that both the federal parliament (with regard to related federal matters) and the provincial legislatures (with regard to related matters within provincial jurisdictions) are ultimately sovereign over these affairs. In practice, however, section 33 lacks wide public legitimacy and is often viewed by critics as a political "dead letter." Indeed, since the charter's enactment in 1982, there have only been five significant instances (and only two of those outside Quebec) where governments have either invoked or attempted to invoke this clause.

Like the Canadian Charter of Rights and Freedoms, both of Israel's new Basic Laws protecting a number of fundamental rights and liberties contain a limitation clause forbidding infringement of the declared rights, "except by a statute that befits the values of the State of Israel, for a worthy purpose, and not exceeding what is necessary." Moreover, in 1994, two years after its enactment, Basic Law: Freedom of Occupation was amended by the Knesset (the Israeli parliament) in the spirit of the Canadian "notwithstanding" override clause to allow for future modifications by ordinary laws in the instance of an absolute majority of Knesset members declaring support for the amendment. Similarly, the rights protected by the 1996 South African Constitution are fully entrenched but are subject to a general limitations clause, section 36(1), which is largely modeled on similar provisions in other international human rights texts and national bills of rights (such as section 1 of the Canadian Charter).

Other innovative mechanisms for mitigating the tension between judicial review and parliamentary supremacy are found in New Zealand and Britain. These two countries use what I call the *preferential* model of judicial review. This compromise model, which has been established over the past decade in several common-law countries with a long tradition of parliamentary supremacy, gives preference to legislation or a court judgment that is consistent with the bill of rights over one that is not,

and instructs legislators to avoid enacting laws that contradict, prima facie, constitutional provisions protecting basic rights. This model enables a limited judicial review on the one hand and on the other accords with the parliamentary tradition of these countries.

Unlike most catalogues of rights adopted over the past few decades, the New Zealand Bill of Rights Act 1990 (NZBORA) is an ordinary statute that does not formally empower the courts to nullify legislation inconsistent with its provisions. Nevertheless, the operational provisions of the bill were designed to reduce the likelihood of legislation unreasonably infringing the rights protected by the NZBORA. In practice, this has set the stage for active judicial policymaking in New Zealand. In a landmark decision in 1994, for example, the New Zealand Court of Appeal observed that lack of entrenched status "makes no difference to the strength of the Bill of Rights where it is to be applied" (*Simpson* 1994, 706). Section 7 of the NZBORA requires the attorney general to advise the House of Representatives whenever he or she believes that any provision in a bill introduced to parliament would infringe a right. This procedure has been invoked several times since 1990, and, with only one exception, has prevented the provision from being enacted.

The British Human Rights Act 1998, which came into effect in October 2000, presents another version of the preferential model of judicial review. The act requires the courts to interpret existing and future legislation as far as possible in accordance with the European Convention on Human Rights. According to the act, if the higher courts in Britain decide that an act of Parliament prevents someone exercising their human rights, judges make what is termed a "statement of compatibility." Such a declaration would put ministers under political pressure to change the law (or so it is hoped). Formally, the European Convention does not override existing acts of Parliament, but ministers have to state whether each new piece of legislation they introduce complies with the European Convention on Human Rights.

Foundational Cases and the Establishment of Judicial Review

As in early nineteenth-century America, the legitimacy of judicial review in postwar Europe was often established through *Marbury v. Madison*–like manifestations of judicial activism. Four well-known examples of such foundational moments of judicial activism in Western Europe are the German Federal Constitutional Court ruling in the *Southwest* case (1951)—involving a constitutional challenge to the federal government's attempt to redraw the boundaries of three of Germany's *Länder* (constitutionally recognized states); the French *Conseil Constitutionnel*'s *Decision on Association* (1971)—involving a successful challenge by opposition parties to a bill proposed by the government that would have banned any associations appearing to have "an immoral or illicit purpose"; the Italian Constitutional Court's inaugural ruling in the *Security Law* case (1956)—retroactively invalidating a public security law of fascist vintage (and in the process, indirectly invalidating an entire corpus of similar laws) on the grounds that it contravened the freedom of expression and press provisions of the Italian Constitution; and the European Court of Justice's landmark *Van Gend*

and Loos (1963) and *Costa v. ENEL* (1964) decisions—which declared that European law was supreme to national law, thereby creating an obligation for national courts to enforce EU law over conflicting national laws.

The establishment of judicial review through foundational cases has certainly not been limited to leading European polities. National high courts in other parts of the new constitutionalism world have been called on by constituent assemblies and legislatures to establish their authority over the political sphere by means of foundational judgments. In other countries, manifestations of judicial activism have brought about popular political backlashes, legislative override of controversial rulings, and "court packing" attempts by political power holders. Sometimes they have even resulted in constitutional crises leading to the dissolution of high courts.

Consider, for example, the newly established South African Constitutional Court's profound (and invited) involvement in the very certification of the final South African Constitution of 1996—an involvement that has no equivalent in the history of modern constitutionalism. After a long and arduous political battle, the South African Constitutional Assembly voted in May 1996 in favor of a new constitutional text, which was to form the basis of the final constitution. Following its adoption by the Constitutional Assembly, the new constitutional text was submitted to the Constitutional Court for certification to ensure that it complied with the constitutional principles agreed on in multiparty negotiations in 1993.

In its landmark certification decision delivered in September 1996, the Constitutional

Court identified nine elements of the new text that failed to comply with certain constitutional principles. The draft constitution was therefore sent back to the Constitutional Assembly so that certain provisions could be reworked. Following the refusal of the court to certify the draft constitution, the Constitutional Assembly was recalled in an attempt to pass an amended text that would satisfy the constitutional principles. In October 1996, barely a month after the first certification judgment was handed down, the South African Constitutional Assembly passed an amended text addressing all of the concerns raised by the Constitutional Court in the first certification hearing. In December 1996, the court approved the amended text in the second certification hearing.

The initial certification judgment represented the first time a court had refused to accept a national constitutional text drafted by a representative constitution-making body. Moreover, the initial certification hearing took place fewer than eighteen months after the inauguration of the Constitutional Court. Its relative youth notwithstanding, none of the political actors and parties questioned the legitimacy of either the certification process itself or the particular decisions taken by the Constitutional Court during that process. By the end of the certification process, the transformation of the court into a pivotal decision maker in constituting the new South Africa was complete.

Consider the convoluted establishment of full-scale judicial review in Israel through two foundational cases, *Meatrael Ltd. v. Minister of Religious Affairs* (1993) and *United Mizrahi Bank v. Migdal* (1995). The first case dealt with the review of an administrative act, and the second with a request for the nullification of a statute. Like many other formerly British-ruled territories, Israel inherited the British common-law tradition with its strong emphasis on parliamentary supremacy; it thus remains without a written constitution or entrenched bill of rights contained in one document. Instead, a web of eleven Basic Laws serves as the formal core of Israeli constitutional law. Some fundamental provisions of this set of laws are immune from manipulation by a simple parliamentary majority. Until 1992, the Basic Laws did not include an entrenched law regarding civil liberties and human rights. In the absence of a necessary constitutional framework for actively reviewing primary legislation, the Supreme Court was limited in the era before 1992 to judicial review of administrative acts, informed by an "implied bill of rights" doctrine.

The constitutional landscape in Israel was altered in the early 1990s when a group of prominent Knesset members representing a primarily secular, neoliberal ideological agenda reacted to the continuous decline in their popular support by initiating and carrying out an institutional empowerment of the judiciary (Hirschl 2000). This initiative, tacitly supported by Israel's judicial elite, culminated in the 1992 enactment of two basic rights and liberties laws—Basic Law: Human Dignity and Liberty and Basic Law: Freedom of Occupation. Although these two new human rights Basic Laws do not constitute an official bill of rights, they are widely understood to fulfil the functions of such a bill.

Meatrael reached the Israeli Supreme Court several months after the introduction of the two new Basic Laws. It raised a prima facie contradiction between the constitutional right to freedom of occupation and Israel's primary character as a Jewish state. Meatrael, a private company that intended to import nonkosher meat products to Israel, appealed to the Supreme Court against the Ministry of Religious Affairs' refusal to license the company to do so. The company argued that the ministry's refusal violated its constitutional right to freedom of occupation. The ministry's refusal was based on the claim that Israel's Jewish character was one of the state's foundational norms, and thus had priority over any other constitutional provision. In its first decision in the case, the court declared the ministry's refusal unconstitutional because it stood in contradiction to the principles of the new Basic Law, and thus infringed the company's right to engage in any legal economic initiative. Under pressure from the religious parties, the Basic Law was then amended, to allow for future modifications by ordinary laws endorsed by an absolute majority of Knesset members. Such a law, forbidding the import of nonkosher meat, was subsequently enacted in 1994.

Based on the new 1994 "meat law," the government renewed its refusal to license the import of nonkosher meat. In reaction, the company appealed once again to the Supreme Court, arguing both for its right to engage in any legal economic initiative and for the unconstitutionality of the "meat law." This time, the court ruled against the company based on the reasonableness of the new law, given the conditions for modification mentioned in the Basic Law. However, behind this decision and the formal rhetoric used by the court, there was immense political pressure on the court not to allow any further erosion of the con-struction of "Israel as a Jewish state" as the most fundamental norm on which Israel was built. In spite of its somewhat anticlimactic ending—the legislature ultimately managed to circumvent judicial scrutiny of its decision—the *Meatrael* affair clearly illustrates the impact of the new Basic Laws on the constitutional discourse in Israel, even to the extent of nullifying statutes. Before the new Basic Laws, it would have been unthinkable that the legislature might have to scramble to assert its will and obviate a constitutional crisis in the courts.

Encouraged by its effect on Israel's political sphere during the *Meatrael* saga, in November 1995 the Israeli Supreme Court released its historic ruling in the previously mentioned *United Mizrahi Bank* case—the "Israeli *Marbury v. Madison*," as observers of the Israeli legal system have described it. The court drew on the constitutional entrenchment of the right to property, as specified in Article 3 of the Basic Law: Human Dignity and Liberty, to virtually invalidate—for the first time in Israel's constitutional history—a Knesset law that was aimed at erasing the heavy financial debts owed to major banks by collective agricultural settlements in Israel. Several banks filed a petition arguing that the new law was inconsistent with the property rights provisions of Basic Law: Human Dignity and Liberty. Sitting in an expanded panel of nine judges, the court declared that the property rights of creditors had constitutional priority over primary legislation enacted by the Knesset. The court used this decision to firmly establish its power to declare unconstitutional acts and statutes that did not comply with the standards set out in the new Basic Laws. The majority of justices held that the two Basic Laws had indeed ushered in a new era in the historic quest for a comprehensive constitutional catalogue of rights and active judicial review in Israel. It was recognized that these laws had formal constitutional status and were therefore superior to any ordinary legislation.

The expansion of judicial power through foundational court rulings in the new constitutionalism world has extended beyond "standard" controversies over the scope of powers of legislatures and executives to include judicial appraisal of the very constitutionality and democratic legitimacy of newly installed political regimes (Hirschl 2002). Examples of this emerging pattern of foundational cases include the Fijian Court of Appeal's landmark ruling in *Fiji v. Prasad* (2001)—the first time in the history of modern constitutionalism that a polity's high court restored a constitution and the democratic system of government created by it following a constitutionally illegitimate *coup d'état*; the 1993 ruling by the reinstalled Supreme Court of Pakistan nullifying a presidential decree that ordered the dissolution of Pakistan's National Assembly, thereby restoring the democratically elected government of Nawaz Sharif; and the recent landmark ruling by the same court affirming the constitutionality of the military *coup d'état* of 1999, led by Pervez Musharraf, while ordering Musharraf to restore democratic order in Pakistan no later than October 2002.

Recognizing the crucial political significance of the Supreme Court, Pakistan's political leaders have repeatedly tried to control the judicial appointments process. In late 1997, for example, a serious rift developed between Prime Minister Sharif and the chief justice of the Supreme Court, Sajjad Ali Shah, over the appointment of new judges to the court. The constitutional crisis came to a dramatic end when the chief justice was suspended from office by rebel members of the supreme court. A crisis of a similar nature occurred in January 2000, when General Musharraf insisted that all members of the supreme court pledge allegiance to the military administration. The judges who refused to take the oath were expelled from the court.

Indeed, not all the groundbreaking manifestations of judicial activism in the new constitutionalism world have survived popular political backlashes and reactive pressures by influential political actors whose institutional room for political maneuvering had been curtailed by judicial review. In some cases, legislators have bowed to popular political pressure by enacting laws that override controversial high court rulings. In other countries, political backlashes against excessive judicial activism have culminated in constitutional revolution.

A good example of legislative override of a controversial high court decision in the new constitutionalism world is the 1985 Indian Supreme Court *Shah Bano* ruling and its political aftermath. Shah Bano, a seventy-three-year-old Muslim Indian woman, was unilaterally divorced by her husband by way of a Muslim *talaq* divorce after forty-three years of marriage (Shachar 2001, 81–83). She then turned to a magistrate's court to obtain state-decreed alimony payments from her ex-husband, although according to a standard reading of Muslim personal law she was only entitled to alimony for the first three months following the dissolution of the marriage. When the case reached the Supreme Court of

India, it imposed on Shah Bano's ex-husband monthly maintenance payments for as long as she had not remarried and was unable to maintain herself. The court held that the state-defined statutory right of a neglected wife to maintenance stood regardless of the personal law applicable to the parties. This decision had potentially far-reaching implications for India's long-standing practice of Muslim self-jurisdiction in core religious matters. Traditionalist representatives of the Muslim community considered this to be proof of Hindu homogenizing trends that threatened to weaken Muslim identity. In 1986, a year after the Supreme Court handed down its controversial decision, the Indian parliament bowed to massive political pressure by conservative Muslims and overruled the court's decision in *Shah Bano* by passing the Muslim Women's (Protection of Rights of Divorce) Act. This new bill, its reassuring title notwithstanding, undid the court's ruling by removing the rights of Muslim women to appeal to state courts for postdivorce maintenance payments. It also exempted Muslim ex-husbands from other postdivorce obligations (Shachar 2001, 83).

Several new national high courts in former Eastern Bloc countries also had to endure a series of direct challenges to their authority and independence by political elites and power holders. Such challenges confronted the newly established national high courts in Albania (the 1998 suspension of the Albanian Constitutional Court, the arrest of its chair, and the adoption of a constitutional amendment limiting the justices' tenure in office to nine years); Belarus (the referendum crisis of 1996); Bulgaria ("court packing" attempts by the former Communist Party–controlled parliament throughout 1994–1995); Kazakhstan (the dissolution of the initial Constitutional Court following the 1995 election crisis and the inauguration of a new French-style Constitutional Council); Tajikistan (the 1997 parliamentary restriction of the Constitutional Court's jurisdiction after the court declared several parliamentary by-laws unconstitutional); and the 1993 constitutional crisis in Russia—perhaps the most telling illustration of how volatile the status of judges and supreme courts was in the early days of constitutional design in postcommunist societies.

Immediately after its establishment in 1991, the first Russian Constitutional Court found itself entangled in several politically charged cases. These included the *ISS-MVD* case, involving a parliamentary challenge to a presidential decree merging the remnants of the KGB with the Ministry of Interior (MVD), which controlled the police (Schwartz 2000, 118–122); the *Tatarstan* case, in which the court declared unconstitutional a proposed referendum question concerning the Republic of Tatarstan's status within the Russian federation—a ruling that was flagrantly ignored by the Tatar government (Schwartz 2000, 122–125; Sharlet 1993); and the landmark *Communist Party* case 1992, in which the court had to deal with a petition filed by a group of Duma members (mostly former Communist Party officials) challenging the constitutionality of a decree issued by President Boris Yeltsin suspending the Communist Party and taking some of its property in the aftermath of the failed August 1991 *coup*. These proceedings were then turned by anticommunist members of the Duma into a widely publicized counterattack on the Communist Party, resulting in a semiformal judicial inquest by the first Russian Constitutional Court into the alleged "atrocities" committed by the Communist Party during its seventy years of dominance.

In 1993, the involvement of the Constitutional Court in Russia's political sphere brought about its dissolution. By late 1993, the Court's proactive chair, Valerii Zorkin, had become deeply involved in a fierce political struggle over presidential and legislative prerogatives, resulting in President Yeltsin's dissolution of parliament. Throughout the events leading up to the political crisis of 1993, the Court invoked its ex-officio right to initiate constitutional scrutiny of a number of decrees issued by Yeltsin. This led to a split within the Constitutional Court, with the group headed by Zorkin declaring Yeltsin's dissolution of parliament to be unconstitutional. Yeltsin reacted by signing a decree suspending the Constitutional Court until the adoption of a new constitution—an act that marked the demise of the first Constitutional Court and its controversial chair. A new draft constitution granting the president significantly expanded powers (and establishing a new Constitutional Court) was put forward for a national referendum by Yeltsin and adopted by a narrow majority on December 14, 1993. The post-1993 Constitutional Court combined elements of the old court with new provisions. These included keeping all thirteen former members of the first Constitutional Court, who have life tenure until age sixty-five, and adding six new members who are nominated by the president for only one twelve-year term but have a retirement age of seventy (Schwartz 2000, 144–145).

Constitutional Jurisprudence in the New Constitutionalism World

Rights Jurisprudence

The global expansion of judicial review has also generated an impressively rich rights jurisprudence, which often goes unnoticed in the United States. National high courts of most leading constitutional democracies have developed sophisticated constitutional jurisprudence dealing with principles of federalism and the separation of powers, fundamental civil rights and liberties, and a number of social welfare and collective rights. Accordingly, the past few decades of rights jurisprudence in the new constitutionalism world have seen a decline in the traditional reliance on and citation of the U.S. Supreme Court's corpus of civil liberties adjudication and an increased reliance on domestic precedents, as well as more frequent reference to comparative and international case law. Simultaneously, there has been an accelerating trend toward the creation of a globalized, non–United States-centered judicial discourse and intercourt borrowing, described by Mary Ann Glendon as "a brisk international traffic in ideas about rights," (1991, 158) carried on through advanced information technologies by high court judges from different countries. In the *Makwanyane* case (1995), for example, the South African Constitutional Court, in determining the constitutionality of the death penalty, examined in detail landmark rulings from Botswana, Canada, the European Court of Human Rights, Germany, Hong Kong, Hungary, India, Jamaica, Tanzania, the United Nations Committee on Human Rights, the United States, and Zimbabwe (L'Heureux-Dube 2000, 220). In short, as Anne-Marie

Slaughter put it, "Courts are talking to one another all over the world" (1994, 99).

The global trend toward the constitutionalization of rights and fortification of judicial review has not only ushered in a new era in constitutional law and politics worldwide but has also elevated the level of judicial activism and the scope of constitutional rights jurisprudence in numerous new constitutionalism polities to the level and scope seen in the United States during the post-*Brown* era (1954 to the present). However, a closer look at prevalent patterns of judicial interpretation of rights in the United States and abroad suggests that the answer to the question of whether patterns of constitutional rights jurisprudence worldwide are moving toward American-style constitutional rights jurisprudence is more nuanced than it might initially seem.

Over the past two decades, the rights jurisprudence of most constitutional democracies has tended to converge in matters that deal with the Lockean-style "negative liberty" aspects of constitutional rights. Most leading national high courts and supranational tribunals have adopted their U.S. counterpart's traditional conception of constitutional rights as protecting the private sphere (human and economic) from interference by the "collective" (often understood as the state and its regulatory institutions). Accordingly, fundamental civil liberties, economic freedoms, due process rights, and formal equality have been elevated into supreme constitutional norms throughout most of the new constitutionalism world.

In spite of the powerful centripetal forces of convergence found within American and foreign constitutional rights jurisprudence, the global expansion of judicial review has manifested several significant divergences from American constitutional rights jurisprudence. Some important examples are the strict definition of capital punishment as degrading and inhumane by courts throughout the world; the gradual retreat from the "content neutrality" approach prevalent in the U.S. Supreme Court's freedom of expression adjudication toward a more restrictive (if admittedly less intellectually coherent) approach in freedom of expression cases involving the production and dissemination of pornographic material and hate propaganda; or the recent wave of progressive jurisprudence regarding privacy and equality rights in the context of sexual orientation, the stage for which was set by the European Court of Human Rights' landmark 1981 ruling in *Dudgeon v. United Kingdom*, declaring Northern Ireland's "sodomy laws," which prohibited private consenting acts of sodomy between adult males 21 years of age and older, as violating the privacy provision of the European Convention on Human Rights.

Perhaps the most significant contributions of constitutional rights jurisprudence outside the United States is the evolution of relatively rich case law concerning "second generation" rights (traditionally, these consist of social rights such as the universal right to services that meet basic human needs such as health care, basic housing, education, social security and welfare, and an adequate standard of living); and "third generation" group rights (such as minority language and education rights, group rights to self-determination and autonomous jurisdiction over matters pertaining to that group's traditions, or some forms of affirmative action designed to advance the status of historically disenfranchised groups).

Unlike in the United States, the recognition of poverty and socioeconomic living conditions as a "suspect category" in equality rights cases and the struggle to include positive entitlements to subsistence social welfare within the scope of constitutional rights provisions is far from sinking into constitutional oblivion in India, Belgium, Portugal, and South Africa. In its landmark ruling in the *Olga Tellis* case (1986), for example, the Indian Supreme Court held that the right to life, enshrined by Article 21 of the Indian constitution, implies constitutional protection of the right to livelihood and a person's right not to be deprived of his or her right to livelihood to the point of abrogation. Specifically, the court imposed a duty on the Bombay municipality to refrain from evicting [pavement dwellers] without previous notice and without fulfilling stringent conditions, such as providing other sites for resettlement and not expelling people who had lived there for more than twenty years and who had improved their dwellings (Fabre 2000, 162). Evicting those who migrated from the poverty-stricken rural areas to squat on the pavements of Bombay would have the effect of depriving them of their means of livelihood, which would ultimately threaten their lives. In a similar spirit, the Indian Supreme Court went on to rule in the landmark *Unni Krishnan* case (1993) that the right to basic education until the age of fourteen years is embraced within Article 21, thereby elevating the right to education to the status of fundamental right.

The new South African constitutional catalogue of rights explicitly protects positive social and economic rights such as the right to housing; the right to health care, food, water, and social security; and the right to education. These positive rights provisions, however, do not imply a right to housing, health care, or education per se but require that reasonable state measures, within the state's available resources, be taken to make housing, health care, and education available and accessible. What appears to be a turning point in the South African Constitutional Court's interpretation of positive rights provisions is its recent ruling in the *Grootboom* case (2001)—a landmark decision dealing with the enforceability of social and economic rights and redefining the scope of the state's obligations under section 26 of the South African Bill of Rights, which grants everyone the right to access to adequate housing (subject to available resources).

In a unanimous decision, written by Justice Z. M. Yacoob, the court noted that the new South African constitution obliges the state to act positively to ameliorate the plight of the hundreds of thousands of South Africans living in deplorable conditions throughout the country. It must provide access to housing, health care, sufficient food and water, and social security to those unable to support themselves and their dependants. The state must also foster conditions that enable citizens to gain access to land on an equitable basis. Having said this, the court went on to recognize that achieving these goals is an extremely difficult task in the prevailing conditions, and reiterated that the constitution does not oblige the state to go beyond its available resources or to realize these rights immediately.

An equally telling manifestation of judicial activism in the context of positive entitlements can be found in the 1995 *Austerity Package Decisions* (the "Bokros cases") by the Hungarian Constitutional Court. The court drew on the concepts of reliance interest and legal certainty to strike down some twenty-six provisions of a comprehensive economic emergency plan introduced by the government, the major thrust of which was a substantial cut in expenditures on welfare benefits, pension allowances, education, and health care to reduce Hungary's enormous budget deficit and foreign debt. The "austerity package" had been passed in May 1995 on the grounds of economic emergency and was slated to go into effect in July 1995. The court stated that the principle of legal certainty was "the most substantial conceptual element of a state under the rule of law and the theoretical basis of the protection of acquired rights" (Sólyom and Brunner 2000, 325); it also accepted the claim that the proposed reform to Hungary's social security system would violate the legitimate expectations of millions of employees and welfare beneficiaries.

Armed with their newly acquired judicial review powers, courts in "settler societies" have also become active during the past two decades in determining the status of their respective countries' indigenous populations. The New Zealand Court of Appeal, for example, has established itself as one of the major decision makers in dealing with the most fraught issue on New Zealand's public agenda: the recognition and application of Maori rights. As in New Zealand, Australia's High Court and the Supreme Court of Canada have become the central national loci for dealing with aboriginal peoples' claims to identity, land, economic rights, and political voice (Havermann 1999). A notable example of this trend is the Australian High Court's landmark ruling in the *Mabo* case (1992), in which the court rejected the legal doctrine of *terra nullius* (which cate-

gorized Australia as a vacant land before the arrival of white settlers), and found that in principle aboriginal title had not been extinguished by the change of sovereignty. In *Wik* (1996) the High Court went on to hold that leases of pastoral land by the government to third parties did not necessarily extinguish native title. In stark contrast to the gradually expanded recognition of these and other group rights by supreme courts of most ethnically fragmented polities (for example, relatively generous judicial interpretations concerning minority language and education rights have been made in Belgium, Canada, South Africa, Spain, and Switzerland), there has been significant erosion of the U.S. Supreme Court's willingness to recognize and affirm such rights.

Judicial Review and "Political" Jurisprudence

Constitutional scholars, legal practitioners, and political activists critical of the U.S. Supreme Court's crucial role in determining the outcome of the 2000 presidential election regard the *Bush v. Gore* saga as the most glaring example of the judicialization of politics in the United States. Indeed, short of the Supreme Court declaring war, it would be difficult to imagine the Court making a more momentous decision on behalf of the American populace. Although reliance on courts and adjudicative means to resolve contentious moral and political questions is by no means a new phenomenon in the United States, never before had a presidential election hung on the judgment of the U.S. Supreme Court, let alone on a 5–4 decision that split the Court into bitterly opposed and partisan camps. A close comparative look at recent constitutional politics in many other democracies suggests, however, that although the specific details of the courtroom struggle over the fate of the American presidency made it unique, it was anything but an idiosyncratic moment in the recent history of comparative constitutional politics. Rather, it would be more accurate to consider the election judgment as symptomatic of a global trend whereby national high courts and supranational tribunals have become crucial political decision makers.

One of the most significant political consequences of new constitutionalism and the worldwide expansion of judicial review over the past several decades has been the judicialization of politics. Courts throughout the constitutional–democratic world have been gradually eroding the exclusive prerogatives of legislatures and executives to determine a range of matters extending well beyond the now "standard" concept of judge-made policymaking through constitutional rights jurisprudence and judicial redrawing of legislative boundaries between state organs. The judicialization of politics now includes the wholesale transfer to the courts of some of the most pertinent and polemical moral dilemmas and political controversies a democratic polity can contemplate. What has been loosely termed "the judicialization of politics" has in fact taken so many different forms in recent years that it has evolved beyond the existing conventions found in public law and politics literature.

High court interventions and the corresponding judicialization of politics throughout the world of new constitutionalism have recently expanded to include at least four new areas: (1) core executive prerogatives (for example, national security matters and macroeconomic policymaking); (2) formative "nation building"

processes; (3) fundamental restorative justice dilemmas; and (4) political transformation, regime change, and electoral disputes. These emerging areas of judicial intervention expand the boundaries of national high court involvement in the political sphere and take the judicialization of politics to a point that far exceeds any previous limit. It is precisely these groundbreaking, yet rarely acknowledged, scenarios of judicial intervention in the political sphere that make the global expansion of judicial review one of the most significant phenomena of contemporary government.

Consider the increasing intrusion by national high courts and supranational tribunals into core prerogatives of legislatures and executives in foreign, military, and fiscal affairs. This is best exemplified by the gradual erosion of the "political question doctrine" in many constitutional democracies. According to this concept, there are certain kinds of explicitly political questions that a court ought to refuse to rule on, because providing answers to such questions should fall exclusively within the decision-making ambit of the legislative and executive branches of government. The apparent nonjusticiability of a political question is based primarily on the principle of separation of powers and the corresponding ideal of representative, fully accountable, and well-informed decision making, particularly in matters of fiscal policy, foreign affairs, and national security. The political question doctrine is also based on the need to attribute finality to actions of the legislative and executive branches of government and to respect their defined prerogatives.

In spite of its declared adherence to the core concept of the political question doctrine, the U.S. Supreme Court, for example, has on several occasions decided questions concerning the foreign affairs and military powers of the government. The Supreme Court of Canada was quick to reject the political question doctrine following the adoption of the Canadian Charter of Rights and Freedoms in 1982. And as we have seen, courts in Hungary, Pakistan, Israel, and South Africa have also been reluctant to adhere to the political question rationale.

The second Russian Constitutional Court followed suit in the *Chechnya* case (1995), when it agreed to hear petitions by a number of opposition members of the Duma, who challenged the constitutionality of three presidential decrees ordering the Russian military invasion of Chechnya. Rejecting Chechnya's claim to independence and upholding the constitutionality of President Yeltsin's decrees as *intra vires*, the majority of the judges of this court stated that maintaining the territorial integrity and unity of Russia was "[a]n unshakable rule that excludes the possibility of an armed secession in any federative state" (Gaeta 1996, 563). The court found that

the Constitution of the Russian Federation, like the previous constitution of 1978, does not envisage a unilateral resolution of the issue of changing the status of the subject of the Federation and its secession from the Russian Federation. . . . [S]tate integrity is one of the foundations of the Constitutional system of the Russian Federation. . . . [T]he constitutional goal of preserving the integrity of the Russian State accords with the universally recognized principles concerning the right of nations to self-determination. (Gaeta 1996, 563)

The dissenting judges concluded that at least one of the decrees under scrutiny had exceeded Yeltsin's constitutional authority but stressed the justiciablity of presidential decrees pertaining to national security, as well as of the Russian government's policies concerning the Chechnya issue.

Another illustration of the increasingly common involvement of national high courts in core legislative and executive prerogatives can be found in the landmark ruling of the German Federal Constitutional Court in the *Maastricht* case (1993)—where the court drew on Basic Law provisions to determine the status of post-unification Germany with respect to the emerging European supranational polity. Section 38 of the Basic Law confers on German citizens the right to vote for their parliamentary representatives. Article 20(2) of the Basic Law confers on citizen-voters the right to participate in the exercise of state authority through their parliamentary deputies. The petitioners argued that the creation of the EU through the Maastricht treaty of 1992 implied a transfer of policymaking authority from the national level to the supranational level, thereby placing a considerable amount of policymaking authority beyond the ambit of national legislators. Specifically, the transfer of policymaking authority to the EU constituted a relinquishment of power by the Bundestag, thereby infringing on the right of German citizens to influence the exercise of state power through the act of voting. Once again, a national high court was called on to clarify and settle fundamental political controversies, this time relating to the interrelationships between the German voter, the Bundestag, and the emerging supranational European polity.

In its decision, the court addressed at great length the rationale behind the creation of a supranational European community, and stipulated the necessary conditions for generating democratic legitimacy at the supranational level. The court went on to define the legislative purview of member states and national parliaments with regard to the Union, and stated that the Bundestag should retain functions and powers of substantial importance. Moreover, the court stated that

[a]rticle 38 of the Constitution is breached if an act opens up the German legal system to the application of the law of the supra-national European, and if that act does not establish with sufficient certainty what powers are transferred and how they will be integrated. (Kommers 1997, 185–186)

The court also held that fundamental democratic principles of political participation and representation did not jeopardize German membership in the EU as long as the transfer of power to such bodies "remain[ed] rooted in the right of German citizens to vote and thus to participate in the national lawmaking process" (Kommers 1997, 185–186). In other words, the court did not shy away from dealing with an explicitly political question. Rather, it upheld the constitutionality of the Maastricht treaty, specifically placing it under the judgment of German Basic Law and its principles.

Consider the accelerating judicialization of "nation building" processes—the transformation of national high courts into major decision-making bodies dealing with fundamental questions concerning the very definition, or *raison d'être*, of the polity as such. This is common in fragmented polities facing deep ethnic, linguistic, and religious cleavages that may result in political "ungovernability" crises or threats of political breakdown. A few textbook

examples of this increasingly common scenario of political jurisprudence include the previously mentioned constitutional certification saga in South Africa—the first time a court refused to accept a national constitutional text drafted by a representative constitution-making body; the unprecedented involvement of the Canadian judiciary in dealing with the political future of Quebec and the Canadian federation, including the Supreme Court of Canada's landmark ruling in the *Quebec Secession Reference* (1998)—the first time a democratic country had ever tested in advance the legal terms of its own dissolution; the key role the Turkish Constitutional Court has played in preserving the strictly secular nature of Turkey's political system by continually outlawing antisecularist political forces in that country; the crucial role of the Egyptian Supreme Constitutional Court in determining the nature of public life in Egypt as a modern state formally governed by principles of Islamic *Shari'a* laws; the wholesale transfer of the deep religious–secular cleavage in Israeli society to the Israeli judiciary through the judicialization of determining who is a Jew, and the corresponding entanglement of the Israeli Supreme Court in interpreting Israel's fundamental definition as a "Jewish and Democratic State."

A third contested political issue that has been rapidly and excessively judicialized over the past several decades is that of restorative justice. The increasingly common transfer of fundamental moral and political dilemmas concerning extreme injustices and mass atrocities committed against historically disenfranchised groups and individuals from the political sphere to the courts involves a few subcategories that reflect different notions of restorative justice. A few examples include the judicialization of restorative justice in the wake of the mass atrocities of the apartheid era in South Africa; the Pinochet affair as the epitome of the ongoing judicialization of restorative justice in Chile and other postauthoritarian Latin American countries; the major role played by the newly established constitutional courts in postcommunist Europe in confronting their respective countries' pasts; and the previously mentioned judicialization of the battle over the status of indigenous peoples in "settler societies."

In other words, the wave of judicial activism that has swept the world in the past few decades has not bypassed one of the most fundamental issues a democratic polity ought to address: that of coming to terms with its own (often not so admirable) past. None of the recently judicialized questions of restorative justice are uniquely or intrinsically legal. Whereas some recently judicialized questions of restorative justice have certain important constitutional aspects, they are neither purely, nor even primarily, legal dilemmas. As such, they ought to be resolved, at least on the level of principle, through public deliberation in the political sphere. Nonetheless, national high courts throughout the world have gradually become major decision-making bodies for dealing with precisely such restorative justice dilemmas. Fundamental distributive justice questions concerning collective responsibility for crimes against humanity masterminded by political power holders (and tacitly supported by certain of their subjects) and questions of reconciliation and reparative justice have been framed in terms of constitutional claims for rights and entitlements, and as such have rap-

idly found their way to the national high courts.

A fourth emerging scenario germane to judicialized politics is the increasing involvement of national high courts in controversies concerning the legitimacy, procedure, and outcomes of political transformation and regime change. This scenario includes at least three subcategories: legal disputes over election procedures and outcomes (for example, the *Bush v. Gore* saga following the 2000 presidential election in the United States or the Russian Constitutional Court's 1998 ruling to disqualify Boris Yeltsin from seeking a third term as president); frequent courtroom battles over the political future of prominent leaders (think of the widely publicized trials of the Philippines' ex-president Joseph Estrada, Indonesia's ex-president Abdurrahman Wahid, Thailand's prime minister Thaksin Shinawatra, and Pakistan's former prime ministers Benazir Bhutto and Nawaz Sharif, as well as the impeachment trials of Peru's ex-president Alberto Fujimori, Yugoslavia's ex-president Slobodan Milosevic, and the United States' former president Bill Clinton); and judicial review of the constitutionality of regime change (such as the previously mentioned restoration of the 1997 Fijian constitution by the Fijian Court of Appeals in *Fiji v. Prasad* in 2001 and the previously discussed involvement of the Pakistan Supreme Court in political transformation in that country).

Conclusion

The traditional neglect of the study of comparative judicial review and judicial politics is becoming harder and harder to justify. Over the past few years, the world has witnessed an astoundingly rapid transition to "juristocracy." Around the world, in numerous countries and in several supranational entities, fundamental constitutional reform has transferred an unprecedented amount of power to judiciaries. The countries that have hosted this expansion of judicial power stretch from the former Eastern Bloc to Canada, from Latin America to South Africa, and from Britain to Israel. Almost every one of these countries has a recently adopted constitution or constitutional revision that contains a bill of rights and establishes some form of active judicial review. Armed with these judicial review powers, national high courts in these countries have become increasingly important, if not crucial, public policymakers. The increasing power of supranational tribunals such as the European Court of Justice suggests that judicial review is becoming a key factor in international politics as well.

"Anything and everything is justiciable!" Aharon Barak (the proactive chief justice of the Israeli Supreme Court) once said, and this appears to have become a widely accepted motto among many courts and judges worldwide. Throughout the world, there has been a growing legislative deference to the judiciary, an increasing (and at times welcomed) intrusion of the judiciary into the prerogatives of legislatures and executives, and a corresponding acceleration of the process whereby political agendas have been judicialized. Together, these developments have helped bring about a growing reliance on adjudicative means for articulating, framing, and settling fundamental moral controversies and highly contentious political questions, and have transformed numerous national high courts into major loci for dealing with the most salient political contro-

versies a democratic polity can contemplate. Indeed, there is hardly a political controversy in most constitutional democracies that has not sooner or later turned into a judicial one. This global trend toward juristocracy has been arguably one of the most significant developments in late-twentieth- and early-twenty-first-century government.

Most existing studies concerning the sociopolitical origins and consequences of judicial activism are based on the United States' exceptional, if not downright idiosyncratic, constitutional legacy. It is remarkable how rarely works on American constitutional law and politics, for example, refer to public law and judicial politics in other countries. Until recently, it was appropriate to give the American experience of judicial review a privileged position in the study of constitutional politics, primarily because other experiments with written constitutions and judicial review were simply too short to warrant confident predictions as to which, if any, would successfully shape long-term constitutional and sociopolitical evolution (Ackerman 1997, 771). However, as we have seen, the evolution, structure, and practice of judicial review in the new constitutionalism world over the past few decades reflect a tremendously rich array of historical contexts, institutional mechanisms, and constitutional adjudications. Constitutional politics and judicial activism in Hungary, Germany, Russia, Israel, Australia, Pakistan, Britain, India, New Zealand, France, Canada, and South Africa have arisen out of a wide variety of social struggles, legal traditions, and political contexts. Although it is important to emphasize the United States' undisputedly unique legacy of judicial review and its profound implications, I believe it is equally important to place the dramatic manifestations of the expansion of judicial review in one's own country within a broader context of similar developments that have taken place in numerous other constitutional democracies. Such an informed comparative research agenda is likely to yield novel and illuminating insights concerning the political origins, practice, and consequences of judicial review, and to enrich the lively debate concerning the contribution of judicial review to democratic government.

Bibliography

Abraham, Henry. *The Judicial Process.* New York: Oxford University Press, 1986.

Ackerman, Bruce. "The Rise of World Constitutionalism." *Virginia Law Review* 83 (1997): 771.

Baar, Carl. "Social Action Litigation in India: The Operation and Limits of the World's Most Active Judiciary." In *Comparative Judicial Review and Public Policy.* Edited by D. Jackson and C. N. Tate. Westport, Conn.: Greenwood Press, 1992.

Fabre, Cecile. *Social Rights under the Constitution.* Oxford: Clarendon Press, 2000.

Gaeta, Paul. "The Armed Conflict in Chechnya before the Russian Constitutional Court." *European Journal of International Law* (1996): 563.

Glendon, Mary Ann. *Rights Talk: The Impoverishment of Political Discourse.* New York: Free Press, 1991.

Havermann, Paul. "Indigenous Rights in the Political Jurisprudence of Australia, Canada, and New Zealand." In *Indigenous Peoples' Rights in Australia, Canada, and New Zealand.* Edited by Paul Havermann. Auckland: Oxford University Press, 1999.

Hirschl, Ran. "The Political Origins of Judicial Empowerment through the Constitutionalization of Rights: Lessons from Four Polities." *Law and Social Inquiry* 25 (2000): 91–149.

———. "The Global Expansion of Judicial Review: Political Origins and Consequences." *Canadian Journal of Law and Jurisprudence* 15 (2002): 191–218.

———. *Towards Juristocracy: A Comparative Inquiry into the Origins and Consequences of the New Constitutionalism.* Cambridge: Harvard University Press, 2003.

Kommers, Donald. *The Constitutional Jurisprudence of the Federal Republic of Germany.* 2d ed. Durham: Duke University Press, 1997.

L'Heureux-Dube, Clair. "Human Rights: A Worldwide Dialogue." In *Supreme but Not Infallible: Essays in Honour of the Supreme Court of India.* Edited by B. N. Kirpal et al. New Delhi: Oxford University Press, 2000.

Schwartz, Herman. *The Struggle for Constitutional Justice in Post-Communist Europe.* Chicago: University of Chicago Press, 2000.

Shachar, Ayelet. *Multicultural Jurisdictions: Cultural Differences and Women's Rights.* Cambridge: Cambridge University Press, 2001.

Sharlet, Robert. "Russian Chief Justice as Judicial Politician." *East European Constitutional Review* 2 (1993): 32–33.

Slaughter, Anne-Marie. "A Typology of Transjudicial Communities." *University of Richmond Law Review* 29 (1994): 99.

Sólyom, Lázló, and Georg Brunner. *Constitutional Judiciary in a New Democracy: The Hungarian Constitutional Court.* Ann Arbor: University of Michigan Press, 2000.

Tate, C. Neal. "Comparative Judicial Review and Public Policy: Concepts and Overview." In *Comparative Judicial Review and Public Policy.* Edited by D. Jackson and C. N. Tate. Westport, Conn.: Greenwood Press, 1992.

8

Marbury v. Madison as a Model for Understanding Contemporary Judicial Review

RONALD KAHN

Marbury v. Madison (1803) is the most widely cited and studied case in American constitutional law. Nonetheless, the reason for the case's preeminence is murky. Is *Marbury* still good law? Is *Marbury* a case study in the jurisprudence of its time or ours? Is the theory of judicial review at its heart plausible in the twenty-first century? If there has been seemingly unanimous agreement by political scientists and law professors that the case should be studied, there seems to be a wide diversity of views on *how Marbury* should be studied. Is the case best approached through close attention to the internal logic of the argument advanced by Chief Justice John Marshall? Is *Marbury* best approached by focusing on the case's political context, which clearly played some role in the decision?

To answer these questions, one must go beyond *Marbury*. Approaches to *Marbury* reflect views on the nature of Supreme Court decision making. If constitutional principles and legal norms guide or should guide constitutional decision making, focusing on the internal logic of the Court's *Marbury* decision is appropriate. If forces external to the Court tend to drive doctrinal development, then discussing political context becomes a central consideration. *Marbury* can assume the role of a Rorschach test in the American constitutional tradition. In important ways, our contemporary uses of *Marbury* speak to concerns of contemporary Supreme Court decision making and contemporary considerations about judicial review in our constitutional democracy.

Political scientists approach the Supreme Court, constitutional review, and judicial review in two primary ways: via empirical behavioralism and empirical interpretivism. Empirical behavioralism is used by political scientists to explain Supreme Court decision making and judicial review as a consequence of events outside the Court or the attitudes of the justices. Such scholars regard Supreme Court justices as policymakers, not significantly different from elected officials and administrators. Precedents, polity and rights principles, and institutional norms do not have an important causative effect on what justices do or on the development of constitutional law, according to this view.

Empirical interpretivism views polity and rights principles and precedents as important to Court decision making. Polity and rights principles are the basic filters through which doctrines of popular sovereignty and fundamental rights confront each other. Polity principles are deeply held ideas about where the decision-making power should be located when deciding questions of constitutional significance. Polity principles involve beliefs about whether courts or electorally accountable political institutions are the appropriate forums for constitutional decision making and what level of government—state, local, and national—is the proper forum for such decisions. With regard to separation of powers, the major polity principle at the core of *Marbury,* the Marshal Court had to decide what the role of president, Senate, and the Supreme Court is in the interpretation of the Constitution and the role of the Senate, president, Secretary of State, and the Supreme Court in deciding the nature of the appointment process. Rights principles are beliefs about legally enforceable claims of individual powers, privileges, and immunities guaranteed under the Constitution, statutes, and law. Rights may be seen as entitlements or affirmative responsibilities on the part of government or as cocoons that shield a citizen from government intrusion, such as the right of privacy (Kahn 1994, 20–22).

The empirical interpretive approach views judicial review as a process which is explained by the rules and processes internal to Supreme Court decision making, such as the rule that the Court respect precedents made in earlier cases, as it applies polity and rights principles; it is also explained by the social, economic, political, and historical context in which the Supreme Court makes its decisions. Institutional norms, such as the requirement that the Supreme Court respect precedent, rights principles (such as the right to equal protection under the law), and polity (among the presidency, Congress, and Supreme Court), all structure and inform the process of Supreme Court decision making. Empirical interpretivists train empirical attention less on the individual judge or the role of context and norms in shaping the decision *in a single case* and more on the dynamics of long-term constitutional change.

Empirical interpretivists, unlike most law school scholars, do not highlight narrow doctrinal developments or normative arguments. Most law professors explore how rights arguments build from case to case. Many propound constitutional theories in support of such rights. Such analyses are internal-looking and less concerned about the Supreme Court as an institution in American political development. Empirical interpretivists study the Supreme Court and judicial review empirically, not normatively. They see the Court as a political institution. However, like legalists and unlike empirical behavioralists, empirical interpretivists recognize that courts are also legal institutions different from other political and policymaking institutions in important ways. Such an approach yields an understanding of *Marbury* and judicial review that takes law, politics, and society into account by grounding understanding of the case in context. By doing so, the meaning of cases as freestanding rulings can be elaborated, and how cases are constructed over time in altered historical, institutional, and intellectual contexts can be determined. Such an approach highlights changes in interpretative forms and legal arguments and changing normative visions of principles and cases.[1]

One's particular analysis of *Marbury,* its place in the history of judicial review, and its impact on contemporary Supreme Court decision making is directly related to whether one takes an empirical behavioral or empirical interpretive approach to explaining Supreme Court decision making. When an empirical interpretive approach is used, *Marbury* reveals much about the nature of contemporary judicial review. However, a behavioral approach to *Marbury* cannot explain the case or its importance to modern judicial review. Judicial review has changed as a result of the growth of the national economy and the administrative state since the 1890s. Nevertheless, since 1803 when *Marbury* was decided, Supreme Court decision making has exhibited an integrity, importance, and independence from politics. The Supreme Court has always applied polity and rights principles in settling cases. Precedents and institutional norms shape the process. Moreover, in *Marbury* and to the present, the Supreme Court must interpret polity and rights principles through their application in light of the social, political, and economic world outside the Court. What has changed is a great expansion of the factors in the social, economic, and political world that the Court considers and the relationship among such factors, not the nature of the decision-making process itself or some of the basic principles enunciated in *Marbury.*

An Empirical Behavioral Approach to Judicial Review and *Marbury*

For much of the post–World War II period, most political scientists looked at Supreme Court decision making and constitutional doctrine using behavioral concepts—in other words, they studied the Court as scientists might study the natural world, through observation and experimentation, without regard for the special process of decision making that is found within legal institutions, such as the Supreme Court. These understandings conceptualized the Court as a political institution akin to other electorally accountable institutions, peopled by justices viewed as policymakers. Decisions were understood to be determined by the substantive political preferences of the justices, the majority coalition in power, or the presidents who appointed the judicial majority. The empirically oriented behavioralists portrayed the U.S. Supreme Court as a collection of preference-bearing, goal-directed individuals.

Empirical behavioralism has many forms: *Attitudinalism* portrays judges as voting instrumentally in constitutional (and other) cases, consistent with their preexisting political attitudes. In other words, liberal justices decide cases to achieve liberal policy goals. Conservative justices decide cases to achieve conservative policy goals. Behaviorally oriented researchers refined these understandings and explored strategic behavior by judges interested in forming judicial majorities and handing down decisions that would be respected by other political actors. Additional scholarship on judicial behavior further expanded the analysis to help explain factors operating before and after the Supreme Court case itself. Studies of the dynamics of agenda setting and interest-group litigation emphasized how lawyers, advocacy groups, and other actors influenced judicial decision making (Epp 1998; Epstein and Kobylka 1992). Judicial impact studies assessed the real world consequences of judicial decisions (Halpern 1995; Rosenberg 1991). Gerald

Rosenberg (1991) argued that the Supreme Court tends to follow political trends when making landmark decisions and influences public policy only to the degree that politically accountable actors support Court decisions.

Some behavioralists (for example, Adamany 1973; Funston 1975) who rejected the attitudinal approach explained case outcomes tied to changes in the political system. Particular emphasis was placed on political changes associated with the election of new majority coalitions, such as the 1932 and 1936 presidential election of Franklin Delano Roosevelt. Internal decision making, principles, and precedent are not seen as key to Court decision making—only the policy concerns of the justices or the president who appointed the judicial majority. Robert Dahl, in a seminal study, concluded that the Supreme Court was a policymaking institution not very different from an elected legislature or an appointed bureaucracy. For Dahl, the question at issue on the Court is "who gets what and how?" The answer, to Dahl, lies outside the Court, legal principles, and institutional norms. He assumed little difference between law and politics. Dahl viewed the Supreme Court as a political institution rather than a legal one. Dahl (1957, 280) noted that the Supreme Court is built on a "fiction that it is not a political institution but exclusively a legal one." Scholars were naive who took seriously legal principles, precedents, and internal institutional rules as important when explaining Court decision making, according to Dahl.

Empirical interpretivists reject such behavioralist approaches to analyzing the Supreme Court. Studies linking Court action to political changes or critical elections assume legal decision-making processes do not independently affect doctrine. The Court is characterized as responding only to politics rather than relying on precedent and constitutional principles when deciding cases. Prominent scholars of this school see a "deep and ineradicable tension in the American political tradition between the value of electorally accountable policy-making and certain other values and ideas" (Perry 1988, 163). The values that limit raw politics include substantive due process of law, equality and equal protection of the law, and the notion that individuals are responsible only for what they do as individuals and not for what society thinks they might do because of its stereotyped view of the group in which the individual is a member. "This propensity to hold contradictory ideas simultaneously," Robert McCloskey (2000, 7) wrote, "is one of the most significant qualities of the American political mind at all stages of national history, and it helps substantially in explaining the rise to power of the United States Supreme Court."

Howard Gillman (1993) and Keith Whittington (1999, 2000) presented evidence challenging any theory explaining constitutional revolutions as simple responses to external political events. They maintain that early twentieth-century constitutional change can be understood only by looking at the Court as engaged in a dynamic, case-by-case decision-making process in which the justices applied polity and rights principles to political and economic life outside the Court.

Marbury under Empirical Behavioralism

Empirical behavioralists place too sharp a focus on events outside the Court as causative of Supreme Court decision making. They present an approach in which the politics of the world external to the Court is imported essentially unaltered into the Court as a cause for its decision making. In doing so, behaviorism not only skews our understanding of the *Marbury* decision and its place in the study of judicial review, but also results in misunderstanding the impact of courts and law on American political development. Empirical behavioralists study the politics outside the Court and judicial votes rather than the reasoning in judicial opinions. They do not explain *Marbury* in terms of precedents, institutional norms, and principles such as the rule of law. Using this line of reasoning, *Marbury* is explained by Chief Justice Marshall's effort to meet the threatened Jeffersonian assault on the Supreme Court. Behavioralists emphasize that the case is primarily an effort by Marshall to sustain Federalist principles of government and institutions after the Federalists had lost control of the presidency and national legislature. Empirical behavioralists emphasize that Marshall made a decision not to grant the commission to William Marbury (the reason for the case in the first place), knowing full well that the Jefferson administration would not deliver the commission even if so ordered by the Supreme Court.

Empirical behavioralists eschew the importance of legal principles in the Court and the Court itself as an important agent of American political change. They believe that the Court follows politics and elections. However, a major role, polity principle, and institutional norm on the Court is that the Court is to be countermajoritarian (Graber 1993; Kahn 1994, 255–256) especially when institutional and rights principles in the Constitution are abused by government. The Supreme Court periodically takes a strong stand that as an institution it must be countermajoritarian when supporting a constitutional principle, as seen in the abortion rights cases. The notion that the Court is to be countermajoritarian when rights are at issue is demonstrated throughout *Marbury*. Marshall demonstrated this institutional norm when asserting that the failure to deliver the commission to Marbury denied Marbury a right or entitlement to the commission. The entitlement was created by those rules in the Constitution that defined the process of appointment (*Marbury* 1803, 162–163). All procedures were completed with regard to the president's appointment and the Senate's approval of Marbury's appointment. Marshall wrote, "The question, whether a right has vested or not, is, in its nature, judicial, and must be tried by the judicial authority" (*Marbury* 1803, 167).

An Empirical Interpretive Analysis of *Marbury* and Judicial Review

Marbury cannot be understood simply as reflecting the politics of its day. Empirical behavioralism fails to view as important the legal and institutional norms that guided the reasoning in *Marbury* and fails to take seriously the notion that what *Marbury* means today reflects both what it meant in 1803 and how that case has been interpreted in the thousands of cases of judicial review decided afterward elaborating the authority of the Court to interpret the Constitution. To understand and explain the importance of *Marbury* to the process of judicial review and American political development, we need to explore the process of

Supreme Court decision making in a way that acknowledges that the Supreme Court is a legal institution, different from a political or policy-making institution.

Empirical interpretivism emphasizes the essentially dual nature of the task of constitutional interpretation, which involves both fidelity to the Constitution and openness to politics and change. Supreme Court justices adhere to principle and make policy. They do so routinely in response to a steady sequence of concrete constitutional cases. I argue that they do not make policy as articulated by empirical behavioralists. The following principles are at the core of this integrated understanding of constitutional decision making:

1. Constitutional principles, precedents, and constitutional theory are taken seriously. They are not fodder used instrumentally by justices to justify preconceived policy choices.
2. Precedents are important in themselves and as analogies when various social changes raise new constitutional problems.
3. Supreme Court justices follow institutional norms, such as *stare decisis* or respect for precedent. The Supreme Court is relatively independent from the president, Congress, and the direct effects of politics.
4. Justices view law and politics as separate and distinct, even though they bring in outside social, political, and economic factors when they apply polity and rights principles in deciding a case. This respect for legal and institutional norms explains the many cases in which judicial votes are inconsistent with their personal policy preferences.
5. Supreme Court decision-making process is constitutive in nature. The principles in

a case and the construction process in applying principles to the social, economic, and political world outside the Court are just as important to the development of doctrine as are the specific policy outcomes.

Constitutional Interpretation Before 1937: Traditional Originalism

Supreme Court decision making must be situated historically. When explaining what *Marbury teaches* us about Supreme Court decision making, judicial review, and constitutional interpretation—whether we are reading *Marbury* as written in 1803 or in light of present concerns—makes a significant difference. Gillman (1997) highlighted a major shift in approaches to constitutional meaning that took place in the United States beginning in the late nineteenth century. From the founding until the 1890s, traditional originalism predominated as a method of constitutional interpretation. Under traditional originalism, "there was a consensus in court opinions and legal treatises that judges were obliged to interpret the Constitution on the basis of the original meaning of constitutional provisions" (Gillman 1997, 192). Beginning in the 1890s, under the influence of monumental changes in the nature of the nation's political economy, traditional originalism gradually lost its status as a desirable and authoritative approach to the Constitution. This fall of traditional originalism culminated in the Supreme Court's retreat from *Lochner v. New York* (1905) principles in the middle and late 1930s. These included a retreat from such notions as that there is a "right to contract" between employee and employer that government may not violate except for the most compelling reasons, and that manufacturing was a state action and thus subject only to state regulation and that commerce was defined only as the movement of goods, which was to be subject to national government regulation under the Constitution's commerce clause. Under traditional originalism, the *Lochner* Court emphasized that the Constitution had to be interpreted line by line and word by word as the framers would have interpreted it, without regard to the meaning of such principles in light of changing social, economic, and political complexities of the world outside the Court.

Some scholars have labeled this retreat from *Lochner*-era principles in cases in the middle and late 1930s as the New Deal Constitutional Revolution (Ackerman 1991); other scholars (Cushman 1998; Gillman 1997; White 2001) have argued that the decline in originalist interpretations of the Constitution and overturning of *Lochner*-era decisions were not the Court's response to the problems of the New Deal period or to the elections and politics of the 1930s in which demands were made for a new Supreme Court or Constitution, but rather to developments in legal and social thought that began in the 1890s. The arguments for a living Constitution that adapts and changes with the ages through a nonoriginalist process of interpretation simply took root in the 1930s but had been developing since the 1890s. This new outlook came to dominate constitutional thinking for much of the remainder of the twentieth century.

Traditional originalism hewed to an array of interrelated assumptions about American constitutionalism. Many nineteenth-century legalists analogized the Constitution to a statute or a contract. As such, they argued that the Constitution should be interpreted according to prevailing canons governing the interpretation and construction of those documents. Foremost among these was the canon that, as the product of discernible minds (whether legislators, parties to agreements, or constitutional founders), these texts should be interpreted according to their intentions. When changing circumstances made the original purposes obsolete or inconvenient, people could amend or revise their earlier instructions or agreements. Until that happened, the original understanding would be enforced. The judiciary lacked authority to update the rules or establish the terms of the new bargain. Traditional originalism ruled out an evolutionary conception of constitutional meaning (Gillman 1997, 194). The duty of the judge was to give effect, in the context of concrete disputes, to the rules and intentions set out by others whose authority to make laws and agreements was clear.

Gillman (1997, 197–203) noted the principles of traditional originalism are that (1) the Constitution's authority derives from an act of higher law making by a sovereign people; (2) the Constitution is a super-statute that creates and regulates the institutions, procedures, powers, and responsibilities of government; (3) the Constitution was established to be a permanent set of instructions issued by a sovereign people to protect the liberties of citizens; (4) constitutional provisions that listed enumerated powers and prohibitions have permanent fixed meanings not to be changed, except by amendment; (5) to keep these bedrock principles front and center, the Constitution specifically avoids mentioning issues that do not lend themselves to regulation by the Constitution, such as salaries, elections, and the jurisdiction of federal courts; (6) the Constitution, unlike common law, comprises fixed, immutable principles; (7) the Constitution is to be construed by ascertaining the intentions of those who made the Constitution; (8) the bedrock constitutional sovereignty principle of the Constitution is preserved by judicial enforcement of the Constitution as fundamental law; and (9) the Constitution adjusts itself to experience and social change through its law-based, Article V amendment process.[2]

These traditional originalist principles were at the core of Marshall's decision in *Marbury*. They also were at the core of *McCulloch v. Maryland* (1819), in which Marshall discussed how Congress may pursue constitutionally permitted ends. Marshall made clear in *McCulloch* that the original understanding of the national power was the touchstone for constitutional interpretation. Only the means necessary for the execution of those powers, he declared, were at issue. As Gillman (1997, 205) recognized, nothing in the original *McCulloch* opinion supports claims that constitutional meanings change over time.

The writings of the towering nineteenth-century Supreme Court justice and treatise writer Joseph Story are also characteristic of traditional originalism. In his *Commentaries on the Constitution of the United States*, Story (1833, 143) emphasized that the means by which government pursues enumerated and fixed objects

must be subject to perpetual modification, and change; they must be adapted to the existing manners, habits, and institutions of society, which were never stationary; to the pressure of dangers, or necessities; to the ends in view; to general and permanent operations, as well as to fugitive and extraordinary emergencies. In short, if the whole society is not to be revolutionized at every critical period, and remodeled in every generation, there must be left to those, who administer the government, a very large mass of discretionary powers, capable of greater or less expansion according to circumstances, and sufficiently flexible not to involve the nation in utter destruction from the rigid limitations imposed upon it by an improvident jealousy.

At the same time, Story (1833, 144–145) wrote,

a rule of equal importance is, not to enlarge the construction of a given power beyond the fair scope of its terms, merely because the restriction is inconvenient, impolitic, or even mischievous. If it be mischievous, the power of redressing the evil lies with the people in the exercise of the power of amendment. . . . Nor should it ever be lost sight of, that the government of the United States is one of limited and enumerated powers; and that a departure from the true import and sense of its powers is *pro tanto*, the establishment of a new constitution. It is doing for the people, that they have not chosen to do themselves. It is usurping the functions of a legislator, and deserting those of the expounder of the law. Arguments drawn from impolicy or inconvenience ought to be of no weight. . . . Temporary delusions, prejudices, excitements, and objects have irresistible influence on mere questions of policy. . . . The constitution is not to be subject to such fluctuations. It is to have a fixed, uniform, permanent construction. It should be, so far as human infirmity will allow, not dependent upon the passions or parties of particular times, but the same yesterday, to-day, and for ever.

The Constitution at the time of its adoption determined the meaning of the powers of government.

Enumerated powers in nineteenth-century constitutional law were fixed categories that yielded essentially unrevisable decisions about whether particular policies or problems fit with these categories. Social ends (the great objects) to which those powers were related were also fixed (Gillman 1997, 208–209). Formal statutory and constitutional changes in the wake of the Civil War led to a major expansion of judicial power. Nonetheless, even with these political developmental changes, judges and constitutional scholars in the later nineteenth century did not question their traditional originalist approach to constitutional interpretation (Gillman 1997, 214).

Constitutional Interpretation after 1937: The Constitution as Living, Adaptive, and Evolutionary

During the early years of the twentieth century, an insurgent group of progressives in the legal community launched a full-scale assault on the authority of traditional originalism. Judges and legal theorists such as Oliver Wendell Holmes Jr. asserted that the political system needed to be reconfigured so government could cope with revolutionary changes in the nation. The political system needed expanded national government authority and a modern administrative state. Those legal progressives found that national authority and a modern administrative state could not be readily reconciled with the prevailing understanding of traditional originalism. Scholars and judges drew on modern intellectual currents, "including Darwinism, historicism, and pragmatism," to argue that "provisions of the Constitution were designed to adapt to changing environments and social purposes" (Gillman 1997, 193). They won the argument, after long jurisprudential and political battles on and off the Court, that the Constitution could be adapted without formally amending the Constitution. Debates over

whether the Constitution could be changed through interpretation versus the originalist requirement of amendment raged in the 1930s, as did the debate over whether the Constitution and its interpretation were to be viewed as "living" (Gillman 1997, 213–224).

The assault on traditional originalism by Holmes, by treatise writers such as Christopher Tiedeman (1890), by political scientists such as Edward Corwin (1934), and by a whole array of Darwinians (Sumner 1963; Ward 1903) and pragmatists proved devastating. The pragmatists proposed a radical innovation in constitutional theory in the interest of modernization. They asked that there be "a transference of power from traditional popular sovereignty (the people in state constitutional conventions) to contemporary popular majorities. . . ." This was essential, in their view, because, as they saw the world, law would inevitably "reflect current power configurations" (Gillman 1997, 220). In the new political economy, recourse to legislatures was also advisable because legislatures were better than courts at collecting social data, making decisions on public policy, and deciding whether power should be in the hands of state or national governments. These views implicitly called into question the continuing usefulness of traditional original commitments to the separation of powers and federalism. "Once law was viewed as an instrument of evolving social needs and not a fixed instruction from historical legislators," Gillman (1997, 220) wrote, "then it almost followed naturally that judicial power should be contracted and legislative power expanded."

The change necessitated the construction by legal progressives of new justifications for the exercise of judicial review. Harvard law professor Zechariah Chafee Jr. was at the center of this new project in constitutional theory, which eventually replaced traditional originalism with a nonoriginalist approach. Chafee, in his landmark writings (Chafee 1920, 1941) on the freedom of speech, distinguished between broad constitutional principles and the precise policies the framers thought best realized those principles in practice. It was a mistake, according to Chafee, to let the conditions of the eighteenth century fix for all time the division between the lawful and the unlawful. Chafee conceptualized nonoriginalism as fidelity to "immutable concepts of political morality that motivated the framers" (Gillman 1997, 222). The "abstract goals of the framers" under the new nonoriginalism were separated from "their specific intents and purposes" (Gillman 1997, 222).

Nonoriginalism soon influenced Supreme Court decision making. In *Home Building & Loan Association v. Blaisdell* (1934), Justice Benjamin Cardozo drafted a concurrence, later withdrawn, that "reformulat(ed) . . . the key question in constitutional law—from a focus on what the framers actually said to speculation of what the framers would say today in light of our accumulated experiences" (Gillman 1997, 223). Chief Justice Charles Hughes responded to that draft by penning a famed articulation of the new nonoriginalist constitutionalism:

It is no answer to say that this public need was not apprehended a century ago, or to insist that what the provisions of the Constitution meant to the vision of that day it must mean to the vision of our time. If by the statement that what the Constitution meant at the time of its adoption it means to-day, it is intended to say that the great clauses of the Constitution must be confined to the interpretation which the framers, with the

conditions and outlook of their time, would have placed upon them, the statement carries its own refutation. It was to guard against such a narrow conception that Chief Justice Marshall uttered the memorable warning—"We must never forget, that it is a *constitution* we are expounding"—"a constitution intended to endure for ages to come, and consequently, to be adapted to the various *crises* of human affairs." . . . The case before us must be considered in light of our whole experience and not merely in that of what was said a hundred years ago." (*Blaisdell* 1934, 442–443)

In characterizing the nature of the constitutional project this way, Hughes appropriated Marshall's words to the end of vanquishing his constitutional vision. Hughes changed the interpretation of "this is a *constitution* we are expounding" from that of Marshall's traditional originalism. Under nonoriginalism, the interpretation of constitutional principles and the constitutional provisions changed significantly. Progressive legal scholars, government officials, and justices viewed the Constitution as adaptive and the focal point of an evolutionary process of nonoriginalist interpretation that would, in many cases, obviate the need for constitutional amendments. The Court confirmed the decision made in *Blaisdell* in *West Coast Hotel v. Parrish* (1937) when the justices launched a direct assault on the liberty of contract and the notion that the economic system was beyond the police powers of government when the use of such powers violated the limited and enumerated powers set out in the originalist Constitution.

The culmination of these early twentieth-century political and jurisprudential battles was the development of the notion of a "living constitution" that could adapt through interpretation to the changing social, economic, and political world outside the Court. The Constitution was viewed as organic, like a plant, animal, or any living species, which over time may change its color and aspects of its structure in response to changes in the environment in which it lives. This shift to conceiving of the Constitution as adaptive, living, and organic was quite different from how the Constitution was viewed in the age of traditional originalism. Under traditional originalism, the Constitution was viewed as consisting of a set of reliable and durable rules and principles that were to be mechanistically applied by judges not changed through their interpretation. The notion of a Constitution as an organic, living, and adapting document became the conventional way in which contemporary nonoriginalists viewed the Constitution. Even purported originalists arguably see the Constitution and constitutional interpretation as more adaptive than nineteenth-century constitutionalists. Gillman (1997, 241) concluded that post-1937 constitutionalism is based on "the accommodation of political development through the acceptance of the idea of a 'living Constitution.'" "The old constitutionalism," in his view, "was so thoroughly dislodged that with rare exceptions, over the next sixty years no one would use *Lochner*-era jurisprudence as the yardstick for legitimate constitutional interpretation."

Marbury as a Model for Understanding Contemporary Judicial Review

Important similarities in the process of Supreme Court decision making can be detected between 1803 and the present. The Court in every era must interpret the Constitution. The words do not speak for themselves. The Court must determine whether rights have been violated through an application of polity and rights principles to the questions at issue in a case. In other words, the Court must engage in a construction process. The Court must rely on precedents and consider more basic legal principles and practices of law. The Court must make analogies between the facts and issues in a particular case and those of earlier cases. Although past and present practices of judicial review differ in important ways, the commonalities over time are of greater significance when understanding the impact of *Marbury* on judicial review.

The major difference between originalist and nonoriginalist judicial review is the tremendous expansion of the factors included in the construction process. With each passing decade of the twentieth century, the Supreme Court confronted an increasing number of social factors when applying polity and rights principles. What constitutes state action continues to expand into the twenty-first century and, concomitantly, the sphere of human behavior considered pure individual agency has contracted. This expansion of the social construction process yields more expansive readings of equal protection of the law and due process. The number, complexity, and depth of individual rights are increasing. The distinction between judicial review before and after 1937 can be overstated. The primary and important difference between pre- and post-1937 Court decision making is that after 1937 the construction process includes a much deeper look at the political, social, and economic world. Construction took place in 1803—but in a more narrow sense than at present.

Many questions and issues that arise in *Marbury* are similar to those that arise under modern judicial review. A close reading of *Marbury* demonstrates that Chief Justice Marshall had to consider many more questions than the three primary ones listed at the start of the case: "Has the applicant a right to the commission he demands?" If he has a right, and that right has been violated, "do the laws of his country afford him a remedy" and "If they do afford him a remedy, is it a *mandamus* issuing from this Court" (*Marbury* 1803, 153). How the Court answered these questions, the process by which these questions were answered, and the principles used tell us much about contemporary Supreme Court decision making.

Have *Marbury's* Rights Been Violated?

In 1803—as it would today—the Court asked whether Marbury had a right to the commission in question. The Supreme Court had to determine whether individual rights had been violated and the source of those rights. To determine whether a right had been violated, the Court had to decide whether public officials had violated specific limitations on government power or had denied Marbury rights listed in the Constitution. In this case, the Constitution really cannot say directly whether Marbury has a right to the commission. The words of the Constitution cannot speak to all specific acts of public officials, events, and resulting disputes. In 1803, as today, justices had first to read the constitutional provisions relevant to the appointment process. Marshall had to interpret what these words mean:

[The President] shall nominate, and by and with the advice and consent of the senate, shall appoint ambassadors, other public ministers and consuls, judges of the supreme Court, and all other Officers of the United States, whose Appointments are not herein otherwise provided for, and which shall be established by law, but the Congress may by law vest the appointment of such inferior Officers, as they think proper in the President alone, to the Courts of law, or in the heads of Departments. (Article II, Section 2, Clause 2)

Even though Marshall explicitly asked if "Marbury . . . [had] a right to the commission," he was really asking *what* rights were at issue in the case. The decision had to be made on the basis of law and principles. Marshall had to explain why Marbury had a right to the commission.

When he read the Constitution, Marshall found two constitutional appointment processes. Congress by law may require that a nomination be made by the president and consented to by the Senate. Congress may also by law vest the appointment process for inferior officers exclusively in the president.

What Is to Be Left to Politics and What to Law?

A major aspect of judicial review in 1803 and today is a judicial determination about the aspects of official action left to ordinary politics. Such actions are not subject to Court review.[3] The justices must also determine what official actions are required by law, the Constitution, and common-law principles. These are subject to scrutiny by the Court. Marshall had to determine whether the act of delivering the commission was a political act, performed at the discretion of the Jefferson administration, or an official duty. Marshall had to determine whether the act of delivering the commission was an essential part of the appointment process. He had to determine which acts in the appointment process were political and discretionary and which public officials had to perform as a matter of law.

The Court in *Marbury* decided that once a commission is sealed, the act of delivery is required by law and by the Constitution. When the Senate approves a nomination and the president signs a commission, all procedures required under the Constitution are completed. Marbury was constitutionally appointed to a justice of the peace position that was authorized by Congress in 1801. No more politics, discretion, or deliberation is permitted. Marshall noted, "After seal, no other solemnity is required by law—no other act of government is required" (*Marbury* 1803, 159).

Marshall has the important task of determining whether the delivery of the commission to Marbury is a political act or one required by law. Some acts are political and not subject to judicial review. Others are required by the Constitution, as interpreted. Marshall emphasized that the president is invested with certain important political powers, the exercise of which he is to use at his own discretion. For these, executives are accountable only to their country and conscience. Such powers include the president's powers as commander in chief and leader in foreign policy. The Court has no power to control executive discretion in these areas. But the Court must determine the boundaries of executive discretion.

Although *Marbury* was decided under an originalist scheme, Marshall could not simply look at the words of the Constitution. A wide range of materials must be considered. For ex-

ample, when Marshall considered whether delivery is part of the appointment process, he drew on the common law of contract. As in modern judicial review, analogies are made between the act of delivering the commission and delivery of documents under practices long used by the common law. Marshall decided that the lack of delivery does not change the entitlement to the commission. The legal entitlement was established when the secretary of state completed the act required by law to place the seal on the commission, which attested to the completion of the process created by law and the Constitution.

Supreme Court Decisions Based on Principles

The Supreme Court bases decisions on principles. Courts differ from elected bodies. The Supreme Court ensures that public officials do not violate the Constitution as interpreted. Throughout *Marbury* there is a continuing argument about the legal principles necessary to resolve the dispute before the justices. By making principles clear, the Court demonstrated that making a decision by a legal body differs from a decision by a political body. Marshall was aware of the political "delicacy" of the case before the Court. He acknowledged

[t]he peculiar delicacy of this case, the novelty of some of its circumstances, and the real difficulty attending the points which occupy it, require a complete exposition of the principles on which the opinion to be given by the court is founded. (*Marbury* 1803, 154)

This is one of the few places where Marshall referred to politics outside the Court. Still, the Court is charged with making decisions based on principles, not on outcomes an individual justice desires. Moreover, a Court is establishing principles for future generations. The first case in which a federal law is declared unconstitutional requires a decision whose principles can stand the test of time. This general concern with principles is as alive for justices today as it was in 1803.

Fundamental law supports the decision that Marbury had a right to the commission. The Constitution is superior to the political discretion of public officials. The Constitution comes from people in convention, not from the states. This origin provides foundations for insisting that constitutional language and doctrine govern the everyday acts of political leaders. Most modern judicial review is not about the constitutionality of legislation but about whether public officials have abused their authority.

The Supreme Court in 1803, as it does at present, consciously asked what is in the realm of politics and what is in the realm of law. The Court determines what the Constitution leaves to politics and what elected officials must do under the Constitution. This determination by the Court is crucial for maintaining the central theoretical premise of the Constitution: that the people in convention meant to limit politics and government action in specified ways.

To determine whether Marbury had a right to the commission, the Marshall Court invoked separation of powers. Marshall suggested that because the appointment is a product of presidential and Senate action and because the position was created by congressional action, the Jeffersonian decision not to deliver the commission belied the framing decision to provide a joint appointment process and the congressional decision to use that joint

appointment process. The appointment is not just an act of Congress or of the president but an act of both branches. The president lacks the discretion not to act after both branches have performed their legislatively mandated function. Congress has chosen to be part of the appointment process. Not to deliver the commission denies the will of Congress and those processes that allow the congressional will to be known and respected.

Jefferson denied Marbury's individual right to the commission, a right created by the lawful completion of the appointment process. The issue in this case is the protection of a larger principle than the need for the president to follow the words of the appointment clause. Failure to deliver means the president is not following a law. The violation of the polity principle, separation of powers, informs us that Marbury's rights were violated. At the core of an empirical interpretive analysis of Supreme Court decision making is Court determination of the relationship between polity principles in the Constitution and the denial of rights. The structure of the Constitution, not just its words narrowly read, enters court decision making even in the age of traditional originalism.

The Importance of the Rule of Law

The Court explores what constitutes a rule of law. The rule of law is the expectation that public officials will comply with known rules and do their duty under those rules. We see the rule of law notion in the discussion of whether there is and should be a remedy when a right has been violated. Marshall asked that if there were a vested right to the commission as established by law and that right had been violated, did the laws of the country afford Marbury a remedy? The chief justice concluded, "The government of the United States has been emphatically termed a government of laws, and not of men. It will certainly cease to deserve this high appellation if the laws furnish no remedy for the violation of a vested legal right" (*Marbury* 1803, 163).

The rule of law in the United States enables every person to claim the protection of law when injured by government through its failure to do what is required by law. As part of this rule of law, we see another legal principle that Marshall held dear. He wrote, "The very essence of civil liberty certainly consists in the right of every individual to claim the protection of the laws whenever he receives an injury. One of the first duties of government is to afford that protection" (*Marbury* 1803, 163).

The Court in *Marbury* argued that no official of the United States is above the rule of law. A president may not lawfully ignore a commission. In this case, the appointment had already occurred. Delivery is not part of the appointment process, as established by law and the Constitution. Marshall emphasized that the principle that government must comply with its own rules and legal principles dates back to Great Britain. Even the king and the king's men had to comply with a judgment of a court and a lawful writ. When a right has been violated, a remedy must be provided. Marshall wrote, "It is a settled and invariable principle in the laws of England, that every right, when withheld, must have a remedy, and every injury its proper redress" (*Marbury* 1803, 163).

Government must afford a remedy for the violation of rights by government. Marshall

drew on Blackstone to emphasize the point that laws are not self-executing: "It is the general and indisputable rule," the chief justice declared, "that where there is a legal right, there is also a legal remedy by suit, by action at law, or whenever that right is invaded" (*Marbury* 1803, 163). For a right to exist, there must be a remedy to vindicate such rights so government is forced to follow its own rules. Without a remedy to vindicate rights there cannot be a rule of law.

Marshall asked whether the writ of mandamus Marbury applied for is the proper remedy. Mandamus is the proper writ through which the Court determines whether a public official should do his or her duty under the law. That writ in 1803 was used to order an official to do a nondiscretionary act pertaining to a duty required of his office by law. Again we see the clear law and politics distinction and a concern for the rule of law, even though the political situation is difficult. Marshall recognized "[t]he intimate political relation subsisting between the President of the United States and the heads of departments, necessarily renders any legal investigation of the acts of one of those high officials peculiarly irksome, as well as delicate, and excites some hesitation with respect to the propriety of entering into such investigation" (*Marbury* 1803, 169). Nevertheless, he declared, "If one of the heads of departments commits any illegal act, under color of his office, by which an individual sustains an injury, it cannot be pretended that his office alone exempts him from being sued in the ordinary mode of proceeding, and being compelled to obey the judgement of the law."

Marshall understood the injustice done to Marbury. Jefferson violated the rule of law and the separation of powers by failing to deliver the commission. The Court argued that citizens should expect that government will not violate the rules that it sets for itself under a process mandated by the Constitution. Because the appointments process was created by the sovereign people and is based on fundamental law, the denial of the right, the violation of the rule of law is particularly grievous. When government officials can do what they want and not follow the Constitution, government is arbitrary.

The Constitution as Fundamental Law, Elected Bodies, and the Supreme Court

Marshall asked whether the Supreme Court may issue the writ of mandamus. After clearly determining that (1) the writ of mandamus is the proper writ, that (2) Marbury has a right to the commission, and that (3) the role of a court is to protect rights when an officer of government does not do what he is required to do by law, Marshall said that the Supreme Court could not issue the writ. Marshall asked whether an institution of government, in this case Congress, can give the Supreme Court the power to issue the writ of mandamus. He wrote, "If this court is not authorized to issue a writ of *mandamus* to such an officer, it must be because the law is unconstitutional, and therefore, absolutely incapable of conferring the authority, and assigning the duties which its words purport to confer and assign" (*Marbury* 1803, 173). Marshall determined that Congress's conferring on the Supreme Court the power to issue writs of mandamus is unconstitutional. For the Court to issue such a writ in *Marbury* would have added to the Court's original jurisdiction. The Constitution limits original jurisdiction to "cases affecting ambassadors, other public ministers and consuls, and those in which a State shall be a party" (*Marbury* 1803, 174).

Marshall explained why jurisdiction conferred by Congress inconsistent with the Constitution may not be exercised. "The question of whether an act repugnant to the Constitution can become the law of the land," he declared, is "deeply interesting to the United States; but happily, not of an intricacy proportioned to its interest. It seems only necessary to recognize certain principles, supposed to have been long and well established, to decide it" (*Marbury* 1803, 176).

The principles Marshall referred to are that the rights in the Constitution are fundamental, because they proceed from the supreme sovereign authority of the people in convention. We have a written Constitution so the defined limited powers of the legislature are not forgotten. Marshall wrote,

The distinction between a government of limited and unlimited powers is abolished, if those limits do not confine the person on whom they are imposed, and if acts prohibited and acts allowed are of equal obligation. . . . The Constitution is either a superior paramount law, unchangeable by ordinary means, or it is on a level with ordinary legislative acts, and, like other acts, is alterable when the legislature shall please to alter it." (*Marbury* 1803, 176)

To allow legislation to trump the Constitution, the paramount law from the people, undercuts the basic principles of the nation and undermines the rights of its citizens. The Constitution is the supreme law of the land.

What is so fascinating in *Marbury* is the unspoken but clear linkage between the arguments made by Marshall about why Marbury had a right to the commission and why the Constitution must be viewed as paramount, fundamental law. Both aspects of *Marbury* are about the rule of law. Both are of equal importance. They must be read with equal diligence if one is to fully understand Supreme Court decision making and judicial review.

Emphasizing the last section of *Marbury,* which discusses the Constitution as fundamental law, undervalues what Marshall said about why the Supreme Court and judicial review is so central to the United States as a nation. The protection of individual rights and the securing of justice for the nation's citizens are at the core of judicial review. This has been persistent from the founding onwards. An exclusive focus on the last section of *Marbury* also understates the degree to which the Supreme Court, even in the nineteenth century, constructs the world outside the Court when it engages in the process of judicial review.

Modern Judicial Review and the Limits of *Marbury*: The Social Construction of Law

To understand the importance of *Marbury,* and its limits, as an exemplar of contemporary judicial review, we need to explore the aspects of the Court decision making found in *Marbury* that continue to this day, such as the Court's respect for precedent and application of polity and rights principles in light of practices outside the Court. We also must review the place of the norm that the Court must follow the intentions of the founders present in *Marbury*

plays in modern judicial review. Finally, we must document the nature of the social construction process in Supreme Court decision making, which has expanded with each passing decade of the twentieth century and promises to continue in the twenty-first.

Aspects of Marbury *That Continue to This Day*

Many aspects of *Marbury* continue to be important to understand modern Supreme Court decision making and judicial review. These include the Court's reliance on precedent, the need for the Court to see whether a right has been violated, and the focus on the words of the Constitution to decide whether institutional rules have been broken. Legal decision making is a process that does not simply respond to political will but determines whether polity and rights principles in the Constitution have been violated. These practices characterize judicial review under the adaptive, living Constitution, as they did under a Constitution interpreted under pre-1937 originalism.

To decide whether Marbury had a vested right to the commission, the Court had to engage in a construction process. The Constitution does not speak for itself. As in all constitutional law cases, the Court uses a construction process when applying the words of the Constitution and constitutional principles to see whether the government has abused its authority. Marbury was being denied the commission to which he was appointed because the Jefferson administration failed to formally deliver the commission. The Court had to construct the nature of each act in relation to the words in the Constitution, notions of rule of law, and common-law principles and precedents. The Court had to decide the constitutional significance through constructing the process by which Congress created the position, the president nominated a candidate for the position, the Senate gave its consent, the secretary of state placed his seal on the commission, and the administration delivered the commission. The Court had to interpret the Constitution to determine whether the Supreme Court or electorally based institutions have the final authority to interpret the Constitution when disputes arise. These constructions and the changes in the way polity and rights principles are envisioned in a case such as *Marbury* become part of the precedential basis of constitutional law. *Marbury* provides a precedential basis for the concept of executive privilege, the notion that some presidential actions are not subject to either judicial or legislative scrutiny.

The Intention of the Founders in Modern Judicial Review

Although the decision-making process has changed little, interpretive modes have changed a great deal from an age of traditional originalism to an age of nonoriginalism. The Constitution is not now interpreted according to what the framers meant by every word in the text. The Constitution is read in its entirety, rather than line by line or clause by clause. The Constitution is read as a set of principles to be applied, not as a document that must mirror the policies that the framers in 1787 or the drafters of the Civil War Amendments in the 1860s would have approved. This does not mean that what the words of the Constitution meant at their writing is of no importance to contempo-

rary judicial review. The words and open-ended phrases of the Constitution are now viewed as constituting principles, which take more complex forms with each passing decade.

Griswold v. Connecticut (1965) is a clear-cut example of nonoriginalist review. The Supreme Court in that case interpreted the word liberty in the due process clause of the Fourteenth Amendment to include a right to privacy in the Constitution. A Connecticut law denying married couples the right to use contraceptives violated this unenumerated constitutional freedom. The members of the *Griswold* majority found the right to privacy in early- and middle-twentieth-century precedents that detailed such peripheral rights necessary to protect rights explicitly set out in the Bill of Rights. The Court noted precedents in which previous Courts said the right to associate and the right of parents to educate their children as they wish were necessary to ensure the freedom to speak under the First Amendment. The Court invoked the Ninth Amendment for the proposition that citizens have fundamental rights other than those spelled out in the Bill of Rights. Finally, the *Griswold* Court viewed the limitation on the use of contraceptives by married persons as a denial of the equal protection clause of the Fourteenth Amendment because Connecticut had allowed for the sale and use of contraceptives for all citizens for disease control.

The Social Construction Process in Modern Judicial Review

The second major aspect of a living, adaptive Constitution central to modern constitutional interpretation is an exponential growth in the importance of the construction process and the breadth of the social, economic, and political factors that inform the construction process. *Marbury* falls short as a model for contemporary judicial review. The construction process in 1803 was far more limited than would be the case after 1937. With each new decade, the degree to which the construction process in *Marbury* fails to mirror judicial review grows. This is so because it can be argued that the nation has become more complex socially, politically, and economically. The interdependence of such factors is more and more evident to scholars, to the interpretive community, and to the general public. In modern judicial review, the construction process becomes more central to Supreme Court decision making. Only the most conservative contemporary originalist justices reject the place of an expansive construction process.

The concept of a living, adaptive, and evolving Constitution provides a conceptual lift to rights discussed by the Court before 1937, such as the preferred freedoms under the First Amendment. The principle that the equal protection clause protects discrete and insular minorities from the majority, enunciated in 1938, increases the application of the equal protection clause as a basis to scrutinize race and gender classifications in the law. The Constitution is interpreted as protecting discrete and insular minorities against majority will because prejudice limits the capacity of normal political processes to redress constitutional wrongs.[4] This becomes a key constitutional basis for judicial review in the 1950s, 1960s, and 1970s.

The change from a judicial review under traditional originalism to nonoriginalism was not simply a change from the intentions of the framers and the words of the Constitution to a Constitution of principles, broadly interpreted. Modern nonoriginalist interpretation is a process through which the outside social, political, and economic world is brought into Supreme Court decision making through a complex, expanded construction process. This process grows in significance as the principles in the Constitution are defined in more complex ways by contemporary constitutional theory and the interdependencies between social, political, and economic facts of life grow and become known. The growth of these complexities changes notions of what constitutes those state actions that require judicial review to ensure rights are honored. With the growth in the notion of interdependency between government action and individual action, the scope of actions attributed exclusively to individuals is reduced. The need for rights against intrusion by government grows, as the ability of citizens to be left alone decreases with technology.

The Constitution after 1937 was not simply viewed as words and phrases interpreted in line with the intentions of the framers. The Constitution included the general principles envisioned by the framers, not their specific intentions. After 1937 the Court asked what constitutional principles were violated rather than whether the Constitution grants a specific enumerated power or prohibition.

The Social Construction Process and Supreme Court Overturning of Landmark Cases

The joint opinion by Justices Sandra Day O'Connor, Anthony Kennedy, and David Souter in *Planned Parenthood of Southeastern*

Pennsylvania v. Casey (1992) highlights the centrality of the social construction process in contemporary Supreme Court decision making. In that opinion, these justices explained why the right of abortion choice established in *Roe v. Wade* (1973) should not be abandoned, even though the justices in *West Coast Hotel v. Parrish* (1937) overturned *Lochner*-era principles and in *Brown v. Board of Education* (1954) abandoned the state-mandated segregation sustained in *Plessy v. Ferguson* (1896). Contemporary justices, whether they are conservative, moderate, liberal, or originalist, engage in social construction when they decide cases. They differ in the breadth and interdependence of social, political, and economic factors considered when applying constitutional principles. A major difference between the conservative, moderate, and liberal justices in the majority in *Casey* and the justices in dissent is that the dissenters reject the social construction process by which *Roe* was decided. The majority in *Casey* determined that the right to abortion choice was an even more fundamental right in 1992, nineteen years later.

O'Connor, Kennedy, and Souter explained in detail why the principles that justify not overruling *Roe* are consistent with the decision in *West Coast Hotel* to overturn *Adkins v. Children's Hospital* (1923), a case in which a minimum-wage law for women was declared unconstitutional, and the decision in *Brown* to overturn *Plessy*. They asked whether these cases are of "comparable dimension" to *Roe* in "that [they] have responded to national controversies and taken the impress of the controversies addressed" (*Casey* 1992, 861).

The *Casey* joint opinion asserts that at the core of *Adkins* were "fundamentally false fac-

tual assumptions" (*Casey* 1992, 861). The justices in the joint opinion observed that in between *Adkins* and *West Coast Hotel*,

[T]he Depression had come and, with it, the lesson that seemed unmistakable to most people by 1937, that the interpretation of contractual freedom protected in *Adkins* rested on fundamentally false factual assumptions about the capacity of a relatively unregulated market to satisfy minimal levels of human welfare. . . . The facts upon which the earlier case had premised a constitutional resolution of social controversy had proven to be untrue, and history's demonstration of their untruth not only justified but required the new choice of constitutional principle that *West Coast Hotel* announced. (*Casey* 1992, 861–862)

The justices in *Casey* ruefully noted that belated recognition of these social changes harmed the Court's reputation. They noted that the Court's ultimate decision to overrule a line of earlier precedent cost some authority. Nevertheless, they concluded, "[T]he clear demonstration that the facts of economic life were different from those previously assumed warranted the repudiation of the old law" (*Casey* 1992, 862).

The justices writing the joint opinion argued that the Supreme Court in *Brown* "repudiated" the "understanding of the facts and the rule" (*Casey* 1992, 862–863) in *Plessy*. O'Connor, Souter, and Kennedy maintained that the *Plessy* Court rejected the plaintiff's argument "that the enforced separation of the two races stamps the colored race with a badge of inferiority." Justice Henry Brown's infamous opinion declared, "[I]f this be so, it is not by reason of anything found in the act, but solely because the colored race chooses to put that construction upon it" (*Plessy* 1896, 551, as cited in *Casey* 1992, 892). The *Casey* plurality questioned the sincerity of the justices who had made this argument in *Plessy*. Sincere or not, the argument was the foundation of *Plessy*. The facts that underlay that judgment, the *Casey* plurality stated, were expressly repudiated in *Brown*. In *Brown*, the *Casey* plurality observed, the Court rejected the *Plessy* reasoning "on the ground of history and of common knowledge about the facts of life" surrounding the segregation at issue in the case. As the *Casey* justices put it,

The Court in *Brown* addressed these facts of life by observing that whatever may have been the understanding in *Plessy*'s time of the power of segregation to stigmatize those who were segregated with a "badge of inferiority," it was clear by 1954 that legally sanctioned segregation had just such an effect, to the point that racially separate public educational facilities were deemed inherently unequal. Society's understanding of the facts upon which a constitutional ruling was sought in 1954 was thus fundamentally different from the basis claimed for the decision in 1896. While we think *Plessy* was wrong the day it was decided, we must also recognize that the *Plessy* Court's explanation for its decision was so clearly at odds with the facts apparent to the Court in 1954 that the decision to reexamine *Plessy* was, on this ground alone, not only justified but required. (*Casey* 1992, 862–863)

In an extraordinary statement about the importance of social constructions to the Court's making of constitutional law, these moderate and conservative justices make clear that *Plessy* was not just wrong in terms of the rights principles enunciated; *Plessy*, they illustrated, was wrong in terms of its construction of social facts about the nature of the "badge of inferiority" caused by segregation of the races.

Emphasizing what they saw as parallels between the landmark anti-*Lochner* and anti–Jim Crow (*Casey* 1992, 863) decisions, the *Casey* justices wrote, "*West Coast Hotel* and *Brown*

each rested on facts, or an understanding of facts, changed from those which furnished the claimed justifications for the earlier constitutional resolutions." "Each case was comprehensible," they added, "as the Court's response to facts that the country could understand, or had come to understand already, but which the Court of an earlier day, as its own declarations disclosed, had not been able to perceive" (*Casey* 1992, 863). Accordingly, the decisions to repudiate longstanding legal landmarks must be understood "not merely as the victories of one doctrinal school" but as applications of constitutional principle to facts as they had not been seen by the Court before (*Casey* 1992, 864). In constitutional adjudications, as elsewhere in life, "changed circumstances [had] impose[d] new obligations, and the thoughtful part of the Nation could accept each decision to overrule a prior case as a response to the Court's constitutional duty" (*Casey* 1992, 863–864).

Decisions to overrule cases, such as the decisions in the original cases themselves, do not rest simply on rights and polity principles. They also rest on the justices' social construction of the conditions of the times as they apply those principles. The Court might be misguided about the nature of polity and rights principles. Polity or rights principles may remain constant but be applied differently over time. In these decisions we see the Supreme Court's own description of the place of social constructs in Supreme Court decisions: "[C]hanged circumstances may impose new obligations" (*Casey* 1992, 864).

These insights about changing circumstances buttress the holding in *Casey*. The plurality opinion finds that "neither the factual underpinnings of *Roe*'s central holding nor our understanding of it has changed. . . ." They "could not pretend to be reexamining the prior law with any justification beyond a present doctrinal disposition to come out differently from the Court of 1973." "[A] decision to overrule," the justices declared, "should rest on some special reason over and above the belief that a prior case was wrongly decided" (*Casey* 1992, 864). They found no such reason in *Casey*.

To overrule a decision without this "special reason" would come at a serious cost to the Court's legitimacy. Overruling "would seriously weaken the Court's capacity to exercise the judicial power and to function as the Supreme Court of a Nation dedicated to the rule of law" (*Casey* 1992, 865). "The underlying substance of this legitimacy is . . . the warrant for the Court's decisions in the Constitution and the lesser sources of legal principle" (*Casey* 1992, 864). That substance is expressed in the Court's opinions, and our contemporary understanding is such that a decision without principled justification would be no judicial act at all. But even when justification is furnished by apposite legal principle, something more is required. Because not every conscientious claim of principled justification will be accepted as such, the justification claimed must be beyond dispute. The Court must take care to speak and act in ways that allow people to accept its decisions on the terms the Court claims for them, as grounded truly in principle, not as compromises with social and political pressures having, as such, no bearing on the principled choices that the Court is obliged to make. Thus, the Court's legitimacy depends on making legally principled decisions under cir-

cumstances in which their principled character is sufficiently plausible to be accepted by the nation (*Casey* 1992, 865–866).

The justices asked under what circumstances the Supreme Court would "fail to receive the benefit of the doubt in overruling prior cases" (*Casey* 1992, 866). The first circumstance, the justices wrote, is if the Court overruled cases very often. That is "hypothetical." Overrulings are rare. The second is when "the Court decides a case in such a way as to resolve the sort of intensely divisive controversy reflected in *Roe* . . ." (*Casey* 1992, 866). "[W]henever the Court's interpretation of the Constitution calls the contending sides of a national controversy to end their national division by accepting a common mandate rooted in the Constitution," the Court must ensure that judicial decisions are not perceived as giving into political pressure if the Court wants to sustain its legitimacy. The burden of proof is on overturning. "The Court is not asked to do this very often," the *Casey* justices added, "having thus addressed the Nation only twice in our lifetime, in the decisions of *Brown* and *Roe*. But when the Court does act in this way . . . its decision requires an equally rare precedential force to counter the inevitable efforts to overturn it and to thwart its implementation" (*Casey* 1992, 867). The plurality justices continued,

[S]ome of those efforts may be mere unprincipled emotional reactions; others may proceed from principles worthy of profound respect. But whatever the premises of opposition may be, only the most convincing justification under accepted standards of precedent could suffice to demonstrate that a later decision overruling the first was anything but a surrender to political pressure and an unjustified repudiation of the principle on which the Court staked its authority in the first instance. So to overrule under fire in the absence of the most compelling reason to reexamine a watershed decision would subvert the Court's legitimacy beyond any serious question. (*Casey* 1992, 867)

The Court concluded its discussion of the principles used when deciding whether to overturn a controversial landmark decision by writing,

The Court's duty in the present cases is clear. In 1973, it confronted the already-divisive issue of governmental power to limit personal choice to undergo abortion, for which it provided a new resolution based on the due process guaranteed by the Fourteenth Amendment. Whether or not a new social consensus is developing on that issue, its divisiveness is no less today than in 1973, and pressure to overrule the decision, like pressure to retain it, has grown only more intense. A decision to overrule *Roe's* essential holding under the existing circumstances would address error, if error there was, at the cost of both profound and unnecessary damage to the Court's legitimacy, and to the Nation's commitment to the rule of law. It is therefore imperative to adhere to the essence of *Roe's* original decision, and we do so today. (*Casey* 1992, 868–869)

Rights principles central to *Roe* had become even more clearly defined. The concept of privacy found in *Roe* has become a right to "personhood." The factual underpinnings for protecting the privacy of women when deciding whether to abort a fetus strengthened between 1973 and 1992. *Roe* could be overturned only on the ground that the case was wrongly decided, not on a determination that factual premises of that decision had become incorrect over time.

As did *Marbury, Casey* provides evidence that the Court is viewed as legitimate only when the justices make principled decisions. What has changed since *Marbury* is the presence of more open-ended concepts of implied fundamental rights and the importance of what those rights mean through the process of social construction. In *Casey* the Court found that the place of women in the political, social, and economic system has changed substantially. Women's liberty would be even more limited in 1992 than in 1973 should the right of abortion be denied. After 1973, expectations increased that abortion would be available should contraception fail. The right to privacy and the right to abortion choice have expanded since 1973 to apply to unmarried women. Through the social construction of that right, not simply in reference to principles, the Court expanded the right of abortion choice. Moreover, the Court argued that the right to abortion choice is not simply the right to a loosely applied *Griswold* concept of privacy. Instead, the Court in *Casey* wrote in terms of a woman's right to personhood.

One can see the use of social constructions about the nature of the relationship between men and women, and parents and daughters, with regard to abortion choice in the parts of *Casey* where the Court decided whether spousal notification, waiting periods, and parental notification are constitutional. The Court viewed the liberty interests of women most at risk when states are allowed to require spousal notification. This conclusion is based on evidence that such notifications have been flashpoints for domestic violence. The plurality opinion concluded that parental notification, with a judicial bypass and a twenty-four-hour waiting period, do not unduly burden the right of a woman to choose an abortion.

These social constructs play key roles in constitutive Supreme Court decision making. The development of social constructs, when they fit with change in the world outside, add legitimacy to Court decision making among the interpretive community and wider public. When the social construct in a doctrinal area is so out of kilter with social, political, and economic structures, the doctrine is ripe for overturning. The best way to see the role of social constructs in the development of constitutional law is by comparing social constructs within doctrinal areas.

The primary objective of empirical interpretivists is to be empirical; it is not to evaluate which social constructs are good or bad. A key objective is to identify social constructs in key doctrinal areas of constitutional law and to determine what patterns of social construction lead the Court to support or overturn landmark decisions. Once these patterns are identified and compared across doctrinal areas, normative implications may be explored. One can then gain a more precise understanding of the role of constitutional theory in influencing the development of constitutional law.

Conclusion

In *Marbury* we see a construction process, important to the case but of more limited breadth than is found in modern judicial review. The most important change in judicial review since *Marbury* is the expansion of the construction process to look at a far wider set of social, economic, and political facts. Social constructs occur within doctrinal areas and help justices make sense of how they should view a doctrinal issue in a new case. Because new cases come at later times in history, nonoriginalist justices must look at the social constructs of earlier cases in light of new social, economic, and political facts.

Justices and judges are neither simply doctrinal nor logical in the application of principles. They ask how this case is similar or different from earlier cases while still supporting a strong notion of a rule of law in a constitutive decision-making process. The justices in *Brown* abandoned the civil–social distinction in *Plessy* that justified state-mandated segregation in general and state-mandated school segregation in particular.

Brown gets its moral force from a social construct that offers a clearer definition of the state's role in the development of citizens. In a broad sense, social constructs are drawn from a linking of fundamental rights and polity principles in the Constitution to recognized social, economic, and political structural inequalities. These external practices redefined polity and rights principles, which in turn modified or reconstructed social constructs. *Brown* gets its moral force from the distinction between sociological, economic, or political facts as simple facts and the concept of social constructs.

Social constructs include various social "facts" about the structural inequalities. In *Plessy* blacks were deemed responsible for the feelings of inferiority generated by government-enforced segregation of races. In *Brown*, that social construct is no longer valid, not simply because the role of education has changed but because equal protection is no longer possible for blacks when the tasks of being a citizen in a changing society require public education.

By centering on social constructions in precedents and lines of cases, we move beyond the idea of social facts as reality and the use of facts in one case at a time. We study the progression from a social construction in a case to a social construction that becomes central to a doctrinal area. As in *Marbury*, the construction process is a key element in a constitutive preference formation process central to Supreme Court decision making since the birth of the nation. In *Marbury*, Marshall was wide-ranging in the construction process for his age. With the development of the "living Constitution" in the twentieth century, the construction process has dramatically changed. With this change the social, economic, and political world outside the Supreme Court is brought into its decision making in a far more expansive way. The polity and rights principles in the Constitution continue to have resonance and legitimacy today in the far more complex society in which we live. When social constructions are so out of kilter with the social, political, and economic structures that affect the lives of citizens, landmark cases are ripe for overturning.

Bibliography

Ackerman, Bruce. *We the People. Vol. 1. Foundations.* Cambridge: Harvard University Press, 1991.

Adamany, David. "Legitimacy, Realigning Election, and the Supreme Court." *Wisconsin Law Review* (1973): 790–845.

Chafee, Jr., Zechariah. *Freedom of Speech.* New York: Harcourt, Brace and Howe, 1920.

_____. *Free Speech in the United States.* Cambridge: Harvard University Press, 1941.

Corwin, Edward. *The Twilight of the Supreme Court.* New Haven: Yale University Press, 1934.

Cushman, Barry. *Rethinking the New Deal Court: The Structure of a Constitutional Revolution.* New York: Oxford University Press, 1998.

Dahl, Robert. "Decision-making in a Democracy: The Supreme Court as a National Policy-Maker." *Journal of Public Law* 6 (fall 1957): 279–295.

Epp, Charles. *The Rights Revolution: Lawyers, Activists, and Supreme Courts in Comparative Perspective.* Chicago: University of Chicago Press, 1998.

Epstein, Lee, and Gary King. "Rules of Inference." *The University of Chicago Law Review* 69 (winter 2002): 1–133.

Epstein, Lee, and Joseph F. Kobylka. *The Supreme Court and Legal Change: Abortion and the Death Penalty.* Chapel Hill: University of North Carolina Press, 1992.

Funston, Richard Y. "The Supreme Court and Critical Elections." *American Political Science Review* 69 (1975): 795–811.

Gillman, Howard. "The Collapse of Constitutional Originalism and the Rise of the Notion of a 'Living Constitution' in the Course of American State-Building." *Studies in American Political Development* 11 (fall 1997): 191–247.

_____. *The Constitution Besieged.* Durham: Duke University Press, 1993.

Graber, Mark A. "The Non-majoritarian Difficulty: Legislative Deference to the Judiciary." *Studies in American Political Development* 7 (1993): 35–73.

Gustafson, Thomas. *Representative Words: Politics, Literature, and the American Language, 1776–1865.* Cambridge: Cambridge University Press, 1992.

Halpern, Stephen C. *On the Limits of the Law.* Baltimore: Johns Hopkins University Press, 1995.

Kahn, Ronald. *The Supreme Court and Constitutional Theory, 1953–1993.* Lawrence: University Press of Kansas, 1994.

Kammen, Michael. *A Machine That Would Not Go of Itself: The Constitution in American Culture.* New York: Knopf, 1986.

McCloskey, Robert G. *The American Supreme Court.* 3d ed., rev. Edited by Sanford Levinson. Chicago: University of Chicago Press, 2000.

Perry, Michael J. *Morality, Politics and Law.* New York: Oxford University Press, 1988.

Rosenberg, Gerald. *The Hollow Hope: Can Courts Bring about Social Change?* Chicago: University of Chicago Press, 1991.

Story, Joseph. *Commentaries on the Constitution of the United States.* Boston: Hilliard, Gray, 1833.

Sumner, William Graham. *Social Darwinism: Selected Essays.* Englewood Cliffs, N.J.: Prentice-Hall, 1963.

Tiedeman, Christopher Gustavus. *The Unwritten Constitution of the United States: A Philosophical Inquiry Into the Fundamentals of American Constitutional Law.* New York. G. P. Putnam's Sons, 1890.

Ward, Lester Frank. *Pure Sociology: A Treatise on the Origin and Spontaneous Development of Society.* New York: Macmillan, 1903.

White, Edward G. *The Constitution and the New Deal.* Cambridge: Harvard University Press, 2001.

Whittington, Keith. *Constitutional Construction.* Cambridge: Harvard University Press, 1999.

————. "Review Essay: Once More unto the Breach: Post-Behavioralist Approaches to Judicial Politics." *Law and Social Inquiry* 25 (2000): 601–632.

Notes

1. See Epstein and King (2002, 1–133) and responding articles for a spirited debate on the quality of empirical analysis in law reviews.
2. Article V of the Constitution:

   The Congress, whenever two thirds of both Houses shall deem it necessary, shall propose Amendments to this Constitution, or, on the Application of the Legislatures of two thirds of the several States, shall call a Convention for proposing Amendments, which, in either Case, shall be valid to all Intents and Purposes, as part of this Constitution, when ratified by the Legislatures of three fourths of the several States, or by Conventions in three fourths thereof, as the one or the other Mode of Ratification may be proposed by the Congress; Provided that no Amendment which may be made prior to the Year One thousand eight hundred and eight shall in any manner affect the first and fourth Clauses in the Ninth Section of the First Article; and that no State, without its Consent, shall be deprived of its equal Suffrage in the Senate.

3. These might include decisions by the president as to whether to recognize a foreign government, dispatch troops to a foreign land, determine the make-up of the budget that he sends to Congress, or choose who are to be members of his personal staff in the White House.
4. Also, the principle that the equal protection clause protects discrete and insular minorities was first enunciated in the most famous footnote in Supreme Court history, footnote 4 of Chief Justice Stone's majority opinion in *United States v. Carolene Products Co.* (1938).

9 Judicial Power and Popular Sovereignty

JEREMY WALDRON

When the Supreme Court in *Marbury v. Madison* (1803) set out its answer to the question "whether an act, repugnant to the constitution, can become the law of the land," Chief Justice John Marshall began from the following premise, which I shall call the principle of *popular sovereignty*: "[T]he people have an original right to establish, for their future government, such principles as, in their opinion, shall most conduce to their own happiness. . ." (*Marbury* 1803, 176). What is the relationship between this principle and the power that the Court said was vested in the judiciary—the power to interpret the Constitution and to strike down legislation at odds with the Constitution as it interprets it? In this chapter, I would like to investigate various understandings of judicial review in light of the principle of popular sovereignty. I am interested particularly in what commentators refer to as "judicial supremacy"—the idea that the courts have a privileged position in the constitutional scheme and that other branches of government should always defer to the courts' interpretations of the Constitution, even when their interpreta-

tions are controversial and even when they implicate important issues of national policy. I shall argue that judicial supremacy sits ill with the American commitment to popular sovereignty and sometimes comes dangerously close to a mythic identification of the Supreme Court with the sovereign entity—the people—who are supposed to be the source of all constitutional authority.

The argument I shall make is not intended as a repetition of the familiar democratic case against judicial review. What Alexander Bickel (1986, 16) referred to, delicately but misleadingly, as "the counter-majoritarian difficulty" remains one of the central points of debate in American constitutional theory, but it is not my subject here. Democracy is not the same as popular sovereignty, and the tension I see between popular sovereignty and judicial supremacy is independent of—though it nicely complements—the arguments we hear every day about the affront to democracy in allowing a measure passed by an elected legislature to be struck down by a handful of unelected and unaccountable judges. I have argued elsewhere

An earlier version of this chapter was presented as a James Madison Lecture at Princeton University in December 2000. I am grateful to George Kateb, Henry Monaghan, and Robert George for comments on that earlier version.

(Waldron 1999) that when a community is divided about whether a legislative measure infringes fundamental rights, the matter should be settled by deliberation and majority voting among the people or their representatives and not by deliberation and majority voting among nine unelected justices. In this chapter, I will suspend that attack. Accepting the legitimacy of judicial review (for the sake of argument), I want to ask whether a particular form of that practice—a form pervaded by assertions of and deference to judicial supremacy—can be reconciled with the popular-sovereignty foundations of American constitutionalism.

Popular Sovereignty in Political Theory

Popular sovereignty is not the same as democracy. A legislature is democratic when it comprises representatives chosen in regular elections on the basis of universal suffrage and when its members legislate on the basis of majority voting among themselves. The executive is democratic when it is staffed at the highest level by individuals elected on the basis of universal suffrage. In both branches, democratic elections are a means whereby citizens acting together can exercise fair control over the policies pursued in their society. In some countries, political institutions do not have these characteristics. Executive power may be in the hands of a hereditary monarch or it may be seized and exercised by a military strongman; and laws may be enacted by decree or by a chamber of legislators appointed on some nonelective basis. We fancy that these alternatives are widely discredited these days and that in all but a few cases nondemocratic institutions are temporary

expedients or relics destined for overthrow and replacement. Still, acceptance of this optimistic view does not mean the end of controversy about forms of government. Democratic forms admit of innumerable variations, and among these variations there is considerable contestation as to which are "more authentically democratic." Even the institutional characteristics that everyone agrees are important for democracy are all matters of degree: frequency of elections, size of constituencies, exact extent of the suffrage, and so on. To establish a system of government is to make choices along all of these dimensions, taking sides in various controversies about the detail of political arrangements.

The principle of popular sovereignty requires that the most important of these choices be made *by the people*. We may hope that they will choose democracy. But even if a nondemocratic form of government or a compromised or limited version of democracy is chosen, it is possible that such choice can be attributed to the people and made legitimate on that basis. No doubt suspicion will attach to the claim that such a nondemocratic constitution is legitimized by popular choice. Although democracy cannot be inferred from the principle of popular sovereignty, there are important continuities between them. Popular sovereignty betokens a recognition of some level of political competence among the people, and that surely belies certain rationales for their exclusion from ordinary politics. (If they can be trusted with something as important as the choice of a constitution, why can they not be trusted with the choice of representatives?) We know, moreover, that power holders will almost always *claim* legitimacy on the basis of popular sovereignty even when such claims are preposterous.

Still, the combination of popular sovereignty and nondemocratic institutions is not out of the question. The point is illustrated vividly in the mythology of political theory. The great philosophers of the social contract all imagined that the people might choose to vest lawmaking authority or executive authority (or both) in a monarch. Thomas Hobbes (1651/1983) argued that that would be the most prudent option (though he acknowledged the impossibility of demonstrating the point). John Locke (1689/1988, 329–330, 354–356) may have thought it more sensible to establish a large representative body as a legislature, but he too wrote that this was ultimately a matter for the people not the theorist and that the legislature was "sacred and inalterable in the hands where the Community have once placed it" (1689/1988, 356). Even Jean-Jacques Rousseau (1762/1997, 89–99), who balked at the idea of the most fundamental laws being enacted otherwise than by *la volonté générale* (the general will) believed that it was perfectly sensible for the people to establish a nondemocratic form of administration. There are all sorts of respectable reasons why nondemocratic forms might be chosen. People may have less time, energy, and inclination to devote to day-to-day politics than participatory theories of democracy presuppose. Even if popular rule is possible, one might argue along Hobbesian lines (Hobbes 1651/1983, 136–138; see also Waldron 1999, 52) that nevertheless monarchies are more stable, less turbulent, and more efficient than democracies.

Though respect for popular sovereignty is compatible with all sorts of constitutional choices, it is by no means true that every system of government is legitimized by the principle. Even a democracy may be set up on a basis that is not legitimized by popular sovereignty: A country's democratic institutions may represent unilateral concessions made by its king, or a departing colonial power may impose a democratic constitution (as the British did in regard to their former possessions in Africa). Though the revolutionary generation in America looked back to Greece and Rome as exemplars of the sort of foundation they were contemplating (Arendt 1977, 196), they were well aware that the constitutions of many of the ancient republics were supposed to have been established by great lawgivers, like Solon or Lycurgus, rather than by an exercise of popular choice: "What degree of agency these reputed lawgivers might have in their respective establishments, or how far they might be clothed with the legitimate authority of the people, cannot in every instance be ascertained" (Hamilton, Madison, and Jay 1787–1788/1987, 248). The ambiguous character of "the lawgiver" in Rousseau's *Social Contract* (1762/1997, 68–73) is a tribute to the doubts that are felt on this matter even by the most fervent partisan of popular sovereignty, even in his most utopian work.

Popular Sovereignty and Real-World Politics

What happens when we turn from political mythology to political reality, from the neat but fictional chronology of the social contract story—individuals get together to form a people; the people choose a constitution; their rulers govern them under that constitution—to the messy processes of real-world constitutional formation? Can a distinction between popular sovereignty and political democracy still be sustained?

The question is complicated by two aspects of the theory of popular sovereignty. First, it is part of the theory that popular sovereignty should be an infrequently exercised power. Though Chief Justice Marshall said the people have an original right to constitute their polity as they see fit, he acknowledged that because "[t]he exercise of this original right is a very great exertion," it cannot "nor ought it to be frequently repeated" (*Marbury* 1803, 176). That sounds as though the people have to go rest for a generation or two after each exercise, lest they tire themselves out. But the real reason is not ergonomic. The exercise of popular sovereignty is supposed to create a set of institutions that are capable of housing the ordinary operations of government on an indefinite basis. We should surely treat as a failure a constitution that required regular wholesale revision to suit the different conceptions of each generation. Of course it is never enough to satisfy the principle of popular sovereignty that the people are governed under a constitution that was acceptable to their ancestors. Each generation has its rights. The point about durability has to be driven in the other direction. An exercise of popular sovereignty by any generation is futile unless conditions are such, and the constitution established by the founding generation is such, that their descendants will rest largely content with it for a generation or two. If the founding generation does not establish something that is really acceptable to later generations—even if that real acceptance is expressed only tacitly—then it will have failed (Arendt 1977, 197–205). Now, assuming we accept this, we have to acknowledge an

unavoidable real-world difficulty in saying that a long-established constitution is or is not legitimate in terms of popular sovereignty at any particular time. We cannot require an explicit affirmation by the people; we must expect a healthy constitution to rest for a long period on a foundation of *tacit* popular support. But it is also true that a constitution opposed by the people may remain in existence because those who would otherwise rise up to change it are cowed or coerced into silence. Accordingly, the truth of the proposition that a constitution enjoys tacit popular support is always a matter of judgment—a matter of how one reads the quiescence of the people in regard to existing constitutional arrangements.

Suppose, on the other hand, that a constitution changes over time. How in the real world are we to distinguish changes that result from genuine exercises of popular sovereignty from changes that represent the usurpation of the rights of the people by a faction of power holders in the society? In this instance the problem derives from the logic of popular sovereignty. Although institutional provision may be made for its occasional action, the popular sovereign always reserves the right to break the bounds of that provision and to exercise itself in a less orderly and formalized manner. This is not a matter of the inherent unruliness of the people. It is a reflection of the basic difference between what is regarded as the active constituting power in the society (*le pouvoir constituant* in the language of European constitutionalism) and the forms and institutions that that power has constituted (*les pouvoirs constitués*). Now a formal procedure for constitutional amendment like the one set out in Article V of the U.S. Constitution may be intended to cabin the exercise of popular sovereignty subsequent to 1787. But its status is still that of *un pouvoir constitué*. It is something that the primal constitutive power has wrought, rather than something that defines what the primal constitutive power now amounts to. Remember that popular sovereignty is not just a convenient fiction; it is supposed to provide a convincing answer to the question of the legitimacy of the constitution, which is something it cannot do except in a question-begging way if its own nature and exercise is pinned down entirely to a particular constitutionally defined structure. Once again there is an interpretive problem. The tendency of *le pouvoir constituant* to break its constitutional bounds makes it much harder to discern when popular sovereignty has been exercised and when it has not. If it were just a matter of ascertaining whether the Article V procedure had been followed, things would be straightforward enough. But once we admit the possibility that popular sovereignty may be exercised in undefined ways, it becomes a matter of political judgment to say that certain events amount or do not amount to its exercise.

The Sièyes Principles

The previous section mentioned the distinction, familiar to European constitutionalists, between the entity by whose authority the constitution of a society is set up and amended (*le pouvoir constituant*) and the institutions whose authority is constituted by that entity (*les pouvoirs constitués*). In the theory of popular sovereignty, *le pouvoir constituant* is the people and *les pouvoirs constitués* include the familiar branches of government: the legislative institutions, the executive and its agencies, and the courts. The relationship between the two types of power is obviously very important for the integrity of a constitutional regime. Those who inhabit *les pouvoirs constitués* must understand that theirs are subordinate powers—subordinate to the constitutive power that set them up—and that they are limited by the terms of the constitution in what they do and what they can claim for themselves. They must respect the people as *le pouvoir constituant* and not try to imitate or supplant its sovereignty.

L'Abbé Emmanuel Joseph Sièyes, "the great constitutional architect of revolutionary France" (McCormick 1997, 243, quoting Carl Schmitt), is one of the earliest theorists of the relationship between *le pouvoir constituant* and *les pouvoirs constitués*. In his pamphlet, *What Is the Third Estate?*, Sièyes (1788/1964, 133) identified the French people as a whole with the sovereign that was entitled to give France a constitution. As a sovereign nation, the people are supposed to make a constitution to structure and limit the powers they set up for their governance. But they do not constitute *themselves*, by which Sièyes (1788/1964, 125–126) meant that they are not to subject their own power to a constituted form: "It would be ridiculous to suppose that the nation itself could be constricted by the procedures or the constitution to which it had subjected its mandatories" (125–126).

The proposition that the constitutive power of the popular sovereign defies constitution and may be exercised in any manner and through any channels that the people choose, I shall call *the positive Sièyes principle*. It has inspired a number of political thinkers, most notably the German theorist Carl Schmitt, who took it as the basis of his theory of constitutional crisis and populist dictatorship (1928, 1933). Some (Baker 1989, 321) have described Sièyes's positive principle as inherently destabilizing; and because its most direct impact has been on the thought of one of the few reputable political theorists associated with Nazism, Carl Schmitt, it may seem inappropriate to try connecting it with American constitutional ideas (Arato 2000, 1741). But in fact something like the positive principle can be associated with the determination of the Federalists to appeal for the legitimacy of their constitution to the American people (Hamilton, Madison, and Jay 1787–1788/1987, 184), even when such an appeal was, strictly speaking, illegitimate relative to the ground rules laid down for the Constitutional Convention. In 1790 James Wilson (1967, 93) described popular sovereignty as "the vital principle" of American government. "[T]he supreme or sovereign power of the society," he said, "resides in the citizens at large; and . . . they always retain the right of abolishing, altering, or amending their constitution, at whatever time, and in whatever manner, they shall deem it expedient." He went on to state his position in terms that matched Sièyes's formulation more or less exactly: "As our constitutions are superior to our legislatures, so our people are superior to our constitutions" (Morgan 1988, 2881, quoting James Wilson). Sièyes's principle, or something like it, has had an impact on modern constitutional theory in the United States as well: Bruce Ackerman (1991, 40–57; 1998, 99–119), for example, in spite of his professed disdain for applying the doctrines of European thinkers to help explain American constitu-

tionalism to itself (1991, 3), is really invoking the positive principle when he insists on the importance of constitutional moments that are inherently irregular relative to existing constitutional arrangements.

Sièyes (1788/1964, 122ff) also articulated a second principle, which I shall call *the negative Sièyes principle*: A constitutional system must be ordered in such a way as to prohibit (and reduce the prospect and plausibility of) any constituted power taking on itself the mantle of *le pouvoir constituant*. The idea is that no constituted power may be identified—or identify itself—directly or indirectly with the people or claim the credentials of the popular sovereign. This is the principle I need for my argument about judicial supremacy. The point of Sièyes's negative principle is partly to vindicate the unique right of the people to speak in their capacity as popular sovereign. But it is also a matter of maintaining balance and integrity in the constitutional scheme: We want to avoid a situation in which any one institution claims a preeminent place by virtue (say) of its representative or directly elective character. Of course, if the popular sovereign has constituted a democracy, then some of *les pouvoirs constitués* will be elective or representative, and it may be tempting to say that their voice is the voice of the people. It is important to avoid this impression, according to Sièyes's negative principle, particularly if the claim goes beyond simply asserting a popular mandate for some policy or legislative program. The legislature may be representative in character, but if it speaks for the people (in relation to legislative matters), it does so only according to its constituted procedures. As Sièyes (1788/1964, 123) put it, "the Assembly of Representatives which is entrusted with the legislative power . . . exists only in the form which the nation has chosen to give it. It is nothing outside the articles of its constitution; only through its constitution can it act, conduct its proceedings and govern."

Politically, the point was a delicate one for Sièyes, for he envisaged the possibility that the popular sovereign might have to do its work through a special assembly of representatives (1788/1964, 130). Such a convention of extraordinary representatives might closely resemble a representative legislature; and precisely for that reason it was crucial to insist on the distinction. Again, this is partly an application of Sièyes's positive principle:

[A]n extraordinary representative body is different from the ordinary legislature. . . . The latter can move only according to prescribed forms and conditions. The former is not subjected to any procedure whatsoever: it meets and debates as the nation itself would do if we assumed a nation consisting of a tiny population that wanted to give its government a constitution. (1788/1964, 132)

But the negative side of the position was also important to Sièyes's political purposes in 1788. Though he was willing to concede for the sake of argument that France might have appointed as its legislature an institution ordered by estates—nobles, clergy, and others—it was unthinkable that France itself (that is, the popular sovereign) should be conceived in this way. It was therefore unthinkable, according to Sièyes, that a constitutional convention should be assembled on any other basis than the plenary representation of ordinary citizens.

The negative Sièyes principle is clearly reflected in the architecture of American constitutionalism. The framers were adamant that

from the fact that the Constitution was premised on popular sovereignty, nothing could be inferred about the popular character of its institutions. Thus Madison insisted that a republic is not the same as a democracy and that there was no reason to make a republic democratic simply because it was a people's republic (in the constitutive sense; Hamilton, Madison, and Jay 1787–1788/1987, 126). He was equally anxious to avoid any inferences in the opposite direction. From the fact that some—but not others—of the instituted branches of government were elective or representative, it was important not to infer anything about their special status in the constitutional scheme. This helps explain why Madison insisted on a form of election to the presidency that would be indirect (at best) rather than directly populist and why at least initially he thought it unwise to have direct elections to the national legislature—giving up the point (in the case of the House of Representatives) only when it became clear that the national legislature would have to compete for legitimacy with directly elected state legislatures (Morgan 1988, 167–177).

The discussion so far about the application of the negative Sièyes principle to elective institutions leads us naturally to expect that the principle's main implication for the debate about judicial review will be to undermine some of the claims that are made on behalf of legislatures. One sometimes hears it said that judicial review deprives the people of their fundamental right to govern themselves. Lincoln (1861/1991), for example, said that

if the policy of the Government upon vital questions affecting the whole people is to be irrevocably fixed by decisions of the Supreme

Court, the instant they are made in ordinary litigation between parties in personal actions, *the people* will have ceased to be their own rulers, having to that extent practically resigned their Government into the hands of that eminent tribunal [emphasis added].

But the negative Sièyes principle prohibits the identification of "the Government" in this assertion with "the people." The people are those who constitute the institutions of government; but the institutions of government are not the sovereign people, not even when they are elective and act responsively to popular opinion. Nothing equivalent to "the will of the sovereign people" emerges through ordinary legislative processes and so legislation cannot be defended against judicial attack on that basis. Indeed there is a strong case—which, as we shall see, Chief Justice Marshall made in *Marbury*—that if considerations of popular sovereignty have weight in the argument about judicial review, they weigh in favor of the practice not against it. It is surely no accident that Sièyes (1793/1939) argued in the 1790s for the institution of a constitutional jury with power to annul acts that were contrary to the Constitution.

However, the negative Sièyes principle does not apply only to elective or representative institutions. It applies to all *les pouvoirs constitués*. It applies, for instance, to the army, which in some countries and in some revolutionary situations has been known to take on the mantle of the people and to claim a unique or ultimate right to speak and act for national salvation in the name of the popular sovereign (see Finer 1962). It applies also to political parties. Certain political parties have been known to regard themselves not just as one competitor among others in electoral politics but as "the

revolutionary party"—the party whose organization, determination, and sacrifices led the nation to the possibility of liberty and a constitution in the first place. On that basis they assert a special claim to the support of the voters and special privileges in the organization of the state. Readers should not need reminding that claims of this sort have been made not only by the Bolshevik Party in Russia and by communist parties in East Asia and Central and Eastern Europe but also by revolutionary parties in our own hemisphere (by the Partido Revoluncionairo Institucional in Mexico, for example). Of course what I would like to consider in this chapter is the application of the negative Sièyes principle to the judiciary as *un pouvoir constitué*. Even if we cannot argue—against judicial review—that the legislature speaks for the people, still we may ask the following question: To what extent are the courts claiming to speak for the people (and thus violating the negative Sièyes principle) in the way they exercise their powers of judicial review? To what extent are they taking on the mantle of the people when they set up their own interpretations and repudiate interpretations of the Constitution that emanate from the other branches?

Popular Sovereignty and Judicial Review

Like any constitutional arrangement, the practice of judicial review of legislation may be made legitimate by the fact that it enjoys popular support. (I do not mean popular support for the way it is exercised; I mean popular support for the very existence of the power.) It is not implausible to suppose that judicial review of legislation in the United States falls into this category, despite widespread grumbling about activist judges and so forth. Like everything else about popular sovereignty, this is a matter of interpretation; but as far as one can tell the American people seem to value the arrangement, and I suspect that most of them would be very uneasy if the legislative authority of either Congress or the state assemblies were made unreviewable. The fact that the practice of judicial review enjoys this level of popular support does not of course dispose of the democratic objection that I mentioned earlier. Once again, popular sovereignty is not the same as democracy. We know that the people are capable of giving genuine endorsement to undemocratic constitutional arrangements, and such arrangements do not become democratic merely because they enjoy popular support (Waldron 1999, 255–257). What we should say is that the fact that something is democratic or undemocratic might be a reason for the sovereign people to give or withhold their endorsement. Those (like me) who argue against judicial review on the grounds that it is undemocratic are best read as trying to persuade the people to withdraw their support from the practice for this reason.

There is also a more direct route from popular sovereignty to judicial review. In *Marbury,* the Supreme Court argued that judicial review of legislation is necessary to give effect to the people's constitutional choices. The "original and supreme will" of the American people, said Chief Justice Marshall, has structured a form of government, assigned powers to its various branches, and, most important, established certain limits on the exercise of those powers (*Marbury* 1803, 176). These limits are to be taken as seriously as any other aspect of the constitutional scheme, and taking them seriously means they must be regarded as controlling any legislative act repugnant to them. Like the rest of the Constitution, the limits on legislative power are to be treated by all the branches of the government as *law* and (by the logic of limited government) as law that prevails over ordinary legislation. Accordingly, Marshall argued, when a legislative measure is challenged in court on constitutional grounds, the court has no choice but to review it, to consider whether it is repugnant to the limits that the Constitution imposes, and, if it is, to deny any effect to it as law. To refuse to do this, to refuse to countenance a challenge to the constitutionality of a legislative measure, to refuse to consider whether the Constitution prohibits the passage of a measure of this kind, or to give effect to the measure notwithstanding the Court's perception that it is repugnant to the Constitution would be to reduce the constitutional scheme and the expression of popular will that it embodies to nothing.

I think this is the best interpretation of the case made by Marshall. I can imagine though that someone might offer a more modest reconstruction that gave popular sovereignty a less prominent place as a premise. Although the principle of popular sovereignty is presented initially as a premise of Chief Justice Marshall's argument, most of his argument proceeds on the basis of the importance of a written constitution. That the Constitution is written, said Marshall, is "what we have deemed the greatest improvement on political institutions" (*Marbury* 1803, 178).

Certainly all those who have framed written constitutions contemplate them as forming the fundamental and paramount law of the nation, and consequently the theory of every such government must be, that an act of the legislature repugnant to the constitution is void. This theory is essentially attached to a written constitution, and is consequently to be considered by this court as one of the fundamental principles of our society. (*Marbury* 1803, 177)

However, it would be uncharitable to make the fact that the material is *written,* in and of itself, the key to the argument. Had the country been granted a written constitution by Great Britain (in the way the United Kingdom assigned written constitutions to some of its former colonies in the 1960s), there might have been a formalistic argument for judicial review along the lines just intimated. But the argument would have had none of the force that Marshall assigned to it. It is not merely the fact that the American people have found themselves with a piece of parchment imposing limits on the powers assigned to various agencies of government that led Marshall to regard those limits as forming part of "the fundamental and paramount law of the nation" (*Marbury* 1803, 177). It is the fact that the document in question is the expression of a solemn exercise of will by the American people themselves, an exercise of their "original right to establish, for their future government, such principles as, in their opinion, shall most conduce to their own happiness" (*Marbury* 1803, 176). Marshall perhaps made a plausible case that the element of writing is necessary. But I do not think he regarded it as sufficient. What matters is that *the people* have chosen to commit their basic principles of government to writing. Even "writing" does not quite get at it. It is not just a matter of the people having kept a written record of how they proposed to govern themselves. It is a matter of their hav-

ing chosen a mode of exercise of popular sovereignty that is deliberately law-like in form. It is text rather than mere record, and in its textuality it is normative rather than merely descriptive of its authors' ruminations on constitutional structure. Above all, it is performative text—written to be executed as a solemn charter, to reflect not the authority or standing of its immediate authors but with a view to a form of ratification that might plausibly be imputed to the people of the whole society.

I have said several times in this chapter that popular sovereignty is not the same as democracy; it is worth observing that although popular sovereignty is an important premise in *Marbury*, democracy (or the principle of representative government) does not feature in Chief Justice Marshall's argument at all. He does not try to argue, like some modern defenders of judicial review (Dworkin 1996), that the practice really is democratic. Nor does he try to defend it against democratic critique. In considering the implications of the existence of constitutional limits on the exercise of legislative authority and the responsibility of the federal courts to police those limits, he pays no attention to the legislature in its character as an elective body (in his day an imperfectly elective body) or as a body of representatives. For him it was enough that the legislature, whatever its character, was subject to legal limitations. Nor did he lose any sleep over the proposition that the community might be divided on the question of what those legislative limits amount to. For him it was sufficient that judges have a sworn duty to call it as they see it— "[i]t is emphatically the province and the duty of the judicial department to say what the law is" (*Marbury* 1803, 172)—whatever the state of opinion in the community at large, and to cast their votes against applying a piece of legislation to the case in front of them when they are convinced that it violates the Constitution.

From Judicial Review to Judicial Supremacy

Marbury used to be regarded as authority for the proposition that the judicial branch has a unique and preeminent responsibility to interpret the Constitution. The language of the Supreme Court in *Cooper v. Aaron* (1958, 18) is typical:

In 1803, Chief Justice Marshall, speaking for a unanimous Court, referring to the Constitution as "the fundamental and paramount law of the nation," declared in the notable case of *Marbury v. Madison* . . . that "It is emphatically the province and duty of the judicial department to say what the law is." This decision declared the basic principle that the federal judiciary is supreme in the exposition of the law of the Constitution, and that principle has ever since been respected by this Court and the Country as a permanent and indispensable feature of our constitutional system.

But of course *Marbury* would be authority for that proposition only if it had been necessary for the Supreme Court in 1803 to determine whether an interpretation of the Constitution by the federal judiciary should prevail over interpretations of the Constitution by other branches. In fact no such determination was necessary. Chief Justice Marshall was not facing an interpretation of the Constitution by another branch of government; he was facing actions by other branches of government (which they may or may not have been willing to describe as the exercise of their assigned powers); and the question he had to decide

was whether the courts were competent to determine the constitutionality of such exercises. He held that they were: The Constitution is paramount law and if a question is properly posed about whether it permits the passage of a given piece of legislation, it is inescapably the duty of the judiciary to answer that question, a duty that necessarily involves the judiciary in saying what the paramount law is. But the proposition that a constitutional duty is inescapable so far as the judicial branch of government is concerned does not at all imply that that duty is not to be performed by any other branch or that if it is performed by another branch, its performance by that branch is to be subordinate to its performance by the judicial branch. Indeed part of the argument for Marshall's conclusion in *Marbury* is that the courts have the same responsibility to interpret the constitution as any other branch: Justices are bound, just like legislators, to carry out their duties "agreeably to the constitution and laws of the United States" (*Marbury* 1803, 180). Marshall is in fact arguing that their duties in respect to the Constitution are *no less than* the legislators', not that they are inherently superior.

What then does judicial supremacy amount to? The term has no canonical definition—and we are going to wrestle with it for a few pages—but I assume that it should not be regarded as synonymous with "judicial review" as that is ordinarily understood in the United States. I know that judges in other countries have powers of judicial review that fall somewhat short of the U.S. model. For example, the Human Rights Act of 1998, which came into force in the United Kingdom in October 2001, provides that judges may review the compatibility of any provision of a statute with the fundamental rights and freedoms of the European Convention on Human Rights, and, "[i]f the court is satisfied that the provision is incompatible with a Convention right," to make "a declaration of that incompatibility" (chap. 42, § 4 (2)). The act provides that such declaration "does not affect the validity, continuing operation or enforcement of the provision in respect of which it is given; and . . . is not binding on the parties to the proceedings in which it is made" (chap. 42, § 4 (6)). But still it has some effect: A minister may use such a declaration as an authorization to initiate a fast-track legislative procedure to remedy the incompatibility (chap. 42, § 10). (This is a power the minister would not have but for the process of judicial review that led to the declaration in the first place.) Thus in Britain there is a power of "judicial review," even though judges there wield much less power when they exercise it than their counterparts in the federal courts of the United States. But this is not the contrast between judicial review and judicial supremacy that I want to explore. In the United States and in more informal constitutionalist discourse around the world, judicial supremacy means something more than the power (which British courts lack) to refuse to apply the provisions of an unconstitutional statute to the case in front of them.

For similar reasons I shall not adopt the definition of judicial supremacy that Barry Friedman provides. Judicial supremacy, said Friedman (1998, 352), means "that a Supreme Court interpretation binds parties beyond those to the instant case, including other state and national governmental actors." The idea seems to be that a court has supremacy whenever its determination of the constitutionality of a legislative measure in a particular case, has force beyond that particular case. It would seem, on this definition, that we have to be willing to talk about judicial supremacy whenever judicial interpretations are cited as authoritative for cases other than those in which they are issued. If a federal court in a second case defers to the decision of a higher (or, for that matter, a coordinate) court in the first case concerning the constitutionality of the legislation, that would seem to satisfy Friedman's definition. This is unsatisfactory for two reasons.

First, as judicial review is ordinarily understood, a decision in the first case to the effect that the legislation is unconstitutional has the effect of "striking down" the legislation and preventing it (or the part of it that has been found unconstitutional in the first case) from having any effect in any other case. Strictly speaking, that is a misconception. A U.S. court has no power to remove a law from the statute books or to enter a judgment against a statute; even in the case of a facial challenge, the court has no power formally to repeal the measure or (as in some continental systems) to order anyone to repeal the measure. The legislation remains formally on the books and the prudent statute compiler will even include it in subsequent editions (see Fallon 2000, 1339). If there is any meaning to the popular notion of a statutory provision being "struck down" by the courts, it is that subsequent courts (in subsequent cases) will follow the court in the first case in refusing to apply the legislation in the cases that come respectively before them. Because this is ordinary judicial review as it is commonly understood, I think we may infer that the first case's operation as a precedent cannot define judicial *supremacy*.

The other reason concerns the relational aspect of judicial supremacy. Judicial supremacy is not just a matter of what a court does and what it says; it is also a matter of how the things it does and says are received by other actors in the political system. There can be no judicial supremacy without deference, and so to define judicial supremacy we must ask over whom the court in question is supreme—in other words, who it is that is deferring to the power that it purports to exercise. The trouble with the Friedman definition is that it seems to suggest that judicial supremacy is displayed whenever one group of judges defers to another group of judges. But in fact none of those who oppose judicial supremacy deny that our federal courts are and ought to be organized hierarchically nor that there is and ought to be some deference by courts at a given level to decisions taken by courts at a higher level. Supremacy in that sense, then, is not the issue. Judicial supremacy is usually understood as a relationship between the judiciary, on the one hand, and officials, institutions, and branches of government outside the judiciary, on the other.

Can we define judicial supremacy politically, in terms of the overall impact of decisions by the courts? As previously mentioned, Lincoln observed that certain forms of assertiveness on the part of the judiciary might have the effect of taking national policy out of the hands of the people, and I criticized this for its inherent equation of "the people" and "the government." But if we leave that particular point aside, Lincoln (1861/1991, 58) does seem to suggest an important contrast. On the one

hand, there are decisions by the Supreme Court in particular cases, which Lincoln acknowledged "must be binding . . . upon the parties to a suit as to the object of that suit." On the other hand, there is the prospect that "the policy of the Government upon vital questions affecting the whole people is to be irrevocably fixed by decisions of the Supreme Court." The distinction here seems to be one of scope: particular decisions (perhaps elaborated one case at a time through precedent) versus general policy. Can we say, then, that we are dealing with an aspiration to judicial supremacy whenever the court goes beyond case-by-case decision making at a "micro" level and seeks to engage with broader issues of policy? Perhaps we can, but then we will have to acknowledge that judicial supremacy, in this sense, may be something commanded by the Constitution (see Dworkin 1985, 69). It may be that the provisions of the Constitution lay down certain broad principles of public policy. The First Amendment prohibition on the establishment of a national religion and the Thirteenth Amendment ban on slavery are the clearest examples. The Constitution takes sides on large issues, and it seems to require those whose actions it structures and authorizes to take those sides also. If in some case a court discerns that the legislature has committed the country to a broad policy path that the Constitution clearly prohibits, then the court has no option but to give effect to the prohibition in every case that comes before it; and citizens concerned about the path to which the legislature has committed the country might quite reasonably devise litigation strategies that would amplify and maximize the political effect of the courts' doing their duty under *Marbury* in particular cases.

This seems to indicate that a political impact test, though perhaps necessary, might not be sufficient to define judicial supremacy. What more do we need, then, to pin down the meaning of "judicial supremacy"? I believe that supremacy has to do with the posture that the courts adopt—and the deference that is accorded to that posture—when the demands of the Constitution are unclear. Those familiar with Lincoln's first inaugural address will remember that he prefaced the remarks we have been considering with some observations on the indeterminacy of the U.S. Constitution on important issues about slavery.

[N]o organic law can ever be framed with a provision specifically applicable to every question which may occur in practical administration. No foresight can anticipate nor any document of reasonable length contain express provisions for all possible questions. Shall fugitives from labor be surrendered by national or by State authority? The Constitution does not expressly say. May Congress prohibit slavery in the Territories? The Constitution does not expressly say. Must Congress protect slavery in the Territories? The Constitution does not expressly say. (Lincoln 1861/1991, 57–58)

Lincoln's point about not having the Supreme Court settle great issues of national policy had to do with issues like these, issues to which the Constitution of the United States says nothing explicit. Now let us approach this slowly. The fact that the Constitution "does not expressly say" how a given issue should be resolved does not mean that read carefully it might not have a bearing on the way the issue should be resolved. Values and principles enshrined in the text may have what Ronald Dworkin (1977, 110–115) has called "gravitational force" as well as "enactment force," and a judicial mind accustomed to grappling with

statutes and case law on that basis may be naturally inclined to try out its talents on the Constitution. For example, maybe in the early nineteenth century one could make a case that taking the slavery provisions of the Constitution seriously required one to acknowledge the legitimacy of extending the peculiar institution into the territories. Still, if one pursued this line, one would have to face up to two issues. First, one would have to face up to the fact that reasonable people might engage in a similar exercise to opposite effect: They might argue, for example, that the unusual nature of the provision made for slavery in the Constitution indicates that it is to be treated as a strictly bounded exception to more general principles of liberty. Second, one would have to recognize that opinions might differ about whether inferences of this sort can legitimately be used as a basis for striking down legislative or executive measures. Two people who agreed about the gravitational force of the slavery clauses might disagree under this second heading—one thinking that power of judicial review should be used only in the clearest cases of repugnancy between constitutional and legislative provisions, the other thinking that the duty laid down in *Marbury*—the duty to say what the law is and act on it—does not run out in hard or challenging cases.

We might define "judicial supremacy," then, as a particular set of responses to these misgivings. We might call it the posture of a court that was prepared to reason in this way and strike down legislation on the basis of its reasoning, even when it knew that that reasoning was controversial and even though it knew that there was disagreement in the constitutional community about whether courts should be permitted to strike down legislation in such circumstances of controversy.

We are not quite finished yet, for there is *still* a sense in which judicial supremacy, as I have just defined it, may seem inevitable rather than an optional posture that the courts might be criticized for adopting in their exercise of judicial review. The point can be stated as follows: Except in cases in which Congress or a state assembly actually legislates in the precise form that the Constitution forbids, judicial review is always a matter of interpretation. Though we talk sometimes of "facial" challenges (challenges that allege that the very text of a legislative enactment shows that it is unconstitutional), legislative measures are seldom facially unconstitutional in the crude sense of a "religious establishment act" or an "uncompensated takings of property act." Usually it is a matter of judgment rather than simple textual comparison to establish that a particular legislative measure runs foul of a constitutional provision—the claim that the provision prohibits the legislation is always a matter of how one interprets the provision in the first place (and also, of course, of how one interprets the legislation).

However, it is one thing to undertake this interpretive exercise in a case where a legislature has been careless or disingenuous about the constitutional standing of a given piece of legislation; it is quite another to undertake it in circumstances where it might reasonably be said that the whole society faces an important choice about how a constitutional provision shall be understood. I have in mind cases in which one understanding of a particular provision, which makes it incompatible with the legislation in question, is going to take the na-

tion in one broad direction, while a different yet still plausible interpretation of the provision, which allows the legislation to stand, is going to take the nation in a different direction. This is where the political impact test, mentioned earlier, does its work. We are to imagine a subset of the cases requiring constitutional interpretation, a subset in which the issues for decision represent major watersheds in national policy. I use *policy* here in a broad sense: The watershed choices I am referring to include not only choices about overall social and economic direction, like the choices posed in *Lochner v. New York* (1905) and *West Coast Hotel v. Parrish* (1937), but also choices about the general character of our principled commitments to rights—cases such as *Dred Scott v. Sanford* (1857), the *Slaughterhouse Cases* (1872), *Brown v. Board of Education* (1954), *Roe v. Wade* (1973), and *Employment Division v. Smith* (1990). I believe it makes sense to talk of judicial supremacy in circumstances where the courts insist on deciding some issue despite the fact that the constitutional text does not speak to it directly and despite their recognition of the very high stakes for the nation in the decision they are proposing to make or in a series of decisions of which the case before them is a prominent member.

I have been struggling throughout this section to find a definition of judicial supremacy that would not make it coextensive with judicial review as that is usually understood or with the simple exercise of the duty laid down in *Marbury*. It might be said yet again that the definition I have proposed still falls foul of that specification. If a party who has been charged or who is otherwise adversely affected under a particular legislative measure claims before a federal court that this legislation is incompatible with a particular provision of the Constitution, surely the court has the inescapable duty to adjudicate that claim, however difficult and controversial it may be and however high the stakes for the nation might appear to be. It seems a bit unfair to call a judge a judicial supremacist simply because he or she faces up to that duty.

However, a judge who is aware that the choice facing him or her represents a major watershed of national policy may reasonably wonder whether he or she should proceed purely on the basis of his or her own reasoning about the gravitational force of such material in the Constitution as bears on the matter. The judge may reasonably wonder whether he or she should take notice of thoughts and conclusions reached by other officials elsewhere in the polity. One can imagine, perhaps, a severely textualist judge trying to make a decision of this kind by him- or herself without reference to any extraneous materials—just the texts of the Constitution and the statute at issue and perhaps a couple of dictionaries. But in fact this is not how judges usually proceed. They refer to other interpretations in earlier cases. They cite doctrines and principles that have grown up as part of the judiciary's collective understanding of what the Constitution means. And they use all that to help them figure out the bearing that the Constitution may have on the important issue that faces them. So far these are intrajudicial materials: They are drawn entirely from the past activity of the judicial branch. That, it seems to me, is the key to the issue of judicial supremacy. Judicial supremacy may be represented as the posture of a court that refuses to look beyond judicial ma-

terials. It is the posture of a court that refuses to take any guidance from the legislature or from the executive or from plebiscitary resolutions of the people about how the choice that faces the court should be resolved.

Here is an example to illustrate. Consider *Employment Division v. Smith*, a watershed case in which the Supreme Court changed the way the U.S. Constitution's guarantee of religious freedom is understood. Liberal philosophers have long been torn between two conceptions of religious freedom (see Waldron 1993, 103–107, 145–153): (1) It is a right to be free from legislation that is intended to burden religious practice; and (2) it is a right to be free from legislation that burdens one's religious practice, whether such burden is intended or not. The text of the Constitution is noncommittal on these options, but any society that respects religious freedom has to make a choice between them. Before *Smith*, it seemed that the American courts were committed to something like the second option (*Sherbert v. Verner*, 1963), but the majority in *Smith* seems to have turned its back on the second option and adopted the less generous interpretation of religious freedom—the first option. The Court did so partly because of the apprehension by a majority of justices about the impact that the second option will have on legislation and regulation in the modern state (*Smith* 1990, 885–889). The legislature had its own view on the matter, however. In 1993, in response to the decision in *Smith*, the U.S. Congress passed the Religious Freedom Restoration Act (42 U.S.C. § 2000bb et seq., tit. 42, chap. 21b), which stated that the second option was the better understanding of religious freedom. Four years later, however, when the issue came before the Supreme Court again, in *City of Boerne v. Flores* (1997), the Supreme Court stuck to its determination to adopt the first approach, brushing aside Congress's view, in the following terms:

Our national experience teaches that the Constitution is preserved best when each part of the Government respects both the Constitution and the proper actions and determinations of the other branches. When the Court has interpreted the Constitution, it has acted within the province of the Judicial Branch, which embraces the duty to say what the law is. *Marbury v. Madison*, 1 Cranch, at 177, 2 L. Ed. 60. When the political branches act against the background of a judicial interpretation of the Constitution already issued, it must be understood that in later cases or controversies the Court will treat its precedents with the respect due to them under settled principles, including stare decisis, and contrary expectations must be disappointed. The Religious Freedom Restoration Act was designed to control cases and controversies, such as the one before us; but as the provisions of the federal statute are beyond congressional authority, it is this Court's precedent, not RFRA, which must control. (*Boerne* 1997, 535–536)

That is what I mean by an assertion of judicial supremacy: The nation faces an important choice about how to conceive a core value; the constitutional text offers no explicit guidance (and this is not simply because the meaning of a phrase is unclear but because the Constitution leaves unresolved a major watershed issue in the philosophy of the modern liberal state); in the series of cases I have mentioned the courts find themselves faced with the issue; as that series of cases unfolds, the national legislature debates the issue and offers its view; but although that opinion by the legislature plays an important role in the national debate on a watershed issue, the highest court holds

that it is *its own reasoning* and *its own precedents* and *its own doctrine* that should prevail; an important matter that had never been explicitly settled in the Constitution is now to be settled decisively and exclusively by the reasoning of a court.

What would be the alternative? I have said several times, following *Marbury*, that courts have an inescapable duty to answer the constitutional questions put to them in the proper course of litigation. So surely they have to reserve for themselves the last word on the issue. Even if Congress puts in its two cents, must not a judge faced with the issue who does not find the congressional interpretation persuasive call the matter as he or she sees it and render judgment on that basis? I wonder. In fact, courts—even supreme courts—are often in the position of deferring to opinions held by others, opinions that they would not find persuasive in their own right. Justice Anthony Kennedy in *City of Boerne* (1997, 536) said that "the Court will treat its precedents with the respect due to them under settled principles, including *stare decisis*"—which if it means anything means that sometimes the Court will properly adopt a position on the basis of deference to authority, a position that it would not have adopted apart from the authority. Of course Kennedy meant deference to other judicial opinions, indeed previous decisions by the Supreme Court. But the broader point applies: Deference per se is not an evasion of the courts' role in the constitutional scheme. So then it is just a matter of determining to whom one defers. If the courts never defer on matters of this kind to anyone or anything except past decisions by the courts, and if other actors in the political system accept that, then we have a situation of judicial supremacy. If on the other hand the courts are willing to give some weight to voices other than their own on matters like these then the accusation of judicial supremacy cannot be sustained. It will not do, of course, for a court to infer an opinion from every exercise of legislative power that it reviews and then defer to it: That *would* be a violation of the duty laid down in *Marbury*. But it is different where what confronts the Court is not an implicit interpretation of the Constitution by the legislature on some matter that the Court thinks is perfectly clear but an explicit contribution by the legislature to a national debate about what the Constitution should be taken to mean in circumstances in which its unclarity poses a watershed choice. For the courts to refuse ever to defer to such a contribution is for them to insist that serious constitutional choices are to be made by them— all by themselves.

Conclusion

We come finally to the question that I raised at the beginning of this chapter. Earlier I defined a negative principle of constitutional structure, formulated by l'Abbé Sièyes, as follows: No branch of government should ever be able to claim the credentials of popular sovereignty or identify itself directly or indirectly with the sovereign people. Do assertions of judicial supremacy count as violations of that principle?

The quick answer is "not necessarily." Whether the Sièyes principle is violated is not just a matter of what *un pouvoir constitué* does but also of the costume in which it does it: The principle insists that no constituted power should try to do the things that *le pouvoir con-stituant* is supposed to do, but it also insists that no constituted power should try to legitimize whatever it does by taking on itself the mantle of *le pouvoir constituant*. Also, as I have said several times in this chapter, judicial supremacy is displayed not merely in the courts' assertions but by the deference that is given to those assertions elsewhere in the political system. The same is true of violations of the Sièyes principle: Whether a constituted branch wears the mantle of *le pouvoir constituant* is not just a matter of how it parades itself but also of how others see it.

Thus it is possible to imagine rationalizations of judicial supremacy that involve no attempt to identify the Supreme Court with the sovereign people. Larry Alexander and Fred Schauer (1997, 1359, 1379) argued for something like judicial supremacy on the ground that the legal system needs certain matters to be settled definitively, for the sake of certainty, coordination, and the other advantages of authority. They acknowledged in a footnote that this is not necessarily an argument for *judicial* supremacy; it might equally be an argument for legislative supremacy, provided that legislative supremacy also satisfied the function of "a single authoritative interpreter to which others must defer" (1377, n. 80). [If their argument is about sovereignty, it is about what A. V. Dicey (1982, 27ff.) called "legal sovereignty"—like the sovereignty of Parliament in the United Kingdom—as opposed to the "political sovereignty," which is implicated in our discussion of *le pouvoir constituant*.]

Other rationalizations of judicial supremacy may look innocuous, so far as the Sièyes principle is concerned, but raise serious questions once they are subject to scrutiny. In *Casey v.*

Planned Parenthood (1992, 868), for example, the Supreme Court presented judicial supremacy as a symbol of the rule of law:

Like the character of an individual, the legitimacy of the Court must be earned over time. So, indeed, must be the character of a Nation of people who aspire to live according to the rule of law. Their belief in themselves as such a people is not readily separable from their understanding of the Court invested with the authority to decide their constitutional cases and speak before all others for their constitutional ideals.

The idea seems to be that the supremacy of the judiciary represents the special constitutional role of law in a way that could not possibly be associated with the supremacy of any other branch of government. But in fact uncontrolled decision making by the courts where there is no clearly applicable legal provision has as often afforded a symbol of "the rule of men" as a symbol of the rule of law; indeed the rule of law is often invoked to condemn such decision making. People do not think the rule of law is satisfied simply because decisions are made by judges; they think it is satisfied only if decisions are made by judges according to law, and in constitutional contexts—where striking down legislation is an issue—only if decisions are made by judges according to the higher law of the Constitution. Because that law acquires its higher status by virtue of its emanation from "the people," there is a natural worry that the court is putting itself into the people's shoes when, although it acknowledges that the constitutional text does not speak directly to an issue, it maintains nevertheless that its own tendentious opinions should have the sort of priority over ordinary legislation that is usually accorded to the higher constitutional law. As stated earlier,

the cases that should particularly concern us in this regard are cases in which the Constitution is unclear, and there is serious division in the society about which of two paths should be taken so far as the nation's future orientation toward rights and constitutional structure is concerned. For example, how should we think about federalism in the twenty-first century? Which of the traditionally defined options for religious freedom in a liberal society should we adopt, given the extent of social regulation in the modern state? How should campaign finance be regulated in a modern electoral system? These are all issues on which the constitutional text has a bearing, but on none of them is the text decisive among the major options that the community faces. The choices that have to be faced go to the heart of what it is to maintain a liberal democracy in the modern world, and so they *are* appropriate for constitutional decision. The question is simply whether that constitution making should be dominated exclusively by the opinions of a court or whether it should be open to a more inclusive constituent process.

For his part, Sieyès was adamant. Though he believed that there should be an institution—a constitutional jury—to enforce the clear provisions of the constitution on the other powers (1788/1964, 119, 135), he denied that this or any other constituted body should have the function of deciding new directions for the constitutional structure: "In every free nation, . . . there is only one way of settling disputes about the constitution. One must not call upon the Notables, but upon the nation itself." The popular sovereign "cannot absolve itself from the responsibility of giving certainty to a disputed constitution."

It is a further question about what forms and procedures the people should use to address these issues. As Sièyes emphasized in his positive principle and as Ackerman (1991, 1998) and others have argued, it is wrong and unrealistic to suppose that this decision making always has to take place in a formally constituted convention or through the exercise of formally constituted amendment powers. All that the negative thesis prohibits is the decision being made by one constituted body to the exclusion of all others on the ground that that one body is the preeminent guardian of the people's will. If the process of constitutional change is informal, the negative thesis does not require that *les pouvoirs constitués* play no role; it requires only that none of them (no *one* of them) purport to play the role of the people. So the negative principle does not mean that the courts may not play a part in constitutional change or clarification, where it is an informal exercise rather than an exercise cabined within Article V powers. But if they do play a part, they must do so as if their opinions were a contribution to a wider political debate—which amounts in its entirety to deliberation by the people—rather than as if their opinions were supposed to definitively settle the matter.

Let me connect this finally with some points about constitutional growth. A dominant idea in modern constitutional jurisprudence is that the Constitution should not be thought of as, in Justice William Brennan's words, "a stagnant, archaic, hidebound document steeped in the prejudices and superstitions of a time long past" (1989, 141); it should be seen as a living charter, growing, changing, and adapting to the times. The idea of "a living Constitution" has sometimes been used as a basis for oppos-

ing judicial review altogether: The courts should stand back and let the Constitution grow and not try to thwart that growth by striking down the new types of legislation that emanate from it (see Horwitz 1993, 51–56). Nowadays, however, it tends to be used as a way of defending judicial power. By its adeptness in the use of interpretive methods, by its ability to adapt the formulations of the past to new realities and discern the bearing of old values on new issues, the judiciary can bring the Constitution up to date, treating it in its decisions "as a living evolving document that must be read anew for our time" (Brennan 1989, 433). To some (Rehnquist 1976, 698), this is a nightmare prospect:

Once we have abandoned the idea that the authority of the courts to declare laws unconstitutional is somehow tied to the language of the Constitution that the people adopted, a judiciary exercising the power of judicial review appears in a quite different light. Judges then are no longer the keepers of the covenant; instead they are a small group of fortunately situated people with a roving commission to second-guess Congress, state legislatures, and state and federal administrative officers concerning what is best for the country.

But even those who do not find the notion of "a living Constitution" viscerally repugnant may still recoil—on exactly the sort of grounds we have been considering—from various ways in which the judiciary might perform this function of keeping the Constitution up to date. Justice Brennan in his account of the living Constitution associated it with a process of dialogue between the courts and the other branches, in which the court functions as "the calmer, cooler party to a dialogue from which the community benefits over time" (Brennan

1989, 433). His particular model of dialogue perhaps depends too much on the courts having the last word—and the legislature being eventually grateful for it (like a grown-up reflecting on his or her childhood piano lessons). Still the idea of a dialogue in these circumstances is quite attractive. When the citizens in general and all the branches of their government are aware that there are new and major choices to be made so far as the Constitution of their society is concerned, they may talk to one another and express various opinions about the desirability of the various constitutional options and listen to one another in a spirit that indicates that these are choices the polity must somehow face together if the option that is eventually chosen is to have the legitimacy usually associated with constitutional law.

But the idea of judicial supremacy that we discussed earlier is directly at odds with this. It seems to proceed on the basis that because the courts have a plain responsibility to apply the provisions of the Constitution when the Constitution is clear, they also have a preeminent responsibility to develop and articulate the provisions of the Constitution when they are unclear or when they leave certain choices open. Just as they should not be distracted by the protestations of the other branches in their performance of the former function, so they should exclude or refuse ever to defer to the voices of the other branches in their performance of the latter function. That analogy fails, as we saw in our discussion of the rule of law, because there is clear law in the one case and nothing but the enterprise of law-*making* in the other. So we may ask, "By what right does a court refuse to listen or defer to the views of the other branches when it faces—as sometimes it is bound to face—constitutional choices that are genuinely open?" If the open choices were being addressed by a constitutional convention, it might be appropriate to exclude the voices of *les pouvoirs constituès*: When the nation speaks through its extraordinary representatives, the ordinary representatives and the ordinary institutions must fall silent (Sièyes 1788/1964, 130–131). That is the worry—that the Court is putting itself in the special position that a constitutional convention would occupy and using that and the aura of legality that surrounds its own ordinary operation to silence other voices in the extraordinary decision making that it engages in.

There are some, no doubt, for whom such a posture is attractive. Hannah Arendt once wrote that the Supreme Court is "the true seat of authority in the American Republic," adding that "this authority is exerted in a kind of continuous constitution-making, for the Supreme Court is indeed, in Woodrow Wilson's phrase, 'a kind of Constitutional Assembly in continuous session'" (Arendt 1977, 200). Others of us, however, find it deeply disturbing, and I hope that in these ruminations on the principle of popular sovereignty and on the constitutionalism of Sièyes I have been able to go some distance toward helping to explain why.

Bibliography

Ackerman, Bruce. *We the People. Vol. 1. Foundations.* Cambridge: Harvard University Press, 1991.

———. *We the People. Vol. 2. Transformations.* Cambridge: Harvard University Press, 1998.

Alexander, Larry, and Fred Schauer. "On Extrajudicial Constitutional Interpretation." *Harvard Law Review* 110 (1997): 1359–1387.

Arato, Andrew. "Carl Schmitt and the Revival of the Doctrine of the Constituent Power in the United States." *Cardozo Law Review* 21 (2000): 1739–1747.

Arendt, Hannah. *On Revolution.* Harmondsworth: Penguin Books, 1977.

Baker, Keith M. "Sièyes." In *A Critical Dictionary of the French Revolution.* Edited by François Furet and Mana Ozouf. Cambridge: Harvard University Press, 1989.

Bickel, Alexander. *The Least Dangerous Branch: The Supreme Court at the Bar of Politics.* 2d ed. New Haven: Yale University Press, 1986.

Brennan, William. "Why Have a Bill of Rights?" *Oxford Journal of Legal Studies* 9 (1989): 425–447.

Constant, Benjamin. *Political Writings.* Edited by Biancamaria Fontana. Cambridge: Cambridge University Press, 1988.

Dicey, A. V. *Introduction to the Study of the Law of the Constitution.* 8th edition of 1915. Indianapolis: Liberty Classics, 1982.

Dworkin, Ronald. *Taking Rights Seriously.* Rev. ed. London: Duckworth, 1977.

———. *A Matter of Principle.* Cambridge: Harvard University Press, 1985.

———. *Freedom's Law: The Moral Reading of the Constitution.* Cambridge: Harvard University Press, 1996.

Fallon, Richard H. "As-Applied and Facial Challenges and Third-Party Standing." *Harvard Law Review* 113 (2000): 1321–1370.

Finer, S. E. *The Man on Horseback: The Role of the Military in Politics.* New York: Praeger, 1962.

Friedman, Barry. "The History of the Counter-majoritarian Difficulty. Part 1: The Road to Judicial Supremacy." *New York University Law Review* 73 (1998): 333–433.

Hamilton, Alexander, James Madison, and John Jay. *The Federalist Papers.* Edited by Isaac Kramnick. Harmondsworth: Penguin Books, 1987.

Hobbes, Thomas. *De Cive: The English Version.* Edited and translated by Howard Warrender. 1651. Reprint, Oxford: Clarendon Press, 1983.

Horwitz, Morton J. "The Constitution of Change: Legal Fundamentality without Fundamentalism." *Harvard Law Review* 107 (1993): 30–116.

Lincoln, Abraham. *Great Speeches.* Edited by Jon Grafton. New York: Dover, 1991.

Locke, John. *Two Treatises of Government.* Edited by Peter Laslett. 1689. Reprint, Cambridge: Cambridge University Press, 1988.

McCormick, John P. *Carl Schmitt's Critique of Liberalism.* Cambridge: Cambridge University Press, 1997.

Morgan, Edmund S. *Inventing the People: The Rise of Popular Sovereignty in England and America.* New York: W. W. Norton, 1988.

Rawls, John. *A Theory of Justice.* Cambridge: Harvard University Press, 1971.

Rehnquist, William. "The Notion of a Living Constitution." *Texas Law Review* 54 (1976): 693–706.

Rousseau, Jean Jacques. *Rousseau: The Social Contract and Other Later Political Writings.* Edited and translated by Victor Gourevitch. 1762. Reprint, Cambridge: Cambridge University Press, 1997.

Schmitt, Carl. *Die Diktatur (The Dictator).* Munich: Duncker and Humboldt, 1928.

———. *Verfassungslehre (Constitutional Doctrine).* Munich: Duncker and Humboldt, 1933.

Sièyes, Emmanuel Joseph. *Les discours de Sièyes dans les débats constitutionnels de l'an III, 2 et 18 thermidor* (The Speeches of Sièyes in the Constitutional Debates of the 2nd and 18th of the month Thermidor in Year III). 1793. Reprint, Paris: Hachette, 1939.

———. *What Is the Third Estate?* Translated by M. Blondel. 1788. Reprint, New York: Praeger, 1964.

Waldron, Jeremy. *Liberal Rights: Collected Papers, 1981–91.* Cambridge: Cambridge University Press, 1993.

———. *Law and Disagreement.* Oxford: Clarendon Press, 1999.

Wilson, James. *The Works of James Wilson. Vol. 1.* Edited by Robert Green McCloskey. 1790. Reprint, Cambridge: Harvard University Press, 1967.

List of Documents

Introduction to the Documents

Marbury v. Madison can be fully appreciated and understood only in light of an historical survey that ranges from practices in ancient Athens to contemporary decisions by the United States Supreme Court. The historical precedents for judicial review, whether judicial review was intended by the framers of the Constitution, the role it played in both the legal practices of the 1790s and the politics of the 1800s, and its evolution after *Marbury,* have all inspired substantial scholarly investigation and debate. The materials that follow do not provide conclusive answers to various controversies over *Marbury*, though in some cases they provide more support for some positions than for others. The documents are presented to help readers make more intelligent judgments about the past, present, and future of the political practices that either vest justices with the power to ignore laws believed unconstitutional when adjudicating cases (judicial review) or the power to determine what the Constitution means (judicial supremacy).

Readers interested in additional biographical information about the individuals discussed may consult the sources provided in the headnotes of relevant documents or use the multivolume *Dictionary of American Biography* (New York: Charles Scribner's Sons, 1964).

Section I (Documents 1–18): Historical Foundations

Judicial review did not emerge fully formed from the head of John Marshall in 1803 or from the collective wisdom of the framers of the Constitution of the United States in 1787.

The practice had several distinct historical foundations. Numerous regimes from the Athenian polity to Stuart England had legal practices that resembled judicial review. Legal actors for two millennia typically found ways of ignoring statutes or official decrees deemed particularly unjust or incoherent, even if those means did not require the legal decision maker to declare that the law violated some provision in a written constitution. Political philosophers during the Enlightenment debated at some length whether legislative power could be limited and, if so, what institutions would best limit that power. These political thinkers rarely discussed judicial power, but they bequeathed to the nascent United States the general principle of limited government that would later be used to justify judicial review. American thinkers before and immediately after the Revolution spoke specifically of courts as the appropriate institutions for limiting government. Many prominent state justices declared that state laws violated either the state constitution or some equally fundamental legal principle. These foreign practices, political treatises, and state court decisions influenced the debates both over whether to ratify the Constitution and, later, over what powers the Constitution had granted the judiciary.

Documents 1–4: Legal Antecedents

Judicial review has preconstitutional roots that go back at least two thousand years. Demosthenes in ancient Athens and Lord Chief Justice Edward Coke in seventeenth-century England are among the many participants in legal disputes who claimed that courts should ignore certain laws inconsistent with more fundamental laws. The Athenian polity had a well-established practice that required legal decisions nullifying certain laws.

Indictments for illegality are the earliest practice analogous to judicial review. Athenian law declared that statutes passed by the assembly were superior to mere decrees related to specific persons or events. Athenians further established a legal procedure for determining whether a decree was illegal or, in Demosthenes's words, "unconstitutional." In what were called "indictments for illegality," any citizen of Athens could charge a legislator with misleading the assembly of the polis, or city, into adopting an illegal decree. If the prosecution was successful the offending legislator could be fined, jailed, or executed.

The historical examples or precursors of judicial review in England provide more immediate legal sources for Chief Justice John Marshall's argument in *Marbury v. Madison*. In a handful of cases prior to the Glorious Revolution of 1688, members of England's highest courts declared several acts of Parliament null and void. Judges in other English cases claimed the theoretical power to declare legislative acts null and void, without actually doing so. By the early 1700s, English justices had abandoned the practice of judicial review in favor of parliamentary supremacy.

English courts prior to the Glorious Revolution occasionally declared parliamentary acts void. These practices and others presented below resemble judicial review as practiced in the United States, but important differences exist. Fundamental law was not conceptualized in terms of a written constitution that represented the highest expression of the people's sovereignty. Prominent jurists argued that a particular statute was either inconsistent with certain general principles, deemed fundamental, or inconsistent with another body of law deemed to have higher legal status. No judicial tribunal before the American Revolution declared a judicial power to void laws inconsistent with the written constitution of that polity.

Documents 5–11: Philosophical Background

Judicial review received very little attention from those political philosophers who, during the sixteenth and seventeenth centuries, articulated the crucial principles underlying liberal democracy and liberal constitutionalism. Prominent intellectuals from Hugo Grotius to John Locke did discuss at great length questions associated with sovereignty and fundamental law. Central to these Enlightenment debates was whether the legislative power in a society was limited by some combination of natural or positive law. Those philosophers who maintained that fundamental law limited legislative power provided crucial jurisprudential foundations for the later development of judicial review, even though their works rarely if ever commented on the actual practice of judicial review.

Documents 12–18: Preconstitutional American Thought and Legal Practice

American constitutionalists during the decades before the Constitution was framed and ratified enthusiastically endorsed and elaborated on previous suggestions that government was limited by certain fundamental tenets and by whatever principles a people might choose to place in a constitution. Unlike their European predecessors, colonial and postcolonial Americans thought more seriously about the governing institutions necessary to ensure that legislation did not violate these higher political principles. Some suggested that the judicial branch of government could best enforce natural and constitutional limits on legislative power by declaring null and void all government acts that violated those limits.

Several American judges before the Revolution and before the ratification of the Constitution asserted the power to declare legislation null and void. The number of cases in which this power was considered is sufficient to support the inference that most political elites by 1787 were aware that some lawyers were asserting and some state judges were exercising a power to strike down legislative and executive acts perceived to be inconsistent with natural rights or the state constitution. The number of cases is not sufficient to support the inference that judicial review was a common and generally accepted practice at the time the Constitution was framed and ratified. Only a few courts had declared laws void. Those decisions were often exceptionally controversial; justices who struck down laws during the 1780s risked being turned out of office.

1   Ancient Athens: Demosthenes

Demosthenes (384–322 B.C.) is widely considered to have been the finest Athenian orator of his day. Demosthenes was born into a wealthy family, but his father died when he was young and his legal guardians squandered away his estate. Upon reaching adulthood, Demosthenes gained a reputation for being an excellent orator. He was soon hired to draft speeches for others, eventually including some of the richest men in Athens. He became involved in public affairs and brought several indictments for illegality against various political leaders in Athens. Demosthenes was a leader of the Athenian opposition to Macedon during the Lamian War. Upon the war's end, he took his own life.

For more biographical information, see Ian Worthington, ed. Demosthenes: Statesman and Orator (London: Routledge, 2000).

The excerpt below is an abridged copy of a speech by Demosthenes supporting an indictment for illegality. Charidemus was a well-known mercenary leader who had been given substantial benefits by the Athenians for his involvement in negotiating the peace of Chares. Several years later, Aristocrates, a prominent Athenian, proposed to the Senate that anyone who killed Charidemus should be summarily arrested, and that any state or individual harboring an assassin of Charidemus should be excluded from all treaties with Athens. After the decree had passed the Senate, Euthycles, another Athenian citizen, brought an indictment for illegality against Aristocrates. He retained Demosthenes to draft the following speech for him. For background information on this political struggle see T. H. Vince, Demosthenes: Against Meidias, Androtion, Aristocrates, Timocrates, Aristogeiton (Cambridge: Harvard University Press, 1956), 212.

. . . I have undertaken to prove three propositions,—first that the decree is unconstitutional, secondly that it is injurious to the common weal, and thirdly that the person in whose favour it has been moved is unworthy of such privilege. . . .

Now take and read the actual statutes, that I may prove thereby the illegality of their proposal.

. . . In the statute it is provided that the Council shall take cognizance of homicide, intentional wounding, arson, and poisoning, if a man kills another by giving him poison. The legislator, while he presumes the killing, has nevertheless directed a judicial inquiry before specifying what is to be done to the culprit, and thereby has shown a just respect . . . for the religious feeling of the whole city. . . . So much for the legislator; but what of the author of the decree? "If any man kill Charidemus," he says. So he defines the injury in the same phrase, "if any man kill," as the legislator; but the sequel is not the same. He struck out submission to trial, and made the culprit liable to immediate seizure; he passed by the tribunal appointed by law, and handed over to the accusers, to be dealt with as they chose, a man

untried, a man whose guilt is not yet proven. When they have got him, they are to be allowed to torture him, or maltreat him, or extort money from him. Yet the next ensuing statute directly and distinctly forbids such treatment even of men convicted and proved to be murderers. . . .

STATUTE

It shall be lawful to kill murderers in our own territory, or to arrest them as directed on the first turning-table, but not to maltreat or amerce them. . . .

. . . He uses the term "murderers"; but in the first place you see that by murderer he means a man found guilty by verdict; for no man comes under that designation until he has been convicted and found guilty. . . . Well, what does he direct? That it shall be lawful to kill them and to put them under arrest. Does he say that they are to be taken to the house of the prosecutor, or as he pleases? No, indeed. How are they to be arrested? . . . The judicial archons are there authorized to punish with death persons who have gone into exile on a charge of murder. . . . It is to the archons, then, that the murderer is to be taken on arrest; and that differs from being taken to the house of the prosecutor in this respect. . . , that the captor who carries a man to the judges gives control of the malefactor to the laws, while the captor who takes him home gives such control to himself. . . . Note that in this manner the law lays down not only how the murderer or convict is to be punished, but also where, for it specifies the country of the person injured, and it directly prescribes that the penalty is to be inflicted in that way and in no other, in that place and in no other. Yet the author of the decree is far indeed from making this distinction,—his proposals are exactly contrary. After the words, "if anyone shall kill Charidemus," he adds, "he shall be liable to seizure everywhere."—What do you mean, sir? The laws do not allow even convicted criminals to be arrested elsewhere than in our own country, and do you propose that a man shall be liable to seizure without trial in any allied territory? And when the laws forbid seizure even in our own territory, do you permit seizure? Indeed, in making a man liable to seizure you have permitted everything that the law has forbidden,—extortion of blood-money, maltreatment and misusage of a living man, private custody and private execution. How could a man be convicted of a more clearly unconstitutional proposal, or of drafting a resolution more outrageously than in this fashion? . . . You have eliminated the intermediate process, for between accusation and conviction comes a trial.—There is not a word about trial in the decree proposed by the defendant.

. . . Though the law so clearly gives permission to slay, and states under what conditions, the defendant ignores all those conditions, and has drawn his penal clause without any suggestion as to the manner of the slaying. . . . When there are so many conditions that justify the slaying of anyone else, it is monstrous that that man should be the only man in the world whom, even under those conditions, it is to be unlawful to slay.

. . . The law permits homicide in immediate self-defence; but Aristocrates has made no such exception. He says, without qualification, "if anyone ever kills,"—that is, even if he kill righteously, or as the laws permit. . . . The slaying of Charidemus is forbidden even on those terms,—if even though he be iniquitously plundering another man's property, his slayer is to be liable to seizure, though the statute ordains that he who takes life under such conditions shall have impunity.

. . . [A]s every citizen has an equal share in civil rights, so everybody should have an equal share in the laws; and therefore he moved that it should not be lawful to propose a law affecting any individual, unless the same applied to all Athenians. Now seeing that it is agreed that the drafting of decrees must conform to the law, a man who draws a decree for the special benefit of Charidemus, such as is not applicable to all the rest of you, must evidently be making a proposal in defiance of this statute also; of course what it is unlawful to put into a statute cannot legitimately be put into a decree. . . .

I say that I do not expect that Aristocrates will be able to deny that he has moved a decree in open violation of all the laws; but before now. . . I have seen a man contesting an indictment for illegal measures, who, though convicted by law, made an attempt to argue that his proposal had been to the public advantage, and insisted strongly on that point. . . . Admit a man's proposition to be in every other respect advantageous; it is still disadvantageous in so far as he begs you, who are sworn to give judgement according to law, to ratify a decree which he himself cannot prove to have been honestly drawn, seeing that every man is bound to set the highest value upon fidelity to his oath. At the same time the plea, though impertinent, has reason in it; but not a reason which Aristocrates will be able to submit to you. Entirely opposed as his decree is to the laws, it is not less pernicious than illegal. . . .

Source: Demosthenes, *Demosthenes: Against Meidias, Androtion, Aristocrates, Timocrates, Aristogeiton* (Cambridge: Harvard University Press, 1956), 215, 223–235, 247–249, 251–257, 275, 285, 365–367.

2
Ancient Rome: Code of Justinian

In 527 A.D. Justinian (483–565 A.D.) succeeded his uncle Justin as emperor of Byzantium, the eastern half of the former Roman Empire. Roman law was in a state of confusion at the time of Justinian's accession to the throne. The laws and legal opinions of Rome had never been systematically published. Instead, they were spread throughout several thousand books. During his first year in office, Justinian organized a commission to systematize and codify Roman law. The resulting product, finished in 529 A.D., was the Code of Justinian.

The following excerpt from the code indicates that judges were "admonished" to determine whether rescripts, or particular decrees of the emperor, were contrary "to general law or to public utility," and, if so, not to "permit" them. This practice anticipates judicial review. Late Roman law recognized a hierarchy of laws. Some laws, constituting the general law, were superior to others—the decrees of the emperor. Judicial officials were authorized to determine the meaning of the more fundamental law and whether official decrees were inconsistent with that law.

. . ."We admonish all judges of every administration, greater or less, in our whole commonwealth that in the trial of every sort of litigation, they permit no rescript, no pragmatic sanction and no imperial adnotation to be alleged before them, which seems to be adverse to general law or to public utility; but that they have no doubt that general imperial constitutions are to be observed in every way."

. . . "We command that rescripts which are obtained from us *contra jus* shall be rejected by all judges unless perchance there be something therein which injures not another and profits him who seeks it, or gives pardons for crime to the suppliants." . . .

Source: Brinton Coxe, *An Essay on Judicial Power and Unconstitutional Legislation, Being a Commentary on Parts of the Constitution of the United States* (Philadelphia: Kay and Brother, 1893), 108–109.

3
Papal Italy: *Ghisilardi's Case*

Throughout much of the Middle Ages popes exercised temporal power in central Italy. Such pontifical states as Bologna were authorized to draft legislative statutes, but those measures did not have the status of law until confirmed by the pope. Although canonical law was committed to papal supremacy, papal acts were sometimes interpreted—or more accurately interpreted away—in light of perceived principles of fundamental law. The excerpt below summarizes a 1638 case decided by the court of the Rota Romana, the highest within the Roman Catholic Church at that time. The justices in that case declared that certain legislative acts approved by two different popes, Leo X and Clement VII, were not to be considered valid because they impaired an individual's "well-acquired right" to operate a mill, established by a previous enactment of the government of Bologna and Pope Sixtus IV. The acts in question were not explicitly declared void or unconstitutional. Anticipating a practice commonly adopted in American courts, the justices declared that because Popes Leo and Clement were not aware that the legislation in question was hostile to the rights of the existing mill owner, the legislation would not be interpreted as abridging those rights. Ghisilardi's Case highlights how constitutional principles or principles of fundamental law may influence how legislation is interpreted, as well as whether courts declare legislation unconstitutional.

. . . In a case decided in 1638, the Court of the Rota Romana held that certain legislative acts of two popes as princes, expressly made in the plenitude of power, were not to be accounted good against a third party because they impaired or prejudiced his well-acquired right under a contract with the government of Bologna. . . .

In 1466, the Cardinal Legate at Bologna with the consent and will of the members of the government of Bologna granted to Batholomew Ghisilardi, the elder, and his heirs and successors the faculty of building a mill beyond the walls of the city. . . . After the mill had been constructed, Sixtus IV, after diligent examination, confirmed the grant and . . . granted it anew, in 1473. Batholomew and his heirs and successors continued in quiet possession of the mill and the rights and business belonging to it until 1520. In that year the government of Bologna made a statute providing that the bakers of the city should not be permitted to have their corn ground outside of its walls. This statute was confirmed by Leo X. . . . The prohibition of the statute so confirmed was one gravely injuring the business of the mill. In consequence . . . a suit was brought by An-

thony Ghisilardi, nephew of the deceased grantee. . . . Pending this suit, the government of Bologna sought and obtained another and a similar confirmation of its statute from Clement VII. In its supplication or request therefore, no mention of any pending suit was made.

The auditor, or judge who heard the suit, stated a *dubitatur* to the whole court as to whether the letters of patent of Leo X. and Clement VII. were to be accounted good against the Ghisilardi and it was answered that both were not. . . .

. . . The pope was ignorant of the contract between them and the government of Bologna, which gave them such a right. The presumption must therefore be made that the letters patent confirming the statute had emanated at the suggestion of one party only and that the pope had been circumvented under cover of words, for he had no intention of prejudicing a third party. . . . The pontiff, although he can do such a thing, was never held to wish to destroy a well-acquired right. . . .

Every thing said concerning the letters patent of Leo X. . . . was held to apply to those of Clement VII. . . .

Source: Brinton Coxe, *An Essay on Judicial Power and Unconstitutional Legislation, Being a Commentary on Parts of the Constitution of the United States* (Philadelphia: Kay and Brother, 1893), 129–132.

4

England: *Dr. Bonham's Case* (1610)

Dr. Bonham's Case *is probably the most important judicial precursor of Marbury v. Madison. The precise issue litigated concerned the power of the Royal College of Physicians. The law empowered the Royal College to govern all matters pertaining to the practice of medicine in London. Part of this governance entailed examining medical practitioners to determine whether they were sufficiently trained in the medical sciences. If an individual was found deficient, the college could impose a fine, half of which went to the king and half of which went to the college. Much of the court's opinion explores whether persons who received medical degrees from other universities could legally practice temporarily in London without a license from the Royal College. On this statutory matter, the justices concluded that Thomas Bonham, a graduate of the University of Cambridge, was a competent physician who was legally entitled to practice medicine for less than a month without the requisite credentials.*

The most famous passages in Dr. Bonham's Case *were not strictly necessary to the resolution of the case (another facet of* Bonham *that anticipates* Marbury*). After ruling that Bonham had a statutory right to practice medicine, the justices considered whether Parliament had the power to vest the col-*

lege with the power to judge whether an individual was qualified to practice medicine and the right to receive half the fine administered as a penalty if he was not. Dr. Bonham's Case concludes that Parliament lacked such power. Lord Chief Justice Edward Coke asserted a judicial power to rule that legislatures could not violate certain fundamental principles of common law. The most famous passage in his opinion declares:

> it appears in our books, that in many cases, the common law will control Acts of Parliament, and sometimes adjudge them to be utterly void: for when an Act of Parliament is against common right and reason, or repugnant, or impossible to be performed, the common will control it, and adjudge such Act to be void.

Although this passage appears to suggest a legal limit on state power, some scholars think Coke was merely claiming a judicial power to interpret laws as consistent with natural right and reason.

Lord Chief Justice Edward Coke (1552–1634) of the Court of Common Pleas was one of the most eminent jurists in the entire history of English law. Coke was educated at the University of Cambridge, elected to Parliament in 1589, selected as solicitor general in 1592, chosen as Speaker of the House of Commons in 1593, and promoted to attorney general in 1594. Coke earned a reputation as a dogged champion of the crown, then occupied by King James I. In 1606 Coke became chief justice of the Court of Common Pleas. He proceeded to champion the common law against all other sources of authority, including that of the king and Parliament. In 1613 King James I, in an effort to limit Coke's influence, "promoted" him to chief justice of the King's Bench. Coke continued to defy royal prerogative. Attorney General Francis Bacon, no doubt at the instigation of King James, brought several minor charges against Coke, among which was "disrespect to the King." These allegations led to Coke's dismissal from the bench in 1616. Coke was then elected to Parliament, where he emerged as a leader in the oppositions to Kings James I and Charles I.

For biographical information, see Catherine Drinker Bowen, The Lion and the Throne: The Life and Times of Sir Edward Coke (London: Hamish Hamilton, 1957).

. . . He who practises physic in London doth not offend the statute by his practise, unless he practices it by the space of a month. But the clause . . . doth not prescribe any certain time, but at what time soever he ministers physic . . . he shall be punished by the said second branch: and the law hath great reason in making this distinction, for divers nobles, gentlemen, and others, come upon divers occasions to London, and when they are here they become subject to diseases, and thereupon they send for their physicians in the country, who know their bodies, and the cause of their diseases; now it was never the meaning of the Act to bar any one of his own physicians; and when he is here he may practise and minister to another by two or three weeks, &c. without any forfeiture; for any one who practises physic . . . in London though he has not taken any degree in any of the universities shall forfeit nothing unless he practises it by the space of a month; and that was the reason that the time of a month was put in the Act. . . .

. . . The censors cannot be judges, ministers, and parties; judges to give sentence or judgment; ministers to make summons; and parties to have the moiety of the forfeiture. . . . And it appears in our books, that in many cases, the common law will controul Acts of Parliament, and sometimes adjudge them to be utterly void: for when an Act of Parliament is against common right and reason, or repugnant, or impossible to be performed, the common law will controul it, and adjudge such Act to be void; and therefore . . . some statutes are made against law and right which those who made them perceiving, would not put them in execution. . . .

Source: *Dr. Bonham's Case* (1610): 651–652.

5   Hugo Grotius

Hugo Grotius (1583–1645) was a lawyer, writer, politician, and diplomat. Born in the Netherlands, Grotius completed his studies at the University of Leiden at sixteen and began a career as a lawyer. Despite a flourishing legal practice, during the next eight years Grotius found time to write a history of the Dutch Republic, a comparative study of constitutions, and a legal treatise on maritime law. In 1606 Grotius was named attorney general of Holland. He held various political and diplomatic positions over the next ten years, including envoy to England and governor of Rotterdam. When civil war erupted in Holland in 1617 Grotius supported the losing side. He was subsequently arrested and sentenced to life imprisonment. Two years into his sentence, Grotius escaped and fled to France, where he wrote The Law of War and Peace.

    Scholars regard The Law of War and Peace *as the seminal work of international law. Crucial passages maintain that governing authorities have no power to pass laws that violate natural law or the constitution—a claim that would be repeated by many later political thinkers. In time, some commentators would conclude that courts were the appropriate institution for ensuring that legislation did not violate natural law or the constitution.*

    For more biographical information, see Hamilton Vreeland, Hugo Grotius: The Father of the Modern Science of International Law *(Oxford: Oxford University Press, 1917); and Christian Gellinek,* Hugo Grotius *(New York: Twayne Publishers, 1983).*

. . . [I]f a people has placed a king in power without absolute authority, but subject to certain laws, his acts contrary to those laws can be rendered void by them, either wholly or in part, because to that extent the people has preserved its own right. The acts of kings who rule with absolute power but do not hold their kingdoms as proprietary owners, acts by which the kingdom, or a part of the kingdom, or its revenues are alienated, we have treated above; and we have shown that by the very law of nature such acts are null and void, just as if they had been performed in respect to the property of another. . . .

Source: Hugo Grotius, *The Law of War and Peace,* trans. Francis W. Kelsey (Indianapolis: Bobbs-Merrill, 1925), 138, 381–382.

6   Thomas Hobbes

Thomas Hobbes (1588–1679) was an English philosopher and political theorist. After studying classics at the University of Oxford, he found lifelong employment first as a tutor to William Cavendish, the eventual Earl of Devonshire, and then to Cavendish's son. Hobbes traveled throughout Europe with his pupils, meeting many intellectual luminaries of his day, including the Italian astronomer Galileo Galilei and the French philosopher René Descartes. Hobbes sided with the crown in its ongoing struggle with Parliament. In 1640 he circulated a comprehensive defense of royal prerogative, titled The Elements of Law. *Fearing possible retribution from Parliament, Hobbes voluntarily exiled himself to France, where he remained for the next eleven years. During this time, Hobbes wrote* De Cive, *or* On Citizenship, *and* Leviathan, *his most important works of political theory.*

    Leviathan *defends the absolute power of the sovereign. Hobbesian rulers were vested with the power to make any law and take any action they believed in the national interest. Subjects could not call rulers to account for perceived violations of natural law or the constitution. Individuals in the political universe elaborated by* Leviathan *had rights only by sufferance of the authorities. This absolutism, while written in defense of monarchy, would provide strong intellectual foundations for legislative supremacy.*

For more biographical information, see Noel Malcolm, "A Summary Biography of Hobbes," in Tom Sorell, ed., The Cambridge Companion to Hobbes *(Cambridge: Cambridge University Press, 1996), 13–44); and A. P. Martinich,* Thomas Hobbes *(New York: St. Martin's Press, 1997), 3–23.*

. . . [B]ecause every subject is by this institution author of all the actions and judgements of the sovereign instituted, it follows that whatsoever he doth, can be no injury to any of his subjects; nor ought he to be by any of them accused of injustice. For he that doth anything by authority from another doth therein no injury to him by whose authority he acteth: but by this institution of a Commonwealth every particular man is author of all the sovereign doth; and consequently he that complaineth of injury from his sovereign complaineth of that whereof he himself is author, and therefore ought not to accuse any man but himself; no, nor himself of injury, because to do injury to oneself is impossible. It is true that they that have sovereign power may commit iniquity, but not injustice or injury in the proper signification. . . .

Source: Thomas Hobbes, *Leviathan* (New York: Oxford University Press, 1996), 117–119.

---

7 **Samuel Pufendorf**

Samuel Pufendorf (1632–1694) was a German political theorist and historian. The son of a Lutheran clergyman, Pufendorf studied law and political theory at the University of Leipzig, where he read the works of Hugo Grotius and Thomas Hobbes. Pufendorf served as a professor of law at the University of Heidelberg from 1661 until 1670, then taught jurisprudence at the University of Lund until 1677. He completed his most influential writing, De Jure Naturae et Gentium, *or* Of the Law of Nature and Nations, *while teaching at Lund in 1672. For the remainder of his life he worked as the royal historian for the king of Sweden and the elector of Brandenburg.*

Of the Law of Nature and Nations was an attempt to reconcile Grotius and Hobbes on the issue of sovereignty. Pufendorf insisted that a people could choose between an absolute Hobbesian sovereign and a more limited monarchy of the sort detailed by Grotius. Absolute monarchs reigned without legal restraint; at most, subjects had a right to rebel against decrees they perceived to be inconsistent with fundamental law. More limited monarchs, however, were legally or constitutionally obligated to obey those fundamental laws laid down as a condition of their rule. Pufendorf believed that a legislative assembly rather than the judiciary was the appropriate institution for ensuring that a monarch obeyed the fundamental law of the land.

For more biographical information, see Craig L. Carr, ed., The Political Writings of Samuel Pufendorf *(Oxford: Oxford University Press, 1994), 3–4.*

. . . [I]t lies entirely within the will of free peoples, when they grant a king sovereignty, as to whether they wish it to be absolute or restricted by certain laws, provided, of course, such laws have in them nothing impious, and do not obstruct the end of sovereignty itself. For although at the first men enjoyed liberty to come together into a civil society, yet they were still subject to natural law, and so were obligated, of course, to draw up only such rules of sovereignty and civil disobedience as were agreeable to that law and the lawful end of states. . . .

The sovereignty of a king is more strictly limited, if, at its transfer, an express convention is entered into between king and citizens that he will exercise it in accordance with certain basic laws, and on affairs, over the disposal of which he has not been accorded absolute power, he will consult with an assembly of the people or council of nobles, and that without the consent of one of the last two he will make no decision; and that if he does otherwise, the citizens will not be bound by his commands on such affairs. The people that has set a king over them in this way is not understood to have promised to obey him absolutely and in all things, but in so far as his sovereignty accords with their bargain and the fundamental laws, while whatever acts of his deviate from them, are thereby void and without force to obligate citizens. . . .

. . . [I]f a king should promise that he will not levy new taxes without consulting the representatives of the people, I should judge that any levy which he made on his own decision would be void. . . .

But for the more thorough understanding of the nature of limited monarchies, we should know that the matters which come up in the administration of a state are usually of two kinds. For some can be decided in advance, by reason of the fact that whenever they arise they are of the same nature, while on others a judgement as to whether or not they are to the advantage of the state can be reached only at the time they arise, because it cannot be foreseen what circumstances will attend them. With both of these kinds a people which has decided upon a limited monarchy could take due precautions that no hurt be done the state; in the case of the former kind of business, by pass-ing permanent laws which the king would be required to observe, in the latter kind, by specifying that he consult with the assembly of the people, or the council of nobles. . . .

But a monarchy is actually limited when the citizens have conferred it upon a king, with the condition that in certain spheres of action he confer with a council of the estates, without whose consent no decrees of the king will be valid. Although the king ought still to be empowered to call and dissolve that council, and to present to it the matters to be discussed in it, unless we wish to leave him the mere name of king, or to form an irregular state. And even if such orders when summoned may on their own initiative offer some suggestions looking to the kingdom's safety, yet their decrees on such matters will secure force only from the king's ratification. Such estates differ from counselors properly speaking in this, that, although both can treat with the king only through advice and suggestion, he can reject the suggestions of the latter but not those of the former. Nor will a king take it as an affront, if the estates do not accept some of his proposals, for he has promised always to hold before his eyes the welfare of the state, on which the judgement of a number of picked men is presumed to be better than that of one. Therefore, in case the estates happen to differ with him, the king may blame his own imprudence, or base passions, or the unhappy state of the commonwealth. . . .

. . . [T]he supreme sovereign can rightfully force citizens to all things which he judges to be of any advantage to the public good. But to force citizens to such things as are repugnant to the safety of a state, or opposed to natural laws, should be a thing never even contemplated, and if he has undertaken any such enormity, he oversteps without a doubt the limits of his power.

Source: Samuel Pufendorf, *De Jure Naturae et Gentium: Libri Octo,* trans. C. H. Oldfather and W. A. Oldfather (New York: Oceana Publications, 1964), 1068–1072, 1074–1077.

8

John Locke

John Locke (1632–1704) was an English physician and political theorist. The son of an attorney, Locke was educated at the University of Oxford, where he studied medicine. In 1666 Locke befriended Lord Anthony Ashley Cooper, the eventual Earl of Shaftesbury, and thenceforth served as his personal physician, special adviser, and confidante. Lord Ashley, intimately connected with the parliamentary opposition to the Stuart kings, was accused of conspiracy and imprisoned in 1681. Soon thereafter he escaped and fled to Holland. Because of his close ties to Lord Ashley, Locke joined him in exile. While in Holland Locke wrote several books, including his most influential work, Two Treatises of Government. *Upon the accession of William and Mary to the crown following the Glorious Revolution of 1688, Locke returned to England and published his political writings.*

Two Treatises had a substantial impact on American constitutional thinking, although the precise nature of that impact is subject to debate. That work provided crucial premises that would later be used both to defend and to attack judicial review. Locke plainly asserted that sovereignty was limited: no legislature had the power to violate certain fundamental rights. Locke also denied that any legal or other institution had special authority to prevent legislatures from violating fundamental rights. Rebellion was the appropriate Lockean response to laws inconsistent with natural rights or the social contract.

For more biographical information, see Maurice Cranston, John Locke: A Biography *(London: Longmans, Green & Company, 1957).*

. . . This legislative is not only the supreme power of the common-wealth, but sacred and unalterable in the hands where the community have once placed it; nor can any edict of any body else, in what form soever conceived, or by what power soever backed, have the force and obligation of a law, which has not its sanction from that legislative which the public has chosen and appointed: for without this the law could not have that, which is absolutely necessary to its being a law, the consent of the society, over whom no body can have a power to make laws, but by their own consent, and by authority received from them; and therefore all the obedience, which by the most solemn ties any one can be obliged to pay, ultimately terminates in this supreme power, and is directed by those laws which it enacts: nor can any oaths to any foreign power whatsoever, or any domestic subordinate power, discharge any member of the society from his obedience to the legislative, acting pursuant to their trust; nor oblige him to any obedience contrary to the laws so enacted, or farther than they do allow; it being ridiculous to imagine one can be tied ultimately to obey any power in the society, which is not the supreme.

. . .Though the legislative, whether placed in one or more, whether it be always in being, or only by intervals, though it be the supreme power in every common-wealth; yet:

First, It is not, nor can possibly be absolutely arbitrary over the lives and fortunes of the people. . . . A man, as has been proved, cannot subject himself to the arbitrary power of another; and having in the state of nature no arbitrary power over the life, liberty, or possession of another, but only so much as the law of nature gave him for the preservation of himself, and the rest of mankind; this is all he doth, or can give up to the common-wealth, and by it to the legislative power, so that the legislative can have no more than this. Their power, in the utmost bounds of it, is limited to the public good of the society. It is a power, that hath no other end but preservation, and therefore can never have a right to destroy, enslave, or designedly to impoverish the subjects. . . . Thus the law of nature stands as an eternal rule to all men, legislators as well as others.

The rules that they make for other men's actions, must, as well as their own and other men's actions, be conformable to the law of nature, i.e. to the will of God, of which that is a declaration, and the fundamental law of nature being the preservation of mankind, no human sanction can be good, or valid against it.

. . . Secondly, The legislative, or supreme authority, cannot assume to itself a power to rule by extemporary arbitrary decrees, but is bound to dispense justice, and decide the rights of the subject by promulgated standing laws, and known authorized judges. . . .

. . . Absolute arbitrary power, or governing without settled standing laws, can neither of them consist with the ends of society and government, which men would not quit the freedom of the state of nature for, and tie themselves up under, were it not to preserve their lives, liberties and fortunes, and by stated rules of right and property to secure their peace and quiet. It cannot be supposed that they should intend, had they a power so to do, to give to any one, or more, an absolute arbitrary power over their persons and estates, and put a force into the magistrate's hand to execute his unlimited will arbitrarily upon them.

. . . If a controversy arise betwixt a prince and some of the people, in a matter where the law is silent, or doubtful, and the thing be of great consequence, I should think the proper umpire, in such a case, should be the body of the people: for in cases where the prince hath a trust reposed in him, and is dispensed from the common ordinary rules of the law; there, if any men find themselves aggrieved, and think the prince acts contrary to, or beyond that trust, who so proper to judge as the body of the people—who, at first, lodged that trust in him—how far they meant it should extend? But if the prince, or whoever they be in the administration, decline that way of determination, the appeal then lies no where but to heaven; force between either persons, who have no known superior on earth, or which permits no appeal to a judge on earth, being properly a state of war, wherein the appeal lies only to heaven; and in that state the injured party must judge for himself, when he will think fit to make use of that appeal, and put himself upon it.

Source: John Locke, *Two Treatises of Government*, ed. Thomas I. Cook (New York: Hafner Press, 1997), 188–191, 207, 245–246.

9

Charles Louis de Secondat, Baron de Montesquieu

Charles Louis de Secondat (1689–1755), more commonly referred to as Montesquieu, was a French writer and political philosopher. When he was only eleven, Secondat was sent to study at the College of Juilly, then studied law at the University of Bordeaux. Secondat's uncle, the baron de Montesquieu, died in 1716, leaving Secondat a sizeable estate, his title as baron, and his office as president of the Bordeaux parliament. The new Baron de Montesquieu could now devote much of his time to travel, research, and writing. Montesquieu in 1721 anonymously published his Persian Letters. That work, which mocked the lifestyle of the wealthy French, was enormously successful, enjoying ten printings within its first year of publication alone. The Spirit of Laws, published in 1748, was less of a popular success but had far more historical influence.

The Spirit of the Laws was the first major work to emphasize the separation of powers as a means for preserving fundamental rights. Montesquieu claimed that legislating, executing, and judging were distinct governmental functions that required distinct and independent government institutions. He did not claim that the judiciary should have the power to declare legislative or executive acts unconstitu-

tional: courts were expected to apply the law faithfully to individual cases, and laws were made exclusively by the legislature. If laws were perceived to be too harsh, he claimed, the executive could exercise the pardoning power.

For biographical information, see Robert Shackleton, Montesquieu: A Critical Biography *(Oxford: Oxford University Press, 1961).*

. . . In every government there are three sorts of power: the legislative; the executive in respect to things dependent on the law of nations; and the executive in regard to matters that depend on the civil law.

By virtue of the first, the prince or magistrate enacts temporary or perpetual laws, and amends or abrogates those that have been already enacted. By the second, he makes peace or war, sends or receives embassies, establishes the public security, and provides against invasions. By the third, he punishes criminals, or determines the disputes that arise between individuals. The latter we shall call the judiciary power, and the other simply the executive power of the state. . . .

Again, there is no liberty, if the judiciary power be not separated from the legislative and executive. Were it joined with the legislative, the life and liberty of the subject would be exposed to arbitrary control; for the judge would be then the legislator. Were it joined to the executive power, the judge might behave with violence and oppression. . . .

The judiciary power ought not to be given to a standing senate; it should be exercised by persons taken from the body of the people at certain times of the year, and consistently with a form and manner prescribed by law, in order to erect a tribunal that should last only so long as necessity requires.

By this method the judicial power, so terrible to mankind, not being annexed to any particular state or profession, becomes, as it were, invisible. People have not then the judges continually present to their view; they fear the office, but not the magistrate. . . .

But though the tribunals ought not to be fixed, the judgments ought; and to such a degree as to be ever conformable to the letter of the law. Were they to be the private opinion of the judge, people would then live in society, without exactly knowing the nature of their obligations. . . .

Of the three powers above mentioned, the judiciary is in some measure next to nothing. . . .

It is possible that the law, which is clear sighted in one sense, and blind in another, might, in some cases, be too severe. But as we have already observed, the national judges are no more than the mouth that pronounces the words of the law, mere passive beings, incapable of moderating either its force or rigor. That part, therefore, of the legislative body, which we have just now observed to be a necessary tribunal on another occasion, is also a necessary tribunal in this; it belongs to its supreme authority to moderate the law in favor of the law itself, by mitigating the sentence.

Source: Baron de Montesquieu, *The Spirit of the Laws,* trans. Thomas Nugent (New York: Hafner Publishing, 1949), 151–154, 156, 159.

10

Emerich de Vattel

Emerich de Vattel (1714–1767) was a Swiss philosopher and lawyer. After studying philosophy at the Universities of Basel and Geneva, he obtained a position from Augustus III, elector of Dresden, as minister to Bern. This post did not demand much of Vattel's time, enabling him to concentrate on research and writing. Vattel wrote several works during this period, the most famous of which, The Law of Nations, *was published in 1758.*

The Law of Nations contains the first clear statement that a positive constitution was fundamental law that limited the power of legislative bodies. Legislation was not simply limited by natural law but by whatever rules people chose to embody in a constitution. Vattel, however, did not think any governing body was authorized to declare legislation unconstitutional. As did Locke, he thought that "the great body of the people" determined whether a constitution had been violated, not the national judiciary or any other governing institution.

. . . The fundamental law which determines the manner in which the public authority is to be exercised is what forms the *constitution of the State.* In it can be seen the organization by means of which the Nation acts in quality of a political body; how and by whom the people are to be governed, and what are the rights and duties of those who govern. This constitution is nothing else at bottom than the establishment of the system, according to which a Nation proposes to work in common to obtain the advantages for which the political society is formed. . . .

The constitution of a State and its laws are the foundation of public peace, the firm support of political authority, and a security for the liberty of the citizens. But this constitution is a mere dead letter, and the best laws are useless if they be not sacredly observed. It is therefore the duty of a Nation to be ever on the watch that the laws be equally respected, both by those who govern and by the people who are to be ruled by them. To attack the constitution of the State and to violate its laws is a capital crime against society; and if the persons who are guilty of it are those in authority, they add to this crime a perfidious abuse of the power confided to them. A Nation must uniformly put down such violations with all the vigor and vigilance which the importance of the case demand.

. . . It is the body of the Nation alone which has the right to check its rulers when they abuse their power. When the Nation keeps silent and obeys it is regarded as approving the conduct of its rulers, or at least as finding it supportable; and it does not belong to a small number of citizens to endanger the State under a pretence of reforming it.

On the same principles it is questionable that a Nation which finds its very constitution unsuited to it has the right to change it.

. . . It belongs essentially to the social body to make laws concerning the manner in which it is to be governed and the conduct of its citizens. This function is called the *legislative power.* The exercise of it may be confided by the Nation to the Prince, or to an assembly, or to both conjointly; and they are thereby empowered to make new laws and to repeal old ones. The question arises whether their power extends to the fundamental laws, whether they can change the constitution of the State. The principles we have laid down lead us to decide definitely that the authority of these legislators does not go that far, and that the fundamental laws must be sacred to them, unless they are expressly empowered by the nation to change them; for the constitution of a State should possess stability; and since the Nation established it in the first place, and afterwards confided the *legislative power* to certain persons, the fundamental laws are excepted from their authority. It is clear that the society had only in view to provide that the State should be furnished with laws enacted for special occasions, and with that object it gave to the legislators the power to repeal existing civil laws, and such public ones as were not fundamental, and to make new ones. Nothing leads us to think that it wished to subject the constitution itself to their will. In a word, it is from the constitution that the legislators derive their power; how, then, could

they change it without destroying the source of their authority?

We infer . . . that if there arise in the State disputes over the fundamental laws, over the public administration, or over the rights of the various powers which have a share in it, it belongs to the Nation alone to decide them, and to settle them according to its political constitution.

Source: E. de Vattel, *The Law of Nations, or the Principles of Natural Law Applied to the Conduct and to the Affairs of Nations and of Sovereigns,* trans. Charles G. Fenwick (New York: Oceana, 1964), vol. 3: 17–19.

11   William Blackstone

William Blackstone (1723–1780) was an English legal scholar and jurist. He completed his degree in legal studies at the University of Oxford in 1746. His law practice never flourished, but he eventually turned to teaching law, a profession with which he met with more success. His lectures were published in 1756 under the title An Analysis of the Laws of England. *Soon thereafter, Blackstone was invited to serve as the first professor of English law at Oxford. During his tenure, Blackstone wrote and published his* Commentaries on the Laws of England—*a work widely used for more than a century in nearly all programs of legal education throughout England and the United States. In the later part of his life, Blackstone briefly served in Parliament, as a justice on the Court of King's Bench and as a justice on the Court of Common Pleas.*

Commentaries on the Laws of England is the authoritative source for legislative supremacy as practiced in Great Britain. Blackstone thought human laws could not violate the natural law. Nevertheless, he insisted that justices had no power to determine whether a legislative or executive act infringed fundamental principles. When ambiguities existed on the face of a statute, justices were authorized to assume that legislators had not intended to violate fundamental law. Legislatures retained the ultimate authority to determine the nature of fundamental law. When faced with clear legislative commands, courts had no power to rely on higher law, natural law, constitutional law, or some other source of fundamental law.

For biographical information, see David A. Lockmiller, Sir William Blackstone *(Chapel Hill: University of North Carolina Press, 1938).*

. . . This law of nature, being co-eval with mankind and dictated by God himself, is of course superior in obligation to any other. It is binding over all the globe, in all countries, and at all times: no human laws are of any validity, if contrary to this; and such of them as are valid derive all their force, and all their authority, mediately or immediately, from this original. . . .

By the sovereign power, as was before observed, is meant the making of laws; for wherever that power resides, all others must conform to, and be directed by it, whatever appearance the

outward form and administration of the government may put on. For it is at any time in the option of the legislature to alter that form and administration by a new edict or rule, and to put the execution of the laws into whatever hands it pleases: and all the other powers of the state must obey the legislature power in the execution of their several functions, or else the constitution is at an end. . . .

Acts of parliament derogatory from the power of subsequent parliaments bind not. . . . Because the legislature, being in truth the sovereign power, is always of equal, always of absolute authority: it acknowledges no superior upon earth, which the prior legislature must have been, if it's ordinances could bind the present parliament. . . .

Lastly, acts of parliament that are impossible to be performed are of no validity; and if there arise out of them collaterally any absurd consequences, manifestly contradictory to common reason, they are, with regard to those collateral consequences, void. I lay down the rule with these restrictions; though I know it is generally laid down more largely, that acts of parliament contrary to reason are void. But if the parliament will positively enact a thing to be done which is unreasonable, I know of no power that can control it: and the examples usually alleged in support of this sense of the rule do none of them prove, that where the main object of a statute is unreasonable the judges are at liberty to reject it; for that were to set the judicial power above that of the legislature, which would be subversive of all government. But where some collateral matter arises out of the general words, and happens to be unreasonable; there the judges are in decency to conclude that this consequence was not foreseen by the parliament, and therefore they are at liberty to expound the statute by equity, and only *quoad hoc* disregard it. . . .

Source: William Blackstone, *Commentaries on the Laws of England* (Chicago: University of Chicago Press, 1979), vol. 1: 41, 49, 90–91.

12   James Otis

James Otis (1725–1783) was an American lawyer and political leader. Soon after graduating from Harvard College in 1743, Otis began to read law. He became deeply involved in constitutional politics in 1760, when the Superior Court of Massachusetts began issuing writs of assistance. These writs were open-ended, general search warrants authorizing customs officials to search for contraband wherever and whenever they felt necessary. Otis, who was serving as advocate general of the vice-admiralty court, was asked to defend the actions of the customs officials. Believing the writs to be tyrannical, he refused. Otis resigned his post, then defended a merchant whose liberty he felt had been violated by the writs. In the famous Writs of Assistance Case, *or* Paxton v. Gray *(1761), Otis argued that any act of Parliament that violated the natural rights of individuals was void. He lost the case but established his position as a leader in the colonial opposition to England. From that point forward, Otis published many pamphlets and delivered many speeches opposing various British measures. Sadly, Otis was struck on the head during an altercation with an English commissioner of customs in 1769. He never fully recovered.*

The Rights of the British Colonies Asserted and Proved was one of Otis's early pamphlets opposing the writs of assistance and asserting other limits on government power. In the pamphlet he insists on a judicial obligation to strike down government practices inconsistent with fundamental common-law rights. Otis derived this judicial power from Dr. Bonham's Case and other English decisions. Whether he and other colonial Americans correctly interpreted Sir Edward Coke is doubtful. Nevertheless, The Rights of British Colonies clearly expresses the increasingly widespread belief in Revolutionary America that the colonists had judicially enforceable rights against parliamentary practices inconsistent with perceived fundamental rights.

For more background information, see William Tudor, The Life of James Otis *(New York: Da Capo Press, 1970).*

. . . The same law of nature and of reason is equally obligatory on a *democracy,* an *aristoc-* *racy,* and a *monarchy:* Whenever the administrators, in any of those forms, deviate from truth, justice and equity, they verge towards tyranny, and are to be opposed; and if they prove incorrigible, they will be *deposed* by the people, if the people are not rendered too abject. Deposing the administrators of a *simple democracy* may sound oddly, but it is done every day, and in almost every vote. . . .

Every British subject born on the continent of America, or in any other of the British dominions, is by the law of God and nature, by the common law, and by act of parliament . . . entitled to all the natural, essential, inherent and inseparable rights of our fellow subjects in Great Britain. Among those rights are the following, which it is humbly conceived no man or body of men, not excepting the parliament, justly equitably and consistently with their own rights and the constitution, can take away. . . .

The supreme national legislative cannot be altered justly 'till the commonwealth is dissolved, nor a subordinate legislative taken away without forfeiture or other good cause. Nor then can the subjects in the subordinate government be reduced to a state of slavery, and subject to the despotic rule of others. A state has no right to make slaves of the conquered. . . .

To say the parliament is absolute and arbitrary, is a contradiction. The parliament cannot make 2 and 2,5: Omnipotency cannot do it. The supreme power in a state strictly speaking, belongs alone to God. Parliaments are in all cases to *declare* what is for the good of the whole; but it is not the *declaration* of parliament that makes it so: There must be in every instance, a higher authority, viz. GOD. Should an act of parliament be against any of *his* natural laws, which are *immutably* true, their declaration would be contrary to eternal truth, equity and justice, and consequently void: and so it would be adjudged by the parliament itself, when convinced of their mistake. Upon this great principle, parliaments repeal such acts, as soon as they find they have been mistaken, in having declared them to be for the public good, when in fact they were not so. When such mistake is evident and palpable, as in the instances in the appendix, the judges of the executive courts have declared the act "of a whole parliament void." . . . The supreme *legislative*, and the supreme *executive*, are a perpetual check and balance to each other. If the supreme executive errs, it is informed by the supreme legislative in parliament: if the supreme legislative errs, it is informed by the supreme executive in the King's courts of law. Here, the King appears, as represented by his judges, in the highest lustre and majesty, as supreme executor of the commonwealth; and he never shines brighter, but on his throne, at the head of the supreme legislative. . . .

Source: James Otis, "The Rights of the British Colonies Asserted and Proved," *University of Missouri Studies* 4 (1929): 47, 55, 57, 70, 78–79.

---

13   John Adams

John Adams (1735–1826) was an American political theorist and politician. Born and raised in what is now Quincy, Massachusetts, he graduated from Harvard College in 1755. Adams, an early proponent of American independence from England, signed the Declaration of Independence and served in the First and Second Continental Congresses. Recognized as one of the ablest thinkers on matters of constitutional design, Adams was flooded with questions about the best way to structure state constitutional institutions. He responded by writing his brief Thoughts on Government, *which he later expanded into* A Defense of the Constitutions of Government of the United States. *During the Revolutionary War and immediately following, Adams served in various overseas diplomatic positions. After ratification of the Constitution, he was elected vice president under George Washington and president in 1796. In 1800 Adams lost his bid for reelection to Thomas Jefferson. One of his last acts before leaving office was to appoint his secretary of state, John Marshall, as chief justice of the Supreme Court. Adams lived the remainder of his life in Massachusetts, dying on July 4, 1826. Thomas Jefferson, the primary author of the declaration, died on the same day, several hours earlier.*

Thoughts on Government highlights the near universal consensus in preconstitutional American thought on the merits of the separation of powers and a strong judiciary. This clear consensus on the need for judicial power did not reflect agreement on judicial review: Thoughts on Government does not vest the judiciary with the power to declare laws unconstitutional. Adams recommended that legislative power be limited by an appointive council armed with the power to void on any ground laws passed by the representative assembly.

For more biographical information, see John Ferling, John Adams: A Life *(Knoxville: University of Tennessee Press, 1992); and David McCulloch,* John Adams *(New York: Simon & Schuster, 2001).*

. . . A representation of the people in one assembly being obtained, a question arises, whether all the powers of government, legislative, executive, and judicial, shall be left in this body? I think a people cannot be long free, nor ever happy, whose government is in one assembly. . . .

1. A single assembly is liable to all the vices, follies, and frailties of an individual; subject to fits of humor, starts of passion, flights of enthusiasm, partialities, or prejudice, and consequently productive of hasty results and absurd judgments. . . .

4. A representative assembly, although extremely well qualified, and absolutely necessary, as a branch of the legislative, is unfit to exercise the executive power, for want of two essential properties, secrecy and despatch.

5. A representative assembly is still less qualified for the judicial power, because it is too numerous, too slow, and too little skilled in the laws.

6. Because a single assembly, possessed of all the powers of government, would make arbitrary laws for their own interest, execute all laws arbitrarily for their own interest, and adjudge all controversies in their own favor. . . .

The dignity and stability of government in all its branches, the morals of the people, and every blessing of society depend so much upon an upright and skillful administration of justice, that the judicial power ought to be distinct from both the legislative and executive, and independent upon both, that so it may be a check upon both, as both should be checks upon that. The judges, therefore, should be always men of learning and experience in the laws, of exemplary morals, great patience, calmness, coolness, and attention. Their minds should not be distracted with jarring interests; they should not be dependent upon any man, or body of men. To these ends, they should hold estates for life in their offices; or, in other words, their commissions should be during good behavior, and their salaries ascertained and established by law. . . .

Source: John Adams, *The Revolutionary Writings of John Adams*, ed. C. Bradley Thompson (Indianapolis: Liberty Fund, 2000), 288–290, 291–292.

14 *Commonwealth v. Caton* (1782)

In 1782 John Caton, James Lamb, and Joshua Hopkins were convicted of treason by a Virginia court and sentenced to death. Virginia statutory law at that time forbade gubernatorial pardons for this offense. The relevant statute declared, "[t]he governor . . . shall in no wise have or exercise a right of granting pardon to any person or persons convicted [of treason], but may suspend the execution until the meeting of the general assembly, who shall determine whether such person or persons are proper objects of mercy or not, and order accordingly." The three prisoners subsequently petitioned the Virginia House of Delegates for a pardon. The House of Delegates voted for a pardon and forwarded its resolution to the Senate for its concurrence. The Senate rejected the pardoning resolution. Caton, Lamb, and Hopkins claimed that the pardon granted by the House of Delegates was sufficient to secure their release. The state constitution, their attorney pointed out, declared that "[the governor] shall, with the advice of the Council of State, have the power of granting reprieves or pardons, except where the prosecution shall have been carried on by the House of Delegates, or the law shall otherwise particularly direct; in which case, no reprieve or pardon shall be granted, but by resolve of the House of Delegates." The prisoners insisted that Virginia law violated the state constitution by vesting the power to pardon treason in the general assembly rather than solely in the House of Delegates. As such, the prisoners concluded, courts in Virginia must treat that law as null and void. For background information, see William Michael Treanor, "The Case of the Prisoners and the Origins of Judicial Review," University of Pennsylvania Law Review (December 1994).

The justices sitting on the Court of Appeals of Virginia rejected the appeal but apparently accepted the claim that state courts had the power to declare laws unconstitutional. The justices who clearly considered the question of judicial power explicitly asserted that courts were authorized to strike down any statute inconsistent with the state constitution. A unanimous court agreed that the state law at issue was consistent with the state constitution. The Virginia Constitution, the justices concluded, did not require that pardons in treason cases be vested exclusively in the House of Delegates. The clause "or the law shall otherwise particularly direct" was interpreted as permitting the state assembly to vest the pardoning power in both houses of the Virginia legislature.

Opinion of Judge Wythe

I have heard of an english chancellor who said, and it was nobly said, that it was his duty to protect the rights of the subject, against the encroachments of the crown; and that he would do it, at every hazard. But if it was his duty to protect a solitary individual against the rapacity of the sovereign, surely, it is equally mine, to protect one branch of the legislature, and, consequently, the whole community, against the usurpations of the other: and, whenever the proper occasion occurs, I shall feel the duty; and, fearlessly, perform it. Whenever traitors shall be fairly convicted, by the verdict of their peers, before the competent tribunal, if one branch of the legislature, without the concurrence of the other, shall attempt to rescue the offenders from the sentence of the law, I shall not hesitate, sitting in this place, to say, to the general court, *Fiat justitia, ruat coelum*; and, to the usurping branch of the legislature, you attempt worse than a vain thing; for, although, you cannot succeed, you set an example, which may convulse society to its centre. Nay more, if the whole legislature, an event to be deprecated, should attempt to overleap the bounds, prescribed to them by the people, I, in administering the public justice of the country, will meet the united powers, at my seat in this tribunal; and, pointing to the constitution, will say, to them, here is the limit of your authority; and, hither, shall you go, but no further. . . .

Opinion of Pendleton

I shall pass to the two great points into which the question has been divided, whether, if the constitution of government and the act declaring what shall be treason are at variance on this subject, which shall prevail and be the rule of judgment? And then, whether they do contravene each other? The constitution of other governments in Europe or elsewhere, seem to throw little light upon this question, since we have a written record of that which the citizens of this state have adopted as their social compact; and beyond which we need not extend our researches. It has been very properly said, on all sides, that this act, declaring the rights of the citizens, and forming their government, divided it into three great branches, the legislative, executive, and judiciary, assigning to each its proper powers, and directing that each shall be kept separate and distinct, must be considered as a rule obligatory upon every department, not to be departed from on any occasion. But how far this court, in whom the judiciary powers may in some sort be said to be concentrated, shall have power to declare the nullity of a law passed in its forms by the legislative power, without exercising the power of that branch, contrary to the plain terms of that constitution, is indeed a deep, important, and I will add, a tremendous question, the decision of which might involve consequences to which gentlemen may not have extended their ideas. I am happy in being of opinion there is no occasion to consider it upon this occasion; and still more happy in the hope that the wisdom and prudence of the legislature will prevent the disagreeable necessity of ever deciding it, by suggesting the propriety of making the principles of the constitution the great rule to direct the spirit of their laws.

Opinion of Chancellor Blair and Others

Chancellor Blair and the rest of the judges, were of opinion, that the court had power to declare any resolution or act of the legislature, or of either branch of it, to be unconstitutional and void.

Source: Commonwealth v. Caton (1782): 5, 7–13, 20.

---

15   *Rutgers v. Waddington* (1784)

Elizabeth Rutgers was the owner of a brewery and malt house in New York City. During at least a portion of the Revolutionary War, Joshua Waddington, a British subject, occupied Rutgers's brewery and malt house under authority of British military authorities. In March 1783, the state of New York passed legislation providing that individuals who had been displaced from their homes or businesses during the war should be entitled to collect damages from those who had occupied their property. Rutgers subsequently sued Waddington to recover damages. The treaty ending the Revolutionary War, ratified by the Continental Congress on January 4, 1784, included a provision that barred claims by citizens of the United States against the subjects of Britain for certain actions that occurred during the war. Alexander Hamilton, serving as a defense attorney for Waddington, argued that the state law was contrary both to the peace treaty, as ratified under the power granted to the Continental Congress by the Articles of Confederation, and to the law of nations. The justices of the Mayor's Court first indicated that federal treatises made under the Articles of Confederation were superior to state law, but they did not rule on that ground. After suggesting that courts had no power to void laws passed by a legislative body, the justices asserted a power to disregard the natural import of laws when doing so would prevent substantial injustice.

For background information, see William Crosskey, Politics and the Constitution in the History of the United States *(Chicago: University of Chicago Press, 1953), vol. 2: 962–963.*

. . . We must acknowledge there appears to us very great force in the observation arising from the federal compact. By this compact these States are bound together as one great independent nation; and with respect to their common and national affairs, exercise a joint sovereignty, whose will can only be manifested by the acts of their delegates in Congress assembled. As a nation they must be governed by one common law of nations; for on any other principles how can they act with regard to foreign powers; and how shall foreign powers act towards them? It seems evident that abroad they can only be known in their federal capacity. What then must be the effect? What the confusion? if each separate State should arrogate to itself a right of changing at pleasure those laws, which are received as a rule of conduct, by the common consent of the greatest part of the civilized world.

We shall deduce only one inference from what hath been here observed—that to abrogate or alter any one of the known laws or usages of nations, by the authority of a single State, must be contrary to the very nature of the confederacy, and the evident intention of the articles, by which it is established, as well as dangerous to the Union itself.

. . . Our Union, as has been properly observed, is known and legalized in our Constitution, and adopted as a fundamental law in the first Act of our Legislature. The federal compact hath vested Congress with full and exclusive powers to make peace and war. This treaty they have made and ratified, and rendered its obligation perpetual.

And we are clearly of opinion, that no State in this Union can alter or abridge, in a single point, the federal articles or the treaty.

Source: Rutgers v. Waddington (1784).

But the operation and effects of the treaty, within our own State, are fit subjects of inquiry and decision: according to its spirit and true meaning we must determine our judgment; nor shall any man, by any act of ours, be deprived of the benefits which, on a fair and reasonable construction, he ought to derive from it. . . .

[T]he uncontrollable power of the legislature, and the sanctity of its laws, have been earnestly pressed by the counsel for the plaintiff; and a great number of authorities have been quoted to establish an opinion, that the courts of justice in no case ought to exercise a discretion in the construction of a statute.

However contradictory these authorities may appear to superficial observers, they are not only capable of being reconciled, but the result of the whole will appear to be wise, suited to human imperfection and easily explained.

The supremacy of the legislature need not be called into question; if they think fit positively to enact a law, there is no power which can control them. When the main object of such a law is clearly expressed, and the intention manifest, the judges are not at liberty . . . to reject it. . . .

But when a law is expressed in general words, and some collateral matter, which happens to arise from those general words, is unreasonable, there the judges are in decency to conclude, that the consequences were not foreseen by the legislature; and therefore they are at liberty to expound the statute by equity, and only *quoad hoc* to disregard it.

When the judicial make these distinctions, they do not control the legislature; they endeavor to give their intention its proper effect. . . .

16 *Trevett v. Weeden* (1786)

In 1786 Rhode Island imposed a penalty on individuals who refused to accept the state's paper money. Guilt under this law was determined without the benefit of a jury trial. John Trevett brought an action against John Weeden for refusing to accept paper money as payment. Weeden employed General James M. Varnum, a political leader of Rhode Island and a well-respected lawyer, as his defense attorney. Varnum argued that trial by jury was a fundamental constitutional right and that the legislation in question was unconstitutional and void. A short article from the Providence Gazette *of October 7, 1786, reported that, in deciding this case, several justices of the Superior Court of Judicature of Rhode Island declared the legislation in question was "repugnant and unconstitutional." The general assembly of Rhode Island responded to Trevett by summoning the justices to explain their actions. Legislators by a close vote rejected a measure to remove the justices from office.*

For more background information, see Charles Warren, "Earliest Cases of Judicial Review of State Legislation by Federal Courts," Yale Law Journal *(November 1922): 16–22.*

. . . John Trevett against John Weeden, for refusing to receive the paper bills of this State, in payment for meat sold in market, equivalent to silver or gold; and upon the day following, the court delivered the unanimous opinion of the judges, that the information was not cognizable before them. . . .

. . . Weeden, being demanded and present in court, made the following answer: "That it appears by the Act of the General Assembly, whereon said information is founded, that the said Act hath expired, and hath no force: also, for that by the said Act the matters of complaint are made triable before special courts, uncontrollable by the Supreme Judiciary Court of the State; and also for that the court is not, by said Act, authorized and empowered to impanel a jury to try the facts charged in the information; and so the same is unconstitutional and void." . . .

. . . [U]pon the next succeeding week a summons was issued from both Houses of Assembly, requiring an immediate attendance of the judges, "to render their reasons for adjudging an Act of the General Assembly unconstitutional, and so void." . . . This circumstance induced the Assembly to dismiss them at that time, but they were directed to appear at the October session next following. . . .

Certain ceremonies being adjusted, and the records of the court produced, the Honor-

able . . . Howell . . . addressed himself to the Assembly in a very learned, sensible, and elaborate discourse. . . .

Under the first head, the honorable gentleman pointed out the objectionable parts of the Act upon which the information was founded, and most clearly demonstrated, by a variety of conclusive arguments, that it was unconstitutional, had not the force of a law, and could not be executed. His arguments were enforced by many authorities of the first eminence, in addition to those produced upon the trial. But as this part of the subject hath in a great measure been anticipated, we shall not enter into a further detail, concluding that the legal defence of the court, in showing "that they were not accountable to the legislature for the reasons of their judgment," will be more interesting to the public. . . .

If it be conceded, that the equal distribution of justice is as requisite to answer the purposes of government as the enacting of salutary laws, it is evident that the judiciary power should be as independent as the legislative. And consequently the judges cannot be answerable for their opinion, unless charged with criminality. . . .

A motion was then made, and seconded, "for dismissing the judges from their office." . . .

The only question remaining was, whether the judges should be discharged from any further attendance upon the General Assembly, as no accusation appeared against them? The question was put, and decided by a very great majority, "that as the judges are not charged with any criminality in rendering the judgment, upon the information, Trevett against Weeden, they are therefore discharged from any further attendance upon this Assembly, on that account."

Source: Trevett v. Weeden (1786).

---

17   *Bayard v. Singleton* (1787)

In 1785 the North Carolina legislature mandated that state courts immediately dismiss, without regard to the merits of the cases at hand, any action seeking to recover lands under the previously enacted revolutionary confiscation act. In the 1787 case Bayard v. Singleton, *the defendant moved to have his case dismissed. The court delayed a decision and attempted to secure a compromise between the two parties that would avoid any conflict between the state's constitution and the law. During this delay, the judges were summoned to appear before the state legislature to explain their actions. They were subsequently charged with disregarding an act of the legislature and making remarks derogatory of its supreme authority. Found guilty of these charges, the judges were nevertheless discharged without penalty, since they had not actually been found guilty of malpractice in office. Defendant Singleton renewed his motion to dismiss the case, and the following decision declaring a state law unconstitutional was rendered.*

For background information, see William Crosskey, Politics and the Constitution in the History of the United States *(Chicago: University of Chicago Press, 1953), vol. 2: 971–972.*

Opinion of Judges Ashe, Williams, and Spencer

. . . That by the constitution every citizen had undoubtedly a right to a decision of his property by a trial by jury. For that if the Legislature could take away this right, and require him to stand condemned in his property without a trial, it might with as much authority require his life to be taken away without a trial by jury, and that he should stand condemned to die, without the formality of any trial at all: that if the members of the General Assembly could do this, they might with equal authority, not only render themselves the Legislators of the State for life, without any further election of the people, from thence transmit the dignity and authority of legislation down to their heirs male forever.

But that it was clear, that no act they could pass, could by any means repeal or alter the constitution, because if they could do this, they would at the same instant of time, destroy their own existence as a Legislature, and dissolve the government thereby established. Consequently the constitution (which the judicial power was bound to take notice of as much as of any other law whatever,) standing in full force as the fundamental law of the land, notwithstanding the act on which the present motion was grounded, the same act must of course, in that instance, stand as abrogated and without any effect.

Source: Bayard v. Singleton (1787): 5, 6–7 .

18   Spaight–Iredell Correspondence, August 1787

Bayard v. Singleton *inspired an important correspondence on the merits of judicial review between Richard Dobbs Spaight, a member of the Philadelphia convention, and James Iredell, a prominent North Carolina jurist. Their discussion provides the most detailed analysis of judicial power that took place during the late eighteenth century and highlights numerous themes that would be discussed during and after the Marbury litigation. Both letters were written while the Constitutional Convention was meeting. In his letter, Spaight argued that judges should not have the power of judicial review. He believed that judicial decisions declaring laws unconstitutional usurped legislative power and that constitutional limitations were best protected by annual legislative elections. Iredell, however, defended judicial review. More so than Chief Justice Marshall had done in 1803, Iredell in 1787 emphasized the importance of judicial review as a means for protecting individual right from "occasional majorities."*

Richard Dobbs Spaight (1758–1802) was born in North Carolina and orphaned at the age of eight. He was educated in Ireland and eventually completed his advanced studies at the University of Glasgow in Scotland. Spaight returned to North Carolina in 1778 and was promptly elected to the House of Commons, where he would serve intermittently for the next ten years. In 1785 Spaight was chosen Speaker of the House of Commons and in 1787 selected as a delegate to the Philadelphia convention. After the convention, Spaight actively fought for ratification of the Constitution. Following an unsuccessful bid for election to the United States Senate in 1789, Spaight temporarily retired from politics because of ill health. In 1792 he was elected governor of North Carolina and subsequently reelected twice. Spaight was then elected to the House of Representatives, serving as a Jeffersonian Republican from 1798 until 1801. In 1802 Spaight was killed in a duel with John Stanly, a prominent Federalist leader.

James Iredell (1751–1799) was born in England, the son of a British merchant. At the age of seventeen he was appointed comptroller of customs for Edenton, North Carolina. Between 1774 and 1776, Iredell served as collector of the port, a position that exposed him to the growing conflict between England and the colonies. In 1776 Iredell turned his full attention to the practice of law. He began to write essays supporting the revolutionary cause, without calling for colonial independence. Iredell was elected attorney general in 1779 and to the Council of State in 1787. He actively supported ratification of the proposed constitution, publishing a series of letters under the pseudonym "Marcus" arguing for its adoption. Iredell also was a prominent member of the North Carolina state ratifying convention. In 1790 President George Washington appointed Iredell associate justice of the United States Supreme Court. Iredell was only thirty-eight years old, but the exhausting task of riding circuit soon took its toll on his health. He died in 1799, after less than ten years on the bench.

For more biographical information, see Griffith J. McRee, Life and Correspondence of James Iredell, One of the Associate Justices of the Supreme Court of the United States *(New York: P. Smith, 1857).*

Spaight to Iredell, August 12, 1787

. . . It cannot be denied, but that the Assembly have passed laws unjust in themselves, and militating in their principles against the Constitution, in more instances than one, and in my opinion of a more alarming and destructive nature than the one which the judges, by their own authority, thought proper to set aside and declare void. . . . [I]t is immaterial what law they have declared void; it is their usurpation of the authority to do it, that I complain of, as I do most positively deny that they have any such power; nor can they find any thing in the Constitution, either directly or impliedly, that will support them, or give them any color of right to exercise that authority. Besides, it would have been absurd, and contrary to the practice of all the world, had the Constitution vested such powers in them, as they would have operated as an absolute negative on the proceedings of the Legislature, which no judiciary ought ever to possess: and the State, instead of being governed by the representatives in general Assembly, would be subject to the will of three individuals. . . . If they possessed the power, what check or control would there be to their proceedings? or who is there to take the same liberty with them, that they have taken with the Legislature, and declare their opinions to be erroneous? none that I know of. In consequence of which, whenever the judges should become corrupt, they might at pleasure set aside every law, however just or consistent with the Constitution, to answer their designs; and the persons and property of every individual would be completely at their disposal. Many instances might be brought to show the absurdity and impropriety of such a power being lodged with the judges.

It must be acknowledged that our Constitution, unfortunately, has not provided a sufficient check to prevent the intemperate and unjust proceedings of our Legislature, though such a check would be very beneficial, and, I think, absolutely necessary to our well-being: the only one that I know of, is the annual election, which, by leaving out such members as have supported improper measures, will in some degree remedy, though it cannot prevent, such evils as may arise.

Iredell to Spaight, August 26, 1787

. . . I confess it has ever been my opinion, that an act inconsistent with the Constitution was void; and that the judges, consistently with their duties, could not carry it into effect. The Constitution appears to me to be fundamental law, limiting the powers of the Legislature, and with which every exercise of those powers must, necessarily, be compared. Without an express Constitution the powers of the Legislature would undoubtedly have been absolute . . . and any act passed, *not inconsistent with natural justice* . . . would have been binding on the people. The experience of the evils which the American war fully disclosed, attending an absolute power in a legislative body, suggested the propriety of a real, original contract between the people and their future Government, such, perhaps, as there has been no instance of in the world in America. . . . In a republican Government (as I conceive) *individual liberty* is a matter of the utmost moment, as, if there be no check upon the public passions, it is in the greatest danger. The majority having the rule in their own hands, may take care of themselves; but in what condition are the minority, if the power of the other is without limit? These considerations, I suppose, or similar ones, occasioned such express provisions for the personal liberty of each citizen, which the citizens, when they formed the Constitution, chose to reserve as an unalienated right, and not to leave at the mercy of any Assembly whatever. . . . The Constitution, therefore, *being a fundamental law*, and a law *in writing* of the solemn nature I have mentioned. . ., the judicial power, in the exercise of their authority, must take notice of it as the groundwork of that as well as of all other authority; and as no article of the Constitution can be repealed by a Legislature, which derives its whole power from it, it follows either that the *fundamental unrepealable* law must be obeyed, by the rejection of an act unwarranted by and inconsistent with it, or you must obey an act founded on an authority not given by the people, and to which, therefore, the people owe no obedience. It is not that the judges are appointed arbiters, and to determine as it were upon any application, whether the Assembly have or have not violated the Constitution; but when an act is necessarily brought in judgment before them, they must, unavoidably, determine one way or another. . . . It really appears to me, the exercise of the power is unavoidable, the Constitution not being a mere imaginary thing, about which ten thousand different opinions may be formed, but a written document to which all may have recourse, and to which, therefore, the judges cannot wilfully blind themselves. . . . In any other light than as I have stated it, the greater part of the provisions of the Constitution would appear to me to be ridiculous, since in my opinion nothing could be more so than for the representatives of a people solemnly assembled to form a Constitution, to set down a number of political dogmas, which might or might not be regarded; whereas it must have been intended, as I conceive, that it should be a system of authority, not depending on the casual whim or accidental ideas of a majority either in or out of doors for the time being; but to remain in force until by a similar appointment of deputies specially appointed for the same important purpose; and alterations should be equal solemnity and deliberation made.

. . . In all doubtful cases, to be sure, the Act ought to be supported: it should be unconstitutional beyond dispute before it is pronounced such. I conceive the remedy by a new election to be of very little consequence, because this would only secure the views of a majority; whereas every citizen in my opinion should have a surer pledge for his constitutional rights than the wisdom and activity of any occasional majority of his fellow-citizens, who, if their own rights are in fact unmolested, may care very little for his. . . .

Source: Griffith J. McRee, *Life and Correspondence of James Iredell, One of the Associate Justices of the Supreme Court of the United States* (New York: P. Smith, 1857), 169–170, 172–1776.

Section II (Documents 19–33):
Constitutional Foundations

The persons responsible for framing and ratifying the Constitution of the United States provided more immediate foundations than foreign practices, Enlightenment political theory, and previous state court decisions had done for *Marbury v. Madison* and the American practice of judicial review. Members of the framing and state ratifying conventions were authorized to decide whether past practices that resembled judicial review would be emulated, expanded, modified, limited, or altogether abandoned. Their decisions influenced both the capacity and authority of federal courts to declare federal and state laws unconstitutional. The American practice of judicial review has been structured by the general principles underlying the 1787 constitution, the specific declarations about judicial power set out in Articles III and VI, and those provisions in Article III designed to secure justices the independence necessary to exercise their constitutional powers.

Founding conceptions continue influencing judicial practice. Courts claim their authority to declare laws unconstitutional derives from the constitutional provisions ratified in 1789. The federal judiciary is staffed by the life-tenured justices mandated in Article III and, with the exception of the Eleventh Amendment, federal court jurisdiction in constitutional cases is rooted in the provisions ratified by the framers. Many Americans in the late eighteenth, nineteenth, twentieth, and early twenty-first centuries maintain that the judiciary should exercise those powers and only those powers that the framers intended the judiciary to exercise. Commentators scour the original debates over the Constitution to determine whether the framers intended courts to have the power to declare laws unconstitutional, how and when that power could be exercised, and whether the framers also intended that courts would have the final authority to determine what the Constitution means.

These original historical materials are sparse. The framers were committed to limited government, but they did not regard judicial review as the most important practice for limiting government. Debate in both the framing and ratifying conventions was over the structure of the elected branches of government and the powers vested in the national government. When persons commented on the judicial power to declare laws unconstitutional, those comments were typically made during debates on other subjects. As a result, determining the precise powers a particular commentator thought the judiciary should possess or what understandings about the federal judiciary were broadly shared is difficult. The weight of the evidence and most contemporary scholarship suggest that most, not all, persons responsible for the Constitution assumed that justices would have the power to declare laws unconstitutional. The precise contours of that power cannot be assessed with any meaningful reliability.

Documents 19–22:
The Constitutional Convention of 1787

By the mid-1780s, many distinguished political leaders throughout the thirteen colonies were convinced that the Articles of Confederation did not provide the federal government with sufficient powers to accomplish vital national purposes. They also believed, because of the requirement for unanimity, that the Articles could not be amended to rectify various deficiencies. When delegates from twelve states—Rhode Island did not participate—met in Philadelphia in the summer of 1787, they promptly decided to replace, rather than merely amend, the Articles. For the best recent work on the framing and ratifying conventions see Jack N. Rakove, *Original Meanings: Politics and Ideas in the Making of the Constitution* (New York: Alfred A. Knopf, 1996).

When debating various proposals, the delegates discussed the separation of powers, checks and balances, federalism, and representation at length. The structure of the elected branches of national government was subject to extensive scrutiny, but not the structure of the national judiciary. The delegates quickly agreed to establish a Supreme Court staffed by life-tenured justices and to vest Congress with the power to establish lower federal courts staffed by life-tenured justices. Judicial review was discussed only incidentally to other subjects, most notably the proposed council of revision and the proposed power of the national legislature to veto state laws. Most delegates who mentioned judicial power assumed that courts would have the power to declare laws unconstitutional; some prominent framers bluntly rejected that power. These diverging views were never explicitly resolved during the Philadelphia convention.

Documents 23–33:
The Ratification Debate

The ink was hardly dry on the proposed constitution when a contentious debate broke out over whether the document should be adopted. Thousands of letters, articles, and pamphlets were written and published throughout the thirteen states. While several states easily ratified the Constitution, the contest was more heated and discussion far more lengthy in such crucial battlegrounds as New York, Virginia, and Massachusetts. Federalists triumphed in the end, but only after promising to add amendments during the First Congress that would further limit national power. Two states, North Carolina and Rhode Island, did not ratify the Constitution until after President George Washington took office. For more information on the ratification struggles in each state, see Michael Allen Gillespie and Michael Lienesch, eds., *Ratifying the Constitution* (Lawrence, Kan.: University Press of Kansas, 1989).

The ratification debates, for the most part, paid no more attention to the federal judiciary than the framing debates had done. The main bones of contention between Federalists and Anti-Federalists were the powers granted the federal government, the structure of representation, and the absence of a bill of rights. Still, in the pamphlet wars and at the various state ratifying conventions, many prominent political leaders, including future chief justice of the United States John Marshall, commented on the judicial power to declare laws unconstitutional.

Those Federalists who discussed the matter explicitly stated that the judiciary had the power to declare laws unconstitutional, but they did elaborate on how they anticipated that power would be exercised. Anti-Federalists who mentioned the subject agreed that the Constitution vested the judiciary with the power to declare laws unconstitutional. Prominent opponents of the Constitution worried that the federal judiciary would overwhelm the states or not be strong enough to resist attempts by the national legislature to overwhelm the states.

19   The Virginia Plan, May 29, 1787

From the very beginning of the convention prominent framers declared their intention to abandon the Articles of Confederation for a constitution that granted far more power to the national government than previously held. The Virginia Plan called for a national legislature directly elected by the people of each state that would appoint members to both the second legislative branch of the national government and the executive branch. Two provisions of the Virginia Plan proved particularly controversial and inspired debates that frequently touched on questions of judicial power. The first was the provision giving the national government power "to legislate in all cases to which the separate States are incompetent" and to reject any state law deemed inconsistent with the Constitution. The second was the provision establishing a "council of revision" composed of the president and some federal justices authorized to prevent any measure passed by the national legislature from becoming law. Both the national veto and the council of revision were eventually rejected. The framers did, however, adopt the Virginia Plan's proposals about the national judiciary almost verbatim.

6. Resolved. . . ; that the National Legislature ought to be impowered . . . to negative all laws passed by the several States, contravening in the opinion of the National Legislature the articles of Union. . . .

8. Resd. that the Executive and a convenient number of the National Judiciary, ought to compose a Council of revision with authority to examine every act of the National Legislature before it shall operate, & every act of a particular Legislature before a Negative thereon shall be final; and that the dissent of the said Council shall amount to a rejection, unless the Act of the Na-

tional Legislature be again passed, or that of a particular Legislature be again negatived by _____ of the members of each branch.

9. Resd. that a National Judiciary be established to consist of one or more supreme tribunals, and of inferior tribunals to be chosen by the National Legislature, to hold their offices during good behaviour; and to receive punctually at stated times fixed compensation for their services, in which no increase or diminution shall be made so as to affect the persons actually in office at the time of such increase or diminution.

Source: Max Farrand, ed., *The Records of the Federal Convention of 1787* (New Haven: Yale University Press, 1937), vol. 1: 20–22.

20 Debate over the Council of Revision

James Madison fought hard at the Constitutional Convention for a council of revision, composed of the president and some federal justices, that would have the right to reject every national law passed by the national legislature. That proposal was never accepted. Several delegates at the convention claimed that the Constitution vested the justices of the Supreme Court with the power to declare laws unconstitutional in the normal course of judicial business. Other delegates insisted that justices should not have that power. The framers resolved the controversy over the council of revision when they rejected that proposal in favor of a qualified presidential veto over national legislation. The framing convention did not explicitly determine whether courts would have the power to declare laws unconstitutional in the normal course of judicial business.

June 4, 1787:

Mr. GERRY doubts whether the Judiciary ought to form a part of it, as they will have a sufficient check agst. encroachments on their own department by their exposition of the laws, which involved a power of deciding on their Constitutionality. In some States the Judges had actually set aside laws as being agst. the Constitution. This was done too with general approbation. . . .

Mr. KING . . . observ[ed] that the Judges ought to be able to expound the law as it should come before them, free from the bias of having participated in its formation.

Mr. WILSON thinks neither the original proposition nor the amendment go far enough. If the Legislative Exetv & Judiciary ought to be distinct & independent. . . . He was for varying the proposition in such a manner as to give the Executive & Judiciary jointly an absolute negative. . . .

Mr. BEDFORD was opposed to every check on the Legislative, even the Council of Revision first proposed. He thought it would be sufficient to mark out in the Constitution the boundaries to the Legislative Authority, which would give all the requisite security to the rights of the other departments. The Representatives of the people were the best Judges of what was for their interest, and ought to be under no external controul whatever. . . .

[Mr. MADISON.] The Judicial ought to be introduced in the business of Legislation—they will protect their Department, and united [with] the Executive render their Check or negative more respectable. . . .

We must introduce the Checks, which will destroy the measures of an interested majority—in this view a negative in the Ex[ecutive] is not only necessary for its safety, but for the safety of a minority in Danger of oppression from an unjust and interested majority—The independent condition of the Ex[ecutive] who has the Eyes of all nations on him will render him a just Judge—add the Judiciary and you increase the respectability. . . .

Mr. Dickinson could not agree with Gentlemen in blending the national Judicial with the Executive, because the one is the expounder, and the other the Executor of the Laws.

July 21, 1787:

Mr. WILSON. . . . The Judiciary ought to have an opportunity of remonstrating agst. projected encroachments on the people as well as on themselves. It had been said that the Judges, as expositors of the Laws would have an opportunity of defending their constitutional rights. There was weight in this observation; but this power of the Judges did not go far enough. Laws may be unjust, may be unwise, may be dangerous, may be destructive; and yet may not be so unconstitutional as to justify the Judges in refusing to give them effect. Let them have a share in the Revisionary power, and they will have an opportunity of taking notice of these characters of a law, and of counteracting, by the weight of their opinions the improper views of the Legislature. . . .

Mr. GHORUM did not see the advantage of employing the Judges in this way. As Judges they are not to be presumed to possess any peculiar knowledge of the mere policy of public measures. Nor can it be necessary as a security for their constitutional rights. . . . He thought it would be best to let the Executive alone be responsible, and at most to authorize him to call on Judges for their opinions.

Mr. ELSEWORTH. . . . The aid of the Judges will give more wisdom & firmness to the Executive. They will possess a systematic and accurate knowledge of the Laws, which the Executive can not be expected always to possess. The law of Nations also will frequently come into question. Of this the Judges alone will have competent information.

Mr. MADISON. . . . It would be useful to the Judiciary departmt. by giving it an additional opportunity of defending itself agst. Legislative encroachments; It would be useful to the Executive, by inspiring additional confidence & firmness in exerting the revisionary power. . . . Experience in all the States had evinced a powerful tendency in the Legislature to absorb all power into its vortex. This was the real source of danger to the American Constitutions; & suggested the necessity of giving every defensive authority to the other departments that was consistent with republican principles.

Mr. GERRY. . . . The motion was liable to strong objections. It was combining & mixing together the Legislative & the other departments. It was establishing an improper coalition between the Executive & Judiciary departments. It was making Statesmen of the Judges; and setting them up as the guardians of the Rights of the people. . . .

Mr. STRONG thought with Mr. Gerry that the power of making ought to be kept distinct from that of expounding, the laws. No maxim was better established. The Judges in exercising the function of expositors might be influenced by the part they had taken, in framing the laws.

Mr. Govr. MORRIS. Some check being necessary on the Legislature, the question is in what hands it should be lodged. . . . He did not think that an Executive appointed for 6 years, and impeachable whilst in office wd. be a very effectual check. On the other side it was urged that he ought to be reinforced by the Judiciary department. Agst. this it was objected that Expositors of laws ought to have no hand in making them, and arguments in favor of this had been drawn from England. . . . The interest of our Executive is so inconsiderable & so transitory, and his means of defending it so feeble, that there is the justest ground to fear his want of firmness in resisting incroachments. He was extremely apprehensive that the auxiliary firmness & weight of the Judiciary would not supply the deficiency. . . .

Mr. L. MARTIN. Considered the association of the Judges with the Executive as a dangerous innovation; as well as one which could not produce the particular advantage expected from it. A knowledge of Mankind, and of Legislative affairs cannot be presumed to belong in a higher . . . degree to the Judges than to the Legislature. And as to the Constitutionality of laws, that point will come before the Judges in their proper official character. In this character they have a negative on the laws. Join them with the Executive in the Revision and they will have a double negative. It is necessary that the Supreme Judiciary should have the confidence of the people. This will soon be lost, if they are employed in the task of remonstrating agst. popular measures of the Legislature. Besides in what mode & proportion are they to vote in the Council of Revision?

Mr. MADISON could not discover in the proposed association of the Judges with the Executive in the Revisionary check on the Legislature any violation of the maxim which requires the great departments of power to be kept separate & distinct. . . . If a Constitutional discrimination of the departments on paper were a sufficient security to each agst. encroachments of the others, all further provisions would indeed be superfluous. But experience had taught us a distrust of that security; and that it is necessary to introduce such a balance of powers and interests, as will guarantee the provisions on paper. . . . The objection agst. a union of the Judiciary & Executive branches in the revision of the laws, had either no foundation or was not carried far enough. If such a Union was an improper mixture of powers, or such a Judiciary check on the laws, was inconsistent with the Theory of a free Constitution, it was equally so to admit the Executive to any participation in the making of laws; and the revisionary plan ought to be discarded altogether.

Col. MASON. . . . It had been said [by Mr. L. Martin] that if the Judges were joined in this check on the laws, they would have a double negative, since in their expository capacity of Judges they would have one negative. He would reply that in this capacity they could impede in one case only, the operation of laws. They could declare an unconstitutional law void. But with regard to every law however unjust oppressive or pernicious, which did not come plainly under this description, they would be under the necessity as Judges to give it a free course. He wished the further use to be made of the Judges, of giving aid in preventing every improper law. Their aid will be the more valuable as they are in the habit and practice of considering laws in their true principles, and in all their consequences. . . .

Mr. GERRY had rather give the Executive an absolute negative for its own defence than thus to blend together the Judiciary & Executive departments. . . .

Mr. GHORUM. All agree that a check on the Legislature is necessary. But there are two objections agst. admitting the Judges to share in it which no observations on the other side seem to obviate. the 1st. is that the Judges ought to carry into the exposition of the laws no prepossessions with regard to them. 2d. that as the Judges will outnumber the Executive, the revisionary check would be thrown entirely out of the Executive hands, and instead of enabling him to defend himself, would enable the Judges to sacrifice him.

Mr. RUTLIDGE thought the Judges of all men the most unfit to be concerned in the revisionary Council. The Judges ought never to give their opinion on a law till it comes before them. . . .

August 15, 1787:

Mr. MADISON moved that all acts before they become laws should be submitted both to the Executive and Supreme Judiciary Departments. . . .

Mr. PINKNEY opposed the interference of the Judges in the Legislative business: it will involve them in parties, and give a previous tincture to their opinions.

Mr. MERCER heartily approved the motion. It is an axiom that the Judiciary ought to be separate from the Legislative: but equally so that it ought to be independent of that department. . . . He disapproved of the Doctrine that the Judges as expositors of the Constitution should have authority to declare a law void.

Mr. DICKENSON was strongly impressed with the remark of Mr. Mercer as to the power of the Judges to set aside the law. He thought no such power ought to exist. He was at the same time at a loss what expedient to substitute. The Justiciary of Arragon he observed became by degrees, the lawgiver.

Mr. Govr. MORRIS, suggested the expedient of an absolute negative in the Executive. He could not agree that the Judiciary which was part of the Executive, should be bound to say that a direct violation of the Constitution was law. A controul over the legislature might have its inconveniences. But view the danger on the other side. . . .

Mr. SHERMAN. Can one man be trusted better than all the others if they all agree? This was neither wise nor safe. He disapproved of Judges meddling in politics and parties. We have gone far enough in forming the negative as it now stands.

Source: Max Farrand, ed., *The Records of the Federal Convention of 1787* (New Haven: Yale University Press, 1937), vol. 1: 97–98, 100–101, 108, 110; vol. 2: 73–80, 298, 299–300.

21

Debate over the Legislative Veto of State Laws and Supremacy Clause

James Madison thought the Constitution would survive only if the national government could veto all state laws deemed inconsistent with the Constitution or the national interest. He repeatedly urged the framing convention to adopt his proposed national veto, only to fail on all occasions. Madison believed that the national legislature should be the institution initially responsible for voiding unconstitutional state laws. Several delegates who spoke against the national veto maintained that the judiciary was better suited for determining whether state laws were unconstitutional. Immediately after the national veto was voted down, Luther Martin proposed what would later become the supremacy clause. That provision in Article VI quite clearly authorizes state courts to declare state laws unconstitutional.

July 17, 1787:

Mr. SHERMAN thought it unnecessary, as the Courts of the States would not consider as valid any law contravening the Authority of the Union, and which the legislature would wish to be negatived. . . .

Mr. MADISON, considered the negative on the laws of the States as essential to the efficacy & security of the Genl. Govt. . . . Confidence can not be put in the State Tribunals as guardians of the National authority and interests. In all the States these are more or less dependt. on the Legislatures. In Georgia they are appointed annually by the Legislature. In R. Island the Judges who refused to execute an unconstitutional law were displaced, and others substituted, by the Legislature who would be willing instruments of the wicked & arbitrary plans of their masters. A power of negativing the improper laws of the States is at once the most mild & certain means of preserving the harmony of the system. . . .

Mr. Govr. MORRIS. . . . A law that ought to be negatived will be set aside in the Judiciary de-

partmt. and if that security should fail; may be repealed by a Nationl. law. . . .

August 23, 1787:

Mr. C- PINKNEY moved to add as an additional power to be vested in the Legislature of the U.S. "To negative all laws passed by the several States interfering in the opinion of the Legislature with the general interests and harmony of the Union; provided that two thirds of the members of each House assent to the same.". . .

MR. SHERMAN thought it unnecessary; the laws of the General Government being Supreme & paramount to the State laws according to the plan, as it now stands. . . .

Mr. WILSON considered this as the key-stone wanted to compleat the wide arch of Government, we are raising. . . . The firmness of Judges is not of itself sufficient. Something further is requisite. It will be better to prevent the passage of an improper law, than to declare it void when passed.

Source: Max Farrand, ed., *The Records of the Federal Convention of 1787* (New Haven: Yale University Press, 1937), vol. 2: 27–29, 390, 391.

22

Debate over the Mode of Ratification, July 23, 1787

The framers of the Constitution insisted that the text be ratified by specially elected conventions rather than by existing state legislatures. This mode of ratification was deemed a necessary expression of the founding belief that, as constitutions were designed to limit government power, constitutions had to be ratified by the people rather than by existing government institutions. Both James Madison and Gouverneur Morris declared that ratification by the people provided crucial foundations for the judicial power to void legislation not authorized by the populace who approved the Constitution. Had the Constitution been ratified by state legislatures, those legislators might have claimed authority to alter their constitutional powers or to determine what the Constitution meant.

Col. MASON considered a reference of the plan to the authority of the people as one of the most important and essential of the Resolutions. The Legislatures have no power to ratify it. They are the mere creatures of the State Constitutions, and can not be greater than their creators. . . .

Mr. Govr. MORRIS. . . . Legislative alterations not conformable to the federal compact, would clearly not be valid. The Judges would consider them as null & void. Whereas in case of an appeal to the people of the U.S., the supreme authority, the federal compact may be altered by a *majority of them*; in like manner as the Constitution of a particular State may be altered by a majority of the people of the State. . . .

Mr. MADISON thought it clear that the Legislatures were incompetent to the proposed changes.

These changes would make essential inroads on the State Constitutions, and it would be a novel & dangerous doctrine that a Legislature could change the constitution under which it held its existence. . . . He considered the difference between a system founded on the Legislatures only, and one founded on the people, to be the true difference between a *league* or *treaty*, and a *Constitution*. . . . In point of *political operation*, there were two important distinctions in favor of the latter. A law violating a treaty ratified by a preexisting law, might be respected by the Judges as a law, though an unwise or perfidious one. A law violating a constitution established by the people themselves, would be considered by the Judges as null & void. . . .

Source: Max Farrand, ed., *The Records of the Federal Convention of 1787* (New Haven: Yale University Press, 1937), vol. 2: 88–89, 92–93.

23

The Federalist Papers

The Federalist Papers is generally considered the most important contemporaneous exposition of the Constitution. Written primarily by Alexander Hamilton and James Madison for the immediate purpose of securing ratification in New York, the eighty-five essays written under the pseudonym "Publius" were republished throughout the United States. Of particular importance are Madison's essays on how a large republic could prevent the tyranny of the majority (i.e., Federalist No. 10) and Hamilton's essays on the need to give government the powers necessary to secure vital national ends (i.e., Federalist No. 23). Hamilton discussed judicial issues at length in Federalist Nos. 78 through 83, and other papers touched on judicial power incidentally. Federalist No. 78 defends judicial review in de-

tail and Federalist No. 44 indicates that Madison as well as Hamilton thought courts had the power to declare laws unconstitutional. As John Marshall would later claim in Marbury, Hamilton in Federalist No. 78 asserted that the judicial power to declare laws unconstitutional was inherent in a written constitution. The Federalist Papers is less clear on how judicial power should be exercised. An ongoing debate exists over precisely what Hamilton meant when he declared that courts have a "duty . . . to declare all acts contrary to the manifest tenor of the constitution void." That passage might be broadly interpreted as authorizing decisions based on the spirit as well as the letter of constitutional provisions or, more narrowly, as authorizing only judicial decisions striking down laws no reasonable person would think constitutional.

Hamilton thought the Constitution vested both state and federal courts with the power to declare state, as well as federal, laws unconstitutional. Rather than enforce federal law through a federal military presence or mere requisitions, Federalist No. 16 suggests a system of federal courts would provide the national institutional presence necessary to exact obedience to the Constitution and federal legislation. Still, as Federalist No. 44 indicates, judicial review was not deemed the primary means for preventing unconstitutional legislation. Constitutional limits in 1787 were thought best protected by a government structured to facilitate the election of officials who would not violate constitutional rights.

Alexander Hamilton (1757–1804) was born in the British colony of Nevis and orphaned at the age of eleven. His aunts sent him to the American colonies to receive a college education. He began his studies at King's College (now Columbia University) in 1773, but his work was soon interrupted by the Revolutionary War. Hamilton was an early supporter of colonial independence, publishing anonymous pamphlets in late 1774 and early 1775 arguing that cause. When war broke out Hamilton volunteered to serve in the Continental Army. General George Washington, impressed with Hamilton's writing skills, made Hamilton his aide-de-camp. After the war, Hamilton began a legal practice in New York and served for a short time in the Continental Congress. He attended the Constitutional Convention of 1787 but played no role in the drafting of the Constitution. Hamilton did play an important leadership role in the New York state ratification convention, however, and after ratification became secretary of the treasury in the new federal government under now-president Washington. In this position, Hamilton pushed a policy of protection for manufacturing interests and fought to establish the national bank. Because of personal financial difficulties, Hamilton resigned his office in 1795. In 1804 Vice President Aaron Burr, who with some reason blamed Hamilton for his defeat in the 1800 presidential election and 1804 gubernatorial election in New York, challenged Hamilton to a duel. Hamilton reluctantly accepted and was subsequently mortally wounded by Burr. For more biographical information, see Richard Brookhiser, Alexander Hamilton, American (New York: Free Press, 1999).

James Madison (1751–1836) was born in Virginia. He was tutored during his formative years, and he enrolled in the College of New Jersey (now known as Princeton University) in 1769. Madison considered a career in divinity or law before finally settling upon politics. He was elected to the Committee of Safety for Orange County, to the convention that framed the new state constitution, to the governor's council, and then to the Continental Congress. Upon returning to Virginia in 1784, Madison was immediately elected to the House of Delegates. Madison in the 1780s became convinced that a new, more powerful national government was needed to replace the one enacted by the Articles of Confederation, and he worked hard to achieve that end. He played a prominent role at the Philadelphia convention, earning him modern praise as the "father of the Constitution." Following the Philadelphia convention, Madison was elected a delegate to the Virginia state ratifying convention. His arguments are credited with helping secure ratification by the narrow margin of eighty-nine votes to seventy-nine. During the first session of Congress Madison was the principle advocate for adopting a bill of rights. When Thomas Jefferson was elected president in 1800, Madison became secretary of state. At the end of his second term, Jefferson anointed Madison as his chosen successor. Madison easily won election as the fourth president of the United States and was just as easily reelected in 1812. He retired to Montpelier, his Virginia estate, and lived until 1836, the last survivor of the founding fathers.

Federalist No. 16

But if the execution of the laws of the national government should not require the intervention of the State legislatures, if they were to pass into immediate operation upon the citizens themselves, the particular governments could not interrupt their progress without an open and violent exertion of an unconstitutional power. . . . An experiment of this nature would always be hazardous in the face of a constitution in any degree competent to its own defense, and of a people enlightened enough to distinguish between a legal exercise and an illegal usurpation of authority. The success of it would require not merely a factious majority in the legislature, but the concurrence of the courts of justice and of the body of the people. If the judges were not embarked in a conspiracy with the legislature, they would pronounce the resolutions of such a majority to be contrary to the supreme law of the land, unconstitutional, and void. If the people were not tainted with the spirit of their State representatives, they, as the natural guardians of the Constitution, would throw their weight into the national scale and give it a decided preponderancy in the contest. . . .

Federalist No. 44

If it be asked what is to be the consequence, in case the Congress shall misconstrue this part of the Constitution, and exercise powers not warranted by its true meaning, I answer, the same as if they should misconstrue or enlarge any other power vested in them. . . . In the first instance, the success of the usurpation will depend on the executive and judiciary departments, which are to expound and give effect to the legislative acts; and in the last resort a remedy must be obtained from the people who can, by the election of more faithful representatives, annul the acts of the usurpers. . . .

Federalist No. 78

. . . [T]he judiciary is beyond comparison the weakest of the three departments of power; . . . it can never attack with success either of the other two; and . . . all possible care is requisite to enable it to defend itself against their attacks. . . . [T]hough individual oppression may now and then proceed from the courts of justice, the general liberty of the people can never be endangered from that quarter; I mean so long as the judiciary remains truly distinct from both the legislature and the Executive. . . .

The complete independence of the courts of justice is peculiarly essential in a limited Constitution. By a limited Constitution, I understand one which contains certain specified exceptions to the legislative authority; such, for instance, as that it shall pass no bills of attainder, no ex-post-facto laws, and the like. Limitations of this kind can be preserved in practice no other way than through the medium of courts of justice, whose duty it must be to declare all acts contrary to the manifest tenor of the Constitution void. Without this, all the reservations of particular rights or privileges would amount to nothing.

Some perplexity respecting the rights of the courts to pronounce legislative acts void, because contrary to the Constitution, has arisen from an imagination that the doctrine would imply a superiority of the judiciary to the legislative power. It is urged that the authority which can declare the acts of another void, must necessarily be superior to the one whose acts may be declared void. . . .

There is no position which depends on clearer principles, than that every act of a delegated authority, contrary to the tenor of the commission under which it is exercised, is void. No legislative act, therefore, contrary to the Constitution, can be valid. . . .

If it be said that the legislative body are themselves the constitutional judges of their own powers, and that the construction they put upon them is conclusive upon the other departments, it may be answered, that this cannot be the natural presumption, where it is not to be collected from any particular provisions in the Constitution. It is not otherwise to be supposed, that the Constitution could intend to enable the representatives of the people to substitute their WILL to that of their constituents. It is far more rational to suppose, that the courts were designed to be an intermediate body between the people and the legislature, in order, among other things, to keep the latter within the limits assigned to their authority. The interpretation of the laws is the proper and peculiar province of the courts. A constitution is, in fact, and must be regarded by the judges, as a fundamental law. It therefore belongs to them to ascertain its meaning, as well as the meaning of any particular act proceeding from the legislative body. If there should happen to be an irreconcilable variance between the two, that which has the superior obligation and validity ought, of course, to be preferred; or, in other words, the Constitution ought to be preferred to the statute, the intention of the people to the intention of their agents.

Nor does this conclusion by any means suppose a superiority of the judicial to the legislative power. It only supposes that the power of the people is superior to both; and that where the will of the legislature, declared in its statutes, stands in opposition to that of the people, declared in the Constitution, the judges ought to be governed by the latter rather than the former. They ought to regulate their decisions by the fundamental laws, rather than by those which are not fundamental.

This exercise of judicial discretion, in determining between two contradictory laws, is exemplified in a familiar instance. . . . The rule which has obtained in the courts for determining their relative validity is, that the last in order of time shall be preferred to the first. . . . They thought it reasonable, that between the interfering acts of an EQUAL authority, that which was the last indication of its will should have the preference.

But in regard to the interfering acts of a superior and subordinate authority, of an original and derivative power, the nature and reason of the thing indicate the converse of that rule as proper to be followed. They teach us that the prior act of a superior ought to be preferred to the subsequent act of an inferior and subordinate author-

ity; and that accordingly, whenever a particular statute contravenes the Constitution, it will be the duty of the judicial tribunals to adhere to the latter and disregard the former.

It can be of no weight to say that the courts, on the pretense of a repugnancy, may substitute their own pleasure to the constitutional intentions of the legislature. . . . The courts must declare the sense of the law; and if they should be disposed to exercise WILL instead of JUDGMENT, the consequence would equally be the substitution of their pleasure to that of the legislative body. The observation, if it prove any thing, would prove that there ought to be no judges distinct from that body. . . .

This independence of the judges is equally requisite to guard the Constitution and the rights of individuals from the effects of those ill humors, which the arts of designing men, or the influence of particular conjunctures, sometimes disseminate among the people themselves, and which, though they speedily give place to better information, and more deliberate reflection, have a tendency, in the meantime, to occasion dangerous innovations in the government, and serious oppressions of the minor party in the community. Though I trust the friends of the proposed Constitution will never concur with its enemies, in questioning that fundamental principle of republican government, which admits the right of the people to alter or abolish the established Constitution, whenever they find it inconsistent with their happiness, yet it is not to be inferred from this principle, that the representatives of the people, whenever a momentary inclination happens to lay hold of a majority of their constituents, incompatible with the provisions in the existing Constitution, would, on that account, be justifiable in a violation of those provisions; or that the courts would be under a greater obligation to connive at infractions in this shape, than when they had proceeded wholly from the cabals of the representative body. Until the people have, by some solemn and authoritative act, annulled or changed the established form, it is binding upon themselves collectively, as well as individually; and no presumption, or even knowledge, of their sentiments, can warrant their representatives in a departure from it, prior to such an act. But it is easy to see, that it would require an uncommon portion of fortitude in the judges to do their duty as faithful guardians of the Constitution, where legislative invasions of it had been instigated by the major voice of the community. . . .

. . . That inflexible and uniform adherence to the rights of the Constitution, and of individuals, which we perceive to be indispensable in the courts of justice, can certainly not be expected from judges who hold their offices by a temporary commission. Periodical appointments, however regulated, or by whomsoever made, would, in some way or other, be fatal to their necessary independence. If the power of making them was committed either to the Executive or legislature, there would be danger of an improper complaisance to the branch which possessed it; if to both, there would be an unwillingness to hazard the displeasure of either; if to the people, or to persons chosen by them for the special purpose, there would be too great a disposition to consult popularity, to justify a reliance that nothing would be consulted but the Constitution and the laws.

Source: Alexander Hamilton, James Madison, and John Jay, *The Federalist Papers* (New York: New American Library, 1961), 117, 285–286, 465–471.

---

24   James Wilson, Pennsylvania Convention

James Wilson (1742–1798) was born in Scotland. He secured a position at the College of Philadelphia as a Latin tutor after arriving in the American colonies in 1765. Wilson soon became interested in a legal career and began reading law in the office of John Dickinson. He published a pamphlet in 1774, Considerations on the Nature and Extent of the Legislative Authority of the British Parliament, arguing that Parliament had no authority over the American colonies. The pamphlet was widely read in the colonies and established Wilson's reputation as a distinguished legal scholar. In 1775 Wilson was elected to the Second Continental Congress, and in subsequent years he held various political positions. In 1787 he attended the Constitutional Convention as a delegate from Pennsylvania. Despite some qualms about the final product, Wilson signed the Constitution and urged ratification in speeches made before and during the Pennsylvania state ratifying convention. President George Washington in 1789 successfully nominated Wilson to be an associate justice of the Supreme Court. Wilson's tenure was not a happy one, owing largely to substantial debts accrued during land speculations. In 1798, after a period of mental illness, Wilson passed away.

Next to The Federalist Papers, Wilson's speeches and writings were considered the most influential works favoring ratification. His argument that a bill of rights was unnecessary for a democratic government became a staple of Federalist rhetoric. Unlike Hamilton, Wilson typically assumed, rather than defended, judicial review. The following brief excerpts demonstrate his belief that the Constitution vested the judiciary with the power to declare laws unconstitutional, but they say little on how Wilson believed that power should be exercised.

December 1, 1787:

. . . I say, under this Constitution, the legislature may be restrained, and kept within its prescribed bounds, by the interposition of the judicial department. . . . I had occasion, on a former day, to state that the power of the Constitution was paramount to the power of the legislature acting under that Constitution; for it is possible that the legislature, when acting in that capacity, may transgress the bounds assigned to it, and an act may pass, in the usual *mode*, notwithstanding that transgression; but when it comes to be discussed before *the judges*,—when they consider its principles, and find it to be incompatible with the superior power of the Constitution,—it is their duty to pronounce it *void*; and judges independent, and not obliged to look to every session for a continuance of their salaries, will behave with intrepidity, and refuse to the act the sanction of judicial authority. . . .

December 4, 1787:

The last observation respects the judges. It is said that if they dare to decide against the law, one house will impeach them, and the other will convict them. [*Note:* John Smilie had earlier insisted, "(w)e have not every security from the judiciary department. The judges, for disobeying a law, may be impeached by one house, and tried by another" (Jensen 1978, vol. 2: 466). For an account of the debate between Smile and Wilson in the December 8, 1787, edition of the *Pennsylvania Herald*, see Jensen vol. 2: 524–525.] . . . The judges are to be impeached because they decide an act null and void that was made in defiance of

the Constitution! What House of Representatives would dare to impeach, or Senate to commit judges for the performance of their duty?

December 7, 1787

. . . Controversies may certainly arise under this Constitution and the laws of the United States, and is it not proper that there should be judges to decide them? The honorable gentleman from Cumberland (Mr. Whitehill) says that laws may be made inconsistent with the Constitution; and that therefore the powers given to the judges are dangerous. For my part, Mr. President, I think the contrary inference true. If a law should be made inconsistent with those powers vested by this instrument in Congress, the judges, as a consequence of their independence, and the particular powers of government being defined, will declare such law to be null and void; for the power of the Constitution predominates. Any thing, therefore, that shall be enacted by Congress contrary thereto, will not have the force of law.

Source: Merrill Jensen, ed., *The Documentary History of the Ratification of the Constitution* (Madison: State Historical Society of Wisconsin, 1978), vol. 2: 450–451, 466, 492, 517, 524–525.

---

25   John Dickinson, "Letters of Fabius"

John Dickinson (1732–1808) was born into a relatively wealthy family and received his early education at home by tutor. From 1753 until 1757 Dickinson studied at Middle Temple in London, then returned to Philadelphia to establish a law practice. He was elected to the state assembly of Delaware and, later, to the Pennsylvania legislature. In 1765 Dickinson published a pamphlet, The Late Regulations Respecting the British Colonies . . . Considered, that vigorously opposed the Sugar and Stamp Acts. Additional pamphlets opposing English rule followed. In the mid-1770s Dickinson was elected to the First and Second Continental Congresses. Hoping for a peaceful resolution of the conflict between the American colonies and England, he voted against issuing the Declaration of Independence. During the Revolutionary War and immediately following, Dickinson served intermittently as a member of Congress from Delaware and Pennsylvania. Dickinson attended the Constitutional Convention as a delegate of Delaware. After the convention, he wrote a series of letters under the pseudonym "Fabius" that urged the adoption of the Constitution. For the remainder of his life, Dickinson held no political office but remained active in politics.

The following brief excerpt from the "Letters of Fabius" is another example of a prominent framer who assumed that courts had the power to declare laws unconstitutional. That Dickinson made this assumption may be particularly significant: in the framing convention he indicated that he did not support judicial review.

Our government under its proposed confederation, will be guarded by a repetition of the strongest cautions against excesses. In the senate the sovereignties of the several states will be equally represented; in the house of representatives, the people of the whole union will be equally represented; and, in the president, and the federal independent judges, so much concerned in the execution of the laws, and in the determination of their constitutionality, the sovereignties of the several states and the people of the whole union, may be considered as conjoined represented.

Source: Merrill Jensen, ed., *The Documentary History of the Ratification of the Constitution* (Madison: State Historical Society of Wisconsin, 1978), vol. 17: 182.

---

26   Robert Yates, "Essays of Brutus"

Robert Yates (1738–1801) was born and raised in Schenectady, New York. He read law in the office of William Livingston and, in 1760, was admitted to the bar. He served on the Albany Board of Alderman from 1771 until 1775, and in the provincial congress of New York from 1775 until 1777, when he was appointed an associate justice of the state's supreme court. He was a supporter of Governor George Clinton, and by the mid-1780s a leader of the state's Anti-Federalist wing. In 1787 Yates was appointed to represent New York at the Constitutional Convention in Philadelphia. He left when he recognized that the convention was not amending the Articles of Confederation but was writing an entirely new constitution. When the Constitution was sent to the states for debate, Yates argued against ratification in a series of letters under the pseudonym "Brutus." In the years following, Yates twice ran for governor of New York but lost to George Clinton and John Jay, respectively. He resigned from the state supreme court at the required age of sixty and died three years later.

The "Essays of Brutus" contain the most sustained attack on federal judicial review made during the debates over the Constitution. Yates opposed vesting federal courts with the right to declare laws unconstitutional. His essays praised previous state court decisions declaring state laws unconstitutional and maintained that state courts should be trusted to void state laws that were inconsistent with the Constitution. When attacking the Constitution for sanctioning judicial review, Yates recognized that the Constitution, perhaps wrongly, vested federal justices with the authority to declare laws unconstitutional. As a supporter of state power, Yates did not oppose federal judicial review because he feared federal courts would declare federal laws unconstitutional. He worried that federal justices would have a tendency to construe federal powers liberally at the expense of the states.

In my last, I shewed, that the judicial power of the United States under the first clause of the second section of article eight, would be authorized to explain the constitution, not only according to its letter, but according to its spirit and intention; and having this power, they would strongly incline to give it such a construction as to extend the powers of the general government, as much as possible, to the diminution, and finally to the destruction, of that of the respective states. . . .

. . . [I]is easy to see, that in their adjudications they may establish certain principles, which being received by the legislature, will enlarge the sphere of their power beyond all bounds. . . .

It is to be observed, that the supreme court has the power, in the last resort, to determine all questions that may arise in the course of legal discussion, on the meaning and construction of the constitution. This power they will hold under the constitution, and independent of the legislature. The latter can no more deprive the former of this right, than either of them, or both of them together, can take from the president, with the advice of the senate, the power of making treaties, or appointing ambassadors.

In determining these questions, the court must and will assume certain principles, from which they will reason, in forming their decisions. These principles, whatever they may be, when they become fixed, by a course of decisions, will be adopted by the legislature, and will be the rule by which they will explain their own powers. This appears evident from this consideration, that if the legislature pass laws, which, in the judgment of the court, they are not authorised to do by the constitution, the court will not take notice of them; for it will not be denied, that the constitution is the highest or supreme law. And the courts are vested with the supreme and uncontroulable power, to determine, in all cases that come before them, what the constitution means; they cannot, therefore, execute a law, which, in their judgment, opposes the constitution, unless we can suppose they can make a superior law give way to an inferior. The legislature, therefore, will not go over the limits by which the courts may adjudge they are confined. And there is little room to doubt but that they will come up to those bounds, as often as occasion and opportunity may offer, and they may judge it proper to do it. For as on the one hand, they will not readily pass laws which they know the courts will not execute, so on the other, we may be sure they will not scruple to pass such as they know they will give effect, as often as they may judge it proper. . . .

. . . [N]o doubt can remain, but that the great end of the constitution, if it is to be collected from the preamble, in which its end is declared, is to constitute a government which is to extend to every case for which any government is instituted, whether external or internal. The courts, therefore, will establish this as a principle in expounding the constitution, and will give every part of it such an explanation, as will give latitude to every department under it, to take cognizance of every matter, not only that affects the general and national concerns of the union, but also of such as relate to the administration of private justice, and to regulating the internal and local affairs of the different parts.

Such a rule of exposition is not only consistent with the general spirit of the preamble, but it will stand confirmed by considering more minutely the different clauses of it. . . .

The first object declared to be in view is, "To form a perfect union." . . . The courts therefore will establish it as a rule in explaining the constitution to give it such a construction as will best tend to perfect the union or take from the state governments every power of either making or executing laws. The second object is "to establish justice." . . . And under this the courts will in their decisions extend the power of the government to all cases they possibly can, or otherwise they will be restricted in doing what appears to be the intent of the constitution they should do, to wit, pass laws and provide for the execution of them, for the general distribution of justice between man and man. Another end declared is "to insure domestic tranquility." This comprehends a provision against all private breaches of the peace, as well as against all public commotions or general insurrections; and to attain the object of this clause fully, the government must exercise the power of passing laws on these subjects, as well as of appointing magistrates with authority to execute them. And the courts will adopt these ideas in their expositions. . . .

This same manner of explaining the constitution, will fix a meaning, and a very important one too, to the [18th] . . . clause of the same section, which authorises the Congress to make all laws which shall be proper and necessary for carrying into effect the foregoing powers, &c. . . . [T]his will undoubtedly be an excellent auxilliary to assist the courts to discover the spirit and reason of the constitution, and when applied to any and every of the other clauses granting power, will operate powerfully in extracting the spirit from them. . . .

It is obvious that these courts will have authority to decide upon the validity of the laws of any of the states, in all cases where they come in question before them. Where the constitution gives the general government exclusive jurisdiction, they will adjudge all laws made by the states, in such cases, void ab initio. Where the constitution gives them concurrent jurisdiction, the laws of the United States must prevail, because they are the supreme law. In such cases, therefore, the laws of the state legislatures must be repealed, restricted, or so construed, as to give full effect to the laws of the union on the same subject. From these remarks it is easy to see, that in proportion as the general government acquires power and jurisdiction, by the liberal construction which the judges may give the constitution, will those of the states lose its rights, until they become so trifling and unimportant, as not to be worth having. . . .

These extraordinary powers in this court are the more objectionable because there does not appear the least necessity for them, in order to secure a due and impartial distribution of justice.

. . . It is true in some of the states, paper money has been made, and the debtor authorised to discharge his debts with it, at a depreciated value, in others, tender laws have been passed, obliging the creditor to receive on execution other property than money in discharge of his demand, and in several of the states laws have been made unfavorable to the creditor and tending to render property insecure. . . .

But these evils have not happened from any defect in the judicial departments of the states; the courts indeed are bound to take notice of these laws, and so will the courts of the general government be under obligation to observe the laws made by the general legislature not repugnant to the constitution; but so far have the judicial been from giving undue latitude of construction to laws of this kind, that they have invariably strongly inclined to the other side. All the acts of our legislature, which have been charged with being of this complexion, have uniformly received the strictest construction by the judges, and have been extended to no cases but to such as came within the strict letter of the law. In this way, have our courts, I will not say evaded the law, but so limited it in its operation as to work the least possible injustice: the same thing has taken place in Rhode-Island, which has justly rendered herself

infamous, by her tenaciously adhering to her paper money system. The judges there gave a decision, in opposition to the words of the Statute, on this principle, that a construction according to the words of it, would contradict the fundamental maxims of their laws and constitution.

No pretext therefore, can be formed, from the conduct of the judicial courts which will justify giving such powers to the supreme general court, for their decisions have been such as to give just ground of confidence in them, that they will firmly adhere to the principles of rectitude, and there is no necessity of lodging these powers in the courts, in order to guard against the evils justly complained of, on the subject of security of property under this constitution. For it has provided, "that no state shall emit bills of credit, or make any thing but gold and silver coin a tender in payment of debts." It has also declared, that "no state shall pass any law impairing the obligation of contracts." —These prohibitions give the most perfect security against those attacks upon property which I am sorry to say some of the states have but too wantonly made, by passing laws sanctioning fraud in the debtor against his creditor. For "this constitution will be the supreme law of the land, and the judges in every state will be bound thereby; any thing in the constitution and laws of any state to the contrary notwithstanding."

The courts of the respective states might therefore have been securely trusted, with deciding all cases between man and man, whether citizens of the same state or of different states, or between foreigners and citizens, and indeed for ought I see every case that can arise under the constitution or laws of the United States, ought in the first instance to be tried in the court of the state, except those which might arise between states, such as respect ambassadors, or other public ministers, and perhaps such as call in question the claim of lands under grants from different states. . . .

. . . I question whether the world ever saw, in any period of it, a court of justice invested with such immense powers, and yet placed in a situation so little responsible. . . .

. . . The judges under this constitution will controul the legislature, for the supreme court are authorised in the last resort, to determine what is the extent of the powers of the Congress; they are to give the constitution an explanation, and there is no power above them to set aside their judgment. . . .

. . . [T]hey have made the judges *independent*, in the fullest sense of the word. There is no power above them, to controul any of their decisions. There is no authority that can remove them, and they cannot be controuled by the laws of the legislature. In short, they are independent of the people, of the legislature, and of every power under heaven. Men placed in this situation will generally soon feel themselves independent of heaven itself. . . .

. . . There is no power above them that can correct their errors or controul their decisions— The adjudications of this court are final and irreversible, for there is no court above them to which appeals can lie, either in error or on the merits. . . .

. . . The power of this court is in many cases superior to that of the legislature. I have shewed, in a former paper, that this court will be authorised to decide upon the meaning of the constitution, and that, not only according to the natural and ob[vious] meaning of the words, but also according to the spirit and intention of it. In the exercise of this power they will not be subordinate to, but above the legislature. For all the departments of this government will receive their powers, so far as they are expressed in the constitution, from the people immediately, who are the source of power. The legislature can only exercise such powers as are given them by the constitution, they cannot assume any of the rights annexed to the judicial, for this plain reason, that the same authority which vested the legislature with their powers, vested the judicial with theirs—both are derived from the same source, both therefore are equally valid, and the judicial hold their powers independently of the legislature, as the legislature do of the judicial.—The supreme court then have a right, independent of the legislature, to give a construction to the constitution and every part of it, and there is no power provided in this system to correct their construction or do it away. If, therefore, the legislature pass any laws, inconsistent with the sense the judges put upon the constitution, they will declare it void; and therefore in this respect their power is superior to that of the legislature. . . .

Perhaps nothing could have been better conceived to facilitate the abolition of the state governments than the constitution of the judicial. They will be able to extend the limits of the general government gradually, and by insensible degrees, and to accommodate themselves to the temper of the people. . . . [T]he general legislature, might pass one law after another, extending the general and abridging the state jurisdictions, and to sanction their proceedings would have a course of decisions of the judicial to whom the constitution has committed the power of explaining the constitution.—If the states remonstrated, the constitutional mode of deciding upon the validity of the law, is with the supreme court, and neither people, nor state legislatures, nor the general legislature can remove them or reverse their decrees.

Had the construction of the constitution been left with the legislature, they would have explained it at their peril; if they exceed their powers, or sought to find, in the spirit of the constitution, more than was expressed in the letter, the people from whom they derived their power could remove them, and do themselves right; and indeed I can see no other remedy that the people can have against their rulers for encroachments of this nature. A constitution is a compact of a people with their rulers; if the rulers break the compact, the people have a right and ought to remove them and do themselves justice; but in order to enable them to do this with the greater facility, those whom the people chuse at stated periods, should have the power in the last resort to determine the sense of the compact; if they determine contrary to the understanding of the people, an appeal will lie to the people at the period when the rulers are to be elected, and they will have it in their power to remedy the evil; but when this power is lodged in the hands of men independent of the people, and of their representatives, and who are not, constitutionally, accountable for their opinions, no way is left to controul them but *with a high hand and an outstretched arm.*

Source: Herbert Storing, ed., *The Complete Anti-Federalist* (Chicago: University of Chicago Press, 1981), vol. 2: 422–427, 435–437, 438–442.

---

27   Samuel Adams, February 1, 1788

Samuel Adams (1722–1803) was born in Boston, Massachusetts, to the socially prominent Adams family. He graduated from Harvard College in 1740 and in 1765 was elected to the Massachusetts House of Representatives. He was continuously reelected until 1774, and over time emerged as a leader of the growing opposition to English rule. Adams was intimately involved with planning the Boston Tea Party, selected a delegate to the First and Second Continental Congresses, and voted for and signed the Declaration of Independence. Adams served in the U.S. Congress until 1781, when he returned to Boston and private life. Adams originally opposed adopting the Constitution during the Massachusetts state ratifying convention but eventually supported ratification with proposed amendments. Adams failed in his bid to win election to Congress in 1788 and instead served as lieutenant governor to John Hancock until 1794. He became governor that year after Hancock's death. Adams served for three years and then retired from political life for good.

As was the case with many proponents and opponents of the Constitution, Adams assumed that the Constitution vested the Supreme Court with the power to declare laws unconstitutional. His speech, briefly excerpted below, expresses the concern many Americans shared that the proposed constitution granted too much power to the federal government. One virtue of a clearer stipulation that federal power was limited, Adams claimed, was that justices would gain the power to strike down national laws not justified by the constitutional text.

Your excellency's first proposition is, "that it be explicitly declared, that all powers not expressly delegated to Congress are reserved to the several states, to be by them exercised." This appears, to my mind, to be a summary of a bill of rights, which gentlemen are anxious to obtain. It removes a doubt which many have entertained respecting the matter, and gives assurance that, if any law made by the federal government shall be extended beyond the power granted by the proposed Constitution, and inconsistent with the constitution of this state, it will be an error, and adjudged by the courts of law to be void.

Source: Jonathan Elliot, ed., *The Debates in the Several State Conventions on the Adoption of the Federal Constitution, as Recommended by the General Convention at Philadelphia in 1787,* 2d ed. (Philadelphia: J. B. Lippincott, 1836), vol. 2: 131.

28

Oliver Ellsworth, January 7, 1788

Oliver Ellsworth (1745–1807) was born in Windsor, Connecticut. After graduating from the College of New Jersey (now Princeton University), he was admitted to the bar in 1771 and quickly recognized as a leading lawyer in Connecticut. In 1777 Ellsworth was appointed state's attorney for Hartford County. Three years later, Ellsworth was appointed to be a member of the Governor's Council. When the council was made a supreme court in 1784, Ellsworth became one of the judges. He served in the Continental Congress from 1777 until 1783 and attended the Constitutional Convention of 1787. Ellsworth played an important role at the convention and afterwards actively sought ratification. When the new government was formed, Ellsworth was elected by the Connecticut state legislature to the U.S. Senate. He served as a senator until 1796, when he was appointed chief justice of the Supreme Court by President George Washington. In 1799 President John Adams appointed Ellsworth as an envoy to France. While in France, Ellsworth's health deteriorated and he subsequently resigned his position as chief justice. Upon returning to the United States, Ellsworth retired from an active role in politics.

The following excerpt is yet another instance of a prominent framer asserting that justices under the proposed constitution would have the power to declare both federal and state laws unconstitutional. That Ellsworth made this assumption may be particularly important. He was the second chief justice of the United States and, when in the Senate, drafted what became the Judiciary Act of 1789. That measure (Document 34) established the federal judicial system and assumed a judicial power to declare laws unconstitutional.

. . . This Constitution defines the extent of the powers of the general government. If the general legislature should at any time overleap their limits, the judicial department is a constitutional check. If the United States go beyond their powers, if they make a law which the Constitution does not authorize, it is void; and the judicial power, the national judges, who, to secure their impartiality, are to be made independent, will declare it to be void. On the other hand, if the states go beyond their limits, if they make a law which is a usurpation upon the general government, the law is void, and upright, independent judges will declare it to be so. . . .

Source: Merrill Jensen, ed., *The Documentary History of the Ratification of the Constitution* (Madison: State Historical Society of Wisconsin, 1978), vol. 3: 553.

29

Patrick Henry, Speeches

Patrick Henry (1736–1799) turned to the law after failing at several business ventures. He soon gained a reputation as a highly skilled lawyer, and his practice boomed. He was elected in 1765 to the Virginia House of Burgesses, where he immediately rose to a leadership position. Henry was an ardent supporter of American independence from England, and his assertion, "give me liberty or give me death," became a rallying cry for American patriots. In 1774 Henry was selected a delegate to the First Continental Congress. During the Revolutionary War, Henry was elected governor of Virginia. He served for five terms, retiring in 1786. The next year Henry was selected a member of Virginia's delegation to the Constitutional Convention, but he declined to attend. At the Virginia state ratifying convention, Henry was the acknowledged leader of those opposing adopting the Constitution. In his final years, Henry became reconciled to the Constitution.

Henry at the ratification convention was more concerned with judicial weakness than judicial strength. He endorsed Virginia court decisions declaring state laws unconstitutional and approved vesting the Supreme Court of the United States with the power to declare federal laws unconstitutional. He feared that federal justices, while having the power to declare laws unconstitutional in theory, lacked the independence necessary to exercise that power in practice.

June 9, 1788:

. . . If there be a real check intended to be left on Congress, it must be left in the State Government(s). There will be some check, as long as the Judges are uncorrupt. As long as they are upright, you may preserve your liberty. But what will the Judges determine when the State and Federal authority come to be contrasted? Will your liberty then be secure, when the Congressional laws are declared paramount to the laws of your State, and the Judges are sworn to support them?

June 12, 1799:

The honorable gentleman did our judiciary honor in saying that they had firmness to counteract the legislature in some cases. Yes, sir, our judges opposed the acts of the legislature. We have this landmark to guide us. They had fortitude to declare that they were the judiciary, and would oppose unconstitutional acts. Are you sure that your federal judiciary will act thus? Is that judiciary as well constructed, and as independent of the other branches, as our state judiciary? Where are your landmarks in this government? I will be bold to say you cannot find any in it. I take it as the highest encomium on this country, that the acts of the legislature, if unconstitutional, are liable to be opposed by the judiciary.

June 20, 1788:

. . . When the Congress, by virtue of this sweeping clause, will organize these courts, they cannot depart from the Constitution; and their laws in opposition to the Constitution would be void. If Congress, under the specious pretence of pursuing this clause, altered it, and prohibited appeals as to fact, the federal judges, if they spoke the sentiments of independent men, would declare their prohibition nugatory and void. . . .

Source: Merrill Jensen, ed., *The Documentary History of the Ratification of the Constitution* (Madison: State Historical Society of Wisconsin, 1978), vol. 9: 1070; vol. 10: 1219, 1420–1421.

30   Edmund Pendleton, Speeches

Edmund Pendleton (1721–1803) was born in Caroline County, Virginia. At fourteen he was apprenticed to Colonel Benjamin Robinson, the clerk of the court of Caroline County. In 1751 he was made a county justice of the peace. The next year Pendleton was elected to the Virginia House of Burgesses, where he remained an active member for many years. When the Virginia government was reorganized in 1776, Pendleton became the Speaker of the House of Delegates. In 1779 Pendleton was made president of the newly created Supreme Court of Appeals. He would serve in this post until his death.

During the Virginia state ratifying convention, Pendleton was a strong advocate for adopting the Constitution. Both Patrick Henry and Pendleton supported vesting courts with the power to declare laws unconstitutional. Both praised Virginia courts for previously declaring that state laws violated the state constitution. Unlike Henry, Pendleton and other Virginia Federalists insisted that federal courts were sufficiently independent to strike down federal laws that were inconsistent with the Constitution.

June 12, 1788:

I believe every Gentleman will see that it is unconstitutional to condemn any man without a fair trial. Such a condemnation is repugnant to the principles of justice. It is contrary to the Constitution, and the spirit of the common law. Look at the Bill of Rights. You find there, that no man should be condemned without being confronted with his accusers and witnesses—that every man has a right to call for evidence in his favor, and above all, to a speedy trial by an impartial jury of the vicinage, without whose unanimous consent he cannot be found guilty.—These principles have not been attended to. An instance have been mentioned already, where they have been in some degree violated. . . . My brethren in that department (*the judicial*) felt great uneasiness in their minds, to violate the Constitution by such a law. They have prevented the operation of some unconstitutional acts. Notwithstanding those violations, I rely upon the principles of the Government—that it will produce its own reforms, by the responsibility resulting from frequent elections.

June 20, 1788:

His [Patrick Henry's] next objection was to the first two clauses—cases arising under the Constitution, and the laws made in pursuance thereof. Are you to refer these to the state courts? Must not the judicial powers extend to enforce the federal laws, govern its own officers, and confine them to the line of their duty? Must it not protect them, in the proper exercise of duty, against all opposition, whether from individuals or state laws? No, say gentlemen, because the legislature may make oppressive laws, or partial judges may give them a partial interpretation. This is carrying suspicion to an extreme which tends to prove there should be no legislative or judiciary at all. The fair inference is, that oppressive laws will not be warranted by the Constitution, not attempted by our representatives, who are selected for their ability and integrity, and that honest independent judges will never admit an oppressive construction.

Source: Merrill Jensen, ed., *The Documentary History of the Ratification of the Constitution* (Madison: State Historical Society of Wisconsin, 1978), vol. 10: 1197, 1426–1427.

---

31   Edmund Randolph, Speeches

Edmund Randolph (1753–1813) was born in Williamsburg, Virginia. He attended the College of William and Mary and studied law with his father, John Randolph. When the Revolutionary War broke out, John Randolph sided with the loyalists and fled to England. Edmund joined his uncle, Peyton Randolph, an influential lawyer and politician, who advocated independence. After a short stint in the Continental army, Randolph entered Virginia politics. He represented Virginia in the Continental Congress and, in 1786, became governor of that state. Randolph was elected to the Philadelphia convention, where he formally proposed the Virginia Plan. Finding various defects in the final draft, Randolph refused to sign the constitution that emerged from the framing convention. Nevertheless, he voted for ratification in the Virginia state convention, hoping for future amendments. After ratification, Randolph became the first attorney general of the United States and then secretary of state. Forced into retirement by scandal or rumors of scandal, Randolph reemerged politically in 1807 when he served as defense counsel to Aaron Burr. Shortly thereafter, he became ill and died in 1813.

Randolph's comments at the Virginia ratification convention highlight how judicial review was only one of many safeguards for constitutional rights. One advantage of the separation of powers, he and other Federalists believed, was that numerous independent government institutions would exist that would be capable of checking the unconstitutional schemes of other governing institutions. His comments on a bill of rights also support judicial review, but they highlight an ambiguity in framing thought. What would happen, Randolph asked, if a constitutional power conflicted with a provision in the Bill of Rights? Contemporary Americans are confident that the justices should rely on the provision in the Bill of Rights. Randolph's comments suggest that this was not the clear consensus view of the founding generation.

June 9, 1788:

. . . Virginia has a Bill of Rights, but it is no part of the Constitution. By not saying whether it is paramount to the Constitution or not, it has left us in confusion. Is the Bill of Rights consistent with the Constitution? Why then is it not inserted in the Constitution? Does it add any thing to the Constitution? Why is it not the Constitution? Does it except any thing from the Constitution; why not put the exceptions in the Constitution? Does it oppose the Constitution? This will produce mischief. The Judges will dispute which is paramount: Some will say, the Bill of Rights is paramount: —Others will say, that the Constitu-tion being subsequent in point of time, must be paramount.

———————

June 17, 1788:

That general warrants are grievous and oppressive, and ought not to be granted, I fully admit. I heartily concur in expressing my detestation of them. We do not rely on the integrity of any one particular person or body; but on the number and different orders of the Members of the Government: Some of them having necessarily the same feelings with ourselves. Can it be believed, that the Federal Judiciary would not be independent enough to prevent such oppressive practices?

Source: Merrill Jensen, ed., *The Documentary History of the Ratification of the Constitution* (Madison: State Historical Society of Wisconsin, 1978), vol. 9: 1085; vol. 10: 1351–1352.

32   **George Mason, June 17, 1788**

George Mason (1725–1792) was born into one of the oldest and most distinguished families in Virginia. Mason eschewed public office throughout most of his life, preferring to exercise influence by publishing various pamphlets and through close friendships with such influential revolutionaries as George Washington. Mason was an active participant in the convention that framed the Virginia Constitution of 1776. He drafted many constitutional provisions and was the primary author of the famed Virginia Declaration of Rights. After retiring from politics, Mason was chosen to represent Virginia at the framing convention of 1787. He frequently participated in debates over the structure of the national government but eventually decided not to sign the final document. Mason objected to the absence of a bill of rights, the constitutional protection for the slave trade, and the extensive powers of the general government. Next to Patrick Henry, Mason was the leader of the opposition forces at the Virginia convention. He died shortly after the Constitution was ratified.

Mason was concerned with federal power, not with judicial review per se. He believed the Constitution imposed too many restrictions on the states. The federal judicial power to declare state laws unconstitutional, Mason believed, was another practice that would lead to the subjugation of local governments. The problem was not the practice of judicial review, but the constitutional provisions Mason maintained the judiciary would be obligated to enforce. Such provisions as the contracts and ex post facto clauses, he thought, would allow the federal judiciary to strike down economic measures deemed vital by local governments.

. . . Whatever it may be at the bar, or in a professional line, I conceive, that according to the common acceptation of the words, *ex post facto* laws, and retrospective laws, are synonymous terms. Are we to trust business of this sort to technical definitions? . . . When this matter comes before the Federal Judiciary, they must determine according to this Constitution. It says expressly, that they shall not make *ex post facto* laws. Whatever may be the professional meaning, yet the general meaning of *ex post facto* law, is, an act having a retrospective operation. This construction is agreeable to its primary etymology. Will it not be the duty of the Federal Court to say, that such laws are prohibited?—This goes to the destruction and annihilation of all the citizens of the United States, to enrich a few.

Source: Merrill Jensen, ed., *The Documentary History of the Ratification of the Constitution* (Madison: State Historical Society of Wisconsin, 1978), vol. 10: 1361.

33   John Marshall, June 20, 1788

John Marshall (1755–1835) was born and raised in the wilderness of western Virginia. When armed conflict with England began, Marshall quickly joined the revolutionary cause. When his enlistment expired in 1779, Marshall attended a course of lectures given by George Wythe at the College of William and Mary. Shortly thereafter, he was elected to the state assembly. There, he helped lead the successful fight to send the proposed constitution to the state ratifying convention free from any legislative instructions. At the ratifying convention, Marshall emerged as a strong speaker for adopting the Constitution. By the mid-1790s, Marshall was a recognized leader of the Federalist Party of Virginia. He was frequently asked to join the cabinet or the federal judiciary but refused. He finally agreed to become secretary of state late in the Adams administration. After Marshall served in this position for less than a year, Adams nominated him to replace Oliver Ellsworth as chief justice of the Supreme Court, where he served until his death in 1835. During that time, Marshall wrote the opinion for the Court in such seminal cases as Marbury v. Madison (1803); Fletcher v. Peck (1810), which applied the contracts clause to state contracts; Dartmouth College v. Woodward (1819), which applied the contracts clause to corporate charters; McCulloch v. Maryland (1819), which sustained the constitutionality of the national bank; and Gibbons v. Ogden (1824), which defined the federal commerce power to include navigation and all forms of commercial intercourse that involve more than one state. Many regard Marshall as the greatest chief justice in American history.

Marshall at the Virginia ratification convention was an outspoken proponent of judicial review. His speeches asserted the judicial power he would later defend at length in Marbury v. Madison. While Marshall was defending judicial power as early as 1788, his defense was too brief to determine the conditions under which he thought courts were authorized to declare laws unconstitutional.

. . . Has the government of the United States power to make laws on every subject? Does he [George Mason] understand it so? Can they make laws affected the mode of transferring property, or contracts, or claims, between citizens of the same state? Can they go beyond the delegated powers? If they were to make a law not warranted by any of the powers enumerated, it would be considered by the judges as an infringement of the Constitution which they are to guard. They would not consider such a law as coming under their jurisdiction. They would declare it void. . . . To what quarter will you look for protection from an infringement on the Constitution, if you will not give the power to the Judiciary? There is no other body that can afford such a protection.

Source: Merrill Jensen, ed., *The Documentary History of the Ratification of the Constitution* (Madison: State Historical Society of Wisconsin, 1978), vol. 10: 1431, 1432.

Section III (Documents 34–63): Early Practice

Some form of judicial review enjoyed fairly broad support among American political and legal elites during the period between the ratification of the Constitution and *Marbury v. Madison*. Elected officials who spoke on judicial power generally assumed that courts had the power to declare federal and state laws unconstitutional. Debate in Congress centered on whether legislators, in addition to justices, were authorized to make constitutional decisions. State and federal justices declared laws unconstitutional. No justice rejected the power to declare laws unconstitutional, though several asserted the power should be exercised only when the government had clearly violated constitutional norms.

This consensus that courts had the power to declare laws unconstitutional was neither broad, deep, nor detailed. Most constitutional cases in the eighteenth century involved relatively minor controversies, of little interest to anyone but the parties in the case. Prominent Federalists and Jeffersonians supported judicial review, confident that the courts would decide in their favor when more salient constitutional issues arose. No clear consensus developed or extensive debate took place over whether courts could strike down only the most flagrant constitutional violations. This position, that courts could declare unconstitutional only laws no reasonable person would think constitutional, was asserted more often in federal than in state courts. No agreement existed on the extent to which government officials should defer to judicial interpretation. The ma-

jority position for most of the eighteenth century seems to have been that courts had the power to declare laws unconstitutional—judicial review—and the power to provide the standards that other governing officials used when making constitutional decisions—judicial supremacy. The issue, however, was rarely debated. Claims about judicial supremacy tended to be tangential remarks in speeches devoted to other matters, and judicial power in constitutional cases became a major political issue in the United States only after 1799, when the justices of the Supreme Court on circuit sustained the Sedition Act.

Documents 34–48:
Legislative and Executive Statements

Members of Congress and other governing officials occasionally alluded to judicial review during the first decade of the Constitution's existence. Many national legislators briefly stated that courts had the power to void unconstitutional legislation. Although the precise nature of the judicial power was rarely discussed at length, some national legislators spoke as if they believed the Supreme Court was the ultimate expositor of the Constitution. Prominent members of Congress from 1789 until 1801 advocated both judicial review and judicial supremacy. Other prominent members of Congress seemed to reject judicial supremacy, calling on the national legislature to participate more aggressively in constitutional decision making. No national official during the eighteenth century rejected the judicial authority to declare laws unconstitutional.

Until 1800 members of the emerging Jeffersonian coalition were as likely as the Federalists to speak in ways that implied a commitment to judicial supremacy. The judicial willingness to sustain the Sedition Act inspired a change in Jeffersonian attitudes toward judicial power. After the election of Thomas Jefferson, his supporters were far less inclined than previously to champion the courts as having the final authority to determine constitutional meaning.

For more information on the constitutional debates discussed in this section, see David P. Currie, *The Constitution in Congress: The Federalist Period, 1789–1810* (Chicago: University of Chicago Press, 1997).

Legal Precedents

State and federal justices from 1789 until 1803 occasionally considered whether justices had the right to declare laws unconstitutional. Virtually all justices who considered the matter favored exercising the power of judicial review. Federal justices, with some exceptions, tended to claim that only clearly unconstitutional statutes should be struck down. State justices, with some exceptions, did not articulate this limit on judicial power. Some federal and state justices indicated that courts could declare laws that violated fundamental rights unconstitutional, even when those rights were not explicitly mentioned by the Constitution. No firm consensus developed before *Marbury* on whether courts could strike down only clearly unconstitutional laws or on the use of fundamental rights analysis when doing constitutional adjudication.

Judicial discussions of judicial review before *Marbury* took place for the most part in fairly obscure cases. Even when the Supreme Court apparently declared unconstitutional a federal law mandating that justices help determine recipients of Revolutionary War pensions, the matter did not attract much political attention or interest. The judiciary first became embroiled in more partisan conflicts during the final years of the eighteenth century. Much to the distress of some Jeffersonians, federal justices declared constitutional such Federalist measures as the Sedition Act. These decisions inspired a political reaction that provided crucial background elements of *Marbury v. Madison*.

Documents 49–53: State Precedents

State courts reviewed the constitutionality of state legislation with increasing frequency during the years between the ratification of the Constitution and *Marbury v. Madison*. State justices who discussed judicial review consistently declared their power to declare state laws unconstitutional and sometimes exercised that power. South Carolina, Virginia, and Kentucky justices exercised the power to declare laws unconstitutional with some vigor. The South Carolina Supreme Court went further, asserting that courts could strike down laws inconsistent with certain fundamental rights not explicitly mentioned in the state constitution. Courts in Maryland and Pennsylvania maintained that courts had the power to declare laws unconstitutional but did not exercise that authority.

Unlike the years before ratification, judicial review in the states seems to have been generally accepted after 1787. Courts declared minor laws unconstitutional free from legislative interference. Virginia representatives in Congress would celebrate Virginia decisions declaring laws unconstitutional during the debates over the repeal of the Judiciary Act of 1801.

Documents 54–63: Federal Precedents

Until the late nineteenth century, justices of the United States Supreme Court had two opportunities to exercise the power of judicial review. The first came when riding circuit, fulfilling their obligation under the Judiciary Act of 1789 to preside over the various federal circuit courts located throughout the nation; the second came when sitting as justices of the Supreme Court. From 1789 until 1801, Supreme Court opinions were delivered *seriatim,* with each justice expressing his distinctive grounds for deciding the case before the Court.

Supreme Court justices before *Marbury* discussed and exercised the power to declare laws unconstitutional when riding circuit and when sitting as Supreme Court justices. The justices uniformly assumed they had the power to declare federal and state laws unconstitutional. Some debate existed over whether federal justices could declare that state laws violated the state constitution. Most federal justices, Justices Samuel Chase and William Paterson in particular, indicated that justices should void only clearly unconstitutional laws. In at least one instance, *United States v. Yale Todd* (1794), the justices appear to have declared a federal law unconstitutional.

34   The Judiciary Act of 1789

The framers left most details of federal judicial power to future congressional discretion. Article III of the Constitution vests Congress with the power to establish lower federal courts and, subject to important exceptions, the power to determine the conditions under which the Supreme Court hears appeals from lower federal and state courts. The First Congress quickly moved to establish a federal judicial system. Drafted largely by future chief justice Oliver Ellsworth, the Judiciary Act of 1789 was the first major piece of legislation passed by Congress and signed into law by President George Washington. The measure provided for a Supreme Court with one chief justice and five associate justices; three circuit courts of appeals presided over by two justices from the Supreme Court and one district judge; and thirteen district courts, one in each state, each with a single presiding judge. The act strongly implied, but did not explicitly state, that the Supreme Court had the power to declare federal and state laws unconstitutional. Section 25 gave that tribunal the jurisdiction to hear appeals from state court decisions declaring federal laws unconstitutional or rejecting claims of federal constitutional right. When resolving those cases, the justices would consider whether the state court had correctly interpreted the Constitution. Section 34, which declares that federal courts must follow the Constitution when constitutional provisions conflict with state procedures for holding trials, implies a judicial power to declare state laws unconstitutional. An obscure provision in Section 13 might be read as vesting the Supreme Court with the authority to issue writs of mandamus when exercising original jurisdiction. This provision, not commented on at the time, became a crucial bone of contention in Marbury.

Little survives of the congressional debate responsible for the Judiciary Act. No recorded statement outlines how any national legislator in 1789 conceived of judicial review, other than the text of Sections 25 and 34.

For more information on the Judiciary Act of 1789, see Maeva Marcus, ed., Origins of the Federal Judiciary: Essays on the Judiciary Act of 1789 (New York: Oxford University Press, 1992).

CHAP. XX.—*An Act to establish the Judicial Courts of the United States.*

SECTION 1. *Be it enacted by the Senate and House of Representatives of the United States of America in Congress assembled,* That the supreme court of the United States shall consist of a chief justice and five associate justices, any four of whom shall be a quorum, and shall hold annually at the seat of government two sessions, the one commencing the first Monday of February, and the other the first Monday of August. . . .

SEC. 13. *And be it further enacted.* . . . The Supreme Court shall also have appellate jurisdiction from the circuit courts and courts of the several states, in the cases herein after specially provided for; and shall have power to issue writs of prohibition to the district courts, when proceeding as courts of admiralty and maritime jurisdic-

tion, and writs of *mandamus,* in cases warranted by the principles and usages of law, to any courts appointed, or persons holding office, under the authority of the United States. . . .

SEC. 25. *And be it further enacted,* That a final judgment or decree in any suit, in the highest court of law or equity of a State in which a decision in the suit could be had, where is drawn in question the validity of a treaty or statute of, or an authority exercised under the United States, and the decision is against their validity; or where is drawn in question the validity of a statute of, or an authority exercised under any State, on the ground of their being repugnant to the constitution, treaties or laws of the United States, and the decision is in favour of such their validity, or where is drawn in question the construction of any clause of the constitution, or of a treaty, or statute of, or commission held under the United

States, and the decision is against the title, right, privilege or exemption specially set up or claimed by either party, under such clause of the said Constitution, treaty, statute or commission, may be re-examined and reversed or affirmed in the Supreme Court of the United States upon a writ of error, the citation being signed by the chief justice, or judge or chancellor of the court rendering or passing the judgment or decree complained of, or by a justice of the Supreme Court of the United States, in the same manner and under the same regulations, and the writ shall have the same effect, as if the judgment or decree complained of had been rendered or passed in a circuit court, and the proceeding upon the reversal shall also be the same, except that the Supreme Court, instead of remanding the cause for a final decision as be-

fore provided, may at their discretion, if the cause shall have been once remanded before, proceed to a final decision of the same, and award execution. But no other error shall be assigned or regarded as a ground of reversal in any such case as aforesaid, than such as appears on the face of the record, and immediately respects the before mentioned questions of validity or construction of the said constitution, treaties, statutes, commissions, or authorities in dispute. . . .

SEC. 34. *And be it further enacted*, That the laws of the several states, except where the constitution, treaties or statutes of the United States shall otherwise require or provide, shall be regarded as rules of decision in trials at common law in the courts of the United States in cases where they apply.

Source: U.S. Statutes at Large. 1789. Vol. 1: 73, 81, 85–87, 92.

---

35 Debate over the Bill of Rights

The First Congress framed the first ten amendments to the Constitution, now known as the Bill of Rights. With the prominent exception of James Madison, very few members of the national legislature expressed much interest in provisions that many twentieth-century constitutionalists view as central to the American political order. Debates over the Bill of Rights and particular provisions were brief and often desultory, providing later scholars with little idea of the specific limits various amendments were expected to place on government action. The persons responsible for the Bill of Rights paid even less attention to the judicial responsibility for protecting fundamental freedoms. Thomas Jefferson wrote to Madison while the Constitution was being debated that he believed courts would enforce the liberties protected by the Bill of Rights. Madison, in his speech proposing those amendments, similarly predicted that courts would protect the fundamental freedoms being appended to the Constitution. Neither Madison nor any other participant in the limited debates over the Bill of Rights detailed the nature of the expected judicial protection. Madison regarded judicial review as only one institutional protection for fundamental rights. State legislatures, he believed, would play an even greater role in ensuring that the national government protected fundamental freedoms. Madison also emphasized before Congress that a bill of rights would promote liberty more by fostering a public opinion favorable to protecting rights than by providing a judicial check should majorities violate minority rights.

Thomas Jefferson to James Madison, March 15, 1789

In the arguments in favor of a declaration of rights, you omit one which has great weight with

me, the legal check which it puts into the hands of the judiciary. This is a body, which if rendered independent, and kept strictly to their own department merits great confidence for their learning and integrity. In fact what degree of confidence would be too much for a body composed of such men as Wythe, Blair, and Pendleton?

Speech of James Madison

It may thought that all paper barriers against the power of the community are too weak to be worthy of attention. I am sensible they are not so strong as to satisfy gentlemen of every description who have seen and examined thoroughly the texture of such a defence; yet, as they have a tendency to impress some degree of respect for them, to establish the public opinion in their favor, and rouse the attention of the whole community, it may be one means to control the majority from those acts to which they might be otherwise inclined. . . .

It has been said that it is unnecessary to load the constitution with this provision, because it was not found effectual in the constitution of the particular States. It is true, there are a few particular States in which some of the most valuable articles have not, at one time or other, been violated; but it does not follow but they may have, to a certain degree, a salutary effect against the abuse of power. If they are incorporated into the constitution, independent tribunals of justice will consider themselves in a peculiar manner the guardians of those rights; they will be an impenetrable bulwark against every assumption of power in the legislative or executive; they will be naturally led to resist every encroachment upon rights expressly stipulated for in the constitution by the declaration of rights. Besides this security, there is a great probably that such a declaration in the federal system would be enforced; because the State Legislatures will jealously and closely watch the operations of this Government, and be able to resist with more effect every assumption of power, than any other power on earth can do; and the greatest opponents to a Federal Government admit the State Legislatures to be sure guardians of the people's liberty.

Sources: Thomas Jefferson, *The Portable Thomas Jefferson*, ed. Merrill D. Peterson (New York: Penguin Books, 1975), 438; *Annals of Congress*, 1st Cong., 2d Sess., 455, 456–57 (1790).

36 Debate over Removals

The first extensive constitutional debate after ratification was over presidential power to remove executive branch officials. The Constitution requires that certain executive branch officials be appointed with the "advise and consent" of the Senate but does not explicitly mandate how those officials may be removed. A bill in the First Congress declared that the head of the proposed Department of Foreign Affairs was "to be removable from office by the President of the United States." A heated controversy over this measure took place during the week of June 15, 1789. Opponents of the measure claimed that the Constitution required that removals as well as appointments be approved by the Senate.

Notions of judicial review and judicial supremacy were discussed at length in the debates over removal. Some opponents of the proposed clause claimed that the House of Representatives had no right even to express an opinion on the constitutional issue, that only the federal judiciary was empowered to resolve constitutional questions. Other legislators indicated that, while Congress was entitled to express an opinion on the constitutional matter, the opinion was subject to reversal by the Supreme Court. James Madison indicated that the legislature might have the final authority to determine the constitutional procedure for removing executive branch officials. His speeches in this debate are often interpreted as advocating what is known as "departmentalism," the view that each department has an equal right to interpret the Constitution. When his words are read closely, however, Madison appears to have been claiming only that elected officials have the final authority to interpret the Constitution when the dispute concerns the constitutional balance of power between the elected branches of the national government.

The eighteenth-century constitutional debates over removals took place entirely within Congress. The Supreme Court of the United States did not resolve the major constitutional questions associated with how executive branch officials could be removed until the twentieth century. Excerpts from those cases, Myers v. United States (1926) and Humphrey's Executor v. United States (1935), are reprinted in Documents 89 and 90.

Mr. Smith:

. . . [T]he words should be struck out, and the question of right, if it is one, left to the decision of the Judiciary. It will be time enough to determine the question when the President shall remove an officer in this way. I conceive it can properly be brought before that tribunal; the officer will have a right to mandamus to be restored to his office, and the judges would determine whether the President exercised a constitutional authority or not.

Mr. Madison:

. . . I suppose an exposition of the constitution may come with as much propriety from the Legislature, as any other department of the Government. If the power naturally belongs to the Government, and the constitution is undecided as to the body which is to exercise it, it is likely that it is submitted to the discretion of the Legislature, and the question will depend upon its own merits.

Mr. White:

. . . I would rather the Judiciary should decide the point, because it is more properly within their department. . . .

Let us, then, leave the constitution to a free operation, and let the President, with or without the Senate, carry it into execution. Then if any one supposes himself injured by the determination, let him have recourse to the law, and its decision will establish the true construction of the constitution.

Mr. Boudinot:

I conceive it will be improper to leave the determination of this question to the judges. There

will be some indelicacy in subjecting the executive action in this particular to a suit at law; and there may be much inconvenience if the President does not exercise the prerogative until it is decided by the courts of justice.

Mr. Smith:

Gentlemen have said that it is proper to give a legislative construction of the constitution. I differ with them on this point. I think it an infringement of the powers of the Judiciary. . . . A great deal of mischief has arisen in the several States, by the Legislatures undertaking to decide constitutional questions. Sir, it is the duty of the Legislature to make laws; your judges are to expound them.

Mr. Gerry:

. . . Why then should we interfere in the business? Are we afraid that the President and the Senate are not sufficiently informed to know their respective duties . . . If the fact is, as we seem to suspect, they do not understand the constitution, let it go before the proper tribunal; the judges are the constitutional umpires on such questions.

Mr. Ames:

. . . It therefore appears to me proper for the House to declare what is their sense of the constitution. If we declare justly on this point, it will serve for a rule of conduct to the Executive Magistrate; if we declare improperly, the judiciary will revise our decision.

Mr. Livermore:

. . . But gentlemen say it is inconsistent with the constitution to make this declaration; that, as the constitution is silent, we ought not to be explicit. The constitution has expressly pointed out several matters which we can do, and some which we cannot do; but in other matters it is silent, and leaves them to the discretion of the Legislature. . . . I look upon it that the Legislature have therefore a right to exercise their discretion on such questions. . . .

Mr. Lawrence:

With respect to this and every case omitted, but which can be collected from the other provisions made in the constitution, the people look up to the Legislature, the concurrent opinion of the two branches, for their construction; they conceive those cases proper subjects for legislative wisdom, they naturally suppose, where provisions are to be made, they ought to spring from this source, and this source alone. . . .

I take it, Mr. Chairman, that it is proper for the Legislature to speak their sense upon those points on which the constitution is silent. I believe the judges will never decide that we are guilty of a breach of the constitution, by declaring a legislative opinion in cases where the constitution is silent. If the laws shall be in violation of any part of the constitution, the judges will not hesitate to decide against them; where the power is incident to the Government, and the constitution is silent, it can be no impediment to a legislative grant; I hold it necessary in such cases to make provision. In the case of removal, the constitution is silent; the wisdom of the Legislature should therefore declare where the power resides.

Mr. Stone:

. . . I do not think it would do to leave it to the determination of courts of law hereafter. It should be our duty, in cases like the present, to give our opinion on the construction of the constitution.

Mr. Madison:

. . . I acknowledge, in the ordinary course of Government, that the exposition of the laws and constitution devolves upon the Judiciary. But, I beg to know, upon what principle it can be contended, that any one department draws from the constitution greater powers than another, in marking out the limits of the powers of the several departments? The constitution is the charter of the people to the Government; it specifies certain great powers as absolutely granted, and marks out the departments to exercise them. If the constitutional boundary of either be brought into question, I do not see that any one of these independent departments has more right than another to declare their sentiments on that point.

Perhaps this is an omitted case. There is not one Government on the face of the earth, so far as I recollect, there is not one in the United States, in which provision is made for a particular authority to determine the limits of the constitutional divisions of power between the branches of the Government. . . . It is therefore a fair question, whether this great point may not as well be decided, at least by the whole Legislature as by a part, by us as well as by the Executive or Judiciary. As I think it will be equally constitutional, I cannot imagine it will be less safe, that the exposition should issue from the legislative authority than any others: and the more so, because it involves in the decision the opinions of both departments, whose powers to be affected by it. Besides, I do not see in what way this question would come before the judges, to obtain a fair and solemn decision; but even if it were the case that it could, I should suppose, at least while the Government is not led by passion, disturbed by faction, or deceived by any discolored medium of sight, but while there is a desire in all to see and be guided by the benignant ray of truth, that the decision may be made with the most advantage by the Legislature itself.

Mr. Gerry:

. . . If it is an omitted case, an attempt in the Legislature to supply the defect, will be in fact an attempt to amend the constitution. But this can only be done in the way pointed out by the fifth article of that instrument. . . .

. . . It was said, that the judges could not have the power of deciding on this subject, because the constitution is silent; but I ask, if the judges are not *ex officio* judges of the law; and whether they would not be bound to declare the law a nullity, if this clause is continued in it, and is inconsistent with the constitution? There is a clause in this system of government that makes it their duty. I allude to that which authorizes the President to obtain the opinions of the heads of departments in writings; so the President and Senate may require the opinion of the judges respecting this power, if they have any doubts concerning it.

Mr. Benson:

. . . Does he suppose, whenever a doubt arises in this House, (and it will be a doubt if an individual doubts,) with respect to the meaning of any part of the constitution, we must take that mode? Or does he really suppose that we are never to take any part of the constitution by construction. This I conceive to be altogether inadmissible; for it is not in the compass of human wisdom to frame a system of Government so minutely, but that a construction will, in some cases, be necessary. This is such a case; and we ought most assuredly to declare our sentiments on the occasion.

Mr. Smith:

. . . It has been said, that the Legislature may give their opinion on the constitution. I agree with gentlemen if they mean that, as an individual, we may give our single opinions; but I never can admit it to be right in our legislative capacity to influence the judges, and throw our weight into either scale to warp their decision. I think it highly criminal to attempt to bias their judgment in any way. . . .

An honorable gentlemen has said, he did not see how this case could be brought before a court of justice in order to obtain their decision. That gentlemen is no stranger to a just and venerable maxim. Wherever a man has a right, he has a remedy: if he suffers a wrong, he can have a re-

dress; he would be entitled to damages for being deprived of his property in his office.

Mr. White:

. . . I imagine the Legislature may construe the constitution with respect to the powers annexed to their department, but subject to the decision of the judges. The same with regard to the Executive: the President and Senate may construe the power in question, and as they determine respecting the mode of removal, so they may act, but liable also to the decision of the Judiciary.

Mr. Boudinot:

. . . [F]or what purpose shall Congress refuse a legislative declaration of the constitution, and leave it to remain a doubtful point. Because, if Congress refuses to determine, we cannot conceive that others will be more entitled to decide upon it than we are. This will appear to give ground for what the gentlemen have asserted, that we are afraid to carry the constitution into effect. This, I apprehend, would not be doing our duty.

Mr. Madison:

. . . I think this branch of the Legislature is as much interested in the establishment of the true meaning of the constitution, as either the President or Senate. . . . And have we not as good a right as any branch of the Government to declare our sense of the meaning of the constitution.

Nothing has yet been offered to invalidate the doctrine, that the meaning of the constitution may as well be ascertained by the legislative as by the judicial authority. When the question emerges as it does in this bill, and much seems to depend on it, I should conceive it highly proper to make a legislative construction. . . .

Mr. Page:

I wish to strike out the clause, sir, because we shall leave the constitution to the proper expositors of it.

Mr. Baldwin:

Gentlemen say it properly belongs to the Judiciary to decide this question. Be it so. It is their province to decide upon our laws; and if they find this clause to be unconstitutional, they will not hesitate to declare it so; and it seems to be a very difficult point to bring it before them in any other way. Let gentlemen consider themselves in the tribunal of justice, called upon to decide this question on a mandamus. What a situation! almost too great for human nature to bear, they would feel great relief in having had the question decided by the representatives of the people. Hence I conclude, they also will receive our opinion kindly.

Mr. Sylvester:

Surely it will not be any longer contended that we have no right to give our sentiments? We certainly have that right, for without such a power we could pass no law whatever. It is certain that the Judiciary will be better able to decide the question of constitutionality in this way than any other. If we are wrong, they can correct our error. . . .

Mr. Gerry:

. . . [T]he judges are the expositors of the constitution and the acts of Congress. Our exposition, therefore, would be subject to their reversal. In this way the constitutional balance would be destroyed; the Legislature, with the Judiciary, might remove the head of the Executive branch. But a further reason why we are not the expositors is, that the Judiciary may disagree with us, and undo what all our efforts have labored to accomplish. A law is a nullity, unless it can be carried into execution; in this case, our law will be suspended. Hence, all construction of the meaning of the constitution is dangerous or unnatural, and therefore ought to be avoided.

Source: Annals of Congress, 1st Cong., 1st Sess., 477, 479, 484–486, 488–492, 496, 500, 503, 505, 511, 520–521, 523–525, 528–530, 537, 539, 568, 572, 582, 584–585, 596.

37   Debate over the National Bank

The 1791 legislative proposal that the federal government incorporate a national bank launched a constitutional controversy that lasted until the Civil War. President George Washington asked each member of his cabinet to write a memorandum on the constitutional issues raised by the bank proposal. Alexander Hamilton's bold defense of the bank is the seminal state paper championing broad constructions of federal power, and Thomas Jefferson's sharp attack is the seminal state paper favoring narrow constructions of federal power. Congressional debate also highlighted constitutional issues. Legislators paid substantial attention both to how constitutional powers should be construed and to more general principles of constitutional interpretation.

The participants in the debate over the national bank disputed whether the federal government was constitutionally authorized to incorporate a national bank, not which branch of government was authorized to determine that question. Several defenders of the national bank did maintain that the Supreme Court had the power to determine whether the bank bill was constitutional and had the final authority to settle all constitutional debates over the national bank. More than a quarter century after the first bank of the United States was incorporated, the Supreme Court in McCulloch v. Maryland (1819) ruled that Congress had the power to incorporate a national bank. That decision, however, did not end the constitutional dispute. Both Presidents Andrew Jackson and John Tyler later vetoed efforts to recharter a national bank on the ground that they believed the bank bill unconstitutional.

Mr. Lawrence:

It is said we must not pass a problematical bill, which is liable to a supervision by the Judges of the Supreme Court; but he conceived there was no force in this, as those Judges are invested by the Constitution with a power to pass their judgment on all laws that may be passed.

Mr. Boudinot:

The last objection was that, by adopting this bill we exposed the measure to be considered and defeated by the Judiciary of the United States, who might adjudge it to be contrary to the Constitution, and therefore void; and not lend their aid to carry it into execution. This, he alleged, gave him no uneasiness. He was so far from controverting this right in the Judiciary, that it was his boast and his confidence. It led him to greater decision on all subjects of a constitutional nature, when he reflected that if, from inattention, want of precision, or any other defect, he should do wrong, that there was a power in the Govern-

ment which could constitutionally prevent the operations of such a wrong measure from effecting his constituents. He was legislating for a nation, and, for thousands unborn; and it was the glory of the Constitution that there was a remedy even for the failures of the supreme Legislature itself.

Mr. Smith:

If, in such cases, it appeared to them, on solemn deliberation, that the measure was not prohibited by any part of the Constitution, was not a violation of the rights of any State or individual, and was peculiarly necessary and proper to carry into operation certain essential powers of the Government, it was then not only justifiable on the part of Congress, but it as even their duty to adopt such measure. That, nevertheless, it was still within the province of the Judiciary to annul the law, if it should be by them deemed not to result by fair construction from the powers vested by the Constitution.

Source: Annals of Congress, 2d Cong., 1st Sess., 1916, 1927, 1937.

---

38   Debate over the Post Office

In 1791 Congress debated whether the national government had the power to authorize vehicles transporting mail to carry passengers, even when such practices were forbidden by state law. Opponents of the bill maintained that such a law was not warranted by the postal power and, if passed, should be declared unconstitutional by the Supreme Court.

Mr. Niles:

But, sir, the question is simply, whether Congress have a right to authorize the carrier of the mail to carry passengers, on hire, through those States where an exclusive right of carrying passengers for hire has been granted by the State Government and still exists. You are empowered by the Constitution to establish post offices and post roads, and to do whatever may be *necessary* and *proper* to carry that power into effect. Now,

sir, is it necessary in order to the transportation of your mail, that you should erect state-coaches for the purpose of transporting passengers? What has your mail to do with passengers transported for hire? Why, sir, nothing more than this—by granting to the carrier of your mail a right to carry passengers for hire, the carriage of the mail may be a little less expensive. Does this consideration render it *necessary* and *proper* for you to violate the laws of the States? If not, you will, by so doing, violate their rights, and overleap the bounds of your own. This matter may occasion a legal adjudication, in order to which the Judiciary must determine, whether you have a *constitu-* *tional right* to establish this regulation, and this will depend on the question whether it be *necessary* and *proper*.

Source: *Annals of Congress*, 2d Cong., 1st Sess., 308–309.

39 Debate over the Jay Treaty

The proposed peace treaty with Great Britain negotiated by Chief Justice John Jay provoked a national debate that hardened emerging party differences between Federalists and the Jeffersonian Republicans. Elected officials and their partisans debated the merits of the treaty, whether the treaty was constitutional, whether the House of Representatives was constitutionally obligated to pass laws implementing the treaty, and whether a branch of Congress could require the president to make public various papers concerning the negotiations responsible for the treaty. Several participants in the debate over the Jay Treaty alluded to judicial power, though none did so at length. Some claimed that the judiciary had the final authority to determine all constitutional issues raised by treaties and all other government actions. Others, most notably Abraham Baldwin of Georgia, indicated that constitutional interpretation was a shared responsibility of all branches of the national government.

Mr. Smith:

. . . Mr. S. referred to the proceedings of the Supreme Court in the case lately argued of the carriage tax and just decided; how did the Court proceed? Did they call for the journals of the two Houses, or the report of the Committee of Ways and Means, in which the law originated, or the debates of the House on passing the law? What impression would such call have made on the public mind? Would it have enhanced in the public opinion either the dignity or wisdom of that tribunal? They took the Constitution in their hand, and tested the act by that standard, and by that alone has their decision been governed.

Mr. Harper:

Every branch of the Government, in extreme cases, has a right to oppose itself, to the other branches, and arrest the progress of destructive measures. The Judicial power might make a stand, and refuse to execute a law. This discretion, he trusted, would never be used. It must, in-

deed, be a desperate case which would justify its use.

Mr. Baldwin:

And how, he asked, are such questions between different constituent parts of the Government to be settled, but for each branch to deliberate with calmness and moderation in their own sphere, and come to a mutual result? It must indeed be a fearful, trembling loyalty, that should prevent so important a branch of the Government as that House from even presuming to deliberate on the very important considerations which have been addressed to them. It was not a new case, or peculiar to that House; there can be no doubt but it will be well received by the other branches of the Government, with the exception of but few individuals. The President had not hesitated to send back to them their laws when he thought them against the Constitution, and they had given way to his reasons. The Judges had refused to execute a law intruding upon their department; it was repealed, and they passed another on the subject. . . .

Mr. Gilbert:

. . . The legislature could check the Judiciary; so the Judiciary might, in some cases, in order to guard the Constitution, check the Legislature.

Mr. Harper:

The second position which the honorable member from Pennsylvania [Mr. Gallatin] had attempted to establish was, that Treaties cannot repeal existing laws. . . . [I]t ought to be remarked, that this was purely a judicial question. The business of the Legislature was to make laws of the President and Senate to make Treaties; but it belonged to the Judicial power to decide about the effect of laws and Treaties after they should be made. He had great doubts, he said, about this question; and should always think it proper to remove any laws out of the way of a Treaty by formal repeal; but still if a case should occur in which a Treaty stood opposed to a law, the Courts of Justice must decide which would supercede the other.

Source: Annals of Congress, 4th Cong., 1st Sess., 441–443, 463, 538, 539, 682, 754–755.

40   Debate on Foreign Intercourse

The House of Representatives in 1798 debated whether Congress was obligated to appropriate money to pay the salaries of persons appointed by the president to foreign ministries. Much discussion centered on the appropriate constitutional roles of the executive and legislative branches. Both Jeffersonians who believed Congress had a constitutional right not to appropriate money for salaries and Federalists who believed Congress was constitutionally obligated to appropriate money for salaries agreed that the judicial power to declare laws unconstitutional was a legitimate constitutional check on the power of elected officials.

Mr. Nicholas:

Was it true, Mr. N. asked, according to the practice of the Government, that the departments had no check upon each other? Did not the Judiciary consider the acts of the Executive and Legislature? Certainly they did. There were instances in which the judges had decided upon the Constitution and laws of the country, and in one instance he believed they had determined for them, and in another against them.

Source: Annals of Congress, 5th Cong., 2d Sess., 924.

41   Debate over the Sedition Act

The Sedition Act of 1798 inspired an intense, bitter debate over federal power and the rights guaranteed by the First Amendment. The central provision of that measure criminalized "any false, scandalous and malicious writing or writings against the government of the United States, or either house of the Congress of the United States, or the President of the United States." Federalists said the law was a constitutional effort to preserve the public peace and the reputation of the national government, while Jeffersonians claimed it was an unconstitutional endeavor to preserve the Federalist Party. While disputing the constitutionality of the Sedition Act, both proponents and opponents of the measure agreed in 1798 that the federal judiciary had the power to determine whether the Sedition Act was constitutional.

Passage of the Sedition Act inspired the Kentucky and Virginia Resolutions of 1798 and 1799 (see Documents 42–44). These legislative declarations became the seminal state papers on strict constructionism and state rights. Kentucky and Virginia legislators did not discuss the judicial power to declare laws unconstitutional: both asserted the right of states to oppose unconstitutional laws. Kentucky in 1799 claimed that each state had the right to "nullify" unconstitutional laws, and the Virginia Resolution spoke more vaguely about a state right "to interpose for arresting the progress of [unconstitutional laws]." Virtually every northern state that responded to the resolutions insisted that only the federal judiciary was authorized to declare laws unconstitutional (see Document 45). James Madison's subsequent report for the Virginia legislature reaffirmed the resolutions but acknowledged the judicial power to declare laws unconstitutional (see Document 46). Several passages suggest he now believed that the judiciary had the last word for the federal government on issues of constitutional meaning. Nevertheless, Madison insisted that judicial decisions sustaining national legislation did not bar state efforts to have offending laws repealed, to pass constitutional amendments, and to take other unspecified steps to protect liberty. Later in his life, Madison insisted that neither the Virginia resolutions nor his report were intended in any way to sanction nullification.

Mr. Bayard:

Even the Judges, the gentleman said, are a check upon the Legislature. . . . If the Legislature transgress the bounds of their authority, their acts are void, and neither the people nor the Judges are bound by them.

Mr. Gallatin:

But Mr. G. would go further, and say that the States and the State Judiciary would, indeed they must, consider the law as a mere nullity, they must declare it to be unconstitutional.

Mr. Harper:

But the gentleman from Pennsylvania says, that, if this law were to pass, the courts of justice would declare it to be unconstitutional. If so then, according to his own opinion, the law would become a dead letter. He did not know what the de-

cision of the judicial power would be. Whatever it might be, he should submit to it.

Mr. Kittera:

. . . There is a Judicial power which will sit in judgment upon our acts; but to call upon the people to resist the law, was a doctrine big with mischief. If a law be unconstitutional, the Judges will refuse to execute it.

Mr. Allen:

But, sir, in the same speech the people are instructed that opposition to the laws, that insurrection is a duty; whenever they think we exceed our Constitutional powers; but I ask the gentleman, who shall determine that point? I thought the Constitution had assigned the cognizance of that question to the Courts, and so it has.

Mr. Gallatin:

. . . He meant only to state that, notwithstanding that conviction, his opinion was that an appeal must be made to another tribunal, to the Judiciary in the first instance, on the subject of a supposedly unconstitutional law; and that even where no redress could be obtained, he did not think that law alone, and in itself, sufficient to justify resistance and opposition even in those who thought it unconstitutional.

Mr. Bayard:

. . . [H]e believed the effect of this amendment would be, to put it into the power of a jury to declare that this is an unconstitutional law, instead of leaving this to be determined, where it ought to be determined, by the Judiciary.

Mr. Macon:

. . . [H]e was convinced that Congress does not possess the power to pass a law like the present; but if there be a majority determined to pass it, he could only hope that the Judges would exercise the power placed in them of determining the law an unconstitutional law, if, upon scrutiny, they find it to be so.

Source: Annals of Congress, 5th Cong., 2d Sess., 1221, 1991, 2016, 2096, 2111, 2136, 2152.

42 Kentucky Resolutions of 1798

1. *Resolved,* That . . . whensoever the general government assumes undelegated powers, its acts are unauthoritative, void, and of no force: that to this compact each State acceded as a State, and is an integral part, its co-States forming, as to itself, the other party: that the government created by this compact was not made the exclusive or final judge of the extent of the powers delegated to itself; since that would have made its discretion, and not the Constitution, the measure of its powers; but that, as in all other cases of compact among powers having no common judge, *each party has an equal right to judge for itself, as well of infractions as of the mode and measure of redress.*

Source: Jonathan Elliot, ed., *The Debates in the Several State Conventions on the Adoption of the Federal Constitution, as Recommended by the General Convention at Philadelphia in 1787,* 2d ed. (Philadelphia: J. B. Lippincott, 1836), vol. 4: 540.

43   Virginia Resolutions of 1798

That this Assembly doth explicitly and peremptorily declare, that it views the powers of the federal government, as resulting from the compact, to which the states are parties; as limited by the plain sense and intention of the instrument constituting the compact; as no further valid that they are authorized by the grants enumerated in that compact; and that in case of a deliberate, palpable, and dangerous exercise of other powers, not granted by the said compact, the states who are parties thereto, have the right, and are in duty bound, to interpose for arresting the progress of the evil, and for maintaining within their respective limits, the authorities, rights and liberties appertaining to them.

Source: Jonathan Elliot, ed., *The Debates in the Several State Conventions on the Adoption of the Federal Constitution, as Recommended by the General Convention at Philadelphia in 1787,* 2d ed. (Philadelphia: J. B. Lippincott, 1836), vol. 4: 528.

44   Kentucky Resolution of 1799

. . . That the several states who formed that instrument, being sovereign and independent, have the unquestionable right to judge of its infraction; and *That a nullification, by those sovereignties, of all unauthorized acts done under color of that instrument, is the rightful remedy. . . .*

Source: Jonathan Elliot, ed., *The Debates in the Several State Conventions on the Adoption of the Federal Constitution, as Recommended by the General Convention at Philadelphia in 1787,* 2d ed. (Philadelphia: J. B. Lippincott, 1836), vol. 4: 545.

45   Answers

State of Rhode Island and Providence Plantations

1. *Resolved,* That, in the opinion of this legislature, the second section of the third article of the Constitution of the United States . . . vests in the federal courts, exclusively, and in the Supreme Court of the United States ultimately, the authority of deciding on the constitutionality of any act or law of the Congress of the United States.

2. *Resolved,* that for any state legislature to assume that authority would be—

1st. Blending together legislative and judicial powers; . . .

3d. Submitting most important questions of law to less competent tribunals. . . .

Commonwealth of Massachusetts

. . . [T]his legislature are persuaded that the decision of all cases in law and equity arising under the Constitution of the United States, and the construction of all laws made in pursuance thereof, are exclusively vested by the people in the judicial courts of the United States.

State of New York

. . . [W]hereas the judicial power extends expressly to all cases of law and equity arising under the Constitution and the laws of the United States; whereby the interference of the legislatures of the particular states in those cases is manifestly excluded.

State of New Hampshire

. . . That the state legislatures are not the proper tribunals to determine the constitutionality of the laws of the general government; that the duty of such decision is properly and exclusively confided to the judicial department. . . .

State of Vermont

. . . It belongs not to state legislatures to decide on the constitutionality of laws made by the general government; this power being exclusively vested in the judiciary courts of the Union.

Source: Jonathan Elliot, ed., *The Debates in the Several State Conventions on the Adoption of the Federal Constitution, as Recommended by the General Convention at Philadelphia in 1787*, 2d ed. (Philadelphia: J. B. Lippincott, 1836), vol. 4: 533, 536, 537, 539.

46   Madison's Report on the Virginia Resolutions

. . . [I]t is objected, that the judicial authority is to be regarded as the sole expositor of the Constitution in the last resort. . . .

. . . [T]he proper answer to the objection is, that the resolution of the General Assembly relates to those great and extraordinary cases, in which all the forms of the Constitution may prove ineffectual against infractions dangerous to the essential rights of the parties to it. The resolution supposes that dangerous powers, not delegated, may not only be usurped and executed by the other departments, but that the judicial department, also, may exercise or sanction dangerous powers beyond the grant of the Constitution; and, consequently, that the ultimate right of the parties to the Constitution, to judge whether the compact has been dangerously violated, must extend to violations by one delegated authority as well as by another—by the judiciary as well as by the executive, or the legislature.

However true, therefore, it may be, that the judiciary department is, in all questions submitted to it by the forms of the Constitution, to decide in the last resort, this resort must necessarily be deemed the last in relation to the authorities of the other departments of the government; not in relation to the rights of the parties to the constitutional compact, from which the judicial, as well as the other departments, hold their delegated trusts. . . .

It has been said that it belongs to the judiciary of the United States, and not the state legislatures, to declare the meaning of the Federal Constitution.

But a declaration that proceedings of the federal government are not warranted by the Constitution, is a novelty neither among the citizens nor among the legislatures of the states; nor are the citizens or the legislature of Virginia singular in the example of it.

Nor can the declarations of either, whether affirming or denying the constitutionality of measures of the federal government, or whether made before or after judicial decisions thereupon, be deemed, in any point of view, an assumption of the office of the judge. The declarations in such cases are expressions of opinion, unaccompanied with any other effect than what they may produce on opinion, by exciting reflection. . . .

And if there be no impropriety in declaring the unconstitutionality of proceedings in the federal government, where can there be the impropriety of communicating the declaration to other states and inviting their concurrence in a like declaration? . . .

Source: Jonathan Elliot, ed., *The Debates in the Several State Conventions on the Adoption of the Federal Constitution, as Recommended by the General Convention at Philadelphia in 1787,* 2d ed. (Philadelphia: J. B. Lippincott, 1836), vol. 4: 549–550, 568, 578.

---

47   Debate over Judicial Organization

During the first decade of the Constitution's existence, members of the federal judiciary played many roles. John Jay negotiated the peace treaty with Great Britain while he was chief justice of the United States, and Oliver Ellsworth negotiated a treaty with France while he held that office. Congress also passed laws authorizing the justices to determine who was eligible for military pensions. Many officials thought these practices compromised judicial independence. Prominent members of Congress went further and sought, unsuccessfully, to pass a constitutional amendment or federal statute that would ban persons serving as federal justices from holding any other national office. One reason they gave was that a president who could offer justices prestigious and lucrative offices might influence judicial rulings on the constitutionality of laws. Charles Pinkney's speech defending this proposal includes the only clear congressional assertion before the election of 1800 that justices ought not have the power to declare laws unconstitutional.

Mr. Pinkney:

The Constitution contemplates an independent Judiciary. The public, therefore, will expect and have a right to demand, upon all questions, a fair and impartial trial by Judges, whose minds are open to conviction, and unprejudiced by party opinions; by men who have not been concerned in forming a law or treaty, but who are totally unfettered by the recollection of what passed at the negotiation, or what might have been wished or expected by either party, as judges, candidly and impartially to determine upon every question that may come before them.

. . . It is our duty to guard against any addition to this bias, which a Judge, from the nature of his appointment, must inevitably feel in favor of the President. It is more particularly incumbent on us when we recollect that our Judges claim the dangerous right to question the constitutionality of the laws; and either to execute them or not, as they think proper; a right in my judgment as unfounded and as dangerous as any that was ever attempted in a free government; they however do exercise it, and while they are suffered to do so, it is impossible to say to what extent it might be carried. What might be the consequences if the President could at any time get rid of obnoxious laws by persuading or influencing the Judges to decide that they were unconstitutional, and ought not to be executed?

Source: Annals of Congress, 6th Cong., 1st Sess., 97, 98, 101.

48   Debate over Extending the Sedition Act

The original Sedition Act, passed in 1798, expired the day the president elected in 1800 took office. After the election of 1800, Congress debated whether to extend the measure. Remarkably, many Federalists who supported it when John Adams was in office continued to do so knowing that Thomas Jefferson was about to take office. Many Jeffersonians took an equally principled stance, opposing a sedition law they would now have the power to enforce. The debate over extension highlighted increased Republican suspicion of the Supreme Court. Some Republicans in 1798, quoted in Document 41, declared that the federal judiciary had the ultimate authority to determine whether such laws as the Sedition Act were constitutional. Supreme Court justices on circuit had declared the act constitutional. Responding to these decisions and increasingly concerned about a Federalist-dominated judiciary, Jeffersonians in 1801 for the first time raised substantial questions about judicial review and judicial supremacy.

Mr. Davis:

. . . But a Judge of the United States having determined the law to be Constitutional, did not bring conviction to his mind. He still entertained the same opinion he had formerly entertained, and he believed it would be difficult to persuade the American people that the law was either Constitutional or expedient.

Mr. Randolph:

He would not enter into a view of the unconstitutionality of the law. How strongly soever the gentleman supposed the question to have been decided by the Congress who passed the law, he would tell that gentlemen and all his adherents, that he had a still higher tribunal to appeal to—one higher than they could produce: he meant the American people. Their voice was more powerful than that of the courts and the President. . . .

Mr. Griswold:

. . . The Judiciary had decided it to be a law effectually within the Constitution. There might be some other quorum to which gentlemen would wish to appeal; perhaps they might be better satisfied by appealing to the people, but he could not be. He believed the decision to be made in a Constitutional mode, and was desirous of giving it his decided support.

Mr. Rutledge:

Respecting the constitutionality of this law, I will only observe that our Judiciary (and they are the only appropriate judges of its constitutionality) have decided, and repeatedly decided, that it was Constitutional. An honorable gentleman from Virginia has told us that a more high and respectable tribunal—the people—had declared it unconstitutional. Sir, I am not so good a Democrat, nor so diffident of myself, as to have a recourse to the people on the passage of every law to inquire of them if it be Constitutional. As a legislator, it is sufficient for me that, with the best understanding I can obtain of the Constitution, I take care not to violate it, and to know that, if through error of judgment, I travel beyond the sphere of the Constitution, my errors will immediately be checked by a mound and barrier which cannot be overleaped. If any proceeding of the Legislature be unconstitutional, I have the consolation of knowing the Judiciary will declare it so; and to the decisions of our venerable and profoundly learned Judges I look up for information whenever the constitutionality of a law is questioned, and not to the resolutions of popular and tumultuous meetings. If, upon every Constitutional doubt, we are to have recourse to the people, there is an end to representative Government.

Source: Annals of Congress, 6th Cong., 2d Sess., 917–918, 919–920, 921, 932.

49   *Cases of the Judges* (1788)

In 1788 the Virginia legislature passed an act requiring judges on the state court of appeals to pre-side over newly created district courts. The judges were not given a salary increase to compensate them for this additional responsibility. Sitting judges in Virginia objected to this law. They refused to appoint the clerks necessary to hold district courts and prepared a remonstrance for the state legisla-ture requesting that the offending measure be repealed. The remonstrance asserted that the law obli-gating justices on the court of appeals to sit as district court justices was unconstitutional. The imposi-tion of additional duties without a corresponding increase in salary, the Virginia justices claimed, threatened the judicial independence guaranteed by the state constitution. The first legislative re-sponse to the remonstrance failed to allay judicial concerns. Foreshadowing themes that would be raised during the debates over the repeal of the Judiciary Act of 1801, the Virginia justices objected to a state law combining several state courts on the ground that the measure deprived justices of the abolished courts of their office in violation of the constitutional requirement of good behavior. Matters were not fully resolved until the Virginia legislature passed new laws, satisfactory to the judges, that reorganized the state judiciary.

Remonstrance of the Judges, April 1788

. . . [T]hey found it unavoidable to consider more important questions, viz: Whether the principles of this act do not violate those of the constitution or form of government, . . . and, if such violation were apparent, whether they had power, and it was their duty to declare that the act must yield to the constitution?

. . . [T]he constitution and the act are in oppo-sition and cannot exist together; and that the for-mer must control the operation of the latter. If this opinion, declaring the supremacy of the constitu-tion, needed any support, it may be found in the opinion of the legislature themselves, who have, in several instances, considered the constitution as prescribing limits to their powers, as well as to those of the other departments of government.

. . . The propriety and necessity of the inde-pendence of the judges is evident in reason and the nature of their office; since they are to decide between government and the people, as well as between contending citizens; and, if they be de-pendent on either, corrupt influence may be ap-prehended, sacrificing the innocent to popular prejudice; and subjecting the poor to oppression and persecution by the rich. . . .

. . . [T]he act now under consideration pre-senting a system, which assigns, to the judges of the chancery and admiralty, jurisdiction in com-mon law cases: which so far may be considered as a new office, the labour of which would greatly exceed that of the former: without a correspon-dent reward; and to the judges of the general court, duties, which, though not changed as to their subjects, are yet more than doubled, without any increase of salary, appeared so evident an at-tack upon the independency of the judges, that they thought it inconsistent with a conscientious discharge of their duty to pass it over. For vain would be the precautions of the founders of our government to secure liberty, if the legislature, though restrained from changing the tenure of ju-dicial offices, are at liberty to compel a resigna-tion by reducing salaries to a copper, or by mak-ing it a part of the official duty to become hewers of wood, and drawers of water: Or, if, in case of a contrary disposition, they can make salaries ex-orbitant; or, by lessening the duties, render offices, almost, sinecures: the independence of the judici-ary is, in either case, equally annihilated. . . .

To obviate a possible objection, that the court, while they are maintaining the independency of the judiciary, are countenancing encroachments of that branch upon the department of others, and assuming a right to control the legislature, it may be observed, that when they decide between an act of the people, and an act of the legislature, they are within the line of their duty, declaring what the law is, and not making a new law. And ever disposed to maintain harmony with other members of government, so necessary to promote the happiness of society, they most sincerely wish, that the present infraction of the constitution may be remedied by the legislature themselves; and thereby all further uneasiness on the occasion be prevented. But should their wishes be disappointed by the event, they see no other alternative for a decision between the legislature and judiciary, than an appeal to the people, whose servants both are; and for whose sakes both were created, and who may exercise their original and supreme power, whenever they think proper. To that tribunal, therefore, the court, in that case, commit themselves, conscious of perfect integrity, in their intentions, however they may have been mistaken in their judgment.

Source: Cases of the Judges of the Court of Appeal, (1788): 135, 142–143, 145–146.

---

50   *Ham v. M'Claws* (1789)

On March 28, 1787, the general assembly of South Carolina passed an act that prohibited the importation of slaves but exempted individuals with slaves who came into the state to take up residence. In late August or early September, the M'Claw family, along with their seven slaves, left the English colony on the Bay of Honduras en route to South Carolina, where they intended to settle. Unbeknownst to the M'Claws, on November 4, 1788, the general assembly of South Carolina passed a new act that prohibited the importation of all slaves before January 1, 1793. That act made no exemption for persons intending to reside in the state. A few days after that act became law, the M'Claws arrived in South Carolina. They were immediately prosecuted for importing slaves in violation of the law passed on November 4. They challenged the constitutionality of the law as applied to them, claiming that application violated fundamental principles of justice.

The Supreme Court of South Carolina agreed that the M'Claws could not be punished for violating the ban on imported slaves. The justices refused to apply the 1788 law that apparently governed the case. After asserting a judicial power to declare "null and void" a "statute passed against the plan and obvious principle of common right," they concluded that the legislature could not have intended forfeiture in this case, even though forfeiture was required by the "strict letter of the law." This decision is an early example of statutory misinterpretation as a means for avoiding an asserted judicial power to declare laws unconstitutional.

It is clear, that statutes passed against the plain and obvious principles of common right, and common reason, are absolutely null and void, as far as they are calculated to operate against those principles. In the present instance, we have an act before us, which, were the strict letter of it applied to the case of the present claimants, would be evidently against common reason. But we would not do the legislature who passed this act, so much injustice, as to sit here and say that it was their intention to make a forfeiture of property brought in here as this was. We are, therefore, bound to give such a construction to this enacting clause of the act of 1788, as will be consistent with justice, and the dictates of natural reason, though contrary to the strict letter of the law; and this construction is, that the legislature never had it in their contemplation to make a forfeiture of the negroes in question, and subject the parties to so heavy a penalty for bringing slaves into the state, under the circumstances and for the purposes, the claimants have proved.

Source: Ham v. M'Claws (1789): 93, 98.

51   *Bowman v. Middleton* (1792)

In 1677 Roger Nicholls was granted a large tract of land along the Ashley River in South Carolina. In 1701 John Cattel was granted property along the same river. When the plots of land were surveyed, 140 acres of the land granted to Cattel appeared to be part of the land previously granted to Nicholls. An act of the state legislature was passed in 1712 confirming the title to the disputed land to Cattel's heirs.

Bowman v. Middleton rejects legislative power to resolve land disputes. Controversies over land titles, the South Carolina Supreme Court asserted, could constitutionally be resolved only by civil trials. The legislative declaration confirming Cattel's title was a taking of private property and, for that reason, void. The opinion refers to "common right" and "magna charta," making no mention of the South Carolina or United States Constitutions.

. . . [T]he plaintiffs could claim no title under the act in question, as it was against common right, as well as against magna charta, to take away the freehold of one man and vest it in another, and that, too, to the prejudice of third persons, without any compensation, or even a trial by the jury of the country, to determine the right in question. That the act was, therefore, ipso facto, void. That no length of time could give it validity, being originally founded on erroneous principles.

Source: Bowman v. Middleton (1792): 252, 254–255.

52   *Kamper v. Hawkins* (1793)

The Virginia legislature in 1792 attempted to combine two judicial offices, the district court and the court of chancery, into a single tribunal. The relevant act declared that district court justices would have the power to issue injunctions. This power was traditionally exercised only by chancery courts. Shortly after the law was passed, Mary Hawkins asked a district court judge for an injunction against Peter Kamper, forbidding Kamper to carry out a legal decision he had won against Hawkins the previous year. Kamper appealed to the Supreme Court of Appeals, claiming that the Virginia legislature could not constitutionally combine common law and equity courts.

The state court unanimously found for Kamper. The five justices of the Virginia Supreme Court of Appeals delivered separate opinions, each declaring that courts had the power to declare laws unconstitutional and that the Virginia law was unconstitutional. The justices disputed the precise grounds of unconstitutionality. Several justices declared that Virginia could never vest the same justices with common law and equitable power. Others thought Virginia could, but that a separate appointment was necessary. Kamper is most notable for the extensive analysis of judicial review in each opinion. Justice Spencer Roane, who delivered a detailed justification for the power of state courts to declare state laws unconstitutional, would later become a staunch opponent of vesting federal courts with the power to declare state laws unconstitutional.

Opinion of Justice Nelson

. . . The present question is whether an act of the legislature contrary to it, be valid? . . .

It is confessedly the assent of the people which gives validity to a Constitution. . . .

Who then can change it? —I answer, the people alone.

But it has been supposed that the legislature can do this.

To decide this question, I have already stated that the legislature derived their existence from the Constitution. . . .

And can the legislature impugn that charter under which they claim, and to which by their acts they themselves have acknowledged an obligation? I apprehend not, nor can any argument against this position be drawn from an acquiescence in some acts which may be unconstitutional. . . .

But the greatest objection still remains, that the judiciary, by declaring an act of the legislature to be no law, assumes legislative authority, or claims a superiority over the legislature.

In answer to this, . . . when the cases of individuals are brought before them judicially, they are bound to decide. . . .

Nor is it a novelty for the judiciary to declare, whether an act of the legislature be in force or not in force, or in other words, whether it be a law or not.

In many instances one statute is virtually repealed by another, and the judiciary must decide which is the law, or whether both can exist together.

The only difference is, that in one instance that which was once in existence is carried out of existence, by a subsequent act virtually contrary to it, and in the other the prior fundamental law has prevented its coming into existence as a law.

With respect to the idea that for the judiciary to declare an act of the legislature void, is to claim a superiority to the legislature, —if the legislative authority is derived from the constitution,

and such a decision be a judicial act . . . this objection seems to be refuted.

For the reasons which I have given, I am of opinion that the fundamental act of government controls the legislature, who owe their existence and powers to it. . . .

Opinion of Judge Roane

. . . I now think that the judiciary may and ought not only to refuse to execute a law expressly repugnant to the Constitution; but also one which is, by a plain and natural construction, in opposition to the fundamental principles thereof. . . .

A very important question now occurs, viz. whose province it is to decide in such cases. It is the province of the judiciary to expound the laws, and to adjudge cases which may be brought before them. . . . In expounding laws, the judiciary considers every law which relates to the subject: would you have them to shut their eyes against that law which is of the highest authority of any, or against a part of that law, which either by its words or by its spirit, denies to any but the people the power to change it? . . .

From the above premises I conclude that the judiciary may and ought to adjudge a law unconstitutional and void, if it be plainly repugnant to the letter of the Constitution, or the fundamental principles thereof. By fundamental principles I understand, those great principles growing out of the Constitution, by the aid of which, in dubious cases, the Constitution may be explained and preserved inviolate; those landmarks, which it may be necessary to resort to, on account of the impossibility to foresee or provide for cases within the spirit, but without the letter of the Constitution. . . .

Opinion of Judge Henry

. . . If a chancellor in any case must be chosen by ballot, be commissioned and hold his office during good behavior, surely it is proper, it is necessary in all cases, that every judge shall be so chosen, shall be so commissioned, and hold his office so long as he behaves well. The business of hearing causes originating in that court by injunction, is of a permanent nature. To exercise this duty without the appointment and commission prescribed by the constitution, would be an exercise of a power according to the will of the legislature, who are servants of the people, not only without, but expressly against the will of the people. This would be a solecism in government, —establishing the will of the legislature, servants of the people, to control the will of their masters, if the word may be permitted. Till the appointment is made agreeable to the directions of the constitution, I cannot think myself duly authorized to take upon me the office.

Opinion of Judge Tyler

. . . What is the Constitution but the great contract of the people, every individual whereof having sworn allegiance to it? —A system of fundamental principles, the violation of which must be considered as a crime of the highest magnitude. —That this great and paramount law should be faithfully and rightfully executed, it is divided into three departments, to wit: the legislative, the executive, and judiciary, with an express restraint upon all, so that neither shall encroach on the rights of the other. —In the Bill of Rights many things are laid down, which are reserved to the people—trial by jury, on life and death, liberty of conscience, &c. Can the legislature rightfully pass a law taking away these rights from the people? Can the judiciary pass sentence without a conviction of a citizen by twelve of his peers? Can the executive do any thing forbidden by this bill of rights, or the constitution? In short, can one branch of the government call upon another to aid in the violation of this sacred letter? The answer to these questions must be in the negative.

But who is to judge of this matter? the legislature only? I hope not. —The object of all government is and ought to be, the faithful administration of justice. —It cannot, I hope, be less the object of our government, which has been founded on principles very different from any we read of in the world. . . .

I will not in an extra-judicial manner assume the right to negative a law, for this would be as dangerous as the example before us; but if by any legal means I have jurisdiction of a cause, in which it is made a question how far the law be a violation of the constitution, and therefore of no obligation, I shall not shrink from a comparison of the two, and pronounce sentence as my mind may receive conviction. —To be made an agent, therefore, for the purpose of violating the constitution, I cannot consent to. . . .

Opinion of Judge Tucker

. . . The government . . . and all its branches must be governed by the constitution. Hence it becomes the first law of the land, and as such must be resorted to on every occasion, where it becomes necessary to expound what the law is. This exposition it is the duty and office of the judiciary to make; our constitution expressly declaring that the legislative, executive, and judiciary, shall be separate and distinct, so that neither exercise the powers properly belong to the other. Now since it is the province of the legislature to make, and of the executive to enforce obedience to the laws, the duty of expounding must be exclusively vested in the judiciary. But how can any just exposition be made, if that which is the supreme law of the land be withheld from their view? Suppose a question had arisen on either of the acts before cited, which the legislature have discovered to be unconstitutional, would the judiciary have been bound by the act, or by the constitution?

But that the constitution is a rule to all the departments of the government, to the judiciary as well as to the legislature. . . .

. . . [T]he judiciary are bound to take notice of the constitution, as the first law of the land; and that whatsoever is contradictory thereto, is not the law of the land. . . .

Source: Kamper v. Hawkins (1788): 20, 23, 35–42, 46–48, 53, 58–61, 63–64, 77–81, 89.

53   *Whittington v. Polk* (1802)

In November 1797 the state assembly of Maryland passed an act that commissioned William Whittington chief justice of the county courts for Caroline, Dorchester, Somerset, and Worcester Counties. The act directed that justices of the county courts hold their offices during good behavior. In November 1801 the general assembly of Maryland repealed the previous act and authorized the commission of new justices for the county courts. Under this legislation, William Polk was duly commissioned chief justice of the county courts for the same counties. Whittington brought suit against Polk, arguing that the 1801 act was unconstitutional. The state constitution, he declared, authorized all judges to hold their offices during good behavior.

The three judges of the Maryland Court of Appeals dismissed Whittington's specific allegation of unconstitutionality. The Maryland Constitution, they ruled, did not require justices to hold office during good behavior. The judges did defend at length the judicial power to declare laws unconstitutional.

. . 1st. That an act of assembly repugnant to the constitution is void.

2d. That the court have a right to determine an act of assembly void, which is repugnant to the constitution.

3d. That the act of assembly passed in 1801, *ch.* 74, entitled, "An act relative to the administration of justice in this state, and to repeal the acts of assembly therein mentioned," so far as respects the plaintiff, is unconstitutional and void. . . .

The *two first points* were conceded by the counsel for the defendant; indeed they have not been controverted in any of the cases which have been brought before this court. . . .

The legislature, being the creature of the constitution, and acting within a circumscribed sphere, is not omnipotent, and cannot rightfully exercise any power, but that which is derived from that instrument.

The constitution having set certain limits or land marks to the power of the legislature, whenever they exceed them they act without authority, and such acts are mere nullities, not being done in pursuance of power delegated to them: Hence the necessity of some power under the constitution to restrict the acts of the legislature within the limits defined by the constitution.

The power of determining finally on the validity of the acts of the legislature cannot reside with the legislature, because such power would defeat and render nugatory, all the limitations and restrictions on the authority of the legislature, contained in the bill of rights and form of government, and they would become judges of the validity of their own acts, which would establish a despotism, and subvert that great principle of the constitution, which declares that the powers of making, judging, and executing the law, shall be separate and distinct from each other.

This power cannot be exercised by the people at large, or in their collective capacity, because they cannot interfere according to their own compact, unless by elections, and in such manner as the constitution has prescribed, and because there is no other mode ascertained by which they can express their will. . . .

The interference of the people by elections cannot be considered as the proper and only check and a suitable remedy, because in the interval of time, between the elections of the members who compose the different legislatures, the law may have had its full operation, and the evil arising from it become irremediable; nor is it probable that the elections will be made with the view to afford redress in such particular case, and if they were, and the law should be repealed, it would not be an adequate remedy. . . .

It is the office and province of the court to decide all questions of law which are judicially brought before them, according to the established mode of proceeding, and to determine whether an act of the legislature, which assumes the appearance of a law, and is clothed with the garb of authority, is made pursuant to the power vested by the constitution in the legislature; for if it is not the result or emanation of authority derived from the constitution, it is not law, and cannot influence the judgment of the court in the decision of the question before them. . . .

To do right and justice according to the law, the judge must determine what the law is, which necessarily involves in it the right of examining the constitution, (which is the supreme or paramount law, and under which the legislature de-

rive the only authority they are invested with, of making laws), and considering whether the act passed is made pursuant to the constitution, and that trust and authority which is delegated thereby to the legislative body.

. . . The legislature are the trustees of the people, and, as such, can only move within those lines which the constitution has defined as the boundaries of their authority, and if they should incautiously, or unadvisedly transcend those limits, the constitution has placed the judiciary as the barrier or safeguard to resist the oppression, and redress the injuries which might accrue from such inadvertent, or unintentional infringements of the constitution. . . .

Source: Whittington v. Polk (1802): 236, 241–246, 249.

---

54   *Vanhorne's Lessee v. Dorrance* (1795)

The Pennsylvania legislature attempted to settle a land dispute between state residents and out-of-state purchasers from Connecticut by passing a law vesting title to the disputed property in the out-of-state purchasers. State residents with bona fide claims were compensated with an equivalent tract. Several Pennsylvania residents sued, claiming that the legislative resolution of the land dispute deprived them of their vested rights and right to a jury trial.

Justice William Paterson, serving on the Circuit Court for the Pennsylvania District, supported the Pennsylvania claimants. His charge to the jury defended the judicial power to declare laws unconstitutional. Paterson concluded that the Pennsylvania "quieting and confirming act" violated the Pennsylvania and United States Constitutions. Vanhorne's Lessee may be the first instance in which a federal court held state legislation unconstitutional.

. . . What is a constitution? It is the form of government, delineated by the mighty hand of the people, in which certain first principles of fundamental laws are established. The constitution is certain and fixed; it contains the permanent will of the people, and is the supreme law of the land; it is paramount to the power of the legislature, and can be revoked or altered only by the authority that made it. The life-giving principle and the death-doing stroke must proceed from the same hand. What are legislatures? Creatures of the con-

stitution; they owe their existence to the constitution: they derive their powers from the constitution: It is their commission; and, therefore, all their acts must be conformable to it, or else they will be void. The constitution is the work or will of the people themselves, in their original, sovereign, and unlimited capacity. Law is the work or will of the legislature in their derivative and subordinate capacity. The one is the work of the creator, and the other of the creature. The constitution fixes limits to the exercise of legislative authority, and prescribes the orbit within which it must move. In short . . . the constitution is the sun of the political system, around which all legislative, executive and judicial bodies must revolve. Whatever may be the case in other countries, yet in this there can be no doubt, that every act of the legislature, repugnant to the constitution, is absolutely void.

. . . I take it to be a clear position; that if a legislative act oppugns a constitutional principle, the former must give way, and be rejected on the score of repugnance. I hold it to be a position equally clear and sound, that, in such case, it will be the duty of the court to adhere to the constitution, and to declare the act null and void. The constitution is the basis of legislative authority; it lies at the foundation of all law, and is a rule and commission by which both legislators and judges are to proceed. It is an important principle, which, in the discussion of questions of the present kind, ought never to be lost sight of, that the judiciary in this country is not a subordinate, but co-ordinate, branch of the government. . . .

Source: Vanhorne's Lessee v. Dorrance (1795): 1012, 1013–1015, 1018–1020.

55 *Minge v. Gilmour* (1798)

In 1779 David Minge conveyed some lands to Charles Gilmour and William Hendric. Minge's son later claimed the property on the ground that his father had a tenancy in tail. An estate in tail at common law could not be sold but had to be passed to the owner's eldest son. The junior Minge insisted that the North Carolina law recognizing his father's sale and outlawing tenancy in tail deprived him of property rights guaranteed by the North Carolina Constitution and natural justice. Presiding over the Circuit Court for the North Carolina District, Justice James Iredell rejected both claims. His opinion strongly defended the right of judges to declare legislation unconstitutional but rejected any claim that justices may void statutes on grounds of natural justice. Neither issue was actually relevant to that case. Justice Iredell made clear that the North Carolina legislature had the constitutional power to pass laws outlawing estates in tail and that such legislation was consistent with natural justice.

. . . The constitution is a law of the land, as well as an act of assembly, with this difference: that the former is a supreme law, paramount to all acts of assembly, and unrepealable by any. As in case there is a dispute whether one act of assembly is in force or another, the judges must decide this, and when the latter law is inconsistent with a former, say the latter is in force, because it has repealed the former, having authority to repeal it. So when the constitution says one thing and an act of assembly another, the judges must say the former law is in force and not the latter, because the former is a supreme law unrepealable and uncontrolable by the authority which enacted the latter. . . .

It is, however, further urged by the counsel for the plaintiff that this act is contrary to natural justice, and therefore void. Some respectable authorities do, indeed, countenance such a doctrine—that an act against natural justice is void. Others maintain a different one, with at least an equal claim to respect. . . . I confess I think no court is authorized to say that an act is absolutely void merely because, in the opinion of the court, it is contrary to natural justice.

Two principles appear to me to be clear: If an act be unconstitutional, it is void. If it be constitutional, it is valid. In the latter case it must be admitted that the legislature have exercised a trust confided to them by the people. . . . The words "against natural justice" are very loose terms, upon which very wise and upright members of the legislature and judges might differ in opinion. If they did, whose opinion is properly to be regarded—those to whom the authority of passing such an act is given, or a court to whom no authority, in this respect, necessarily results? This case is surely different from an unconstitutional act which the courts must certainly declare to be void, because passed without any authority whatever. The constitution, by saying that the legislature shall have authority in certain cases, but shall not have in others, as plainly declares everything valid done in pursuance of the first provision, as everything void that is done in contradiction of the last; and it may surely be inferred that if, in addition to other restrictions on the legislative power, such a restriction as that in question was intended, so as to leave it to the courts, in all instances, to say whether an act was agreeable to natural justice or not, this restriction would have been inserted, together with others. All courts, indeed, as being bound to give the most reasonable construction to acts of the legislature, will, in construing an act, do it as consistently with their notions of natural justice (if there appears any incompatibility) as the words and context will admit; it being most probable that, by such construction, the true design of the legislature will be pursued; but, if the words are too plain to admit of more than one construction, and the provisions be not inconsistent with any articles of the constitution, I am of opinion, for the reason I have given, that no court has authority to say the act is void because in their opinion it is not agreeable to the principles of natural justice.

Source: Minge v. Gilmour (1798): 440, 442, 443–444.

---

56   *United States v. Callender* (1800)

In 1800 James Callender, a notorious late-eighteenth-century pamphleteer, was charged with violating the Sedition Act for making such claims as "[t]he reign of Mr. [John] Adams has been one continued tempest of malignant passions." During the course of the trial, his counsel asserted that the Sedition Act was unconstitutional and that juries had the right to determine the constitutionality of federal laws. Justice Samuel Chase immediately interrupted. He ruled that juries were not empowered to decide the constitutionality of legislation: that was a matter for judicial determination. Justice Chase in Callender *and other cases maintained that the Sedition Act was constitutional. These decisions and other pro-Federalist rulings from justices on the federal bench led many Jeffersonians to question their previous commitment to judicial supremacy or judicial review.*

Argument of Mr. Hay

. . . [H]e had long ago formed a determination to appear in behalf of the first man who should be indicted in this state for a libel under the sedition law. He had formed this resolution because he was convinced, after the most mature deliberation, preceded by a calm and temperate investigation of the subject with gentlemen who differed from him in political sentiment, but were of the first characters for talents, that the second section of the sedition law was unconstitutional.

Colloquoy between Mr. Wirt and Justice Chase

Mr. Wirt.—Gentlemen of the jury. . . . If, then, a jury in a court of the state would have a right to decide the law and the fact, so have you. The federal constitution is the supreme law of the land; and a right to consider the law, is a right to consider the constitution: if the law of congress under which we are indicted, be an infraction of the constitution, it has not the force of a law, and if you were to find the traverser guilty, under such an act, you would violate your oaths.

Here CHASE, Circuit Justice. . . . Since I came into the commonwealth, I understood that this question would be stirred, and that the power of a jury to determine the validity or nullity of a law would be urged. I have, therefore, deliberately considered the subject, and I am ready to explain my reasons for concluding that the petit jury have not a right to decide on the constitutionality of a law, and that such a power would be extremely dangerous.

Argument of Mr. Nicholas

First, that a law contrary to the constitution is void; and, secondly, that the jury have a right to consider the law and the fact. First, it seems to be admitted on all hands, that, when the legislature exercise a power not given them by the constitution, the judiciary will disregard their acts. The second point, that the jury have a right to decide the law and the fact, appears to me equally clear. In the exercise of the power of determining law and fact, a jury cannot be controlled by the court. . . .

. . . [I]f an act of congress contravene the constitution of the United States, a jury have a right to say that it is null, and that they will not give the efficacy of a law to an act which is void in itself; believing it to be contrary to the constitution, they will not convict any man of a violation of it; if this jury believed that the sedition act is not a law of the land, they cannot find the defendant guilty. The constitution secures to every man a fair and impartial trial by jury, in the district where the fact shall have been committed: and to preserve this sacred right unimpaired, it should never be interfered with. If ever a precedent is established, that the court can control the jury so as to prevent them from finding a general verdict, their important right, without which every other right is of no value, will be impaired, if not absolutely destroyed. Juries are to decide according to the dictates of conscience and the laws of the country, and to control them would endanger the right of this most invaluable mode of trial.

Opinion of Justice Chase

. . . The petit jury, to discharge their duty, must first inquire, whether the traverser committed all or any of the facts alleged in the indictment to have been done by him, some time before the indictment. If they find that he did commit all or any of the said facts, their next inquiry is, whether the doing such facts have been made criminal and punishable by the statute of the United States, on which the traverser is indicted. . . . By this provision, I understand that a right is given to the jury to determine what the law is in the case before them; and not to decide whether a statute of the United States produced to them, is a law or not, or whether it is void, under an opinion that it is unconstitutional, that is, contrary to the constitution of the United States. . . . It is one thing to decide what the law is, on the facts proved, and another and a very different thing, to determine that the statute produced is no law. . . .

. . . Was it ever intended, by the framers of the constitution, or by the people of America, that it should ever be submitted to the examination of a jury, to decide what restrictions are expressly or impliedly imposed by it on the national legislature? I cannot possibly believe that congress intended, by the statute, to grant a right to a petit jury to declare a statute void. . . .

. . . If a petit jury can rightfully exercise this power over one statute of congress, they must have an equal right and power over any other statute, and indeed over all the statutes; for no line can be drawn, no restriction imposed on the exercise of such power; it must rest in discretion only. If this power be once admitted, petit jurors will be superior to the national legislature, and its laws will be subject to their control. The power to abrogate or to make laws nugatory, is equal to the authority of making them. The evident consequences of this right in juries will be, that a law of congress will be in operation in one state and not in another. A law to impose taxes will be obeyed in one state, and not in another, unless force be employed to compel submission. The doing certain acts will be held criminal, and punished in one state, and similar acts may be held innocent, and even approved and applauded in another. The effects of the exercise of this power by petit jurors may be readily conceived. It appears to me that the right now claimed has a direct tendency to dissolve the union of the United States, on which, under Divine Providence, our political safety, happiness, and prosperity depend.

No citizen of knowledge and information, unless under the influence of passion or prejudice, will believe, without very strong and indubitable proof, that congress will, intentionally, make any law in violation of the federal constitution, and their sacred trust. I admit that the constitution contemplates that congress may, from inattention or error in judgment, pass a law prohibited by the constitution; and, therefore, it has provided a peaceable, safe, and adequate remedy. If such a case should happen, the mode of redress is pointed out in the constitution, and no other mode can be adopted without a manifest infraction of it. Every man must admit that the power of deciding the constitutionality of any law of the United States, or of any particular state, is one of the greatest and most important powers the people could grant. Such power is restrictive of the legislative power of the Union, and also of the several states; not absolute and unlimited, but confined to such cases only where the law in question shall clearly appear to have been prohibited by the federal constitution, and not in any doubtful case. . . .

From these considerations I draw this conclusion, that the judicial power of the United States is the only proper and competent authority to decide whether any statute made by congress (or any of the state legislatures) is contrary to, or in violation of, the federal constitution. . . . No position can be more clear than that all the federal judges are bound by the solemn obligation of religion, to regulate their decisions agreeably to the constitution of the United States, and that it is the standard of their determination in all cases that come before them. I believe that it has been the general and prevailing opinion in all the Union,

that the power now wished to be exercised by a jury, properly belonged to the federal courts. It was alleged that the tax on carriages was considered by the people of this commonwealth to be unconstitutional, and a case was made to submit the question to the supreme court of the United States, and they decided that the statute was not unconstitutional, and their decision was acquiesced in. I have seen a report of a case (*Kamper v. Hawkins*), decided in 1793, in the general court of this commonwealth, respecting the constitutionality of a law which gave the district courts a power of granting injunctions in certain cases, in which case the judges of the general court (four to one) determined that the law was unconstitutional and void. On yesterday I saw the record of another case, in the court of appeals of this commonwealth (in 1788), on which it appears that the general assembly passed "An act to establish district courts," and the judges (ten being present), adjudged "that the constitution and the said act were in opposition, and could not exist together, and that the court ought not to do anything officially in the execution of an act, which appeared to be contrary to the spirit of the constitution." . . . From these two decisions, in the two highest courts of justice in this state, I may fairly conclude, that, at that period, it was thought that the courts of justice were the proper judicature to determine the constitutionality of the laws of this commonwealth. It is now contended, that the constitutionality of the laws of congress should be submitted to the decision of a petit jury. May I ask, whence this change of opinion? I declare that the doctrine is entirely novel to me, and that I never heard of it before my arrival in this city. It appears to me to be not only new, but very absurd and dangerous, in direct opposition to, and a breach of the constitution. . . . It must be evident, that decisions in the district or circuit courts of the United States will be uniform, or they will become so by the revision and correction of the supreme court; and thereby the same principles will pervade all the Union; but the opinions of petit juries will very probably be different in different states.

The decision of courts of justice will not be influenced by political and local principles, and prejudices. If inferior courts commit error, it may be rectified; but if juries make mistakes, there can be no revision or control over their verdicts, and therefore, there can be no mode to obtain uniformity in their decisions. Besides, petit juries are under no obligation by the terms of their oath, to decide the constitutionality of any law; their determination, therefore, will be extra judicial. . . .

I have consulted with my brother, Judge GRIF-FIN, and I now deliver the opinion of the court,

"That the petit jury have no right to decide on the constitutionality of the statute on which the traverser is indicted; and that, if the jury should exercise that power, they would thereby usurp the authority entrusted by the constitution of the United States to this court." Governed by this opinion, the court will not allow the counsel for the traverser to argue before the petit jury, that they have a right to decide on the constitutionality of the statute, on which the traverser stands indicted. . . .

Source: United States v. Callender (1800): 239, 252–258.

57

Hayburn's Case (1792)

In 1792 Congress passed an act requiring the circuit courts of the United States to determine who was eligible for pensions based upon their service in the Revolutionary War. These names were then subject to review by either Congress or the secretary of war. Supreme Court justices riding circuit uniformly agreed that the act was unconstitutional. Chief Justice John Jay, Justice William Cushing, and Judge James Duane, members of the Circuit Court for the New York District, ruled that Congress could not constitutionally assign such responsibilities to the judiciary and that judicial decisions could not constitutionally be subject to review by the national legislature or by an executive officer. They nevertheless agreed to make pension decisions in an extrajudicial capacity as commissioners. Justice James Wilson, Justice John Blair, and Judge Richard Peters, members of the Circuit Court for the North Carolina District, sent a letter to President George Washington informing him that they also believed the assignment of such duties to the circuit courts was "unwarranted by the Constitution." They did not take any additional action because no applications for pensions were pending in their district. Justice James Iredell and Judge John Sitgreaves, members of the Circuit Court for the Pennsylvania District, sent a similar letter to President Washington. They then refused to act when veteran William Hayburn applied for a pension. Attorney General Edmund Randolph appealed to the Supreme Court to issue a writ of mandamus compelling the judges to act. After hearing arguments, the Supreme Court postponed a decision to the next term. Congress then amended the legislation in question, providing an alternative method for determining the eligibility of veterans for pensions. For more information on Hayburn's Case, see Maeva Marcus and Robert Teir, "Hayburn's Case: A Misinterpretation of Precedent," 1988 Wisconsin Law Review (1988): 527.

Opinion of Chief Justice Jay, Justice Cushing, and Judge Duane

. . . That neither the Legislative nor the Executive branches, can constitutionally assign to the Judicial any duties, but such as are properly judicial, and to be performed in a judicial manner.

That the duties assigned to the Circuit courts, by this act, are not of that description; and that the act itself does not appear to contemplate them as such; in as much as it subjects the decisions of these courts, made pursuant to those duties, first to the consideration and suspension of the Secretary of War, and then to the Secretary of the Legislature; whereas by the Constitution, neither the Secretary at War, nor any other Executive officer, nor even the Legislature, are authorized to sit as a court of errors on the judicial acts or opinions of this court.

As, therefore, the business assigned to this court, by the act, is not judicial, nor directed to be performed judicially, the acts can only be considered as appointing commissioners for the purposes mentioned in it, by official instead of personal descriptions. . . .

That as the objects of this act are exceedingly benevolent, and do real honor to the humanity and justice of Congress; and as the Judges desire to manifest, on all proper occasions, and in every proper manner, their high respect for the National Legislature, they will execute this act in the capacity of commissioners.

Justice Wilson, Justice Blair, and Judge Peters to George Washington, April 18, 1792

. . . Upon due consideration, we have been unanimously of opinion, that, under this act, the Circuit court held for the Pennsylvania district could not proceed;

1st. Because the business directed by this act is not of a judicial nature. It forms no part of the power vested by the Constitution in the courts of the United States; the Circuit court must, consequently, have proceeded without constitutional authority.

2d. Because, if, upon that business, the court had proceeded, its judgments (for its opinions are its judgments) might, under the same act, have been revised and controuled by the legislature, and by an officer in the executive department.

Source: Hayburn's Case (1792): 409, 410–414.

Such revision and controul we deemed radically inconsistent with the independence of that judicial power which is vested in the courts.

Justice Iredell and Judge Sitgreaves to George Washington, June 8, 1792

. . . 4. That whatever doubt may be suggested, whether the power in question is properly of a judicial nature, yet inasmuch as the decision of the court is not made final, but may be least suspended in its operation by the Secretary at War, if he shall have cause to suspect imposition or mistake; this subjects the decision of the court to a mode of revision which we consider to be unwarranted by the Constitution; for, though Congress may certainly establish, in instances not yet provided for, courts of appellate jurisdiction, yet such courts must consist of judges appointed in the manner the Constitution requires, and holding their offices by no other tenure than that of their good behaviour, by which tenure the office of Secretary of War is not held. And we beg leave to add, with all due deference, that no decision of any court of the United States can, under any circumstances, in our opinion, agreeable to the Constitution, be liable to a reversion, or even suspension, by the Legislature itself, in whom no judicial power of any kind appears to be vested, but the important one relative to impeachments.

These, sir, are our reasons for being of opinion, as we are at present, that this Circuit court cannot be justified in the execution of that part of the act, which requires it to examine and report an opinion on the unfortunate cases of officers and soldiers disabled in the service of the United States. . . .

58   *United States v. Yale Todd* (1794)

United States v. Yale Todd *was a second test case challenging the Pension Act of 1792. Veteran Yale Todd applied for and was granted a pension by Chief Justice John Jay, Justice William Cushing, and Judge Richard Law. Rather than acting in their official judicial capacity, Jay, Cushing, and Law claimed they were merely acting in an extrajudicial capacity, as commissioners. The attorney general challenged that ruling before the Supreme Court. The justices in an unpublished opinion ruled that Todd was not entitled to a pension. Many years later, Chief Justice Roger Taney rediscovered the opinion in* United States v. Yale Todd. *He published a summary as a note to* United States v. Ferreira *(1851).*

Yale Todd *appears to have declared unconstitutional the Pension Act of 1792. The crucial premise of the decision was that justices could act only in their judicial capacity. Congress, the Court held, could not constitutionally pass a law authorizing justices on the Supreme Court to act as commissioners or behave in some other nonjudicial capacity.* Yale Todd *is also interesting because the Court without commentary assumed that Congress could vest the justices with original jurisdiction to resolve the constitutionality of the Pension Act. A decade later, Chief Justice John Marshall in* Marbury *would declare unconstitutional such legislative efforts to expand the original jurisdiction of the Supreme Court.*

Note by Chief Justice Taney

The result of the opinions expressed by the judges of the Supreme Court of that day in the note to Hayburn's case, and in the case of the *United States* v. *Todd*, is this:

1. That the power proposed to be conferred on the Circuit Courts of the United States by the act of 1792 was not judicial power within the meaning of the Constitution, and was, therefore, unconstitutional, and could not lawfully be exercised by the courts.

2. That as the act of Congress intended to confer the power on the courts as a judicial function, it could not be construed as an authority to the judges composing the court to exercise the power out of court in the character of commissioners.

. . . In the early days of the Government, the right of Congress to give original jurisdiction to the Supreme Court, in cases not enumerated in the Constitution, was maintained by many jurists, and seems to have been entertained by the learned judges who decided Todd's case. But discussion and more mature examination has settled the question otherwise; and it has long been the established doctrine, and we believe now assented to by all who have examined the subject, that the original jurisdiction of this court is confined to the cases specified in the Constitution, and that Congress cannot enlarge it. In all other cases its power must be appellate.

Source: United States v. Ferreira (1851): 40, 53.

59
Ware v. Hylton (1796)

Before the Revolutionary War Virginians Daniel Hylton and Francis Epps owed a debt to Englishmen Joseph Farrel and William Jones. After the outbreak of hostilities, the Virginia legislature passed an act providing that debts owed by citizens of Virginia to subjects of England could be discharged if the money owed was paid into the loan office of the state. Hylton took advantage of this provision and paid the money owed Farrel and Jones to the loan office. He then received a state discharge of his debt. Several years later, Virginia passed a law confiscating all moneys that had been paid into the loan office. After the war, Jones's heirs sued to recover the money owed. They first asserted that Virginia had no right under international law to confiscate debts. They then claimed the Virginia seques- tration and confiscation laws were voided by the peace treaty signed in 1783. Article 4 of the Treaty of Peace between the United States and England stated that "creditors, on either side, shall meet with no lawful impediment to the recovery of the full value, in sterling money, of all bona fide debts hereto- fore contracted." Article VI of the Constitution of the United States provides that "all Treaties made, or which shall be made, under authority of the United States, shall be the supreme Law of the Land." De- fense counsel, which included future chief justice John Marshall, responded that the peace treaty was void: Great Britain had violated crucial provisions, and Article 4 unconstitutionally violated property rights. Even if the treaty were valid, Marshall and cocounsel declared, Article 4 did not grant these British creditors a right to recover from Hylton.

The judicial majority in Ware *concluded that the Virginia sequestration and confiscation laws were inconsistent with the treaty and thus were void. The justices unanimously concluded that Virginia be- fore ratification could confiscate British debts and that federal justices had the right to strike down all state laws inconsistent with federal treaties. Four justices concluded that the Virginia law conflicted with the peace treaty. In their view, the Virginia sequestration and confiscation laws were "lawful im- pediments to the recovery" of "bona fide debts." Justice William Cushing rejected this suggestion. He maintained that the debt had been discharged by payment to Virginia; therefore, the British creditors no longer had a right against Hylton but had to sue Virginia for recover of their money.*

Several opinions in Hylton v. Ware *considered whether courts had the power to strike down federal treaties. Justice Samuel Chase indicated such power might exist when a treaty very clearly violated constitutional norms. Justice James Iredell asserted that courts had no power to declare a treaty uncon- stitutional and no power to determine when a treaty had been violated by another nation. Elected offi- cials, in his view, bore sole responsibility for abrogating agreements with other countries.*

Justice Chase

. . . Virginia had a right, as a sovereign and inde- pendent nation, to confiscate any British property within its territory; unless she had before dele- gated that power to Congress. . . .

. . . The question then may be stated thus: Whether the 4th article of the said treaty nullifies the law of Virginia, passed on the 20th of Octo- ber, 1777; destroys the payment made under it; and revives the debt, and gives a right of recovery thereof, against the original debtor?

It was doubted by . . . the Defendants in error . . . whether Congress has a power to make a

treaty, that could operate to annul a legislative act of any of the states, and to destroy rights acquired by, or vested in individuals, in virtue of such acts. . . . Defendant[] expressly, and with great zeal, de- nied that Congress possessed such power. . . .

If doubts could exist before the establishment of the present national government, they must be entirely removed by the 6th article of the Consti- tution, which provides "That all treaties made, or which shall be made, under the authority of the United States, shall be the supreme law of the land; and the Judges in every State shall be bound thereby, any thing in the Constitution, or laws, or any State to the contrary notwithstanding." There can be no limitation on the power of the people of the United States. By their authority the State Constitutions were made, and by their authority the Constitution of the United States was established; and they had the power to change or abolish the State Constitutions, or to make them yield to the general government, and to treaties made by their authority. A treaty cannot be the supreme law of the land, that is of all the United States, if any act of a State Legislature can stand in its way. If the Constitution of a State (which is the fundamental law of the State, and paramount to its Legislature) must give way to a treaty, and fall before it; can it be questioned, whether the less power, an act of the State Legislature, must not be prostrate? It is the declared will of the people of the United States that every treaty made, by the authority of the United States, shall be superior to the Constitution and laws of any individual State; and their will alone is to decide. —If a law of a State, contrary to a treaty, is not void, but voidable only by a repeal, or nullification by a State Legislature, this certain consequence follows, that the will of a small part of the United States may controul or defeat the will of the whole. The people of America have been pleased to declare, that all treaties made before the establishment of the National Constitution, or laws of any of the States, contrary to a treaty, shall be disregarded. . . .

The argument, that Congress had not power to make the 4th article of the treaty of peace, if its intent and operation was to annul the laws of any of the States, and to destroy vested rights . . . was unnecessary. . . . Whether this court constitutionally possess such a power is not necessary now to determine, because I am fully satisfied that Congress were invested with the authority to make the stipulation in the 4th article. If the court possess a power to declare treaties void, I shall never exercise it, but in a very clear case indeed. . . .

Justice Iredell

. . . It is a part of the law of nations, that if a treaty be violated by one party, it is at the option of the other party, if innocent, to declare, in consequence of the breach, that the treaty is void.

If Congress, therefore, (who, I conceive, alone have such authority under our Government) shall make such a declaration, in any case like the present, I shall deem it my duty to regard the treaty as void, and then to forbear any share in executing it as a Judge.

But the same law of nations tells me, that until that declaration be made, I must regard it (in the language of the law) valid and obligatory. . . .

Judge Wilson

But even if Virginia had the power to confiscate, the treaty annuls the confiscation. . . .

Justice Cushing

. . . The treaty, then, as to the point in question, is of equal force with the constitution itself; and certainly, with any law whatsoever. And the words, "shall meet with no lawful impediment," &c. are as strong as the wit of man could devise, to avoid all effects of sequestration, confiscation, or any other obstacle thrown in the way, by any law, particularly pointed against the recovery of such debts.

. . . When these general words, therefore, can comprehend so many cases, all reasonable objects of the article, I cannot think I am compelled as a Judge, and therefore I ought not to do so, to say that the general words of this article, shall extinguish private as well as public rights.

I hold public faith so sacred, when once pledged either to citizens or to foreigners, that a violation of that faith is never to be inferred as even in contemplation, but when it is impossible to give any other reasonable construction to a public act. I do not clearly see that it was intended in the present instance. I cannot therefore bring myself to say, that the present Defendant having once lawfully paid the money, shall pay it over again. If the matter be only doubtful, I think the doubt should incline in favour of an innocent individual, and not against him. I should hope that the present Plaintiff will still receive his money, as his right to the money certainly has not been divested, but I think for all the reasons I have given, he is not entitled to recover it from the present Defendant.

Source: Ware v. Hylton (1796): 199, 222–223, 229–230, 235–238, 242–245, 260–261, 265–266, 270, 276–277, 279–282, 284.

60 *Hollingsworth v. Virginia* (1798)

In Chisholm v. Georgia *(1793), the Supreme Court interpreted the Judiciary Act of 1789 as authorizing federal courts to adjudicate lawsuits between citizens of one state against another state. In response, Congress proposed and the states ratified the Eleventh Amendment, which declared, "The Judicial power of the United States shall not be construed to extend to any suit in law or equity, commenced or prosecuted against one of the United States by Citizens of another State. . . ." The Congress that proposed the Eleventh Amendment did not repeal any provision of the Judiciary Act. Counsel for Hollingsworth insisted that federal courts after ratification of the Eleventh Amendment still had power to hear lawsuits brought by citizens of one state against another state, if those suits had been instituted before ratification. Charles Lee, the attorney general of the United States (and, later, lawyer for William Marbury), disagreed. He informed the Supreme Court that "[t]he amendment is paramount to all the laws of the union; and if any part of the judicial acts is in opposition to it, that part must be expunged."*

The Supreme Court unanimously rejected jurisdiction. Given that the law authorizing jurisdiction in Chisholm *was technically still on the federal books, some scholars believe that* Hollingsworth *ought to be considered an instance where the federal judiciary implicitly declared a federal law unconstitutional. See David P. Currie,* The Constitution in the Supreme Court: The First Hundred Years, 1789–1888 *(Chicago: University of Chicago Press, 1985), 20–23.*

Argument of Mr. Lee

. . . [T]he amendment being constitutionally adopted, there could not be exercised any jurisdiction, in any case, past or future, in which a state was sued by the citizens of another state, or by citizens, or subjects, of any foreign state.

Hollingsworth v. Virginia (1798): 378, 382.

61 *Hylton v. United States* (1796)

In 1794 Congress passed an act imposing a duty on carriages. Daniel Hylton, a citizen of Virginia, refused to pay. He claimed that the duty was a direct tax, which the Constitution required to be apportioned among the states according to the census. In what was almost certainly an arranged case, the United States sued to recover damages.

The Supreme Court supported the government's position that the tax was constitutional. The difficulty of apportioning a tax on carriages between the states according to population, given great dis-

parities in the number of carriages possessed in different states, convinced the justices that the carriage tax was better classified as an indirect tax constitutionally mandated to be uniform throughout the United States than a direct tax constitutionally mandated to be apportioned between the states. Hylton was the first case in which the United States Supreme Court explicitly declared a federal statute constitutional. The justices discussed the constitutional issues on the merits but did not state explicitly whether they had the power to declare federal laws unconstitutional.

Justice Chase

By the case stated, only one question is submitted to the opinion of this court;—whether the law of Congress, of the 5th of June, 1794, entitled, "An act to lay duties upon carriages, for the conveyance of persons," is unconstitutional and void?

. . . The deliberate decision of the National Legislature, (who did not consider a tax on carriages a direct tax, but thought it was within the description of a duty) would determine me, if the case was doubtful, to receive the construction of the Legislature: But I am inclined to think, that a tax on carriages is not a direct tax, within the letter, or meaning, of the Constitution. . . .

As I do not think the tax on carriages is a direct tax, it is unnecessary, at this time, for me to determine, whether this court, constitutionally possesses the power to declare an act of Congress void, on the ground of its being made contrary to, and in violation of, the Constitution; but if the court have such power, I am free to declare, that I will never exercise it, but in a very clear case.

Justice Paterson

The question is, whether a tax upon carriages be a direct tax? If it be a direct tax, it is unconstitutional because it has been laid pursuant to the rule of uniformity, and not to the rule of apportionment. . . .

Source: Hylton v. United States (1796): 171, 172, 173, 175, 176.

---

62 *Calder v. Bull* (1798)

In 1793 the Court of Probate for Harford, Connecticut, disapproved the will of Norman Morrison. The Connecticut legislature two years later passed a law setting aside that decree and granting a new hearing. At this second hearing, the court approved the original will, which left Morrison's estate to his grandson, Caleb Bull. The Calder family, who stood to inherit under the first probate decision, appealed to the United States Supreme Court. They maintained that the legislation setting aside the first probate ruling was an ex post facto law, prohibited by the Connecticut and United States Constitutions.

The Supreme Court unanimously rejected the claim. All four justices who heard the case agreed that the ex post facto clause only banned retrospective criminal laws and not laws adjusting property rights. Justices Samuel Chase and James Iredell engaged in an important debate over the role of natural law in constitutional decision making. Justice Iredell asserted that courts had no business striking down laws solely on the ground that the legislation was inconsistent with natural justice. Justice Chase maintained that no people would empower a legislature to violate certain fundamental rights and that constitutions should be interpreted as protecting those rights. Chase did not make clear whether he believed that fundamental law merely provided a standard justices should use when interpreting the Constitution (i.e., a presumption exists that a constitution does not give the legislature power to violate fundamental rights) or whether he believed fundamental law provided an independent ground for ju-

dicial decisions to void legislation (i.e., courts should void laws that violate fundamental rights, even when the Constitution explicitly sanctions that violation). Although the justices had previously done so, Justice Chase in his Calder *opinion also claimed that Supreme Court justices should not determine whether state laws violated the state constitution.*

Justice Chase

. . . I cannot subscribe to the omnipotence of a State Legislature, or that it is absolute and without controul; although its authority should not be expressly restrained by the Constitution, or fundamental law, of the State. The people of the United States erected their Constitutions, or forms of government, to establish justice, to promote the general welfare, to secure the blessings of liberty; and to protect their persons and property from violence. The purposes for which men enter into society will determine the nature and terms of the social compact; and as they are the foundation of the legislative power, they will decide what are the proper objects of it: The nature, and ends of legislative power will limit the exercise of it. This fundamental principle flows from the very nature of our free Republican governments, that no man should be compelled to do what the laws do not require; nor to refrain from acts which the laws permit. There are acts which the Federal, or State, Legislature cannot do, without exceeding their authority. There are certain vital principles in our free Republicans governments, which will determine and over-rule an apparant and flagrant abuse of legislative power; as to authorize manifest injustice by positive law; or to take away that security for personal liberty, or private property, for the protection whereof the government was established. An ACT of the Legislature (for I cannot call it a law) contrary to the great first principles of the social compact, cannot be considered a rightful exercise of legislative authority. The obligation of a law in governments established on express compact, and on republican principles, must be determined by the nature of the power, on which it is founded. . . .

Without giving an opinion, at this time, whether this Court has jurisdiction to decide that any law made by Congress, contrary to the Constitution of the United States, is void; I am fully satisfied that this court has no jurisdiction to determine that any law of any state Legislature, contrary to the Constitution of such state, is void. Further, if this court had such jurisdiction, yet it does not appear to me, that the resolution (or law) in question, is contrary to the charter of Connecticut, or its constitution, which is said by counsel to be composed of its acts of assembly, and usages, and customs. I should think, that the courts of Connecticut are the proper tribunals to decide, whether laws, contrary to the constitution thereof, are void. . . .

Justice Iredell

. . . It is true, that some speculative jurists have held, that a legislative act against natural justice must, in itself, be void; but I cannot think that, under such a government, any Court of Justice would possess a power to declare it so. . . .

. . . If any act of Congress, or of the Legislature of a state, violates . . . constitutional provisions, it is unquestionably void; though, I admit, that as the authority to declare it void is of a delicate and awful nature, the Court will never resort to that authority, but in a clear and urgent case. If, on the other hand, the Legislature of the Union, or the Legislature of any member of the Union, shall pass a law, within the general scope of their constitutional power, the Court cannot pronounce it to be void, merely because it is, in their judgment, contrary to the principles of natural justice. The ideas of natural justice are regulated by no fixed standard: the ablest and the purest men have differed upon the subject; and all that the Court could properly say, in such an event, would be, that the Legislature (possessed of an equal right of opinion) had passed an act which, in the opinion of the judges, was inconsistent with the abstract principles of natural justice. There are then but two lights, in which the subject can be viewed: 1st. If the Legislature pursue the authority delegated to them, their acts are valid. 2d. If they transgress the boundaries of that authority, their acts are invalid. In the former case, they exercise the discretion vested in them by the people, to whom alone they are responsible for the faithful discharge of their trust: but in the latter case, they violate a fundamental law, which must be our guide, whenever we are called upon as judges to determine the validity of a legislative act.

Source: Calder v. Bull (1798): 386, 387–389, 392–393, 398–399.

---

63   *Cooper v. Telfair* (1800)

In 1782 the Georgia legislature passed an act banishing and confiscating the property of several named persons who had supported the British during the Revolutionary War. Basil Cooper was one loyalist specifically mentioned in the Georgia decree. Fifteen years later, he sued to recover damages. His central claim was that the confiscation statute, by denying him a trial by jury, violated the provision in the Georgia Constitution that declared "[t]he legislative, executive, and judiciary, departments shall be separate and distinct, so that neither exercise the powers properly belonging to the other."

The Supreme Court rejected this appeal. Each justice who participated in the decision claimed that federal courts had the power to declare state laws unconstitutional. Several declared that this power should be exercised only when the law was clearly unconstitutional. Cooper did not meet that standard. Justices Bushrod Washington and Samuel Chase maintained the Georgia Constitution required trial by jury only for offenses committed in Georgia. Cooper had not claimed his alleged offenses were committed in that state. Justices William Paterson and William Cushing ruled that legislatures had a right to banish citizens who had fought against their home state during the revolution. Justice Chase added that government actions taken before the Constitution of the United States was ratified could not be declared unconstitutional on federal grounds.

Justice Washington

. . . If the plaintiff in error had shown, that the offence, with which he was charged, had been committed in any county of Georgia, he might have raised the question of conflict and collision, between the constitution and the law: but as that fact does not appear, there is no ground on which I could be prepared to say, that the law is void. The presumption, indeed, must always be in favour of the validity of laws, if the contrary is not clearly demonstrated.

Justice Chase

. . . It is, indeed, a general opinion . . . that the Supreme Court can declare an act of congress to be unconstitutional, and, therefore, invalid; but there is no adjudication of the Supreme Court itself upon the point [at this place in the opinion, Chase or the Supreme Court reporter later inserted a footnote declaring, "the point has since been decided affirmatively by the Supreme Court in *Marbury v. Madison*"]. I concur, however, in the general sentiment, with reference to the period, when the existing constitution came into operation; but whether the power, under the existing constitution, can be employed to invalidate laws previously enacted, is a very different question. . . .

Justice Paterson

. . . [T]o authorise this Court to pronounce any law void, it must be a clear and unequivocal breach of the constitution, not a doubtful and argumentative implication.

Justice Cushing

Although I am of opinion, that this Court has the same power, that a Court of the state of Georgia

Source: Cooper v. Telfair (1800): 14, 18, 19, 20.

would possess, to declare the law void, I do not think that the occasion would warrant an exercise of the power. The right to confiscate and banish, in the case of an offending citizen, must belong to every government. . . .

Section IV (Documents 64–82):
Immediate Background and Aftermath

Marbury v. Madison played an important role in the struggle for control over the federal judiciary that took place after the national election of 1800. Few people, including perhaps William Marbury and James Madison, really cared whether Marbury was entitled to his commission as a justice of the peace for the District of Columbia. American elites cared whether the Federalists appointed to the federal judgeships established by the Judiciary Act of 1801 were entitled to their offices after the new Jeffersonian legislative majority repealed that measure in 1802. All parties to *Marbury* recognized that the political stakes in the case concerned the relationship between a Federalist-dominated judiciary and the Jeffersonian-controlled elected branches of government.

Marbury was shaped by the partisan competition that took place during the first years of the nineteenth century. The election of 1800 gave Jeffersonians a working majority in all elected branches of the national government. After the results of the election were known, but before the newly elected Jeffersonians took office, the lame-duck Federalist majority in Congress passed the Judiciary Act of 1801. That measure dramatically increased the jurisdiction of federal courts and created sixteen new circuit court positions. President John Adams immediately appointed and Federalists in Congress promptly confirmed prominent Federalist politicians to occupy those new offices. The first major legislative act of the new Jeffersonian majority repealed the Judiciary Act of 1801. Leading Fed-

eralist politicians and Federalists appointed to the new justiceships created in 1801 maintained that the repeal was unconstitutional. Numerous efforts were made to have the repeal voided.

The lame-duck Federalist Congress also passed a law that organized the District of Columbia. Section 11 authorized the president to appoint an unspecified number of justices of the peace. Adams nominated Marbury to one of those new justiceships. The Senate confirmed his appointment the day before Jeffersonians took control of the national government. Marbury's commission entitling him to the justiceship was signed and sealed but not delivered during the haste and confusion that marked the last hours of the Adams administration. Thomas Jefferson, outraged by this and other last-minute appointments, ordered that the leftover commissions remain undelivered. Determined to hold office, Marbury in December 1801 asked the Supreme Court for a writ of mandamus ordering Jefferson's secretary of state, James Madison, to deliver his commission. The central issue of the *Marbury* litigation was thought to be whether the justices could order the executive to deliver the commission, not whether the justices had the power to declare laws unconstitutional. The test of judicial review, most at the time thought, would take place when the Supreme Court was confronted with a challenge to the law repealing the Judiciary Act of 1801.

Federalists failed to preserve their circuit court justiceships or secure Marbury his office.

They neither persuaded elected officials to restore the Judiciary Act of 1801 nor convinced the Supreme Court to declare the repeal unconstitutional, and Marbury never obtained his commission. The only apparent Federalist successes in the struggle over the judiciary were the Supreme Court's affirmation of judicial review in *Marbury* and the congressional failure to impeach Federalist justices. Judicial review, however, proved more ambiguous than Federalists expected. The Marshall Court in 1803 was willing to assert the power to declare laws unconstitutional, a power at that time being championed far more enthusiastically by Federalists than by Jeffersonians. Nevertheless, the Marshall Court refused to use the power of judicial review to strike down Jeffersonian measures, the expectation of which was the main reason why in 1803 Federalists were far more enthusiastic about judicial review than Jeffersonians were. When the Supreme Court began exercising judicial review more aggressively during the second decade of the nineteenth century, many Republicans had come to endorse and Federalists to oppose the nationalistic doctrines articulated by the Marshall Court.

Election of 1800

Jefferson claimed the "revolution of 1800" was as important to American political development as the "revolution of 1776." The Federalist Party had controlled both houses of Congress and the presidency during the last decade of the eighteenth century. The fall election returns gave Jeffersonian Republicans control over the presidency, the House of Representatives, and the Senate. For the first time in history, a political party was removed from office by election. The identity of the new Republican president was not immediately clear. During the first four presidential elections, electors cast their ballots for two candidates. The result in 1800 was that the two Republicans running in the national election, Jefferson and Aaron Burr, got the same number of electoral votes. After much controversy, the House of Representatives chose Jefferson, in part because Alexander Hamilton preferred Jefferson, whom he found politically obnoxious, to Burr, whom he found personally obnoxious.

The election results seemed ominous for the Federalist-controlled judiciary. Although Republicans had originally given both judicial review and judicial supremacy the same passing support as Federalists, many Jeffersonians after 1799 expressed second thoughts. Federalist judicial appointees during the late eighteenth century behaved as Federalists. Supreme Court justices supported the policies of the Adams administration during the undeclared war against France and on circuit sustained the Sedition Act. Many delivered partisan political speeches when charging grand juries. Jeffersonians victimized by these practices rejected the nonpartisan image of the judiciary zealously being propagated by Federalists. When Jefferson took office prominent Republicans maintained that their constitutional vision was best advanced and maintained by Republican-elected officials.

The emerging political crisis was compounded by constitutional rules that permitted lame-duck Federalists to retain control of national institutions until March 1801. A Federalist-controlled House of Representatives determined whether Jefferson or Burr would become president. Lame-duck Federalists in their last days reconstructed federal judiciary power in ways they hoped would enable their party to control one branch of the national government while Jefferson was in power.

Document 64: The Judiciary Act of 1801

Supreme Court justices and their supporters throughout the 1790s frequently complained that having justices ride circuit in addition to sitting on the Supreme Court was inefficient and ungainly. As early as George Washington's first term, proposals were made to abolish circuit riding. None became law. In 1799 President John Adams again urged Congress to reform the federal judiciary. Congress debated his proposal during the following session, but no action was taken. After Republicans won their overwhelming victory in the national election of 1800, lame-duck Federalists quickly and successfully reintroduced legislation restructuring the federal judiciary.

The Judiciary Act of 1801 reconstructed the entire federal judiciary (Document 64). Congress abolished circuit riding. The bill established five circuit courts, each with three new circuit court judges, and a sixth circuit court composed of one new circuit court justice and the existing district court judges from Tennessee and Kentucky. Federal jurisdiction was substantially expanded. Anticipating an increase in the caseload of the Supreme Court, the Judiciary Act required that tribunal to have sessions in both June and December. The number of justices on the Supreme Court was reduced from six to five. This change, ostensibly made to lessen the chance of a tie vote, denied the incoming president, Jefferson, the opportunity to replace the next justice who left the

bench. The Judiciary Act swiftly moved through Congress. In straight party votes, the measure passed the House of Representatives on January 20, 1801, and the Senate the next week. Adams signed the bill on February 13, then immediately nominated prominent Federalists to the new circuit court judgeships. These so-called "midnight justices" were quickly confirmed by the Senate.

The Judiciary Act of 1801 inspired no debate over judicial review. Public debate was over whether the new judgeships were necessary, given the volume of business in the federal courts, and over the relative merits of federal and state courts. Both Federalists and Jeffersonians recognized that the Federalist Party was seeking a beachhead in the federal judiciary to be used for defeating certain Jeffersonian ambitions. The extent to which prominent politicians at that time thought Federalists justices would limit Jeffersonian power by declaring laws unconstitutional is unclear.

For more information on the Judiciary Act of 1801, see Kathryn Turner, "Federalist Policy and the Judiciary Act of 1801," *William and Mary Quarterly* 22 (1965): 3.

Documents 65–69: Marbury's Commission

The records of the Executive Journal of the Senate indicate that John Adams on March 2, 1802, nominated William Marbury (misspelling his name) to be a justice of the peace for the District of Columbia (Document 65). Marbury and others nominated on that day were confirmed by the Senate the following day, the day before Thomas Jefferson took office (Document 66). John Marshall, then acting as both secretary of state and chief justice, delivered many commissions to last-minute nominees, but Marbury's commission remained in the State Department. Marshall later explained that the messenger was unavailable, and he gave first priority to commissions he thought revocable at the will of the president (Document 67). Jefferson refused to deliver the remaining commissions, maintaining that they were not valid until delivered and accepted (Document 68). Marbury then asked the Supreme Court of the United States for a writ of mandamus, obligating the State Department to deliver his commission. In his view, persons had a right to judgeships once their commissions were signed and sealed. When no member of the Jefferson administration attended the initial hearing on Marbury's lawsuit, the Marshall Court issued a show-cause order to the secretary of state, James Madison—misspelling his name—requiring him to explain why Marbury was not entitled to his commission (Document 69). The Marshall Court decision to issue that show-cause order may have convinced Jeffersonians that the Judiciary Act of 1801 had to be repealed.

Documents 70–71:
Repeal of the Judiciary Act of 1801

The first order of business for the Seventh Congress was the repeal of the Judiciary Act of 1801. Angered by the Federalist effort to pack the judiciary with persons hostile to the Jefferson administration and the judicial decision to issue the show-cause order in *Marbury*, Jeffersonians sought to prevent Federalist justices from further interfering with Republican policies. Federalists maintained that the repeal was

unconstitutional. The constitutional requirement that federal justices hold their office for life during good behavior, they maintained, forbade legislation abolishing judicial offices. Jeffersonians responded that the congressional power to establish lower federal courts entailed the congressional power to abolish lower federal courts.

The repeal of the Judiciary Act of 1801 sparked the first extensive debate on judicial review in American history (Documents 70 and 71). Federalists uniformly insisted that courts had to remain independent of the judiciary in order to exercise the power to declare laws unconstitutional. Opponents of the repeal measure defended judicial review at length and, more so than had previously been the case, asserted that the judicial power to declare laws unconstitutional was the primary means of preserving constitutional rights and limitations. The Federalist constitution of 1801 vested the judiciary with the ultimate authority to determine what the document meant. No Federalist who spoke during the debates over repeal maintained that courts should strike down only clearly unconstitutional laws. Jeffersonians during the debates over repeal spoke less on judicial review and did not adopt a common position. Most rejected judicial supremacy. Several prominent Republicans claimed that justices when deciding cases should ignore laws believed unconstitutional, but that judicial decisions on constitutional questions did not bind elected officials. Some Jeffersonians rejected judicial review entirely, insisting that such a power would make the judiciary more powerful than the people's elected representatives. Others insisted that the power of judicial review was not an issue in the debate, that no effort was being made to interfere with the Supreme Court. That tribunal, in their view, remained sufficiently independent to exercise whatever judicial power was warranted by the Constitution. No Jeffersonian claimed that judicial review was a necessary means for preserving constitutional rights. Several who supported some version of that practice declared that justices should declare laws unconstitutional only when the constitutional violation was very clear.

The *Marbury* litigation played a minor role in the debates over repeal. Jeffersonians declared the show-cause order revealed a Court bent on usurping political power. Federalists responded that the order demonstrated the virtues of an independent judiciary. During the debates, a Jeffersonian representative suggested that Congress had no power to expand the original jurisdiction of the Supreme Court. Federalists responded by claiming that past practice established that the justices had the necessary jurisdiction to issue a writ of mandamus in *Marbury*.

Documents 72–73: Judiciary Act of 1802

Jeffersonians after repealing the Judiciary Act of 1801 reorganized the federal judicial system. The Judiciary Act of 1802 reestablished, with some modifications, the federal court system that had existed before 1801, required Supreme Court justices to ride circuit, transferred all cases assigned to the circuit courts established by the act of 1801 to the circuit courts reconstituted in 1802, and provided that the Supreme Court would sit for only one term a year, beginning in February. Federalists in Congress charged that the purpose of this last provision was to prevent the federal judiciary from

determining whether the repeal of the Judiciary Act of 1801 was constitutional. Jeffersonians responded that the Supreme Court, which had only eight cases pending at the time, did not do enough business to warrant sitting for two sessions a year. The judicial power to declare laws unconstitutional was only briefly alluded to in the debates over the Judiciary Act of 1802. Federalists defended judicial supremacy, as they had done in their unsuccessful fight against repeal. Those Jeffersonians who conceded the judicial power to declare laws unconstitutional insisted that the new judiciary bill would not inhibit the exercise of that judicial prerogative (Documents 72 and 73).

Documents 74–78: The Midnight Justices Respond

The Federalist justices whose offices were abolished when the Judiciary Act of 1801 was repealed made several organized attempts to maintain their positions. After four "midnight justices" met on July 7, 1802, Judge Richard Bassett published a lengthy pamphlet designed to rally legal elites to the cause of his judicial brethren (Document 74). His essay defended judicial review, claimed that Congress had no constitutional power to abolish the circuit court justiceships, and called on members of the Supreme Court who thought the repeal unconstitutional not to ride circuit as required by the Judiciary Act of 1802. Eleven dispossessed federal justices met on November 20, 1802, and drafted a memorial to Congress, asking that they be assigned judicial duties and paid their judicial salaries (Document 75).

The petition proved unavailing. The House of Representatives dismissed it on a party-line vote. The Senate, for unknown reasons, appointed a committee of three Federalists—Gouverneur Morris, Jonathan Dayton, and James Ross—to report on the merits of the memorial. That committee recommended that the Senate ask the executive branch of government to initiate a court action for the purpose of determining whether the justices had been unconstitutionally deprived of their offices (Document 76). Unsurprisingly, the same Senate majority that voted to repeal the Judiciary Act of 1801 voted against having the president challenge the constitutionality of the repeal in court.

The debate over the memorial reiterated many themes played during the debate over the Repeal Act (Documents 77 and 78). Federalists emphasized that the federal judiciary was the ultimate interpreter of the Constitution. Morris made the interesting suggestion that the Supreme Court would not declare the Repeal Act unconstitutional but, following a judicial practice discussed earlier, would rule that Congress had not intended to deprive the midnight justices of their offices. Jeffersonians continued to be ambivalent on judicial power. Some denounced judicial review in any form; others were reconciled to judicial review but not to judicial supremacy. No Jeffersonian thought Congress had any business asking the president to bring a test case that challenged the Repeal Act or the Judiciary Act of 1802.

For more information on the response of the midnight justices (and the justices of the Supreme Court) to the Repeal Act, see Wythe Holt, " '[I]f the Courts have firmness enough to render the decision': Egbert Benson and the Protest of the 'Midnight Justices' Against Repeal of the Judiciary Act of 1801," *Egbert Ben-*

son: First Chief Judge of the Second Circuit (1801–1802) (Second Circuit Committee on the Bicentennial of the United States Constitution, 1987).

Documents 79–80: Senate Debate over Marbury's Request for a Certificate

William Marbury sought to obtain a certificate from the Senate stating that he had been nominated and confirmed to a justiceship of the peace (Document 79). Marbury planned to use it in his litigation as evidence that he was entitled to a judicial commission. Confirmations at that time were done in an executive session, not open to the public. Jeffersonians claimed that the material in the Senate Executive Journal was secret. The Senate, they further insisted, should not assist Marbury in his effort to embarrass the president. Prominent Jeffersonians also claimed that the certificate was not adequate legal evidence that Marbury was entitled to a judicial commission. Federalists supported giving Marbury the document. In their view, people had a right to examine government records and to use those records in lawsuits. Whether the certificate was good evidence was for the judiciary to decide. By a party-line vote, the Senate refused Marbury his certificate. The Senate Executive Journal would not be made public until 1828 (Document 80).

Documents 81–82: The Justices of the Supreme Court Respond

Federalists hoped that the Supreme Court would vindicate the dispossessed midnight justices by not holding circuit court during the fall of 1802 and by declaring unconstitutional the repeal of the Judiciary Act of 1801. Several prominent Federalists, after private communications with Chief Justice John Marshall, thought they had assurances that the justices would be supportive. Marshall privately questioned whether the Constitution permitted justices to serve on both the Supreme Court and circuit courts. Justice Samuel Chase called on the justices to strike down the Repeal Act in toto. Nevertheless, after corresponding with each other, the justices backed down (Document 81). Marshall and his brethren concluded that past precedent established that justices could constitutionally sit on the Supreme Court and ride circuit. Their decision to hold circuit courts, the justices agreed, did not express a judgment on whether the Repeal Act was constitutional. This private agreement to hold circuit courts was confirmed in *Stuart v. Laird* (1803) (Document 82). In that case, Justice William Paterson spoke for a unanimous court. Without discussing the repeal of the Judiciary Act, he ruled that Congress could require Supreme Court justices to ride circuit.

64   An Act to Provide for the More Convenient Organization of the Courts of the United States

SECTION 1. That from and after the next session of the Supreme Court of the United States, the said court shall . . . have two sessions in each and every year thereafter, to commence on the first Monday of June and December respectively. . . .

SEC. 3. That from and after the next vacancy that shall happen in the said court, it shall consist of five justices only; that is to say, of one chief justice, and four associate justices. . . .

SEC. 6. That the said districts shall be classed into six circuits. . . .

SEC. 7. That there shall be in each of the aforesaid circuits, except the sixth circuit, three judges of the United States, to be called circuit judges, . . . and in the sixth circuit, by a circuit judge, and the judges of the district courts of Kentucky and Tennessee. . . .

SEC. 11. That the said circuit courts respectively shall have cognizance of all crimes and offences cognizable under the authority of the United States, and committed within their respective districts, or upon the high seas; and also of all cases in law or equity, arising under the constitution and laws of the United States, and treaties made, or which shall be made, under their authority. . . .

65   Marbury's Nomination

JOHN ADAMS.
United States, March 2d, 1801
Gentlemen of the Senate:

I nominate . . . [t]he Hon. Thomas Sire Lee, the Hon. Tristam Dalton, the Hon. Benjamin Stoddert, the Hon. Uriah Forest, Daniel Carroll, John Mason, James Barry, Thomas Beall, William Thornton, Daniel Reintzell, Robert Brent, Thomas Peter, William Marberry, Thomas Addison, John Laird, Richard Forest, Cornelius Cunningham, Marsham Waring, John Threlkeld, Lewis Deblois, William Hammond Dorsey, Joseph Sprigg Belt, Abraham Boyd, Esquires, to be justices of the peace for the County of Washington, in the District of Columbia.

William Fitzhugh, Robert Townsend Hooe, Richard Conway, Charles Alexander, George Gilpin, Francis Peyton, George Taylor, Dennis Ramsay, Simon Summers, John Potts, Jonah Thompson, William Harper, Jonathan Swift, Abraham Faw, Charles Alexander, Jr., John Herbert, Cuthbert Powell, Jacob Houghman, and Cleon Moore Esquires, to be justices of the peace for the County of Alexandria.

Source: Journal of the Executive Proceedings of the Senate of the United States of America (Washington: Duff Green, 1828), vol. 1: 388.

66   Marbury's Confirmation, March 3, 1801

. . . The Senate proceeded to consider the message of the President of the United States, of the 2d instant, and the nominations contained therein, of Jonathan Russell, and others. Whereupon,

Resolved, That they do advise and consent to the appointments, agreeably to the nominations respectively. . . .

Source: Journal of the Executive Proceedings of the Senate of the United States of America (Washington: Duff Green, 1828), vol. 1: 390.

67   John Marshall to James M. Marshall, March 18, 1801

. . . I did not send out the commissions because I apprehended such as were for a fixd time to be completed when signd & seald & such as depended on the will of the President might at any time be revokd. To withhold the commission of the Marshal is equal to displacing him which the President I presume has the power to do, but to withhold the commission of the Justices is an act of which I entertaind no suspicion. I shoud however have sent out the commissions which had been signd & seald but for the extreme hurry of the time & the absence of Mr. Wagner who had been calld on by the President to act as his private Secretary. . . .

Source: John Marshall, *The Papers of John Marshall*, ed. Charles F. Hobson (Chapel Hill: University of North Carolina Press, 1990), vol. 6: 90.

68   Thomas Jefferson's Response

Thomas Jefferson to General Henry Knox, March 27, 1801

. . . In the class of removals, however, I do not rank the new appointments which Mr. A. crowded in with whip and spur from the 12th of December, when the event of the election was known, and, consequently, that he was making appointments, not for himself, but his successor, until 9 o'clock of the night, at 12 o'clock of which he was to go out of office. This outrage on decency should not have its effect, except in the life appointments which are irremovable; but as to the others I consider the nominations as nullities, and will not view the persons appointed as even candidates for *their* office, much less as possessing it by any title meriting respect. . . .

Thomas Jefferson to Justice William Johnson, June 12, 1823

. . . Among the midnight appointments of Mr. Adams, were commissions to some federal justices of the peace for Alexandria. These were signed and sealed by him, but not delivered. I found them on the table of the department of State, on my entrance into office, and forbade their delivery. . . . For if there is any principle of law never yet contradicted, it is that delivery is one of the essentials to the validity of the deed. Although signed and sealed, yet as long as it remains in the hands of the party himself, it is in *fieri* only, it is not a deed, and can be made so only by its delivery.

Sources: Thomas Jefferson, *The Writings of Thomas Jefferson,* ed. Andrew A. Lipscomb (Washington, D.C.: Thomas Jefferson Memorial Association, 1903), 247; Thomas Jefferson, *Writings,* ed. Merrill D. Peterson (New York: Library of America, 1984), 1474.

69 Show-Cause Order, December 18, 1801

. . . On the motion of William Marbury for a rule upon James Maddison Secretary of State of the United States to shew cause why a Mandamus should not be Issued to said James Maddison Secretary of State of the United States to be directed commanding him to cause to be delivered to the said William Marbury a Commission to be Justice of peace in the County of Washington in the District of Columbia it appearing to this Court that notice of this Motion has been given to the said James Maddison Secretary of State to the United States, and it further appearing by the affidavit of the said William Marbury that he has been credibly informed and verily believes that John Adams, President of the United States nominated the said William Marbury to the Senate of the United States for their advice and consent to be a Justice of the peace in the County of Washington in the District of Columbia and that the Senate aforesaid, Advised and Consented to the appointment of the said William Marbury to the Office aforesaid, and that a Commission having been made Out in due form was signed by the President aforesaid appointing him to the said office and that the great Seal of the United States was after the signature aforesaid, of the President aforesaid, affixed to the said Commission, by the Secretary of State of the United States, and that the said William Marbury has requested of the said James Maddison, Secretary of State of the United States, aforesaid that the said Commission should be delivered to him the said William Marbury, and that the said James Maddison Secretary of State aforesaid, hath not complied with the said request, and that the said Commission is withheld from the said William Marbury, and it further appearing by the affidavit aforesaid that application has been made to the said James Maddison Secretary of State of the United States at his office for information whether the Commission aforesaid was signed by the President aforesaid and sealed with the seal of the United States that explicit, and satisfactory information has not been given in answer to the said inquiry, either by the said Secretary of State or any officer in the Department of State, and it further appearing by the affidavit aforesaid that application has been made to the Secretary of State the Senate for his Certificate of the nomination of the said William Marbury by the aforesaid President, and of the advice and consent of the Senate that the said William Marbury should be appointed to the said office, and that the said Secretary has declined giving such a Certificate. It is ruled and ordered that on the fourth day of the next term James Maddison Secretary of State of the United States shew cause if any he hath why a mandamus should not be awarded by this Court to the said James Maddison Secretary of State of the United States commanding and requiring him to cause to be delivered unto the said William Mar-bury the Commission aforesaid of a Justice of the peace in the County of Washington in the District of Columbia.

Source: Erwin C. Surrency, ed., "The Minutes of the Supreme Court of the United States–1789–1806," *American Journal of Legal History* 8 (1964): 326, 340–341.

70   Senate Debate over the Repeal Act

SPEECH OF MR. BRECKENRIDGE:

. . . 1st. . . . No increase of courts or judges could be necessary or justifiable, unless the existing courts and judges were incompetent to the prompt and proper discharge of the duties consigned to them. To hold out a show of litigation, when in fact little exists, must be impolitic; and to multiply expensive systems, and create hosts of expensive officers, without having experienced an actual necessity for them, must be a wanton waste of the public treasury. . . .

. . . [T]he time never will arrive when America will stand in need of thirty-eight federal judges. . . .

I will now inquire into the power of Congress to put down these additional courts and judges.

First, as to the courts. . .

. . . It would, therefore, in my opinion, be a perversion, not only of language, but of intellect, to say that although Congress may, from time to time, establish inferior courts, yet, when established, that they shall not be abolished by a subsequent Congress possessing equal powers. It would be a paradox in legislation.

2d. As to the judges. . . .

But because the Constitution declares that a judge shall hold his office during good behaviour, can it be tortured to mean, that he shall hold his office after it is abolished? Can it mean, that his tenure should be limited by behaving well in an office which did not exist, although its duties are extinct? . . .

. . . [A]s no government can, I apprehend, seriously deny that this Legislature has a right to re-peal a law enacted by a preceding one, we will, in any event, discharge our duty by repealing this law; and thereby doing all in our power to correct the evil. If the judges are entitled to their salaries under the Constitution, our repeal will not affect them; and they will, no doubt, resort to their proper remedy. For where there is a Constitutional right, there must be a Constitutional remedy.

SPEECH OF MR. J. MASON:

. . . [T]he people, in forming their Constitution, meant to make the judges as independent of the Legislature as of the Executive. Because the duties which they have to perform, call upon them to expound not only the laws, but the Constitution also; in which is involved the power of checking the Legislature in case it should pass any laws in violation of the Constitution. For this reason it was more important that the judges in this country should be placed beyond control of the Legislature, than in other countries where no such power attaches to them. . . .

Mr. Mason knew that a Legislative body was occasionally subject to the dominance of violent passions; he knew that they might pass unconstitutional laws; and that the judges, sworn to support the Constitution, would refuse to carry them into effect; and he knew that the Legislature might contend for the execution of their statutes: Hence the necessity of placing the judges above the influence of these passions; and for these reasons the Constitution had put them out of the power of the Legislature.

SPEECH OF MR. MORRIS:

. . . Did the people of America vest all powers in the Legislature? No, they had vested in the judges a check intended to be efficient—a check of the first necessity, to prevent an invasion of the Constitution by unconstitutional laws—a check which might prevent any faction from intimidating or annihilating the tribunals themselves. . . .

. . . It is admitted that no power derived from the Constitution can deprive him of the office, and yet it is contended that by repeal of the law that office may be destroyed. Is not this absurd? . . .

SPEECH OF MR. JACKSON:

. . . [W]hy are the peculiar and exclusive powers of the Supreme Court designated in the following section of the Constitution, but because the Constitution considered that tribunal as absolutely established; while it viewed the inferior tribunals as dependent upon the will of the Legislature? And that this was the case was evident from the conduct of the Supreme Court on the pension act, which that court had some time since declared unconstitutional; and which declaration, he was convinced, would not have been hazarded by an inferior tribunal. . . .

SPEECH OF MR. TRACY:

. . . Our powers are limited, many acts of sovereignty are prohibited to the National Government, and retained by the States, and many restraints are imposed upon State sovereignty. If either, by accident or design, should exceed its powers, there is the utmost necessity that some timely checks, equal to every exigency, should be interposed. The Judiciary is established by the Constitution for that valuable purpose.

. . . In the United States, the caution must be applied to the existing danger; the Judiciary are to be a check on the Executive, but most emphatically on the Legislature of the Union, and those of the several States. What security is there to an individual, if the Legislature of the Union or any particular State, should pass a law, making any of his transactions criminal which took place anterior to the date of the law? None in the world but by an appeal to the Judiciary of the United States, where he will obtain a decision that the law itself is unconstitutional and void, or by a resort to revolutionary principles, and exciting a civil war. . . .

The danger in our Government is; and always will be, that the Legislative body will become restive, and perhaps unintentionally break down the barriers of our Constitution. . . .

. . . I apprehend the repeal of this law will involve in it the total destruction of our Constitution. It is supported by three independent pillars; the Legislative, Executive and Judiciary; and if any rude hand should pluck either of them away, the beautiful fabric must tumble into ruins. The Judiciary is the center pillar, and a support to each by checking both; on the one side is the sword, and on the other is the wealth of the nation; and it has no inherent capacity to defend itself. . . .

SPEECH OF MR. MASON OF VIRGINIA:

. . . [I]t is important, in a well regulated Government, that the judicial department should be independent. But I have never been among those who have carried this idea to the extent which seems at this day to be fashionable. Though of opinion that each department ought to discharge its proper duties free from the fear of the others, yet I have never believed that they ought to be independent of the nation itself. Much less have I believed it proper, or that our Constitution authorizes our courts of justice to control the other departments of the Government.

. . . Suppose, then, Congress should establish special tribunals to continue for three, four, or five years, to settle these claims [over land titles]. Judges would be appointed. They would be the judges of an inferior court. If the construction of the Constitution now contended for be established, what would the judges say, when the period for which they were appointed expired? . . . Would they not say, in the language of the gentleman from New York, though the law that creates us is temporary, we are in by the Constitution? Have we not heard this doctrine supported in the memorable case [*Marbury*] of the mandamus, lately before the Supreme Court? Was it not there said that, though the law had a right to establish the office of a justice of the peace, yet it had not a right to abridge its duration to five years; that it was a right in making the justices, but unconstitutional in limiting their periods of office; that being a judicial officer, he had a right to hold his office during life—or, what is the same thing—during good behavior, in despite of the law which created him, and in the very act of creation limiting his official life to five years. . . .

I fear . . . that if you take away from these judges that which they ought officially to do, they will be induced, from the want of employment, to do that which they ought not to do. . . . They may, as gentlemen have told us, hold the Constitution in one hand, and the law in the other, and say to the departments of Government, so far shall you go and no farther. This independence of the Judiciary, so much desired, will, I fear sir, if encouraged or tolerated, soon become something like supremacy. They will, indeed, form the main pillar of this goodly fabric; they will soon become the only remaining pillar, and they will presently, become so strong as to crush and absorb all the others into their solid mass.

Speech of Mr. Stone:

. . . Suppose the Legislature to have interests distinct from the people, and the judges to stand in the way of executing any favorite measure—Can anything be more easy than for the Legislature to declare that the courts, instead of being held semi-annually, or oftener, shall be held only once in six, eight, ten, or twenty years? Or in order to free themselves from the opposition of the present Supreme Court, to declare, that courts shall hereafter be held by thirteen judges. An understanding between the President and the Senate would make it practicable to fill the new offices with men of different views and opinions from those now in office. . . . I cannot conceive the Constitution intended so feeble a barrier; a barrier so easily evaded. . . .

The objects of courts of law, as I understand them, are, to settle questions of right between suitors; to enforce obedience to the laws, and to protect the citizens against the oppressive use of power in the Executive offices. Not to protect them against the Legislature, for that I think I have shown to be impossible, with the powers which the Legislature may safely use and exercise; and because the people have retained, in their own hands, the power of controlling and directing the Legislature, by their immediate and mediate elections of President, Senate, and House of Representatives. . . .

Speech of Mr. Cocke:

. . . We have been told that the nation is to look up to these immaculate judges to protect their liberties; to protect the people against themselves. This was novel, and what result did it lead to? He shuddered to think of it. . . .

Speech of Mr. Morris:

. . . Suppose, in the omnipotence of your Legislative authority, you trench upon the rights of your fellow citizens, by passing an unconstitutional law. If the judiciary department preserve its vigor, it will stop you short. Instead of a resort to arms, there will be a happier appeal to argument. . . .

. . . In so far as [the Supreme Court] may be busied with the great mischief of checking the Legislative or Executive departments in any wanton invasion of our rights, I shall rejoice in that mischief. . . . [I]f ever the occasion calls for it, I trust the Supreme Court will not neglect doing the great mischief of saving this Constitution, which can be done much better by their deliberations, than by resorting to what are called revolutionary measures. . . .

. . . What but this compact—what but this specific part of it, can save us from ruin? The Judicial power; that fortress of the Constitution, is now to be overturned. . . .

Speech of Mr. Baldwin:

. . . [I]f it had been intended to convey those distinguished powers which have lately been claimed in their favor, it might naturally have been expected that it would have been done in very conspicuous characters, and not left to be obscurely explored by construction, not enlightened by the least recollection from anybody. . . .

SPEECH OF MR. WRIGHT:

. . . He admitted, with the gentleman from New York [Morris], that judges ought to be guardians of the Constitution, so far as questions were constitutionally submitted to them; but he held the Legislative, Executive, and Judiciary, each severally the guardians of the Constitution, so far as they were called on in their several departments to act; and he had not supposed the judges were intended to decide questions not judicially submitted to them, or to lead the public mind in Legislative or Executive questions; and he confessed he had greater confidence in the security of his liberty in the trial by jury, which had in all times been considered as the palladium of liberty, than in the decision of judges who had at some time been corrupt. For his part, he did not wish to break down the judiciary or the judges, or to violate the Constitution, though he confessed he should feel as secure in the decision of the State judges in even federal questions, with an appeal to the Supreme Federal Court, as in the present judges. . . .

SPEECH OF MR. CHIPMAN:

. . . But to what purpose are the powers of Congress limited by that instrument? To what purpose is it declared to be the supreme law of the land, and as such, binding on the courts of the United States, and of the several States, if it may not be applied to the derivative laws to test their constitutionality? Shall it be only called in to enforce obedience to the laws of Congress, in opposition to the acts of the several States, and even to their rightful powers! Such cannot have been the intention. But, sir, it will be in vain long to expect from the judges, the firmness and integrity to oppose a Constitutional decision to a law, either of the national Legislature, or to a law of any of the powerful States, unless it should interfere with a law of Congress; if such a decision is to be made at the risk of office and salary, of public character, and the means of subsistence. . . .

SPEECH OF MR. ROSS:

. . . [I]t would have been preposterous to subject the courts to those whose acts they are directed to interpret and correct. . . .

The gentlemen ought to recollect that there is no analogy in this respect between our national Government and that of Great Britain. There an act of Parliament can change the constitution. Here the written Constitution, established by the people, restrains the Legislature to the exercise of delegated power, and fixes immutably certain bounds which it may not pass. If it should rashly exceed the delegated power, our Judiciary, sworn to support the Constitution, must declare that the great *irrepealable statute* made by the people shall restrain and control the unauthorized acts of agents who have exceeded the limits of a special authority. . . .

By this horrid doctrine, Congress erects itself into a complete tyranny. All the judges of your civil and criminal courts hold their offices at the will of the Legislature. A majority of the two Houses is in reality the national Judiciary. "During good behaviour" means as long as the prevailing party in Congress choose to continue one of their own laws. When parties change, the judges must all go out. What can our citizens, what can strangers expect from such courts? If you can pass laws impairing the obligations of contracts, or violating our public faith, or *ex post facto* in their operation, will our courts have enough to obey the Constitution and their oaths, by declaring such acts void? If you infringe the right of a State, or deny the privileges secured to it by the Constitution, what remedy, what hope has the State? Will the judges dare to resist your law, or refuse to execute it? If they do, their doom is certain; you sweep away their offices by a law, and appoint others to their duty; or you nominally erect new courts with the same jurisdiction, and leave the Executive to hunt for more pliant men. . . .

SPEECH OF MR. OGDEN:

. . . Suffer me further to observe, that our Government is one of checks; that the power given by the Constitution to the Legislature is not general, but special; that it is not omnipotent, but limited; and that, therefore, necessarily a check against it must somewhere exist. Suppose the Legislature should pass bills of attainder, or an unconstitutional tax, where can an oppressed citizen find protection but in a court of justice firmly denying to carry into execution an unconstitutional law? What power else can protect the State sovereignties, should the other branches combine against them? And let me ask, where can such power be more safely lodged than in that branch of the Government, which, holding neither the sword nor the purse of a nation, cannot have either the ambition or the means of subverting, to their own benefit, the provisions of our Constitution?....

SPEECH OF MR. BRECKENRIDGE:

. . . It is said that the different departments of Government are to be checks on each other, and that the courts are to check the Legislature. If this be true, I would ask where they got that power, and who checks the courts when they violate the Constitution? Would they not, by this doctrine, have the absolute direction of the Government? To whom are they responsible? But I deny the power which is so pretended. If it is derived from the Constitution, I ask gentlemen to point out the clause which grants it. I can find no such grant. Is it not extraordinary, that if this high power was intended, it should nowhere appear? Is it not truly astonishing that the Constitution, in its abundant care to define the powers of each department, should have omitted so important a power as that of the courts to nullify all the acts of Congress, which, in their opinion, were contrary to the Constitution?

Never were such high and transcendent powers in any Government . . . claimed or exercised by construction only. The doctrine of constructions, not warranted by the letter of an instrument, is dangerous in the extreme. . . .

To make the Constitution a practical system, this pretended power of the courts to annul the laws of Congress cannot possibly exist. . . . That those who made the laws are presumed to have

an equal attachment to, and interest in the Constitution; are equally bound by oath to support it, and have an equal right to give a construction to it. That the construction of one department of the powers vested in it, is of higher authority than the construction of any other department; and that, in fact, it is competent to that department to which powers are confided exclusively to decide upon the proper exercise of those powers: that therefore the Legislature have the exclusive right to interpret the Constitution, in what regards the law-making power, and the judges are bound to execute the laws they make. For the Legislature would have at least an equal right to annul the decisions of the courts, founded on their construction of the Constitution, as the courts would have to annul the acts of the Legislature, founded on their construction.

Although, therefore, the courts may take upon them to give decisions which impeach the constitutionality of a law, and thereby, for a time, obstruct its operations, yet I contend that such a law is no the less obligatory because the organ through which it is to be executed has refused its aid. A pertinacious adherence of both departments to their opinions, would soon bring the question to issue, in whom the sovereign power of legislation resided, and whose construction of the law making power should prevail.

If the courts have a right to examine into, and decide upon the constitutionality of laws, their decision ought to be final and effectual. . . . It is making, in my opinion, a mockery of the high powers of legislation. I feel humbled by the doctrine, and enter my protest against it. . . .

SPEECH OF MR. MORRIS:

. . . [H]e asks where the judges got their pretended power of deciding on the constitutionality of laws? If it be in the Constitution (says he) let it be pointed out. I answer they derived that power from authority higher than this Constitution. They derive it from the constitution of man, from the nature of things, from the necessary progress of human affairs. When you have enacted a law, when process thereon has been issued, and suit brought, it becomes eventually necessary that the judges decide on the case before them, and declare what the law is. They must, of course, determine whether that which is produced and relied on, has indeed the binding force of law. The decision of the Supreme Court is, and, of necessity must be final. This,

Sir, is the principle, and the source of the right for which we contend. . . .

SPEECH OF MR. JACKSON:
. . . The gentleman therefore may dismiss his fears, as to what may be done by the inferior courts, for there is always an appeal to the Supreme Court. . . .

Source: Annals of Congress, 7th Cong., 1st Sess., 25–30, 32–34, 38, 39, 48, 50, 56–59, 61–63, 73–75, 83, 89, 91, 105, 115–116, 131–132, 163–167, 171, 175–176, 178–182.

71   House Debate over the Repeal Act

SPEECH OF MR. HENDERSON:
. . . If Congress, who have the power of making laws, can also displace their judges by repealing that which creates the offices they fill, the irresistible consequence is, that whatever law is passed the judges must carry into execution, or they will be turned out of office. . . . Whatever the Legislature declares to be law must be obeyed. The Constitutional check which the judges were to be on the Legislature is completely done away. . . . All the ramparts which the Constitution has erected around the liberties of the people, are prostrated at one blow by the passage of this law. The monstrous and unheard of doctrine which has been lately advanced, that the judges have not the right of declaring unconstitutional laws void, will be put into practice by the adoption of this measure. New offenses may be created by law. Associations and combinations may be declared treason, and the affrighted and appalled citizen may in vain seek refuge in the independence of your courts. In vain may he hold out the Constitution and deny the authority of Congress to pass a law of such undefined signification, and call upon the judges to protect him; he will be told that the opinion of Congress now is, that we have no right to judge of their authority; this will be the consequence of concentrating

Judicial and Legislative power in the same hands. It is the very definition of tyranny. . . .

SPEECH OF MR. R. WILLIAMS:
. . . That there must be some place where the true meaning of the Constitution must be determined, all would agree. . . . The people have constituted two departments of authority, the Executive and Legislative, emanating directly from the people; and have directed them to form another, further removed from the people. Are we then to be told there is more safety in confiding this important power to the last department, so far removed from the people, than in departments flowing directly from the people, responsible to and returning at short intervals into the mass of the people.

. . . If this doctrine is to extend to the length gentlemen contend, then is the sovereignty of the Government to be swallowed up in the vortex of the Judiciary. Whatever the other departments of the Government may do, they can undo. You may pass a law, but they can annul it. Will not the people be astonished to hear that their laws depend upon the will of the judges, who are themselves independent of all law? . . .

I will agree that there are times when checks and balances are useful. Legislative bodies may occasionally, in a gust of passion, pass improper laws; but because in a solitary instance we may pass such laws, shall we pass all authority into the hands of a few men, who, gentlemen say, know none of these passions, who are calm, cool, and wise men, who know no interests of their own, but are totally absorbed in that of the people? Suppose in our construction we should err, the evil can last no longer than two, at most six years, which are the durations of our office. The people will then dismiss us. But how can the judge be checked, or the evil he commits be remedied? In no way but by a recurrence to revolutionary principles. . . .

SPEECH OF MR. HEMPHILL:

. . . If Congress, in coming here, and carrying with them the sentiments of the people, and as their immediate representatives, can do everything which may appear to them for the good of the people, under every change of circumstances, a written Constitution would be useless. . . .

. . . It is said that the Judiciary is a subordinate and not a co-ordinate branch of the Government, that the judges have no right to declare a law to be unconstitutional; that no such power is given to that branch in the Constitution. Why, sir, it is nowhere declared that Congress have a right to exercise their judgment, or to consider the expediency of a measure; the Judiciary, from the nature of their institution, are to judge of the law and what is the law. The Constitution is paramount and supreme. The judge is bound by oath to support it. The Legislature have a right to exercise their judgment as to the constitutionality of a law on its passage; but the Judiciary decide at last, and their decision is final. . . .

. . . [I]t is they who wish that a construction be put upon the Constitution by Congress, which shall be considered as the Constitution itself; and are unwilling that there should be any check to oppose it; and of course, every construction put on it by the different Legislatures, will exhibit the appearance of a new Constitution, a constitution to be tossed and blown about by every political breeze. The powers of Congress will be equal to the powers of the English Parliament, transcendant, splendid, and without control. . . .

SPEECH OF MR. THOMPSON:

. . . Give this Judiciary this check upon the Legislature, allow them the power to declare your laws null and void; . . . and in vain have the people placed you upon this floor to legislate; your laws will be nullified, your proceedings will be checked. . . . I have, sir, looked into the Constitution with a scrutinizing eye, to discern, if possible, whence these pretensions are derived. There are but two clauses of the Constitution, which can even give a pretence for the power which is contended for. The first is [Article III, Section 2].

To declare a law null and void is certainly not such a case, either in law or equity, arising under the Constitution, as was contemplated to be embraced by the paragraph I have cited. . . . The other clause of the Constitution is [Article VI, Section 2.]

This, certainly, from the words with which it concludes, was intended as an instruction or direction to the judges of the State courts; and if they were transposed perhaps, would more fully communicate the intention of their framers, reading in this form: "The judges in any State shall be bound by this Constitution," &c. Is there any reasonable person, sir, after this explanation, will say that by either or both of these clauses a power is given to your Judiciary to declare your laws null and void? They may, to be sure, for a while impede the passage of a law, by a decision against its constitutionality; yet, notwithstanding the law is in force, is not nullified, and will be acted upon whenever there is a change in opinion. The Legislative, Executive, and Judicial departments should be kept separate and distinct. . . . Yet, I inquire, will this be the case if you allow to the Judiciary the power to annul your laws. . . . I am persuaded you thereby concentrate all power in one department. . . .

SPEECH OF MR. DAVIS:

. . . But it is said the law of last session is admitted to be Constitutional, and that we have no power to repeal it. Look at the second section of the law, and compare it with the Constitution, and no candid man will declare it Constitutional. The original jurisdiction given by that section to the judges of the Supreme Court exceeds those intended by the Constitution. . . . I found my opinion of the expedience of repealing the Judiciary law, on another reason in addition to that of the courts being unnecessary; I mean the power they declare they have, in the language of Judge Patterson, to "declare a law null and void." Never can I believe the Judiciary paramount to both branches of the Legislature. . . . In the present state of things, how will it affect us? The minority possessing one department of Government, completely frustrates the views of the other two, and governs the nation against the will of the people and the Legislative and Executive power. I am willing to admit the Judiciary to be coordinate with the Legislature in this respect, to wit, that judges thinking a law unconstitutional are not bound to execute it; but not to declare it null and void. That power rests alone with the Legislature. But we are told this Judiciary is necessary to check this House and the Senate, and to protect the people against their worst enemies. This is saying to the people, you are incapable of governing yourselves, your representatives are incapable of doing it; in the Judiciary alone you find a safe deposit for your liberties; and saying also, that the Judiciary is the vitals of the nation, wherein all power, all safety dwells; that the Legislature is subordinate thereto and a mere nominal thing, a shadow without substance, its acts are perfectly within the control of the Judiciary. I tremble at such ideas. The sooner we put men out of power, who we find determined to act in this manner, the better; by doing so we preserve the power of the Legislature, and save our nation from the ravages of an uncontrolled Judiciary.

SPEECH OF MR. T. MORRIS:

. . . We find, sir, the ablest judges who have graced the bench of Virginia, deliberately declaring acts of the Legislature of that State unconstitutional. . . . Why then . . . are most of the gentlemen who rep-

resent that State, anxious to divest the General Government of a privilege so highly valued in their own State? . . . A State Judiciary, according to the opinions of the Virginia judges, has to protect a citizen against the Government as well as to decide between citizen and citizen. What have the national tribunals to do? Why, sir, they have not only to protect a citizen against a State government, not only to protect him also against the General Government, but, sir, they may be even called upon to decide between a State and the General Government. These are the great purposes for which your Constitution has vested your Judiciary with powers independent of other departments of the Government, that it may effectually interpose between the meanest of your citizens and secure them against the oppression either of an arbitrary Legislature or a tyrannical Executive. . . .

SPEECH OF MR. STANLEY:

. . . First, then, that the Judiciary are a check on the Legislature. In the Constitution, we find they are prohibited from exercising certain powers. . . . Should, unhappily, a Legislature be found who, from weakness or wickedness, or the union of both, should transgress the bounds prescribed, what is the security of the citizen? . . . The Judiciary are our security. The Legislature may enact penalties, and denounce punishments against those who do not yield obedience to their unconstitutional acts; their penalties cannot be exacted, nor punishments inflicted without the judgment of a court. The judges are to expound the law, and that fundamental, paramount law, the Constitution. To this purpose they are sworn to support the Constitution. While the Judiciary firmly, independently, and uprightly, discharge their duty and declare the act of the Legislature contrary to the Constitution, to be void, the Legislature are checked and the citizen shielded from oppression and persecution. . . .

SPEECH OF MR. GILES:

. . . The judges have determined that they are judges in the last resort upon the constitutionality of your laws. He proposed not to discuss this question because he did not think it pertinent to the question before us. He only mentioned it to show their unlimited claims to power. . . . They have sent a mandamus process, or process leading to a mandamus, into the Executive cabinet, to examine its concerns. Does this, in the judges, seem unambitious. . . .

SPEECH OF MR. BAYARD:

. . . [T]he proceeding which has taken place, is no more than notice of the application for justice made to the court and allows the party to show, either that no wrong has been committed, or that the court has no jurisdiction over the subject. Even, sir, if the rule were made absolute, and the mandamus issued, it would not be definitive, but it would be competent for the Secretary in a return to the writ, to justify the act which has been done, or to show that it is not a subject of judicial cognizance.

. . . In this transaction, so far from seeing anything culpable in the conduct of your judges, I think, sir, that they have given a strong proof of the value of that Constitutional provision which makes them independent. They are not terrified by the frowns of Executive power, and dare to judge between the rights of a citizen and the pretensions of a President. . . .

. . . The Legislative power of the Government is not absolute, but limited. If it be doubtful whether the Legislature can do what the Constitution does not explicitly authorize; yet there can be no question that they cannot do what the Constitution expressly prohibits. To maintain, therefore, the Constitution, the judges are a check upon the Legislature. . . .

. . . Of what importance is it to say, Congress are prohibited from doing certain acts, if no legitimate authority exists in the country to decide whether an act done is a prohibited act? Do gentlemen perceive the consequences which would follow from establishing the principle, that Congress have the exclusive right to decide upon their own powers? This principle admitted, does any

Constitution remain? . . . They do what is not authorized, they do what is inhibited, nay, at every step they trample the Constitution under foot; yet their acts are lawful and binding, and it is treason to resist them. . . . They tell us they are friendly to the existence of the States; that they are the friends of a federative, but the enemies of a consolidated, General Government, and yet, sir, to accomplish a paltry object, they are willing to settle a principle which, beyond all doubt, would eventually plant a consolidated Government, with unlimited power, upon the ruins of the State governments. Nothing can be more absurd than to contend that there is a practical restraint upon a political body who are answerable to none but themselves for the violation of the restraint, and who can derive from the very act of violation, undeniable justification of their conduct.

If . . . you mean to have a Constitution, you must discover a power to which the acknowledged right is attached of pronouncing the invalidity of the acts of the Legislature which contravene the instrument. Does the power reside in the States? . . . This would be erring upon the opposite extreme. It would be placing the General Government at the feet of the State governments. It would be allowing one member of the Union to control all the rest. It would inevitably lead to civil dissension and a dissolution of the General Government. Will it be pretended that the State courts have the exclusive right of deciding upon the validity of our laws? I admit that they have the right to declare an act of Congress void. But this right they enjoy in practice, and it ever essentially must exist, subject to the revisions and control of the courts of the United States. If the State courts definitively possessed the right of declaring the invalidity of laws of the Government, it would bring us in subjection to the States. The judges of those courts, being bound by the laws of the State, if a State declared an act of Congress unconstitutional, the law of the State would oblige its courts to determine the law invalid. This principle would also destroy the uniformity of obligation upon all the States which should attend every law of this Government. If a law were declared void in one

State, it would exempt the citizens of that State from its operation, whilst obedience was yielded to it in the other States. . . . Let me now ask if the power to decide upon the validity of our laws resides with the people? Gentlemen cannot deny this right to the people. I admit that they possess it. But if, at the same time, it does not belong to the courts of the United States, where does it lead the people? It leads them to the gallows. Let us suppose that Congress, forgetful of the limits of their authority, pass an unconstitutional law. They lay a direct tax upon one State and impose none upon the others. The people of the State taxed contest the validity of the law. They forcibly resist its execution. They are brought by the Executive authority before the courts upon charges of treason. The law is unconstitutional, the people have done right, but the court are bound by the law, and obliged to pronounce upon them the sentence which it inflicts. Deny to the courts of the United States the power of judging upon the constitutionality of our laws, and it is vain to talk of its existing elsewhere. . . .

. . . I say, in the nature of things, the dependence of the judges upon the Legislature, and their right to declare the acts of the Legislature void, are repugnant and cannot exist together. The doctrine, sir, supposes two rights—first, the right of the Legislature to destroy the office of the judge, and the right of the judge to vacate the act of the Legislature. You have a right to abolish, by a law, the offices of the judges of the circuit court; they have a right to declare the law void. It unavoidably follows, in the exercise of these rights, either that you destroy their rights, or that they destroy yours. This doctrine is not an harmless absurdity, it is a most dangerous heresy. It is a doctrine which cannot be practised without producing not discord only, but bloodshed. If you pass the bill upon your table the judges have a Constitutional right to declare it void. I hope they will have the courage to exercise that right; and if, sir, I am called upon to take my side, standing acquitted in my conscience and before my God, of all motives but the support of the Constitution of my country, I shall not tremble at the consequences.

. . . The independence of the Judiciary was the felicity of our Constitution. It was this principle which was to curb the fury of party upon sudden changes. The first moments of power, gained by a struggle, are the most vindictive and intemperate. Raised above the storm, it was the Judiciary which was to control the fiery zeal, and to quell the fierce passions of a victorious faction. . . .

SPEECH OF MR. RANDOLPH:
. . . But, sir, if you pass the law, the judges are to put their veto upon it by declaring it unconstitutional. Here is a new power, of a dangerous and uncontrollable nature, contended for. The decision of a Constitutional question must rest somewhere. Shall it be confided to men immediately responsible to the people, or to those who are irresponsible? for the responsibility by impeachment is little less than a name. From whom is a corrupt decision most to be feared? To me it appears that the power which has the right of passing, without appeal, on the validity of your laws, is your sovereign. But an extreme case is put; a bill of attainder is passed; are the judges to support the Constitution or the law? Shall they obey God or Mammon? Yet you cannot argue from such cases. . . . But, sir, are we not as deeply interested in the true exposition of the Constitution as the judges can be? With all the deference to their talents, is not Congress as capable of forming a correct opinion as they are? Are not its members acting under a responsibility to public opinion, which can and will check their aberration from duty? Let a case, not an imaginary one, be stated. Congress violate the Constitution by fettering the press; the judicial corrective is applied to; far from protecting the liberty of the citizen, or the letter of the Constitution, you find them outdoing the Legislature in zeal. . . .

. . . [Y]ou may invade the press; the courts will support you, will outstrip you in zeal to further their great object; your citizens may be imprisoned and amerced, the courts will take care to see it executed; the helpless foreigner may, contrary to the express letter of your Constitution, be deprived of compulsory process for obtaining witnesses in his defence; the courts, in their extreme humility, cannot find authority for granting it; but touch one cent of their salaries, abolish one sinecure office which the judges hold, and they are immediately arrayed against the laws, as the champions of the Constitution. Lay your hands on the liberties of the people, they are torpid, utterly insensible; but affect their peculiar interest, and they are all nerve. . . . Grant this authority, sir, to your judges, and you will have a Constitution which gentlemen who are such enemies to dumb legislation may indeed approve, because it is the very reverse of that which has been the object of their animadversions. To you will indeed belong the right of discussing—there ends your power; the judges are to decide, and without appeal. In their inquisitorial capacity, the Supreme Court, relieved from the tedious labor of investigating judicial points by the law of the last session, may easily direct the Executive by mandamus, in what mode it is their pleasure that he should execute his functions. They will also have more leisure to attend to the Legislature, and forestall, by inflammatory pamphlets, their decisions on all important questions; whilst, for the amusement of the public, we shall retain the right of debating but not of voting. . . .

SPEECH OF MR. HUGER:

. . . From an *ex post facto* law, from a bill of attainder, or from any other act of violence, however unconstitutional, on the part of the Executive and Legislature, where are we to look for relief? To what tribunal are we to apply for the protection of our persons and our rights against the predominant faction, or leaders of a faction—against the rage and violence of party zeal and party animosity—if this tribunal, instead of being a barrier, behind which the weak may take shelter, is to become the tool of those in power, and to be made use of as the instrument of their persecution and oppression? . . . . And I hesitate not in saying that, between an independent Judiciary, constituting a tribunal which can control the unconstitutional attempts of the other two branches of the Government, which dares, without dread or fear, to deal out justice, with an impartial hand, between the weak and the strong, the great and the small; between such a tribunal and the bayonet there remains no resource or alternative. . . .

. . . [The persons responsible for the constitution] foresaw that popular branches by uniting might overpower the Executive; or the Executive might, by corruption, induce them to favor his views; or, finally, from whatever cause, these two branches might come to an understanding and unite in a common interest. They . . . well knew that, if these two branches were by any means induced to unite in a common cause, they would construe the Constitution as might best suit their purposes, and all power would of course be in their hands. . . . [O]ne only alternative, hitherto-fore unknown or untried by other nations presented itself to them. This was to establish a third co-ordinate and equal branch in the Government—an independent Judiciary, which, without interfering in the peculiar duties of either of the other two, without having anything to do either in making the laws, or when made, in calling forth the force necessary to carry them into execution, should serve as a protecting shield, as well to individual citizens as the States themselves, against the encroachments and attacks of either or both these branches, acting either separately or in union; should keep each of them in its proper sphere, and check the career or one or both, when stepping beyond the limits which had been assigned to them; when trampling on the Constitution, under which the people had authorized them to act, they undertook to extend their powers at pleasure, and to make their will, instead of the written will of the people, the criterion by which their powers were to be judged. . . .

. . . They neither wield the sword, nor have the purse-strings at their command. They cannot move until the other two branches have acted. They can neither say what laws are to be made, or direct what measures must be pursued. Their whole power consists in assisting to carry the laws and measures, adopted by the other two branches, into operation; in dealing out justice, protecting the weak against the strong, and restraining and checking the unconstitutional attempts of the Government. Their only shield is the Constitution; their only force, argument. . . .

SPEECH OF MR. SMITH:

. . . Gentlemen say, the Constitution authorizes the judges to decide your laws unconstitutional, and they are to hold their offices independent of the Legislature, to give greater efficiency to this salutary check. I beg leave to inform gentlemen, the Constitution has established no such principle. It is true your judges have authority, derived from the nature of their power as judges, to decide in this way; but the clause which the gentleman speaks of has nothing to do with this question. Whether the judge holds his office at the will of the President, or for one year, or during good behaviour, it is equally his duty to decide a law void, which directly infringes the Constitution. . . . [P]rudent judges will exercise this right with great caution, knowing the Legislature has an equal right to put constructions; they will also consider the Legislature are obliged to precede them in their construction. . . . Why is it thought that the barriers which the Constitution has opposed to the passage of hasty, inconsiderate laws, are not sufficiently multiplied? Here is a House of Representatives composed of about one hundred members, coming from every part, and representing every interest in the United States; on every law which passes this House, the different interests and feelings of its members are rallied to guard this passage. The other branch is composed of members different in number, in years, and the interests they represent. All calculated to impose a restraint on such interests and passions which, from any circumstance, might have found way for a bill through this body. It is finally to be presented to the President, who represents the entire interest of the people of the United States; and is accountable to them by an election every fourth year; if he dissents, it must be re-enacted by two thirds of both Houses. What further checks can be wanting? There is a point of precaution, beyond which it would not be salutary to go. If the framers of the Constitution contemplated your judges as the great safeguards against the encroachments of the Legislature in passing unconstitutional laws, I ask, how does it happen that the Constitution does not provide, that every bill, previous to becoming a law, should be laid before the judges of the Supreme Court, for them to decide on its constitutionality? . . .

. . . [G]entlemen say, their construction of the Constitution alone will give firmness to the judges in checking the unconstitutional acts of the Legislature. Can they entertain an opinion of their judges so unfavorable? Will the judges, under an apprehension of removal from office by the Legislature, under the pretext of a law for the better and more perfect organization of courts, give up all their independence of opinion? Will they forget their oaths? Will they forget everything which constitutes the excellency of a judge, for the paltry considerations of a salary, which, gentlemen say, is no more than adequate to their services? . . . It is in vain we talk of independence of judges, whilst the rod of chastisement hangs over them. Let us suppose a law in which this struggle between the Legislature and courts is most likely to be put to the test. In some great national emergency the Legislature pass a law which, in their opinion, is highly promotive of the public good; the safety of the country, in the opinion of the Legislature, depends on its execution; your judges paralyze the operations of Government in deciding that law unconstitutional. Here is a collision of opinion destructive in its nature, and for which a remedy must be devised. The Legislature have decided it compatible with the Constitution; your judges the reverse; here is an impeachment fact; an impeachment is ordered. Gentlemen will say, the safety of the judges is in the purity of their intentions; I answer, I have seen with what facility gentlemen can impeach motives; I have seen it here; I have seen it in solemn trials at the bar. . . .

SPEECH OF MR. GODDARD:

. . . Gentlemen ask, where we find in the Constitution a power given to the judges to decide against the constitutionality of laws? I answer in the sixth article. . . . The judges are not only sworn to support the Constitution, but their oath of office binds them to judge "agreeably to the Constitution and the laws." The expression, "supreme law of the land," imports inferior and subordinate laws. What are those laws, unless acts of Congress? The expression respecting laws made pursuant to the Constitution, necessarily implies that laws may be made which will not be pursuant to that instrument. Such are not the supreme law of the land. They are not law. Shall not the judges when called upon to decide if, in their opinion, a bill should be passed by Congress against the Constitution which assumes the form of a law, declare it, I will not say null and void, if gentlemen dislike those terms, but to be no law?— not being made pursuant to the power delegated to the Congress by the Constitution. . . .

. . . And let us arrogate to ourselves as much wisdom as we please, who, let me ask, are the most competent to decide correctly important questions arising under the Constitution, our judges or our legislators? Legislatures will, in violent times, enact laws manifestly unjust, oppressive, and unconstitutional; and that, too, under the specious pretext of reliving the burdens of the people. Such laws, it is the business of the judges, elevated above the influence of party, to control. . . .

. . . In America the Judicial power was designed as a Constitutional check upon both the Executive and Legislature; but gentlemen on the other side, deprecating all control, are for prostrating the check imposed by the people on their Representatives, and the destruction of which will make them omnipotent. . . .

. . . [W]e do not wish to guard the Constitution by appeals to the people; we will do nothing calculated to produce insurrection; we do not want to protect the great charter of our rights by the bayonet. No sir, we rely on honest and legitimate means of defence; we wish to check these gentlemen only with Constitutional checks. The people of America say in their Constitution, the Judiciary is designed as a check upon the Legislature and Executive, and as a barrier between the people and the Government. . . . The Judiciary is the ballast of the national ship; throw it overboard and she must upset. . . .

SPEECH OF MR. RUTLEDGE:

. . . [S]uppose Congress should pass an *ex post facto* law, or legislate upon any other subject which is prohibited to them, where are the people of this country to seek redress? Who are to decide between the Constitution and the acts of Congress? Who are to pronounce on the laws? Who will declare whether they be unconstitutional? . . .

. . . We are asked by the gentleman from Virginia if the people want judges to protect them? Yes, sir, in popular governments Constitutional checks are necessary for their preservation; the people want to be protected against themselves; no man is so absurd as to suppose the people collectively will consent to the prostration of their liberties; but if they be not shielded by some Constitution checks they will suffer them to be destroyed; to be destroyed by demagogues, who filch the confidence of the people by pretending to be their friends; demagogues who, at the time they are soothing and cajoling the people, with bland and captivating speeches, are forging chains for them; demagogues who carry daggers in their hearts, and seductive smiles in their hypocritical faces; who are dooming the people to despotism, when they profess to be exclusively the friends of the people. Against such designs and artifices were our Constitutional checks made to preserve the people of this country. . . .

SPEECH OF MR. GRISWOLD:

. . . It is well known to every member of this Committee, that the right of the courts to decide on the constitutionality of your laws, has been recognized in your laws themselves; has been exercised by the courts; your laws have been pronounced unconstitutional and void, and that decision has not only been acquiesced in by the Legislature, but the act itself has been removed from your code of statutes. Nor is this principle peculiar to your national Government; it exists, and is exercised under every State Government, where the powers of the Legislature have been limited by a written Constitution. The principle not only exists, and results from the nature of this Government, but is provided for by the terms of the Constitution itself. The words declare that the Constitution shall be supreme law and the judges are not only bound to respect it as such, but have sworn to support it, and they would be guilty of perjury if they should knowingly decide for the execution of an act which the Constitution did not warrant. Nor can any embarrassment result from the execution of this principle; the judges must pronounce your laws generally; they find two statutes in your law book which are repugnant to each other; they must decide which of the statutes shall bind; they find the law of the Constitution and the law of the Legislature clashing with each other; they know the first is paramount, and limits as well the power of the Legislature as the power of the court, and they must decide either that the law of the Constitution or the law of the Legislature is void. In such a case there is nothing left to discretion, the Constitution is peremptory and commands the obedience of every department. . . .

Sir, if there is no power to check the usurpations of the Legislature, the inevitable consequence must be that the Congress of the United States becomes truly omnipotent. All power must be concentrated here, before which every department and all State authorities must fall prostrate. . . .

. . . The Legislature itself is responsible to the Judiciary department for the constitutionality of its acts, and those acts . . . may be declared void, if they are not warranted by the Constitution, and the members of the Legislature are responsible to the people upon the return of every new election. . . .

. . . The Legislature may pass unconstitutional laws, depriving the people of rights which the Constitution has guarantied; but these laws can never be executed so long as an enlightened and independent court remains to expound them. . . .

SPEECH OF MR. NICHOLSON:
. . . Give them the powers and the independence now contended for, and they will require nothing more; for your Government becomes a despotism, and they become your rulers. They are to decide upon the lives, the liberties, and the property of your citizens; they have an absolute veto upon your laws by declaring them null and void at pleasure. . . . If all this be true; if this doctrine be established in the extent which is now contended for, the Constitution is not worth the time we are spending upon it. It is, as it has been called by its enemies, mere parchment. For these judges thus rendered omnipotent, may overleap the Constitution and trample on your laws; they may laugh the Legislature to scorn, and set the nation at defiance. . . .

SPEECH OF MR. DENNIS:
. . . Congress, sir, are the attorneys of the people, and to them, the people, who are our principals, have not given an unlimited but a special authority to do certain things, and have expressly forbidden them from doing certain other things. We, however, not only do things not within our commission, but something expressly forbidden, and the judges are called on to decide between the people, their principals and us, their agents; and we are told they are bound to decide, in this case, in favor of the usurped authority of the agent.

. . . Let us, sir, be more just to that enlightened and patriotic Convention who formed that instrument, than to suppose they meant to guard only against the remoter evils of Executive influence, and leave your Judiciary to the varying dominance of alternate Legislative factions. No sir, they read of Legislative attainders, Legislative confiscations, and Legislative banishments, and therefore declared, "no bill of attainder, or *ex post facto* laws, shall be made." Nor were they such mere novices in political science, and the knowledge of human nature, as not to know, that these paper restrictions were of little avail without the practical means of giving efficacy to these declarations. And it was for that purpose that they rendered the Judiciary a co-ordinate department of our Government. . . .

SPEECH OF MR. HILL:

. . . Should the Legislature even surmount the barrier of the Constitution, it is the duty of the judges to repel it back within the bounds which limit its power. Were they not independent, would they be equal to this duty? Could they perform it—dare they perform it, if, on the Legislature they were dependent? . . .

SPEECH OF MR. CUTLER:

. . . By making the Judiciary, equally with the other branches, a component part, a check was formed, not less necessary to the security and freedom of the people, than any other contained in the Constitution. This check erects a barrier between the Government and the people, and becomes the bulwark of equal justice and equal liberty. It is the only effectual security against the encroachments of the Legislature upon the Constitutional rights of the people, and forming a wise and free Government, it will forever be a *desideratum* to establish, immoveably, an impartial, inflexible and sacred administration of justice. . . .

. . . It is not in my power to conceive that elections are a remedy for every encroachment the Legislature may make on the Constitution. It must be a very uncertain corrective in instances of the most flagrant violations, and in smaller ones, it is none at all. There is not responsibility enough attached to the individual members of this House to render elections a sufficient corrective for the abuse of power. If the acts of the Legislature, which shall violate the most plain and positive provision of the Constitution, can only be corrected by an appeal to the opinion of the people, to be manifested by the exercise of their right of election, we lose the advantages we expect to derive from a written Constitution. And public opinion, which can never be accurately ascertained, and which is continually liable to fluctuation and change, will be our political constitution. If the time should come, which I hope has not yet arrived, when public opinion is to be the only corrective of the abuse of power, Constitutional rights will be reduced to a phantom, and the fair fabric of our national independence, liberty, and safety, will be levelled with the dust.

SPEECH OF MR. HOLLAND:

. . . [I]f they have a right to judge of the constitutionality of law, they will continue unimpaired to have the same right, and in every respect remain in their Constitutional independence. . . .

SPEECH OF MR. GREGG:

. . . Responsibility in public agents I have always considered as the best, the only security the people have against imposition. While that is preserved they are in great danger; destroy it, and where is their security? If the judges of even inferior courts are to be so independent, as that their offices must be sacred, and beyond the reach of the Legislature, and if their power in deciding on the constitutionality of laws, is to be unlimited, and without any qualification, the Legislature is but a subordinate branch of the Government— the Judiciary is paramount—the supreme power is in their hands. Such a doctrine appears to me repugnant to common sense, to the vital principles of our Government, and to the plain and obvious meaning of the Constitution.

SPEECH OF MR. HASTINGS:

. . . It is possible that a Legislature may sometimes be under the influence of popular passions, and that the Executive may not be wholly free from them; to gratify popular clamor, laws may be enacted unconstitutional and oppressive. What power, then, to check the Legislature in their wild career, but an upright and firm Judiciary, that is not dependent upon popular will? Judges who are independent, holding their offices during good behaviour, and who, uninfluenced by popular or party views, will operate as a check upon those, who, in factious times, may attempt to break down the barriers of the Constitution, and by the exercise of this Constitutional power, preserve the liberty, freedom, and independence of their Government and country?

. . . [W]e are told by an honorable member of the Committee, that, if we pass this bill, and thereby violate the Constitution, it will only be for two years; in two years the people may send other Representatives, and restore the law; and this, it is said, is the corrective principle in the Constitution. But if this doctrine be true, if the Judiciary power has no Constitutional check upon the acts and doings of the Legislature, Congress may pass an *ex post facto* law by which I may be deprived of my estate or life, before this correcting principle can operate and have effect. . . .

Speech of Mr. Dana:

. . . [Mr. Davis] has charged the act with being unconstitutional, because it authorized the Supreme Court to issue writs of mandamus. . . . There is no novelty, sir, in allowing to the Supreme Court the power of issuing writs of mandamus. A provision to this effect is found in the thirteenth section of the original Judicial act, passed in 1789. Applications have been repeatedly made to the Supreme Court for such writs. . . .

When such has been the unquestioned usage heretofore, it is not extraordinary that there has not been prudence enough to say less about the case of Marbury against the Secretary of State? In this case, however, no writ of mandamus has been issued; although there has been a preparatory process of an inferior nature. . . . By a rule to show cause, the court has required that notice shall be given of the purpose for which Mr. Marbury has made his appeal to them. This was not a mandate sent into the Executive cabinet, as has been represented. . . . [T]hat a Secretary of State is amenable to a writ of mandamus from the Supreme Court, is a position clearly warranted by principle and precedent. . . .

The President, indeed, may put his negative upon acts of Congress. The Senate may refuse to advise and consent to an appointment where the President has made a nomination. The Judiciary may say that unconstitutional acts are not obligatory. . . .

It is for the judges faithfully to administer justice according to the Constitution and laws. No menacing power should exist to bias their decisions by the influence of personal hopes and fears. They are undoubtedly to give effect to acts of Congress in pursuance of the Constitution. But the Constitution, which granted to Congress their Legislative powers, is the supreme law; and the judges, from the very nature of the case, must pronounce on the validity of acts of Congress, as compared with the imperative provisions of the Constitution. When they are called to decide a cause, if they find on the one side an act of Congress, and on the other, the Constitution of the United States, when they find these placed in opposition to each other, where is their duty? Are they not to obey their oath, and judge accordingly? If so, they necessarily decide, that your act is of no force; for they are sworn to support the Constitution. . . .

Say gentlemen, Congress must be answerable at the period of elections. This is all admitted. But why would you stake the whole control of their power merely on elections? On our part it is said, let there be all the security which elections can give; but let there be at the same time the further security of the judicial power. If there can be no regular decision of Constitutional questions by judicial authority, if there can be no check except elections, what effectual check will finally exist? . . .

Will gentlemen say, the Government cannot go on if there should be this check against unconstitutional acts? This might be pronounced a bold assertion, when it is remembered, that the Government has gone on, and gone on for twelve years, in the exercise of its acknowledged powers with this principle uniformly admitted in practice, any of the people being at liberty as freemen to object, in court, against any act as unconstitutional; and yet laws have been enacted, and carried into full effect.

If any unconstitutional act is passed, what must be done for relief against it, according to the plan of the gentlemen who advocate the bill on the table? . . . Must persons be subjected to the operation of an unconstitutional act until the period of elections comes round, and in the mean time be sending from State to State with a view to influence the electors not to vote for such representatives again?

Instead of all this sufferance, instead of all these efforts, which may at length be found wholly ineffectual for obtaining redress, especially under the present apportionment of representatives, why may not the injured citizen appear before wise and upright judges, and present to them the Constitution of his country, and receive from their decisions that relief to which he is justly entitled? While there are judges who are dependent on no party, but dependent on the fidelity with which they exercise their functions, men of learning and wisdom, who are placed under no bias from persons in power, but act according to the impulse of duty alone, I should suppose that they might be trusted to expound your laws, and guard the Constitution. . . .

A number of interesting questions might be expected to arise, when the Constitution was formed. . . . Controversies were known to exist between particular States, and others might be expected to arise, as well as controversies between a State and the United States. The parties in such controversies would be so powerful; each might put armed forces in motion. When provision was to be made for questions of this nature, who could hesitate to acknowledge the importance of establishing an impartial tribunal, beyond the immediate control of either party? A tribunal, the constitution of which might inspire general confidence, and thereby prevent the recourse to a very different mode of deciding conflicting pretensions. And how were the restrictions on the powers of Congress to be rendered effectual, except by the intervention of such a tribunal? In what other mode could a fair construction of the Constitution be uniformly secured to the respective citizens and to the several States? This impartial tribunal, independent of party, and placed beyond suspicion of undue in-

fluence, should be formed into a Supreme Court, vested by the Constitution with power to decide in the last resort. Will you say that Congress may give a construction to the Constitution? So, too, a State Legislature may give it, and there might be as many constructions as there are State Legislatures. Will you then say, that the State Legislatures shall submit without reserve, to any constructions that may be given by Congress? The members of the State Legislatures are bound to support the Constitution; and may they not judge of their duty as well as yourselves? Will you force them to submit? Remember the particular States divide the power of the militia with the Government of the United States. With respect to the acts of Congress, and of the State Legislatures, as compared to the acts of particular States, when in opposition to each other, who shall decide questions so interesting as these? The Constitution has provided for having them determined by a Supreme Court of the United States. . . .

. . . The principle, sir, of an impartial tribunal to decide questions respecting the fundamental rights of the society and Government, is an original principle of this Country. When adopted in the United States, it was a novelty in the history of nations. The experiment thus far has been successful. To have established this principle of Constitutional security is the particular glory of the American people. It enables the respective parts of the country to assert their Constitutional rights, and at the same time secures internal tranquility. If you now destroy it, will not the people of particular States have cause to complain that they have been deceived, in the event, and that their property and liberties are not secured according to their just expectations? When the Constitution was adopted, was it not right to expect, that the observance of it would be guarded by the judicial authority, which might hold in check the Legislature and the Executive, if ever they should unfortunately be disposed to overleap the established barriers? Without this, what is the protection for the feeble States, if any of the large and powerful States should influence Congress and the President to concur in unconstitutional acts, and to raise armies, and to draw forth the treasure of the United States, to confirm their usurpations.

SPEECH OF MR. PLATTER:

. . . I consider the judicial department as the protector of the Constitution; it stands between the people and the Legislature to check the abuse of a trust committed to them; it is a particular province to determine the constitutionality of all laws—the case may arise wherein it will become the duty of the Judiciary to decide between the Legislature and the President. Should the judges be dependent on either, great apprehension might exist; they would lean to that side on which their dependency existed. And should the Legislature and Executive unite to invade this Constitution, we should be left without a tribunal to give us impartial and disinterested decision. Thus, sir, you are dispensing with the only check to the oppression of an uncontrolled and unlimited power. . . .

SPEECH OF MR. TALLMADGE:

. . . [T]he Judiciary from its very nature, being the most feeble, if unprotected by the others cannot long endure. Whenever a predominant faction shall exist . . . and your Judiciary shall interpose to arrest its progress towards any unconstitutional end, how unsafe and precarious must be our situation! . . . [E]very attempt to prostrate the dignity and independence of the Judiciary system, is an attack upon an important constituent branch of your Government, and ought to be resisted. Encroachments by the Legislature are perhaps the most dangerous, because the least suspected and accompanied by the most power. . . .

In the present constitution of human nature, Government and efficient laws are absolutely necessary; in the structure of which passion and party views too frequently mislead the judgment and obscure the understanding. A sober and dispassionate corrective becomes, therefore, absolutely necessary. Your tribunals of justice afford the necessary relief. Here the rich and the poor, the strong and the weak, meet on equal ground;

and what I claim to be a principal excellence, inherent in their very nature, may here be found, viz, a right to decide between the Constitution and the law. However terrific this may appear to some gentlemen, who advocate the omnipotence of the Legislature, I consider the power which the Judges from the very nature of their office possess, of declaring a law null and void which contravenes the Constitution, to be of the highest importance, and attended with the happiest effects. What safety is there to any individual, or even to the community at large, if this Constitutional check should be removed! If the Legislature are to judge in the last resort on the constitutionality of their laws, what hope can there be entertained of redress, even should they violate the principles of the Constitution in the most flagrant manner. A consolidated Government is the direct result of Legislative and Judicial powers being vested in the same body. No people can long remain free, whose Legislature assumes the right first to enact and then to expound her laws. . . . If a law should be declared unconstitutional by a court, it would by no means follow from thence, that they claimed superiority over the Legislature; but that in the exercise of their functions, they pronounce the sovereign will of the people, expressed or implied in the Constitution, which is superior to both. . . .

SPEECH OF MR. VARNUM:

. . . And sir, notwithstanding the entire dependence on the Legislature [of New Hampshire] for the existence of the court of common pleas, I cannot imagine that the independence of the judges has ever been affected by it. There is an honorable gentleman from that State now on this floor, a judge of one of those courts, who, with his associates, had the independence since the adoption of the Constitution, in their official capacity, to declare an act of the Legislature unconstitutional. This is a demonstration that the independence of the judge does not, in all cases, depend on the certainty of holding their offices, or on receiving the emoluments thereof for life. . . .

SPEECH OF MR. BACON:

. . . I may not deny but must frankly acknowledge the right of judicial officers of every grade to judge for themselves of the constitutionality of every statute on which they are called to act in their respective spheres. This is not only their right, but it is their indispensable duty thus to do. Nor is this the exclusive right and indispensable duty of the Judiciary department. It is equally the inherent and the indispensable duty of every officer, and I believe I may add, of every citizen of the United States. The Constitution is emphatically the law of the land. It certainly cannot be less so than the statute made present pursuant thereto. It is indeed paramount with us to all other human laws that can be made. In whatever capacity I may be called to act, where the law is the rule of my conduct, if two laws are found to clash with each other, in such case I cannot be governed by them both. Of necessity, therefore, I must either not act at all, or reject both, or else determine which shall give way. Should the Constitution and statute be found to contradict each other, the former, with me, must be preferred. . . .

The Judiciary are so far independent of the Legislative and Executive departments of the Government, that these, neither jointly or separately, have a right to prescribe, direct, or control its decisions. . . . The Judiciary have no more right to prescribe, direct or control the acts of the other departments of the Government, than the other departments of the Government have to prescribe or direct those of the Judiciary.

Source: Annals of Congress, 7th Cong., 1st Sess., 529–533, 536, 542–544, 552–554, 556–558, 567–568, 574–576, 595–596, 614–615, 645–648, 650, 661–662, 689–691, 698–702, 727–728, 739–741, 743, 747–748, 754–757, 759–760, 783–787, 823–824, 826, 841–842, 859, 861, 865–866, 875, 876, 879–881, 884, 903–905, 918–932, 935, 940–941, 947–948, 973, 982–983.

72 Congressional Debate over the Judiciary Act of 1802

SPEECH OF MR. GILES:

. . . No man values more highly than I do the independence of the judges; but the question is a question of supremacy; they are to be made supreme! They are to control all your laws!

SPEECH OF MR. BAYARD:

. . . The effect of the present bill will be, to have no court for fourteen months. Is this Constitutional? . . . Are gentlemen afraid of the judges? Are they afraid that they will pronounce the repealing law void? If gentlemen think they have no such power, they will conclude that any interposition of the judges will be rejected by the good sense of the people; and if they have such a power, are they prepared, on a mere political pretense, to deprive them of it? . . .

SPEECH OF MR. NICHOLSON:

I have no hesitation to declare, that I am not afraid of the exercise of any Constitutional authority of the judges. Such authority can be exercised in February as in June. . . . As far as regards myself, I care not whether they pronounce the repealing law unconstitutional or not, though I should regret such an act, as I wish harmony to prevail between all the departments of the Government. . . .

SPEECH OF MR. GRISWOLD:

. . . I cannot believe that this House is afraid of having a session of the Supreme Court in June. . . . For my part, I have strong reasons for wishing a session in June. I believe the repealing act is a usurpation of power by the Legislature;

and, whenever I see a usurpation, I think the speedier it is checked the better. . . .

SPEECH OF MR. BACON:
I apprehend the gentleman need not labor very hard to dispel the fears entertained by a sitting of the Supreme Court. I apprehend there is no cause of fear. . . . [I]f the repealing act be unconstitutional, it is no law, and not in the way of their meeting. If it is so considered by the judges, they will meet together, of course. . . .

Source: *Annals of Congress*, 7th Cong., 1st Sess., 1222, 1229–1230.

---

73   An Act to Amend the Judicial System of the United States

[SEC. 1.] . . . That from and after the passing of this act, the Supreme Court of the United States . . . shall have one session in each and every year, to commence on the first Monday of February annually. . . .

SEC. 9. That all actions, causes, pleas, process and other proceedings relative to any cause, civil or criminal, which shall be returnable to, or depending in the several circuit or district courts of the United States on the first day of July next, shall be and are hereby declared to be respectively transferred, returned and continued to the several circuit and district courts constituted by this act. . . .

Source: *U.S. Statutes at Large*. 1802. Vol. 2: 156, 163.

---

74   Protest of Richard Bassett, 1802

. . . [T]hose acts of the 8th of March and 29th April, 1802, have *not abolished the offices of the judges of the Circuit Courts of the United States*, created and perfected under the act of February, 1801; but that they do exist in full force, as at first, protected against legislative destruction, by the CONSTITUTION OF THE UNITED STATES. . . .

. . . [T]he judges of the United States cannot be deprived of their offices by the *legislative* body; or in any other way than by *impeachment* before the Senate, or on conviction of MISBEHAVIOUR in office. . . .

It was easy to perceive, that a legislative body, which held in its hands the *offices and livings* of those who were to decide whether their acts were contrary to the constitutional law, would at any time command the constitution, and make it yield to their wishes and views. If their law was resisted by the judiciary, as violating the superior law of the constitution, there would be no difficulty in asserting, that the obnoxious judges were *unnecessary*, or too *expensive*, or that a *better system* could be framed:—And *judges* would soon be found more pliant to the governing powers. . . .

It has been made a question, whether the judiciary can lawfully decide, that a legislative act is contrary to the constitution, and, for that reason, hold it void. It has been said, that it must be obeyed; that the judges of the United States are bound to yield to it and execute it. . . .

If, then, the *constitution*, is the *supreme law*, the *judicial* department, in whom is vested, by the same instrument, the *right* and *duty* of expounding and enforcing the law, must necessarily be governed by it.

Whenever any question, however, or wherever it may originate, comes before the judges, they must *decide* according to *law*.

If the controversy happen to turn upon the *opposing* terms of the *constitution*, and the *act* of the legislative body, still the judges must decide, and decide *according to law*.

The executive, or legislative, may err; they may, like other men, from inadvertency, from error of opinion, from some too prevalent bias, or from design, commit an *unconstitutional act*. Every citizen, and every state is entitled to the benefits of the constitution, which is declared the supreme law, and the judicial power of the United States, is that organ, and independent branch of the government whose duty and right it is, to pronounce and execute the *laws*. . . .

If one side insists upon the *act of congress*, and the other upon the *act of the people*, as contained in the constitution, the judges are required, by the nature of their office, by a positive *oath*, and by *express articles* in the latter instrument, to support it as the *supreme* or governing law; and to reject and declare void whatever is contrary to it in the act of the legislature body, or other authority, subordinate to the constitution.

It can be said, that the judges may err, and determine measures and acts to be contrary to the constitution which are not so.

Certainly the judicial department *may* decide wrong. All human tribunals are liable to error. The executive may err, and the legislative often err. But there must be *somewhere* a power to determine what *is the law* of the land, and thereby to settle and quiet, whether right or wrong, legal *rights* and *constructions*. Force and the sword, or some CIVIL JURISDICTION must finally adjust these domestic controversies.

Wise and free people, with free forms of government, have confided this important, but *essential* power, to their JUDICIAL institutions.

. . . [B]ecause there *must* be some *umpire*, to settle "*what is law*," the judicial branch, in the last resort, is that which decides without appeal.

The people, indeed, by a constitutional act, may, if the occasion demands it, correct an error even here. But until then, every department, every officer, every citizen of the United States, is bound to yield to the sentence of the judicial department, judicially declaring what *is the law*. . . .

The judges, who are called in to execute such an act in *any* way, are bound to consider, whether it was constitutional. If they are of opinion it was not, then they are to refuse any *co-operation*, which would effectuate, or tend to effectuate the consequences and designs proposed by the prohibited act of the legislature. . . .

Source: Richard Bassett, *The Protest of the Hon. Richard Bassett* (Philadelphia: Bronson and Chauncey, 1802), 5–6, 7–8, 17, 20–21, 29–34, 40–44.

---

75 Petition of the Judges

. . . [T]he undersigned, after the most deliberate consideration, are compelled to represent it as their opinion, that the rights secured to them by the Constitution, as members of the Judicial department, have been impaired.

With this sincere conviction, and influenced by a sense of public duty, they most respectively request of Congress to review the existing laws which respect the office in question, and to define the duties to be performed by the undersigned, by such provisions as shall be consistent with the Constitution, and the convenient administration of justice.

The right of the undersigned to their compensations, they sincerely believe to be secured by the Constitution, notwithstanding any modification of the Judicial Department, which, in the opinion of Congress, public convenience may recommend. This right, however, involving a personal interest, will be cheerfully submitted to judicial examination and impartiality, in such manner as the wisdom and impartiality of Congress may prescribe.

That judges should not be deprived of their offices or compensations without misbehaviour appears to the undersigned, to be among the first and best established principles in the American constitutions; and in the various reforms they have undergone, it has been preserved and guarded with increased solicitude. . . .

Source: Annals of Congress, 7th Cong., 2d Sess., 30–31.

76 Committee Report

That the petitioners were judges of certain courts, inferior to the Supreme Court, constituted by an act of the 13th of February, 1801, and duly commissioned to hold their offices during good behaviour.

That, while holding and exercising their offices, an act was passed on the 8th of March, last, to repeal the said act of the 13th February, 1801, and transfer the duties of the said judges from them to others.

That a question has arisen whether, by reason of the premises, the said petitioners be deprived of their offices.

That this question, depending on the construction of the laws and Constitution of the United States, is not properly cognizable by the Senate.

The committee, therefore, conceive it improper either to give reasons or express opinions; but they consider it as a question of high and serious import, and believe that a speedy investigation and final decision is of great moment to the commonwealth.

Wherefore, they submit the following resolution:

Resolved, That the President of the United States be requested to cause an information . . . to be filed by the Attorney General against Richard Bassett . . . for the purpose of deciding judicially on their claims.

Source: Annals of Congress, 7th Cong., 2d Sess., 51–52.

77   **Senate Debate on the Judges' Petition**

SPEECH OF MR. MORRIS:

. . . Gentlemen will perceive that the question which the memorialists have submitted to our investigation is, whether the law of last session has deprived them of their office of judge. Your committee consider this question as not being cognizable by the Senate. It is not for the Senate, nor the Representatives, nor both combined, to interpret their own acts. . . .

. . . They consider this question as cognizable by the Judiciary alone. It is gone from us forever; and is, from the nature of things, before the Judiciary, in common with all other laws. . . .

. . . Will the judges rudely declare that you have violated the Constitution unmindful of your duty, and regardless of your oath? No. . . . They will never presume to believe, much less to declare, that you meant to violate the Constitution. . . . They will declare, that in assigning duties to one officer, and taking them from another, you have to consult only your own convictions of what the interest or convenience of the people may require.— They will modestly conclude, that you did not mean to abolish the offices which the Constitution had forbidden you to abolish; and therefore, finding that it was not your intention to abolish, they will declare that the offices still exist. . . .

. . . There was a time when the American Legislature submitted their acts to Judicial decision. At that time Washington presided. . . .

SPEECH OF MR. COCKE:

. . . [W]e have no right as a part of the Executive, to order or request the President to do this. . . .

. . . The people don't want these judges as guardians to protect them from the other House, nor from this House, nor any body else. . . .

SPEECH OF MR. WRIGHT:

. . . Have the Senate any authority to advise him as to the faithful execution of the laws? . . . If the courts have power to try the validity of laws of Congress, they can exercise that power as well without the authority of this resolution as with it. If they have not the power, neither this House nor the Legislature can give it [to] them.

SPEECH OF MR. OGDEN:

. . . [T]he Senate, in this resolution, do not advise the President. He is only requested to procure for the Senate judicial information and a legal decision upon a matter in controversy from a forum which is competent to decide in a case where the discussion here would be improper and out of order. . . .

. . . [T]he people do need a protection against Government, and that courts are their shields against oppression, as well as swords for the execution of the law. The hand of Government is large and broad, and heavy; courts are necessary to defend the people, against its violence; they stand between the people and the Government— through this medium only, can the rights of the citizen be assailed while even a semblance of the Constitution remains. . . .

SPEECH OF MR. JACKSON:

. . . The courts have no power to control the proceedings of the legislature or the Executive. . . .

. . . But I contend further, sir, that if we should even adopt this resolution and the President should instruct the Attorney General to file the information, the Supreme Court have no power to decide the controversy. By turning to that common law which the gentlemen think so highly of, will be seen that, in England, the judges cannot control an act of Parliament. . . .

SPEECH OF MR. ROSS:

. . . [I]t was with infinite surprise and regret, that . . . he had heard this authority of the courts questioned and denied by men of high influence in the national councils. In his apprehension, this new doctrine was not only incorrect, but of the most dangerous tendency. . . .

. . . Suppose such laws pass in direct violation of the Constitution, where is the remedy if the gentleman's doctrine of Legislative supremacy be right? Not in Congress, for they are the wrong-doers; not in the President, for he is the organ to execute, not to interpret, the laws; not in the States, for they might so differ that no two would exactly agree, and this would lead to the most furious and destructive disputes; not in the people, for there is no mode of collecting their opinions. The Judiciary, then, seems to be the only body to which we could look to protection from such laws; their agency becomes necessary to give the laws complete effect upon individuals. The Constitution is the supreme law: it is the duty of a judge to compare acts of the Legislature with this great charter, and pronounce whether the special delegated power has been exceeded or not. The Constitution expressly directs them to take cognizance of all cases arising under the Constitution and laws of the United States. If, then, a citizen be sued before a court of the United States for a tax imposed upon the produce of his farm when exported: if he be prosecuted under an *ex post facto* law; or arrested under a bill of attainder, will any Senator rise and say, that a court sworn to support the Constitution, is nevertheless bound to give judgment for the prohibited tax, and to send the man to execution who has been attainted without a trial? Either the law or the Constitution is a nullity. If the new doctrine be true the law must prevail. If so, why provide any prohibitions or exceptions in a Constitution, and why ask any solemn pledge to support it? The court, when pressed for its judgment, must declare which shall prevail, and if they do their duty they will certainly say, that a law at variance with the Constitution is utterly void; it is made without authority and cannot be executed. By doing so the court do not control or prostrate the just authority of Congress. It is the will of the people expressed in the Constitution which controls them. . . .

. . . We are not the legal tribunal for trying the rights of citizens. Send it then to the courts. . . .

SPEECH OF MR. MORRIS:
. . . I am not now competent to decide on that law. This is the province and the duty of the judge. I feel it my duty, as a citizen, to obey; and believe that all of us owe to our fellow-citizens an example of obedience, of respect, and submission. . . .

SPEECH OF MR. JACKSON:
. . . judges have no power to control the acts and laws of the Legislature. . . .

Source: Annals of Congress, 7th Cong., 2d Sess., 53, 55–58, 60, 62–64, 66, 69–72, 75–77.

78   House Debate on the Judges' Petition

SPEECH OF MR. RANDOLPH:
. . . It is a broad Constitutional question. He was, therefore, in favor of having it examined, where it must eventually be settled, in the House. . . .

SPEECH OF MR. GRISWOLD:
. . . It is the opinion of some very respectable legal characters that though Congress may deprive the judges of all their powers, yet they cannot deprive them of their offices, and their char-

acters of judges, and that they are still entitled to their salaries. . . . [A]nd so long as such opinions are entertained, an impartial tribunal ought to be established to decide the question. I cannot see any objection to such a tribunal. . . . I have no objection to the reference of this question to the Supreme Court. . . .

SPEECH OF MR. T. MORRIS:
. . . The repealing law may be Constitutional or not. Why, then, refuse to refer the decision to an impartial tribunal? . . .

SPEECH OF MR. JOHN C. SMITH:
. . . He said it would be remembered that, at a certain period the judges of the Supreme Court were directed by an act of Congress to receive on their circuits the evidence of claims to invalid pensions, and report their evidence to the Secretary of War for his ultimate determination. Some one or more of the judges considered the act unconstitutional, as requiring them to perform a service not within the sphere of their official duties, and refused to execute it; the others discharged the duty enjoined, but under the title of commissioners. A question arose whether the proceedings of these commissioners were valid so as to entitle the claimants to the provision contemplated by the act. How was this question disposed of? Instead of putting an end at once to all doubts on the subject by a legislative decision, Congress directed the Secretary of War, in conjunction with the Attorney General, to take such measures as might be necessary to obtain an adjudication of the Supreme Court of the United States on the validity of any such rights as were claimed under that act. Here, said Mr. S., is a precedent for the measure now proposed, produced by an occasion of infinitely less importance, in his opinion, than the present. He considered the judges as standing on at least as high ground as ordinary claimants. . . .

SPEECH BY MR. SMILIE:
Mr. Smilie would ask whether the Supreme Court in such a case as this would be denominated an impartial tribunal? . . .

SPEECH BY MR. NICHOLSON:
. . . The resolution contemplated giving the power to try the right of the judges to their claims; but the great object in reality was to authorize the judges of the Supreme Court to decide upon the unconstitutionality of the repealing act. Let this object, then, be avowed; let it be so declared openly, and not introduced in this incidental manner. From the remarks made last year by gentlemen on the other side of the House, it was a little surprising that this application should be made, for it was then strenuously contended that the Supreme Court had the right to decide upon the constitutionality of all laws. Why, then, ask for it? If they have this right we need not confer it; if they have it not, we cannot give it them. If the petitioning judges can bring their case before the Supreme Court, let them do so; my consent shall never authorize it. If the Supreme Court shall arrogate this power to themselves, and declare our law to be unconstitutional, it will then behoove us to act. Our duty is defined. . . .

SPEECH OF MR. DANA:
. . . Why object, then, in a case where there was a difference of opinion, to refer the decision to an impartial tribunal? . . .

Source: Annals of Congress, 7th Cong., 2d Sess., 428, 434–438.

79

Petition of William Marbury and Others, January 28, 1803

To the Honorable the Senate of the United States of America, the petition of William Marbury, Robert Townsend Hooe, and Dennis Ramsay, most respectfully showeth:

That your petitioners have been informed and verily believe that John Adams, while President of the United States, nominated to the Senate of the United States, for their advice and consent, your petitioner William Marbury, to be a justice of the peace. . .; that the said nominations were duly taken into consideration by the Senate . . . were pleased to give their advice and consent that your petitioners should be severally appointed to the offices aforesaid; that commissions were accordingly in due form signed by the said President, and directed to be sent to your petitioners by the Secretary of State, but that your petitioners, from some cause have been deprived of their commissions, and are reduced to the necessity of asserting their rights to the same in a judicial course of

proceeding, in which, as they are advised, it will be requisite to produce satisfactory evidence of the advice and consent of the Senate to the appointment of your petitioners to be justices of the peace as aforesaid in the District of Columbia. Application has been made to the Secretary of the Senate for his certificate that the advice and consent of the Senate was given in consequence of the nominations aforesaid, that your petitioners should be appointed to be justices of the peace in the District of Columbia aforesaid, which your Secretary has declined giving without the leave of the Senate. Your petitioners pray the promises may be taken into consideration, and that your Secretary may be permitted to give to your petitioners a certificate in usual form, setting forth that your petitioners having been nominated by the President of the United States to the aforesaid offices severally and respectively of justices of the peace in the District of Columbia, the Senate advised and consented to their appointment. . . .

Source: Annals of Congress, 7th Cong., 2d Sess., 32–33.

80

Senate Debate on Marbury's Petition

SPEECH OF MR. JACKSON:
. . . He considered it now, as he then did, an attack upon the Executive Department of Government, and as such should be prepared to oppose it, as often, and in whatever shape it might present itself.

SPEECH OF MR. MASON:
. . . Publicity of record was a Constitutional provision, and a check in favor of the people. It was

a right belonging to the meanest citizen to inspect the records of the Government, unless the divulging of these records would be inconsistent with the public safety and interest. . . . This request is so accordant with a common sense of justice, that he had no doubt the mere exemplification of a record, or a certified copy, in itself not improper to be made public, would be granted by one enemy to another, in an enemy's country. Mr. M was at a loss to know what possible injury could arise by giving a copy of a fact as notorious, and he hoped therefore the parties would be indulged.

SPEECH OF MR. BRECKENRIDGE:

. . . The Executive Journal is kept only for the private use of the Senate and there is an express rule that extracts should not be given without the order of the House. . . . As to the case in question, to grant the prayer of the petition would, he said, administer to the means of assailing the Executive Department of the Government. He considered the President as in some measure a party to the Executive Journal, and therefore an extract of it ought not to be communicated without his consent. The Senate ought to protect the dignity of that branch in which they participate. The suit is now pending on a mandamus to the Secretary of State. The Senate ought not to aid the Judiciary in their invasion of the rights of the Executive. . . .

SPEECH OF MR. MORRIS:

. . . [H]e considered the application of a suitor for evidence to support his right, as of a very serious nature. A denial of that evidence might amount to a denial of justice. . . .

SPEECH OF MR. WRIGHT:

. . . The Senate had by a specific rule declared the Executive records a secret. But he could not conceive what benefit they (the petitioners) could derive from an extract if they obtained it. They ask that the Secretary of the Senate may be allowed to certify facts from the Executive record; but the Supreme Court, nor no court, would admit such a certificate as testimony, because the Secretary has no seal. . . . It was well known why this certificate was requested. It was to aid in an audacious attempt to pry into Executive secrets, by a tribunal which had no authority to do any such thing: and to enable the Supreme Court to assume an unheard of and unbounded power, if not despotism. It was to enable the Judiciary to exercise an authority over the President, which he could never consent to. It was well known that

the persons applying were enemies to the President, and that the court were not friendly to him, and, under these circumstances, to interfere in the business would be making the Senate a party. No court on earth could control the Legislature, and yet it had been held here on this floor that they could, and this was a part of the same attempt to set the court above the President, and to cast a stigma upon him. The President had a right to withhold the commissions from these justices, because they did not hold their offices *de bene merito*, but *de bene placito*.

SPEECH OF MR. HILLHOUSE:

. . . It is said there is a cause pending before the Supreme Court of the United States, in which it is important to ascertain the fact, that the Senate did advise and consent to the appointment of the individuals named in this application to be justices of the peace for this territory, and a copy of the journal of the Senate is requested for that purpose—the journals of the Senate being the only evidence of the fact, can that evidence with propriety be withheld? . . .

SPEECH OF MR. JACKSON:

. . . But he thought the commission of the President was the only evidence of an appointment and in all cases conclusive. And he would never lend his aid to set the Judiciary above the Executive. . . .

SPEECH OF MR. BRECKENRIDGE:

. . . That the Senate should not countenance the Judiciary in their attack on the Executive power, which is not constitutionally amenable to the judges. . . . That it was dangerous to countenance the pretensions set up by the judges to examine into the conduct of other branches of the Government; for that, if they had a right to examine, they must have, as a necessary incident, the right to control, the other departments of Government. That such right was inconsistent with every idea of good government, and must necessarily degrade those branches which the Judiciary should thus undertake to direct. The present suit was therefore levelled at the dignity of the first Executive Magistrate, and as he thought the Senate bound to protect that dignity, he should vote against the resolution.

SPEECH OF MR. TRACY:

. . . He could not possibly discover the reason of all the ferment and sensibility about the President. Was he in danger, or could he be in danger from it? If an improper attack was made upon the President, he would agree that so far from assisting in it the Senate should rally in his defence.

. . . The court was authorized by statute of Federal Legislature, among other things, to issue writs of mandamus, in cases warranted by the principles and usages of law, to any courts appointed, or persons holding offices under the authority of the United States. . . .

He was clear in the position that, in the case stated, the petitioners would stand in need of the extract requested, and that they had a right to it; that granting it would do no harm, and withholding it would be an arbitrary denial of justice. He therefore should vote for the resolution.

SPEECH OF MR. BALDWIN:

. . . That the present case was an application for a *mandamus* to the Secretary of State, by persons conceiving or stating themselves to be justices of the peace; that, even if they could obtain the extract they ask for, it would not answer their purpose; for, although the Senate approved of an officer when nominated by the President, it did not follow that the President would make the appointment—circumstances might arise to alter his opinion. . . .

SPEECH OF MR. MORRIS:

. . . [T]he gentlemen say the dignity of the President is involved, and that we are in duty bound to protect his dignity. But how? What have the petitioners asked? They have asked the evidence of a fact. And how are we to protect the Presi-

dent's dignity? By withholding that evidence. And are gentlemen then of opinion that the disclosure of facts will impair the dignity of our First Magistrate? Sir, I have no such apprehension. I trust that our President has acted properly, and that a full inquiry into facts must redound to his honor. Those who oppose this resolution seem to think otherwise. But I ask, are they prepared by their vote to declare that injurious opinion? Is there a gentleman in this Senate, who, when the yeas and nays are called, will record his opinion that the dignity of our President can only be preserved by withholding the evidence of facts? . . .

. . . It appears to me, sir, that this Senate is not the proper tribunal, either to examine the merits of the cause, or the validity and weight of the evidence. These are proper subjects of inquiry elsewhere. . . .

. . . I hope that when the rights of American citizens are invaded, not only the Supreme Court of the United States, but the lowest county court of the most remote district will dare to examine, to judge, and to redress. . . .

SPEECH OF MR. CLINTON:

. . . The Executive Journal from the very nature of it was always secret. This secrecy never ought to be violated, unless some useful purpose was thereby to be attained. In the present case it was very evident to him that the copy prayed for could be of no real use to the petitioners. Giving them a copy of the Journal would, however, be an expression of the Senate's opinion that the testimony would be proper and useful in the suit of the petitioners. By a side-wind the Senate would thus be drawn to give their weight to one side of the cause. . . .

SPEECH OF MR. ROSS:

. . . There was an end of all free and regular Government, if a commission from the President was conclusive evidence of a right to office against the journals of the Senate. There was an end to the Constitutional power of legislation, if the President's proclamation of treaties constituted the supreme law of the land, when the journals of the Senate showed that more than one-third of the Senate had voted against the acceptance and ratification of the treaty. . . .

Source: *Annals of Congress*, 7th Cong., 2d Sess., 34, 35–37, 40, 42, 44, 46–50.

81

Chief Justice Marshall and Justices Paterson, Cushing, and Chase

John Marshall to William Paterson, April 19, 1802

. . . I hope I need not say that no man in existence respects more than I do, those who passd the original law concerning the courts of the United States, & those who first acted under it. So highly do I respect their opinions that I had not examined them & shoud have p(roceed)ed without a doubt on the subject, to perform the duties assignd to me if the late discussions had not unavoidably produced an investigation of the subject which from me it woud not otherwise have received. The result of this investigation has been an opinion which I cannot conquer that the constitution requires distinct appointments & commissions for the Judges of the inferior courts from those of the supreme court. It is however my duty & my inclination in this as in all other cases to be bound by the opinion of the majority of the Judges & I shoud therefore have proceeded to execute the law so far as that task may be assigned to me; had I not supposd it possible that the Judges might be inclind to distinguish between the original case of being appointed to duties markd out before their appointments & of having the duties of administering justice in new courts imposd after their appointments. . . .

Samuel Chase to John Marshall, April 24, 1802

. . . It is a *great doubt* with me, whether the Circuit Courts, established by the Law, can be *abolished*; but I have *no doubt*, that the Circuit Judges cannot, *directly*, or *indirectly*, be deprived of their *Offices*, or *Commissions*, or *Salaries*, during their *lives*; unless only on impeachment for, and conviction of, high Crimes and Misdemeanours, as prescribed in the Constitution. As the Act of Congress evidently intended to *remove* the Circuit Judges from their Offices, and to take away their Salaries, I am of opinion that it is *void*. The distinction of taking the Office from the Judge, and not the Judge from the Office, I consider as puerile, and nonsensical. . . .

. . . The Constitution of the United States is certainly a *limited* Constitution; because (in Art. 1 s. 9.) it *expressly prohibits* Congress from making *certain enumerated Laws*; and also from doing certain specified Acts, in *many* cases; and it is very evident that these restrictions on the *Legislative* power of Congress would be entirely nugatory, and merely waste paper, if there exists no power, under the Constitution, to declare Acts made, *contrary to these express prohibitions*, null and void. It is equally clear that the *limitations* of the power of Congress can only be preserved by the *Judicial* power. There can be no other rational, peaceable and secure barrier against violations of the Constitution by the Legislature, or against encroachments by it on the Executive, or on the *Judiciary* branches of our Government. . . . It appears to me, that the repealing Act, *so far*, as it contemplates to affect the appointment, commission, and office, or Salary of any of the Judges of the Circuit Courts, is contrary to the Constitution, and is therefore, *so far*, void. . . .

I have *three* objections to the Judges of the supreme Court holding the Circuit Courts. First.

If the repealing Law has not *abolished* the Circuit Courts . . . and if the repealing Act has not destroyed the Office of the Judges appointed, commissioned and qualified under the Law repealed; it follows that the Offices of these Judges are *now full*; and consequently no Judge of the Supreme Court . . . holding this opinion can exercise the Office of a Judge of such Courts, without violating the Constitution. Secondly—If the repealing Act be void, *so* far, as it intends to destroy the Office of the Judges under the Law repealed, and a Judge of the Supreme Court . . . should hold the Circuit Court, I think he would, thereby, be *instrumental* to carry into effect an *unconstitutional* Law. . . .

[Thirdly] . . . I think . . . that a Judge of the Supreme Court cannot accept, and act under, a Commission, as *Judge* of a *Circuit Court*. . . . Congress cannot, by Law, give the Judges of the Supreme Court, *original* Jurisdiction of the *same* Cases of which it *expressly* gives them *appellate* Jurisdiction. . . .

Unless the sentiments of my Brethren should induce me to change my present opinion, I shall certainly decline to take the Circuit assigned me. . . .

William Cushing to Samuel Chase, n.d.

. . . [C]an we, after Eleven years of practical exposition of the Laws & Constitution by all federal Judges, now say, that Congress has not power to direct a Judge of the Sup Court to act with a Dt Judge in an inferiour Court, with or without a Commission, yet making one of the Sup bench to hold appellate Jurisdiction? I think

we cannot. As to being instrumental (by taking the Circuits) in violating the rights of the Judges & the Constitution. I do not see that it carries that inference. It is not in our power to restore to them their Salaries or them to the exercise of their Offices. Declining the Circuits will have no tendency to do either. We violate not the Constitution. We only do duties assigned us by Constitutional authority. . . .

William Paterson to John Marshall, n.d.

. . . On the constitutional right of the Judges of the supreme court to sit as circuit court judges, my opin[i]on coincides with Judge Washington's. Practic[e] has fixed construction, which it is too late to disturb. If open for discussion, it would merit serious consideration; but the practical exposition is too old and strong & obstinate to be shaken or controled.

John Marshall to William Paterson, May 3, 1802

. . . Mr. Washington also states it as his opinion that the question respecting the constitutional right of the Judges of the supreme court to sit as circuit Judges ought to be considered as settled & shoud not again be movd. I have no doubt myself but that policy dictates this decision to us all. Judges however are of all men those who have the least right to obey her dictates. I own I shall be privately gratified if such shoud be the opinion of the majority & I shall with much pleasure acquiesce in it; tho, if the subject has never been discussd, I shoud feel greatly embarasd about it myself.

Source: John Marshall, *The Papers of John Marshall*, ed. Charles F. Hobson (Chapel Hill: University of North Carolina Press, 1990) vol. 6: 108–109, 116–118, 118 n. 6, 166 n. 5.

82

Stuart v. Laird (1803)

John Laird successfully sued Hugh Stuart for breach of contract in the federal circuit court of Virginia established by the Judiciary Act of 1801. Before Laird could have that judgment executed, the Judiciary Act of 1801 was repealed and new federal circuit courts were established by the Judiciary Act of 1802. Stuart claimed that his case could not be transferred to the new circuit courts. Charles Lee, who represented both Stuart and William Marbury, asserted that the courts established by the Judiciary Act of 1802 were unconstitutional. The Repeal Act, he maintained, unconstitutionally deprived the justices appointed under the Judiciary Act of 1801 of their offices, and the Judiciary Act of 1802 unconstitutionally required Supreme Court justices to serve as circuit court justices. Other Federalist lawyers litigating in the federal courts during the fall of 1802 made similar arguments. These claims were typically withdrawn after private consultations with the Supreme Court justice riding the local circuit. Chief Justice John Marshall was the exception. Acting as a circuit court justice, Marshall decided and rejected Stuart's claim without issuing an opinion. Stuart then appealed to the Supreme Court.

The Court unanimously decided that Laird was entitled to judgment. Stuart v. Laird holds that Congress may transfer cases from one federal court to another, and that past practice established the constitutionality of Supreme Court justices riding circuit. The justices did not determine whether Congress could repeal the Judiciary Act of 1801. Marshall Court justices never publicly commented on whether the Repeal Act was constitutional.

Opinion of Mr. Justice Paterson

. . . Congress have constitutional authority to establish from time to time such inferior tribunals as they may think proper; and to transfer a cause from one such tribunal to another. In this last particular, there are no words in the constitution to prohibit or restrain the exercise of legislative power. . . .

. . . Another reason for reversal is, that the judges of the supreme court have no right to sit as judges, not being appointed as such, or in other words, that they ought to have distinct commissions for that purpose. To this objection, which is of recent date, it is sufficient to observe, that practice and acquiescence under it for a period of several years, commencing with the organization of the judicial system, affords an irresistable answer, and has indeed fixed the construction. It is a contemporary interpretation of the most forcible nature. This practical exposition is too strong and obstinate to be shaken or controlled. Of course, the question is at rest, and ought not now to be disturbed.

Source: Stuart v. Laird, 5 U.S. 299, 308–309.

Section V (Documents 83–99):
The Legal History of Marbury

Marbury v. Madison has lived many legal lives. Before the Civil War, that decision was almost exclusively cited in cases concerning federal civil procedure. This *Marbury* was about the constitutional rules governing the jurisdiction of the Supreme Court and the conditions under which that tribunal could issue various writs to other governing officials. From the Civil War to the New Deal, Chief Justice John Marshall's opinion continued to be cited in cases concerning federal civil procedure and was also prominently featured in cases involving federal office holding. This *Marbury* was about the conditions under which the president could fire various civil servants and government officials. From the late 1950s until the present, what Marshall called the "mandamus case" was less frequently cited in litigation concerning federal civil procedure and office holding but cited constantly in cases concerning judicial review and federal judicial authority to remedy constitutional wrongs. This contemporary *Marbury*, a *Marbury* born in *Cooper v. Aaron* (1958), is about the scope and significance of the judicial power to declare laws unconstitutional.

The frequency with which Supreme Court justices cite *Marbury* has changed over time. *Marbury* was not considered an important case before the Civil War. That decision was cited an average of only once every three years, typically in minor cases. The citation rate increased to almost once a year between 1860 and 1910, reflecting the greater presence of both the federal judiciary and *Marbury* in po-

litical life. The justices reverted to earlier citation patterns for the next three decades, citing *Marbury* only once every three years, and rarely in important cases. *Marbury* was only cited once in judicial opinions handed down between 1933 and 1942, a time when judicial decisions declaring major New Deal initiatives unconstitutional sparked an intense debate over the proper exercise of judicial review in a democracy. At the close of World War II, the citation rate for *Marbury* returned to late-nineteenth-century levels before increasing dramatically during the 1960s. More than 60 percent of all opinions citing *Marbury* were written between 1960 and 2002. *Marbury* was not cited in any opinion discussing judicial review written between 1803 and 1886, cited only seven times in opinions discussing judicial review written between 1887 and 1957, but cited seventy-two times in opinions discussing the topic in decisions written between 1958 and 2002.

Judicial citations to *Marbury* come in various shapes and sizes. The vast majority are to the *Marbury* opinion, but some refer to other aspects of the case. Justice Antonin Scalia cited *Marbury* in *Rutan v. Republican Party* (1990), noting that presidents use partisan criteria when making judicial appointments. Most citations play little role in the legal argument of the opinion, referring to generally agreed-upon principles established by *Marbury*. Numerous contemporary opinions cite *Marbury* as holding that courts have the power to declare laws unconstitutional, without saying more about that judicial prerogative. Several citations are part of judicial arguments that criticize or modify aspects of _Marbury_. Chief Justice Salmon Chase, for example, in _Ex parte Yerger_ (1868) questioned Marshall's conclusion that the justices lacked the jurisdiction necessary to issue the requested writ of mandamus. Many judicial citations to _Marbury_ interpret that opinion. Marshall and Justice William Johnson disputed the proper interpretation of _Marbury_ in _Ex parte Bollman_ (1807) when debating whether the Supreme Court in that case was exercising original or appellate jurisdiction.

The proper interpretation of _Marbury_ has been the subject of controversy for two hundred years. One bone of contention is the legal significance of various claims in that opinion. In _Cohens v. Virginia_ (1821), Marshall declared that the law of _Marbury_ consisted only of those legal claims in the opinion necessary to the outcome of that case. Other assertions in _Marbury_, he claimed, could be disregarded as the justices

saw fit. Prominent justices at the turn of the twentieth century claimed that, because the Supreme Court in _Marbury_ concluded that the justices lacked jurisdiction to issue a writ of mandamus, that part of the opinion discussing Marbury's right to a commission was unnecessary to the ultimate resolution of the case and not binding law. Contemporary justices dispute the proper interpretation of the judicial power to declare laws unconstitutional asserted in the case. _Marbury_ is the citation of choice for justices who support and justices who oppose various exercises of judicial review. Chief Justice Earl Warren's _Marbury_ is the case that established judicial supremacy and judicial review. Justice Hugo Black's _Marbury_ is the case that definitely rejected the use of natural law when interpreting constitutional norms. Numerous other versions of _Marbury_ appear in the excerpts below. How contemporary constitutionalists understand the proper judicial role in constitutional cases can usually be determined from how they interpret _Marbury v. Madison_.

83   *Ex parte Bollman* (1807)

In January 1807 Erick Bollman and Samuel Swartwout were arrested and charged with treason for allegedly playing prominent roles in Aaron Burr's scheme to form a new republic west of the Mississippi River. The federal court in the District of Columbia ordered that they be detained before trial without bail. Bollman and Swartwout asked the Supreme Court for a writ of habeas corpus challenging the legality of their confinement. The Court, incurring the displeasure of President Thomas Jefferson, granted the writ. Chief Justice John Marshall asserted that Marbury authorized the justices to grant various writs when exercising appellate jurisdiction. The writ was appropriate in Bollman, he claimed, because the justices were reviewing the lower court's decision to refuse bail. Justice William Johnson in dissent maintained that the writ could not constitutionally be granted consistently with Marbury. Bollman, Johnson argued, was a case of original or concurrent jurisdiction. The justices were not reviewing a lower court decision but were for the first time determining whether Bollman and Swartwout were entitled to the writ of habeas corpus. Johnson's dissent is notable both as the first judicial opinion to quote Marbury and for pointing out that the justices before 1803 had without constitutional objection taken jurisdiction in cases similar to Marbury.

Opinion of Chief Justice Marshall

... In the mandamus case, (... *Marbury*) it was decided that this court would not exercise original jurisdiction except so far as that jurisdiction was given by the constitution. But so far as that case has distinguished between original and appellate jurisdiction, that which the court is now asked to exercise is clearly appellate. It is the revision of a decision of an inferior court, by which a citizen has been committed to jail....

Dissenting Opinion of Justice Johnson

... The original jurisdiction of this court is restricted to cases affecting ambassadors or other public ministers, and consuls, and those in which a state shall be a party. In all other cases within the judicial powers of the union, it can exercise only an appellate jurisdiction. The former it possesses independently of the will of any other constituent branch of the general government. Without a violation of the constitution, that division of our jurisdiction can neither be restricted or extended. In the latter its powers are subjected to the will of the legislature of the union, and it can exercise appellate jurisdiction in no case, unless expressly authorised to do so by the laws of congress. If I understand the case of *Marbury*, it maintains this doctrine in its full extent....

... The claim of the prisoners, as founded on precedent, stands thus. The case of [*United States v.*] *Hamilton* [(1795)] was strikingly similar to the present. The prisoner had been committed by order of the district judge on a charge of high treason. A writ of habeas corpus was issued by the supreme court, and the prisoner bailed by their order....

It appears to my mind that the case of *Hamilton* bears upon the face of it evidence of its being entitled to little consideration, and that the authority of it was annihilated by the very able decision in *Marbury*. In this case it was decided that congress could not vest in the supreme court any original powers beyond those to which this court is restricted by the constitution. That an act of congress vesting in this court the power to issue a writ of mandamus in a case not within their original jurisdiction, and in which they were not called upon to exercise an appellate jurisdiction, was unconstitutional and void. In the case of *Hamilton*, ... it is fair to presume that they adopted the idea ... that this court possessed a concurrent power with the district court in admitting to bail. Now a concurrent power in such a case must be an original power, and the principle in *Marbury* applies as much to the issuing of a habeas corpus in a case of treason, as to the issuing of a mandamus in a case not more remote from the original jurisdiction of this court. . . .

. . . The 14th section of the judiciary act, so far as it has relation to this case, is in these words:— "All the beforementioned courts (of which this is one) of the United States shall have power to issue writs of scire facias, habeas corpus, and all other writs not specially provided for by statute, which may be necessary for the exercise of their respective jurisdictions, and agreeable to the

principles and usages of law." . . . If the power to issue the writs of scire facias and habeas corpus be not restricted to the cases within the original or appellate jurisdiction of this court, the case of *Marbury* rejects the clause as unavailing; and if it relate only to cases within their jurisdiction, it does not extend to the case which is now moved for. . . .

On considering this act it cannot be denied that if it vests any power at all, it is an original power. "It is the essential criterion of appellate jurisdiction, that it revises and corrects the proceedings in a cause already instituted." I quote the words of the court in the case of *Marbury*. . . .

Source: Ex parte Bollman (1808): 75, 100, 103–106.

84
Cohens v. Virginia (1821)

In 1820 brothers Mendes and Philip Cohen, both Maryland merchants, were convicted of violating a Virginia law that banned the sale of out-of-state lottery tickets. They appealed to the Supreme Court, claiming that the state law unconstitutionally discriminated against interstate commerce and was inconsistent with federal law. The state of Virginia asserted that the Supreme Court had no power to hear an appeal from a state criminal conviction. The Marshall Court unanimously declared that the Supreme Court had jurisdiction to hear the appeal but that Congress had not intended that congressionally sanctioned lottery tickets be sold in all jurisdictions.

In Cohens v. Virginia, Chief Justice John Marshall renounced some claims he had made in Marbury. His Marbury opinion maintained that the original and appellate jurisdictions of the Supreme Court were constitutionally exclusive. If the Constitution vested the justices with one kind of jurisdiction in particular cases, he had claimed, then the justices could not constitutionally exercise the other kind of jurisdiction in those cases. Article III explicitly vests the Supreme Court with original jurisdiction in cases such as Cohens where a state is a party. Marshall nevertheless justified the judicial exercise of appellate jurisdiction by noting that Article III entitled the Court to exercise appellate jurisdiction in cases arising under the Constitution or laws of the United States. Cohens was a case in which a constitutional ground existed for exercising original jurisdiction and a separate constitutional ground existed for exercising appellate jurisdiction. Under these circumstances, Marshall concluded, Congress could vest the Court with either original or appellate jurisdiction. Words to the contrary in Marbury were erroneous dicta that the Court had no legal obligation to follow in subsequent cases.

Opinion of Chief Justice Marshall

. . . This observation is not made for the purpose of contending, that the legislature may "apportion the judicial power between the Supreme and inferior Courts according to its will." That would be, as was said by this Court in the case of Mar-

bury, to render the distributive clause "mere surplusage," to make it "form without substance." This cannot, therefore, be the true construction of the article. . . . The original jurisdiction of this Court cannot be enlarged, but its appellate jurisdiction may be exercised in every case cognizable under the third article of the constitution, in the federal Courts, in which original jurisdiction cannot be exercised; and the extent of this judicial power is to be measured, not by giving the affirmative words of the distributive clause a negative operation in every possible case, but by giving their true meaning to the words which define its extent.

The counsel for the defendant in error urge, in opposition to this rule of construction, some dicta of the Court, in the case of *Marbury*.

It is a maxim not to be disregarded, that general expressions, in every opinion, are to be taken in connection with the case in which those expressions are used. If they go beyond the case, they may be respected, but ought not to control the judgment in a subsequent suit when the very point is presented for decision. The reason of this maxim is obvious. The question actually before the Court is investigated with care, and considered in its full extent. Other principles which may serve to illustrate it, are considered in their relation to the case decided, but their possible bearing on all other cases is seldom completely investigated.

In the case of *Marbury*, the single question before the Court, so far as that case can be applied to this, was, whether the legislature could give this Court original jurisdiction in a case in which the constitution had clearly not given it, and in which no doubt respecting the construction of the article could possibly be raised. The Court decided, and we think very properly, that the legislature could not give original jurisdiction in such a case. But, in the reasoning of the Court in support of this decision, some expressions are used which go far beyond it. The counsel for Marbury had insisted on the unlimited discretion of the legislature in the apportionment of the judicial power; and it is against this argument that the reasoning of the Court is directed. They say that, if such had been the intention of the article, "it would certainly have been useless to proceed farther than to define the judicial power, and the tribunals in which it should be vested." The Court says, that such a construction would render the clause, dividing the jurisdiction of the Court into original and appellate, totally useless; that "affirmative words are often, in their operation, negative of other objects than those which are affirmed; and, in this case, (in the case of *Marbury*) a negative or exclusive sense must be given to them, or they have no operation at all." "It cannot be presumed," adds the Court, "that any clause in the constitution is intended to be without effect; and, therefore, such a construction is inadmissible, unless the words require it."

The whole reasoning of the Court proceeds upon the idea that the affirmative words of the clause giving one sort of jurisdiction, must imply a negative of any other sort of jurisdiction, because otherwise the words would be totally inoperative, and this reasoning is advanced in a case to which it was strictly applicable. If in that case original jurisdiction could have been exercised, the clause under consideration would have been entirely useless. Having such cases only in its view, the Court lays down a principle which is generally correct, in terms much broader than the decision, and not only much broader than the reasoning with which that decision is supported, but in some instances contradictory to its principle. The reasoning sustains the negative operation of the words in that case, because otherwise the clause would have no meaning whatever, and because such operation was necessary to give effect to the intention of the article. The effort now made is, to apply the conclusion to which the Court was conducted by that reasoning in the particular case, to one in which the words have their full operation when understood affirmatively, and in which the negative, or exclusive sense, is to be so used as to defeat some of the great objects of the article.

To this construction the Court cannot give its assent. The general expressions in the case of *Marbury* must be understood with the limitations which are given to them in this opinion; limitations which in no degree affect the decision in that case, or the tenor of its reasoning. . . .

Source: Cohens v. Virginia (1821): 264, 394, 399–402.

85

Mississippi v. Johnson (1866)

Lawyers for the state of Mississippi asked the Supreme Court to issue an injunction forbidding President Andrew Johnson from implementing allegedly unconstitutional laws passed by Congress during Reconstruction. Counsel cited Marbury as supporting the judicial power to issue writs to executive officials. A unanimous Supreme Court rejected this appeal, holding that courts had no power to issue injunctions forbidding the president from executing a law. Chief Justice Salmon P. Chase distinguished Marbury. His opinion interpreted Marbury as holding that courts could order executive officials to perform only purely ministerial acts. Presidents, Chase maintained, exercised discretion when deciding how to execute laws. Johnson is a good example of the conditions under which Marbury has been interpreted as supporting and not supporting judicial decisions issuing writs to elected officials. Many scholars think Marbury, other cases decided during President Thomas Jefferson's first term, Johnson, and other cases decided during Reconstruction are also good examples of a judicial tendency to manipulate procedural rules to avoid challenging powerful political forces.

Opinion of Chief Justice Chase

. . . A ministerial duty, the performance of which may, in proper cases, be required of the head of a department, by judicial process, is one in respect to which nothing is left to discretion. It is a simple, definite duty, arising under conditions admitted or proved to exist, and imposed by law.

. . . *Marbury* furnishes an illustration. A citizen had been nominated, confirmed, and appointed a justice of the peace for the District of Columbia, and his commission had been made out, signed, and sealed. Nothing remained to be done except delivery, and the duty of delivery was imposed by law on the Secretary of State. It was held that the performance of this duty might be enforced by mandamus issuing from a court having jurisdiction. . . .

Very different is the duty of the President in the exercise of the power to see that the laws are faithfully executed, and among these laws the acts named in the bill. By the first of these acts he is required to assign generals to command in the several military districts, and to detail sufficient military force to enable such officers to discharge their duties under the law. By the supplementary act, other duties are imposed on the several commanding generals, and these duties must necessarily be performed under the supervision of the President as commander-in-chief. The duty thus imposed on the President is in no just sense ministerial. It is purely executive and political.

An attempt on the part of the judicial department of the government to enforce the performance of such duties by the President might be justly characterized, in the language of Chief Justice Marshal, as "an absurd and excessive extravagance." . . .

Source: Mississippi v. Johnson (1866): 475, 498–499.

86   *Ex parte Yerger* (1868)

Defendant Edward Yerger asked the Supreme Court for a writ of habeas corpus, denying the jurisdiction of a military commission in Mississippi to try him for murder. Congress had recently repealed the Judiciary Act of 1867 authorizing the Supreme Court to hear appeals from lower federal courts in habeas corpus cases. The constitutionality of that repeal was sustained in Ex parte McCardle *(1867). Yerger claimed he retained the right under the Judiciary Act of 1787 to have the Supreme Court hear his case on a direct petition from the states.*

The Supreme Court agreed that the justices had the necessary jurisdiction. Chief Justice Salmon P. Chase concluded that the federal law repealing the Judiciary Act of 1867 did not repeal the habeas corpus provisions in the Judiciary Act of 1789. His opinion is notable for claiming that, while Marbury was binding precedent, the decision when first made was probably wrong to conclude that Congress could not add to the original jurisdiction of the Supreme Court.

Opinion of Chief Justice Chase

. . . If the question were a new one, it would, perhaps, deserve inquiry whether Congress might not, under the power to make exceptions from this appellate jurisdiction, extend the original jurisdiction to other cases than those expressly enumerated in the Constitution; and especially, in view of the constitutional guaranty of the writ of habeas corpus, to cases arising upon petition for that writ.

But, in the case of *Marbury*, it was determined, upon full consideration, that the power to issue writs of mandamus, given to this court by the 13th section of the Judiciary Act, is, under the Constitution, an appellate jurisdiction, to be exercised only in the revision of judicial decisions. And this judgment has ever since been accepted as fixing the construction of this part of the Constitution. . . .

Source: Ex parte Yerger *(1868): 85, 97.*

87   *Mugler v. Kansas* (1887)

In 1881 Peter Mugler, a brewery owner, was arrested for violating a Kansas law that banned the manufacture and sale of intoxicant liquors. He appealed his state conviction to the Supreme Court, claiming that the Fourteenth Amendment protected his right to operate a brewery. The Court upheld his conviction, ruling that there was no constitutional right to manufacture or sell alcohol. Justice John Marshall Harlan's opinion for the Court is the first judicial statement after Marbury to interpret that decision as asserting a general judicial power to declare laws unconstitutional.

Opinion of Justice Harlan

. . . While every possible presumption is to be indulged in favor of the validity of a statute . . . , the courts must obey the Constitution rather than the law-making department of government, and must, upon their own responsibility, determine whether, in any particular case, these limits have been passed. "To what purpose," it was said in *Marbury* . . ., "are powers limited, and to what purpose is that limitation committed to writing, if these limits may, at any time, be passed by those intended to be restrained? The distinction between a government with limited and unlim-

ited powers is abolished, if those limits do not confine the persons on whom they are imposed, and if acts prohibited and acts allowed are of equal obligation." . . .

Source: Mugler v. Kansas (1887): 623, 661.

---

88   *Myers v. United States* (1926)

Frank Myers was appointed in 1917 to serve a four-year term as a postmaster in Portland, Oregon. Three years later, he was removed from office by President Woodrow Wilson. Myers sued for back salary, pointing out that postmasters under the relevant federal law could be removed from office only with the "advise and consent" of the Senate. The Court of Claims rejected his lawsuit, and an appeal was taken to the Supreme Court.

The Court sustained the lower court decision, declaring unconstitutional the federal statute requiring Senate consent for the removal of postmasters. The majority and dissenting opinions in Myers contain the most detailed discussion of Marbury in the U.S. Reports. Chief Justice William Howard Taft's majority opinion asserted that the discussion of federal office holding in Marbury was either dicta, erroneous, or overruled by Parsons v. United States (1897). Presidents, in his view, were constitutionally authorized to remove for any reason all executive branch employees. Justices Louis Brandeis and James McReynolds disagreed. Their dissenting opinions claimed that William Marbury's entitlement to his commission was part of the holding of Marbury v. Madison, that the case was correctly decided, and that Congress could limit the president's removal power.

Opinion of Chief Justice Taft

. . . The words of a second great constitutional authority, quoted as in conflict with the Congressional decision, are those of Chief Justice Marshall. They were used by him in his opinion in *Marbury*. . . . The judgment in that case is one of the great landmarks in the history of the construction of the Constitution of the United States, and is of supreme authority, first, in respect of the power and duty of the Supreme Court and other courts to consider and pass upon the validity of acts of Congress enacted in violation of the limitations of the Constitution, when properly brought before them in cases in which the rights of the litigating parties require such consideration and decision, and, second, in respect of the lack of power of Congress to vest in the Supreme Court original jurisdiction to grant the remedy of

mandamus in cases in which by the Constitution it is given only appellate jurisdiction. But it is not to be regarded as such authority in respect of the power of the President to remove officials appointed by the advice and consent of the Senate, for that question was not before the Court.

. . . The rule was discharged by the Supreme Court for the reason that the Court had no jurisdiction in such a case to issue a writ for mandamus. . . .

While everything that the great Chief Justice said, whether obiter dictum or not, challenges the highest and most respectful consideration, it is clear that the mere statement of the conclusion made by him, without any examination of the discussion which went on in the First Congress, and without reference to the elaborate arguments there advanced to maintain the decision of 1789, can not be regarded as authority in considering the weight to be attached to that decision—a decision, which as we shall see, he subsequently recognized as a well-established rule of constitutional construction.

In such a case we may well recur to the Chief Justice's own language in *Cohens v. Virginia*, . . . in which, in declining to yield to the force of his previous language in *Marbury*, which was unnecessary to the judgment in that case and was obiter dictum. . . .

The weight of this dictum of the Chief Justice as to a Presidential removal, in *Marbury*, was considered by this Court in *Parsons v. United States.* . . .

The language of the Court in *Marbury*, already referred to, was pressed upon this Court to show that Parsons was entitled, against the Presidential action of removal, to continue in office. If it was authoritative and stated the law as to an executive office, it ended the case; but this Court did not recognize it as such, for the reason that the Chief Justice's language relied on was not germane to the point decided in *Marbury*. If his language was more than a dictum, and was a decision, then the Parson's case overrules it.

Another distinction, suggested by Mr. Justice Peckham in Parson's case was that the remarks of the Chief Justice were in reference to an office in the District of Columbia, over which . . . Congress had exclusive jurisdiction in all cases, and might not apply to offices outside of the District in respect to which the constant practice and the Congressional decision had been the other way. . . . How much weight should be given to this distinction, which might accord to the special exclusive jurisdiction conferred on Congress over the District power to ignore the usual constitutional separation between the executive and legislative branches of the Government, we need not consider.

If the Chief Justice, in *Marbury* intended to express an opinion for the Court inconsistent with the legislative decision of 1789, it is enough to observe that he changed his mind; for otherwise it is inconceivable that he should have written and printed his full account of the discussion and decision in the First Congress and his acquiescence in it, to be found in his *Life of Washington*. . . .

"After an ardent discussion which consumed several days, the committee divided; and the amendment [i.e. to strike out from the original bill the words 'to be removable by the President'] was negatived by a majority of thirty-four to twenty. The opinion thus expressed by the house of representatives did not explicitly convey their sense of the Constitution. Indeed the express grant of the power to the president, rather implied a right in the legislature to give or withhold it at their discretion. To obviate any misunderstanding of the principle on which the question had been decided, Mr. Benson [later] moved in the house, when the report of the committee of the whole was taken up, to amend the second clause in the bill so as clearly to imply the power of removal to be solely in the president. He gave notice that if he should succeed in this, he would move to strike out the words which had been the subject of debate. If those words continued, he said the power of removal by the president might hereafter appear to be exercised by virtue of a legislative grant only and consequently be subjected to legislative instability; when he was well satisfied in his own mind, that it was by fair construction, fixed in the constitution. The motion was seconded by Mr. Madison, and both amendments were adopted. As the bill passed into a law, it has ever been considered as a full expression of the sense of the legislature on this important part of the American constitution."

This language was first published in 1807, four years after the judgment in *Marbury*. . . .

. . . Mr. Webster denied that the vesting of the executive power in the President was a grant of power. It amounted, he said, to no more than merely naming the department. Such a construction, although having the support of as great an expounder of the Constitution as Mr. Webster, is not in accord with the usual canon of interpretation of that instrument, which requires that real effect should be given to all the words it uses. *Marbury*. . . .

. . . We come now to consider an argument advanced and strongly pressed on behalf of the complainant, that this case concerns only the removal of a postmaster; that a postmaster is an inferior officer; that such an office was not included within the legislative decision of 1789, which related only to superior officers to be appointed by the

President by and with the advice and consent of the Senate. This, it is said, is the distinction which Chief Justice Marshall had in mind in *Marbury*, in the language already discussed in respect of the President's power to remove a District of Columbia justice of the peace appointed and confirmed for a term of years. We find nothing in *Marbury* to indicate any such distinction. It can not be certainly affirmed whether the conclusion there stated was based on a dissent from the legislative decision of 1789, or on the fact that the office was created under the special power of Congress exclusively to legislate for the District of Columbia, or on the fact that the office was a judicial one or on the circumstance that it was an inferior office. In view of the doubt as to what was really the basis of the remarks relied on, and their obiter dictum character, they can certainly not be used to give weight to the argument that the 1789 decision only related to superior officers. . . .

Dissenting Opinion of Justice McReynolds

. . . Act of July 2, 1836 . . . is the first Act which permitted appointment of any postmaster by the President; the first also which fixed terms for them. It was careful to allow removals by the President, which otherwise, under the doctrine of *Marbury* . . . would have been denied him. . . .

Rightly understood the debate and Act of 1789 and subsequent practice afford no support to the claim now advanced. In *Marbury* . . . this court expressly repudiated it, and that decision has never been overruled. . . .

These great expounders had no knowledge of any practical construction of the Constitution sufficient to support the theory here advanced. This court knew nothing of it in 1803 when it decided *Marbury*. . . .

The claim advanced for the United States is supported by no opinion of this court, and conflicts with *Marbury* . . . concurred in by all, including Mr. Justice Paterson, who was a conspicuous member of the Constitutional Convention and, as Senator from New Jersey, participated in the debate of 1789 concerning the power to re-

move and supported the bill to establish the Department of Foreign Affairs.

By an original proceeding here Marbury sought a mandamus requiring Mr. Madison, then Secretary of State, to deliver a commission signed by President Adams which showed his appointment (under the Act of February 27, 1801) as Justice of the Peace for the District of Columbia, "to continue in office five years." The Act contained no provision concerning removal. [At this point, Justice McReynolds quoted at length the passages in *Marbury* on Marbury's right to the commission]. . . .

The point thus decided was directly presented and essential to proper disposition of the cause. If the doctrine now advanced had been approved there would have been no right to protect and the famous discussion and decision of the great constitutional question touching the power of the court to declare an Act of Congress without effect would have been wholly out of place. . . . The sometime suggestion, that the Chief Justice indulged an obiter dictum, is without foundation. The court must have appreciated that unless it found Marbury had the legal right to occupy the office irrespective of the President's will there would be no necessity for passing upon the much-controverted and far-reaching power of the judiciary to declare an Act of Congress without effect. . . .

But, assuming that it was unnecessary in *Marbury* to determine the right to hold the office, nevertheless this Court deemed it essential and decided it. . . .

We are asked by the United States to treat the definite holding in *Marbury* that the plaintiff was not subject to removal by the President at will as mere dictum—to disregard it. But a solemn adjudication by this Court may not be so lightly treated. For a hundred and twenty years that case has been regarded as among the most important ever decided. It lies at the very foundation of our jurisprudence. Every point determined was deemed essential, and the suggestion of dictum, either idle or partisan exhortation, ought not to be tolerated. . . .

At the outset it became necessary to determine whether Marbury had any legal right which could, prima facie at least, create a justiciable or actual case arising under the laws of the United States. Otherwise, there would have been nothing more than a moot cause; the proceeding would have been upon an hypothesis; and he would have shown no legal right whatever to demand an adjudication on the question of jurisdiction and constitutionality of the statute. The court ... emphatically declared, not by way of argument or illustration, but as definite opinion, that the appointment of Marbury "conferred on him a legal right to the office for the space of five years," beyond the President's power to remove; and, plainly on this premise, it thereupon proceeded to consider the grave constitutional question. Indeed, if *Marbury* had failed to show a legal right to protect or enforce, it could be urged that the decision as to invalidity of the statute lacked force as a precedent, because rendered upon a mere abstract question raised by a moot case. . . .

Although he was intensely hostile to *Marbury*, and refused to recognize it as authoritative, I do not find that Mr. Jefferson ever controverted the view that an officer duly appointed for a definite time, without more, held his place free from arbitrary removal by the President. . . .

. . . The judges did not disclaim all cognizance of the cause—they were called upon to determine the question irrespective of the result reached—and, whether rightly or wrongly, they distinctly held that actual delivery of the commission was not essential. That question does not now arise—

here the commission was delivered and the appointee took office. . . .

. . . [N]o removals of such duly commissioned officers were made prior to 1820; and *Marbury* expressly affirms that this could not lawfully be done. . . .

. . . If the framers of the Constitution had intended "the executive power," in Art. II, Sec. 1, to include all power of an executive nature, they would not have added the carefully defined grants of Sec. 2. . . . "Affirmative words are often, in their operation, negative of other objects than those affirmed; and in this case, a negative or exclusive sense must be given to them, or they have no operation at all. It cannot be presumed that any clause in the Constitution is intended to be without effect; and, therefore, such a construction is inadmissible, unless the words require it." *Marbury*. . . .

Dissenting Opinion of Justice Brandeis

. . . In *Marbury*. . . , it was assumed, as the basis of decision, that the President, acting alone, is powerless to remove an inferior civil officer appointed for a fixed term with the consent of the Senate; and that case was long regarded as so deciding. In no case, has this Court determined that the President's power of removal is beyond control, limitation, or regulation by Congress. Nor has any lower federal court ever so decided. . . . We are requested to disregard the authority of *Marbury* and to overturn this long established constitutional practice. . . .

Source: Myers v. United States (1926): 52, 139–144, 151–152, 158, 190, 202, 203, 215–222, 226, 228–229, 242–244.

89

Humphrey's Executor v. United States (1935)

In 1931 President Herbert Hoover appointed William Humphrey to a seven-year term as a commissioner of the Federal Trade Commission. Two years later, President Franklin Roosevelt removed Humphrey from office. The Federal Trade Commission Act of 1925 declared that commissioners could be removed by the president only for specific cause. President Roosevelt conceded that he had no statutory cause for removing Humphrey but claimed a general presidential power under Myers v. United States _(1926) to remove federal bureaucrats._

The Supreme Court rejected this presidential claim. Justice George Sutherland's opinion cited Marbury _for the proposition that, while officers who directly served the president could be removed at the will of the president, justices of the peace, members of the civil service, and others who did not hold "purely executive office(s)" were subject to removal only under conditions laid down by Congress. Sutherland also cited_ Marbury _when claiming that dictum to the contrary in_ Myers _(which claimed that most of_ Marbury _was dictum) was not an authoritative source of law._

Opinion of Justice Sutherland

. . . A like situation was presented in the case of _Cohens v. Virginia_, . . . in respect of certain general expressions in the opinion in _Marbury_. Chief Justice Marshall, who delivered the opinion in the _Marbury_ case, speaking again for the court in the _Cohens_ case, said:

"It is a maxim, not to be disregarded, that general expressions, in every opinion, are to be taken in connection with the case in which those expressions are used. If they go beyond the case, they may be respected, but ought not to control the judgment in a subsequent suit, when the very point is presented for decision. The reason of this maxim is obvious. The question actually before the Court is investigated with care, and considered in its full extent. Other principles which may serve to illustrate it, are considered in their relation to the case decided, but their possible bearing on all other cases is seldom completely investigated."

And he added that these general expressions in the case of _Marbury_ were to be understood with the limitations put upon them by the opinion in the _Cohens_ case. . . .

In _Marbury_. . . , it is made clear that Chief Justice Marshall was of opinion that a justice of the peace for the District of Columbia was not removable at the will of the President; and that there was a distinction between such an officer and officers appointed to aid the President in the performance of his constitutional duties. In the latter case, the distinction he saw was that "their acts are his acts" and his will, therefore, controls; and, by way of illustration, he adverted to the act establishing the Department of Foreign Affairs, which was the subject of the "decision of 1789." . . .

Source: Humphrey's Executor v. United States (1935): 602, 627, 631.

90   *Cooper v. Aaron* (1958)

The Supreme Court in Brown v. Board of Education I *(1954) declared racially segregated public schools unconstitutional. In* Brown v. Board of Education II *(1955), the justices ordered all communities to desegregate their public schools with "all deliberate speed." Massive resistance followed. In Little Rock, Arkansas, federal troops were needed to protect the few African American children attending a formerly all-white high school. Fearing more violence and chaos, a federal district court ordered that the local desegregation plan be suspended for two and one-half years. That order was reversed by a federal court of appeals, and an appeal was taken to the Supreme Court.*

The Supreme Court agreed that the desegregation plan had to be reinstated immediately. In an unprecedented opinion, signed by every member of the Court, the justices declared that Brown I *and II were the law of the land and that all elected officials were obligated to obey the Constitution as interpreted by the Supreme Court.* Cooper *is the first case that explicitly interprets* Marbury *as establishing judicial supremacy as well as judicial review. Judicial decisions, the justices bluntly declared, bind all elected officials, even those who were not parties to the case before the Court. The judicial power articulated in* Marbury, *all nine justices agreed, required all officials to treat the legal principles announced in Supreme Court decisions as constitutionally authoritative.*

Per Curiam Opinion

. . . Article VI of the Constitution makes the Constitution the "supreme Law of the Land." In 1803, Chief Justice Marshall, speaking for a unanimous Court, referring to the Constitution as "the fundamental and paramount law of the nation," declared in the notable case of *Marbury* that "It is emphatically the province and duty of the judicial department to say what the law is." This decision declared the basic principle that the federal judiciary is supreme in the exposition of the law of the Constitution, and that principle has ever since been respected by this Court and the Country as a permanent and indispensable feature of our constitutional system. It follows

that the interpretation of the Fourteenth Amendment enunciated by this Court in the *Brown* case is the supreme law of the land, and Art. VI of the Constitution makes it of binding effect on the States "any Thing in the Constitution or Laws of any State to the Contrary notwithstanding." . . .

No state legislator or executive or judicial officer can war against the Constitution without violating his undertaking to support it. Chief Justice Marshall spoke for a unanimous Court in saying that: "If the legislatures of the several states may, at will, annul the judgments of the courts of the United States, and destroy the rights acquired under those judgments, the constitution itself becomes a solemn mockery. . . ."

Source: Cooper v. Aaron (1958): 1, 18.

91   *Bell v. Maryland* (1964)

Twelve African American students were arrested in Baltimore in 1960 for refusing to leave a restaurant that served only white patrons. They claimed their arrest for trespass violated the equal protection and due process clauses of the Fourteenth Amendment. The Supreme Court reversed those convictions on a legal technicality. Justices William O. Douglas, Arthur Goldberg, and Hugo Black, each writing separately, all scorned this attempt to avoid, on dubious legal grounds, a judicial decision on an important constitutional question. Their Marbury required the Court to resolve all constitutional questions necessary to resolve the lawsuit before the justices.

Concurring Opinion of Justice Douglas

. . . Much of our history has shown that what Marshall said of the encroachment of legislative power on the rights of the people is true also of the encroachment of the judicial branch, as where state courts use unconstitutional procedures to convict people or make criminal what is beyond the reach of the States. I think our approach here should be that of Marshall in *Marbury* . . . where the Court spoke with authority though there was an obviously easy way to avoid saying anything. . . .

Concurring Opinion of Justice Goldberg

. . . In my view the Fourteenth Amendment resolved this issue in favor of the right of petitioners to public accommodations and it follows that in the exercise of that constitutionally granted right they are entitled to the "law's protection." Today, as long ago, "the very essence of civil liberty certainly consists in the right of every individual to claim the protection of the laws . . ." *Marbury*. . . .

Dissenting Opinion of Justice Black

. . . Since *Marbury* . . . it has been this Court's recognized responsibility and duty to decide constitutional questions properly and necessarily before it. That case and others have stressed the duty of judges to act with the greatest caution before frustrating legislation by striking it down as unconstitutional. We should feel constrained to decide this question even if we thought the state law invalid. In this case, however, we believe that the state law is a valid exercise of state legislative power, that the question is properly before us, and that the national interest imperatively calls for an authoritative decision of the question by this Court. Under these circumstances we think that it would be an unjustified abdication of our duty to leave the question undiscussed. This we are not willing to do. . . .

Source: Bell v. Maryland (1964): 226, 244–245, 312, 323.

92
United States v. Nixon (1974)

During the trial of several Watergate defendants, a federal district court issued a subpoena to President Richard Nixon that ordered him to turn various tapes and documents over to the court. Nixon refused on the ground that the court order violated executive privilege. The district court rejected his claim and the matter was appealed to the Supreme Court.

The Court also rejected the claim that the president had the right to reject a subpoena for any reason. Chief Justice Warren Burger's opinion cited Marbury *for the principle that presidential claims of executive privilege raised constitutional questions that could authoritatively be resolved only by the Court.* Nixon *sealed the fate of the Nixon presidency. Shortly after that decision was handed down, Nixon resigned from office.*

Opinion of Chief Justice Burger

. . . The President's counsel . . . reads the Constitution as providing an absolute privilege of confidentiality for all Presidential communications. Many decisions of this Court, however, have unequivocally reaffirmed the holding of *Marbury* . . . that "[it] is emphatically the province and duty of the judicial department to say what the law is." . . .

Notwithstanding the deference each branch must accord the others, the "judicial Power of the United States" vested in the federal courts by Art. III, § 1, of the Constitution can no more be shared with the Executive Branch than the Chief Executive, for example, can share with the Judiciary the veto power, or the Congress share with the Judiciary the power to override a Presidential veto. Any other conclusion would be contrary to the basic concept of separation of powers and the checks and balances that flow from the scheme of a tripartite government. . . . We therefore reaffirm that it is the province and duty of this Court "to say what the law is" with respect to the claim of privilege presented in this case. *Marbury.* . . .

Source: United States v. Nixon (1974): 683, 703–705.

93
Butz v. Economou (1978)

Arthur Economou, a commodities trader, claimed that Earl Butz, secretary of agriculture during the Nixon administration, violated his free speech and due process rights when Butz launched an investigation of Economou's business after the trader had criticized administration policy. Butz claimed that executive officials could not be personally sued for any official conduct. A district court agreed that executive officials were immune from a lawsuit. That decision was reversed by a federal court of appeals, and an appeal was taken to the Supreme Court.

The Court ruled that federal officials did not have absolute liability for actions performed when in office. Marbury *was the citation of choice both for the justices who rejected and those who supported official immunity. Justice Byron White interpreted* Marbury *as defending the principle that executive department officials were not above the law and that courts should find remedies for federal rights violations. Justice William Rehnquist, in dissent, interpreted* Marbury *as supporting his claim that constitutional violations were best remedied by means other than lawsuits against government officials for damages.*

Opinion of Justice White

. . . In _Bivens v. Six Unknown Fed. Narcotics Agents_. . . , the victim of an arrest and search claimed to be violative of the Fourth Amendment brought suit for damages against the responsible federal agents. Repeating the declaration in _Marbury v. Madison_. . . , that " '[the] very essence of civil liberty certainly consists in the right of every individual to claim the protection of the laws,' " . . . and stating that "[historically,] damages have been regarded as the ordinary remedy for an invasion of personal interests in liberty," . . . we rejected the claim that the plaintiff's remedy lay only in the state court under state law, with the Fourth Amendment operating merely to nullify a defense of federal authorization. We held that a violation of the Fourth Amendment by federal agents gives rise to a cause of action for damages consequent upon the unconstitutional conduct. . . .

Our system of jurisprudence rests on the assumption that all individuals, whatever their position in government, are subject to federal law:

"No man in this country is so high that he is above the law. No officer of the law may set that law at defiance with impunity. All the officers of the government, from the highest to the lowest, are creatures of the law, and are bound to obey it." _United States v. Lee_. . . .

See also _Marbury_. . . .

Dissenting Opinion of Justice Rehnquist

. . . The Court purports to find support for this distinction, and therefore this result, in the principles supposedly underlying _Marbury_. . . , and the fact that cognate state officials are not afforded absolute immunity for actions brought under 42 U. S. C. § 1983. Undoubtedly these rationales have some superficial appeal, but none withstands careful analysis. _Marbury_. . . leaves no doubt that the high position of a Government official does not insulate his actions from judicial review. But that case, like numerous others which have followed, involved equitable-type relief by way of mandamus or injunction. In the present case, respondent sought damages in the amount of $32 million. There is undoubtedly force to the argument that injunctive relief, in these cases where a court determines that an official defendant has violated a legal right of the plaintiff, sets the matter right only as to the future. But there is at least as much force to the argument that the threat of injunctive relief without the possibility of damages in the case of a Cabinet official is a better tailoring of the competing need to vindicate individual rights, on the one hand, and the equally vital need, on the other, that federal officials exercising discretion will be unafraid to take vigorous action to protect the public interest. . . .

Source: Butz v. Economou (1978): 478, 485–486, 506, 523–524 (1978).

_94_

Nixon v. Fitzgerald (1982)

In 1970 Air Force analyst A. Ernest Fitzgerald lost his job after testifying before Congress about cost overruns on military projects. The Civil Service Commission found that this dismissal violated federal law. Fitzgerald sued President Richard Nixon for damages, noting that the president in a press conference had claimed personal responsibility for firing him. A federal district court ruled that Fitzgerald had a legal right to sue the president for damages. That ruling was sustained by the court of appeals.

The Supreme Court reversed these lower court rulings, holding that presidents could not be sued for any official act performed when in office. The meaning of Marbury _was at the core of the judicial dispute. Justice Lewis Powell and Chief Justice Warren Burger claimed that the principles underlying_ Marbury _did not justify suing a president for damages in order to vindicate a federal right. Justices_

Byron White and Harry Blackmun, in separate dissents, interpreted Marbury *as establishing that the president was subject to law and that a legal remedy should exist for any legal wrong done by the president.*

Opinion of Justice Powell

. . . Even the case on which JUSTICE WHITE places principal reliance, *Marbury* . . . , provides dubious support at best. The dissent cites *Marbury* for the proposition that "[the] very essence of civil liberty certainly consists in the right of every individual to claim the protection of the laws, whenever he receives an injury." . . . Yet *Marbury* does not establish that the individual's protection must come in the form of a particular remedy. Marbury, it should be remembered, lost his case in the Supreme Court. The Court turned him away with the suggestion that he should have gone elsewhere with his claim. In this case it was clear at least that Fitzgerald was entitled to seek a remedy before the Civil Service Commission—a remedy of which he availed himself. . . .

Concurring Opinion of Chief Justice Burger

. . . Even prior to the adoption of our Constitution, as well as after, judicial review of legislative action was recognized in some instances as necessary to maintain the proper checks and balances. Cf. *Marbury*. . . . However, the Judiciary always must be hesitant to probe into the elements of Presidential decisionmaking, just as other branches should be hesitant to probe into judicial decisionmaking. . . .

. . . Nothing in the Court's opinion is to be read as suggesting that a constitutional holding of this Court can be legislatively overruled or modified. *Marbury*. . . .

Dissenting Opinion of Justice White

. . . In *Marbury*, . . . the Court, speaking through The Chief Justice, observed that while there were "important political powers" committed to the President for the performance of which neither he nor his appointees were accountable in court, "the question, whether the legality of an act of the head of a department be examinable in a court of justice or not, must always depend on the nature of that act." The Court nevertheless refuses to follow this course with respect to the President. It makes no effort to distinguish categories of Presidential conduct that should be absolutely immune from other categories of conduct that should not qualify for that level of immunity. . . .

In *Marbury*, the Chief Justice, speaking for the Court, observed: "The Government of the United States has been emphatically termed a government of laws, and not of men. It will certainly cease to deserve this high appellation, if the laws furnish no remedy for the violation of a vested legal right." Until now, the Court has consistently adhered to this proposition. . . .

The principle that should guide the Court in deciding this question was stated long ago by Chief Justice Marshall: "The very essence of civil liberty certainly consists in the right of every individual to claim the protection of the laws, whenever he receives an injury." *Marbury*. . . .

I find it ironic, as well as tragic, that the Court would so casually discard its own role of assuring "the right of every individual to claim the protection of the laws," *Marbury*, . . . in the name of protecting the principle of separation of powers. . . .

Dissenting Opinion of Justice Blackmun

. . . [N]o man, not even the President of the United States, is absolutely and fully above the law. See . . . *Marbury*. . . . Until today, I had thought this principle was the foundation of our national jurisprudence. It now appears that it is not. . . .

Source: Nixon v. Fitzgerald (1982): 731, 754, 755 n. 37, 761, 763 n. 7 , 766, 768, 783, 789, 797–798.

95   *Lujan v. Defenders of Wildlife* (1992)

In 1986 Donald Hodel, the secretary of the interior under President Ronald Reagan, ruled that the Endangered Species Act (ESA) of 1973 applied only to regulations implemented in the United States and on the high seas. Environmental groups claimed that the act also limited American policy in foreign countries. A federal district court ruled that environmentalists lacked standing to bring a lawsuit challenging the secretary's interpretation of federal law. That decision was reversed by a federal court of appeals, and an appeal was taken to the Supreme Court.

The Court reversed the court of appeals, declaring unconstitutional the federal statute authorizing environmental groups to challenge regulations made under the ESA. The proper constitutional rules for standing, justices in the majority and minority agreed, turned on the proper interpretation of Marbury. Justice Antonin Scalia's majority opinion interpreted Marbury as limiting judicial review to cases where litigants had suffered a particular injury. Justice Anthony Kennedy's concurring opinion noted how standing law had been influenced by changes in litigation practices from the time when William Marbury sued to get his commission to the present day. Justice Harry Blackmun, in dissent, emphasized Marbury's promise that legal remedies would exist for federal wrongs.

Opinion of Justice Scalia

. . . Whether the courts were to act on their own, or at the invitation of Congress, in ignoring the concrete injury requirement described in our cases, they would be discarding a principle fundamental to the separate and distinct constitutional role of the Third Branch—one of the essential elements that identifies those "Cases" and "Controversies" that are the business of the courts rather than of the political branches. "The province of the court," as Chief Justice Marshall said in *Marbury v. Madison*, . . . "is, solely, to decide on the rights of individuals." Vindicating the *public* interest (including the public interest in Government observance of the Constitution and laws) is the function of Congress and the Chief Executive. . . .

Concurring Opinion of Justice Kennedy

. . . As Government programs and policies become more complex and far reaching, we must be sensitive to the articulation of new rights of ac-

tion that do not have clear analogs in our common-law tradition. Modern litigation has progressed far from the paradigm of Marbury suing Madison to get his commission, *Marbury v. Madison*. . . . In my view, Congress has the power to define injuries and articulate chains of causation that will give rise to a case or controversy where none existed before, and I do not read the Court's opinion to suggest a contrary view. . . . In exercising this power, however, Congress must at the very least identify the injury it seeks to vindicate and relate the injury to the class of persons entitled to bring suit. . . .

Dissenting Opinion of Justice Blackmun

. . . I cannot join the Court on what amounts to a slash-and-burn expedition through the law of environmental standing. In my view, "the very essence of civil liberty certainly consists in the right of every individual to claim the protection of the laws, whenever he receives an injury." *Marbury v. Madison*. . . .

Source: Lujan v. Defenders of Wildlife (1992): 555, 576, 580, 606.

96 *United States v. Lopez* (1995)

Alfonso Lopez, a twelfth-grader in San Antonio, Texas, was arrested and convicted for violating a federal law that criminalized gun possession in or near schools. His conviction was overturned by a federal court of appeals on the ground that the commerce power did not authorize Congress to ban guns near schools. The United States appealed this ruling to the Supreme Court.

The Court sustained the court of appeals, declaring unconstitutional the law under which Lopez was convicted. Lopez was the first case in fifty years that asserted a constitutional limit on any federal power enumerated in Article I. Marbury was central to this exercise of conservative judicial policymaking. Chief Justice William Rehnquist and Justice Anthony Kennedy each interpreted that decision as establishing the judicial power to determine the extent of congressional power under the interstate commerce clause.

Opinion of Chief Justice Rehnquist

. . . But, so long as Congress' authority is limited to those powers enumerated in the Constitution, and so long as those enumerated powers are interpreted as having judicially enforceable outer limits, congressional legislation under the Commerce Clause always will engender "legal uncertainty." . . . The Constitution mandates this uncertainty by withholding from Congress a plenary police power that would authorize enactment of every type of legislation. . . . Congress has operated within this framework of legal uncertainty ever since this Court determined that it was the Judiciary's duty "to say what the law is." *Marbury*. . . .

Concurring Opinion of Justice Kennedy

. . . Judicial review is also established beyond question, *Marbury* . . . and though we may differ when applying its principles . . . ., its legitimacy is undoubted. . . .

Our ability to preserve this principle under the Commerce Clause has presented a much greater challenge. . . . "This clause has throughout the Court's history been the chief source of its adjudications regarding federalism," and "no other body of opinions affords a fairer or more revealing test of judicial qualities." . . . . But as the branch whose distinctive duty it is to declare "what the law is," *Marbury* . . . we are often called upon to resolve questions of constitutional law not susceptible to the mechanical application of bright and clear lines. . . .

Source: United States v. Lopez (1995): 549, 566, 575, 579.

97 *City of Boerne v. Flores* (1997)

The Supreme Court in Oregon v. Smith (1990) ruled that the free exercise clause of the First Amendment forbade only laws that intentionally discriminated against religious groups. Congress responded by passing the Religious Freedom Restoration Act (RFRA), which required states to accommodate religious belief unless doing so threatened a compelling state interest. Congress claimed power to pass RFRA under Section 5 of the Fourteenth Amendment, which declares that "Congress shall have power to enforce, by appropriate legislation, the provisions of this article." Soon afterwards, the city of Boerne, Texas, denied a request to expand a church on the ground that the church was an historic landmark. The local archbishop sued, claiming the decision violated RFRA.

The Supreme Court declared RFRA unconstitutional. The Rehnquist Court was as united in City of Boerne *as the Warren Court was in* Cooper v. Aaron *(1958) that* Marbury *established both judicial review and judicial supremacy. Justice Anthony Kennedy's majority opinion frequently cited* Marbury *as supporting his claim that the judiciary had the final authority to interpret what the Fourteenth Amendment and other constitutional provisions mean. Congress, he declared, could protect only those rights the Supreme Court believed to be guaranteed by the Fourteenth Amendment, not those that elected officials believed were protected by the Fourteenth Amendment. Justices Sandra Day O'Connor and Harry Blackmun dissented, but their opinions disputed only whether Kennedy correctly interpreted the First Amendment. All nine justices in* City of Boerne *endorsed Kennedy's understanding of the judicial authority to settle constitutional controversies for the entire political system.*

Opinion of Justice Kennedy

. . . The judicial authority to determine the constitutionality of laws, in cases and controversies, is based on the premise that the "powers of the legislature are defined and limited; and that those limits may not be mistaken, or forgotten, the constitution is written." *Marbury*. . . .

If Congress could define its own powers by altering the Fourteenth Amendment's meaning, no longer would the Constitution be "superior paramount law, unchangeable by ordinary means." It would be "on a level with ordinary legislative acts, and, like other acts, . . . alterable when the legislature shall please to alter it." *Marbury*. . . . Under this approach, it is difficult to conceive of a principle that would limit congressional power. . . .

Our national experience teaches that the Constitution is preserved best when each part of the government respects both the Constitution and the proper actions and determinations of the other branches. When the Court has interpreted the Constitution, it has acted within the province of the Judicial Branch, which embraces the duty to say what the law is. *Marbury*. . . .

It is for Congress in the first instance to "determine whether and what legislation is needed to secure the guarantees of the Fourteenth Amendment," and its conclusions are entitled to much deference. . . . Congress' discretion is not unlimited, however, and the courts retain the power, as they have since *Marbury*, . . . to determine if Congress has exceeded its authority under the Constitution. Broad as the power of Congress is under the Enforcement Clause of the Fourteenth Amendment, RFRA contradicts vital principles necessary to maintain separation of powers and the federal balance. . . .

Source: City of Boerne v. Flores (1997): 507, 516, 529, 535–536.

98 *United States v. Morrison* (2000)

In 1995 Christy Brzonkala sued Antonio Morrison in federal court, claiming he had raped her when both were students at Virginia Polytechnic Institute. She based her lawsuit on the Violence Against Women Act (VAWA), which declared a federal right against gender-motivated violence. The lower federal courts declared VAWA unconstitutional, asserting that neither the commerce clause nor the Fourteenth Amendment vested Congress with the power to punish gender-motivated violence.

The Supreme Court agreed that VAWA was unconstitutional. The meaning of Marbury was again disputed by the justices in the majority and minority. Reversing the roles commonly taken in many controversial Warren Court decisions, in Morrison the more conservative justices interpreted Marbury as authorizing the exercise of judicial review, while the more liberal justices denied that Marbury supported a judicial decision declaring VAWA unconstitutional. Chief Justice William Rehnquist's majority opinion claimed that Congress was not constitutionally authorized to determine the meaning of the Fourteenth Amendment or the commerce clause: the Supreme Court, as established by Marbury, determined the scope of federal power. Justice David Souter disagreed with this use of the case. His dissent claimed the principles set out in Marbury permitted congressional assessment of what actions had a sufficient impact on interstate commerce to warrant federal regulation.

Opinion of Chief Justice Rehnquist

. . . Every law enacted by Congress must be based on one or more of its powers enumerated in the Constitution. "The powers of the legislature are defined and limited; and that those limits may not be mistaken or forgotten, the constitution is written." *Marbury.* . . .

. . . Under our written Constitution, however, the limitation of congressional authority is not solely a matter of legislative grace. See . . . *Marbury.* . . .

Dissenting Opinion of Justice Souter

. . . The majority tries to deflect the objection that it blocks an intended political process by explaining that the Framers intended politics to set the federal balance only within the sphere of permissible commerce legislation, whereas we are looking to politics to define that sphere (in derogation even of *Marbury.*) . . . But we all accept the view that politics is the arbiter of state interests only within the realm of legitimate congressional action under the commerce power. . . . Politics has legitimate authority, for all of us on both sides of the disagreement, only within the legitimate compass of the commerce power. The majority claims merely to be engaging in the judicial task of patrolling the outer boundaries of that congressional authority. . . . That assertion cannot be reconciled with our statements of the substantial effects test, which have not drawn the categorical distinctions the majority favors. . . . The majority's attempt to circumscribe the commerce power by defining it in terms of categorical exceptions can only be seen as a revival of similar efforts that led to near tragedy for the Court and incoherence for the law. If history's lessons are accepted as guides for Commerce Clause interpretation today, as we do accept them, then the subject matter of the Act falls within the commerce power and the choice to legislate nationally on that subject, or to except it from national legislation because the States have traditionally dealt with it, should be a political choice and only a political choice. . . .

Source: United States v. Morrison (2000): 598, 607, 616, 651 n. 19.

99

Dickerson v. United States (2000)

In Miranda v. Arizona (1966), the Supreme Court held that police officers had to give specific warnings before a custodial confession could constitutionally be admitted into evidence during a criminal trial. Language in Miranda suggested that these warnings were not required by the Fifth Amendment but were judicially contrived rules for ensuring that all confessions received in evidence were voluntarily made. Congress in 1968 passed a law requiring courts to admit into evidence any confession that was voluntarily made, even if the appropriate Miranda warnings were not given. Nearly thirty years later, Charles Dickerson successfully had his confession to bank robberies in Virginia and Maryland suppressed because he had not been given Miranda warnings. A federal court of appeals, resurrecting the 1968 statute, overturned the trial court decision to exclude the confession.

The Supreme Court reversed the decision of the court of appeals. Chief Justice William Rehnquist's majority opinion, without citing Marbury, declared that Miranda announced a "constitutional rule" that Congress could not overturn by legislation. Justice Antonin Scalia disagreed. His dissent asserted that if Miranda warnings were merely judicially contrived rules, then Congress was free to pass contrary legislation. Scalia repeatedly cited Marbury as authorizing judicial review only when national legislation violated the Constitution. Marbury, in his view, permitted Congress to challenge judicial rules designed to prevent police from obtaining or using involuntary confessions, as long as legislation did not violate the Fifth Amendment by authorizing the police to obtain or use involuntary confessions.

Dissenting Opinion of Justice Scalia

... _Marbury_ ... held that an Act of Congress will not be enforced by the courts if what it prescribes violates the Constitution of the United States. That was the basis on which _Miranda_ was decided. ... [T]o justify today's agreed-upon result, the Court must adopt a significant new, if not entirely comprehensible, principle of constitutional law. As the Court chooses to describe that principle, statutes of Congress can be disregarded, not only when what they prescribe violates the Constitution, but when what they prescribe contradicts a decision of this Court that "announced a constitutional rule.". ...

The power we recognized in _Marbury_ will thus permit us, indeed require us, to "disregard" § 3501, a duly enacted statute governing the admissibility of evidence in the federal courts, only if it "be in opposition to the constitution"— here, assertedly, the dictates of the Fifth Amendment.

... [W]hat is most remarkable about the _Miranda_ decision—and what made it unacceptable as a matter of straightforward constitutional interpretation in the _Marbury_ tradition—is its palpable hostility toward the act of confession per se, rather than toward what the Constitution abhors, compelled confession. ...

As the Court today acknowledges, since _Miranda_ we have explicitly, and repeatedly, interpreted that decision as having announced, not the circumstances in which custodial interrogation runs afoul of the Fifth or Fourteenth Amendment, but rather only "prophylactic" rules that go beyond the right against compelled self-incrimination. ... The Court has squarely concluded that it is possible—indeed not uncommon—for the police to violate _Miranda_ without also violating the Constitution. ...

Source: Dickerson v. United States (2000): 428, 445, 446–447, 449–451.

Appendix A:
The Annotated *Marbury v. Madison*

General Information

William Marbury (1762–1835) was a wealthy businessman and active Federalist. His life story until 1803 is well told by David F. Forte in "Marbury's Travail: Federalist Politics and William Marbury's Appointment as Justice of the Peace," Catholic University Law Review 45, no. 2 (1996). James Madison (1751–1836) was the nominal defendant in Marbury v. Madison. As secretary of state, Madison was responsible for delivering judicial commissions. President Thomas Jefferson had previously ordered that the commission not be delivered. (See Document 68.)

The United States Reports *is the official source for Supreme Court opinions. "5 U.S. 137" means the decision in* Marbury v. Madison *can be found in the fifth volume of the* United States Reports *beginning on page 137. Throughout most of the nineteenth century, the Supreme Court reporter was responsible for putting together the decisions and opinions of the Supreme Court. Volumes were named after the Court reporter. 1 Cranch 137 is the first volume of the reports edited by William Cranch.*

The best analysis of Marbury *is William W. Van Alstyne, "A Critical Guide to Marbury v. Madison," Duke Law Journal 1969 (1969): 1. The standard source for legal terminology is Bryan A. Garner, ed., Black's Law Dictionary, 7th ed. (St. Paul, Minn.: West Group, 1999). The following annotations make liberal use of these sources.*

Background and Arguments of Counsel

Supreme Court reporters during the late eighteenth and nineteenth centuries often included lengthy summaries of the earlier legal history of the case and the arguments made by counsel before the Supreme Court. Charles Lee (1758–1815), William Marbury's attorney, argued that President John Adams had appointed Marbury as a justice of the peace, that Marbury's commission had been signed and sealed, that the Judiciary Act of 1789 authorized the Supreme Court to issue writs of mandamus in appropriate cases, that Marbury had a right to such a writ ordering the secretary of state to deliver his judicial commission, and that past judicial decisions had established the authority of the Supreme Court to issue writs of mandamus when exercising original jurisdiction.

Levi Lincoln, the attorney general at the time, was summoned as a witness to the present whereabouts of Marbury's commission (he claimed not to know where the commission was). Neither Lincoln nor any other member of the Jefferson administration presented a legal argument in Marbury.

Introduction

OPINION: **Afterwards, on the 24th of February the following opinion of the court was delivered by the chief justice.**

Opinion of the court.

[1] At the last term on the affidavits then read and filed with the clerk, a rule was granted in this case, requiring the secretary of state to show cause why a mandamus should not issue, directing him to deliver to William Marbury his commission as a justice of the peace of the county of Washington, in the district of Columbia.

["A rule to show cause" is a court order requiring a person to appear in court and either justify a particular action or explain why the court should not issue a certain order. A writ of mandamus orders a government official to perform a certain act. In this case, the writ would order James Madison to deliver the judicial commission to William Marbury. A commission authorizes a person to perform official duties. If anyone were to question whether William Marbury was a justice of the peace, he could prove his authority by showing his commission. A justice of the peace is typically given the authority to decide minor criminal and civil disputes.]

[2] No cause has been shown, and the present motion is for a mandamus. The peculiar delicacy of this case, the novelty of some of its circumstances, and the real difficulty attending the points which occur in it, require a complete exposition of the principles, on which the opinion to be given by the court, is founded.

[Other justices have thought that in cases of political delicacy, the less said the better.]

[3] These principles have been, on the side of the applicant, very ably argued at the bar. In rendering the opinion of the court, there will be some departure in form, though not in substance, from the points stated in that argument.

[The opinion does follow Charles Lee until paragraph 117. Lee asserted that the Supreme Court had power to issue writs of mandamus when exercising original jurisdiction. The justices in Marbury

disagreed. The discussion of judicial review that starts on paragraph 132 lacked the benefit of argument by counsel.]

[4] In the order in which the court has viewed this subject, the following questions have been considered and decided.

[5] 1st. Has the applicant a right to the commission he demands?

[6] 2dly. If he has a right, and that right has been violated, do the laws of his country afford him a remedy?

[7] 3dly. If they do afford him a remedy, is it a mandamus issuing from this court?

[Courts normally resolve jurisdictional questions (paragraph 7) before resolving questions of substantive law (paragraphs 5–6). If the Supreme Court had no power to issue a writ of mandamus to James Madison, then the discussion whether Marbury would be entitled to that writ in some other legal proceeding was unnecessary. See paragraphs 88–89. The Supreme Court in Myers v. United States (1926) (Document 88) maintained that every assertion in the following section had no legal standing because, lacking jurisdiction, the Supreme Court was not authorized to determine whether William Marbury had a right to a judicial commission.]

The Right to the Commission

[8] The first object of enquiry is,

[9] 1st. Has the applicant a right to the commission he demands?

[10] His right originates in an act of congress passed in February, 1801, concerning the district of Columbia.

[11] After dividing the district into two counties, the 11th section of this law, enacts, "that there shall be appointed in and for each of the said counties, such number of discreet persons to be justices of the peace as the president of the United States shall, from time to time, think expedient, to continue in office for five years."

[12] It appears, from the affidavits, that in compliance with this law, a commission for William Marbury as a justice of peace for the county of Washington, was signed by John Adams, then president of the United States; after

which the seal of the United States was affixed to it; but the commission has never reached the person for whom it was made out.

[The seal of the United States is a sign or impression that establishes an official document of the United States. John Marshall, acting as secretary of state under President John Adams, failed to deliver Marbury's commission before President Thomas Jefferson took office. Jefferson then refused to deliver all commissions Adams had signed but that had not yet been delivered. See Documents 67–68.]

[13] In order to determine whether he is entitled to this commission, it becomes necessary to enquire whether he has been appointed to the office. For if he has been appointed, the law continues him in office for five years, and he is entitled to the possession of those evidences of office, which, being completed, became his property.

[Paragraph 13 assumes without argument that the law establishing the office of justice of the peace, quoted in paragraph 11, does not entitle the president to remove William Marbury or other justice of the peace before their term expires. Crucial passages in Marbury (paragraphs 30, 52, 64, 79) depend on Marbury having a proprietary right to public office for five years. The Supreme Court in Myers v. United States (1926) asserted that Marbury was mistaken, that President Jefferson had a constitutional right to remove William Marbury from office at any time.]

[14] The 2d section of the 2d article of the constitution, declares, that "the president shall nominate, and, by and with the advice and consent of the senate, shall appoint ambassadors, other public ministers and consuls, and all other officers of the United States, whose appointments are not otherwise provided for."

[15] The third section declares, that "he shall commission all the officers of the United States."

[16] An act of congress directs the secretary of state to keep the seal of the United States, "to make out and record, and affix the said seal to all civil commissions to officers of the United States, to be appointed by the President, by and with the consent of the senate, or by the President alone; provided that the said seal shall not be affixed to any commission before the same shall have been signed by the President of the United States."

[Paragraph 16 claims that the secretary of state acts as an agent of Congress, not the president, when sealing and recording commissions. This assertion provides crucial support for later claims that the president's role in the appointments process ends when the commission is signed, that the president has no authority over the sealing, recording, and delivering of commissions, and that the secretary of state has no discretion when sealing, recording, and delivering commissions. See paragraphs 30, 33–34, 43, 100, and 103.]

[17] These are the clauses of the constitution and laws of the United States, which affect this part of the case. They seem to contemplate three distinct operations:

[18] 1st, The nomination. This is the sole act of the President, and is completely voluntary.

[19] 2d. The appointment. This is also the act of the President, and is also a voluntary act, though it can only be performed by and with the advice and consent of the senate.

[20] 3d. The commission. To grant a commission to a person appointed, might perhaps be deemed a duty enjoined by the constitution. "He shall," says that instrument, "commission all the officers of the United States."

[21] The acts of appointing to office, and commissioning the person appointed, can scarcely be considered as one and the same; since the power to perform them is given in two separate and distinct sections of the constitution. The distinction between the appointment and the commission will be rendered more apparent, by adverting to that provision in the second section of the second article of the constitution, which authorizes congress "to vest, by law, the appointment of such inferior officers, as they think proper, in the President alone, in the courts of law, or in the heads of departments;" thus contemplating cases where the law may direct the President to commission an officer appointed by the courts, or by the heads of departments. In such a case, to issue a commission would be apparently a duty distinct from the appointment, the performance of which, perhaps, could not legally be refused.

[22] Although that clause of the constitution which requires the President to commission all

the officers of the United States, may never have been applied to officers appointed otherwise than by himself, yet it would be difficult to deny the legislative power to apply it to such cases. Of consequence the constitutional distinction between the appointment to an office and the commission of an officer, who has been appointed, remains the same as if in practice the President had commissioned officers appointed by an authority other than his will.

[23] It follows too, from the existence of this distinction, that, if an appointment was to be evidenced by any public act, other than the commission, the performance of such public act would create the officer; and if he was not removable at the will of the President, would either give him a right to his commission, or enable him to perform the duties without it.

[24] These observations are premised solely for the purpose of rendering more intelligible those which apply more directly to the particular case under consideration.

[Paragraphs 17–24 distinguish between the presidential power to appoint and the presidential power to commission. The president exercises discretion when deciding who should be appointed to public office but is constitutionally obligated to commission all persons validly appointed to office.]

[25] This is an appointment by the President, by and with the advice and consent of the senate, and is evidenced by no act but the commission itself. In such a case therefore the commission and the appointment seem inseparable; it being almost impossible to show an appointment otherwise than by proving the existence of a commission; still the commission is not necessarily the appointment; though conclusive evidence of it.

[Paragraph 25 notes the difficulty distinguishing between an exercise of the appointment power and an exercise of the commissioning power when, as is the case with William Marbury and other persons appointed to office by the president, the commission is the evidence of the appointment.]

[26] But at what state does it amount to this conclusive evidence?

[27] The answer to this question seems an obvious one. The appointment being the sole act of the President, must be completely evidenced, when it is shown that he has done every thing to be performed by him.

[28] Should the commission, instead of being evidence of an appointment, even be considered as constituting the appointment itself; still it would be made when the last act to be done by the President was performed, or, at furthest, when the commission was complete.

[29] The last act to be done by the President, is the signature of the commission. He has then acted on the advice and consent of the senate to his own nomination. The time for deliberations has then passed. He has decided. His judgment, on the advice and consent of the senate concurring with his nomination, has been made, and the officer is appointed. This appointment is evidenced by an open, unequivocal act; and being the last act required from the person making it, necessarily excludes the idea of its being, so far as respects the appointment, an inchoate and incomplete transaction.

[Paragraphs 27–29 maintain that the appointment process ends when the president signs the commission.]

[30] Some point of time must be taken when the power of the executive over an officer, not removable at his will, must cease. That point of time must be when the constitutional power of appointment has been exercised. And this power has been exercised when the last act, required from the person possessing the power, has been performed. This last act is the signature of the commission. This idea seems to have prevailed with the legislature, when the act passed, converting the department of foreign affairs into the department of state. By that act it is enacted, that the secretary of state shall keep the seal of the United States, "and shall make out and record, and shall affix the said seal to all civil commissions to officers of the United States, to be appointed by the President:" "Provided that the

said seal shall not be affixed to any commission, before the same shall have been signed by the President of the United States; nor to any other instrument or act, without the special warrant of the President therefor."

[Paragraph 30 highlights the important assumptions made in paragraphs 13 and 16. Presidential discretion whether to appoint William Marbury ended when President John Adams signed his commission. Thereafter, Marbury could not lawfully be removed from office by the president before his five-year term expired. Another official, the secretary of state, was legislatively entrusted with responsibility for sealing, recording, and delivering signed commissions.]

[31] The signature is a warrant for affixing the great seal to the commission; and the great seal is only to be affixed to an instrument which is complete. It asserts, by an act supposed to be of public notoriety, the verity of the Presidential signature.

[32] It is never to be affixed till the commission is signed, because the signature, which gives force and effect to the commission, is conclusive evidence that the appointment is made.

[33] The commission being signed, the subsequent duty of the secretary of state is prescribed by law, and not to be guided by the will of the President. He is to affix the seal of the United States to the commission, and is to record it.

[34] This is not a proceeding which may be varied, if the judgment of the executive shall suggest one more eligible; but is a precise course accurately marked out by law, and is to be strictly pursued. It is the duty of the secretary of state to conform to the law, and in this he is an officer of the United States, bound to obey the laws. He acts, in this regard, as has been very properly stated at the bar, under the authority of law, and not by the instructions of the President. It is a ministerial act which the law enjoins on a particular officer for a particular purpose.

[Paragraphs 33–34 make clear that the secretary of state acts as an agent of Congress, not the president, when sealing and recording signed commissions. The secretary must seal and record all signed commissions. The duty is ministerial, not involving any discretion or choice. The moment his judicial

commission was signed by the president, William Marbury gained the legal right to have that commission sealed, recorded, and delivered by the secretary of state.]

[35] If it should be supposed, that the solemnity of affixing the seal, is necessary not only to the validity of the commission, but even to the completion of an appointment, still when the seal is affixed the appointment is made, and the commission is valid. No other solemnity is required by law; no other act is to be performed on the part of government. All that the executive can do to invest the person with his office, is done; and unless the appointment be then made, the executive cannot make one without the co-operation of others.

[36] After searching anxiously for the principles on which a contrary opinion may be supported, none have been found which appear of sufficient force to maintain the opposite doctrine.

[37] Such as the imagination of the court could suggest, have been very deliberately examined, and after allowing them all the weight which it appears possible to give them, they do not shake the opinion which has been formed.

[38] In considering this question, it has been conjectured that the commission may have been assimilated to a deed, to the validity of which, delivery is essential.

[39] This idea is founded on the supposition that the commission is not merely evidence of an appointment, but is itself the actual appointment; a supposition by no means unquestionable. But for the purpose of examining this objection fairly, let it be conceded, that the principle, claimed for its support, is established.

[Paragraphs 38–39 note a possible objection to the conclusions reached in paragraph 34. The transfer of property is valid when the beneficiary receives the deed, not when the deed is signed.]

[40] The appointment being, under the constitution, to be made by the President personally, the delivery of the deed of appointment, if necessary to its completion, must be made by the

President also. It is not necessary that the livery should be made personally to the grantee of the office: It never is so made. The law would seem to contemplate that it should be made to the secretary of state, since it directs the secretary to affix the seal to the commission after it shall have been signed by the President. If then the act of livery be necessary to give validity to the commission, it has been delivered when executed and given to the secretary for the purpose of being sealed, recorded, and transmitted to the party.

[41] But in all cases of letters patent, certain solemnities are required by law, which solemnities are the evidences of the validity of the instrument. A formal delivery to the person is not among them. In cases of commissions, the sign manual of the President, and the seal of the United States, are those solemnities. This objection therefore does not touch the case.

[42] It has also occurred as possible, and barely possible, that the transmission of the commission, and the acceptance thereof, might be deemed necessary to complete the right of the plaintiff.

[43] The transmission of the commission, is a practice directed by convenience, but not by law. It cannot therefore be necessary to constitute the appointment which must precede it, and which is the mere act of the President. If the executive required that every person appointed to an office, should himself take means to procure his commission, the appointment would not be the less valid on that account. The appointment is the sole act of the President; the transmission of the commission is the sole act of the officer to whom that duty is assigned, and may be accelerated or retarded by circumstances which can have no influence on the appointment.

[Paragraphs 40–43 claim that, should delivery be necessary for the validity of a commission, delivery occurs when the president presents the signed commission to the secretary of state. The secretary of state acts as an agent for both Congress and the appointed official when sealing, recording, and delivering the commission.]

[44] A commission is transmitted to a person already appointed; not to a person to be appointed or not, as the letter enclosing the commission should happen to get into the post-office and reach him in safety, or to miscarry.

[45] It may have some tendency to elucidate this point, to enquire, whether the possession of the original commission be indispensably necessary to authorize a person, appointed to any office, to perform the duties of that office. If it was necessary, then a loss of the commission would lose the office. Not only negligence, but accident or fraud, fire or theft, might deprive an individual of his office. In such a case, I presume it could not be doubted, but that a copy from the record of the office of the secretary of state, would be, to every intent and purpose, equal to the original. The act of congress has expressly made it so. To give that copy validity, it would not be necessary to prove that the original had been transmitted and afterwards lost. The copy would be complete evidence that the original had existed, and that the appointment had been made, but, not that the original had been transmitted. If indeed it should appear that the original had been mislaid in the office of state, that circumstance would not affect the operation of the copy. When all the requisites have been performed which authorize a recording officer to record any instrument whatever, and the order for that purpose has been given, the instrument is, in law, considered as recorded, although the manual labor of inserting it in a book kept for that purpose may not have been performed.

[46] In the case of commissions, the law orders the secretary of state to record them. When therefore they are signed and sealed, the order for their being recorded is given; and whether inserted in the book or not, they are in law recorded.

[47] A copy of this record is declared equal to the original, and the fees, to be paid by a person requiring a copy, are ascertained by law. Can a keeper of a public record, erase therefrom a commission which has been recorded? Or can he refuse a copy thereof to a person demanding it on the terms prescribed by law?

[48] Such a copy would, equally with the original, authorize the justice of peace to proceed in the performance of his duty, because it would, equally with the original, attest his appointment.

[Paragraphs 44–48 claim that persons have a right to hold public office once their commissions are signed by the president and delivered to the secretary of state. Should the original copy of their commission be lost, William Marbury and other persons appointed to public office have the statutory right to ask the secretary of state for a copy of the original commission.]

[49] If the transmission of a commission be not considered as necessary to give validity to an appointment; still less is its acceptance. The appointment is the sole act of the President; the acceptance is the sole act of the officer, and is, in plain common sense, posterior to the appointment. As he may resign, so may he refuse to accept: but neither the one, nor the other, is capable of rendering the appointment a non-entity.

[50] That this is the understanding of the government, is apparent from the whole tenor of its conduct. A commission bears date, and the salary of the officer commences from his appointment; not from the transmission or acceptance of his commission. When a person, appointed to any office, refuses to accept the office, the successor is nominated in the place of the person who has declined to accept, and not in the place of the person who had been previously in office, and had created the original vacancy.

[Paragraphs 49–50 reassert that persons have a right to a public office once their commission is signed by the president and delivered to the secretary of state. William Marbury's right to a salary began when his commission was signed, not when it was delivered.]

[51] It is therefore decidedly the opinion of the court, that when a commission has been signed by the President, the appointment is made; and that the commission is complete, when the seal of the United States has been affixed to it by the secretary of state.

[52] Where an officer is removable at the will of the executive, the circumstance which com-pletes his appointment is of no concern; because the act is at any time revocable; and the commission may be arrested, if still in the office. But when the officer is not removable at the will of the executive, the appointment is not revocable, and cannot be annulled. It has conferred legal rights which cannot be resumed.

[Paragraph 52 reemphasizes that the president had no statutory right to remove justices of the peace from office. Had the president this power, President Jefferson might have legally revoked William Marbury's commission.]

[53] The discretion of the executive is to be exercised until the appointment has been made. But having once made the appointment, his power over the office is terminated in all cases, where, by law, the officer is not removable by him. The right to the office is then in the person appointed, and he has the absolute, unconditional, power of accepting or rejecting it.

[54] Mr. Marbury, then, since his commission was signed by the President, and sealed by the secretary of state, was appointed; and as the law creating the office, gave the officer a right to hold for five years, independent of the executive, the appointment was not revocable; but vested in the officer legal rights, which are protected by the laws of his country.

[55] To withhold his commission, therefore, is an act deemed by the court not warranted by law, but violative of a vested legal right.

[Paragraphs 54–55 conclude that William Marbury had a right to hold a justiceship of the peace for five years. The failure to deliver his commission violated this vested legal right.]

The Right to a Remedy

[56] This brings us to the second enquiry; which is,

[57] 2dly. If he has a right, and that right has been violated, do the laws of his country afford him a remedy?

[58] The very essence of civil liberty certainly consists in the right of every individual to claim

the protection of the laws, whenever he receives an injury. One of the first duties of government is to afford that protection. In Great Britain the king himself is sued in the respectful form of a petition, and he never fails to comply with the judgment of his court.

[59] In the 3d vol. of his commentaries, p. 23, Blackstone states two cases in which a remedy is afforded by mere operation of law.

"In all other cases," he says, "it is a general and indisputable rule, that where there is a legal right, there is also a legal remedy by suit or action at law, whenever that right is invaded."

[60] And afterwards, p. 109, of the same vol. he says, "I am next to consider such injuries as are cognizable by the courts of the common law. And herein I shall for the present only remark, that all possible injuries whatsoever, that did not fall within the exclusive cognizance of either the ecclesiastical, military, or maritime tribunals, are for that very reason, within the cognizance of the common law courts of justice; for it is a settled and invariable principle in the laws of England, that every right, when withheld, must have a remedy, and every injury its proper redress."

[61] The government of the United States has been emphatically termed a government of laws, and not of men. It will certainly cease to deserve this high appellation, if the laws furnish no remedy for the violation of a vested legal right.

[62] If this obloquy is to be cast on the jurisprudence of our country, it must arise from the peculiar character of the case.

[63] It behooves us then to enquire whether there be in its composition any ingredient which shall exempt it from legal investigation, or exclude the injured party from legal redress. In pursuing this enquiry the first question which presents itself is, whether this can be arranged with that class of cases which comes under the description of damnum absque injuria—a loss without an injury.

[Paragraphs 57–63 assert that persons whose vested rights are violated are generally entitled to legal remedies, but that circumstances exist where

persons suffer losses without having legally cognizable injuries.]

[64] This description of cases never has been considered, and it is believed never can be considered, as comprehending offices of trust, of honor or of profit. The office of justice of peace in the district of Columbia is such an office; it is therefore worthy of the attention and guardianship of the laws. It has received that attention and guardianship. It has been created by special act of congress, and has been secured, so far as the laws can give security to the person appointed to fill it, for five years. It is not then on account of the worthlessness of the thing pursued, that the injured party can be alleged to be without remedy.

[Paragraph 64 asserts that illegal deprivation of a public office is a legally cognizable injury that entitles the right holder to a legal remedy. This claim that public office is a species of private property is central to Marbury. *See comments after paragraph 93.]*

[65] Is it in the nature of the transaction? Is the act of delivering or withholding a commission to be considered as a mere political act, belonging to the executive department alone, for the performance of which, entire confidence is placed by our constitution in the supreme executive; and for any misconduct respecting which, the injured individual has no remedy.

[66] That there may be such cases is not to be questioned; but that every act of duty, to be performed in any of the great departments of government, constitutes such a case is not to be admitted.

[67] By the act concerning invalids, passed in June, 1794, vol. 3. p. 112, the secretary of war is ordered to place on the pension list, all persons whose names are contained in a report previously made by him to congress. If he should refuse to do so, would the wounded veteran be without remedy? Is it to be contended that where the law in precise terms, directs the performance of an act, in which an individual is interested, the law is incapable of securing obedience to its mandate?

Is it on account of the character of the person against whom the complaint is made? Is it to be contended that the heads of departments are not amenable to the laws of their country?

[68] Whatever the practice on particular occasions may be, the theory of this principle will certainly never be maintained. No act of the legislature confers so extraordinary a privilege, nor can it derive countenance from the doctrines of the common law. After stating that personal injury from the king to a subject is presumed to be impossible, Blackstone, vol. 3. p. 255, says, "but injuries to the rights of property can scarcely be committed by the crown without the intervention of its officers; for whom, the law, in matters of right, entertains no respect or delicacy; but furnishes various methods of detecting the errors and misconduct of those agents, by whom the king has been deceived and induced to do a temporary injustice."

[69] By the act passed in 1796, authorizing the sale of the lands above the mouth of Kentucky river (vol. 3d. p. 299) the purchaser, on paying his purchase money, becomes completely entitled to the property purchased; and on producing to the secretary of state, the receipt of the treasurer upon a certificate required by the law, the president of the United States is authorized to grant him a patent. It is further enacted that all patents shall be countersigned by the secretary of state, and recorded in his office. If the secretary of state should choose to withhold this patent; or the patent being lost, should refuse a copy of it; can it be imagined that the law furnishes to the injured person no remedy?

[70] It is not believed that any person whatever would attempt to maintain such a proposition.

[Paragraphs 65–70 assert that persons sometimes receive legally cognizable injuries when government officials engage in misconduct or fail to perform certain duties. Persons who suffer legally cognizable injuries at the hands of government officials have a right to legal remedies.]

[71] It follows then that the question, whether the legality of an act of the head of a department

be examinable in a court of justice or not, must always depend on the nature of that act.

[72] If some acts be examinable, and others not, there must be some rule of law to guide the court in the exercise of its jurisdiction.

[Paragraphs 71–72 emphasize that only some official wrongs create legally cognizable injuries.]

[73] In some instances there may be difficulty in applying the rule to particular cases; but there cannot, it is believed, be much difficulty in laying down the rule.

[74] By the constitution of the United States, the President is invested with certain important political powers, in the exercise of which he is to use his own discretion, and is accountable only to his country in his political character, and to his own conscience. To aid him in the performance of these duties, he is authorized to appoint certain officers, who act by his authority and in conformity with his orders.

[75] In such cases, their acts are his acts; and whatever opinion may be entertained of the manner in which executive discretion may be used, still there exists, and can exist, no power to control that discretion. The subjects are political. They respect the nation, not individual rights, and being entrusted to the executive, the decision of the executive is conclusive. The application of this remark will be perceived by adverting to the act of congress for establishing the department of foreign affairs. This office, as his duties were prescribed by that act, is to conform precisely to the will of the President. He is the mere organ by whom that will is communicated. The acts of such an officer, as an officer, can never be examinable by the courts.

[Paragraphs 73–75 claim that discretionary acts performed by government officials never create legally cognizable legal injuries. Personal losses suffered as a result of such acts are never remedial by a court of law. The Constitution vests the president with political powers whose exercise requires discretion. When members of the cabinet act as an agent of the president, they are entitled to exercise that discretion and their actions cannot create

legally cognizable injuries. Their conduct may be judged only by the president and by the general electorate.]

[76] But when the legislature proceeds to impose on that officer other duties; when he is directed peremptorily to perform certain acts; when the rights of individuals are dependent on the performance of those acts; he is so far the officer of the law; is amenable to the laws for his conduct; and cannot at his discretion sport away the vested rights of others.

[Paragraph 76 notes that the personal losses that result when cabinet officials fail to perform statutorily prescribed duties are legally cognizable injuries remedial by courts of law.]

[77] The conclusion from this reasoning is, that where the heads of departments are the political or confidential agents of the executive, merely to execute the will of the President, or rather to act in cases in which the executive possesses a constitutional or legal discretion, nothing can be more perfectly clear than that their acts are only politically examinable. But where a specific duty is assigned by law, and individual rights depend upon the performance of that duty, it seems equally clear that the individual who considers himself injured, has a right to resort to the laws of his country for a remedy.

[Paragraph 77 concludes that executive officials cause legally cognizable injuries when they fail to perform legal duties mandated by Congress, but never cause legally cognizable injuries when making discretionary choices acting as an agent of the president.]

[78] If this be the rule, let us enquire how it applies to the case under the consideration of the court.

[79] The power of nominating to the senate, and the power of appointing the person nominated, are political powers, to be exercised by the President according to his own discretion. When he has made an appointment, he has exercised his whole power, and his discretion has been completely applied to the case. If, by law, the officer be removable at the will of the President, then a new appointment may be immediately made, and the rights of the officer are terminated. But as a fact which has existed cannot be made never to have existed, the appointment cannot be annihilated; and consequently if the officer is by law not removable at the will of the President; the rights he has acquired are protected by the law, and are not resumeable by the President. They cannot be extinguished by executive authority, and he has the privilege of asserting them in like manner as if they had been derived from any other source.

[80] The question whether a right has vested or not, is, in its nature, judicial, and must be tried by the judicial authority. If, for example, Mr. Marbury had taken the oaths of a magistrate, and proceeded to act as one; in consequence of which a suit had been instituted against him, in which his defence had depended on his being a magistrate; the validity of his appointment must have been determined by judicial authority.

[81] So, if he conceives that, by virtue of his appointment, he has a legal right, either to the commission which has been made out for him, or to a copy of that commission, it is equally a question examinable in a court, and the decision of the court upon it must depend on the opinion entertained of his appointment.

[82] That question has been discussed, and the opinion is, that the latest point of time which can be taken as that at which the appointment was complete, and evidenced, was when, after the signature of the president, the seal of the United States was affixed to the commission.

[83] It is then the opinion of the court,

[84] 1st. That by signing the commission of Mr. Marbury, the president of the United States appointed him a justice of peace, for the county of Washington in the district of Columbia; and that the seal of the United States, affixed thereto by the secretary of state, is conclusive testimony of the verity of the signature, and of the completion of the appointment; and that the appointment conferred on him a legal right to the office for the space of five years.

[85] 2dly. That, having this legal title to the office, he has a consequent right to the commission; a refusal to deliver which, is a plain violation of that right, for which the laws of his country afford him a remedy.

[Paragraphs 79–85 conclude that William Marbury had a legal right to a remedy for the illegal withholding of his judicial commission. The secretary of state had a legal obligation mandated by Congress to deliver the commission, and was not acting as an agent of the president when refusing to perform that legal duty. The Supreme Court may examine whether cabinet officials have fulfilled legal obligations mandated by Congress, and may remedy James Madison's failure to fulfill his legal obligation to deliver Marbury's judicial commission.]

The Right to Mandamus

[86] It remains to be enquired whether,

[87] 3dly. He is entitled to the remedy for which he applies. This depends on,

[88] 1st. The nature of the writ applied for, and,

[89] 2dly. The power of this court.

[Contrary to paragraphs 88–89, courts typically determine whether they are empowered to issue a writ before deciding whether the writ is the appropriate remedy. See comments after paragraphs 5–7.]

[90] 1st. The nature of the writ.

[91] Blackstone, in the 3d volume of his commentaries, page 110, defines a mandamus to be, "a command issued in the King's name from the court of King's Bench, and directed to any person, corporation, or inferior court of judicature within the King's dominions, requiring them to do some particular thing therein specified, which appertains to their office and duty, and which the court of King's Bench has previously determined, or at least supposed, to be consonant to right and justice."

[92] Lord Mansfield, in 3d Burrows 1266, in the case of the King v. Baker, et al. states with much precision and explicitness the cases in which this writ may be used.

[93] "Whenever," says that very able judge, "there is a right to execute an office, perform a service, or exercise a franchise (more specifically if it be in a matter of public concern, or attended with profit) and a person is kept out of the possession, or dispossessed of such right, and has no other specific legal remedy, this court ought to assist by mandamus, upon reasons of justice, as the writ expresses, and upon reasons of public policy, to preserve peace, order and good government." In the same case he says, "this writ ought to be used upon all occasions where the law has established no specific remedy, and where in justice and good government there ought to be one."

[Paragraphs 90–93 describe a writ of mandamus (see comment to paragraph 1) and assert that writs of mandamus were issued in England when persons had a right to hold a particular office. Offices under feudal English law were closely connected to property holdings and were commonly understood to be a form of property. Another justice might wonder whether, under a democratic constitution, public offices are appropriately analogized to private property.]

[94] In addition to the authorities now particularly cited, many others were relied on at the bar, which show how far the practice has conformed to the general doctrines that have been just quoted.

[95] This writ, if awarded, would be directed to an officer of government, and its mandate to him would be, to use the words of Blackstone, "to do a particular thing therein specified, which appertains to his office and duty and which the court has previously determined, or at least supposes, to be consonant to right and justice." Or, in the words of Lord Mansfield, the applicant, in this case, has a right to execute an office of public concern, and is kept out of possession of that right.

[96] These circumstances certainly concur in this case.

[97] Still, to render the mandamus a proper remedy, the officer to whom it is directed, must be one to whom, on legal principles, such writ may be directed; and the person applying for it

must be without any other specific and legal remedy.

[Paragraph 97 states that William Marbury and other persons seeking a writ of mandamus must establish that the writ may legally be delivered to the public officer in question and that they have no other legal remedy. Monetary damages are the traditional legal remedy for legal injuries. Persons are entitled to a writ of mandamus only when their injury cannot be remedied monetarily.]

[98] 1st. With respect to the officer to whom it would be directed. The intimate political relation, subsisting between the president of the United States and the heads of departments, necessarily renders any legal investigation of the acts of one of those high officers peculiarly irksome, as well as delicate; and excites some hesitation with respect to the propriety of entering into such investigation. Impressions are often received without much reflection or examination, and it is not wonderful that in such a case as this, the assertion, by an individual, of his legal claims in a court of justice; to which claims it is the duty of that court to attend; should at first view be considered by some, as an attempt to intrude into the cabinet, and to intermeddle with the prerogatives of the executive.

[Jeffersonians very explicitly declared that Marbury was an effort to intermeddle with the executive. (See Documents 77–78.) That William Marbury, after his defeat in Marbury, never asked a lower federal court for a writ of mandamus provides more evidence that his primary purpose was to embarrass the Jefferson administration, not to gain an office or a salary.]

[99] It is scarcely necessary for the court to disclaim all pretensions to such a jurisdiction. An extravagance, so absurd and excessive, could not have been entertained for a moment. The province of the court is, solely, to decide on the rights of individuals, not to enquire how the executive, or executive officers, perform duties in which they have a discretion. Questions, in their nature political, or which are, by the constitution and laws, submitted to the executive, can never be made in this court.

[Paragraph 99 repeats the claim made in paragraphs 73–75 that courts do not investigate how governmental officials perform their discretionary duties.]

[100] But, if this be not such a question; if so far from being an intrusion into the secrets of the cabinet, it respects a paper, which, according to law, is upon record, and to a copy of which the law gives a right, on the payment of ten cents; if it be no intermeddling with a subject, over which the executive can be considered as having exercised any control; what is there in the exalted station of the officer, which shall bar a citizen from asserting, in a court of justice, his legal rights, or shall forbid a court to listen to the claim; or to issue a mandamus, directing the performance of a duty, not depending on executive discretion, but on particular acts of congress and the general principles of law?

[Paragraph 100 reemphasizes that when sealing, recording, and delivering commissions, the secretary of state is not acting as an agent of the president and has no legal discretion. The law gives William Marbury and other persons in similar positions a right to a copy of their commissions.]

[101] If one of the heads of departments commits any illegal act, under the color of his office, by which an individual sustains an injury, it cannot be pretended that his office alone exempts him from being sued in the ordinary mode of proceeding, and being compelled to obey the judgment of the law. How then can his office exempt him from this particular mode of deciding on the legality of his conduct, if the case be such a case as would, were any other individual the party complained of, authorize the process?

[102] It is not by the office of the person to whom the writ is directed, but the nature of the thing to be done that the propriety or impropriety of issuing a mandamus, is to be determined. Where the head of a department acts in a case, in which executive discretion is to be exercised; in which he is the mere organ of executive will; it is again repeated, that any application to a court to

control, in any respect, his conduct, would be rejected without hesitation.

[103] But where he is directed by law to do a certain act affecting the absolute rights of individuals, in the performance of which he is not placed under the particular direction of the President, and the performance of which, the President cannot lawfully forbid, and therefore is never presumed to have forbidden; as for example, to record a commission, or a patent for land, which has received all the legal solemnities; or to give a copy of such record; in such cases, it is not perceived on what ground the courts of the country are further excused from the duty of giving judgment, that right be done to an injured individual, than if the same services were to be performed by a person not the head of a department.

[Paragraphs 101–103 reemphasize that William Marbury and other persons may sue cabinet officials when the official fails to perform a duty mandated by Congress.]

[104] This opinion seems not now, for the first time, to be taken upon in this country.

[105] It must be well recollected that in 1792, an act passed, directing the secretary at war to place on the pension list such disabled officers and soldiers as should be reported to him, by the circuit courts, which act, so far as the duty was imposed on the courts, was deemed unconstitutional; but some of the judges, thinking that the law might be executed by them in the character of commissioners, proceeded to act and to report in that character.

[106] This law being deemed unconstitutional at the circuits, was repealed, and a different system was established; but this question whether those persons, who had been reported by the judges, as commissioners, were entitled, in consequence of that report, to be placed on the pension list, was a legal question, properly determinable in the courts, although the act of placing such persons on the list was to be preformed by the head of a department.

[107] That this question might be properly settled, congress passed an act in February, 1793,

making it the duty of the secretary of war, in conjunction with the attorney general, to take such measures, as might be necessary to obtain an adjudication of the supreme court of the United States on the validity of any such rights, claimed under the act aforesaid.

[108] After the passage of this act, a mandamus was moved for, to be directed to the secretary at war, commanding him to place on the pension list, a person stating himself to be on the report of the judges.

[109] There is, therefore, much reason to believe, that this mode of trying the legal right of the complainant, was deemed by the head of a department, and by the highest law officer of the United States, the most proper which could be selected for the purpose.

[110] When the subject was brought before the court the decision was, not that a mandamus would not lie to the head of a department, directing him to perform an act, enjoined by law, in the performance of which an individual had a vested interest; but that a mandamus ought not to issue in that case—the decision necessarily to be made if the report of the commissioners did not confer on the applicant a legal right.

[111] The judgment in that case, is understood to have decided the merits of all claims of that description; and the persons on the report of the commissioners found it necessary to pursue the mode prescribed by the law subsequent to that which had been deemed unconstitutional, in order to place themselves on the pension list.

[112] The doctrine, therefore, now advanced, is by no means a novel one.

[Paragraphs 105–112 highlight a previous instance when members of Congress and the Washington administration encouraged the Supreme Court to issue a writ of mandamus to cabinet officials. This instance, discussed in Documents 52–58, provides more evidence that the judicial power to issue such writs was well accepted by 1803.]

[113] It is true that the mandamus, now moved for, is not for the performance of an act expressly enjoined by statute.

[114] It is to deliver a commission; on which subject the acts of Congress are silent. This difference is not considered as affecting the case. It has already been stated that the applicant has, to that commission, a vested legal right, of which the executive cannot deprive him. He has been appointed to an office, from which he is not removable at the will of the executive; and being so appointed, he has a right to the commission which the secretary has received from the president for his use. The act of congress does not indeed order the secretary of state to send it to him, but it is placed in his hands for the person entitled to it; and cannot be more lawfully withheld by him, than by any other person.

[Paragraph 114 maintains that the secretary of state has a legal obligation to deliver all commissions to the appointed officeholders. As this is a legal duty, a court may issue a writ of mandamus requiring the secretary of state to fulfill that duty.]

[115] It was at first doubted whether the action of detinue was not a specified legal remedy for the commission which has been withheld from Mr. Marbury; in which case a mandamus would be improper. But this doubt has yielded to the consideration that the judgment in detinue is for the thing itself, or its value. The value of a public office not to be sold, is incapable of being ascertained; and the applicant has a right to the office itself, or to nothing. He will obtain the office by obtaining the commission, or a copy of it from the record.

[Paragraph 115 concludes that William Marbury's injury cannot be remedied by money. A monetary value cannot be placed on the right to hold public office. Other justices might think Marbury fully compensated by payment of his salary. This is the standard legal remedy when a person is illegally denied employment.]

[116] This, then, is a plain case for a mandamus, either to deliver the commission, or a copy of it from the record; and it only remains to be enquired.

[Paragraph 116 concludes that William Marbury is legally entitled to a writ of mandamus. Courts are au-

thorized to issue writs of mandamus to executive officials, and no legal remedy other than delivery of the judicial commission will compensate William Marbury for the illegal deprivation of that commission.]

The Constitutionality of Section 13 of the Judiciary Act of 1789

[117] Whether it can issue from this court.

[The constitutional question in Marbury was whether the Supreme Court could exercise original jurisdiction when a citizen of the United States asked the justices to issue a writ of mandamus to a federal official. Courts exercise original jurisdiction when they are the first legal tribunal to decide a lawsuit. Courts exercise appellate jurisdiction when they review previous judicial rulings in a lawsuit.]

[118] The act to establish the judicial courts of the United States authorizes the supreme court "to issue writs of mandamus, in cases warranted by the principles and usages of law, to any courts appointed, or persons holding office, under the authority of the United States."

[Paragraph 118 selectively quotes Section 13 of the Judiciary Act of 1789. The statutory extract quoted is from a paragraph devoted to the appellate jurisdiction of the Supreme Court. This broader context suggests the best or at least reasonable interpretation of the statutory language is that the Supreme Court is authorized to grant writs of mandamus only when exercising appellate jurisdiction. The phrase, "in cases warranted by the principles and usages of law," might be interpreted as vesting the Supreme Court with power to issue writs of mandamus only in cases where the justices had jurisdiction on other grounds. Nothing in the text of Section 13 supports the claim made in the following paragraph that Congress had authorized the Supreme Court to adjudicate any case where a litigant asked the justices to issue a writ of mandamus to any federal official.

This exercise in statutory "misconstruction" is particularly remarkable given the common judicial practice of interpreting statutes, whenever possible, as consistent with constitutional standards. This practice was even more prevalent at the time Marbury was decided. (See Documents 3, 50, 59.) That Chief Justice John Marshall adopted a forced construction of Section 13 in order to declare that statutory provision unconstitutional provides more evidence that he was using Marbury as a vehicle to test whether Jeffersonians objected to judicial re-

view in the abstract. See comments after paragraph 132.]

[119] The secretary of state, being a person holding an office under the authority of the United States, is precisely within the letter of the description; and if this court is not authorized to issue a writ of mandamus to such an officer, it must be because the law is unconstitutional, and therefore absolutely incapable of conferring the authority, and assigning the duties which its words purport to confer and assign.

[Paragraph 119 concludes that Section 13 vests the Supreme Court with original jurisdiction in all cases in which the justices are asked to issue a writ of mandamus to a federal official. Most contemporary commentators, for reasons discussed in the comment to paragraph 118, reject this interpretation of Section 13.]

[120] The constitution vests the whole judicial power of the United States in one supreme court, and such inferior courts as congress shall, from time to time, ordain and establish. This power is expressly extended to all cases arising under the laws of the United States; and consequently, in some form, may be exercised over the present case; because the right claimed is given by a law of the United States.

[121] In the distribution of this power it is declared that "the supreme court shall have original jurisdiction in all cases affecting ambassadors, other public ministers and consuls, and those in which a state shall be a party. In all other cases, the supreme court shall have appellate jurisdiction."

[Paragraphs 120–121 indicate that the Constitution vests the Supreme Court with appellate jurisdiction in lawsuits between a private individual and a government official. Article III, the text notes, declares the Supreme Court has original jurisdiction only in cases involving states or foreign officials. Neither William Marbury nor James Madison was a state or foreign official. Hence, Article III appears to prohibit the Supreme Court from exercising original jurisdiction in Marbury.
Once again, Marbury engages in selection quotation. Paragraph 121 fails to note that after asserting, "[i]n all other cases, the supreme court shall

have appellate jurisdiction," Article III continues, "both as to Law and Fact, with such Exceptions, and under such Regulations as the Congress shall make." Many scholars think that granting original jurisdiction in cases where the Supreme Court was initially vested with appellate jurisdiction is one of the constitutional "exceptions" Congress may make to the appellate jurisdiction of the Supreme Court. This is the argument discussed in paragraph 122.]

[122] It has been insisted, at the bar, that as the original grant of jurisdiction, to the supreme and inferior courts, is general, and the clause, assigning original jurisdiction to the supreme court, contains no negative or restrictive words; the power remains to the legislature, to assign original jurisdiction to that court in other cases than those specified in the article which has been recited; provided those cases belong to the judicial power of the United States.

[123] If it had been intended to leave it to the discretion of the legislature to apportion the judicial power between the supreme and inferior courts according to the will of that body, it would certainly have been useless to have proceeded further than to have defined the judicial powers, and the tribunals in which it should be vested. The subsequent part of the section is mere surplusage, is entirely without meaning, if such is to be the construction. If congress remains at liberty to give this court appellate jurisdiction, where the constitution has declared their jurisdiction shall be original; and original jurisdiction where the constitution has declared it shall be appellate; the distribution of jurisdiction, made in the constitution, is form without substance.

[The Supreme Court in Cohens v. Virginia (1821) (Document 84) recanted the last sentence in paragraph 123. The justices asserted that Congress could vest the Supreme Court with appellate jurisdiction in cases in which the constitution provided for both appellate and original jurisdiction.]

[124] Affirmative words are often, in their operation, negative of other objects than those affirmed; and in this case, a negative or exclusive sense must be given to them or they have no operation at all.

[125] It cannot be presumed that any clause in the constitution is intended to be without effect; and therefore such a construction is inadmissible, unless the words require it.

[126] If the solicitude of the convention, respecting our peace with foreign powers, induced a provision that the supreme court should take original jurisdiction in cases which might be supposed to affect them; yet the clause would have proceeded no further than to provide for such cases, if no further restriction on the powers of congress had been intended. That they should have appellate jurisdiction in all other cases, with such exceptions as congress might make, is no restriction; unless the words be deemed exclusive of original jurisdiction.

[127] When an instrument organizing fundamentally a judicial system, divides it into one supreme, and so many inferior courts as the legislature may ordain and establish; then enumerates its powers, and proceeds so far to distribute them, as to define the jurisdiction of the supreme court by declaring the cases in which it shall take original jurisdiction, and that in others it shall take appellate jurisdiction; the plain import of the words seems to be, that in one class of cases its jurisdiction is original, and not appellate; in the other it is appellate, and not original. If any other construction would render the clause inoperative, that is an additional reason for rejecting such other construction, and for adhering to their obvious meaning.

[Paragraphs 122–127 claim that Congress may not add or subtract from the original or the appellate jurisdiction of the Supreme Court as laid out in Article III. The relevant constitutional provisions would be meaningless if Congress was free to change federal jurisdiction at will.

On another interpretation, Article III declares that Congress may not subtract from the original jurisdiction of the Supreme Court, but may, when making "exceptions" to appellate jurisdiction, add to that original jurisdiction. Paragraph 126 gives reasons why the framers might not have wanted Congress to reduce the original jurisdiction of the Supreme Court. At no point in Marbury is any reason given why the framers would not have wanted Congress to increase the original jurisdiction of the Supreme Court.]

[128] To enable this court then to issue a mandamus, it must be shown to be an exercise of appellate jurisdiction, or to be necessary to enable them to exercise appellate jurisdiction.

[Paragraph 128 insists that the justices may issue a writ of mandamus in Marbury *only if the justices in that case are exercising appellate jurisdiction.]*

[129] It has been stated at the bar that the appellate jurisdiction may be exercised in a variety of forms, and that if it be the will of the legislature that a mandamus should be used for that purpose, that will must be obeyed. This is true, yet the jurisdiction must be appellate, not original.

[130] It is the essential criterion of appellate jurisdiction, that it revises and corrects the proceedings in a cause already instituted, and does not create that cause. Although, therefore, a mandamus may be directed to courts, yet to issue such a writ to an officer for the delivery of a paper, is in effect the same as to sustain an original action for that paper, and therefore seems not to belong to appellate, but to original jurisdiction. Neither is it necessary in such a case as this, to enable the court to exercise its appellate jurisdiction.

[Paragraphs 129–130 reject the possibility that Marbury *might be an exercise of appellate jurisdiction. The Supreme Court was the first tribunal to determine whether William Marbury was entitled to a writ of mandamus. A decision to grant the writ would not revise, correct, or affirm a previous judicial ruling.]*

[131] The authority, therefore, given to the supreme court, by the act establishing the judicial courts of the United States, to issue writs of mandamus to public officers, appears not to be warranted by the constitution; and it becomes necessary to enquire whether a jurisdiction, so conferred, can be exercised.

[Paragraph 131 concludes that Section 13 of the Judicial Act of 1789 is unconstitutional. The national legislature may not vest the Supreme Court with original jurisdiction over cases in which the Constitution vests the justices with appellate jurisdiction.]

Judicial Review

[132] The question, whether an act, repugnant to the constitution, can become the law of the land, is a question deeply interesting to the United States; but, happily, not of an intricacy proportioned to its interest. It seems only necessary to recognize certain principles, supposed to have been long and well established, to decide it.

[Paragraph 132 begins the discussion of judicial review. The question asked is whether justices should give legal effect to a law previously established as unconstitutional. By first determining that Section 13 of the Judiciary Act of 1787 was unconstitutional and only then discussing how courts should treat an unconstitutional law, Marbury sidesteps the most difficult issue. Nothing in the opinion justifies judicial review when controversy exists over whether the law under constitutional attack is constitutional.

The Marbury opinion suggests the legal status of an unconstitutional act is easy to determine. Scott Douglas Gerber in Chapter 1 highlights the numerous cases, many of which are excerpted above, where justices previously asserted the power to declare laws unconstitutional. Supreme Court justices had previously declared unconstitutional a statutory provision requiring the justices to certify whether Revolutionary War veterans were entitled to federal pensions. (See Documents 57–58.) The judicial power to determine what laws are unconstitutional, however, proved quite controversial in the Seventh Congress. (See Documents 70–72.)

The Marbury opinion may have been intended to test whether Jeffersonians opposed judicial review in the abstract, or merely feared that the Marshall Court would use the power to strike down Jeffersonian initiatives. If, as Chief Justice Marshall probably suspected, Jeffersonians had no generalized objections to judicial review, they would not object when the Supreme Court declared an obscure federal law unconstitutional. James M. O'Fallon, in Chapter 2, and Lee Epstein and Jack Knight, in Chapter 3, discuss the political and strategic context of Marbury.]

[133] That the people have an original right to establish, for their future government, such principles as, in their opinion, shall most conduce to their own happiness, is the basis, on which the whole American fabric has been erected. The exercise of this original right is a very great exertion; nor can it, nor ought it to be frequently repeated. The principles, therefore, so established,

are deemed fundamental. And as the authority, from which they proceed, is supreme, and can seldom act, they are designed to be permanent.

[134] This original and supreme will organizes the government, and assigns, to different departments, their respective powers. It may either stop here; or establish certain limits not to be transcended by those departments.

[135] The government of the United States is of the latter description. The powers of the legislature are defined, and limited; and that those limits may not be mistaken, or forgotten, the constitution is written. To what purpose are powers limited, and to what purpose is that limitation committed to writing, if these limits may, at any time, be passed by those intended to be restrained? The distinction, between a government with limited and unlimited powers, is abolished, if those limits do not confine the persons on whom they are imposed, and if acts prohibited and acts allowed, are of equal obligation. It is a proposition too plain to be contested, that the constitution controls any legislative act repugnant to it; or, that the legislature may alter the constitution by an ordinary act.

[136] Between these alternatives there is no middle ground. The constitution is either a superior, paramount law, unchangeable by ordinary means, or it is on a level with ordinary legislative acts, and like other acts, is alterable when the legislature shall please to alter it.

[This claim that the Constitution is "superior, paramount law" plays a crucial role in the Marbury opinion. Some commentators believe that Americans in the eighteenth century understood constitutions as expressing fundamental political principles rather than as establishing legal limitations on government.]

[137] If the former part of the alternative be true, then a legislative act contrary to the constitution is not law: if the latter part be true, then written constitutions are absurd attempts, on the part of the people, to limit a power, in its own nature illimitable.

[138] Certainly all those who have framed written constitutions contemplate them as form-

ing the fundamental and paramount law of the nation, and consequently the theory of every such government must be, that an act of the legislature, repugnant to the constitution, is void.

[139] This theory is essentially attached to a written constitution, and is consequently to be considered, by this court, as one of the fundamental principles of our society. It is not therefore to be lost sight of in the further consideration of this subject.

[Paragraphs 133–139 assert that the purpose of written constitutions is to provide legal limitations on government power. Constitutions are laws, but superior to ordinary legislation. Hence, all government acts inconsistent with written constitutional provisions are void. The precise relationship between writtenness and judicial review is controversial. The first English courts to engage in practices analogous to judicial review declared that certain unwritten common law principles constrained legislatures. (See Document 4.)]

[140] If an act of the legislature, repugnant to the constitution, is void, does it, notwithstanding its invalidity, bind the courts, and oblige them to give it effect? Or, in other words, though it be not law, does it constitute a rule as operative as if it was a law? This would be to overthrow in fact what was established in theory; and would seem, at first view, an absurdity too gross to be insisted on. It shall, however, receive a more attentive consideration.

[141] It is emphatically the province and duty of the judicial department to say what the law is. Those who apply the rule to particular cases, must of necessity expound and interpret that rule. If two laws conflict with each other, the courts must decide on the operation of each.

[Paragraph 141 highlights the importance of the claim made in paragraph 136 that the Constitution is supreme law. Courts when deciding cases are entitled to examine the Constitution because courts are responsible for expounding the law, and the Constitution is law.]

[142] So if a law be in opposition to the constitution; if both the law and the constitution apply to a particular case, so that the court must either decide that case conformably to the law, disregarding the constitution; or conformably to the constitution, disregarding the law; the court must determine which of these conflicting rules governs the case. This is of the very essence of judicial duty.

[143] If then the courts are to regard the constitution; and the constitution is superior to any ordinary act of the legislature; the constitution, and not such ordinary act, must govern the case to which they both apply.

[Paragraphs 142–143 assert that when a constitutional provision is inconsistent with a legislative act, a court of law must be guided by the Constitution because the Constitution is higher law than ordinary legislation.]

[144] Those then who controvert the principle that the constitution is to be considered, in court, as a paramount law, are reduced to the necessity of maintaining that courts must close their eyes on the constitution, and see only the law.

[145] This doctrine would subvert the very foundation of all written constitutions. It would declare that an act, which, according to the principles and theory of our government, is entirely void; is yet, in practice, completely obligatory. It would declare, that if the legislature shall do what is expressly forbidden, such act, notwithstanding the express prohibition, is in reality effectual. It would be giving to the legislature a practical and real omnipotence, with the same breath which professes to restrict their powers within narrow limits. It is prescribing limits, and declaring that those limits may be passed at pleasure.

[146] That it thus reduces to nothing what we have deemed the greatest improvement on political institutions—a written constitution—would of itself be sufficient, in America, where written constitutions have been viewed with so much reverence, for rejecting the construction. But the peculiar expressions of the constitution of the United States furnish additional arguments in favor of its rejection.

[Paragraphs 144–146 assert that giving legal status to laws "expressly forbidden" by the Constitution

would make legislatures omnipotent, thus destroying the entire purpose of written constitutions. Many framers suggested that elections were the primary mechanism for ensuring that government officials respected the constitutional limits on their power. (See Documents 23, 25, 31.)

[147] The judicial power of the United States is extended to all cases arising under the constitution.

[148] Could it be the intention of those who gave this power, to say that, in using it, the constitution should not be looked into? That a case arising under the constitution should be decided without examining the instrument under which it arises?

[Paragraphs 140–148 conclude that justices must ignore unconstitutional laws when resolving cases. Marbury does not explicitly assert that judicial interpretations of the Constitution bind elected officials. Almost two hundred years later, the Supreme Court in Cooper v. Aaron (1958) (Document 90), claimed that Marbury did assert that judicial power. Whether Marbury is best interpreted as asserting judicial supremacy, the Supreme Court is the final interpreter of constitutional meaning, as well as judicial review, the Supreme Court has the authority to ignore unconstitutional laws when deciding cases, is hotly disputed.

The issue of judicial review and judicial supremacy is central to many essays in this volume. Stephen M. Griffin in Chapter 4 questions whether the notion of judicial review set out in Marbury is the same as contemporary notions of judicial review. Robert Lowry Clinton and Keith E. Whittington (Chapters 5 and 6 respectively) detail the evolution of judicial review over time. Jeremy Waldron in Chapter 9 articulates the case against judicial supremacy. In Chapter 7 Ran Hirschl explores the evolution of judicial review and judicial supremacy outside the United States, and in Chapter 8 Ronald Kahn more aggressively defends judicial power.]

[149] This is too extravagant to be maintained.

[150] In some cases then, the constitution must be looked into by the judges. And if they can open it at all, what part of it are they forbidden to read, or to obey?

[151] There are many other parts of the constitution which serve to illustrate this subject.

[152] It is declared that "no tax or duty shall be laid on articles exported from any state." Suppose a duty on the export of cotton, of tobacco, or of flour; and a suit instituted to recover it. Ought judgment to be rendered in such a case? ought the judges to close their eyes on the constitution, and only see the law.

[153] The constitution declares that "no bill of attainder or ex post facto law shall be passed."

[154] If, however, such a bill should be passed and a person should be prosecuted under it; must the court condemn to death those victims whom the constitution endeavors to preserve?

[155] "No person," says the constitution, "shall be convicted of treason unless on the testimony of two witnesses to the fame overt act, or on confession in open court."

[Paragraphs 152–155 list laws that are, by definition, unconstitutional. Some scholars maintain the power of judicial review asserted in Marbury is only the power to declare unconstitutional laws no reasonable person on reflection would think constitutional. Many reasonable persons, however, have thought Section 13 of the Judiciary Act of 1789 was constitutional.]

[156] Here the language of the constitution is addressed especially to the courts. It prescribes, directly for them, a rule of evidence not to be departed from. If the legislature should change that rule, and declare one witness, or a confession out of court, sufficient for conviction, must the constitutional principle yield to the legislative act?

[157] From these, and many other selections which might be made, it is apparent, that the framers of the constitution contemplated that instrument, as a rule for the government of courts, as well as of the legislature.

[Paragraphs 155–157 point out that some constitutional provisions are directed primarily at the judiciary. Hence, the Constitution must presume that courts will enforce those constitutional provisions when they conflict with a legislative act. Some prominent scholars think paragraphs 153 through 157 assert that the Supreme Court has the power to declare only laws of a judiciary nature unconstitutional. On this view, the justices have the power to

strike down federal laws that unconstitutionally interfere with jury trials, a judicial process, but not federal laws that unconstitutionally give the president power to order troops into combat without a congressional declaration of war. This view is defended by Robert Clinton in Chapter 5.]

[158] Why otherwise does it direct the judges to take an oath to support it? This oath certainly applies, in an especial manner, to their conduct in their official character. How immoral to impose it on them, if they were to be used as the instruments, and the knowing instruments, for violating what they swear to support!

[159] The oath of office, too, imposed by the legislature, is completely demonstrative of the legislative opinion on the subject. It is in these words, "I do solemnly swear that I will administer justice without respect to persons, and do equal right to the poor and to the rich; and that I will faithfully and impartially discharge all the duties incumbent on me as according to the best of my abilities and understanding, agreeably to the constitution, and laws of the United States."

[160] Why does a judge swear to discharge his duties agreeably to the constitution of the United States, if that constitution forms no rule for his government? if it is closed upon him, and cannot be inspected by him?

[161] If such be the real state of things, this is worse than solemn mockery. To prescribe, or to take this oath, becomes equally a crime.

[Paragraphs 158–161 assert the judicial oath to obey the Constitution requires justices to be guided by the Constitution when constitutional provisions conflict with legislative acts. Marbury does not acknowledge that other governing officials take a similar oath. Did President George Washington and the members of the First Congress violate their constitu-

tional oaths when they passed Section 13 of the Judiciary Act of 1789? What of William Paterson, who sat on the Court that decided Marbury, but, when in Congress, drafted much of the Judiciary Act of 1789? Does every officer who takes an oath to support the Constitution swear to act on their best interpretation of the Constitution?]

[162] It is also not entirely unworthy of observation, that in declaring what shall be the supreme law of the land, the constitution itself is first mentioned; and not the laws of the United States generally, but those only which shall be made in pursuance of the constitution, have that rank.

[163] Thus, the particular phraseology of the constitution of the United States confirms and strengthens the principle, supposed to be essential to all written constitutions, that a law repugnant to the constitution is void; and that courts, as well as other departments, are bound by that instrument.

[Paragraphs 162–163 interpret the supremacy clause in Article VI as establishing that only federal acts consistent with the Constitution are part of the law of the land that binds all state officials. Whether the claim in paragraph 163 that "courts, as well as other departments, are bound by" the Constitution entails that other departments must be bound by judicial interpretations of the Constitution is controversial. See the discussion after paragraph 148.]

[164] The rule must be discharged.

[Paragraph 164 cancels the order to show cause discussed in paragraph 1. James Madison does not have to explain to the Supreme Court why William Marbury is not entitled a writ of mandamus because the Supreme Court lacks the jurisdiction necessary to issue that writ in this case.]

B

Appendix B:
Supreme Court Opinions Citing and
Quoting *Marbury v. Madison*

Between 1803 (the decision date of Marbury v. Madison) and the end of the 2001–2002 term in June 2002, the Supreme Court cited or referred to Marbury in well over two hundred cases. Below is a listing of these cases, including justice, types of opinions, and citation.

Cooper v. Telfair, 4 U.S. 14 (1800)
(see Document 63)
Justice Chase, *seriatim* opinion: *Marbury* cited as holding that "the Supreme Court may declare an act of Congress to be unconstitutional" (4 U.S. at 19 n. 1). (*Note: Cooper* was decided before *Marbury* but the opinions were not published until after *Marbury* was handed down.)

Ex parte Bollman, 8 U.S. 75 (1807)
(see Document 83)
Chief Justice Marshall, majority opinion: *Marbury* cited as holding that the Supreme Court may issue a writ of mandamus in cases of appellate jurisdiction but not cases of original jurisdiction (8 U.S. at 100–101).

Justice Johnson, dissenting: *Marbury* cited as holding that the original jurisdiction of the Supreme Court "can neither be restricted or extended" by Congress, cited as overruling *United States v. Hamilton* (1795), cited as holding that the Supreme Court may not issue writs of mandamus or habeas corpus when exercising original jurisdiction, cited as holding that Congress may not empower the Court to issue any writ inconsistent with the jurisdictional rules set out in Article III, and

quoted as holding that "[i]t is the essential criterion of appellate jurisdiction, that it revises and corrects the proceedings in a cause already instituted" (8 U.S. at 103–106).

M'Cluny v. Silliman, 15 U.S. 369 (1817)
Per curiam: *Marbury* cited as holding that the Supreme Court may issue a writ of mandamus to a government official only when exercising appellate jurisdiction (15 U.S. at 370 n. 1).

M'Clung v. Silliman, 19 U.S. 598 (1821)
Justice Johnson, unanimous opinion: *Marbury* cited as holding that Congress may vest federal courts with the power to issue writs of mandamus in cases where jurisdiction may be constitutionally exercised (19 U.S. at 604).

Cohens v. Virginia, 19 U.S. 264 (1821)
(see Document 84)
Chief Justice Marshall, unanimous opinion: *Marbury* quoted as holding that no provision in the Constitution is "mere surplusage" or "form without substance," and cited as erroneously asserting in dictum that Congress could not subtract from the original jurisdiction of the Supreme Court (19 U.S. at 394, 399–402).

United States v. Ortega, 24 U.S. 467 (1826)
Justice Washington, unanimous opinion: *Marbury* cited containing dictum "revised" by *Cohens v. Virginia* (24 U.S. at 469).

Ex parte Crane, 30 U.S. 190 (1831)
Justice Baldwin, dissenting: *Marbury* quoted on the proper definition of a writ of mandamus, quoted as holding that the Supreme Court may not issue writs of mandamus in cases of original jurisdiction, and quoted as a holding that the Supreme Court may not order government officials to purely discretionary duties (30 U.S. at 200, 203–217).

United States v. Arredondo, 31 U.S. 691 (1932)
Justice Baldwin, majority opinion: *Marbury* cited as holding that federal courts cannot order executive officials to perform discretionary tasks (31 U.S. at 729).

Ex parte Watkins, 32 U.S. 568 (1833)
Justice Story, majority opinion: *Marbury* cited as holding that Congress may not expand the original jurisdiction of the Supreme Court but may vest the Supreme Court with power to review the decision by a lower federal court to grant a writ of mandamus, as that is an exercise of appellate jurisdiction (32 U.S. at 572–573).

Harrison v. Nixon, 34 U.S. 483 (1835)
Justice Baldwin, dissenting: *Marbury* cited as holding that Congress may not alter the original jurisdiction of the Supreme Court (34 U.S. at 530).

Kendall v. United States, 37 U.S. 524 (1838)
Justice Thompson, majority opinion: *Marbury* cited as holding that the Supreme Court may not issue a writ on mandamus when exercising original jurisdiction, but as not forbidding Congress from vesting federal courts with the power to issue writs of mandamus in other circumstances (37 U.S. at 617, 618, 621).

Justice Barbour dissenting: *Marbury* cited as leaving in place the legislative decision in 1789 that only the Supreme Court would have the power to issue writs of mandamus (37 U.S. at 651).

Justice Catron, dissenting: *Marbury* cited as leaving in place the congressional decisions before and after 1803 not to vest lower federal courts with the power to issue writs of mandamus (37 U.S. at 653).

Decatur v. Paulding, 39 U.S. 497 (1840)
Justice Baldwin, concurring: *Marbury* quoted on the nature of a writ of mandamus, cited as forbidding the Supreme Court to issue writs of mandamus in cases of original jurisdiction, and cited as allowing Congress to permit federal courts to issue that writ in other circumstances (39 U.S. at 602, 608, 610).

In re Metzger, 46 U.S. 176 (1847)
Justice McLean, unanimous opinion: *Marbury* quoted as holding that "Congress have not power to give original jurisdiction to the Supreme Court in other cases than those described in the constitution" (46 U.S. at 191).

United States v. Chicago, 48 U.S. 185 (1849)
Justice Catron, dissenting: *Marbury* cited as holding that Congress cannot add to the original jurisdiction of the Supreme Court (48 U.S. at 197).

Carroll v. Lessee of Carroll, 57 U.S. 275 (1850)
Justice Curtis, unanimous opinion: *Marbury* quoted as an example of an opinion that contained unnecessary dicta that did not bind subsequent judicial decisions (57 U.S. at 287).

Reeside v. Walker, 52 U.S. 272 (1850)
Justice Woodbury, unanimous opinion: *Marbury* cited as holding that a writ of mandamus is appropriate only when no other legal remedy exists (52 U.S. at 291–292).

In re Kaine, 55 U.S. 103 (1852)

Justice Curtis, dissenting: *Marbury* cited as holding that the Supreme Court may not issue a writ of habeas corpus when exercising original jurisdiction, cited as supporting the claim that an immediate review of an executive action issuing a warrant for extradition involves original rather than appellate jurisdiction, and cited as holding that the Supreme Court has no appellate jurisdiction over such executive decisions (55 U.S. at 119, 128).

Florida v. Georgia, 58 U.S. 478 (1854)

Justice Curtis, dissenting: *Marbury* cited as holding that Congress may not add to the original jurisdiction of the Supreme Court and cited as overruling previous Supreme Court decisions to the contrary (58 U.S. at 505, 509).

Ex parte Wells, 59 U.S. 307 (1855)

Justice McLean, dissenting: *Marbury* cited as holding that the Supreme Court may not issue writs of habeas corpus when exercising original jurisdiction (59 U.S. at 317).

Ex parte Vallandigham, 68 U.S. 243 (1863)

Justice Wayne, majority opinion: *Marbury* cited as holding that Congress cannot add to the original jurisdiction of the Supreme Court (68 U.S. at 252 n. 5).

Daniels v. Railroad Company, 70 U. S. 250 (1865)

Justice Swayne, unanimous opinion: *Marbury* cited as holding that the Supreme Court may exercise appellate jurisdiction only when such jurisdiction is provided for by both the Constitution and federal statute (70 U. S. at 254 n. 2).

Mississippi v. Johnson, 71 U.S. 475 (1866) (see Document 85)

Chief Justice Chase, unanimous opinion: *Marbury* quoted as holding that courts may only order executive branch officials to perform ministerial actions (71 U.S. at 498–499).

The William Bagaley, 72 U.S. 377 (1866)

Justice Clifford, unanimous opinion: *Marbury* cited as holding that the Supreme Court has no original jurisdiction in prize cases (72 U.S. at 411 n. 84).

Riggs v. Johnson County, 73 U.S. 166 (1867)

Justice Clifford, majority opinion: *Marbury* cited as holding that the Supreme Court has no power to issue writs of mandamus when exercising original jurisdiction (73 U.S. at 188).

Gaines v. Thompson, 74 U.S. 347 (1868)

Justice Miller, majority opinion: *Marbury* cited as holding that federal courts may issue various writs to executive officials only to compel them to perform ministerial duties, not duties to which executive officers were constitutionally authorized to exercise discretion (74 U.S. at 348–349).

Ex parte Yerger, 75 U.S. 85 (1868) (see Document 86)

Chief Justice Chase, unanimous opinion: *Marbury* cited as establishing, possibly contrary to the original understanding, that the Supreme Court could issue writs of mandamus only when exercising appellate jurisdiction (75 U.S. at 97).

Ex parte Newman, 81 U.S. 152 (1871)

Justice Clifford, unanimous opinion: *Marbury* cited as holding that Congress cannot enlarge the original jurisdiction of the Supreme Court (81 U.S. at 165 n. 11).

Lapeyre v. United States, 84 U.S. 191 (1872)

Justice Hunt, dissenting: *Marbury* cited as holding that a commission is valid when signed and sealed, but not holding that a proclamation was valid when signed, but not published (84 U.S. at 205).

Insurance Company v. Comstock, 83 U.S. 258 (1872)

Justice Clifford, unanimous opinion: *Marbury* cited as holding that courts may issue writs of mandamus to lower federal justices when exercising appellate jurisdiction (83 U.S. at 270 n. 10).

United States v. Boutwell, 84 U.S. 604 (1873)
Justice Strong, unanimous opinion: *Marbury* cited as holding that the Supreme Court cannot issue writs of mandamus when exercising original jurisdiction (84 U.S. at 609 n. 5).

Virginia v. Rives, 100 U.S. 313 (1879)
Justice Field, concurring: *Marbury* cited as holding that the Supreme Court may normally issue writs of mandamus only when exercising appellate jurisdiction, that the Supreme Court may not issue the writ to public officials because that is an exercise of original jurisdiction, and cited as holding that the Supreme Court may not issue the writ when removing a case from a state to a federal court because that is also an exercise of original jurisdiction (100 U.S. at 327–328, 337).

Ex parte Virginia, 100 U.S. 339 (1879)
Justice Strong, majority opinion: *Marbury* cited as holding that the Supreme Court may not issue a writ of mandamus when exercising original jurisdiction, unless a state is a party to the case (100 U.S. at 341).

Ex parte Clarke, 100 U.S. 399 (1879)
Justice Field, dissenting: *Marbury* cited as holding that Congress may not expand the jurisdiction of federal courts (100 U.S. at 408).

United States v. Schurz, 102 U.S. 378 (1880)
Justice Miller, majority opinion: *Marbury* quoted as holding that courts may compel government officials to perform ministerial duties, that land patents are valid when signed and sealed, and that commissions are valid when signed and sealed (102 U.S. at 395, 399, 402).

Louisiana v. Jumel, 107 U.S. 711 (1882)
Justice Field, dissenting: *Marbury* quoted as establishing the conditions under which a writ of mandamus will be granted, as holding that courts will provide legal remedies for violations of vested rights, as holding that citizens may bring lawsuits against governing officials, and as holding that the Supreme Court may issue a writ of mandamus to require a government officer to perform a ministerial duty (107 U.S. at 743–745).

Cunningham v. Macon & B. R. Co., 109 U.S. 446 (1883)
Justice Miller, majority opinion: *Marbury* cited as holding that a writ of mandamus will be granted only when a public officer is asked to perform a ministerial duty (109 U.S. at 453).

Bors v. Preston, 111 U.S. 252 (1884)
Justice Harlan, majority opinion: *Marbury* cited as holding that Congress may give federal district courts original jurisdiction in cases involving foreign consuls (111 U.S. at 258).

Ames v. Kansas, 111 U.S. 449 (1884)
Chief Justice Waite, unanimous opinion: *Marbury* cited as holding that Congress may not add to the original jurisdiction of the Supreme Court, and as containing erroneous dictum suggesting that Congress may not subtract from the original jurisdiction of the Supreme Court (111 U.S. at 466–467).

Poindexter v. Greenhow, 114 U.S. 270 (1885)
Justice Matthews, majority opinion: *Marbury* qutoed as holding that "[t]he Government of the United States has been emphatically termed a government of laws and not of men. It will certainly cease to deserve this high appellation if the laws furnish no remedy for the violation of a vested legal right" (114 U.S. at 298).

Mugler v. Kansas, 123 U.S. 623 (1887)
(see Document 87)
Justice Harlan, majority opinion: *Marbury* quoted as holding that the Supreme Court

has the power to declare federal laws unconstitutional (123 U.S. at 661).

Sabariego v. Maverick, 124 U.S. 261 (1888)
Justice Matthews, unanimous opinion: _Marbury_ cited as holding that federal courts cannot order executive officials to perform discretionary tasks (124 U.S. at 282).

United States ex rel. Dunlap v. Black, 128 U.S. 40 (1888)
Justice Bradley, unanimous opinion: _Marbury_ cited as holding that a writ of mandamus will be granted only to require an officer to perform a ministerial duty (128 U.S. at 44, 49).

Leisy v. Hardin, 135 U.S. 100 (1890)
Justice Gray, dissenting: _Marbury_ cited as containing erroneous dictum (135 U.S. at 135).

United States ex rel. Redfield v. Windom, 137 U.S. 636 (1891)
Justice Lamar, unanimous opinion: _Marbury_ cited as one of the many cases determining the conditions under which courts may issue writs of mandamus to public officers (137 U.S. at 643).

McAllister v. United States, 141 U.S. 174 (1891)
Justice Harlan, majority opinion: _Marbury_ cited as inapplicable when Congress specifies by statute that a territorial judge is removable at the will of the president (141 U.S. at 188–189).

Noble v. Union River Logging R. Co., 147 U.S. 165 (1893)
Justice Brown, unanimous opinion: _Marbury_ cited as holding that courts may not require executive officials to perform discretionary duties (147 U.S. at 171).

United States v. California & Oregon Land Co., 148 U.S. 31 (1893)
Justice Brewer, unanimous opinion: _Marbury_ cited as holding that federal courts cannot order executive officials to perform discretionary tasks (148 U.S. at 43–44).

United States ex rel. International Contracting Co. v. Lamont, 155 U.S. 303 (1894)
Justice White, unanimous opinion: _Marbury_ cited as holding that a writ of mandamus will be granted only to require an officer to perform a ministerial duty (155 U.S. at 308).

California v. Southern Pacific Co., 157 U.S. 229 (1895)
Chief Justice Fuller, majority opinion: _Marbury_ cited as holding that Congress may "neither enlarge nor restrict" the original jurisdiction of the Supreme Court (157 U.S. at 261).

Pollock v. Farmers' Loan & Trust Co., 157 U.S. 429 (1895)
Chief Justice Fuller, majority opinion: _Marbury_ quoted as holding that the Supreme Court has the power to declare federal laws unconstitutional (157 U.S. at 554).

Parsons v. United States, 167 U.S. 324 (1897)
Justice Peckham, unanimous opinion: _Marbury_ quoted as holding that justices of the peace in the District of Columbia were not removable at the will of the president, but as not denying presidential power to remove district attorneys appointed outside of the District before their term of office expired (167 U.S. at 335–337).

Taylor v. Beckham, 178 U.S. 548 (1900)
Justice Harlan, dissenting: _Marbury_ quoted as holding that "(t)he very essence of civil liberty . . . is the right of every individual to claim the protection of the laws, whenever he receives an injury" (178 U.S. at 586).

Fairbank v. United States, 181 U.S. 283 (1901)
Justice Brewer, majority opinion: _Marbury_ quoted at length as holding that courts have

the power to declare laws unconstitutional (181 U.S. at 285–286).

Downes v. Bidwell, 182 U.S. 244 (1901)
Justice White, concurring: *Marbury* cited as holding that "the government of the United States is supreme within its lawful sphere" (182 U.S. at 288–289).

Chief Justice Fuller, dissenting: *Marbury* quoted as holding that the federal government is one of limited powers (182 U.S. at 358–359).

Justice Harlan, dissenting: *Marbury* quoted as holding that the federal government is one of limited powers (182 U.S. at 380–381).

Dooley v. United States, 183 U.S. 151 (1901)
Chief Justice Fuller, dissenting: *Marbury* quoted as holding that "[i]t is declared that 'no tax or duty shall be laid on articles exported from any State.' Suppose a duty on the export of cotton, of tobacco, or of flour; and a suit instituted to recover it. Ought judgment to be rendered in such a case? Ought the judges to close their eyes on the Constitution, and only see the law?" (183 U.S. at 173).

Lottery Case, 188 U.S. 321 (1903)
Chief Justice Fuller, dissenting: *Marbury* quoted as holding that "[t]o what purpose are powers limited, and to what purpose is that limitation committed to writing, if these limits may, at any time, be passed by those intended to be restrained?" (188 U.S. at 372).

Garfield v. United States, 211 U.S. 249 (1908)
Justice Day, unanimous opinion: *Marbury* cited as holding that courts considering whether to issue a writ of mandamus should recognize the distinction between discretionary and ministerial acts (211 U.S. at 261).

In re Winn, 213 U.S. 458 (1909)
Justice Moody, unanimous opinion: *Marbury* cited as holding that the Court may issue a writ of mandamus when exercising appellate jurisdiction (213 U.S. at 465–466).

Muskrat v. United States, 219 U.S. 346 (1911)
Justice Day, unanimous opinion: *Marbury* cited as holding that courts may declare laws unconstitutional only in the context of a genuine case or controversy (219 U.S. at 356–359).

Louisiana v. McAdoo, 234 U.S. 627 (1914)
Justice Lurton, majority opinion: *Marbury* cited as holding that federal courts have authority to issue a writ of mandamus ordering an executive official to perform a ministerial duty (234 U.S. at 633–634).

Pennsylvania v. West Virginia, 262 U.S. 553 (1923)
Justice Brandeis, dissenting: *Marbury* cited as holding that the Court has jurisdiction only over cases or controversies (262 U.S. at 610).

Myers v. United States, 272 U.S. 52 (1926) (see Document 88)
Chief Justice Taft, majority opinion: *Marbury* quoted as declaring in erroneous dictum or in a holding later overruled in *Parsons v. United States* that justices of the peace appointed for a fixed term of years may not be removed by the president (272 U.S. at 139–144, 151–152, 158).

Justice McReynolds, dissenting: *Marbury* quoted as holding that the president has no power to remove a civil officer who enjoys by statute a fixed term of office (272 U.S. at 190, 202, 203, 215–219, 220–222, 226, 228–229).

Justice Brandeis, dissenting: *Marbury* cited as holding that the president has no power to remove a civil officer who enjoys by statute a fixed term of office (272 U.S. at 242–244).

Olmstead v. United States, 277 U.S. 438 (1928)
Justice Butler, dissenting: *Marbury* cited as holding that constitutional provisions pro-

tecting individual rights should be liberally construed (277 U.S. at 487).

Texas & N. O. R. Co. v. Brotherhood of R. & S.S. Clerks, 281 U.S. 548 (1930)
Chief Justice Hughes, unanimous opinion: *Marbury* cited as holding that a remedy exists for every rights violation (281 U.S. at 569–570).

United States v. Smith, 286 U.S. 6 (1932)
Justice Brandeis, unanimous opinion: *Marbury* cited as a case in which a litigant asserted that he had been constitutionally appointed to a government office, and cited as an instance where the president did not regard a signed commission as sufficient to entitle a person to a government office (286 U.S. at 33, 47).

Ex parte United States, 287 U.S. 241 (1932)
Justice Sutherland, unanimous opinion: *Marbury* cited as holding that, unless independent grounds for original jurisdiction exist, the Supreme Court may issue writs of mandamus only when exercising appellate jurisdiction (287 U.S. at 245–246).

Humphrey's Executor v. United States, 295 U.S. 602 (1935) (see Document 89)
Justice Sutherland, majority opinion: *Marbury* cited as holding that the president may not remove government officers appointed for fixed terms who do not have purely executive duties, and cited as containing erroneous dictum (295 U.S. at 627, 631).

Ex parte Republic of Peru, 318 U.S. 578 (1943)
Chief Justice Stone, majority opinion: *Marbury* cited as holding that the Supreme Court may issue writs of mandamus to lower courts only when exercising appellate jurisdiction (318 U.S. at 582).

Switchmen's Union of North America v. National Mediation Bd., 320 U.S. 297 (1943)

Justice Reed, dissenting: *Marbury* cited as holding that a remedy exists for statutory rights violations (320 U.S. at 318).

Stark v. Wickard, 321 U.S. 288 (1944)
Justice Reed, majority opinion: *Marbury* quoted as holding"(b)ut where a specific duty is assigned by law, and individual rights depend upon the performance of that duty, it seems equally clear that the individual who considers himself injured, has a right to resort to the laws of his country for a remedy," and cited as holding that the power of administrative agencies is limited to the powers granted to them by statute (321 U.S. at 304 n. 19, 309 n. 22).

Bell v. Hood, 327 U.S. 678 (1946)
Justice Black, majority opinion: *Marbury* cited as holding that courts should find appropriate remedies for federal rights violations (327 U.S. at 685 n. 6).

Adamson v. California, 332 U.S. 46 (1947)
Justice Black, dissenting: *Marbury* cited as holding that courts have the power to declare laws unconstitutional (332 U.S. at 90–91).

United States v. United States Dist. Court, 354 U.S. 258 (1948)
Justice Douglas, majority opinion: *Marbury* cited as holding that the Supreme Court may issue a writ of mandamus when exercising appellate jurisdiction (354 U.S. at 263).

National Mut. Ins. Co. v. Tidewater Transfer Co., 337 U.S. 582 (1949)
Chief Justice Vinson, dissenting: *Marbury* cited as holding that courts may declare laws unconstitutional only in the context of a regular lawsuit (337 U.S. at 630).

United States v. Commodities Trading Corp., 339 U.S. 121 (1950)
Justice Black, majority opinion: *Marbury* cited as holding that the Supreme Court

must determine whether federal laws violate the Fifth Amendment (339 U.S. at 125 n. 3).

United States ex rel. Touhy v. Ragen, 340 U.S. 462 (1951)

Justice Reed, majority opinion: *Marbury* cited as a case that counsel claimed held that the "[e]xecutive should not invade the Judicial sphere" (340 U.S. at 468–469).

Dalehite v. United States, 346 U.S. 15 (1953)

Justice Reed, majority opinion: *Marbury* cited as holding that courts may not interfere with the exercise of discretionary powers by government officials (346 U.S. at 34 n. 30).

Textile Workers Union v. Lincoln Mills of Alabama, 353 U.S. 448 (1957)

Justice Frankfurter, dissenting: *Marbury* cited as holding that Congress may not "impose[] on the Court powers or functions . . . outside the scope of the 'judicial power' lodged in the Court by the Constitution" (353 U.S. at 464).

Reid v. Covert, 354 U.S. 1 (1957)

Justice Black, plurality opinion: *Marbury* cited as holding that the United States "can only act in accordance with all the limitations imposed by the Constitution" and cited as holding "the supremacy of the Constitution over a treaty" (354 U.S. at 6 n. 4, 17 n. 33).

Panama Canal Co. v. Grace Line, Inc., 356 U.S. 309 (1958)

Justice Douglas, unanimous opinion: *Marbury* cited as holding that the writ of mandamus is normally "restricted . . . to situations where ministerial duties of a nondiscretionary nature are involved" (356 U.S. at 318).

Cooper v. Aaron, 358 U.S. 1 (1958)

(see Document 90)

Per curiam opinion: *Marbury* quoted as holding that "the federal judiciary is supreme in the exposition of the law of the Constitution" (358 U.S. at 18).

United States v. Raines, 362 U.S. 17 (1960)

Justice Brennan, majority opinion: *Marbury* cited as holding that the judicial obligation "to declare Acts of Congress unconstitutional lies in the power and duty of those courts to decide cases and controversies properly before them" (362 U.S. at 20).

Clay v. Sun Ins. Office, Ltd., 363 U.S. 207 (1960)

Justice Black, dissenting: *Marbury* cited as an example where the justices made constitutional rulings not necessary to the decision in the case, and quoted as holding that "(t)he very essence of civil liberty certainly consists in the right of every individual to claim the protection of the laws, whenever he receives an injury. One of the first duties of government is to afford that protection" (363 U.S. at 223, 225 n. 1).

Flemming v. Nestor, 363 U.S. 603 (1960)

Justice Black, dissenting: *Marbury* cited as holding that justices are obligated in appropriate cases to determine whether laws are unconstitutional (363 U.S. at 626).

Cohen v. Hurley, 366 U.S. 117 (1961)

Justice Douglas, dissenting: *Marbury* quoted as a case in which the Attorney General refused to answer "certain questions on the ground that the answers might tend to criminate him" (366 U.S. at 150–151).

Baker v. Carr, 369 U.S. 186 (1962)

Justice Brennan, majority opinion: *Marbury* quoted as holding "(t)he very essence of civil liberty certainly consists in the right of every individual to claim the protection of the laws, whenever he receives an injury" (369 U.S. at 208).

Hutcheson v. United States, 369 U.S. 599 (1962)

Chief Justice Warren, dissenting: *Marbury* cited as holding that "the judiciary [must] insure that no branch of the Government transgresses constitutional limitations" (369 U.S. at 632).

Glidden Co. v. Zdanok, 370 U.S. 530 (1962)

Justice Harlan, plurality opinion: *Marbury* cited as holding that any court over which the Supreme Court exercised appellate jurisdiction was an Article III court (370 U.S. at 554).

Justice Douglas, dissenting: *Marbury* cited as holding that Congress could not expand federal jurisdiction beyond traditional lawsuits and cited as holding that congressional interpretations of Article III are not constitutionally authoritative (370 U.S. at 600 n. 6, 602–603).

Fay v. Noia, 372 U.S. 391 (1963)

Justice Brennan, majority opinion: *Marbury* cited as holding that the Supreme Court could issue writs of habeas corpus only when exercising appellate jurisdiction (372 U.S. at 407).

Wheeldin v. Wheeler, 373 U.S. 647 (1963)

Justice Brennan, dissenting: *Marbury* cited as holding that government officials are accountable, "in damages, . . . for the consequences of [their] wrongdoing" (373 U.S. at 656).

Wesberry v. Sanders, 376 U.S. 1 (1964)

Justice Black, majority opinion: *Marbury* cited as holding that courts have "the power . . . to protect the constitutional rights of individuals from legislative destruction" (376 U.S. at 6).

Aptheker v. Secretary of State, 378 U.S. 500 (1964)

Justice Clark, dissenting: *Marbury* cited as holding that the judicial obligation "to declare Acts of Congress unconstitutional lies in the power and duty of those courts to decide cases and controversies properly before them"(378 U.S. at 521).

Bell v. Maryland, 378 U.S. 226 (1964) (see Document 91)

Justice Douglas, concurring: *Marbury* quoted as holding that the justices have the power and duty to declare laws unconstitutional (378 U.S. at 244–245).

Justice Goldberg, concurring: *Marbury* quoted as holding that "the very essence of civil liberty certainly consists in the right of every individual to claim the protection of the laws" (378 U.S. at 312).

Justice Black, dissenting: *Marbury* cited as holding that the Supreme Court must decide constitutional questions that are properly before the justices and necessary to decide the case (378 U.S. at 323).

Swain v. Alabama, 380 U.S. 202 (1965)

Justice Goldberg, dissenting: *Marbury* cited as holding "when a constitutional claim is opposed by a nonconstitutional one, the former must prevail" (380 U.S. at 344).

Griswold v. Connecticut, 381 U.S. 479 (1965)

Justice Goldberg, concurring: *Marbury* quoted as holding that "it cannot be presumed that any clause in the constitution is intended to be without effect" (381 U.S. 479, 490–491).

Justice Black, dissenting: *Marbury* cited as holding that courts have the power to declare laws unconstitutional (381 U.S. at 513, 525–526).

United States v. Brown, 381 U.S. 437 (1965)

Chief Justice Warren, majority opinion: *Marbury* cited as holding that "Article III" grants "federal courts . . . exclusive authority over certain areas"(381 U.S. at 443).

Chapman v. California, 386 U.S. 18 (1967)

Justice Harlan, dissenting: *Marbury* quoted as holding "(s)o if a law be in opposition to the constitution; if both the law and the constitution apply to a particular case, so that the court must either decide that case conformably to the law, disregarding the constitution; or conformably to the constitution, disregarding the law; the court must determine which of these conflicting rules governs the case. . . ."(386 U.S. at 47).

Flast v. Cohen, 392 U.S. 83 (1968)
Justice Douglas, concurring: *Marbury* quoted as holding that judicial deference to the legislature gives elected officials "a practical and real omnipotence" (392 U.S. at 111).

Hunter v. Erickson, 393 U.S. 385 (1969)
Justice Black, dissenting: *Marbury* cited as holding that the Supreme Court "has power to invalidate state laws that discriminate on account of race" (393 U.S. at 397).

Allen v. State Board of Elections, 393 U.S. 544 (1969)
Justice Black, dissenting: *Marbury* cited as holding that "courts can pass on the constitutionality of state laws already enacted," but not holding that "federal courts or federal executive officers [may] hold up the passage of state laws until federal courts or federal agencies in Washington could pass on them" (393 U.S. at 596).

Desist v. United States, 394 U.S. 244 (1969)
Justice Douglas, dissenting: *Marbury* cited as a case where constitutional claims not strictly necessary to the actual decision were nevertheless considered part of the holding of the case (394 U.S. at 256).

Justice Harlan, dissenting: *Marbury* cited as holding that "(t)his Court is entitled to decide constitutional issues only when the facts of a particular case require their resolution for a just adjudication on the merits" (394 U.S. at 258).

Utah Public Service Comm'n v. El Paso Natural Gas Co., 395 U.S. 464 (1969)
Justice Harlan, dissenting: *Marbury* cited as holding that "is the function of this Court to

decide controversies between parties only when they cannot be settled by the litigants in any other way" (395 U.S. at 476).

Powell v. McCormick, 395 U.S. 486 (1969)
Chief Justice Warren, majority opinion: *Marbury* cited as holding that "(l)egislative immunity does not . . . bar all judicial review of legislative acts," and as holding that the Supreme Court is "the ultimate interpreter of the Constitution" (395 U.S. at 503, 549).

Justice Douglas, dissenting: *Marbury* cited as holding that courts may determine whether Congress has exceeded constitutional authority (395 U.S. at 552 n. 4).

Goldberg v. Kelly, 397 U.S. 254 (1970)
Justice Black, dissenting: *Marbury* cited as holding that "courts must be the final interpreters of the Constitution" (397 U.S. at 274).

Chandler v. Judicial Council of the Tenth Circuit, 398 U.S. 74 (1970)
Chief Justice Burger, majority opinion: *Marbury* cited as holding that the Supreme Court may issue writs of mandamus only when exercising appellate jurisdiction (398 U.S. at 86).

Justice Harlan, concurring: *Marbury* quoted as holding that the Supreme Court may issue writs of mandamus only when exercising appellate jurisdiction (398 U.S. at 95–96).

Justice Douglas, dissenting: *Marbury* quoted as holding that the Supreme Court may issue writs of mandamus only when exercising appellate jurisdiction (398 U.S. at 133).

Oregon v. Mitchell, 400 U.S. 112, 204 (1970)
Justice Harlan, dissenting: *Marbury* quoted as holding that "(i)t is emphatically the province and duty of the judicial department to say what the law is" (400 U.S. at 204).

Younger v. Harris, 401 U.S. 37 (1971)
Justice Black, majority opinion: *Marbury* cited as holding that courts cannot apply an

unconstitutional law when deciding a case or controversy (401 U.S. at 52).

Mackey v. United States, 401 U.S. 667 (1971)

Justice Harlan, concurring: *Marbury* quoted at length and cited as "the classic explanation for the basis of judicial review . . . and from that day to this the sole continuing rationale for the exercise of this judicial power" (401 U.S. at 678).

McGuatha v. California, 402 U.S. 183 (1971)

Justice Brennan, dissenting: *Marbury* quoted as holding that the constitution should be "termed a government of laws, and not of men" (402 U.S. at 250).

Bivens v. Six Unknown Named Agents of Federal Bureau of Narcotics, 403 U.S. 388 (1971)

Justice Brennan, majority opinion: *Marbury* quoted as holding that persons have a right to remedies for violations of their federal rights (403 U.S. at 397).

Justice Harlan, concurring: *Marbury* cited as holding that a remedy should exist for rights violations (403 U.S. at 400–401 n. 3).

Gooding v. Wilson, 405 U.S. 518 (1972)

Chief Justice Burger, dissenting: *Marbury* cited as holding that courts cannot apply an unconstitutional law when deciding a case or controversy (405 U.S. at 531).

Furman v. Georgia, 408 U.S. 238 (1972)

Justice Rehnquist, dissenting: *Marbury* cited as establishing the proper justification for judicial review in a democratic society (408 U.S. at 466).

Doe v. McMillan, 412 U.S. 306 (1973)

Justice Douglas, concurring: *Marbury* cited as holding that "(l)egislative immunity does not . . . bar all judicial review of legislative acts" (412 U.S. at 326).

Justice Blackmun, concurring: *Marbury* cited as holding that the judicial power to declare laws unconstitutional gave courts had no power to suppress legislative publications (412 U.S. at 337–338).

Justice Rehnquist, dissenting: *Marbury* cited as holding that courts have the power "to review [only] the completed acts of the Legislative and Executive Branches" (412 U.S. at 343–344).

Broadrick v. Oklahoma, 413 U.S. 601 (1973)

Justice White, majority opinion: *Marbury* quoted as holding "[s]o if a law be in opposition to the constitution; if both the law and the constitution apply to a particular case, so that the court must either decide that case conformably to the law, disregarding the constitution; or conformably to the constitution, disregarding the law; the court must determine which of these conflicting rules governs the case. This is of the very essence of judicial duty" (413 U.S. at 611).

Mayor of Philadelphia v. Educational Equality League, 415 U.S. 605 (1974)

Justice Powell, majority opinion: *Marbury* cited as a case concerning a discretionary appointment to the executive branch (415 U.S. at 613).

United States v. Richardson, 418 U.S. 166 (1974)

Chief Justice Burger, majority opinion: *Marbury* cited as holding that the "judicial power may be exercised only in a case properly before it—a 'case or controversy'" (418 U.S. at 171).

Justice Powell, concurring: *Marbury* cited as "recogniz[ing]" a "power . . . incompatible with unlimited notions of taxpayer and citizen standing" (418 U.S. at 191).

United States v. Nixon, 418 U.S. 683 (1974)
(see Document 92)

Chief Justice Burger, unanimous opinion: *Marbury* quoted as holding that in general and in cases of executive privilege it "is emphatically the province and duty of the judicial department to say what the law is" (418 U.S. at 703–705).

Regional Rail Reorganization Act Cases, 419 U.S. 102 (1974)

Justice Brennan, majority opinion: *Marbury* cited as holding that special courts in railroad cases need not obey mandatory statutory provisions when doing so will violate constitutional rights (419 U.S. at 142).

United States v. Watson, 423 U.S. 411 (1976)

Justice Marshall, dissenting: *Marbury* cited as holding that justices in constitutional cases must not defer to legislative interpretations of the constitution" (423 U.S. at 442).

United States v. Santana, 427 U.S. 38 (1976)

Justice Marshall, dissenting: *Marbury* cited as holding that justices in constitutional cases must not defer to legislative interpretations of the constitution" (427 U.S. at 46 n. 1).

Nixon v. Administrator of General Services, 433 U.S. 425 (1977)

Justice Powell, concurring: *Marbury* cited as holding it "is emphatically the province and duty of the judicial department to say what the law is" (433 U.S. at 503).

Chief Justice Burger, dissenting: *Marbury* quoted as setting forth an unduly narrow interpretation of a bill of attainder (433 U.S. at 537).

Justice Rehnquist, dissenting: *Marbury* quoted as holding that the justices have an obligation "say what the law is" in all separation of powers cases (433 U.S. at 559 n. 7).

Monell v. Department of Social Services, 438 U.S. 658 (1978)

Justice Powell, concurring: *Marbury* cited as holding that the justices have the power to declare laws unconstitutional, even though that "issue was not argued or briefed" by counsel (438 U.S. at 709 n. 6).

Justice Rehnquist, dissenting: *Marbury* cited as holding that the justices have the power to declare laws unconstitutional, even though that "issue was never actually briefed or argued" by counsel (438 U.S. at 717–718).

Tennessee Valley Authority v. Hill, 437 U.S. 153 (1978)

Chief Justice Burger, majority opinion: *Marbury* quoted as holding that "it is emphatically the province and duty of the judicial department to say what the law is" (437 U.S. at 194).

Butz v. Economou, 438 U.S. 478 (1978) (see Document 93)

Justice White, majority opinion: *Marbury* quoted as holding that the "very essence of civil liberty certainly consists in the right of every individual to claim the protection of the laws," and cited as holding that national officeholders "are subject to federal law") (438 U.S. at 485–486, 506).

Justice Rehnquist, dissenting: *Marbury* cited as holding that government officials are "not insulat[ed] . . . from judicial review," but as not mandating that government officials be subject to lawsuits for damages (438 U.S. at 523–524).

Orr v. Orr, 440 U.S. 268 (1979)

Justice Rehnquist, dissenting: *Marbury* cited as holding that Congress may not add to the jurisdiction of the Supreme Court (440 U.S. at 299).

Cannon v. University of Chicago, 411 U.S. 677 (1979)

Justice Powell, dissenting: *Marbury* quoted as holding that "it is emphatically the province and duty of the judicial department to say what the law is" (411 U.S. at 744).

Davis v. Passman, 442 U.S. 228 (1979)

Justice Brennan, majority opinion: *Marbury* quoted as holding that "(t)he very essence of civil liberty certainly consists in the right of every individual to claim the protection of the laws, whenever he receives an injury. One of the first duties of government is to afford that protection" (442 U.S. at 242).

Goldwater v. Carter, 444 U.S. 996 (1979)
Justice Powell, concurring: *Marbury* quoted as holding that the Supreme Court has a duty "to say what the law is" when the constitutional standards for cases and controversies are met (444 U.S. at 1001).

United States Parole Comm'n v. Geraghty, 445 U.S. 388 (1980)
Justice Powell, dissenting: *Marbury* cited as holding that "Congress may not confer federal-court jurisdiction when Art. III does not" (445 U.S. at 421).

Owen v. Independence, 445 U.S. 622 (1980)
Justice Powell, dissenting: *Marbury* quoted as holding that "[the] province of the court is . . . not to inquire how the executive, or executive officers, perform duties in which they have a discretion," and quoted as holding that justices must be cautious when considering "[questions], in their nature political, or which are, by the constitution and laws, submitted to the executive" (445 U.S. at 668).

Carlson v. Green, 446 U.S. 14 (1980)
Justice Rehnquist, dissenting: *Marbury* cited as an instance of equitable relief, and quoted as holding that "it is emphatically the province and duty of the judicial department to say what the law is" (446 U.S. at 42 n. 8, 51).

Rome v. United States, 446 U.S. 156 (1980)
Justice Rehnquist, dissenting: *Marbury* cited as holding that the Supreme Court bears the ultimate responsibility for determining congressional power to enforce the post–Civil War Amendments (446 U.S. at 207, 210–211).

Diamond v. Chakrabarty, 447 U.S. 303 (1980)
Chief Justice Burger, majority opinion: *Marbury* quoted as holding that "it is 'the province and duty of the judicial department to say what the law is'" (447 U.S. at 315).

Richmond Newspapers, Inc. v. Virginia, 448 U.S. 555 (1980)
Justice Brennan, concurring: *Marbury* quoted as holding that ours is a "government of laws" (448 U.S. at 597).

Justice Rehnquist, dissenting: *Marbury* cited as holding that Supreme Court should not "smother a healthy pluralism" (448 U.S. at 606).

Fullilove v. Klutznick, 448 U.S. 448 (1980)
Justice Powell, concurring: *Marbury* cited as holding that "judicial review [is] the means by which action of the Legislative and Executive Branches [is] required to conform to the Constitution" (448 U.S. at 509–510).

United States v. Will, 449 U.S. 200 (1980)
Chief Justice Burger, unanimous opinion: *Marbury* quoted as holding that "the province and duty of the judicial department to [is] say what the law is" (449 U.S. at 217).

Middlesex County Seweage Auth. v. National Sea Clammers Ass'n, 453 U.S. 1 (1981)
Justice Stevens, dissenting: *Marbury* cited as holding that "where there is a legal right, there is also a legal remedy by suit, or action at law, whenever that right is invaded'" (453 U.S. at 23 n. 2).

Metromedia, Inc. v. City of San Diego, 453 U.S. 490 (1981)
Justice Stevens, dissenting: *Marbury* quoted as holding, '[s]o if a law be in opposition to the constitution; if both the law and the constitution apply to a particular case, so that the court must either decide that case conformably to the law, disregarding the consti-

tution; or conformably to the constitution, disregarding the law; the court must determine which of these conflicting rules governs the case. This is of the very essence of judicial duty." (453 U.S. at 546).

Valley Forge Christian College v. Americans United for Separation of Church & State, 454 U.S. 464 (1982)

Justice Rehnquist, majority opinion: *Marbury* cited as holding that the Supreme Court has the power to declare laws unconstitutional (454 U.S. at 473–474).

City of Mesquite v. Aladdin's Castle, Inc., 455 U.S. 283 (1982)

Justice Stevens, majority opinion: *Marbury* quoted as holding that the United States is "a government of laws, and not of men" (455 U.S. at 290 n. 12).

Merrill Lynch, Pierce, Fenner & Smith, Inc. v. Curran, 456 U.S. 353 (1982)

Justice Stevens, majority opinion: *Marbury* quoted as holding that "[it] is a general and indisputable rule, that where there is a legal right, there is also a legal remedy by suit, or action at law, whenever that right is invaded'" (456 U.S. at 375 n. 54).

Nixon v. Fitzgerald, 457 U.S. 731 (1982) (see Document 94)

Justice Powell, majority opinion: *Marbury* quoted as holding that persons are not entitled to any particular legal remedy for a legal wrong (457 U.S. at 754–755 n. 37).

Chief Justice Burger, concurring opinion: *Marbury* cited as holding that courts should review the constitutionality of some government actions, and cited as not being overruled by a judicial holding that sitting presidents could not be sued for damages (457 U.S. at 761, 763 n. 7).

Justice White, dissenting: *Marbury* quoted as holding that the Supreme Court must review

"the legality" of executive branch actions, cited as holding that the law must provide a remedy for the violation of rights, and cited as holding that all persons are entitled to the protection of the laws (457 U.S. at 766, 768, 783, 789, 797).

Justice Blackmun, dissenting: *Marbury* cited as holding that "no man, not even the President of the United States, is absolutely and fully above the law" (457 U.S. at 797–798).

Mississippi University for Women v. Hogan, 458 U.S. 718 (1982)

Justice O'Connor, majority opinion: *Marbury* cited as holding that courts cannot apply an unconstitutional law when deciding a case or controversy (458 U.S. at 733).

Moses H. Cone Memorial Hosp. v. Mercury Constr. Corp., 460 U.S. 1 (1983)

Justice Rehnquist, dissenting: *Marbury* quoted as holding "[i]t is the essential criterion of appellate jurisdiction, that it revises and corrects the proceedings in a case already instituted" (460 U.S. at 35).

Briscoe v. LaHue, 460 U.S. 325 (1983)

Justice Marshall, dissenting: *Marbury* quoted as holding that "(t)he very essence of civil liberty certainly consists in the right of every individual to claim the protection of the laws, whenever he receives an injury" (460 U.S. at 368).

Maryland v. United States, 460 U.S. 1101 (1983)

Justice Rehnquist, dissenting: *Marbury* quoted as holding that "[t]he province of the court is, solely, to decide on the rights of individuals, not to inquire how the executive, or executive officers, perform duties in which they have a discretion" (460 U.S. at 1105).

Bush v. Lucas, 462 U.S. 367 (1983)

Justice Stevens, majority opinion: *Marbury* cited as holding that "it is the province of the judiciary to fashion an adequate remedy for every wrong that can be proved in a case over which a court has jurisdiction" (462 U.S. at 373).

INS v. Chadha, 462 U.S. 919 (1983)

Chief Justice Burger, majority opinion: *Marbury* cited as holding that judicial review in separation of powers cases is justified even when a president signed the bill allegedly interfering with executive power and when the case has "political implications" (462 U.S. at 942–943).

South Carolina v. Regan, 465 U.S. 367 (1984)

Justice O'Connor, concurring: *Marbury* cited as holding that "Congress is without power to add parties not within the initial grant of original jurisdiction, and as "indicat[ing], in dicta, that Congress may not withdraw that jurisdiction" (465 U.S. at 397).

Secretary of Maryland v. Joseph H. Munson Co., 467 U.S. 947 (1984)

Justice Rehnquist, dissenting: *Marbury* cited as holding that judicial power may be exercised only in a "'flesh and blood' dispute," and quoted as holding "if a law be in opposition to the constitution; if both the law and the constitution apply to a particular case, so that the court must either decide that case conformably to the law, disregarding the constitution; or conformably to the constitution, disregarding the law; the court must determine which of these conflicting rules governs the case. This is of the very essence of judicial duty" (467 U.S. at 976).

Hobby v. United States, 468 U.S. 339 (1984)

Justice Marshall, dissenting: *Marbury* quoted as holding that "(t)he government of the United States has been emphatically termed a government of laws, and not of men. It will certainly cease to deserve this high appellation, if the laws furnish no remedy for the violation of a vested legal right" (468 U.S. at 359 n. 8).

Allen v. Wright, 468 U.S. 737 (1984)

Justice Stevens, dissenting: *Marbury* quoted as holding that it is "emphatically the province and duty of the Judiciary to say what the law is" (468 U.S. at 794).

Segura v. United States, 468 U.S. 796 (1984)

Justice Stevens, dissenting: *Marbury* cited as holding that "[t]he primary responsibility for enforcing the Constitution's limits on government . . . has been vested in the judicial branch" (468 U.S. at 828 n. 22).

United States v. Leon, 468 U.S. 897 (1984)

Justice Stevens, dissenting: *Marbury* cited as holding that "this Court has a duty to face questions of constitutional law when necessary to the disposition of an actual case or controversy" and quoted as holding "(t)he very essence of civil liberty certainly consists in the right of every individual to claim the protection of the laws, whenever he receives an injury" (468 U.S. at 962–963, 978 n. 36).

Garcia v. San Antonio Metro. Transit Auth., 469 U.S. 528 (1985)

Justice Powell, dissenting: *Marbury* quoted as holding that the Supreme Court has the power "to say what the law is" when determining whether federal laws are constitutional (469 U.S. at 567).

Oklahoma City v. Tuttle, 471 U.S. 808 (1985)

Justice Stevens, dissenting: *Marbury* quoted as holding that "the very essence of civil liberty certainly consists in the right of every individual to claim the protection of the laws, whenever he receives an injury. One of the first duties of government is to afford that protection" (471 U.S. at 843 n. 32).

Lowe v. SEC, 472 U.S. 181 (1985)

Justice White, concurring: *Marbury* quoted as holding "it is emphatically the province and duty of the Judiciary to say what the law is" (472 U.S. at 230).

Atascadero State Hospital v. Scanlon, 473 U.S. 234 (1985)

Justice Powell, majority opinion: *Marbury* quoted as holding that the Supreme Court has the duty "to say what the law is" (473 U.S. at 243).

Thomas v. Union Carbide Agricultural Products Co., 473 U.S. 568 (1985)

Justice Brennan, concurring: *Marbury* quoted as holding that "the essential function of the Judiciary is 'to say what the law is'" (473 U.S. at 601 n. 4).

Bender v. Williamsport Area School District, 475 U.S. 523 (1986)

Justice Stevens, majority opinion: *Marbury* cited as holding that "(f)ederal courts . . . have only the power that is authorized by Article III of the Constitution and the statutes enacted by Congress pursuant thereto" (475 U.S. at 541).

Bowen v. Michigan Academy of Family Physicians, 476 U.S. 667 (1986)

Justice Stevens, unanimous opinion: *Marbury* quoted as holding that "the very essence of civil liberty certainly consists in the right of every individual to claim the protection of the laws" (476 U.S. at 670).

INS v. Cardoza-Fonseca, 480 U.S. 421 (1987)

Justice Powell, dissenting: *Marbury* cited in lower federal court opinion as holding that the Board of Immigration Appeals must follow federal judicial interpretation of laws (480 U.S. at 468).

Webster v. Doe, 486 U.S. 592 (1988)

Justice Scalia, dissenting: *Marbury* quoted as holding that "where the head of a department acts in a case, in which executive discretion is to be exercised; in which he is the mere organ of executive will; it is again repeated, that any application to a court to control, in any respect, his conduct, would be rejected without hesitation" (486 U.S. at 609).

Thompson v. Oklahoma, 487 U.S. 815 (1988)

Justice Stevens, plurality opinion: *Marbury* quoted as holding that "it is emphatically the province and duty of the judiciary to say what the law is" (487 U.S. at 833 n. 40).

Jett v. Dallas Independent School District, 491 U.S. 701 (1989)

Justice Brennan, dissenting: *Marbury* cited as holding that "a statute setting forth substantive rights without specifying a remedy contained an implied cause of action for damages incurred in violation of the statute's terms" (491 U.S. at 742).

Webster v. Reproductive Health Services, 492 U.S. 490 (1989)

Justice Scalia, concurring: *Marbury* cited as an example of a case decided "on broader constitutional grounds than absolutely necessary" (492 U.S. at 533).

United States v. Dalm, 494 U.S. 596 (1990)

Justice Stevens, dissenting: *Marbury* cited as holding that "for every right there should be a remedy" (494 U.S. at 616).

United States v. Munoz-Flores, 495 U.S. 385 (1990)

Justice Marshall, majority opinion: *Marbury* cited as holding that "the courts will strike down a law when Congress has passed it in violation of . . . a [constitutional] command" (495 U.S. at 396–397).

American Trucking Ass'ns v. Smith, 496 U.S. 167 (1990)

Justice Scalia, concurring: *Marbury* cited as holding that the "judicial role . . . is to say what the law is, not to prescribe what it shall be" (496 U.S. at 201).

Rutan v. Republican Party, 497 U.S. 62 (1990)
Justice Scalia, dissenting: *Marbury* cited as demonstrating that it is "rare that a federal administration of one party will appoint a judge from another party." (497 U.S. at 93).

Cheek v. United States, 498 U.S. 192 (1991)
Justice Scalia, concurring: *Marbury* cited as holding that persons do not have a "known legal duty" to obey a statute they believe unconstitutional (498 U.S. at 207–208).

James B. Beam Distilling Co. v. Georgia, 501 U.S. 529 (1991)
Justice Scalia, concurring: *Marbury* quoted as holding that courts have the power "to say what the law is" (501 U.S. at 549).

Justice O'Connor, dissenting: *Marbury* quoted as holding that courts have the power "to say what the law is" (501 U.S. at 550).

Harmelin v. Michigan, 501 U.S. 957 (1991)
Justice White, dissenting: *Marbury* quoted as holding "it is emphatically the province and duty of the judiciary to say what the law is" (501 U.S. at 1017).

Franklin v. Gwinnett County Public School, 503 U.S. 60 (1992)
Justice White, majority opinion: *Marbury* quoted as holding that "our Government 'has been emphatically termed a government of laws, and not of men. It will certainly cease to deserve this high appellation, if the laws furnish no remedy for the violation of a vested legal right'" (503 U.S. at 66).

Lujan v. Defenders of Wildlife, 504 U.S. 555 (1992) (see Document 95)
Justice Scalia, majority opinion: *Marbury* quoted as holding that "[t]he province of the court is, solely, to decide on the rights of individuals" (504 U.S. at 576).

Justice Kennedy, concurring: *Marbury* cited as illustrating that "[m]odern litigation has progressed far from the paradigm of Marbury suing Madison to get his commission" (504 U.S. at 580).

Justice Blackmun, dissenting: *Marbury* quoted as holding that "the very essence of civil liberty certainly consists in the right of every individual to claim the protection of the laws, whenever he receives an injury" (504 U.S. at 606).

Franklin v. Massachusetts, 505 U.S. 788 (1992)
Justice Scalia, concurring: *Marbury* cited as leaving open whether the Supreme Court could order the president to perform a ministerial duty (505 U.S. at 827 n. 2).

Planned Parenthood v. Casey, 505 U.S. 833 (1992)
Justice Scalia, dissenting: *Marbury* cited as a case whose holding under the plurality opinion's interpretation of stare decisis might be that "courts [could] review the constitutionality of only those statutes that pertain to the jurisdiction of the courts" (505 U.S. at 993).

Herrera v. Collins, 506 U.S. 390 (1993)
Justice Blackmun, dissenting: *Marbury* quoted as holding that "[t]he government of the United States has been emphatically termed a government of laws, and not of men. It will certainly cease to deserve this high appellation, if the laws furnish no remedy for the violation of a vested legal right" (506 U.S. at 440).

Deal v. United States, 508 U.S. 129 (1993)
Justice Scalia, majority opinion: *Marbury* cited as an example of a case (508 U.S. at 133).

Harper v. Virginia Dep't of Taxation, 509 U.S. 86 (1993)
Justice Scalia, concurring: *Marbury* quoted as holding that "the province and duty of the judiciary to say what the law is" (509 U.S. at 107).

Dalton v. Specter, 511 U.S. 462 (1994)
Chief Justice Rehnquist, majority opinion: *Marbury* cited as not overruled by a judicial decision declaring that Congress could make a political decision a matter of executive discretion (511 U.S. at 477).

Hess v. Port Auth. Trans-Hudson Corp., 513 U.S. 30 (1994)
Justice Stevens, concurring: *Marbury* cited as holding that "there should be a remedy for every wrong" (513 U.S. at 54).

Plaut v. Spendthrift Farm, 514 U.S. 211 (1995)
Justice Scalia, majority opinion: *Marbury* cited as holding that "the province and duty" of courts is "to say what the law is," and holding that courts have "power to disregard an unconstitutional statute" (514 U.S. at 218, 231).

United States v. Lopez, 514 U.S. 549 (1995)
(see Document 96)
Chief Justice Rehnquist, majority opinion: *Marbury* quoted as holding that the Supreme Court has a duty "to say what the law is" (514 U.S. at 566).

Justice Kennedy, concurring: *Marbury* cited as holding that courts have the power of judicial review, and quoted as holding that courts have the power to say "what the law is" (514 U.S. at 575, 579).

Reynoldsville Casket Co. v. Hyde, 514 U.S. 749 (1995)
Justice Scalia, concurring: *Marbury* quoted as holding that when deciding cases, courts should "disregard[].... [unconstitutional] law[s]" (514 U.S. at 760).

Miller v. Johnson, 515 U.S. 900 (1995)
Justice Kennedy, majority opinion: *Marbury* quoted as holding that "it is emphatically the province and duty of the judiciary to say what the law is" (515 U.S. at 922).

Lawrence v. Chater, 516 U.S. 163 (1996)
Justice Scalia, dissenting: *Marbury* quoted as holding that the Supreme Court has to "revise and correct" other governmental decisions (516 U.S. at 190).

Seminole Tribe v. Florida, 517 U.S. 44 (1996)
Chief Justice Rehnquist, majority opinion: *Marbury* cited as holding that "Congress could not expand the jurisdiction of the federal courts beyond the bounds of Article III" (517 U.S. at 65).

Clinton v. Jones, 520 U.S. 681 (1997)
Justice Stevens, majority opinion: *Marbury* quoted as holding that "it is emphatically the province and duty of the judiciary to say what the law is" (520 U.S. at 703).

City of Boerne v. Flores, 521 U.S. 507 (1997)
(see Document 97)
Justice Kennedy, majority opinion: *Marbury* quoted as holding that the powers of the national government are limited, that Congress does not have the final authority to define the limits of its powers, and that the Supreme Court has the final responsibility for determining what the Fourteenth Amendment and other constitutional provisions mean (521 U.S. at 516, 529, 535–536).

Washington v. Glucksberg, 521 U.S. 702 (1997)
Justice Souter, concurring: *Marbury* cited as holding that judicial review of the substance of legislation is "nothing more than what is required by the judicial authority and obligation to construe constitutional text and review legislation for conformity to that text" (521 U.S. at 763).

Raines v. Byrd, 521 U.S. 811 (1997)
Chief Justice Rehnquist, majority opinion: *Marbury* cited as holding that courts have the power to declare laws unconstitutional and that "[t]he irreplaceable value of th[at] power . . . lies in the protection it has af-

forded the constitutional rights and liberties of individual citizens and minority groups against oppressive or discriminatory government action" (521 U.S. at 829).

Justice Souter, concurring: *Marbury* cited as holding that the Supreme Court has the power to declare laws unconstitutional (521 U.S. at 834).

Printz v. United States, 521 U.S. 898 (1997)
Justice Thomas, concurring: *Marbury* quoted as holding that the federal government has limited powers and "[t]hat those limits may not be mistaken, or forgotten, the constitution is written" (521 U.S. at 937).

Gebser v. Lago Vista Independent School District, 524 U.S. 274 (1998)
Justice Stevens, dissenting: *Marbury* quoted as holding that "our Government 'has been emphatically termed a government of laws, and not of men. It will certainly cease to deserve this high appellation, if the laws furnish no remedy for the violation of a vested legal right'" (524 U.S. at 295 n. 3).

National Endowment for the Arts v. Finley, 524 U.S. 569 (1998)
Justice Souter, dissenting: *Marbury* quoted as holding that "it is emphatically the province and duty of the judiciary to say what the law is" (524 U.S. at 604 n. 3).

City of Chicago v. Morales, 527 U.S. 41 (1999)
Justice Scalia, dissenting: *Marbury* cited as holding that "[t]he rationale for our power to review federal legislation for constitutionality . . . was that we had to do so in order to decide the case before us" (527 U.S. at 74).

College Savings Bank v. Florida Prepaid Postsecondary Ed. Expense Bd., 527 U.S. 666 (1999)
Justice Scalia, majority opinion: *Marbury* cited as a case whose holding is supported by

"clear and conclusive" "constitutional tradition and precedent" (527 U.S. at 688).

Alden v. Maine, 527 U.S. 706 (1999)
Justice Souter, dissenting: *Marbury* quoted as holding that "[i]f he has a right, and that right has been violated, . . . the laws of his country afford him a remedy" (527 U.S. at 812).

Williams v. Taylor, 529 U.S. 362 (2000)
Justice Stevens, majority opinion: *Marbury* quoted as holding that "[w]hen federal judges exercise their federal-question jurisdiction under the "judicial Power" of Article III of the Constitution, it is "emphatically the province and duty" of those judges to "say what the law is" (529 U.S. at 378).

United States v. Morrison, 529 U.S. 598 (2000) (see Document 98)
Chief Justice Rehnquist, majority opinion: *Marbury* quoted as holding that the national government has limited powers and the Supreme Court has the final authority for determining those powers (529 U.S. at 607, 616).

Justice Souter, dissenting: *Marbury* cited as consistent with congressional responsibility for determining what practices substantially effect interstate commerce (529 U.S. at 651 n. 19).

Miller v. French, 530 U.S. 327 (2000)
Justice Souter, dissenting: *Marbury* quoted as holding that "[i]t is emphatically the province and duty of the judiciary to say what the law is" (530 U.S. at 352 n. 3).

Dickerson v. United States, 530 U.S. 428 (2000) (see Document 99)
Justice Scalia, dissenting: *Marbury* quoted as holding that justices may strike down only laws that violate the constitution (530 U.S. at 445, 446–447, 449–451).

Bush v. Gore, 531 U.S. 98 (2000)
Justice Stevens, dissenting: *Marbury* quoted as holding that "[i]t is emphatically the province

and duty of the judicial department to say what the law is" (531 U.S. at 128 n. 7).

Legal Services. Corp. v. Velazquez, 531 U.S. 533 (2001)

Justice Kennedy, majority opinion: *Marbury* quoted as holding that "[i]t is emphatically the province and duty of the judicial department to say what the law is" (531 U.S. at 545).

J.E.M. Ag Supply, Inc. v. Pioneer Hi-Bred Int'l, Inc., 534 U.S. 124; 122 S.Ct. 593 (2001)

Justice Thomas, majority opinion: *Marbury* quoted as holding that "it is 'emphatically

the province and duty of the judicial department to say what the law is'" (122 S.Ct. at 598).

Great-West Life & Annuity Ins. Co. v. Knudson, 534 U.S. 204; 122 S.Ct. 708 (2002)

Justice Stevens, dissenting: *Marbury* quoted as holding that "[t]he very essence of civil liberty certainly consists in the right of every individual to claim the protection of the laws, whenever he receives an injury" (122 S.Ct. at 719 n. 2).

Appendix C: Cases Cited

Abingdon School District v. Schempp, 374 U.S. 203 (1963)

Adamson v. California, 332 U.S. 46 (1947)

Adkins v. Children's Hospital of the District of Columbia, 261 U.S. 525 (1923)

Afroyim v. Rusk, 387 U.S. 253 (1957)

A. L. A. Schechter Poultry Corporation v. United States, 295 U.S. 495 (1935)

Alden v. Maine, 527 U.S. 706 (1999)

Allen v. State Board of Elections, 393 U.S. 544 (1969)

Allen v. Wright, 468 U.S. 737 (1984)

Allgeyer v. Louisiana, 165 U.S. 578 (1897)

American Trucking Associations v. Smith, 496 U.S. 167 (1990)

Ames v. Kansas, 111 U.S. 449 (1884)

Aptheker v. Secretary of State, 378 U.S. 500 (1964)

Atascadero State Hospital v. Scanlon, 473 U.S. 234 (1985)

Austerity Package Decisions (e.g., decision 43/1995, June 30, 1995) (Constitutional Court of Hungary)

Baker v. Carr, 369 U.S. 186 (1962)

Bates v. Little Rock, 361 U.S. 516 (1960)

Bayard v. Singleton, 1 N.C. 5 (1787)

Bell v. Hood, 327 U.S. 678 (1946)

Bell v. Maryland, 378 U.S. 226 (1964)

Bender v. Williamsport Area School District, 475 U.S. 523 (1986)

Bivens v. Six Unknown Named Agents of Federal Bureau of Narcotics, 403 U.S. 388 (1971)

Bors v. Preston, 111 U.S. 252 (1884)

Bowen v. Michigan Academy of Family Physicians, 476 U.S. 667 (1986)

Bowman v. Middleton, 1 Bay 252 (1792)

Bowsher v. Synar, 478 U.S. 714 (1986)

Briscoe v. LaHue, 460 U.S. 325 (1983)

Broadrick v. Oklahoma, 413 U.S. 601 (1973)

Brown v. Board of Education, 347 U.S. 483 (1954)

Brown v. Maryland, 25 U.S. 419 (1827)

Brown v. Mississippi, 297 U.S. 278 (1936)

Bush v. Gore, 531 U.S. 98 (2000)

Bush v. Lucas, 462 U.S. 367 (1983)

Bush v. Palm Beach County Canvassing Board, 531 U.S. 70 (2000)

Butz v. Economou, 438 U.S. 478 (1978)

Calder v. Bull, 3 U.S. 386 (1798)

Caldwell v. Commonwealth, 2 Ky. 129 (1802)

Califano v. Goldfarb, 430 U.S. 199 (1970)

California v. Southern Pacific Co., 157 U.S. 229 (1895)

Cannon v. University of Chicago, 411 U.S. 677 (1979)

Carlson v. Green, 446 U.S. 14 (1980)

Carroll v. Carroll, 57 U.S. 275 (1853)

Carroll v. Lessee of Carroll, 57 U.S. 275 (1850)

Carter v. Carter Coal Co., 298 U.S. 238 (1936)

Cases of the Judges of the Court of Appeal, 8 Va. 135 (1788)

Certification of the Amended Text of the Constitution 1997 (2) SA 97 (CC) (Constitutional Court of South Africa)

Certification of the Constitution 1996 (4) SA 744 (CC) (Constitutional Court of South Africa)

Chandler v. Judicial Council of the Tenth Circuit, 398 U.S. 74 (1970)

Chapman v. California, 386 U.S. 18 (1967)

Chechnya case (July 1995) (Constitutional Court of Russia)

Cheek v. United States, 498 U.S. 192 (1991)

City of Boerne v. Flores, 521 U.S. 507 (1997)

City of Chicago v. Morales, 527 U.S. 41 (1999)

City of London v. Wood, 12 Mod. Rep 669 (1701)

City of Mesquite v. Aladdin's Castle, Inc., 455 U.S. 283 (1982)

Civil Rights Cases, 109 U.S. 3 (1883)

Clay v. Sun Ins. Office, Ltd., 363 U.S. 207 (1960)

Clinton v. Jones, 520 U.S. 681 (1997)

Cohen v. Hurley, 366 U.S. 117 (1961)

Cohens v. Virginia, 19 U.S. (6 Wheat.) 264 (1821)

College Savings Bank v. Florida Prepaid Postsecondary Ed. Expense Bd., 527 U.S. 666 (1999)

Commonwealth v. Caton, 8 Va. (4 Call) 5 (Va., 1782)

Communist Party case (November 1992) (Constitutional Court of Russia)

Cooper v. Aaron, 358 U.S. 1 (1958)

Cooper v. Telfair, 4 U.S. 14 (1800)

Costa v. ENEL, ECJ decision 6/64 (1964) ECR 585 (ECJ)

Cunningham v. Macon & B. R. Co., 109 U.S. 446 (1883)

Dalehite v. United States, 346 U.S. 15 (1953)

Dalton v. Specter, 511 U.S. 462 (1994)

Daniels v. Railroad Company, 70 U.S. 250 (1865)

Dartmouth College v. Woodward, 17 U.S. 518 (1819)

Davis v. Passman, 442 U.S. 228 (1979)

Day v. Savage, 80 Eng. Rep. 235, 237 (K.B. 1615)

Deal v. United States, 508 U.S. 129 (1993)

Decatur v. Paulding, 39 U.S. 497 (1840)

Decision on Freedom of Association, CC 71-44 (July 16, 1971) (*Conseil Constitutionnel*, France)

Department of Agriculture v. Moreno, 413 U.S 528 (1973)

Desist v. United States, 394 U.S. 244 (1969)

Diamond v. Chakrabarty, 447 U.S. 303 (1980)

Dickerson v. United States, 530 U.S. 428 (2000)

Doe v. McMillan, 412 U.S. 306 (1973)

Dooley v. United States, 183 U.S. 151 (1901)

Downes v. Bidwell, 182 U.S. 244 (1901)

Dr. Bonham's Case, 77 Eng. Rep. 646

Dred Scott v. Sandford, 60 U.S. 393 (1857)

Dudgeon v. United Kingdom (1991) 4 E.H.H.R. 149 (ECHR)

Enderman v. Ashby, 2 Ky. 53 (1801)

Engle v. Vitale, 370 U.S. 421 (1962)

Ex parte Bollman, 8 U.S. 75 (1807)

Ex parte Clarke, 100 U.S. 399 (1879)

Ex parte Crane, 30 U.S. 190 (1831)

Ex parte McCardle, 73 U.S. 318 (1867)

Ex parte Newman, 81 U.S. 152 (1871)

Ex parte Republic of Peru, 318 U.S. 578 (1943)

Ex parte Siebold, 100 U.S. 371 (1880)

Ex parte United States, 287 U.S. 241 (1932)

Ex parte Vallandigham, 68 U.S. 243 (1863)

Ex parte Virginia, 100 U.S. 339 (1879)

Ex parte Watkins, 32 U.S. 568 (1833)

Ex parte Wells, 59 U.S. 307 (1855)

Ex parte Yerger, 75 U.S. 85 (1868)

Fairbank v. United States, 181 U.S. 283 (1901)

Fay v. Noia, 372 U.S. 391 (1963)

Flast v. Cohen, 392 U.S. 83 (1968)

Flemming v. Nestor, 363 U.S. 603 (1960)

Fletcher v. Peck, 10 U.S. 87 (1810)

Florida v. Georgia, 58 U.S. 478 (1854)

Franklin v. Gwinnett County Public School, 503 U.S. 60 (1992)

Franklin v. Massachusetts, 505 U.S. 788 (1992)

Frontiero v. Richardson, 411 U.S. 677 (1973)

Fullilove v. Klutznick, 448 U.S. 448 (1980)

Furman v. Georgia, 408 U.S. 238 (1972)

Gaines v. Thompson, 74 U.S. 347 (1868)

Garcia v. San Antonio Metro. Transit Authority, 469 U.S. 528 (1985)

Garfield v. United States, 211 U.S. 249 (1908)

Gebser v. Lago Vista Independent School District, 524 U.S. 274 (1998)

Gideon v. Wainwright, 372 U.S. 335 (1963)

Gitlow v. New York, 268 U.S. 652 (1925)

Glidden Co. v. Zdanok, 370 U.S. 530 (1962)

Godden v. Hales, 89 Eng. Rep. 1050 (K.B. 1686)

Goldberg v. Kelly, 397 U.S. 254 (1970)

Goldwater v. Carter, 444 U.S. 996 (1979)

Gooding v. Wilson, 405 U.S. 518 (1972)

Government of RSA v. Grootboom, 2001 (1) SA 46 (CC) (Constitutional Court of South Africa)

Great-West Life & Annuity Insurance Co. v. Knudson, 534 U.S. 204 (2002)

Griswold v. Connecticut, 381 U.S. 479 (1965)

Guinn v. United States, 238 U.S. 347 (1915)

Hague v. Committee for Industrial Organization, 307 U.S. 496 (1939)

Ham v. M'Claws, 1 Bay 93 (S.C. 1789)

Hamilton v. Eaton, 11 Fed. Cas. 336 (C.C.D. N.C. 1796)

Hammer v. Dagenhart, 247 U.S. 251 (1918)

Harmelin v. Michigan, 501 U.S. 957 (1991)

Harper v. Virginia Department of Taxation, 509 U.S. 86 (1993)

Harrison v. Nixon, 34 U.S. 483 (1835)

Hayburn's Case, 2 U.S. 409 (1792)

Herrera v. Collins, 506 U.S. 390 (1993)

Hess v. Port Authority Trans-Hudson Corp., 513 U.S. 30 (1994)

Hobby v. United States, 468 U.S. 339 (1984)

Holden v. Hardy, 169 U.S. 366 (1898)

Hollingsworth v. Virginia, 3 U.S. 378 (1798)

Holmes v. Walton (N.J., 1780)

Home Building and Loan Association v. Blaisdell, 290 U.S. 398 (1934)

Humphrey's Executor v. United States, 295 U.S. 602 (1935)

Hunter v. Erickson, 393 U.S. 385 (1969)

Hutcheson v. United States, 369 U.S. 599 (1962)

Hylton v. United States, 3 U.S. 171 (1796)

Immigration and Naturalization Service v. Cardoza-Fonseca, 480 U.S. 421 (1987)

Immigration and Naturalization Service v. Chadha, 462 U.S. 919 (1983)

In re Debs, 158 U.S. 564 (1895)

In re Kaine, 55 U.S. 103 (1852)

In re Metzger, 46 U.S. 176 (1847)

In re Winn, 213 U.S. 458 (1909)

Insurance Company v. Comstock, 83 U.S. 258 (1872)

ISS-MVD case (January 1992) (Constitutional Court of Russia)

James B. Beam Distilling Co. v. Georgia, 501 U.S. 529 (1991)

J. E. M. Ag Supply, Inc. v. Pioneer Hi-Bred Int'l., Inc., 534 U.S. 124 (2001)

Jett v. Dallas Independent School District, 491 U.S. 701 (1989)

Jimenez v. Weinberger, 417 U.S. 628 (1974)

Josiah Philips's Case (Va., 1778)

Juilliard v. Greenman, 110 U.S. 421 (1884)

Kamper v. Hawkins, 3 Va. 20 (1793)

Kendall v. United States, 37 U.S. 524 (1838)

Lapeyre v. United States, 84 U.S. 191 (1872)

Lawrence v. Chater, 516 U.S. 163 (1996)

Leary v. United States, 395 U.S. 6 (1969)

Legal Services. Corp. v. Velazquez, 531 U.S. 533 (2001)

Leisy v. Hardin, 135 U.S. 100 (1890)

Lindsay v. Commissioners, 2 Bay 38 (S.C. 1796)

Lochner v. New York, 198 U.S. 45 (1905)

Lottery Case, 188 U.S. 321 (1903)

Louisiana v. Jumel, 107 U.S. 711 (1882)

Louisiana v. McAdoo, 234 U.S. 627 (1914)

Lovell v. Griffin, 303 U.S. 444 (1938)

Lowe v. Securities Exchange Commission, 472 U.S. 181 (1985)

Lujan v. Defenders of Wildlife, 504 U.S. 555 (1992)

Maastricht case, BVerfGE 89 (1993) (Federal Constitutional Court of Germany)

Mabo v. Queensland (No. 2) (1992) 175 C.L.R. 1 (High Court of Australia)

Mackey v. United States, 401 U.S. 667 (1971)

Marbury v. Madison, 5 U.S. (1 Cr.) 137 (1803)

Martin v. Hunter's Lessee, 14 U.S. (1 Wheat.) 304 (1816)

Maryland v. United States, 460 U.S. 1101 (1983)

Mayor of Philadelphia v. Educational Equality League, 415 U.S. 605 (1974)

McAllister v. United States, 141 U.S. 174 (1891)

McCulloch v. Maryland, 17 U.S. 316 (1819)

McGuatha v. California, 402 U.S. 183 (1971)

M'Clung v. Silliman, 19 U.S. 598 (1821)

M'Cluny v. Silliman, 15 U.S. 369 (1817)

H.C. 3872/93 *Meatrael Ltd. v. Minister of Religious Affairs,* 47(5) P.D. 485 (Supreme Court of Israel)

H.C. 4676/94 *Meatrael Ltd. v. the Knesset,* 50(5) P.D. 15 (Supreme Court of Israel)

Merrill Lynch, Pierce, Fenner & Smith, Inc. v. Curran, 456 U.S. 353 (1982)

Metromedia, Inc. v. City of San Diego, 453 U.S. 490 (1981)

Meyer v. Nebraska, 262 U.S. 390 (1923)

Middlesex County Sewage Authority v. National Sea Clammers Association, 453 U.S. 1 (1981)

Miller v. French, 530 U.S. 327 (2000)

Miller v. Johnson, 515 U.S. 900 (1995)

Minersville School District v. Gobitis, 310 U.S. 586 (1940)

Minge v. Gilmour, 17 F. Cas. 440 (C.C.D. N.C. 1798)

Mississippi University for Women v. Hogan, 458 U.S. 718 (1982)

Mississippi v. Johnson, 71 U.S. 475 (1866)

Missouri ex rel. Gaines v. Canada, 305 U.S. 337 (1938)

Mohammed Ahmad Kan v. Shah Bano, AIR 1985 SC 945 (Supreme Court of India)

Monell v. Department of Social Services, 438 U.S. 658 (1978)

Monroe v. Pape, 365 U.S. 167 (1961)

Morehead v. People of the State of New York ex rel. Tipaldo, 298 U.S. 587 (1936)

Moses H. Cone Memorial Hospital v. Mercury Construction Corp., 460 U.S. 1 (1983)

Mugler v. Kansas, 123 U.S. 623 (1887)

Muhammad Nawaz Sharif v. President of Pakistan, P.L.D. 1993 S.C. 473 (Supreme Court of Pakistan)

Muller v. Oregon, 208 U.S. 412 (1908)

Murdock v. Pennsylvania, 319 U.S. 105 (1943)

Muskrat v. United States, 219 U.S. 346 (1911)

Myers v. United States, 272 U.S. 52 (1926)

NAACP v. Alabama, 357 U.S. 449 (1958)

NAACP v. Button, 371 U.S. 415 (1963)

National Endowment for the Arts v. Finley, 524 U.S. 569 (1998)

National Labor Relations Board v. Jones & Laughlin Steel Corp., 301 U.S. 1 (1937)

National Mutual Insurance Co. v. Tidewater Transfer Co., 337 U.S. 582 (1949)

Near v. Minnesota, 283 U.S. 697 (1931)

Nebbia v. New York, 291 U.S. 502 (1934)

New State Ice Co. v. Liebmann, 285 U.S. 262 (1932)

New York Times v. Sullivan, 376 U.S. 254 (1964)

Nixon v. Administrator of General Services, 433 U.S. 425 (1977)

Nixon v. Fitzgerald, 457 U.S. 731 (1982)

Nixon v. Herndon, 273 U.S. 536 (1927)

Noble v. Union River Logging R. Co., 147 U.S. 165 (1893)

Norris v. Alabama, 294 U.S. 587 (1935)

Ogden v. Witherspoon, 18 F. Cas. 618 (C.C.D. N.C. 1802)

Oklahoma City v. Tuttle, 471 U.S. 808 (1985)

Olga Tellis v. Bombay Municipal Corporation, AIR 1986 SC 180 (Supreme Court of India)

Olmstead v. United States, 277 U.S. 438 (1928)

Oregon v. Mitchell, 400 U.S. 112 (1970)

Orr v. Orr, 440 U.S. 268 (1979)

Owen v. Independence, 445 U.S. 622 (1980)

Palko v. Connecticut, 302 U.S. 319 (1937)

Panama Canal Co. v. Grace Line, Inc., 356 U.S. 309 (1958)

Parsons v. United States, 167 U.S. 324 (1897)

Pennhallow v. Doane's Administrators, 3 U.S. (3 Dall.) 54 (1795)

Pennsylvania v. West Virginia, 262 U.S. 553 (1923)

Pierce v. Society of Sisters, 268 U.S. 510 (1925)

Planned Parenthood v. Casey, 505 U.S. 833 (1992)

Plaut v. Spendthrift Farm, 514 U.S. 211 (1995)

Plessy v. Ferguson, 163 U.S. 537 (1896)

Poindexter v. Greenhow, 114 U.S. 270 (1885)

Pollock v. Farmer's Loan and Trust Co., 157 U.S. 429 (1895)

Powell v. Alabama, 287 U.S. 45 (1932)

Powell v. McCormick, 395 U.S. 486 (1969)

Printz v. United States, 521 U.S. 898 (1997)

R. v. Oakes (1986) 1 S.C.R. 103 (Supreme Court of Canada)

Railroad Retirement Board v. Alton Railroad Co., 295 U.S. 330 (1935)

Raines v. Byrd, 521 U.S. 811 (1997)

Reeside v. Walker, 52 U.S. 272 (1850)

Reference re Secession of Quebec (1998) 2 S.C.R. 217 (Supreme Court of Canada) (1998)

Regional Rail Reorganization Act Cases, 419 U.S. 102 (1974)

Reid v. Covert, 354 U.S. 1 (1957)

H.C.C.A. 217/2000 *Republic of Fiji v. Chandrika Prasad* (March 1, 2001) (High Court of Fiji)

Respublica v. Duquet, 2 Yeates 493 (1799)

Reynolds v. Sims, 377 U.S. 533 (1964)

Reynoldsville Casket Co. v. Hyde, 514 U.S. 749 (1995)

Richmond Newspapers, Inc. v. Virginia, 448 U.S. 555 (1980)

Riggs v. Johnson County, 73 U.S. 166 (1867)

Robin v. Hardaway, 1 Jeff (Va.) 109 (1772)

Rome v. United States, 446 U.S. 156 (1980)

Rowles v. Mason, 123 Eng. Rep. 892, 895 (C.P. 1612)

Rutan v. Republican Party, 497 U.S. 62 (1990)

Rutgers v. Waddington (Mayor's Court, City of New York, August 27, 1784)

S v. Makwanyane, 1995 (3) SA 391 (CC) (Constitutional Court of South Africa)

Sabariego v. Maverick, 124 U.S. 261 (1888)

Schneider v. Irvington, 308 U.S. 147 (1939)

Secretary of Maryland v. Joseph H. Munson Co., 467 U.S. 947 (1984)

Security Law case, Judgment No. 1 (May 5, 1956) (Italian Constitutional Court)

Segura v. United States, 468 U.S. 796 (1984)

Seminole Tribe v. Florida, 517 U.S. 44 (1996)

Senn v. Tile Layers Union, 301 U.S. 468 (1937)

Shapiro v. Thompson, 394 U.S. 618 (1969)

Simpson v. Attorney General (1994) 3 N.Z.L.R. 667 (Court of Appeal, New Zealand)

Slaughterhouse Cases, 83 U.S. 36 (1873)

South Carolina v. Regan, 465 U.S. 367 (1984)

Southwest case, BVerfGE 14 (1951) (Federal Constitutional Court of Germany)

Stark v. Wickard, 321 U.S. 288 (1944)

Steward Machine Co. v. Davis, 301 U.S. 548 (1937)

Stidger v. Rogers, 2 Ky. 52 (1801)

Strauder v. West Virginia, 100 U.S. 303 (1880)

Stromberg v. California, 283 U.S. 359 (1931)

Stuart v. Laird, 5 U.S. 299 (1803)

Swain v. Alabama, 380 U.S. 202 (1965)

Switchmen's Union of North America v. National Mediation Board, 320 U.S. 297 (1943)

Symsbury Case, 1 Kirby 444 (Conn. 1785)

Tatarstan case (March 1992) (Constitutional Court of Russia)

Taylor v. Beckham, 178 U.S. 548 (1900)

Tennessee Valley Authority v. Hill, 437 U.S. 153 (1978)

Texas & N.O.R. Co. v. Brotherhood of R. & S. S. Clerks, 281 U.S. 548 (1930)

Textile Workers Union v. Lincoln Mills of Alabama, 353 U.S. 448 (1957)

Thomas v. Union Carbide Agricultural Products Co., 473 U.S. 568 (1985)

Thompson v. Oklahoma, 487 U.S. 815 (1988)

Thornhill v. Alabama, 310 U.S. 88 (1940)

Trevett v. Weeden, Superior Court of Judicature of Rhode Island (1786)

C.A. 6821/93 *United Mizrahi Bank v. Migdal,* 49(4) P.D., 195 (Supreme Court of Israel)

United States ex rel. Dunlap v. Black, 128 U.S. 40 (1888)

United States ex rel. International Contracting Co. v. Lamont, 155 U.S. 303 (1894)

United States ex rel. Redfield v. Windom, 137 U.S. 636 (1891)

United States ex rel. Touhy v. Ragen, 340 U.S. 462 (1951)

United States Parole Commission v. Geraghty, 445 U.S. 388 (1980)

United States v. Arredondo, 31 U.S. 691 (1932)

United States v. Bankers' Trust Co., 294 U.S. 240 (1935)

United States v. Boutwell, 84 U.S. 604 (1873)

United States v. Brown, 381 U.S. 437 (1965)

United States v. California & Oregon Land Co., 148 U.S. 31 (1893)

United States v. Callender, 25 F. Cas. 239 (C.C.D. Va. 1800)

United States v. Carolene Products Corp., 304 U.S. 144 (1938)

United States v. Chicago, 48 U.S. 185 (1849)

United States v. Commodities Trading Corp., 339 U.S. 121 (1950)

United States v. Dalm, 494 U.S. 596 (1990)

United States v. Darby, 312 U.S. 100 (1941)

United States v. E. C. Knight Co., 156 U.S. 1 (1895)

United States v. Ferreira, 54 U.S. 40 (1851)

United States v. Leon, 468 U.S. 897 (1984)

United States v. Lopez, 514 U.S. 549 (1995)

United States v. Morrison, 529 U.S. 598 (2000)

United States v. Munoz-Flores, 495 U.S. 385 (1990)

United States v. Nixon, 418 U.S. 683 (1974)

United States v. Ortega, 24 U.S. 467 (1826)

United States v. Raines, 362 U.S. 17 (1960)

United States v. Richardson, 418 U.S. 166 (1974)

United States v. Robel, 389 U.S. 258 (1967)

United States v. Santana, 427 U.S. 38 (1976)

United States v. Schurz, 102 U.S. 378 (1880)

United States v. Smith, 286 U.S. 6 (1932)

United States v. United States District Court, 354 U.S. 258 (1948)

United States v. Watson, 423 U.S. 411 (1976)

United States v. Will, 449 U.S. 200 (1980)

Unni Krishnan v. State of Andhra Pradesh, AIR 1993 SC 2178 (Supreme Court of India)

Utah Public Service Commission v. El Paso Natural Gas Co., 395 U.S. 464 (1969)

Valley Forge Christian College v. Americans United for Separation of Church & State, 454 U.S. 464 (1982)

van Gend and Loos, ECJ decision 26/62 (1963) ECR 1 (ECJ)

Vanhorne's Lessee v. Dorrance, 2 U.S. (2 Dall.) 304 (1795)

Virginia v. Rives, 100 U.S. 313 (1879)

Ware v. Hylton, 3 U.S. 199 (1796)

Washington v. Glucksberg, 521 U.S. 702 (1997)

Webster v. Doe, 486 U.S. 592 (1988)

Webster v. Reproductive Health Services, 492 U.S. 490 (1989)

Wesberry v. Sanders, 376 U.S. 1 (1964)

West Coast Hotel v. Parrish, 300 U.S. 379 (1937)

Wheeldin v. Wheeler, 373 U.S. 647 (1963)

Whittington v. Polk, 1 H. & J. 236 (Md. 1802)

Wickard v. Filburn, 317 U.S. 111 (1942)

Wik Peoples v. Queensland 1996 141 A.L.R. 129 (High Court of Australia)

William Bagaley, 72 U.S. 377 (1866)

Williams v. Taylor, 529 U.S. 362 (2000)

Williamson v. Lee Optical Co., 348 U.S. 483 (1955)

Younger v. Harris, 401 U.S. 37 (1971)

Zafar Ali Shah v. Pervez Musharraf, P.L.D. 2000 S.C. 869 (Supreme Court of Pakistan)

Contributors

About the Editors

Mark A. Graber is professor of government and politics at the University of Maryland, College Park, and adjunct professor at the University of Maryland School of Law. He has published more than two dozen scholarly articles in American political development, political theory, and constitutionalism and is the author of *Rethinking Abortion: Equal Choice, The Constitution, and Reproductive Politics; Transforming Free Speech: The Ambiguous Legacy of Civil Libertarianism;* and the forthcoming *Dred Scott and the Problem of Constitutional Evil.*

Michael Perhac is pursuing his Ph.D. in government and politics at the University of Maryland, College Park.

About the Contributors

Robert Lowry Clinton is professor of political science at Southern Illinois University. He is the author of *Marbury v. Madison and Judicial Review* and *God and Man in the Law: The Foundations of Anglo-American Constitutionalism.*

Lee Epstein is Edward Mallinckrodt Distinguished University Professor of Political Science and professor of law at Washington University in St. Louis. She is the author or co-author of twelve books, including *The Supreme Court and Legal Change, Constitutional Law for a Changing America,* and *The Choices Justices Make.*

Scott Douglas Gerber is law professor at Ohio Northern University. He has published five books, including *Seriatim: The Supreme Court Before John Marshall.* He also has published dozens of scholarly articles, reviews, and op-eds about constitutional law and history and has made numerous television and radio appearances on these subjects.

Stephen M. Griffin is vice dean and Rutledge C. Clement Jr. Professor of Public and Constitutional Law at Tulane Law School. He has published more than twenty scholarly articles and is the author of *American Constitutionalism: From Theory to Politics* and coeditor of *Radical Critiques of the Law.*

Ran Hirschl is assistant professor of political science at the University of Toronto. He has published more than a dozen scholarly articles and book chapters on comparative public law, constitutionalism, and judicial politics. He is currently completing *Towards Juristocracy: A Comparative Inquiry into the Origins and Consequences of the New Constitutionalism.*

Ronald Kahn is James Monroe Professor of Politics and Law at Oberlin College. He is the author of *The Supreme Court and Constitutional Theory, 1953–1993,* and has published scholarly articles on religious freedom, privacy and abortion rights, and Supreme Court decision makings' relationship to institutional norms as well as to the historical, social, and cultural context outside the Court. He is currently coediting a book on the Supreme Court and American political development.

Jack Knight is Sidney W. Souers Professor of Government and department chair of political science at Washington University in St. Louis. He is the author or coauthor of several publications, including *Institutions and Social Conflict, Explaining Social Institutions,* and *The Choices Justices Make.*

James M. O'Fallon is Frank Nash Professor of Law at the University of Oregon School of Law. His scholarly work includes articles on *Marbury v. Madison* and the Missouri Controversy. He is editor of *Nature's Justice: Writings of William O. Douglas.*

Jeremy Waldron is Maurice and Hilda Friedman Professor of Law and director of the Center for Law and Philosophy at Columbia Law School. He is the author or editor of several books, including *The Right to Private Property; Nonsense Upon Stilts: Bentham, Burke, and Marx on the Rights of Man; Liberal Rights: Collected Papers 1981–91; The Dignity of Legislation; Law and Disagreement;* and *God, Locke, and Equality.* He has also written a number of influential articles on constitutional theory.

Keith E. Whittington is associate professor of politics at Princeton University. He is the author of *Constitutional Construction: Divided Powers and Constitutional Meanings* and *Constitutional Interpretation: Textual Meaning, Original Intent, and Judicial Review* and has published articles on American constitutional theory and development, federalism, and the presidency.

Index

Page numbers in italics indicate references to the documents section, which starts on page 203. For court cases, see appendixes A and B, pages 363–402.